SCHAUM'S OUTLINE OF

THEORY AND PROBLEMS

of

OPERATIONS RESEARCH

•

RICHARD BRONSON, Ph.D.

Professor of Mathematics and Computer Science

Fairleigh Dickinson University

SCHAUM'S OUTLINE SERIES

McGRAW-HILL BOOK COMPANY

New York   St. Louis   San Francisco   Auckland   Bogotá   Guatemala   Hamburg   Johannesburg
Lisbon   London   Madrid   Mexico   Montreal   New Delhi   Panama   Paris
San Juan   São Paulo   Singapore   Sydney   Tokyo   Toronto

To Rachel and Eric

RICHARD BRONSON, who is Professor of Mathematics and Computer Science at Fairleigh Dickinson University, received his Ph.D. in applied mathematics from Stevens Institute of Technology in 1968. Dr. Bronson is currently an associate editor of the journal *Simulation*, has served as a consultant to Bell Telephone Laboratories, and has published technical articles and books, the latter including Schaum's Outline of MODERN INTRODUCTORY DIFFERENTIAL EQUATIONS.

Schaum's Outline of Theory and Problems of
OPERATIONS RESEARCH

1 2 3 4 5 6 7 8 9 10 11 12 13 14 15 16 17 18 19 20   SH SH   8 6 5 4 3 2 1

ISBN 0-07-007977-3

Sponsoring Editor, David Beckwith
Editing Supervisor, James Halston
Production Manager, Nick Monti

Library of Congress Cataloging in Publication Data

Bronson, Richard.
  Schaum's outline of theory and problems of operations research.

  (Schaum's outline series)
  Includes index.
  1. Operations research. I. Title. II. Series.
T57.6.B76   001.4′24   81-8276
ISBN 0-07-007977-3   AACR2

Preface

Operations research, which is concerned with the efficient allocation of scarce resources, is both an art and a science. The art lies in the ability to reflect the concepts *efficient* and *scarce* in a well-defined mathematical model of a given situation; the science consists in the derivation of computational methods for solving such models. This book is meant to introduce readers to both aspects of the field.

Each chapter is divided into three sections. The first deals mainly with methodology; the exception is Chapter 1, which is concerned exclusively with the modeling aspects of mathematical programming. The second section consists of completely worked out problems. Besides clarifying the techniques presented in the first section, these problems may expand them and may also provide prototype situations for understanding the art of modeling. Finally, there is a section of problems with answers through which readers can test their mastery of the material.

The book itself is divided into two parts: mathematical programming and probabilistic methods. The first part, Chapters 1 through 15, is comprised solely of deterministic methods in linear, nonlinear, integer, and dynamic programming, along with a chapter on network analysis. A background in matrix algebra is sufficient for most of this material, although some differential calculus is required for the nonlinear search techniques. The second part, Chapters 16 through 24, includes material on stochastic dynamic programming, graph theory, decision theory, Markov chains, and queueing. As its title suggests, this part of the book has a first course in probability as a prerequisite.

Since the optimal allocation of money, manpower, energy, or a host of other scarce factors, is of importance to decision makers in many traditional disciplines, the material in this book will be useful to individuals from a variety of backgrounds. Therefore, this outline has been designed both as a textbook for students wanting an introduction to operations research and as a reference manual from which practitioners can obtain specific procedures.

I should like to thank those people who helped make the book a reality. The valuable suggestions of Natalie Ruber and Donald Bein with respect to Chapters 13 and 19, respectively, are warmly acknowledged, as are the contributions of Fay Klein, who assisted in the typing of the manuscript. David Beckwith of the Schaum's staff, besides editing the manuscript, contributed in several places to the procedures and the problems.

RICHARD BRONSON

Contents

PART I   *Mathematical Programming* 1

Chapter 1   **MATHEMATICAL PROGRAMMING** 1
Optimization problems. Linear programs. Integer programs. Quadratic programs. Problem formulation. Solution convention.

Chapter 2   **LINEAR PROGRAMMING: STANDARD FORM** 17
Nonnegativity conditions. Slack variables and surplus variables. Generating an initial feasible solution. Penalty costs. Standard form.

Chapter 3   **LINEAR PROGRAMMING: THEORY OF SOLUTIONS** 24
Linear dependence and independence. Convex combinations. Convex sets. Extreme-point solutions. Basic feasible solutions.

Chapter 4   **LINEAR PROGRAMMING: THE SIMPLEX METHOD** 32
The simplex tableau. A tableau simplification. The simplex method. Modifications for programs with artificial variables.

Chapter 5   **LINEAR PROGRAMMING: DUALITY** 44
Symmetric duals. Dual solutions. Unsymmetric duals.

Chapter 6   **INTEGER PROGRAMMING: BRANCH-AND-BOUND ALGORITHM** 54
First approximation. Branching. Bounding. Computational considerations.

Chapter 7   **INTEGER PROGRAMMING: CUT ALGORITHMS** 63
The Gomory algorithm. Computational considerations.

Chapter 8   **INTEGER PROGRAMMING: THE TRANSPORTATION ALGORITHM** 70
Standard form. The transportation algorithm. An initial basic solution. Test for optimality. Improving the solution. Degeneracy.

Chapter 9   **INTEGER PROGRAMMING: SCHEDULING MODELS** 84
Production problems. Transshipment problems. Assignment problems. The traveling salesman problem.

Chapter 10   **NONLINEAR PROGRAMMING: SINGLE-VARIABLE OPTIMIZATION** 97
The problem. Local and global optima. Results from calculus. Sequential-search techniques. Three-point interval search. Fibonacci search. Golden-mean search. Convex functions.

CONTENTS

Chapter **11** **NONLINEAR PROGRAMMING: MULTIVARIABLE OPTIMIZATION WITHOUT CONSTRAINTS** **110**

Local and global maxima. Gradient vector and Hessian matrix. Results from calculus. The method of steepest ascent. The Newton-Raphson method. The Fletcher-Powell method. Hooke-Jeeves' pattern search. A modified pattern search. Choice of an initial approximation. Concave functions.

Chapter **12** **NONLINEAR PROGRAMMING: MULTIVARIABLE OPTIMIZATION WITH CONSTRAINTS** **126**

Standard forms. Lagrange multipliers. Newton-Raphson method. Penalty functions. Kuhn-Tucker conditions. Method of feasible directions.

Chapter **13** **QUADRATIC PROGRAMMING** **143**

Standard form. A Kuhn-Tucker system. The method of Frank and Wolfe. An application to portfolio analysis.

Chapter **14** **DETERMINISTIC DYNAMIC PROGRAMMING** **154**

Multistage decision processes. A mathematical program. Dynamic programming. Dynamic programming with discounting.

Chapter **15** **NETWORK ANALYSIS** **169**

Networks. Minimum-span problems. Shortest-route problems. Maximal-flow problems. Finding a positive-flow path.

PART II *Probabilistic Methods* **184**

Chapter **16** **GAME THEORY** **184**

Games. Strategies. Stable games. Unstable games. Solution by linear programming. Dominance.

Chapter **17** **DECISION THEORY** **197**

Decision processes. Naive decision criteria. *A priori* criterion. *A posteriori* criterion. Decision trees. Utility. Lotteries. Von Neumann utilities.

Chapter **18** **STOCHASTIC DYNAMIC PROGRAMMING** **213**

Stochastic multistage decision processes. Policy tables.

Chapter **19** **FINITE MARKOV CHAINS** **224**

Markov processes. Powers of stochastic matrices. Ergodic matrices. Regular matrices.

Chapter **20** **UNBOUNDED HORIZONS** **234**

Optimal policies under stationarity. Discounting. Deterministic processes with discounting. Markov chains with discounting. Expected return per period.

Chapter **21** **MARKOVIAN BIRTH-DEATH PROCESSES** **255**

Population growth processes. Generalized Markovian birth-death processes. Linear Markovian birth processes. Linear Markovian death processes. Linear Markovian birth-death processes. Poisson birth processes. Poisson death processes. Poisson birth-death processes.

CONTENTS

Chapter 22   **QUEUEING SYSTEMS** 266
Introduction.   Queue characteristics.   Arrival patterns.   Service patterns. System capacity.   Queue disciplines.   Kendall's notation.

Chapter 23   **M/M/1 SYSTEMS** 273
System characteristics.   The Markovian model.   Steady-state solutions.   Measures of effectiveness.

Chapter 24   **OTHER SYSTEMS WITH POISSON-TYPE INPUT AND EXPONENTIAL-TYPE SERVICE TIMES** 282
State-dependent processes.   Little's formulas.   Balking and reneging.   M/M/s systems.   M/M/1/K systems.   M/M/s/K systems.

ANSWERS TO SUPPLEMENTARY PROBLEMS 297

INDEX 325

Chapter 1

Mathematical Programming

OPTIMIZATION PROBLEMS

In an *optimization problem* one seeks to maximize or minimize a specific quantity, called the *objective*, which depends on a finite number of input variables. These variables may be independent of one another, or they may be related through one or more *constraints*.

Example 1.1 The problem

$$\text{minimize:} \quad z = x_1^2 + x_2^2$$
$$\text{subject to:} \quad x_1 - x_2 = 3$$
$$x_2 \geq 2$$

is an optimization problem for the objective z. The input variables are x_1 and x_2, which are constrained in two ways: x_1 must exceed x_2 by 3, and also x_2 must be greater than or equal to 2. It is desired to find values for the input variables which minimize the sum of their squares, subject to the limitations imposed by the constraints.

A *mathematical program* is an optimization problem in which the objective and constraints are given as mathematical functions and functional relationships (as they are in Example 1.1). Mathematical programs treated in this book have the form

$$\text{optimize:} \quad z = f(x_1, x_2, \ldots, x_n)$$
$$\text{subject to:} \quad
\left.
\begin{array}{l}
g_1(x_1, x_2, \ldots, x_n) \\
g_2(x_1, x_2, \ldots, x_n) \\
\cdots\cdots\cdots\cdots \\
g_m(x_1, x_2, \ldots, x_n)
\end{array}
\right\}
\begin{array}{c}
\leq \\
= \\
\geq
\end{array}
\left\{
\begin{array}{l}
b_1 \\
b_2 \\
\cdots \\
b_m
\end{array}
\right. \qquad (1.1)$$

Each of the m constraint relationships in (1.1) involves one of the three signs $\leq, =, \geq$. *Unconstrained* mathematical programs are covered by the formalism (1.1) if each function g_i is chosen as zero and each constant b_i is chosen as zero.

LINEAR PROGRAMS

A mathematical program (1.1) is *linear* if $f(x_1, x_2, \ldots, x_n)$ and each $g_i(x_1, x_2, \ldots, x_n)$ $(i = 1, 2, \ldots, m)$ are linear in each of their arguments—that is, if

$$f(x_1, x_2, \ldots, x_n) = c_1 x_1 + c_2 x_2 + \cdots + c_n x_n \qquad (1.2)$$

and

$$g_i(x_1, x_2, \ldots, x_n) = a_{i1} x_1 + a_{i2} x_2 + \cdots + a_{in} x_n \qquad (1.3)$$

where c_j and a_{ij} $(i = 1, 2, \ldots, m; \quad j = 1, 2, \ldots, n)$ are known constants.

Any other mathematical program is *nonlinear*. Thus, Example 1.1 describes a nonlinear program, in view of the form of z.

1

INTEGER PROGRAMS

An *integer program* is a linear program with the additional restriction that the input variables be integers. It is not necessary that the coefficients in (1.2) and (1.3), and the constants in (1.1), also be integers, but this will very often be the case.

QUADRATIC PROGRAMS

A *quadratic program* is a mathematical program in which each constraint is linear—that is, each constraint function has the form (1.3)—but the objective is of the form

$$f(x_1, x_2, \ldots, x_n) = \sum_{i=1}^{n} \sum_{j=1}^{n} c_{ij} x_i x_j + \sum_{i=1}^{n} d_i x_i \tag{1.4}$$

where c_{ij} and d_i are known constants.

The program given in Example 1.1 is quadratic. Both constraints are linear, and the objective has the form (1.4), with $n = 2$ (two variables), $c_{11} = 1$, $c_{12} = c_{21} = 0$, $c_{22} = 1$, and $d_1 = d_2 = 0$.

PROBLEM FORMULATION

Optimization problems most often are stated verbally. The solution procedure is to model the problem with a mathematical program and then solve the program by the techniques described in Chapters 2 through 15. The following approach is recommended for transforming a word problem into a mathematical program:

STEP 1   Determine the quantity to be optimized and express it as a mathematical function. Doing so serves to define the input variables.

STEP 2   Identify all stipulated requirements, restrictions, and limitations, and express them mathematically. These requirements constitute the constraints.

STEP 3   Express any hidden conditions. Such conditions are not stipulated explicitly in the problem but are apparent from the physical situation being modeled. Generally they involve nonnegativity or integer requirements on the input variables.

SOLUTION CONVENTION

In any mathematical program, we seek *a* solution. If a number of equally optimal solutions exist, then any one will do. *There is no preference between equally optimal solutions if there is no preference stipulated in the constraints.*

Solved Problems

1.1   The Village Butcher Shop traditionally makes its meat loaf from a combination of lean ground beef and ground pork. The ground beef contains 80 percent meat and 20 percent fat, and costs the shop 80¢ per pound; the ground pork contains 68 percent meat and 32 percent fat, and costs 60¢ per pound. How much of each kind of meat should the shop use in each pound of meat loaf if it wants to minimize its cost and to keep the fat content of the meat loaf to no more than 25 percent?

The objective is to minimize the cost (in cents), z, of a pound of meat loaf, where

$z \equiv 80$ times the poundage of ground beef used plus 60 times the poundage of ground pork used

Defining

$x_1 \equiv$ poundage of ground beef used in each pound of meat loaf
$x_2 \equiv$ poundage of ground pork used in each pound of meat loaf

we express the objective as

$$\text{minimize:} \quad z = 80x_1 + 60x_2 \tag{1}$$

Each pound of meat loaf will contain $0.20\,x_1$ pound of fat contributed from the beef and $0.32\,x_2$ pound of fat contributed from the pork. The total fat content of a pound of meat loaf must be no greater than 0.25 lb. Therefore,

$$0.20\,x_1 + 0.32\,x_2 \leq 0.25 \tag{2}$$

The poundages of beef and pork used in each pound of meat loaf must sum to 1; hence,

$$x_1 + x_2 = 1 \tag{3}$$

Finally, the butcher shop may not use negative quantities of either meat, so that two hidden constraints are $x_1 \geq 0$ and $x_2 \geq 0$. Combining these conditions with (1), (2), and (3), we obtain

$$\text{minimize:} \quad z = 80x_1 + 60x_2$$
$$\text{subject to:} \quad 0.20\,x_1 + 0.32\,x_2 \leq 0.25 \tag{4}$$
$$x_1 + \quad x_2 = \quad 1$$
$$\text{with:} \quad \text{all variables nonnegative}$$

System (4) is a linear program. As there are only two variables, a graphical solution may be given.

1.2 Solve the linear program (4) of Problem 1.1 graphically.

See Fig. 1-1. The *feasible region*—the set of points (x_1, x_2) satisfying all the constraints, including the nonnegativity conditions—is the heavy line segment in the figure. To determine z^*, the minimal value of z, we arbitrarily choose values of z and plot the graphs of the associated objectives. By choosing $z = 70$ and then $z = 75$, we obtain the objectives

$$70 = 80x_1 + 60x_2 \qquad \text{and} \qquad 75 = 80x_1 + 60x_2$$

respectively. Their graphs are the dashed lines in Fig. 1-1. It is seen that z^* will be assumed at the upper endpoint of the feasible segment, which is the intersection of the two lines

$$0.20\,x_1 + 0.32\,x_2 = 0.25 \qquad \text{and} \qquad x_1 + x_2 = 1$$

Simultaneous solution of these equations gives $x_1^* = 7/12$, $x_2^* = 5/12$; hence,

$$z^* = 80(7/12) + 60(5/12) = 71.67 \, \cent$$

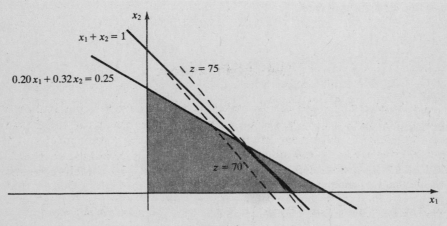

Fig. 1-1

1.3   A furniture maker has 6 units of wood and 28 h of free time, in which he will make decorative screens. Two models have sold well in the past, so he will restrict himself to those two. He estimates that model I requires 2 units of wood and 7 h of time, while model II requires 1 unit of wood and 8 h of time. The prices of the models are $120 and $80, respectively. How many screens of each model should the furniture maker assemble if he wishes to maximize his sales revenue?

The objective is to maximize revenue (in dollars), which we denote as z:

$z \equiv 120$ times the number of model I screens produced plus 80
        times the number of model II screens produced

Letting

$x_1 \equiv$ number of model I screens to be produced
$x_2 \equiv$ number of model II screens to be produced

we express the objective as

$$\text{maximize:} \quad z = 120x_1 + 80x_2 \tag{1}$$

The furniture maker is subject to a wood constraint. As each model I requires 2 units of wood, $2x_1$ units must be allocated to them; likewise, $1x_2$ units of wood must be allocated to the model II screens. Hence the wood constraint is

$$2x_1 + x_2 \le 6 \tag{2}$$

The furniture maker also has a time constraint. The model I screens will consume $7x_1$ hours and the model II screens $8x_2$ hours; and so

$$7x_1 + 8x_2 \le 28 \tag{3}$$

It is obvious that negative quantities of either screen cannot be produced, so two hidden constraints are $x_1 \ge 0$ and $x_2 \ge 0$. Furthermore, since there is no revenue derived from partially completed screens, another hidden condition is that x_1 and x_2 be integers. Combining these hidden conditions with (1), (2), and (3), we obtain the mathematical program

$$\text{maximize:} \quad z = 120x_1 + 80x_2$$
$$\text{subject to:} \quad 2x_1 + \ x_2 \le \ 6 \tag{4}$$
$$7x_1 + 8x_2 \le 28$$
$$\text{with:} \quad \text{all variables nonnegative and integral}$$

System (4) is an integer program. As there are only two variables, a graphical solution may be given.

1.4   Give a graphical solution of the integer program (4) of Problem 1.3.

See Fig. 1-2. The feasible region is the set of integer points (marked by crosses) within the shaded area. The dashed lines are the graphs of the objective function when z is arbitrarily given the values 240, 330, and 380. It is seen that the z-line through the point (3, 0) will furnish the desired maximum; thus, the furniture maker should assemble three model I screens and no model II screens, for a maximum revenue of

$$z^* = 120(3) + 80(0) = \$360$$

Observe that this optimal answer is *not* achieved by first solving the associated linear program (the same problem without the integer constraints) and then moving to the closest feasible integer point. In fact, the feasible region for the associated linear program is the shaded area of Fig. 1-2; so the optimal solution occurs at the circled corner point. But at the closest feasible integer point, (2, 1), the objective function has the value $z = 120(2) + 80(1) = \$320$ or \$40 less than the true optimum.

An alternate solution procedure for Problem 1.3 is given in Problem 7.8.

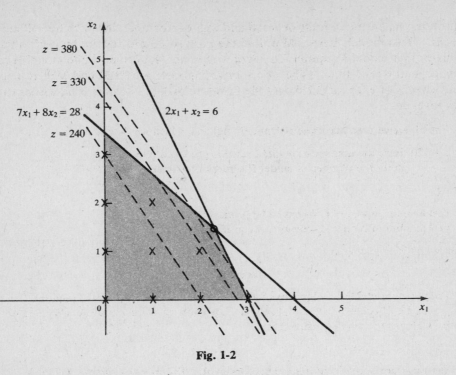

Fig. 1-2

1.5   Universal Mines Inc. operates three mines in West Virginia. The ore from each mine is separated into two grades before it is shipped; the daily production capacities of the mines, as well as their daily operating costs, are as follows:

	High-Grade Ore, tons/day	Low-Grade Ore, tons/day	Operating Cost, $1000/day
Mine I	4	4	20
Mine II	6	4	22
Mine III	1	6	18

Universal has committed itself to deliver 54 tons of high-grade ore and 65 tons of low-grade ore by the end of the week. It also has labor contracts that guarantee employees in each mine a full day's pay for each day or fraction of a day the mine is open. Determine the number of days each mine should be operated during the upcoming week if Universal Mines is to fulfill its commitment at minimum total cost.

Let x_1, x_2, and x_3, respectively, denote the numbers of days that mines I, II, and III will be operated during the upcoming week. Then the objective (measured in units of $1000) is

$$\text{minimize:}\quad z = 20x_1 + 22x_2 + 18x_3 \qquad\qquad (1)$$

The high-grade ore requirement is

$$4x_1 + 6x_2 + x_3 \geq 54 \qquad\qquad (2)$$

and the low-grade ore requirement is

$$4x_1 + 4x_2 + 6x_3 \geq 65 \qquad\qquad (3)$$

As no mine may operate a negative number of days, three hidden constraints are $x_1 \geq 0$, $x_2 \geq 0$, and $x_3 \geq 0$. Moreover, as no mine may operate more than 7 days in a week, three other hidden constraints are $x_1 \leq 7$, $x_2 \leq 7$, and $x_3 \leq 7$. Finally, in view of the labor contracts, Universal Mines has nothing to gain in operating a mine for part of a day; consequently, x_1, x_2, and x_3 are required to be integral. Combining the hidden conditions with (1), (2), and (3), we obtain the mathematical program

$$\text{minimize:} \quad z = 20x_1 + 22x_2 + 18x_3$$

$$\text{subject to:} \quad 4x_1 + 6x_2 + x_3 \geq 54$$

$$4x_1 + 4x_2 + 6x_3 \geq 65$$

$$x_1 \qquad \leq 7 \qquad\qquad (4)$$

$$x_2 \quad \leq 7$$

$$x_3 \leq 7$$

$$\text{with:} \quad \text{all variables nonnegative and integral}$$

System (4) is an integer program; its solution is determined in Problem 7.4.

1.6 A manufacturer is beginning the last week of production of four different models of wooden television consoles, labeled I, II, III, and IV, each of which must be assembled and then decorated. The models require 4, 5, 3, and 5 h, respectively, for assembling and 2, 1.5, 3, and 3 h, respectively, for decorating. The profits on the models are $7, $7, $6, and $9, respectively. The manufacturer has 30 000 h available for assembling these products (750 assemblers working 40 h/wk) and 20 000 h available for decorating (500 decorators working 40 h/wk). How many of each model should the manufacturer produce during this last week to maximize profit? Assume that all units made can be sold.

The objective is to maximize profit (in dollars), which we denote as z. Setting

$x_1 \equiv$ number of model I consoles to be produced in the week
$x_2 \equiv$ number of model II consoles to be produced in the week
$x_3 \equiv$ number of model III consoles to be produced in the week
$x_4 \equiv$ number of model IV consoles to be produced in the week

we can formulate the objective as

$$\text{maximize:} \quad z = 7x_1 + 7x_2 + 6x_3 + 9x_4 \qquad\qquad (1)$$

There are constraints on the total time available for assembling and the total time available for decorating. These are, respectively, modeled by

$$4x_1 + 5x_2 + 3x_3 + 5x_4 \leq 30\,000 \qquad\qquad (2)$$

$$2x_1 + 1.5x_2 + 3x_3 + 3x_4 \leq 20\,000 \qquad\qquad (3)$$

As negative quantities may not be produced, four hidden constraints are $x_i \geq 0$ ($i = 1, 2, 3, 4$). Additionally, since this is the last week of production, partially completed models at the week's end would remain unfinished and so would generate no profit. To avoid such possibilities, we require an integral value for each variable. Combining the hidden conditions with (1), (2), and (3), we obtain the mathematical program

$$\text{maximize:} \quad z = 7x_1 + 7x_2 + 6x_3 + 9x_4$$

$$\text{subject to:} \quad 4x_1 + 5x_2 + 3x_3 + 5x_4 \leq 30\,000$$

$$2x_1 + 1.5x_2 + 3x_3 + 3x_4 \leq 20\,000 \qquad\qquad (4)$$

$$\text{with:} \quad \text{all variables nonnegative and integral}$$

System (4) is an integer program; its solution is determined in Problem 6.4.

1.7 The Aztec Refining Company produces two types of unleaded gasoline, regular and premium, which it sells to its chain of service stations for $12 and $14 per barrel, respectively. Both types are blended from Aztec's inventory of refined domestic oil and refined foreign oil, and must meet the following specifications:

	Maximum Vapor Pressure	Minimum Octane Rating	Maximum Demand, bbl/wk	Minimum Deliveries, bbl/wk
Regular	23	88	100 000	50 000
Premium	23	93	20 000	5 000

The characteristics of the refined oils in inventory are as follows:

	Vapor Pressure	Octane Rating	Inventory, bbl	Cost, $/bbl
Domestic	25	87	40 000	8
Foreign	15	98	60 000	15

What quantities of the two oils should Aztec blend into the two gasolines in order to maximize weekly profit?

Set

$x_1 \equiv$ barrels of domestic blended into regular
$x_2 \equiv$ barrels of foreign blended into regular
$x_3 \equiv$ barrels of domestic blended into premium
$x_4 \equiv$ barrels of foreign blended into premium

An amount $x_1 + x_2$ of regular will be produced and generate a revenue of $12(x_1 + x_2)$; an amount $x_3 + x_4$ of premium will be produced and generate a revenue of $14(x_3 + x_4)$. An amount $x_1 + x_3$ of domestic will be used, at a cost of $8(x_1 + x_3)$; an amount $x_2 + x_4$ of foreign will be used, at a cost of $15(x_2 + x_4)$. The total profit, z, is revenue minus cost:

$$\text{maximize:} \quad z = 12(x_1 + x_2) + 14(x_3 + x_4) - 8(x_1 + x_3) - 15(x_2 + x_4)$$
$$= 4x_1 - 3x_2 + 6x_3 - x_4 \tag{1}$$

There are limitations imposed on the production by demand, availability of supplies, and specifications on the blends. From the demands,

$$x_1 + x_2 \leq 100\,000 \quad \text{(maximum demand for regular)} \tag{2}$$

$$x_3 + x_4 \leq 20\,000 \quad \text{(maximum demand for premium)} \tag{3}$$

$$x_1 + x_2 \geq 50\,000 \quad \text{(minimum regular required)} \tag{4}$$

$$x_3 + x_4 \geq 5\,000 \quad \text{(minimum premium required)} \tag{5}$$

From the availability,

$$x_1 + x_3 \leq 40\,000 \quad \text{(domestic)} \tag{6}$$

$$x_2 + x_4 \leq 60\,000 \quad \text{(foreign)} \tag{7}$$

The constituents of a blend contribute to the overall octane rating according to their percentages by weight; likewise for the vapor pressure. Thus, the octane rating of regular is

$$87\frac{x_1}{x_1 + x_2} + 98\frac{x_2}{x_1 + x_2}$$

and the requirement that this be at least 88 leads to

$$x_1 - 10x_2 \leq 0 \tag{8}$$

Similarly, we obtain:

$$6x_3 - 5x_4 \leq 0 \quad \text{(premium octane constraint)} \tag{9}$$

$$2x_1 - 8x_2 \le 0 \quad \text{(regular vapor-pressure constraint)} \tag{10}$$

$$2x_3 - 8x_4 \le 0 \quad \text{(premium vapor-pressure constraint)} \tag{11}$$

Combining (1) through (11) with the four (hidden) nonnegativity constraints on the four variables, we obtain the mathematical program

$$\text{maximize:} \quad z = 4x_1 - 3x_2 + 6x_3 - x_4$$

$$
\begin{aligned}
\text{subject to:} \quad x_1 + \; x_2 \qquad\qquad\;\; &\le 100\,000 \\
x_3 + \; x_4 &\le 20\,000 \\
x_1 \qquad + \; x_3 \qquad\;\; &\le 40\,000 \\
x_2 \qquad + \; x_4 &\le 60\,000 \\
x_1 - 10x_2 \qquad\qquad\;\; &\le \quad 0 \\
6x_3 - 5x_4 &\le \quad 0 \\
2x_1 - \; 8x_2 \qquad\qquad\;\; &\le \quad 0 \\
2x_3 - 8x_4 &\le \quad 0 \\
x_1 + \; x_2 \qquad\qquad\;\; &\ge 50\,000 \\
x_3 + \; x_4 &\ge \quad 5\,000
\end{aligned}
\tag{12}
$$

with: all variables nonnegative

System (12) is a linear program; its solution is determined in Problem 4.7.

1.8   A hiker plans to go on a camping trip. There are five items the hiker wishes to take with her, but together they exceed the 60-lb weight limit she feels she can carry. To assist herself in the selection process, she has assigned a value to each item in ascending order of importance:

Item	1	2	3	4	5
Weight, lb	52	23	35	15	7
Value	100	60	70	15	15

Which items should she take to maximize the total value without exceeding the weight restriction?

Letting x_i $(i = 1, 2, 3, 4, 5)$ designate the amount of item i to be taken, we can formulate the objective as

$$\text{maximize:} \quad z = 100x_1 + 60x_2 + 70x_3 + 15x_4 + 15x_5 \tag{1}$$

The weight limitation is

$$52x_1 + 23x_2 + 35x_3 + 15x_4 + 7x_5 \le 60 \tag{2}$$

Since an item either will or will not be taken, each variable must be either 1 or 0. Such conditions are enforced if we require each variable to be nonnegative, no greater than 1, and integral. Combining these constraints with (1) and (2), we obtain the mathematical program

$$\text{maximize:} \quad z = 100x_1 + 60x_2 + 70x_3 + 15x_4 + 15x_5$$

$$
\begin{aligned}
\text{subject to:} \quad 52x_1 + 23x_2 + 35x_3 + 15x_4 + 7x_5 &\le 60 \\
x_1 \qquad\qquad\qquad\qquad &\le 1 \\
x_2 \qquad\qquad\qquad &\le 1 \\
x_3 \qquad\qquad &\le 1 \\
x_4 \qquad &\le 1 \\
x_5 &\le 1
\end{aligned}
\tag{3}
$$

with: all variables nonnegative and integral

System (3) is an integer program; its solution is determined in Problem 6.7 and again in Problem 14.16.

1.9 A 24-hour supermarket has the following minimal requirements for cashiers:

Period	1	2	3	4	5	6
Time of day (24-h clock)	3–7	7–11	11–15	15–19	19–23	23–3
Minimum No.	7	20	14	20	10	5

Period 1 follows immediately after period 6. A cashier works eight consecutive hours, starting at the beginning of one of the six periods. Determine a daily employee worksheet which satisfies the requirements with the least number of personnel.

Setting x_i $(i = 1, 2, \ldots, 6)$ equal to the number of cashiers *beginning* work at the start of period i, we can model this problem by the mathematical program

$$\text{minimize:} \quad z = x_1 + x_2 + x_3 + x_4 + x_5 + x_6$$

$$\text{subject to:} \quad
\begin{aligned}
x_1 \phantom{{}+x_2{}} + x_6 &\geq 7 \\
x_1 + x_2 \phantom{{}+x_6} &\geq 20 \\
x_2 + x_3 \phantom{{}+x_6} &\geq 14 \\
x_3 + x_4 \phantom{{}+x_6} &\geq 20 \\
x_4 + x_5 \phantom{{}+x_6} &\geq 10 \\
x_5 + x_6 &\geq 5
\end{aligned}
\qquad (1)$$

$$\text{with:} \quad \text{all variables nonnegative and integral}$$

System (1) is an integer program; its solution is determined in Problem 6.3.

1.10 A cheese shop has 20 lb of a seasonal fruit mix and 60 lb of an expensive cheese with which it will make two cheese spreads, delux and regular, that are popular during Christmas week. Each pound of the delux spread consists of 0.2 lb of the fruit mix and 0.8 lb of the expensive cheese, while each pound of the regular spread consists of 0.2 lb of the fruit mix, 0.3 lb of the expensive cheese, and 0.5 lb of a filler cheese which is cheap and in plentiful supply. From past pricing policies, the shop has found that the demand for each spread depends on its price as follows:

$$D_1 = 190 - 25P_1 \qquad \text{and} \qquad D_2 = 250 - 50P_2$$

where D denotes demand (in pounds), P denotes price (in dollars per pound), and the subscripts 1 and 2 refer to the delux and regular spreads, respectively. How many pounds of each spread should the cheese shop prepare, and what prices should it establish, if it wishes to maximize income and be left with no inventory of either spread at the end of Christmas week?

Let x_1 pounds of delux spread and x_2 pounds of regular spread be made. If all product can be sold, the objective is to

$$\text{maximize:} \quad z = P_1 x_1 + P_2 x_2 \qquad (1)$$

Now, all product will indeed be sold (and none will be left over in inventory) if production does not exceed demand, i.e., if $x_1 \leq D_1$ and $x_2 \leq D_2$. This gives the constraints

$$x_1 + 25P_1 \leq 190 \qquad \text{and} \qquad x_2 + 50P_2 \leq 250 \qquad (2)$$

From the availability of fruit mix,

$$0.2x_1 + 0.2x_2 \leq 20 \tag{3}$$

and from the availability of expensive cheese,

$$0.8x_1 + 0.3x_2 \leq 60 \tag{4}$$

There is no constraint on the filler cheese, since the shop has as much as it needs. Finally, neither production nor price can be negative; so four hidden constraints are $x_1 \geq 0$, $x_2 \geq 0$, $P_1 \geq 0$, and $P_2 \geq 0$. Combining these conditions with (1) through (4), we obtain the mathematical program

$$\text{maximize:} \quad z = P_1 x_1 + P_2 x_2$$

$$
\begin{aligned}
\text{subject to:} \quad 0.2x_1 + 0.2x_2 &\leq 20 \\
0.8x_1 + 0.3x_2 &\leq 60 \\
x_1 \qquad\quad + 25P_1 &\leq 190 \\
x_2 \qquad\quad + 50P_2 &\leq 250
\end{aligned}
\tag{5}
$$

$$\text{with:} \quad \text{all variables nonnegative}$$

System (5) is a quadratic program in the variables x_1, x_2, P_1, and P_2. It can be simplified if we note that for any fixed positive x_1 and x_2 the objective function increases as either P_1 or P_2 increases. Thus, for a maximum, P_1 and P_2 must be such that the constraints (2) become equations, whereby P_1 and P_2 may be eliminated from the objective function. We then have a quadratic program in x_1 and x_2,

$$\text{maximize:} \quad z = (7.6 - 0.04x_1)x_1 + (5 - 0.02x_2)x_2$$

$$
\begin{aligned}
\text{subject to:} \quad 0.2x_1 + 0.2x_2 &\leq 20 \\
0.8x_1 + 0.3x_2 &\leq 60
\end{aligned}
\tag{6}
$$

$$\text{with:} \quad x_1 \text{ and } x_2 \text{ nonnegative}$$

which is easily solved graphically.

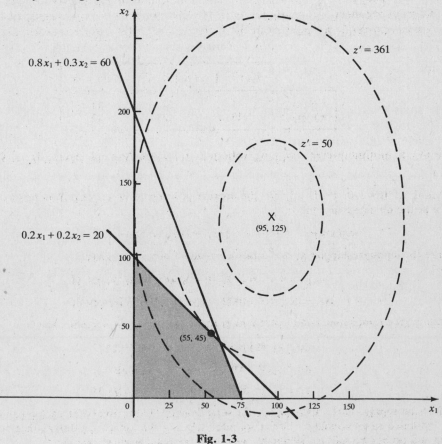

Fig. 1-3

1.11 Give a graphical solution of the quadratic program (6) of Problem 1.10.

For graphing purposes, it is convenient to complete the square in the objective function, yielding

$$\text{maximize:} \quad z = 673.5 - 0.04(x_1 - 95)^2 - 0.02(x_2 - 125)^2$$

which is equivalent to

$$\text{minimize:} \quad z' = 0.04(x_1 - 95)^2 + 0.02(x_2 - 125)^2 \tag{1}$$

Since the constraints are linear, the feasible region is bounded by straight lines; it appears shaded in Fig. 1.3. For any particular value of z', (1) defines an ellipse centered at (95, 125), and two such ellipses are shown in Fig. 1-3 as dashed curves. The minimum value of z' will correspond to that ellipse defined by (1) which is tangent to the line

$$0.2x_1 + 0.2x_2 = 20 \tag{2}$$

To find the point of tangency, we equate the slopes of the line and the ellipse,

$$\frac{dx_2}{dx_1} = -1 \qquad \text{and} \qquad \frac{dx_2}{dx_1} = -\frac{2(x_1 - 95)}{x_2 - 125}$$

obtained by implicit differentiation of (2) and (1), respectively; this gives

$$x_2 = 2x_1 - 65 \tag{3}$$

Solving (2) and (3) simultaneously gives the optimal solution to Problem 1.10:

$$x_1^* = 55 \text{ lb of delux spread} \qquad x_2^* = 45 \text{ lb of regular spread}$$

1.12 A plastics manufacturer has 1200 boxes of transparent wrap in stock at one factory and another 1000 boxes at its second factory. The manufacturer has orders for this product from three different retailers, in quantities of 1000, 700, and 500 boxes, respectively. The unit shipping costs (in cents per box) from the factories to the retailers are as follows:

	Retailer 1	Retailer 2	Retailer 3
Factory 1	14	13	11
Factory 2	13	13	12

Determine a minimum-cost shipping schedule for satisfying all demands from current inventory.

Writing x_{ij} ($i = 1, 2$; $j = 1, 2, 3$) for the number of boxes to be shipped from factory i to retailer j, we have as the objective (in cents):

$$\text{minimize:} \quad z = 14x_{11} + 13x_{12} + 11x_{13} + 13x_{21} + 13x_{22} + 12x_{23}$$

Since the amounts shipped from the factories cannot exceed supplies,

$$x_{11} + x_{12} + x_{13} \leq 1200 \quad \text{(shipments from factory 1)}$$

$$x_{21} + x_{22} + x_{23} \leq 1000 \quad \text{(shipments from factory 2)}$$

Additionally, the total amounts sent to the retailers must meet their demands; hence

$$x_{11} + x_{21} \geq 1000 \quad \text{(shipments to retailer 1)}$$

$$x_{12} + x_{22} \geq 700 \quad \text{(shipments to retailer 2)}$$

$$x_{13} + x_{23} \geq 500 \quad \text{(shipments to retailer 3)}$$

Since the total supply, $1200 + 1000$, equals the total demand, $1000 + 700 + 500$, each inequality constraint can be tightened to an equality. Doing so, and including the hidden conditions that no shipment be negative and no box be split for shipment, we obtain the mathematical program

$$\text{minimize:} \quad z = 14x_{11} + 13x_{12} + 11x_{13} + 13x_{21} + 13x_{22} + 12x_{23}$$

$$
\begin{aligned}
\text{subject to:} \quad & x_{11} + x_{12} + x_{13} && = 1200 \\
& x_{21} + x_{22} + x_{23} = 1000 \\
& x_{11} \qquad\quad + x_{21} \qquad\quad = 1000 \\
& \quad x_{12} \qquad\quad + x_{22} \quad = 700 \\
& \qquad x_{13} \qquad\quad + x_{23} = 500
\end{aligned}
\qquad (1)
$$

with: all variables nonnegative and integral

System (1) is an integer program; its solution is determined in Problem 7.3 and again in Problem 8.6.

1.13   A 400-meter medley relay involves four different swimmers, who successively swim 100 meters of the backstroke, breaststroke, butterfly, and freestyle.   A coach has six very fast swimmers whose expected times (in seconds) in the individual events are given in Table 1-1.

Table 1-1

	Event 1 (backstroke)	Event 2 (breaststroke)	Event 3 (butterfly)	Event 4 (freestyle)
Swimmer 1	65	73	63	57
Swimmer 2	67	70	65	58
Swimmer 3	68	72	69	55
Swimmer 4	67	75	70	59
Swimmer 5	71	69	75	57
Swimmer 6	69	71	66	59

How should the coach assign swimmers to the relay so as to minimize the sum of their times?

The objective is to minimize total time, which we denote as z.   Using double-subscripted variables x_{ij} $(i = 1, 2, \ldots, 6; \; j = 1, 2, 3, 4)$ to designate the number of times swimmer i will be assigned to event j, we can formulate the objective as

$$\text{minimize:} \quad z = 65x_{11} + 73x_{12} + 63x_{13} + 57x_{14} + 67x_{21} + \cdots + 66x_{63} + 59x_{64}$$

Since no swimmer can be assigned to more than one event,

$$
\begin{aligned}
x_{11} + x_{12} + x_{13} + x_{14} &\le 1 \\
x_{21} + x_{22} + x_{23} + x_{24} &\le 1 \\
&\cdots\cdots\cdots\cdots\cdots \\
x_{61} + x_{62} + x_{63} + x_{64} &\le 1
\end{aligned}
$$

Since each event must have one swimmer assigned to it, we also have

$$
\begin{aligned}
x_{11} + x_{21} + x_{31} + x_{41} + x_{51} + x_{61} &= 1 \\
&\cdots\cdots\cdots\cdots\cdots \\
x_{14} + x_{24} + x_{34} + x_{44} + x_{54} + x_{64} &= 1
\end{aligned}
$$

These 10 constraints, combined with the objective and the hidden conditions that each variable be nonnegative and integral, comprise an integer program.   Its solution is determined in Problem 9.4.

1.14   A major oil company wants to build a refinery that will be supplied from three port cities.   Port B is located 300 km east and 400 km north of Port A, while Port C is 400 km east and 100 km south of Port B.   Determine the location of the refinery so that the total amount of pipe required to connect the refinery to the ports is minimized.

The objective is tantamount to minimizing the sum of the distances between the refinery and the three ports.   As an aid to calculating this sum, we establish a coordinate system, Fig. 1-4, with Port A as the origin.   In this system, Port B has coordinates $(300, 400)$ and Port C has coordinates $(700, 300)$.

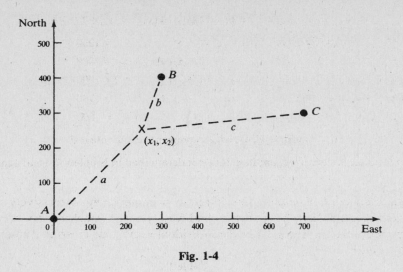

Fig. 1-4

With (x_1, x_2) designating the unknown coordinates of the refinery, the objective is

$$\text{minimize:} \quad z = \sqrt{x_1^2 + x_2^2} + \sqrt{(x_1 - 300)^2 + (x_2 - 400)^2} + \sqrt{(x_1 - 700)^2 + (x_2 - 300)^2} \quad (1)$$

There are no constraints on the coordinates of the refinery nor any hidden conditions; for example, a negative value of x_1 signifies only that the refinery should be placed west of Port A. Equation (1) is a nonlinear, unconstrained, mathematical program; its solution is determined in Problem 11.11. See also Problem 1.26.

1.15 An individual has \$4000 to invest and three opportunities available to him. Each opportunity requires deposits in \$1000 amounts; the investor may allocate all the money to just one opportunity or split the money between them. The expected returns are tabulated as follows.

	Dollars Invested				
	0	1000	2000	3000	4000
Return from Opportunity 1	0	2000	5000	6000	7000
Return from Opportunity 2	0	1000	3000	6000	7000
Return from Opportunity 3	0	1000	4000	5000	8000

How much money should be invested in each opportunity to obtain the greatest total return?

The objective is to maximize total return, denoted by z, which is the sum of the returns from each opportunity. All investments are restricted to be integral multiples of the unit \$1000. Letting $f_i(x)$ ($i = 1, 2, 3$) denote the return (in thousand-dollar units) from opportunity i when x units of money are invested in it, we can rewrite the returns table as Table 1-2.

Table 1-2

f \ x	0	1	2	3	4
$f_1(x)$	0	2	5	6	7
$f_2(x)$	0	1	3	6	7
$f_3(x)$	0	1	4	5	8

Defining x_i ($i = 1, 2, 3$) as the number of units of money invested in opportunity i, we can formulate the objective as

$$\text{maximize:} \quad z = f_1(x_1) + f_2(x_2) + f_3(x_3) \tag{1}$$

Since the individual has only 4 units of money to invest,

$$x_1 + x_2 + x_3 \le 4 \tag{2}$$

Augmenting (1) and (2) with the hidden conditions that x_1, x_2, and x_3 be nonnegative and integral, we obtain the mathematical program

$$\text{maximize:} \quad z = f_1(x_1) + f_2(x_2) + f_3(x_3)$$

$$\text{subject to:} \quad x_1 + x_2 + x_3 \le 4 \tag{3}$$

$$\text{with:} \quad \text{all variables nonnegative and integral}$$

Plotting $f_i(x)$ against x for each function gives a graph that is not a straight line. Therefore, system (3) is a nonlinear program; its solution is determined in Problem 14.1.

Supplementary Problems

Formulate but do not solve mathematical programs that model Problems 1.16 through 1.25.

1.16 Fay Klein had developed two types of handcrafted, adult games that she sells to department stores throughout the country. Although the demand for these games exceeds her capacity to produce them, Ms. Klein continues to work alone and to limit her workweek to 50 h. Game I takes 3.5 h to produce and brings a profit of \$28, while game II requires 4 h to complete and brings a profit of \$31. How many games of each type should Ms. Klein produce weekly if her objective is to maximize total profit?

1.17 A pet store has determined that each hamster should receive at least 70 units of protein, 100 units of carbohydrates, and 20 units of fat daily. If the store carries the six types of feed shown in Table 1-3, what blend of feeds satisfies the requirements at minimum cost to the store?

Table 1-3

Feed	Protein, units/oz	Carbohydrates, units/oz	Fat, units/oz	Cost, ¢/oz
A	20	50	4	2
B	30	30	9	3
C	40	20	11	5
D	40	25	10	6
E	45	50	9	8
F	30	20	10	8

1.18 A local manufacturing firm produces four different metal products, each of which must be machined, polished, and assembled. The specific time requirements (in hours) for each product are as follows.

	Machining, h	Polishing, h	Assembling, h
Product I	3	1	2
Product II	2	1	1
Product III	2	2	2
Product IV	4	3	1

The firm has available to it on a weekly basis 480 h of machine time, 400 h of polishing time, and 400 h of assembly time. The unit profits on the products are $6, $4, $6, and $8, respectively. The firm has a contract with a distributor to provide 50 units of product I and 100 units of any combination of products II and III each week. Through other customers, the firm can sell each week as many units of products I, II, and III as it can produce, but only a maximum of 25 units of product IV. How many units of each product should the firm manufacture each week to meet all contractual obligations and maximize its total profit? Assume that any unfinished pieces can be completed the following week.

1.19 A caterer must prepare from five fruit drinks in stock 500 gal of a punch containing at least 20 percent orange juice, 10 percent grapefruit juice, and 5 percent cranberry juice. If inventory data are as shown below, how much of each fruit drink should the caterer use to obtain the required composition at minimum total cost?

	Orange Juice, %	Grapefruit Juice, %	Cranberry Juice, %	Supply, gal	Cost, $/gal
Drink A	40	40	0	200	1.50
Drink B	5	10	20	400	0.75
Drink C	100	0	0	100	2.00
Drink D	0	100	0	50	1.75
Drink E	0	0	0	800	0.25

1.20 A town has budgeted $250 000 for the development of new rubbish disposal areas. Seven sites are available, whose projected capacities and development costs are given below. Which sites should the town develop?

Site	A	B	C	D	E	F	G
Capacity, tons/wk	20	17	15	15	10	8	5
Cost, $1000	145	92	70	70	84	14	47

1.21 A semiconductor corporation produces a particular solid-state module that it supplies to four different television manufacturers. The module can be produced at each of the corporation's three plants, although the costs vary because of differing production efficiencies at the plants. Specifically, it costs $1.10 to produce a module at plant A, $0.95 at plant B, and $1.03 at plant C. Monthly production capacities of the plants are 7500, 10 000, and 8100 modules, respectively. Sales forecasts project monthly demand at 4200, 8300, 6300, and 2700 modules for television manufacturers I, II, III, and IV, respectively. If the cost (in dollars) for shipping a module from a factory to a manufacturer is as shown below, find a production schedule that will meet all needs at minimum total cost.

	I	II	III	IV
A	0.11	0.13	0.09	0.19
B	0.12	0.16	0.10	0.14
C	0.14	0.13	0.12	0.15

1.22 The manager of a supermarket meat department finds she has 200 lb of round steak, 800 lb of chuck steak, and 150 lb of pork in stock on Saturday morning, which she will use to make hamburger meat, picnic patties, and meat loaf. The demand for each of these items always exceeds the supermarket's supply. Hamburger meat must be at least 20 percent ground round and 50 percent ground chuck (by weight); picnic patties must be at least 20 percent ground pork and 50 percent ground chuck; and meat loaf must be at least 10 percent ground round, 30 percent ground pork, and 40 percent ground chuck. The remainder of each product is an inexpensive nonmeat filler which the store has in unlimited supply. How many pounds of each product should be made if the manager desires to minimize the amount of meat that must be stored in the supermarket over Sunday?

1.23 A legal firm has accepted five new cases, each of which can be handled adequately by any one of its five junior partners. Due to differences in experience and expertise, however, the junior partners would spend varying amounts of time on the cases. A senior partner has estimated the time requirements (in hours) as shown below:

	Case 1	Case 2	Case 3	Case 4	Case 5
Lawyer 1	145	122	130	95	115
Lawyer 2	80	63	85	48	78
Lawyer 3	121	107	93	69	95
Lawyer 4	118	83	116	80	105
Lawyer 5	97	75	120	80	111

Determine an optimal assignment of cases to lawyers such that each junior partner receives a different case and the total hours expended by the firm is minimized.

1.24 Recreational Motors manufactures golf carts and snowmobiles at its three plants. Plant A produces 40 golf carts and 35 snowmobiles daily; plant B produces 65 golf carts daily, but no snowmobiles; plant C produces 53 snowmobiles daily, but no golf carts. The costs of operating plants A, B, and C are respectively $210 000, $190 000, and $182 000 per day. How many days (including Sundays and holidays) should each plant operate during September to fulfill a production schedule of 1500 golf carts and 1100 snowmobiles at minimum cost? Assume that labor contracts require that once a plant is opened, workers must be paid for the entire day.

1.25 The Futura Company produces two types of farm fertilizers, Futura Regular and Futura's Best. Futura Regular is composed of 25% active ingredients and 75% inert ingredients, while Futura's Best contains 40% active ingredients and 60% inert ingredients. Warehouse facilities limit inventories to 500 tons of active ingredients and 1200 tons of inert ingredients, and they are completely replenished once a week.

Futura Regular is similar to other fertilizers on the market and is competitively priced at $250 per ton. At this price, the company has had no difficulty in selling all the Futura Regular it produces. Futura's Best, however, has no competition, and so there are no constraints on its price. Of course, demand does depend on price, and through past experience the company has determined that price P (in dollars) and demand D (in tons) are related by $P = 600 - D$. How many tons of each type of fertilizer should Futura produce weekly in order to maximize revenue?

1.26 *Explain why the following constitutes an analog solution to Problem 1.14.* Imagine that Fig. 1-4 represents the top of a tall table. Small holes are bored through the tabletop at points A, B, and C. The three ends of three lengths of string are joined in a knot, which lies on the tabletop; the three free ends are run through the holes, and, underneath the tabletop, three equal weights are hung from them. Then, assuming negligible friction, the equilibrium position of the knot gives the optimal location of the refinery.

Chapter 2

Linear Programming: Standard Form

A method for solving linear programs involving many variables is described in Chapter 4. To initialize the method, one must transform all inequality constraints into equalities and must know one feasible, nonnegative solution.

NONNEGATIVITY CONDITIONS

Any variable not already constrained to be nonnegative is replaced by the difference of two new variables which are so constrained. (See Problem 2.6.)

Linear constraints (Chapter 1) are of the form:

$$\sum_{j=1}^{n} a_{ij}x_j \sim b_i \tag{2.1}$$

where $\sim$ stands for one of the relations $\leq$, $\geq$, $=$ (not necessarily the same one for each i). The constants b_i may always be assumed nonnegative.

Example 2.1 The constraint $2x_1 - 3x_2 + 4x_3 \leq -5$ is multiplied by -1 to obtain $-2x_1 + 3x_2 - 4x_3 \geq 5$, which has a nonnegative right-hand side.

SLACK VARIABLES AND SURPLUS VARIABLES

A linear constraint of the form $\sum a_{ij}x_j \leq b_i$ can be converted into an equality by adding a new, nonnegative variable to the left-hand side of the inequality. Such a variable is numerically equal to the difference between the right- and left-hand sides of the inequality and is known as a *slack variable*. It represents the waste involved in that phase of the system modeled by the constraint.

Example 2.2 The first constraint in Problem 1.6 is

$$4x_1 + 5x_2 + 3x_3 + 5x_4 \leq 30\,000$$

The left-hand side of this inequality models the total number of hours used to assemble all television consoles, while the right-hand side is the total number of hours available. This inequality is transformed into the equation

$$4x_1 + 5x_2 + 3x_3 + 5x_4 + x_5 = 30\,000$$

by adding the slack variable x_5 to the left-hand side of the inequality. Here x_5 represents the number of assembly hours available to the manufacturer but not used.

A linear constraint of the form $\sum a_{ij}x_j \geq b_i$ can be converted into an equality by subtracting a new, nonnegative variable from the left-hand side of the inequality. Such a variable is numerically equal to the difference between the left- and right-hand sides of the inequality and is known as a *surplus variable*. It represents excess input into that phase of the system modeled by the constraint.

Example 2.3 The first constraint in Problem 1.5 is

$$4x_1 + 6x_2 + x_3 \geq 54$$

The left-hand side of this inequality represents the combined output of high-grade ore from three mines, while the right-hand side is the minimum tonnage of such ore required to meet contractual obligations. This inequality is transformed into the equation

$$4x_1 + 6x_2 + x_3 - x_4 = 54$$

by subtracting the surplus variable x_4 from the left-hand side of the inequality. Here x_4 represents the amount of high-grade ore mined over and above that needed to fulfill the contract.

GENERATING AN INITIAL FEASIBLE SOLUTION

After all linear constraints (with nonnegative right-hand sides) have been transformed into equalities by introducing slack and surplus variables where necessary, add a new variable, called an *artificial variable*, to the left-hand side of each constraint equation that does not contain a slack variable. Each constraint equation will then contain either one slack variable or one artificial variable. A nonnegative initial solution to this new set of constraints is obtained by setting each slack variable and each artificial variable equal to the right-hand side of the equation in which it appears and setting all other variables, including the surplus variables, equal to zero.

Example 2.4 The set of constraints

$$x_1 + 2x_2 \leq 3$$
$$4x_1 + 5x_2 \geq 6$$
$$7x_1 + 8x_2 = 15$$

is transformed into a system of equations by adding a slack variable, x_3, to the left-hand side of the first constraint and subtracting a surplus variable, x_4, from the left-hand side of the second constraint. The new system is

$$
\begin{aligned}
x_1 + 2x_2 + x_3 &= 3 \\
4x_1 + 5x_2 \quad - x_4 &= 6 \\
7x_1 + 8x_2 &= 15
\end{aligned}
\tag{2.2}
$$

If now artificial variables x_5 and x_6 are respectively added to the left-hand sides of the last two constraints in system (2.2), the constraints without a slack variable, the result is

$$
\begin{aligned}
x_1 + 2x_2 + x_3 &= 3 \\
4x_1 + 5x_2 \quad - x_4 + x_5 &= 6 \\
7x_1 + 8x_2 \quad\quad + x_6 &= 15
\end{aligned}
$$

A *nonnegative* solution to this last system is $x_3 = 3$, $x_5 = 6$, $x_6 = 15$, and $x_1 = x_2 = x_4 = 0$. (Notice, however, that $x_1 = 0$, $x_2 = 0$ is *not* a solution to the original set of constraints.)

Occasionally, an initial solution can be generated easily without a full complement of slack and artificial variables. An example is Problem 2.5.

PENALTY COSTS

The introduction of slack and surplus variables alters neither the nature of the constraints nor the objective. Accordingly, such variables are incorporated into the objective function with zero coefficients. Artificial variables, however, do change the nature of the constraints. Since they are added to only one side of an equality, the new system is equivalent to the old system of constraints if and only if the artificial variables are zero. To guarantee such assignments in the optimal solution (in contrast to the initial solution), artificial variables are incorporated into the objective function with very large positive coefficients in a minimization program or very large negative coefficients in a maximization program.   These coefficients, denoted by either M or $-M$, where M is understood to be a large positive number, represent the (severe) penalty incurred in making a unit assignment to the artificial variables.

In hand calculations, penalty costs can be left as $\pm M$.   In computer calculations, M must be assigned a numerical value, usually a number three or four times larger in magnitude than any other number in the program.

STANDARD FORM

A linear program is in *standard form* if the constraints are all modeled as equalities and if one feasible solution is known.   In matrix notation, standard form is

$$\text{optimize:} \quad z = \mathbf{C}^T \mathbf{X}$$

$$\text{subject to:} \quad \mathbf{AX} = \mathbf{B} \tag{2.3}$$

$$\text{with:} \quad \mathbf{X} \geq 0$$

where $\mathbf{X}$ is the column vector of unknowns, including all slack, surplus, and artificial variables; $\mathbf{C}^T$ is the row vector of the corresponding costs; $\mathbf{A}$ is the coefficient matrix of the constraint equations; and $\mathbf{B}$ is the column vector of the right-hand sides of the constraint equations.   [*Note*:   In the remainder of this book, vectors shall normally be represented as one-columned matrices, and we shall simply say "vector" instead of "column vector."   Superscript T designates transposition.]   If $\mathbf{X}_0$ denotes the vector of slack and artificial variables only, then the initial feasible solution is given by $\mathbf{X}_0 = \mathbf{B}$,   where it is understood that all variables in $\mathbf{X}$ not included in $\mathbf{X}_0$ are assigned zero values.

Solved Problems

2.1   Put the following program in standard matrix form:

$$\text{maximize:} \quad z = x_1 + x_2$$

$$\text{subject to:} \quad x_1 + 5x_2 \leq 5$$

$$2x_1 + x_2 \leq 4$$

$$\text{with:} \quad x_1 \text{ and } x_2 \text{ nonnegative}$$

Adding slack variables x_3 and x_4, respectively, to the left-hand sides of the constraints, and including these new variables with zero cost coefficients in the objective, we have

$$\text{maximize:} \quad z = x_1 + x_2 + 0x_3 + 0x_4$$

$$\text{subject to:} \quad x_1 + 5x_2 + x_3 \qquad = 5 \tag{1}$$

$$2x_1 + x_2 \qquad + x_4 = 4$$

$$\text{with:} \quad \text{all variables nonnegative}$$

Since each constraint equation contains a slack variable, no artificial variables are required; an initial feasible solution is $x_3 = 5$, $x_4 = 4$, $x_1 = x_2 = 0$.   System (1) is in the standard form (2.3) if we define

$$\mathbf{X} \equiv [x_1, x_2, x_3, x_4]^T \qquad \mathbf{C} \equiv [1, 1, 0, 0]^T$$

$$\mathbf{A} \equiv \begin{bmatrix} 1 & 5 & 1 & 0 \\ 2 & 1 & 0 & 1 \end{bmatrix} \qquad \mathbf{B} \equiv \begin{bmatrix} 5 \\ 4 \end{bmatrix} \qquad \mathbf{X}_0 \equiv \begin{bmatrix} x_3 \\ x_4 \end{bmatrix}$$

2.2 Put the following program in standard form:

$$\text{maximize:} \quad z = 80x_1 + 60x_2$$

$$\text{subject to:} \quad 0.20x_1 + 0.32x_2 \le 0.25$$

$$x_1 + \quad x_2 = 1$$

$$\text{with:} \quad x_1 \text{ and } x_2 \text{ nonnegative}$$

To convert the first constraint into an equality, add a slack variable x_3 to the left-hand side. Since the second constraint, an equation, does not contain a slack variable, add an artificial variable x_4 to its left-hand side. Both new variables are included in the objective function, the slack variable with a zero cost coefficient and the artificial variable with a very large negative cost coefficient, yielding the program

$$\text{maximize:} \quad z = 80x_1 + 60x_2 + 0x_3 - Mx_4$$

$$\text{subject to:} \quad 0.20x_1 + 0.32x_2 + x_3 \quad\;\; = 0.25$$

$$x_1 + \quad x_2 \quad + x_4 = 1$$

$$\text{with:} \quad \text{all variables nonnegative}$$

This program is in standard form, with an initial feasible solution $x_3 = 0.25$, $x_4 = 1$, $x_1 = x_2 = 0$.

2.3 Redo Problem 2.2 if the objective is to be minimized.

The only change is in the cost coefficient associated with the artificial variable; it becomes $+M$ instead of $-M$.

2.4 Put the following program in standard form:

$$\text{maximize:} \quad z = 5x_1 + 2x_2$$

$$\text{subject to:} \quad 6x_1 + \quad x_2 \ge 6$$

$$4x_1 + 3x_2 \ge 12$$

$$x_1 + 2x_2 \ge 4$$

$$\text{with:} \quad x_1 \text{ and } x_2 \text{ nonnegative}$$

Subtracting surplus variables x_3, x_4, and x_5, respectively, from the left-hand sides of the constraints, and including each new variable with a zero cost coefficient in the objective, we obtain

$$\text{maximize:} \quad z = 5x_1 + 2x_2 + 0x_3 + 0x_4 + 0x_5$$

$$\text{subject to:} \quad 6x_1 + \quad x_2 - x_3 \quad\quad\;\; = 6$$

$$4x_1 + 3x_2 \quad\;\; - x_4 \quad\;\; = 12$$

$$x_1 + 2x_2 \quad\quad\quad - x_5 = 4$$

$$\text{with:} \quad \text{all variables nonnegative}$$

Since no constraint equation contains a slack variable, we next add artificial variables x_6, x_7, and x_8, respectively, to the left-hand sides of the equations. We also include these variables with very large negative cost coefficients in the objective. The program becomes

$$\text{maximize:} \quad z = 5x_1 + 2x_2 + 0x_3 + 0x_4 + 0x_5 - Mx_6 - Mx_7 - Mx_8$$

$$\text{subject to:} \quad 6x_1 + \quad x_2 - x_3 \quad\quad\;\; + x_6 \quad\quad\;\; = 6$$

$$4x_1 + 3x_2 \quad\;\; - x_4 \quad\quad\;\; + x_7 \quad\;\; = 12$$

$$x_1 + 2x_2 \quad\quad\quad - x_5 \quad\quad\;\; + x_8 = 4$$

$$\text{with:} \quad \text{all variables nonnegative}$$

This program is in standard form, with an initial feasible solution $x_6 = 6$, $x_7 = 12$, $x_8 = 4$, $x_1 = x_2 = x_3 = x_4 = x_5 = 0$.

2.5   Put the following program in standard matrix form:

$$\text{minimize:} \quad z = x_1 + 2x_2 + 3x_3$$

$$\text{subject to:} \quad 3x_1 \quad\ \ + 4x_3 \leq 5$$

$$5x_1 + x_2 + 6x_3 = 7$$

$$8x_1 \quad\ \ + 9x_3 \geq 2$$

with: all variables nonnegative

Adding a slack variable x_4 to the left-hand side of the first constraint, subtracting a surplus variable x_5 from the left-hand side of the third constraint, and then adding an artificial variable x_6 only to the left-hand side of the third constraint, we obtain the program

$$\text{minimize:} \quad z = x_1 + 2x_2 + 3x_3 + 0x_4 + 0x_5 + Mx_6$$

$$\text{subject to:} \quad 3x_1 \quad\ \ + 4x_3 + x_4 \qquad\quad = 5$$

$$5x_1 + x_2 + 6x_3 \qquad\qquad\quad = 7$$

$$8x_1 \quad\ \ + 9x_3 \qquad - x_5 + x_6 = 2$$

with: all variables nonnegative

This program is in standard form, with an initial feasible solution $x_4 = 5$, $x_2 = 7$, $x_6 = 2$, $x_1 = x_3 = x_5 = 0$. It has the form of system (2.3) if we define

$$\mathbf{X} \equiv [x_1, x_2, x_3, x_4, x_5, x_6]^T \qquad \mathbf{C} \equiv [1, 2, 3, 0, 0, M]^T$$

$$\mathbf{A} \equiv \begin{bmatrix} 3 & 0 & 4 & 1 & 0 & 0 \\ 5 & 1 & 6 & 0 & 0 & 0 \\ 8 & 0 & 9 & 0 & -1 & 1 \end{bmatrix} \qquad \mathbf{B} \equiv \begin{bmatrix} 5 \\ 7 \\ 2 \end{bmatrix} \qquad \mathbf{X}_0 \equiv \begin{bmatrix} x_4 \\ x_2 \\ x_6 \end{bmatrix}$$

In this case, x_2 can be used to generate the initial solution rather than adding an artificial variable to the second constraint to achieve the same result.   In general, whenever a variable appears in one and only one constraint equation, and there with a positive coefficient, that variable can be used to generate part of the initial solution by first dividing the constraint equation by the positive coefficient and then setting the variable equal to the right-hand side of the equation; an artificial variable need not be added to the equation.

2.6   Put the following program in standard form:

$$\text{minimize:} \quad z = 25x_1 + 30x_2$$

$$\text{subject to:} \quad 4x_1 + 7x_2 \geq \ \ 1$$

$$8x_1 + 5x_2 \geq \ \ 3$$

$$6x_1 + 9x_2 \geq -2$$

Since both x_1 and x_2 are unrestricted, we set $x_1 = x_3 - x_4$ and $x_2 = x_5 - x_6$, where all four new variables are required to be nonnegative.   Substituting these quantities into the given program and then multiplying the last constraint by -1 to force a nonnegative right-hand side, we obtain the equivalent program:

$$\text{minimize:} \quad z = 25x_3 - 25x_4 + 30x_5 - 30x_6$$

$$\text{subject to:} \quad 4x_3 - 4x_4 + 7x_5 - 7x_6 \geq 1$$

$$8x_3 - 8x_4 + 5x_5 - 5x_6 \geq 3$$

$$-6x_3 + 6x_4 - 9x_5 + 9x_6 \leq 2$$

with: all variables nonnegative

This program is converted into standard form by subtracting surplus variables x_7 and x_8, respectively, from the left-hand sides of the first two constraints; adding a slack variable x_9 to the left-hand side of the third constraint; and then adding artificial variables x_{10} and x_{11}, respectively, to the left-hand sides of the first two constraints.   Doing so, we obtain minimize: $z = 25x_3 - 25x_4 + 30x_5 - 30x_6 + 0x_7 + 0x_8 + 0x_9 + Mx_{10} + Mx_{11}$

subject to: $4x_3 - 4x_4 + 7x_5 - 7x_6 - x_7 \qquad + x_{10} \qquad = 1$

$\qquad\qquad 8x_3 - 8x_4 + 5x_5 - 5x_6 \qquad - x_8 \qquad\quad + x_{11} = 3$

$\qquad\qquad -6x_3 + 6x_4 - 9x_5 + 9x_6 \qquad\qquad + x_9 \qquad\qquad = 2$

with: all variables nonnegative

An initial solution to this program in standard form is

$$x_{10} = 1 \qquad x_{11} = 3 \qquad x_9 = 2 \qquad x_3 = x_4 = x_5 = x_6 = x_7 = x_8 = 0$$

Supplementary Problems

Put each of the following programs in matrix standard form.

2.7

minimize: $z = 2x_1 - x_2 + 4x_3$

subject to: $5x_1 + 2x_2 - 3x_3 \geq -7$

$\qquad\qquad 2x_1 - 2x_2 + x_3 \leq 8$

with: x_1 nonnegative

2.8

maximize: $z = 10x_1 + 11x_2$

subject to: $x_1 + 2x_2 \leq 150$

$\qquad\qquad 3x_1 + 4x_2 \leq 200$

$\qquad\qquad 6x_1 + x_2 \leq 175$

with: x_1 and x_2 nonnegative

2.9 Problem 2.8 with the three constraint inequalities reversed.

2.10

minimize: $z = 3x_1 + 2x_2 + 4x_3 + 6x_4$

subject to: $x_1 + 2x_2 + x_3 + x_4 \geq 1000$

$\qquad\qquad 2x_1 + x_2 + 3x_3 + 7x_4 \geq 1500$

with: all variables nonnegative

2.11

minimize: $z = 6x_1 + 3x_2 + 4x_3$

subject to: $x_1 + 6x_2 + x_3 = 10$

$\qquad\qquad 2x_1 + 3x_2 + x_3 = 15$

with: all variables nonnegative

2.12

maximize: $z = 7x_1 + 2x_2 + 3x_3 + x_4$

subject to: $2x_1 + 7x_2 \qquad\qquad = 7$

$\qquad\qquad 5x_1 + 8x_2 \qquad + 2x_4 = 10$

$\qquad\qquad x_1 \qquad + x_3 \qquad = 11$

with: x_1, x_2, and x_3 nonnegative

2.13

$$\text{minimize:} \quad z = 10x_1 + 2x_2 - x_3$$

$$\text{subject to:} \quad x_1 + x_2 \qquad \leq 50$$

$$x_1 + x_2 \qquad \geq 10$$

$$x_2 + x_3 \leq 30$$

$$x_2 + x_3 \geq 7$$

$$x_1 + x_2 + x_3 = 60$$

$$\text{with:} \quad \text{all variables nonnegative}$$

Chapter 3

Linear Programming: Theory of Solutions

LINEAR DEPENDENCE AND INDEPENDENCE

A set of m-dimensional vectors, $\{\mathbf{P}_1, \mathbf{P}_2, \ldots, \mathbf{P}_n\}$, is *linearly dependent* if there exist constants $\alpha_1, \alpha_2, \ldots, \alpha_n$, not all zero, such that

$$\alpha_1 \mathbf{P}_1 + \alpha_2 \mathbf{P}_2 + \cdots + \alpha_n \mathbf{P}_n = \mathbf{0} \qquad (3.1)$$

Example 3.1 The set of 5-dimensional vectors

$$\{[1, 2, 0, 0, 0]^T, [1, 0, 0, 0, 0]^T, [0, 0, 1, 1, 0]^T, [0, 1, 0, 0, 0]^T\}$$

is linearly dependent, since

$$-1\begin{bmatrix}1\\2\\0\\0\\0\end{bmatrix} + 1\begin{bmatrix}1\\0\\0\\0\\0\end{bmatrix} + 0\begin{bmatrix}0\\0\\1\\1\\0\end{bmatrix} + 2\begin{bmatrix}0\\1\\0\\0\\0\end{bmatrix} = \begin{bmatrix}0\\0\\0\\0\\0\end{bmatrix}$$

Theorem 3.1: Every set of $m + 1$ or more m-dimensional vectors is linearly dependent.

A set of m-dimensional vectors, $\{\mathbf{P}_1, \mathbf{P}_2, \ldots, \mathbf{P}_n\}$, is *linearly independent* if the only constants for which (3.1) holds are $\alpha_1 = \alpha_2 = \cdots = \alpha_n = 0$. (See Problems 3.1 and 3.2.)

CONVEX COMBINATIONS

An m-dimensional vector $\mathbf{P}$ is a *convex combination* of the m-dimensional vectors $\mathbf{P}_1, \mathbf{P}_2, \ldots, \mathbf{P}_n$ if there exist nonnegative constants $\beta_1, \beta_2, \ldots, \beta_n$ whose sum is 1, such that

$$\mathbf{P} = \beta_1 \mathbf{P}_1 + \beta_2 \mathbf{P}_2 + \cdots + \beta_n \mathbf{P}_n \qquad (3.2)$$

Example 3.2 The 2-dimensional vector $[5/3, 5/6]^T$ is a convex combination of the vectors $[1, 1]^T$, $[3, 0]^T$, and $[1, 2]^T$ because

$$\begin{bmatrix}5/3\\5/6\end{bmatrix} = \tfrac{1}{2}\begin{bmatrix}1\\1\end{bmatrix} + \tfrac{1}{3}\begin{bmatrix}3\\0\end{bmatrix} + \tfrac{1}{6}\begin{bmatrix}1\\2\end{bmatrix}$$

Given two m-dimensional vectors, $\mathbf{P}_1$ and $\mathbf{P}_2$, we call the set of all convex combinations of $\mathbf{P}_1$ and $\mathbf{P}_2$ the *line segment* between the two vectors. The geometrical significance of this term is apparent in the case $m = 3$.

CONVEX SETS

A set of m-dimensional vectors is *convex* if whenever two vectors belong to the set then so too does the line segment between the vectors.

Example 3.3 The disk shaded in Fig. 3-1(a) is a convex set since the line segment between any two of its points (2-dimensional vectors) is wholly within the disk. Figure 3-1(b) is not convex; although R and S belong

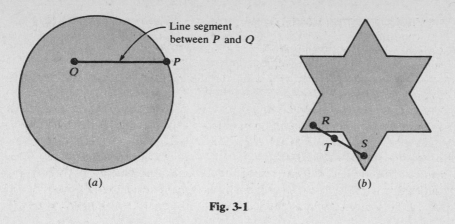

Fig. 3-1

to the shaded set, there exist points, such as T, belonging to the line segment between R and S which are not part of the star.

A vector **P** is an *extreme point* of a convex set if it cannot be expressed as a convex combination of two other vectors in the set; that is, an extreme point does not lie on the line segment between any other two vectors in the set.

Example 3.4   Any point on the circumference of the disk in Fig. 3-1(a) is an extreme point of the disk.

Theorem 3.2:   Any vector in a closed and bounded convex set with a finite number of extreme points can be expressed as a convex combination of the extreme points.

Theorem 3.3:   The solution space of a set of simultaneous linear equations is a convex set having a finite number of extreme points.

EXTREME-POINT SOLUTIONS

Let $\mathscr{S}$ designate the set of all feasible solutions to the linear program in standard form, (2.3); that is, $\mathscr{S}$ is the set of all vectors **X** that satisfy $\mathbf{AX} = \mathbf{B}$ and $\mathbf{X} \geq \mathbf{0}$.   From Theorem 3.3 and from the fact that convex sets intersect in convex sets (Problem 3.11), it follows that $\mathscr{S}$ is a convex set having a finite number of extreme points.

Remark 1:   The objective function attains its optimum (either maximum or minimum) at an extreme point of $\mathscr{S}$, provided an optimum exists.   (See Problem 3.12.)

Remark 2:   If **A** has order $m \times n$ (m rows and n columns), with $m \leq n$, then extreme points of $\mathscr{S}$ have at least $n - m$ zero components.   (See Problem 3.13.)

BASIC FEASIBLE SOLUTIONS

Denote the columns of the $m \times n$ coefficient matrix **A** in system (2.3) by $\mathbf{A}_1, \mathbf{A}_2, \ldots, \mathbf{A}_n$, respectively.   Then the matrix constraint equation $\mathbf{AX} = \mathbf{B}$ can be rewritten in the vector form

$$x_1\mathbf{A}_1 + x_2\mathbf{A}_2 + \cdots + x_n\mathbf{A}_n = \mathbf{B} \qquad (3.3)$$

We emphasize that the **A**-vectors and **B** are known m-dimensional vectors; we wish to find nonnegative solutions for the variables $x_1, x_2, \ldots, x_n$.   We shall suppose that $m \leq n$ and that rank $\mathbf{A} = m$, which means that at least one collection of m **A**-vectors is linearly independent.

A *basic feasible solution* to (3.3) is obtained by setting $n - m$ of the x-variables equal to zero and finding a nonnegative solution for the remaining x-variables, provided the m **A**-vectors corresponding to the x-variables not set equal to zero are linearly independent.   The x-variables not initially set equal to zero are called *basic variables*.   If one or more of the basic variables turns out to be zero, the basic feasible solution is *degenerate*; if all the basic variables are positive, the basic feasible solution is *nondegenerate*.   (See Problems 3.7, 3.8, and 3.9.)

Remarks 1 and 2 above can be strengthened as follows:

Remark 1′:   The objective function attains its optimum at a basic feasible solution.

Remark 2′:   The extreme points of $\mathscr{S}$ are precisely the basic feasible solutions.   (See Problems 3.13 and 3.14.)

It follows that the standard linear program can be solved by seeking among the basic feasible solutions the one(s) at which the objective is optimized.   A computationally efficient procedure for doing so is described in Chapter 4.

Solved Problems

3.1   Determine whether $\{[1, 2]^T, [2, 4]^T\}$ is linearly independent.

Calling the two vectors $\mathbf{P}_1$ and $\mathbf{P}_2$, it is obvious that $\mathbf{P}_2 = 2\mathbf{P}_1$, or

$$2\mathbf{P}_1 + (-1)\mathbf{P}_2 = \mathbf{0}$$

Thus the given set of vectors is linearly dependent (not linearly independent).

3.2   Is $\{[1, 1, 3, 1]^T, [1, 2, 1, 1]^T, [1, 0, 0, 1]^T\}$ linearly independent?

For these vectors, (*3.1*) becomes

$$\alpha_1 \begin{bmatrix} 1 \\ 1 \\ 3 \\ 1 \end{bmatrix} + \alpha_2 \begin{bmatrix} 1 \\ 2 \\ 1 \\ 1 \end{bmatrix} + \alpha_3 \begin{bmatrix} 1 \\ 0 \\ 0 \\ 1 \end{bmatrix} = \begin{bmatrix} 0 \\ 0 \\ 0 \\ 0 \end{bmatrix} \quad \text{or} \quad \begin{aligned} \alpha_1 + \alpha_2 + \alpha_3 &= 0 \\ \alpha_1 + 2\alpha_2 &= 0 \\ 3\alpha_1 + \alpha_2 &= 0 \\ \alpha_1 + \alpha_2 + \alpha_3 &= 0 \end{aligned}$$

The first three equations (the fourth is redundant) have $\alpha_1 = \alpha_2 = \alpha_3 = 0$ as the only solution.   Therefore, the given set of vectors is linearly independent.

3.3   A vector $\mathbf{Q}$ is a *linear combination* of the vectors $\mathbf{Q}_1, \mathbf{Q}_2, \ldots, \mathbf{Q}_n$ if there exist constants $\delta_1, \delta_2, \ldots, \delta_n$ such that

$$\mathbf{Q} = \delta_1 \mathbf{Q}_1 + \delta_2 \mathbf{Q}_2 + \cdots + \delta_n \mathbf{Q}_n$$

Show that the set of vectors $\{\mathbf{P}_1, \mathbf{P}_2, \ldots, \mathbf{P}_n\}$ is linearly dependent if and only if one of the vectors is a linear combination of the rest.

If $\mathbf{P}_i = \delta_1 \mathbf{P}_1 + \cdots + \delta_{i-1}\mathbf{P}_{i-1} + \delta_{i+1}\mathbf{P}_{i+1} + \cdots + \delta_n \mathbf{P}_n$,   in which some or all of the δ's may be zero, then

$$\delta_1 \mathbf{P}_1 + \cdots + \delta_{i-1}\mathbf{P}_{i-1} + (-1)\mathbf{P}_i + \delta_{i+1}\mathbf{P}_{i+1} + \cdots + \delta_n \mathbf{P}_n = \mathbf{0}$$

and so the set is linearly dependent.

On the other hand, if the set is linearly dependent, let α_j be the first nonzero coefficient in (*3.1*).   Then,

$$\mathbf{P}_j = 0\mathbf{P}_1 + \cdots + 0\mathbf{P}_{j-1} + \left(\frac{\alpha_{j+1}}{-\alpha_j}\right)\mathbf{P}_{j+1} + \cdots + \left(\frac{\alpha_n}{-\alpha_j}\right)\mathbf{P}_n$$

i.e., $\mathbf{P}_j$ is a linear combination of the remaining vectors.

3.4   Determine whether $[1, 2, 3]^T$ is a linear combination of

$$[1, 2, 1]^T \qquad [1, 1, 1]^T \qquad [2, 3, 2]^T$$

It is not; any linear combination of the three vectors must have its first and third components equal. (More generally:

$$\begin{bmatrix} 1 \\ 2 \\ 3 \end{bmatrix} = \delta_1 \begin{bmatrix} 1 \\ 2 \\ 1 \end{bmatrix} + \delta_2 \begin{bmatrix} 1 \\ 1 \\ 1 \end{bmatrix} + \delta_3 \begin{bmatrix} 2 \\ 3 \\ 2 \end{bmatrix}, \qquad \text{iff} \qquad \begin{array}{l} \delta_1 + \delta_2 + 2\delta_3 = 1 \\ 2\delta_1 + \delta_2 + 3\delta_3 = 2 \\ \delta_1 + \delta_2 + 2\delta_3 = 3 \end{array}$$

But this second system has no solution.)

3.5   Prove that if $\{\mathbf{P}_1, \mathbf{P}_2, \dots, \mathbf{P}_r\}$ is a linearly independent set of vectors and $\mathbf{P}$ is a vector such that

$$\mathbf{P} = \sum_{j=1}^{r} c_j \mathbf{P}_j \qquad \text{and} \qquad \mathbf{P} = \sum_{j=1}^{r} d_j \mathbf{P}_j$$

then $c_j = d_j$ $(j = 1, 2, \dots, r)$.

Subtracting the two representations, we obtain

$$\sum_{j=1}^{r} (c_j - d_j)\mathbf{P}_j = \mathbf{0}$$

which is (3.1) with $\alpha_j = c_j - d_j$ and $n = r$. Since $\mathbf{P}_1, \mathbf{P}_2, \dots, \mathbf{P}_r$ are linearly independent, it follows that $c_j - d_j = 0$, or $c_j = d_j$ $(j = 1, 2, \dots, r)$.

3.6   Write the constraint equations of the following linear program in the vector form (3.3):

$$\text{minimize:} \quad z = 2x_1 + 3x_2 + x_3 + 0x_4 + Mx_5 + 0x_6$$

$$\text{subject to:} \quad \begin{aligned} x_1 + 2x_2 + 2x_3 - x_4 + x_5 \quad &= 3 \\ 2x_1 + 3x_2 + 4x_3 \qquad\qquad + x_6 &= 6 \end{aligned}$$

$$\text{with:} \quad \text{all variables nonnegative}$$

For this problem, (3.3) becomes

$$x_1 \underset{\substack{\| \\ \mathbf{A}_1}}{\begin{bmatrix} 1 \\ 2 \end{bmatrix}} + x_2 \underset{\substack{\| \\ \mathbf{A}_2}}{\begin{bmatrix} 2 \\ 3 \end{bmatrix}} + x_3 \underset{\substack{\| \\ \mathbf{A}_3}}{\begin{bmatrix} 2 \\ 4 \end{bmatrix}} + x_4 \underset{\substack{\| \\ \mathbf{A}_4}}{\begin{bmatrix} -1 \\ 0 \end{bmatrix}} + x_5 \underset{\substack{\| \\ \mathbf{A}_5}}{\begin{bmatrix} 1 \\ 0 \end{bmatrix}} + x_6 \underset{\substack{\| \\ \mathbf{A}_6}}{\begin{bmatrix} 0 \\ 1 \end{bmatrix}} = \underset{\substack{\| \\ \mathbf{B}}}{\begin{bmatrix} 3 \\ 6 \end{bmatrix}}$$

3.7   Determine whether $[1, 0, 1, 0, 0, 0]^T$ is a basic feasible solution to the linear program given in Problem 3.6.

Although all its components are nonnegative, the proposed solution is not basic. The vectors $\mathbf{A}_1$ and $\mathbf{A}_3$ associated with the x-variables not set equal to zero are not linearly independent (Problem 3.1).

3.8   Determine whether $[1, 0, 0, 0, 2, 4]^T$ is a basic feasible solution to the linear program given in Problem 3.6.

The coefficient matrix $\mathbf{A}$, comprised of the column vectors $\mathbf{A}_1$ through $\mathbf{A}_6$, has order 2×6. Therefore, a basic feasible solution must have at least $6 - 2 = 4$ zero components (variables), which is not the case here.

3.9   Find two different basic feasible solutions to the linear program given in Problem 3.6.

Since $n - m = 4$, a basic feasible solution will have four x-variables set equal to zero. With x_1 through x_4 made zero, the vector constraint equation becomes

$$x_5\begin{bmatrix}1\\0\end{bmatrix} + x_6\begin{bmatrix}0\\1\end{bmatrix} = \begin{bmatrix}3\\6\end{bmatrix}$$

which has the (nonnegative) solution $x_5 = 3$, $x_6 = 6$. Since $\mathbf{A}_5$ and $\mathbf{A}_6$ are linearly independent, the complete solution, $[0, 0, 0, 0, 3, 6]^T$, is basic. Here the basic variables are x_5 and x_6, and since both of them are positive, the solution is also nondegenerate.

To obtain a second basic feasible solution, we set $x_3 = x_4 = x_5 = x_6 = 0$, whereupon the vector constraint equation becomes

$$x_1\begin{bmatrix}1\\2\end{bmatrix} + x_2\begin{bmatrix}2\\3\end{bmatrix} = \begin{bmatrix}3\\6\end{bmatrix}$$

Solving this equation for x_1 and x_2, we find $x_1 = 3$ and $x_2 = 0$. The corresponding A-vectors, $\mathbf{A}_1$ and $\mathbf{A}_2$, are linearly independent, so the complete solution, $[3, 0, 0, 0, 0, 0]^T$, is basic. The basic variables are x_1 and x_2, and since one of them is zero, the solution is degenerate.

3.10 Determine whether the vector $[0, 7]^T$ is a convex combination of the set $\{[3, 6]^T,$ $[-6, 9]^T, [2, 1]^T, [-1, 1]^T\}$.

For these vectors, (*3.2*) becomes

$$\begin{bmatrix}0\\7\end{bmatrix} = \beta_1\begin{bmatrix}3\\6\end{bmatrix} + \beta_2\begin{bmatrix}-6\\9\end{bmatrix} + \beta_3\begin{bmatrix}2\\1\end{bmatrix} + \beta_4\begin{bmatrix}-1\\1\end{bmatrix}$$

or

$$3\beta_1 - 6\beta_2 + 2\beta_3 - \beta_4 = 0$$
$$6\beta_1 + 9\beta_2 + \beta_3 + \beta_4 = 7 \tag{1}$$

To these equations we add a third condition,

$$\beta_1 + \beta_2 + \beta_3 + \beta_4 = 1 \tag{2}$$

We must determine whether there exist *nonnegative* values of β_1, β_2, β_3, and β_4 that simultaneously satisfy (*1*) and (*2*). Solving these equations, we obtain

$$\beta_1 = \tfrac{2}{3} + \tfrac{1}{2}\beta_4 \qquad \beta_2 = \tfrac{1}{3} - \tfrac{5}{16}\beta_4 \qquad \beta_3 = (-19/16)\beta_4$$

with β_4 arbitrary. The choice $\beta_4 = 0$ is forced, giving

$$\beta_1 = \tfrac{2}{3} \qquad \beta_2 = \tfrac{1}{3} \qquad \beta_3 = 0 \qquad \beta_4 = 0$$

as an acceptable set of constants. Thus, $[0, 7]^T$ is a convex combination of the given set of four vectors.

3.11 If $\mathcal{Q}$ and $\mathcal{R}$ are convex sets, show that their intersection $\mathcal{Q} \cap \mathcal{R}$ is a convex set.

Let $\mathbf{X}$ and $\mathbf{Y}$ be any two vectors in $\mathcal{Q} \cap \mathcal{R}$. Then the line segment between $\mathbf{X}$ and $\mathbf{Y}$ is in $\mathcal{Q}$ (because $\mathbf{X}$ and $\mathbf{Y}$ are in $\mathcal{Q}$, and $\mathcal{Q}$ is convex) and it is in $\mathcal{R}$ (similarly). Thus, the line segment is in $\mathcal{Q} \cap \mathcal{R}$; and so $\mathcal{Q} \cap \mathcal{R}$ is convex.

In the case that $\mathcal{Q}$ and $\mathcal{R}$ are convex polyhedra (have finitely many extreme points), it is intuitively obvious that the intersection is also a convex polyhedron.

3.12 Prove that the objective function $z = f(\mathbf{X}) = \mathbf{C}^T\mathbf{X}$ of system (*2.3*) assumes its optimum (say, a minimum) at an extreme point of $\mathcal{S}$, provided a minimum exists and $\mathcal{S}$ is bounded.

If a minimum exists, then there exists a point $\mathbf{X}_0 \in \mathcal{S}$ such that

$$f(\mathbf{X}_0) \leq f(\mathbf{X}) \quad \text{for all } \mathbf{X} \in \mathcal{S} \tag{1}$$

If $\mathbf{X}_0$ is an extreme point of $\mathcal{S}$, we are done. If not, we must produce an extreme point $\mathbf{X}_m$ such that $f(\mathbf{X}_m) = f(\mathbf{X}_0)$.

Now, $\mathcal{S}$ has only a finite number of extreme points: we designate them as $\mathbf{X}_1, \mathbf{X}_2, \ldots, \mathbf{X}_p$. Because $\mathcal{S}$ is bounded (as well as being closed), Theorem 3.2 ensures that $\mathbf{X}_0$ can be written as a convex combination of these extreme points; i.e., there exist nonnegative β_j ($j = 1, 2, \ldots, p$), whose sum is 1, such that

$$\mathbf{X}_0 = \sum_{j=1}^{p} \beta_j \mathbf{X}_j$$

Let the minimum of $f(\mathbf{X})$ over the extreme points be assumed at $\mathbf{X}_m$. By (1), $f(\mathbf{X}_0) \leq f(\mathbf{X}_m)$. But

$$f(\mathbf{X}_0) = f\left(\sum_{j=1}^{p} \beta_j \mathbf{X}_j\right) = \sum_{j=1}^{p} \beta_j f(\mathbf{X}_j) \geq \sum_{j=1}^{p} \beta_j f(\mathbf{X}_m) = f(\mathbf{X}_m) \sum_{j=1}^{p} \beta_j = f(\mathbf{X}_m) \tag{2}$$

Consequently, $f(\mathbf{X}_0) = f(\mathbf{X}_m)$, and so there is an extreme point, namely $\mathbf{X}_m$, at which $f(\mathbf{X})$ assumes its minimum.

According to the fundamental *Weierstrass theorem* (Theorem 11.1), a continuous function—in particular, a linear function such as $f(\mathbf{X})$—actually assumes a minimum value on a closed and bounded region. We conclude that the standard linear program always possesses an extreme-point optimal solution when $\mathscr{S}$ is bounded. If $\mathscr{S}$ is not bounded, the optimum may not exist; however, if it does exist, it is again assumed at an extreme point.

3.13 Prove that every extreme point of $\mathscr{S}$ has at least $n - m$ zero components and is a basic feasible solution.

Let $\mathbf{X} = [x_1, x_2, \ldots, x_n]^T$ be an extreme point of $\mathscr{S}$. Without loss of generality, we can assume that the x-variables have been indexed so that $x_1, x_2, \ldots, x_r$ $(r \leq n)$ are positive and all subsequent components of $\mathbf{X}$, if any, are zero. Since $\mathbf{X} \in \mathscr{S}$, we have $\mathbf{AX} = \mathbf{B}$, which, as a consequence of $x_j = 0$ for $j > r$, can be written in the vector form

$$\sum_{j=1}^{r} x_j \mathbf{A}_j = \mathbf{B} \tag{1}$$

We first show that the vectors $\mathbf{A}_j$ involved in (1) are linearly independent. *Assume they are not.* Then there exist constants $\alpha_1, \alpha_2, \ldots, \alpha_r$, not all zero, such that

$$\sum_{j=1}^{r} \alpha_j \mathbf{A}_j = \mathbf{0} \tag{2}$$

Let θ be a positive number; then (1) and (2) give

$$\sum_{j=1}^{r} (x_j + \theta\alpha_j)\mathbf{A}_j = \mathbf{B} \qquad \text{and} \qquad \sum_{j=1}^{r} (x_j - \theta\alpha_j)\mathbf{A}_j = \mathbf{B} \tag{3}$$

If θ is chosen small enough so that $x_j + \theta\alpha_j$ and $x_j - \theta\alpha_j$ remain positive for all $j = 1, 2, \ldots, r$, then it follows directly from (3) that

$$\mathbf{X}_1 = [x_1 + \theta\alpha_1, x_2 + \theta\alpha_2, \ldots, x_r + \theta\alpha_r, 0, 0, \ldots, 0]^T$$
$$\mathbf{X}_2 = [x_1 - \theta\alpha_1, x_2 - \theta\alpha_2, \ldots, x_r - \theta\alpha_r, 0, 0, \ldots, 0]^T$$

are *distinct* elements of $\mathscr{S}$. But then $\mathbf{X} = \frac{1}{2}\mathbf{X}_1 + \frac{1}{2}\mathbf{X}_2$, which is impossible, since $\mathbf{X}$ is an extreme point of $\mathscr{S}$. Thus, $\{\mathbf{A}_1, \mathbf{A}_2, \ldots, \mathbf{A}_r\}$ must be a linearly independent set.

Since the vectors are m-dimensional, it follows from Theorem 3.1 that there can be no more than m of them which are linearly independent; accordingly, $r \leq m$. But all components of $\mathbf{X}$ past the rth one are zero; hence $\mathbf{X}$ must have at least $n - m$ zero components.

In case $r = m$, the above proof at once establishes that $\mathbf{X}$ is a basic feasible solution. If $r < m$, we can always (supposing rank $\mathbf{A} = m$) identify $m - r$ zero components of $\mathbf{X}$ such that their corresponding $\mathbf{A}$-vectors combine with $\mathbf{A}_1, \mathbf{A}_2, \ldots,$ and $\mathbf{A}_r$ to make up a linearly independent set. Thus, once more, $\mathbf{X}$ is a basic feasible solution.

3.14 Prove that every basic feasible solution is an extreme point of $\mathscr{S}$.

Let $\mathbf{X}$ be a basic feasible solution. Then, $\mathbf{X} \in \mathscr{S}$ and at least $n - m$ of the components of $\mathbf{X}$ are zero. Without loss of generality, we can assume that the x-variables have been indexed so that the positive components of $\mathbf{X}$ appear first:

$$\mathbf{X} = [x_1, x_2, \ldots, x_s, 0, 0, \ldots, 0]^T \tag{1}$$

with $x_j > 0$ $(j = 1, 2, \ldots, s)$ and $s \le m$.   Consequently, the equality $\mathbf{AX} = \mathbf{B}$ can be written in the vector form

$$\sum_{j=1}^{s} x_j \mathbf{A}_j = \mathbf{B}$$

where, as a result of $\mathbf{X}$ being basic, the set $\{\mathbf{A}_1, \mathbf{A}_2, \ldots, \mathbf{A}_s\}$ is linearly independent (see Problem 3.22).

   Assume that $\mathbf{X}$ is not an extreme point of $\mathcal{S}$.   Then $\mathbf{X}$ can be expressed as a convex combination of two other points in $\mathcal{S}$:

$$\mathbf{X} = \beta_1 \mathbf{X}_1 + \beta_2 \mathbf{X}_2 \qquad \text{where} \qquad \mathbf{X}_1 \ne \mathbf{X}_2 \tag{2}$$

Since the components of $\mathbf{X}_1$ and $\mathbf{X}_2$ are nonnegative, and the constants β_1 and β_2 are strictly positive, it follows from (1) and (2) that the last $n - s$ components of $\mathbf{X}_1$ and $\mathbf{X}_2$ also are zero.   Therefore,

$$\mathbf{X}_1 = [c_1, c_2, \ldots, c_s, 0, 0, \ldots, 0]^T \qquad \mathbf{X}_2 = [d_1, d_2, \ldots, d_s, 0, 0, \ldots, 0]^T \tag{3}$$

In view of (3), $\mathbf{AX}_1 = \mathbf{B}$ and $\mathbf{AX}_2 = \mathbf{B}$ take the vector forms

$$\sum_{j=1}^{s} c_j \mathbf{A}_j = \mathbf{B} \qquad \text{and} \qquad \sum_{j=1}^{s} d_j \mathbf{A}_j = \mathbf{B}$$

Using the result of Problem 3.5, we conclude that $c_j = d_j$, whence $\mathbf{X}_1 = \mathbf{X}_2$.   This contradiction establishes that $\mathbf{X}$ is, in fact, an extreme point.

3.15   Show that the initial solution $\mathbf{X}_0$ generated in Chapter 2 is a basic feasible solution.

   The set of $\mathbf{A}$-vectors corresponding to the initial solution are the columns of the $m \times m$ identity matrix, which are linearly independent.

Supplementary Problems

3.16   Determine graphically whether $[1, 2]^T$ is a convex combination of $[1, 1]^T$ and $[2, -1]^T$.

3.17   Write the constraint equations for the following linear program in vector form:

$$\text{minimize:} \quad z = x_1 + 2x_2 + 0x_3 + Mx_4 + 0x_5$$

$$\text{subject to:} \quad \begin{aligned} x_1 + 2x_2 + x_3 \qquad\qquad &= 3 \\ 2x_1 + 4x_2 \qquad - x_4 + x_5 &= 6 \end{aligned}$$

$$\text{with:} \quad \text{all variables nonnegative}$$

3.18   Determine which of the following vectors are basic feasible solutions to the linear program of Problem 3.17.   Are any of the basic feasible solutions degenerate?

(a) $[1, 1, 0, 0, 0]^T$ (b) $[3, 0, 0, 0, 0]^T$ (c) $[0, 0, 3, 0, 6]^T$ (d) $[0, 0, 3, 2, 8]^T$

3.19   Write the constraint equations for the following linear program in vector form:

$$\text{maximize:} \quad z = x_1 + 2x_2 + 3x_3 + 4x_4 + 0x_5 + 0x_6 + 0x_7$$

$$\text{subject to:} \quad \begin{aligned} x_1 + 2x_2 + x_3 + 3x_4 + x_5 \qquad\qquad\quad &= 9 \\ 2x_1 + x_2 \qquad + 3x_4 \qquad + x_6 \quad &= 9 \\ -x_1 + x_2 + x_3 \qquad\qquad\qquad\quad + x_7 &= 0 \end{aligned}$$

$$\text{with:} \quad \text{all variables nonnegative}$$

3.20   Determine which of the following vectors are basic feasible solutions to the linear program of Problem
3.19.   Are any of the basic feasible solutions degenerate?

(a) $[3, 3, 0, 0, 0, 0, 0]^T$ (c) $[0, 0, 0, 3, 0, 0, 0]^T$ (e) $[1, 0, 0, 0, 8, 7, 1]^T$

(b) $[2, 2, 0, 1, 0, 0, 0]^T$ (d) $[0, 0, 0, 0, 9, 9, 0]^T$ (f) $[0, 0, 9, 0, 0, 9, -9]^T$

3.21   Prove that if a linear function assumes its minimum at two different points of a convex set, then it
assumes this minimum on the entire line segment between the points.

3.22   Prove that every nonempty subset of a linearly independent set of vectors is itself linearly independent.

3.23   Prove that any set of vectors containing the zero vector is linearly dependent.

Chapter 4

Linear Programming: The Simplex Method

THE SIMPLEX TABLEAU

The *simplex method* is a matrix procedure for solving linear programs in the standard form

$$\text{optimize:} \quad z = \mathbf{C}^T\mathbf{X}$$

$$\text{subject to:} \quad \mathbf{AX} = \mathbf{B}$$

$$\text{with:} \quad \mathbf{X} \geq \mathbf{0}$$

where $\mathbf{B} \geq \mathbf{0}$ and a basic feasible solution $\mathbf{X}_0$ is known (Problem 3.15). Starting with $\mathbf{X}_0$, the method locates successively other basic feasible solutions having better values of the objective, until the optimal solution is obtained. For minimization programs, the simplex method utilizes Tableau 4-1, in which $\mathbf{C}_0$ designates the cost vector associated with the variables in $\mathbf{X}_0$.

		$\mathbf{X}^T$ $\mathbf{C}^T$	
$\mathbf{X}_0$	$\mathbf{C}_0$	$\mathbf{A}$	$\mathbf{B}$
		$\mathbf{C}^T - \mathbf{C}_0^T\mathbf{A}$	$-\mathbf{C}_0^T\mathbf{B}$

Tableau 4-1

For maximization programs, Tableau 4-1 applies if the elements of the bottom row have their *signs reversed*.

Example 4.1 For the minimization program of Problem 2.5, $\mathbf{C}_0 = [0, 2, M]^T$. Then,

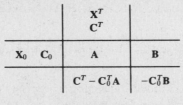

$$\mathbf{C}^T - \mathbf{C}_0^T\mathbf{A} = [1, 2, 3, 0, 0, M] - [0, 2, M]\begin{bmatrix} 3 & 0 & 4 & 1 & 0 & 0 \\ 5 & 1 & 6 & 0 & 0 & 0 \\ 8 & 0 & 9 & 0 & -1 & 1 \end{bmatrix}$$

$$= [1, 2, 3, 0, 0, M] - [10 + 8M, 2, 12 + 9M, 0, -M, M] = [-9 - 8M, 0, -9 - 9M, 0, M, 0]$$

$$-\mathbf{C}_0^T\mathbf{B} = -[0, 2, M]\begin{bmatrix} 5 \\ 7 \\ 2 \end{bmatrix} = -14 - 2M$$

and Tableau 4-1 becomes

		x_1 1	x_2 2	x_3 3	x_4 0	x_5 0	x_6 M	
x_4	0	3	0	4	1	0	0	5
x_2	2	5	1	6	0	0	0	7
x_6	M	8	0	9	0	-1	1	2
		$-9 - 8M$	0	$-9 - 9M$	0	M	0	$-14 - 2M$

32

A TABLEAU SIMPLIFICATION

For each j $(j = 1, 2, \ldots, n)$, define $z_j \equiv C_0^T A_j$, the dot product of C_0 with the jth column of A. The jth entry in the last row of Tableau 4-1 is $c_j - z_j$ (or, for a maximization program, $z_j - c_j$), where c_j is the cost in the second row of the tableau, immediately above A_j. Once this last row has been obtained, the second row and second column of the tableau, corresponding to C^T and C_0, respectively, become superfluous and may be eliminated.

THE SIMPLEX METHOD

STEP 1   Locate the most negative number in the bottom row of the simplex tableau, excluding the last column, and call the column in which this number appears the *work column*. If more than one candidate for most negative number exists, choose one.

STEP 2   Form ratios by dividing each *positive* number in the work column, excluding the last row, into the element in the same row and last column. Designate the element in the work column that yields the *smallest* ratio as the *pivot element*. If more than one element yields the same smallest ratio, choose one. If no element in the work column is positive, the program has no solution.

STEP 3   Use elementary row operations to convert the pivot element to 1 and then to reduce all *other* elements in the work column to 0.

STEP 4   Replace the x-variable in the pivot row and first column by the x-variable in the first row and pivot column. This new first column is the current set of basic variables (see Chapter 3).

STEP 5   Repeat Steps 1 through 4 until there are no negative numbers in the last row, excluding the last column.

STEP 6   The optimal solution is obtained by assigning to each variable in the first column that value in the corresponding row and last column. All other variables are assigned the value zero. The associated z^*, the optimal value of the objective function, is the number in the last row and last column for a maximization program, but the *negative* of this number for a minimization program.

MODIFICATIONS FOR PROGRAMS WITH
ARTIFICIAL VARIABLES

Whenever artificial variables are part of the initial solution X_0, the last row of Tableau 4-1 will contain the penalty cost M (see Chapter 2). To minimize roundoff error (see Problem 4.6), the following modifications are incorporated into the simplex method; the resulting algorithm is the *two-phase method*.

Change 1:   The last row of Tableau 4-1 is decomposed into two rows, the first of which involves those terms not containing M, while the second involves the coefficients of M in the remaining terms.

Example 4.2   The last row of the tableau in Example 4.1 is

$$-9 - 8M \quad 0 \quad -9 - 9M \quad 0 \quad M \quad 0 \quad -14 - 2M$$

Under Change 1 it would be transformed into the two rows

$$-9 \quad 0 \quad -9 \quad 0 \quad 0 \quad 0 \quad -14$$
$$-8 \quad 0 \quad -9 \quad 0 \quad 1 \quad 0 \quad -2$$

Change 2:   Step 1 of the simplex method is applied to the last row created in Change 1 (followed by Steps 2, 3, and 4), until this row contains no negative elements. Then Step 1 is applied to those elements in the next-to-last row that are positioned over zeros in the last row.

Change 3:   Whenever an artificial variable ceases to be basic—i.e. is removed from the first column of the tableau as a result of Step 4—it is deleted from the top row of the tableau, as is the entire column under it. (This modification simplifies hand calculations but is not implemented in many computer programs.)

Change 4:   The last row can be deleted from the tableau whenever it contains all zeros.

Change 5:   If *nonzero* artificial variables are present in the final basic set, then the program has no solution. (In contrast, zero-valued artificial variables may appear as basic variables in the final solution when one or more of the original constraint equations is redundant.)

Solved Problems

4.1

$$\text{maximize:} \quad z = x_1 + 9x_2 + x_3$$

$$\text{subject to:} \quad x_1 + 2x_2 + 3x_3 \le 9$$

$$3x_1 + 2x_2 + 2x_3 \le 15$$

$$\text{with:} \quad \text{all variables nonnegative}$$

This program is put into matrix standard form by first introducing slack variables x_4 and x_5 in the first and second constraint inequalities, respectively, and then defining

$$\mathbf{X} \equiv [x_1, x_2, x_3, x_4, x_5]^T \qquad \mathbf{C} \equiv [1, 9, 1, 0, 0]^T$$

$$\mathbf{A} \equiv \begin{bmatrix} 1 & 2 & 3 & 1 & 0 \\ 3 & 2 & 2 & 0 & 1 \end{bmatrix} \qquad \mathbf{B} \equiv \begin{bmatrix} 9 \\ 15 \end{bmatrix} \qquad \mathbf{X}_0 \equiv \begin{bmatrix} x_4 \\ x_5 \end{bmatrix}$$

The costs associated with the components of $\mathbf{X}_0$, the slack variables, are zero; hence $\mathbf{C}_0 \equiv [0, 0]^T$. Tableau 4-1 becomes

		x_1	x_2	x_3	x_4	x_5	
		1	9	1	0	0	
x_4	0	1	2	3	1	0	9
x_5	0	3	2	2	0	1	15

To compute the last row of this tableau, we use the tableau simplification and first calculate each z_j by inspection: it is the dot product of column 2 and the jth column of $\mathbf{A}$. We then subtract the corresponding cost c_j from it (maximization program). In this case, the second column is zero, and so $z_j - c_j = 0 - c_j = -c_j$. Hence, the bottom row of the tableau, excluding the last element, is just the negative of row 2. The last element in the bottom row is simply the dot product of column 2 and the final, **B**-column, and so it too is zero. At this point, the second row and second column of the tableau are superfluous. Eliminating them, we obtain Tableau 1 as the complete initial tableau.

	x_1	x_2	x_3	x_4	x_5	
x_4	1	2*	3	1	0	9
x_5	3	2	2	0	1	15
$(z_j - c_j)$:	-1	-9	-1	0	0	0

Tableau 1

	x_1	x_2	x_3	x_4	x_5	
x_2	1/2	1	3/2	1/2	0	9/2
x_5	2	0	-1	-1	1	6
	7/2	0	25/2	9/2	0	81/2

Tableau 2

We are now ready to apply the simplex method. The most negative element in the last row of Tableau 1 is -9, corresponding to the x_2-column; hence this column becomes the work column. Forming the ratios $9/2 = 4.5$ and $15/2 = 7.5$, we find that the element 2, marked by the asterisk in Tableau 1, is the pivot element, since it yields the smallest ratio. Then, applying Steps 3 and 4 to Tableau 1, we obtain Tableau 2. Since the last row of Tableau 2 contains no negative elements, it follows from Step 6 that the optimal solution is $x_2^* = 9/2$, $x_5^* = 6$, $x_1^* = x_3^* = x_4^* = 0$, with $z^* = 81/2$.

4.2
$$\text{minimize:}\quad z = 80x_1 + 60x_2$$

$$\text{subject to:}\quad 0.20\,x_1 + 0.32\,x_2 \le 0.25$$

$$x_1 + \quad x_2 = \quad 1$$

$$\text{with:}\quad x_1 \text{ and } x_2 \text{ nonnegative}$$

Adding a slack variable x_3 and an artificial variable x_4 to the first and second constraints, respectively, we convert the program to standard matrix form, with

$$\mathbf{X} \equiv [x_1, x_2, x_3, x_4]^T \qquad \mathbf{C} \equiv [80, 60, 0, M]^T$$

$$\mathbf{A} \equiv \begin{bmatrix} 0.20 & 0.32 & 1 & 0 \\ 1 & 1 & 0 & 1 \end{bmatrix} \qquad \mathbf{B} \equiv \begin{bmatrix} 0.25 \\ 1 \end{bmatrix} \qquad \mathbf{X}_0 \equiv \begin{bmatrix} x_3 \\ x_4 \end{bmatrix}$$

Substituting these matrices, along with $\mathbf{C}_0 \equiv [0, M]^T$, into Tableau 4-1, we obtain Tableau 0. Since the bottom row involves M, we apply Change 1; the resulting Tableau 1 is the initial tableau for the two-phase method.

		x_1	x_2	x_3	x_4	
		80	60	0	M	
x_3	0	0.20	0.32	1	0	0.25
x_4	M	1	1	0	1	1
		$80-M$	$60-M$	0	0	$-M$

Tableau 0

	x_1	x_2	x_3	x_4	
x_3	0.20	0.32	1	0	0.25
x_4	1*	1	0	1	1
$(c_j - z_j)$:	80	60	0	0	0
	-1	-1	0	0	-1

Tableau 1

	x_1	x_2	x_3	
x_3	0	0.12*	1	0.05
x_1	1	1	0	1
	0	-20	0	-80
	0	0	0	0

Tableau 2

Using both Step 1 of the simplex method and Change 2, we find that the most negative element in the last row of Tableau 1 (excluding the last column) is -1, which appears twice. Arbitrarily selecting the x_1-column as the work column, we form the ratios $0.25/0.20 = 1.25$ and $1/1 = 1$. Since the element 1, starred in Tableau 1, yields the smallest ratio, it becomes the pivot. Then, applying Steps 3 and 4 and Change 3 to Tableau 1, we generate Tableau 2. Observe that x_1 replaces the artificial variable x_4 in the first column of Tableau 2, so that the entire x_4-column is absent from Tableau 2. Now, with no artificial variables in the first column and with Change 3 implemented, the last row of the tableau should be all zeros. It is; and by Change 4 this row may be deleted, giving

$$0 \quad -20 \quad 0 \quad -80$$

as the new last row of Tableau 2.

Repeating Steps 1 through 4, we find that the x_2-column is the new work column (recall that the last element in the last row is excluded under Step 1), the starred element in Tableau 2 is the new pivot, and the elementary row operations yield Tableau 3, in which all calculations have been rounded to four significant figures. Since the last row of Tableau 3, excluding the last column, contains no negative elements, it follows from Step 6 that $x_1^* = 0.5833$, $x_2^* = 0.4167$, $x_3^* = x_4^* = 0$, with $z^* = 71.67$. (Compare with Problem 1.2.)

	x_1	x_2	x_3	
x_2	0	1	8.333	0.4167
x_1	1	0	-8.333	0.5833
	0	0	166.7	-71.67

Tableau 3

4.3

$$\text{maximize:} \quad z = 5x_1 + 2x_2$$

$$\text{subject to:} \quad 6x_1 + x_2 \geq 6$$

$$4x_1 + 3x_2 \geq 12$$

$$x_1 + 2x_2 \geq 4$$

$$\text{with:} \quad \text{all variables nonnegative}$$

This program is put into standard form by introducing surplus variables x_3, x_4, and x_5, respectively, in the constraint inequalities, and then artificial variables x_6, x_7, and x_8, respectively, in the resulting equations. Then, applying the two-phase method and rounding all calculations to four significant figures, we generate sequentially the following tableaux, in each of which the pivot element is marked by an asterisk.

	x_1	x_2	x_3	x_4	x_5	x_6	x_7	x_8	
	5	2	0	0	0	$-M$	$-M$	$-M$	
x_6 $-M$	6^*	1	-1	0	0	1	0	0	6
x_7 $-M$	4	3	0	-1	0	0	1	0	12
x_8 $-M$	1	2	0	0	-1	0	0	1	4
$(z_j - c_j)$:	-5	-2	0	0	0	0	0	0	0
	-11	-6	1	1	1	0	0	0	-22

Tableau 1

	x_1	x_2	x_3	x_4	x_5	x_7	x_8	
x_1	1	0.1667	-0.1667	0	0	0	0	1
x_7	0	2.333	0.6668	-1	0	1	0	8
x_8	0	1.833^*	0.1667	0	-1	0	1	3
	0	-1.167	-0.8335	0	0	0	0	5
	0	-4.166	-0.8337	1	1	0	0	-11

Tableau 2

	x_1	x_2	x_3	x_4	x_5	x_7	
x_1	1	0	-0.1819	0	0.09095	0	0.7271
x_7	0	0	0.4546	-1	1.273^*	1	4.181
x_2	0	1	0.09094	0	-0.5456	0	1.637
	0	0	-0.7274	0	-0.6367	0	6.910
	0	0	-0.4548	1	-1.273	0	-4.180

Tableau 3

	x_1	x_2	x_3	x_4	x_5	
x_1	1	0	-0.2144	0.07144*	0	0.4284
x_5	0	1	0.3571	-0.7855	1	3.284
x_2	0	1	0.2858	-0.4286	0	3.429
	0	0	-0.5000	-0.5001	0	9.001
	0	0	-0.0002	0.0001	0	0.0005

Tableau 4

	x_1	x_2	x_3	x_4	x_5	
x_4	14.00	0	-3.001	1	0	6.000
x_5	11.00	0	-2.000	0	1	7.997
x_2	6.000	1	-1.000	0	0	6.001
	7.001	0	-2.001	0	0	12.00

Tableau 5

Tableau 4 is the first tableau containing no artificial variables in its first column, hence, with Change 3 implemented, the last row of the tableau should be zero. To within roundoff errors it is zero, so we delete it from the Tableau. Tableau 5, however, presents a problem that cannot be ignored: the work column is the x_3-column and all the elements in that column are negative! It follows from Step 2 that the original program has no solution. (It is easy to show graphically that the feasible region is infinite and that the objective function can be made arbitrarily large by choosing feasible points with arbitrarily large coordinates.)

4.4

$$\text{maximize:} \quad z = 2x_1 + 3x_2$$

$$\text{subject to:} \quad x_1 + 2x_2 \leq 2$$

$$6x_1 + 4x_2 \geq 24$$

$$\text{with:} \quad \text{all variables nonnegative}$$

This program is put in standard form by introducing a slack variable x_3 to the first constraint, and both a surplus variable x_4 and an artificial variable x_5 to the second constraint. Then Tableau 4-1, with Change 1, becomes Tableau 1.

		x_1	x_2	x_3	x_4	x_5	
		2	3	0	0	$-M$	
x_3	0	1*	2	1	0	0	2
x_5	$-M$	6	4	0	-1	1	24
$(z_j - c_j)$:		-2	-3	0	0	0	0
		-6	-4	0	1	0	-24

Tableau 1

	x_1	x_2	x_3	x_4	x_5	
x_1	1	2	1	0	0	2
x_5	0	-8	-6	-1	1	12
	0	1	2	0	0	4
	0	8	6	1	0	-12

Tableau 2

Applying the two-phase algorithm to Tableau 1 (the pivot element is starred), we generate Tableau 2. Now, there are no negative entries in the last row of Tableau 2, and in the next-to-last row there is no negative entry positioned above a zero of the last row. Thus, the two-phase method signals that optimality has been achieved. But the nonzero artificial variable x_5 is still basic! By Change 5, the original program has no solution. (In this case $\mathscr{S}$ is empty, as the constraint inequalities and the nonnegativity conditions cannot be satisfied simultaneously.)

4.5

maximize: $z = -x_5$

subject to: $3x_1 - 2x_2 - 4x_3 + 6x_4 - x_5 \leq 0$

$-4x_1 + 2x_2 - x_3 - 8x_4 - x_5 \leq 0$

$-3x_2 - 2x_3 - x_4 - x_5 \leq 0$

$x_1 + x_2 + x_3 + x_4 \leq 1$

$-x_1 - x_2 - x_3 - x_4 \leq -1$

with: x_1, x_2, x_3, x_4 nonnegative

Since x_5 is unrestricted, we set $x_5 = x_6 - x_7$, where both x_6 and x_7 are nonnegative; then all variables are nonnegative. We multiply the last constraint by -1, thereby forcing a positive right-hand side. Finally, we achieve standard form by adding slack variables x_8 through x_{11}, respectively, to the left-hand sides of the first four constraints, and subtracting surplus variable x_{12} and adding artificial variable x_{13} to the left-hand side of the last constraint. The initial tableau for the two-phase method is Tableau 1, from which are derived Tableaux $2, 3, \ldots, 6$. From Tableau 3 on, the bottom row is permanently nonnegative, and Step 1 of the simplex method is restricted to those elements of the next-to-last row that are situated above the zeros of the last row. From Tableau 6,

$x_1^* = 0$ $x_2^* = 0.11667$ $x_3^* = 0.7$ $x_4^* = 0.18333$ $x_5^* = x_6^* - x_7^* = -1.93334$

with $z^* = 1.93334$.

| | | x_1 | x_2 | x_3 | x_4 | x_6 | x_7 | x_8 | x_9 | x_{10} | x_{11} | x_{12} | x_{13} | |
		0	0	0	0	-1	1	0	0	0	0	0	$-M$	
x_8	0	3*	-2	-4	6	-1	1	1	0	0	0	0	0	0
x_9	0	-4	2	-1	-8	-1	1	0	1	0	0	0	0	0
x_{10}	0	0	-3	-2	-1	-1	1	0	0	1	0	0	0	0
x_{11}	0	1	1	1	1	0	0	0	0	0	1	0	0	1
x_{13}	$-M$	1	1	1	1	0	0	0	0	0	0	-1	1	1
$(z_j - c_j)$:		0	0	0	0	1	-1	0	0	0	0	0	0	0
		-1	-1	-1	-1	0	0	0	0	0	0	1	0	-1

Tableau 1

	x_1	x_2	x_3	x_4	x_6	x_7	x_8	x_9	x_{10}	x_{11}	x_{12}	x_{13}	
x_1	1	-0.666667	-1.33333	2	-0.333333	0.333333	0.333333	0	0	0	0	0	0
x_9	0	-0.666668	-6.33332	0	-2.333333	2.33333	1.33333	1	0	0	0	0	0
x_{10}	0	-3	-2	-1	-1	1	0	0	1	0	0	0	0
x_{11}	0	1.66667	2.33333*	-1	0.333333	-0.333333	-0.333333	0	0	1	0	0	1
x_{13}	0	1.66667	2.33333	-1	0.333333	-0.333333	-0.333333	0	0	0	-1	1	1
	0	0	0	0	1	-1	0	0	0	0	0	0	0
	0	-1.666667	-2.33333	1	-0.333333	0.333333	0.333333	0	0	0	1	0	-1

Tableau 2

	x_1	x_2	x_3	x_4	x_6	x_7	x_8	x_9	x_{10}	x_{11}	x_{12}	x_{13}	
x_1	1	0.285715	0	1.42857	-0.142857	0.142857	0.142857	0	0	0.571428	0	0	0.571428
x_9	0	3.85715	0	-2.71428	-1.42857	1.42857	0.428571	1	0	2.71427	0	0	2.71427
x_{10}	0	-1.57142	0	-1.85714	-0.714286	0.714286*	-0.285714	0	1	0.857144	0	0	0.857144
x_3	0	0.714288	1	-0.428572	0.142857	-0.142857	-0.142857	0	0	0.428572	0	0	0.428572
x_{13}	0	0	0	0	0	0	0	0	0	-1	-1	1	0
	0	0	0	0	1	-1	0	0	0	0	0	0	0
	0	0	0	0	0	0	0	0	0	1	1	0	0

Tableau 3

	x_1	x_2	x_3	x_4	x_6	x_7	x_8	x_9	x_{10}	x_{11}	x_{12}	x_{13}	
x_4	0.583333	0	0	1	0	0	0.0666667	−0.05	−0.0166668	0.183333	0	0	0.183333
x_2	−0.0833332	1	0	0	0	0	0.133333	0.15	−0.283333	0.116667	0	0	0.116667
x_7	1.33333	0	0	0	−1	1	0.0666671	0.20	0.733334	1.93334	0	0	1.93334
x_3	0.499999	0	1	0	0	0	−0.200000	−0.10	0.300000	0.700000	0	0	0.700000
x_{13}	0	0	0	0	0	0	0	0	0	−1	−1	1	0
	1.33333	0	0	0	0	0	0.0666659	0.20	0.733333	1.93334	0	0	1.93334
	0	0	0	0	0	0	0	0	0	1	1	0	0

Tableau 6

4.6 Solve the following program using the simplex method without any of the modifications (such a procedure is known as the *Big M method*) and show how roundoff could affect the answer:

$$\text{maximize:} \quad z = -8x_1 + 3x_2 - 6x_3$$

$$\text{subject to:} \quad x_1 - 3x_2 + 5x_3 = 4$$

$$5x_1 + 3x_2 - 4x_3 \geq 6$$

$$\text{with:} \quad \text{all variables nonnegative}$$

This program is put in standard form by introducing the surplus variable x_4 in the inequality constraint and then artificial variables x_5 and x_6 in the two equality constraints. Substituting the appropriate coefficients into Tableau 4-1 and then applying the simplex method directly, with all calculations rounded to four significant figures and with the pivot elements designated by stars, we generate successively Tableaux 1 through 4.

		x_1	x_2	x_3	x_4	x_5	x_6	
		−8	3	−6	0	−M	−M	
x_5	−M	1	−3	5	0	1	0	4
x_6	−M	5*	3	−4	−1	0	1	6
$(z_j - c_j)$:		−6M + 8	−3	−M + 6	M	0	0	−10M

Tableau 1

	x_1	x_2	x_3	x_4	x_5	x_6	
x_5	0	−3.6	5.8*	0.2	1	−0.2	2.8
x_1	1	0.6	−0.8	−0.2	0	0.2	1.2
	0	3.6M − 7.8	−5.8M + 12.4	−0.2M + 1.6	0	1.2M − 1.6	−2.8M − 9.6

Tableau 2

	x_1	x_2	x_3	x_4	x_5	x_6	
x_3	0	−0.6207	1	0.03448	0.1724	−0.03448	0.4828
x_1	1	0.1034*	0	−0.1724	0.1379	0.1724	1.586
	0	−0.1033	0	1.172	M − 2.138	M − 1.172	−15.59

Tableau 3

	x_1	x_2	x_3	x_4	x_5	x_6	
x_3	6.003	0	1	−10.00	1.000	10.00	10.00
x_2	9.671	1	0	−1.667	1.334	1.667	15.34
	0.9990	0	0	0.9998	M − 2	M − 0.9998	−14.01

Tableau 4

Since M designates a large positive number, all the entries in the last row of Tableau 4, excluding the entry in the last column, are nonnegative. The optimal solution, therefore, can be read directly from it as $x_3^* = 10.00$, $x_2^* = 15.34$, and all other variables zero, with $z^* = -14.01$.

The quantity M in the previous calculations could be left as a letter only because those calculations were done by hand. Had a computer been used, a large numerical value would necessarily have been substituted for M; say, $M = 10\,000$. Then, assuming again that all numbers are rounded to *four* significant figures, the bottom row of Tableau 1 becomes

$$-60\,000 \qquad -3 \qquad -10\,000 \qquad 10\,000 \qquad 0 \qquad 0 \qquad -100\,000$$

Note that the additive constants $+8$ in the first entry and $+6$ in the third entry are lost in roundoff. The bottom row of Tableau 2 becomes

$$0 \qquad 36\,000 \qquad -58\,000 \qquad -2\,000 \qquad 12\,000 \qquad -28\,000$$

while the bottom row of Tableau 3 is

$$0 \qquad 0 \qquad 0 \qquad 0 \qquad 10\,000 \qquad 10\,000 \qquad 0$$

which signals optimality! The erroneous optimal solution would be read from Tableau 3 as $x_3^* = 0.4828$, $x_1^* = 1.586$, and all other variables zero, with $z^* = 0$.

This roundoff problem does not occur in the two-phase method since the terms that do not involve M are separated from those that do, making it impossible for the M-terms to "swamp" the others.

4.7　　Solve Problem 1.7.

Using the mathematical program defined by system (12) in Problem 1.7, we introduce slack variables x_5 through x_{12}, one each to the first eight inequality constraints; surplus variables x_{13} and x_{14}, one each to the last two inequality constraints; and artificial variables x_{15} and x_{16}, one each to the last two constraints. Entering the appropriate coefficients into Tableau 4-1 and using Change 1, we get Tableau 1. Then, applying the two-phase method, we generate Tableaux 2, ..., 5. The optimal solution is read directly from Tableau 5 as $x_1^* = 37\,727.3$ bbl, $x_2^* = 12\,272.7$ bbl, $x_3^* = 2272.7$ bbl, $x_4^* = 2727.3$ bbl, with $z^* = \$125\,000$.

Under this optimal production schedule, Aztec will produce $x_1^* + x_2^* = 50\,000$ bbl of regular having a vapor pressure of 22.5 and an octane rating of 89.7. It will also produce $x_3^* + x_4^* = 5000$ bbl of premium having a vapor pressure of 19.5 and an octane rating of 93.0. Thus, it will produce exactly the amount needed to meet its minimum supply requirements, and no more. To do so, Aztec will use $x_1^* + x_3^* = 40\,000$ bbl of its domestic inventory—all it has—and $x_2^* + x_4^* = 15\,000$ bbl of its foreign inventory.

		x_1	x_2	x_3	x_4	x_5	x_6	x_7	x_8	x_9	x_{10}	x_{11}	x_{12}	x_{13}	x_{14}	x_{15}	x_{16}	
		4	−3	6	−1	0	0	0	0	0	0	0	0	0	0	−M	−M	
x_5	0	1	1	0	0	1	0	0	0	0	0	0	0	0	0	0	0	100 000
x_6	0	0	0	1	1	0	1	0	0	0	0	0	0	0	0	0	0	20 000
x_7	0	1	0	1	0	0	0	1	0	0	0	0	0	0	0	0	0	40 000
x_8	0	0	1	0	1	0	0	0	1	0	0	0	0	0	0	0	0	60 000
x_9	0	1	−10	0	0	0	0	0	0	1	0	0	0	0	0	0	0	0
x_{10}	0	0	0	6	−5	0	0	0	0	0	1	0	0	0	0	0	0	0
x_{11}	0	2	−8	0	0	0	0	0	0	0	0	1	0	0	0	0	0	0
x_{12}	0	0	0	2	−8	0	0	0	0	0	0	0	1	0	0	0	0	0
x_{15}	−M	1	1	0	0	0	0	0	0	0	0	0	0	−1	0	1	0	50 000
x_{16}	−M	0	0	1	1*	0	0	0	0	0	0	0	0	0	−1	0	1	5 000
$(z_j − c_j)$:		−4	3	−6	1	0	0	0	0	0	0	0	0	0	0	0	0	0
		−1	−1	−1	−1	0	0	0	0	0	0	0	0	1	1	0	0	−55 000

Tableau 1

	x_1	x_2	x_3	x_4	x_5	x_6	x_7	x_8	x_9	x_{10}	x_{11}	x_{12}	x_{13}	x_{14}	x_{15}	
x_5	1	1	0	0	1	0	0	0	0	0	0	0	0	0	0	100 000
x_6	0	0	0	0	0	1	0	0	0	0	0	0	0	1	0	15 000
x_7	1	0	1	0	0	0	1	0	0	0	0	0	0	0	0	40 000
x_8	0	1	−1	0	0	0	0	1	0	0	0	0	0	1	0	55 000
x_9	1	−10	0	0	0	0	0	0	1	0	0	0	0	0	0	0
x_{10}	0	0	11	0	0	0	0	0	0	1	0	0	0	−5	0	25 000
x_{11}	2	−8	0	0	0	0	0	0	0	0	1	0	0	0	0	0
x_{12}	0	0	10	0	0	0	0	0	0	0	0	1	0	−8	0	40 000
x_{15}	1	1*	0	0	0	0	0	0	0	0	0	0	−1	0	1	50 000
x_4	0	0	1	1	0	0	0	0	0	0	0	0	0	−1	0	5 000
	−4	3	−7	0	0	0	0	0	0	0	0	0	0	1	0	−5 000
	−1	−1	0	0	0	0	0	0	0	0	0	0	1	0	0	−50 000

Tableau 2

	x_1	x_2	x_3	x_4	x_5	x_6	x_7	x_8	x_9	x_{10}	x_{11}	x_{12}	x_{13}	x_{14}	
x_5	0	0	0	0	1	0	0	0	0	0	0	0	1	0	50 000
x_6	0	0	0	0	0	1	0	0	0	0	0	0	0	1	15 000
x_1	1	0	0	0	0	0	1	0	0	−0.0909	0	0	0	0.4545	37 727.3
x_8	0	0	0	0	0	0	1	1	0	0	0	0	1	1	45 000
x_9	0	0	0	0	0	0	−11	0	1	1	0	0	−10	−5	85 000
x_3	0	0	1	0	0	0	0	0	0	0.0909	0	0	0	−0.4545	2 272.7
x_{11}	0	0	0	0	0	0	−10	0	0	0.9091	1	0	−8	−4.5455	22 727.2
x_{12}	0	0	0	0	0	0	0	0	0	−0.9091	0	1	0	−3.4545	17 272.7
x_2	0	1	0	0	0	0	−1	0	0	0.0909	0	0	−1	−0.4545	12 272.7
x_4	0	0	0	1	0	0	0	0	0	−0.0909	0	0	0	−0.5455	2 727.3
	0	0	0	0	0	0	7	0	0	0	0	0	3	1	125 000

Tableau 5

4.8   Demonstrate the validity of the simplex method by solving Problem 4.2 algebraically.

The program in standard form is

$$\text{minimize:} \quad z = 80x_1 + 60x_2 + 0x_3 + Mx_4$$

$$\text{subject to:} \quad 0.20x_1 + 0.32x_2 + x_3 \quad\quad = 0.25$$

$$x_1 + \quad x_2 \quad\quad + x_4 = 1 \tag{1}$$

with: all variables nonnegative

Applying the theory developed in Chapter 3 to this system, we have $n = 4$ (variables) and $m = 2$ (constraint equations), so that an extreme point of the feasible region $\mathcal{S}$ must have at least $n - m = 2$ zero components.   Since the minimum must occur at an extreme point, these are the only candidates we need consider.

An initial extreme-point solution to system (1) is $x_1 = x_2 = 0$, $x_3 = 0.25$, $x_4 = 1$.   We determine whether this solution can be improved by writing the objective function solely in terms of those variables currently set equal to zero, here x_1 and x_2.   (We are assured that the constraint equations can be solved for x_3 and x_4 in terms of x_1 and x_2 because our extreme-point solution is a basic feasible solution.)   Solving the second constraint equation for x_4 and substituting in the objective function, we obtain

$$z = (80 - M)x_1 + (60 - M)x_2 + M \tag{2}$$

Compare system (1) with Tableau 0 of Problem 4.2, and note how (2) is given by the bottom row of the tableau.

In the current solution, $x_1 = x_2 = 0$ and, from (2), $z = M$. The objective function can be reduced substantially if either x_1 or x_2 is allowed to become positive; we arbitrarily select x_1. Now, the first constraint in system (1) limits x_1 to no more than $0.25/0.20 = 1.25$ units, if the remaining variables are to remain nonnegative; while the second constraint limits x_1 to no more than 1 unit, for the same reason. Since both constraints must be satisfied, x_1 can be no larger than 1 unit. Setting $x_1 = 1$, which is tantamount to setting $x_2 = x_4 = 0$, we obtain from the constraint equations $x_3 = 0.05$. These values constitute the new extreme-point (basic) solution to the program.

The artificial variable x_4 was introduced initially only to provide a first solution. Ultimately, this variable must be zero. Since we now have a solution to the program in which $x_4 = 0$, we can omit this variable from further consideration and restrict ourselves to the program

$$\text{minimize:} \quad z = 80x_1 + 60x_2 + 0x_3 \tag{3}$$

$$\text{subject to:} \quad 0.20x_1 + 0.32x_2 + x_3 = 0.25 \tag{4}$$

$$x_1 + x_2 \quad = 1 \tag{5}$$

with: all variables nonnegative

of which an extreme-point solution— $x_1 = 1$, $x_2 = 0$, $x_3 = 0.05$ —is known. Observe that this modified program has $n = 3$ variables and $m = 2$ constraint equations, so that extreme points must possess at least $3 - 2 = 1$ zero-valued variables.

To determine whether the starting solution for the new program can be improved, we solve (5)—the equation that restricted x_1—for x_1 and substitute the result into (3) and (4). The program becomes

$$\text{minimize:} \quad z = 0x_1 - 20x_2 + 0x_3 + 80 \tag{6}$$

$$\text{subject to:} \quad 0.12x_2 + x_3 = 0.05 \tag{7}$$

$$x_1 + x_2 \quad = 1 \tag{8}$$

with: all variables nonnegative

Compare this program with Tableau 2 of Problem 4.2.

In the current solution, $x_2 = 0$, and it follows from (6) that $z = 80$. It is obvious from this equation, however, that z will be reduced if x_2 is increased. Constraint (7) limits x_2 to $0.05/0.12 = 5/12$, if the other variables are to remain nonnegative; while (8) limits x_2 to 1. Since both constraints must be obeyed, x_2 cannot be increased beyond $5/12$. Setting $x_2 = 5/12$, which forces $x_3 = 0$, we find from (8) that $x_1 = 7/12$. This is the new extreme-point solution to the program.

To determine whether this solution can be improved, we solve (7)—the equation that restricted x_2—for x_2 and substitute the result in (6) and (8). The program becomes

$$\text{minimize:} \quad z = 0x_1 + 0x_2 + 166.7x_3 + 71.67 \tag{9}$$

$$\text{subject to:} \quad x_2 + 8.333x_3 = 0.4167 \tag{10}$$

$$x_1 - 8.333x_3 = 0.5833 \tag{11}$$

with: all variables nonnegative

Equation (10) is just (7) divided through by 0.12. Compare the form of this program with Tableau 3 of Problem 4.2.

In the current solution, $x_3 = 0$, so it follows from (9) that $z = 71.67$. It also follows from (9) that no positive allocation to x_3 will reduce z below this value. In fact, any such allocation will increase z. Thus, the current solution is an optimal one.

Supplementary Problems

Use the simplex or two-phase method to solve the following problems.

4.9   maximize: $z = x_1 + x_2$

subject to: $x_1 + 5x_2 \le 5$

$2x_1 + x_2 \le 4$

with: x_1, x_2 nonnegative

4.10   maximize: $z = 3x_1 + 4x_2$

subject to: $2x_1 + x_2 \le 6$

$2x_1 + 3x_2 \le 9$

with: x_1, x_2 nonnegative

4.11   minimize: $z = x_1 + 2x_2$

subject to: $x_1 + 3x_2 \ge 11$

$2x_1 + x_2 \ge 9$

with: x_1, x_2 nonnegative

4.12   maximize: $z = -x_1 - x_2$

subject to: $x_1 + 2x_2 \ge 5\,000$

$5x_1 + 3x_2 \ge 12\,000$

with: x_1, x_2 nonnegative

4.13   maximize: $z_i = 2x_1 + 3x_2 + 4x_3$

subject to: $x_1 + x_2 + x_3 \le 1$

$x_1 + x_2 + 2x_3 = 2$

$3x_1 + 2x_2 + x_3 \ge 4$

with: all variables nonnegative

4.14   minimize: $z = 14x_1 + 13x_2 + 11x_3 + 13x_4 + 13x_5 + 12x_6$

subject to: $x_1 + x_2 + x_3 \qquad\qquad = 1200$

$x_4 + x_5 + x_6 = 1000$

$x_1 \qquad + x_4 \qquad = 1000$

$x_2 \qquad\quad + x_5 \quad = 700$

$x_3 \qquad\qquad + x_6 = 500$

with: all variables nonnegative

4.15   Problem 2.8.

4.16   Problem 2.10.

4.17   Problem 2.9.

4.18   Problem 2.11.

4.19   Problem 2.13.

4.20   Problem 1.7, but with inventories of 80 000 bbl of domestic oil and 20 000 bbl of foreign oil.

4.21   Problem 1.17.

4.22   Problem 1.18.

4.23   Problem 1.19.

4.24   Problem 1.22.

Chapter 5

Linear Programming: Duality

Every linear program in the variables $x_1, x_2, \ldots, x_n$ has associated with it another linear program in the variables $w_1, w_2, \ldots, w_m$ (where m is the number of constraints in the original program), known as its *dual*. The original program, called the *primal*, completely determines the form of its dual.

SYMMETRIC DUALS

The dual of a (primal) linear program in the (nonstandard) matrix form

$$\text{minimize:} \quad z = \mathbf{C}^T \mathbf{X}$$
$$\text{subject to:} \quad \mathbf{AX} \geq \mathbf{B} \tag{5.1}$$
$$\text{with:} \quad \mathbf{X} \geq \mathbf{0}$$

is the linear program

$$\text{maximize:} \quad z = \mathbf{B}^T \mathbf{W}$$
$$\text{subject to:} \quad \mathbf{A}^T \mathbf{W} \leq \mathbf{C} \tag{5.2}$$
$$\text{with:} \quad \mathbf{W} \geq \mathbf{0}$$

Conversely, the dual of program (5.2) is program (5.1). (See Problems 5.1 and 5.2.)

Programs (5.1) and (5.2) are symmetrical in that both involve nonnegative variables and inequality constraints; they are known as the *symmetric duals* of each other. The dual variables $w_1, w_2, \ldots, w_m$ are sometimes called *shadow costs*.

DUAL SOLUTIONS

Theorem 5.1 (Duality Theorem): If an optimal solution exists to either the primal or symmetric dual program, then the other program also has an optimal solution and the two objective functions have the same optimal value.

In such situations, the optimal solution to the primal (dual) is found in the last row of the final simplex tableau for the dual (primal), in those columns associated with the slack or surplus variables (see Problem 5.3). Since the solutions to both programs are obtained by solving either one, it may be computationally advantageous to solve a program's dual rather than the program itself. (See Problem 5.4.)

Theorem 5.2 (Complementary Slackness Principle): Given that a pair of symmetric duals have optimal solutions, then if the kth constraint of one system holds as an inequality—i.e., the associated slack or surplus variable is positive—the kth component of the optimal solution of its symmetric dual is zero.

(See Problems 5.11 and 5.12.)

UNSYMMETRIC DUALS

For primal programs in standard matrix form, duals may be defined as follows:

Primal	*Dual*	
minimize: $z = \mathbf{C}^T\mathbf{X}$	maximize: $z = \mathbf{B}^T\mathbf{W}$	
subject to: $\mathbf{AX} = \mathbf{B}$ (5.3)	subject to: $\mathbf{A}^T\mathbf{W} \le \mathbf{C}$	(5.4)
with: $\mathbf{X} \ge 0$		
maximize: $z = \mathbf{C}^T\mathbf{X}$	minimize: $z = \mathbf{B}^T\mathbf{W}$	
subject to: $\mathbf{AX} = \mathbf{B}$ (5.5)	subject to: $\mathbf{A}^T\mathbf{W} \ge \mathbf{C}$	(5.6)
with: $\mathbf{X} \ge 0$		

(See Problems 5.5 and 5.6.)   Conversely, the duals of programs (5.4) and (5.6) are defined as programs (5.3) and (5.5), respectively.   Since the dual of a program in standard form is not itself in standard form, these duals are *unsymmetric*.   Their forms are consistent with and a direct consequence of the definition of symmetric duals (see Problem 5.8).

Theorem 5.1 is valid for unsymmetric duals too.   However, the solution to an unsymmetric dual is not, in general, immediately apparent from the solution to the primal; the relationships are

$$\mathbf{W}^{*T} = \mathbf{C}_0^T\mathbf{A}_0^{-1} \qquad \text{or} \qquad \mathbf{W}^* = (\mathbf{A}_0^T)^{-1}\mathbf{C}_0 \tag{5.7}$$

$$\mathbf{X}^{*T} = \mathbf{B}_0^T(\mathbf{A}_0^T)^{-1} \qquad \text{or} \qquad \mathbf{X}^* = \mathbf{A}_0^{-1}\mathbf{B}_0 \tag{5.8}$$

In (5.7), $\mathbf{C}_0$ and $\mathbf{A}_0$ are made up of those elements of $\mathbf{C}$ and $\mathbf{A}$, in either program (5.3) or (5.5), that correspond to the *basic variables* in $\mathbf{X}^*$; in (5.8), $\mathbf{B}_0$ and $\mathbf{A}_0$ are made up of those elements of $\mathbf{B}$ and $\mathbf{A}$, in either program (5.4) or (5.6), that correspond to the *basic variables* in $\mathbf{W}^*$.   (See Problem 5.7.)

Solved Problems

5.1   Determine the symmetric dual of the program

$$\text{minimize:} \quad z = 5x_1 + 2x_2 + x_3$$

$$\begin{aligned} \text{subject to:} \quad & 2x_1 + 3x_2 + \ x_3 \ge 20 \\ & 6x_1 + 8x_2 + 5x_3 \ge 30 \\ & 7x_1 + \ x_2 + 3x_3 \ge 40 \\ & x_1 + 2x_2 + 4x_3 \ge 50 \end{aligned} \tag{1}$$

with: all variables nonnegative

This program has the form of (5.1).   Its dual, of the form (5.2), is found by taking the opposite optimum, interchanging $\mathbf{B}$ and $\mathbf{C}$, transposing $\mathbf{A}$, and reversing the constraint inequalities:

$$\text{maximize:} \quad z = 20w_1 + 30w_2 + 40w_3 + 50w_4$$

$$\begin{aligned} \text{subject to:} \quad & 2w_1 + 6w_2 + 7w_3 + \ w_4 \le 5 \\ & 3w_1 + 8w_2 + \ w_3 + 2w_4 \le 2 \\ & w_1 + 5w_2 + 3w_3 + 4w_4 \le 1 \end{aligned} \tag{2}$$

with: all variables nonnegative

Note that the primal, program (1), contains three variables and four constraints, while its dual, program (2), contains four variables and three constraints.

5.2 Determine the symmetric dual of the program

$$\text{maximize:} \quad z = 2x_1 + x_2$$

$$\text{subject to:} \quad x_1 + 5x_2 \leq 10$$

$$x_1 + 3x_2 \leq 6 \tag{1}$$

$$2x_1 + 2x_2 \leq 8$$

$$\text{with:} \quad \text{all variables nonnegative}$$

This program has the form (5.2), with x-variables replacing w-variables. Proceeding as in Problem 5.1, we generate its dual, (5.1), with w-variables replacing x-variables:

$$\text{minimize:} \quad z = 10w_1 + 6w_2 + 8w_3$$

$$\text{subject to:} \quad w_1 + w_2 + 2w_3 \geq 2$$

$$5w_1 + 3w_2 + 2w_3 \geq 1 \tag{2}$$

$$\text{with:} \quad \text{all variables nonnegative}$$

5.3 Show that both the primal and dual programs in Problem 5.2 have the same optimal value for z, and that the solution of each is imbedded in the final simplex tableau of the other.

Introducing slack variables x_3, x_4, and x_5, respectively, in the constraint inequalities of program (1) of Problem 5.2, and then applying the simplex method to the resulting program, we generate sequentially Tableaux 1 and 2.

		x_1	x_2	x_3	x_4	x_5	
		2	1	0	0	0	
x_3	0	1	5	1	0	0	10
x_4	0	1	3	0	1	0	6
x_5	0	2*	2	0	0	1	8
$(z_j - c_j)$:		-2	-1	0	0	0	0

Tableau 1

				slack variables			
	x_1	x_2	x_3	x_4	x_5	
x_3	0	4	1	0	$-1/2$	6
x_4	0	2	0	1	$-1/2$	2
x_1	1	1	0	0	1/2	4
	0	1	0	0	1	8

solution to the dual

Tableau 2

The solution to the primal is obtained from Tableau 2 as $x_1^* = 4$, $x_2^* = 0$, with $z^* = 8$. The solution to the dual program is found in the last row of this tableau, in those columns associated with the slack variables for the primal. Here, $w_1^* = 0$, $w_2^* = 0$, and $w_3^* = 1$.

We can solve the dual directly by introducing surplus variables w_4 and w_5, and artificial variables w_6 and w_7, to program (2) of Problem 5.2, and then applying the two-phase method, which generates Tableaux $1', \ldots, 4'$.

		w_1	w_2	w_3	w_4	w_5	w_6	w_7	
		10	6	8	0	0	M	M	
w_6	M	1	1	2	-1	0	1	0	2
w_7	M	5*	3	2	0	-1	0	1	1
$(c_j - z_j)$:		10	6	8	0	0	0	0	0
		-6	-4	-4	1	1	0	0	-3

Tableau 1'

				surplus variables			
	w_1	w_2	w_3	w_4	w_5	
w_5	-4	-5	0	-1	1	1
w_3	1/2	1/2	1	$-1/2$	0	1
	6	2	0	4	0	-8

solution to the primal

Tableau 4'

The solution to the dual is read from Tableau 4' as $w_1^* = w_2^* = 0$, $w_3^* = 1$, with $z^* = -(-8) = 8$. The solution to the primal is found in the last row of this tableau, in those columns associated with the surplus variables. It is the same solution as found previously.

5.4

$$\text{minimize:} \quad z = x_1 + x_2 + x_3 + x_4 + x_5 + x_6$$

$$\text{subject to:} \quad x_1 \qquad\qquad\qquad + x_6 \geq 7$$
$$x_1 + x_2 \qquad\qquad\qquad \geq 20$$
$$x_2 + x_3 \qquad\qquad \geq 14$$
$$x_3 + x_4 \qquad\qquad \geq 20$$
$$x_4 + x_5 \quad\;\; \geq 10$$
$$x_5 + x_6 \geq 5$$

$$\text{with:} \quad \text{all variables nonnegative}$$

To solve this program directly would require the introduction of 12 new variables, six surplus and six artificial, and the application of the two-phase method. A simpler approach is to consider the dual program:

$$\text{maximize:} \quad z = 7w_1 + 20w_2 + 14w_3 + 20w_4 + 10w_5 + 5w_6$$

$$\text{subject to:} \quad w_1 + w_2 \qquad\qquad\qquad \leq 1$$
$$w_2 + w_3 \qquad\qquad \leq 1$$
$$w_3 + w_4 \qquad\qquad \leq 1$$
$$w_4 + w_5 \qquad \leq 1$$
$$w_5 + w_6 \leq 1$$
$$w_1 \qquad\qquad\qquad + w_6 \leq 1$$

$$\text{with:} \quad \text{all variables nonnegative}$$

		w_1	w_2	w_3	w_4	w_5	w_6	w_7	w_8	w_9	w_{10}	w_{11}	w_{12}	
		7	20	14	20	10	5	0	0	0	0	0	0	
w_7	0	1	1	0	0	0	0	1	0	0	0	0	0	1
w_8	0	0	1*	1	0	0	0	0	1	0	0	0	0	1
w_9	0	0	0	1	1	0	0	0	0	1	0	0	0	1
w_{10}	0	0	0	0	1	1	0	0	0	0	1	0	0	1
w_{11}	0	0	0	0	0	1	1	0	0	0	0	1	0	1
w_{12}	0	1	0	0	0	0	1	0	0	0	0	0	1	1
$(z_j - c_j)$:		−7	−20	−14	−20	−10	−5	0	0	0	0	0	0	0

Tableau 1

. . . .

	w_1	w_2	w_3	w_4	w_5	w_6	*slack variables*						
							w_7	w_8	w_9	w_{10}	w_{11}	w_{12}	
w_1	1	0	−1	0	0	0	1	−1	0	0	0	0	0
w_2	0	1	1	0	0	0	0	1	0	0	0	0	1
w_9	0	0	1	0	−1	0	0	0	1	−1	0	0	0
w_4	0	0	0	1	1	0	0	0	0	1	0	0	1
w_{11}	0	0	−1	0	1	0	1	−1	0	0	1	−1	0
w_6	0	0	1	0	0	1	−1	1	0	0	0	1	1
	0	0	4	0	10	0	2	18	0	20	0	5	45

solution to the primal

Tableau 5

This system is put in standard form by introducing only six new variables, all slack. Doing so and then applying the simplex method, we successively generate Tableaux $1, \ldots, 5$. Tableau 5 signals optimality for the dual program, so the optimal solution to the primal is found in the last row of this tableau, in those columns associated with the slack variables. Specifically, $x_1^* = 2$, $x_2^* = 18$, $x_3^* = 0$, $x_4^* = 20$, $x_5^* = 0$, $x_6^* = 5$, with $z^* = 45$.

5.5   Determine the dual of the program

$$\text{maximize:} \quad z = x_1 + 3x_2 - 2x_3$$
$$\text{subject to:} \quad 4x_1 + 8x_2 + 6x_3 = 25$$
$$7x_1 + 5x_2 + 9x_3 = 30$$
$$\text{with:} \quad \text{all variables nonnegative}$$

This program has the form (5.5); its unsymmetric dual is given by (5.6) as

$$\text{minimize:} \quad z = 25w_1 + 30w_2$$
$$\text{subject to:} \quad 4w_1 + 7w_2 \geq 1$$
$$8w_1 + 5w_2 \geq 3$$
$$6w_1 + 9w_2 \geq -2$$

5.6   Determine the dual of the program

$$\text{minimize:} \quad z = 3x_1 + x_2 + 0x_3 + 0x_4 + Mx_5 + Mx_6$$
$$\text{subject to:} \quad x_1 + x_2 - x_3 \qquad + x_5 \qquad = 7$$
$$2x_1 + 3x_2 \qquad - x_4 \qquad + x_6 = 8$$
$$\text{with:} \quad \text{all variables nonnegative}$$

As this program has the form (5.3), its unsymmetric dual is given by (5.4) as

$$\text{maximize:} \quad z = 7w_1 + 8w_2$$
$$\text{subject to:} \quad w_1 + 2w_2 \leq 3$$
$$w_1 + 3w_2 \leq 1$$
$$-w_1 \qquad \leq 0$$
$$- w_2 \leq 0$$
$$w_1 \qquad \leq M$$
$$w_2 \leq M$$

Because the third and fourth constraints are equivalent to $w_1 \geq 0$ and $w_2 \geq 0$, and because the fifth and sixth constraints simply require the variables to be finite (a condition that is always presupposed), the dual program can be simplified to

$$\text{maximize:} \quad z = 7w_1 + 8w_2$$
$$\text{subject to:} \quad w_1 + 2w_2 \leq 3$$
$$w_1 + 3w_2 \leq 1$$
$$\text{with:} \quad w_1 \text{ and } w_2 \text{ nonnegative}$$

5.7   Verify (5.7) and (5.8) for the programs of Problem 5.5.

The primal program can be solved by the two-phase method if artificial variables x_4 and x_5, respectively, are first added to the left-hand sides of the constraint equations. Tableaux $1, \ldots, 4$ result.

		x_1	x_2	x_3	x_4	x_5	
		1	3	-2	$-M$	$-M$	
x_4	$-M$	4	8	6	1	0	25
x_5	$-M$	7	5	9^*	0	1	30
$(z_j - c_j)$:		-1	-3	2	0	0	0
		-11	-13	-15	0	0	-55

Tableau 1

. . . .

	x_1	x_2	x_3	
x_2	0	1	0.1668	1.528
x_1	1	0	1.167	3.193
	0	0	3.668	7.777

Tableau 4

The dual program was put into standard form in Problem 2.6 (with x's replacing w's). Applying the two-phase method to that program, we generate Tableaux $1', \ldots, 3'$. It follows from Tableau 4 that $x_1^* = 3.193$, $x_2^* = 1.528$, $x_3^* = 0$, with $z^* = 7.777$. It follows from Tableau $3'$ that

$$w_1^* = w_3^* - w_4^* = 0.4444 \qquad w_2^* = w_5^* - w_6^* = -0.1111$$

with $z^* = -(-7.778) = 7.778$. Note that the values of the objective for both the primal and the dual are identical except for roundoff error.

		w_3	w_4	w_5	w_6	w_7	w_8	w_9	w_{10}	w_{11}	
		25	-25	30	-30	0	0	0	M	M	
w_{10}	M	4^*	-4	7	-7	-1	0	0	1	0	1
w_{11}	M	8	-8	5	-5	0	-1	0	0	1	3
w_9	0	-6	6	-9	9	0	0	1	0	0	2
$(c_j - z_j)$:		25	-25	30	-30	0	0	0	0	0	0
		-12	12	-12	12	1	1	0	0	0	-4

Tableau 1′

. . . .

	w_3	w_4	w_5	w_6	w_7	w_8	w_9	
w_3	1	1	0	0	0.1389	-0.1944	0	0.4444
w_6	0	0	-1	1	0.2222	-0.1111	0	0.1111
w_9	0	0	0	0	-1.167	-0.1667	1	3.667
	0	0	0	0	3.195	1.528	0	-7.778

Tableau 3′

To verify (5.7), we note that the basic variables in $\mathbf{X}^*$ are x_1 and x_2; hence (5.7) becomes

$$\mathbf{W}^{*T} = [1, 3] \begin{bmatrix} 4 & 8 \\ 7 & 5 \end{bmatrix}^{-1} = [1, 3] \begin{bmatrix} -5/36 & 8/36 \\ 7/36 & -4/36 \end{bmatrix} = [16/36, -4/36] = [0.4444, -0.1111]$$

To verify (5.8), we note that the basic variables in $\mathbf{W}^*$, as given in Tableau $3'$, are w_3, w_6, and w_9; hence (5.8) becomes

$$\mathbf{X}^{*T} = [25, -30, 0] \begin{bmatrix} 4 & -7 & 0 \\ 8 & -5 & 0 \\ -6 & 9 & 1 \end{bmatrix}^{-1} = [25, -30, 0] \begin{bmatrix} -5/36 & 7/36 & 0 \\ -8/36 & 4/36 & 0 \\ 42/36 & 6/36 & 1 \end{bmatrix}$$

$$= [115/36, 55/36, 0] = [3.194, 1.528, 0]$$

5.8 Show that the form of the unsymmetric dual is uniquely determined by the form of the symmetric dual.

Consider program (5.3), with an $m \times n$ matrix $\mathbf{A}$. Since the equality constraint $\mathbf{AX} = \mathbf{B}$ is equivalent to the two inequality constraints $\mathbf{AX} \geq \mathbf{B}$ and $\mathbf{AX} \leq \mathbf{B}$, and since this second inequality can be rewritten as $-\mathbf{AX} \geq -\mathbf{B}$, program (5.3) is equivalent to

$$\text{minimize:} \quad z = \mathbf{C}^T \mathbf{X}$$

$$\text{subject to:} \quad \hat{\mathbf{A}} \mathbf{X} \geq \hat{\mathbf{B}} \tag{1}$$

$$\text{with:} \quad \mathbf{X} \geq 0$$

where

$$\hat{\mathbf{A}} \equiv \begin{bmatrix} \mathbf{A} \\ -\mathbf{A} \end{bmatrix} \qquad \hat{\mathbf{B}} \equiv \begin{bmatrix} \mathbf{B} \\ -\mathbf{B} \end{bmatrix}$$

Program (1) has the form (5.1); its symmetric dual is given by (5.2) (with $\mathbf{U}$ written instead of $\mathbf{W}$) as

$$\text{maximize:} \quad z = \hat{\mathbf{B}}^T \mathbf{U}$$

$$\text{subject to:} \quad \hat{\mathbf{A}}^T \mathbf{U} \leq \mathbf{C} \tag{2}$$

$$\text{with:} \quad \mathbf{U} \geq 0$$

Partitioning $\mathbf{U}$ into two m-dimensional vectors, $\mathbf{U}_1$ and $\mathbf{U}_2$, and using the definitions of $\hat{\mathbf{A}}$ and $\hat{\mathbf{B}}$, we may rewrite (2) as

$$\text{maximize:} \quad z = [\mathbf{B}^T, -\mathbf{B}^T] \begin{bmatrix} \mathbf{U}_1 \\ \mathbf{U}_2 \end{bmatrix} = \mathbf{B}^T (\mathbf{U}_1 - \mathbf{U}_2)$$

$$\text{subject to:} \quad [\mathbf{A}^T, -\mathbf{A}^T] \begin{bmatrix} \mathbf{U}_1 \\ \mathbf{U}_2 \end{bmatrix} = \mathbf{A}^T (\mathbf{U}_1 - \mathbf{U}_2) \leq \mathbf{C} \tag{3}$$

$$\text{with:} \quad \mathbf{U}_1 \geq 0 \quad \text{and} \quad \mathbf{U}_2 \geq 0$$

Finally, defining $\mathbf{W} \equiv \mathbf{U}_1 - \mathbf{U}_2$, and noting that the difference of two nonnegative vectors is not itself restricted in sign, we put (3), which is the dual of program (5.3), into the form

$$\text{maximize:} \quad z = \mathbf{B}^T \mathbf{W}$$

$$\text{subject to:} \quad \mathbf{A}^T \mathbf{W} \leq \mathbf{C} \tag{4}$$

This last system is precisely program (5.4).

Repeating all the above steps with the words "maximize" and "minimize" interchanged and with the inequalities reversed in the main constraints, we may also show that the dual of program (5.5) is program (5.6).

5.9 Prove that if $\mathbf{X}$ is *any* feasible solution to program (5.1) and if $\mathbf{W}$ is *any* feasible solution to program (5.2), then $\mathbf{C}^T \mathbf{X} \geq \mathbf{B}^T \mathbf{W}$.

If $\mathbf{X}$ is a feasible solution to (5.1), then $\mathbf{AX} \geq \mathbf{B}$. Premultiplying this inequality by the nonnegative vector $\mathbf{W}^T$, we obtain $\mathbf{W}^T \mathbf{AX} \geq \mathbf{W}^T \mathbf{B}$, which is equivalent to

$$\mathbf{W}^T \mathbf{AX} \geq \mathbf{B}^T \mathbf{W} \tag{1}$$

since $\mathbf{W}^T \mathbf{B}$ is a scalar.

If $\mathbf{W}$ is a feasible solution of (5.2), then $\mathbf{A}^T \mathbf{W} \leq \mathbf{C}$, or $\mathbf{W}^T \mathbf{A} \leq \mathbf{C}^T$. Postmultiplying by the nonnegative vector $\mathbf{X}$, we obtain

$$\mathbf{W}^T \mathbf{AX} \leq \mathbf{C}^T \mathbf{X} \tag{2}$$

Together, (1) and (2) imply $\mathbf{C}^T \mathbf{X} \geq \mathbf{B}^T \mathbf{W}$.

5.10 Given that $\mathbf{A}$ in program (5.1) is $m \times n$, let $x_{n+1}, x_{n+2}, \ldots, x_{n+m}$ be surplus variables introduced in the program to render the constraints equalities; and let $w_{m+1}, w_{m+2}, \ldots, w_{m+n}$ be slack variables introduced in program (5.2) for the same reason.   Let z_1 and z_2 be the values of the objective functions of programs (5.1) and (5.2), respectively.   Show that

$$\sum_{j=1}^{n} x_j w_{m+j} + \sum_{i=1}^{m} w_i x_{n+i} = z_1 - z_2 \qquad (1)$$

Program (5.1) takes the form

$$\text{minimize:} \quad z_1 = c_1 x_1 + \cdots + c_n x_n + 0 x_{n+1} + 0 x_{n+2} + \cdots + 0 x_{n+m}$$

$$\text{subject to:} \quad a_{11} x_1 + a_{12} x_2 + \cdots + a_{1n} x_n - x_{n+1} \qquad\qquad\quad = b_1$$

$$a_{21} x_1 + a_{22} x_2 + \cdots + a_{2n} x_n \qquad - x_{n+2} \qquad\quad = b_2$$

$$\cdot \quad \cdot \quad \cdot \quad \cdot \quad \cdot \quad \cdot \quad \cdot \quad \cdot \quad \cdot \quad \cdot \quad \cdot \quad \cdot \quad \cdot$$

$$a_{m1} x_1 + a_{m2} x_2 + \cdots + a_{mn} x_n \qquad\qquad\qquad - x_{n+m} = b_m$$

with: all variables nonnegative

Multiplying the ith constraint equation of this program by w_i $(i = 1, 2, \ldots, m)$ and summing the results, we obtain

$$\sum_{i=1}^{m} \sum_{j=1}^{n} a_{ij} x_j w_i - \sum_{i=1}^{m} x_{n+i} w_i = \sum_{i=1}^{m} b_i w_i$$

Subtracting this equation from

$$\sum_{j=1}^{n} c_j x_j = z_1$$

we get

$$\sum_{j=1}^{n} c_j x_j - \sum_{i=1}^{m} \sum_{j=1}^{n} a_{ij} x_j w_i + \sum_{i=1}^{m} x_{n+i} w_i = z_1 - \sum_{i=1}^{m} b_i w_i$$

which can be rewritten as

$$\sum_{j=1}^{n} \left(c_j - \sum_{i=1}^{m} a_{ij} w_i \right) x_j + \sum_{i=1}^{m} x_{n+i} w_i = z_1 - \sum_{i=1}^{m} b_i w_i \qquad (2)$$

Program (5.2) takes the form

$$\text{maximize:} \quad z_2 = b_1 w_1 + \cdots + b_m w_m + 0 w_{m+1} + 0 w_{m+2} + \cdots + 0 w_{m+n}$$

$$\text{subject to:} \quad a_{11} w_1 + a_{21} w_2 + \cdots + a_{m1} w_m + w_{m+1} \qquad\qquad\quad = c_1$$

$$a_{12} w_1 + a_{22} w_2 + \cdots + a_{m2} w_m \qquad + w_{m+2} \qquad\quad = c_2$$

$$\cdot \quad \cdot \quad \cdot \quad \cdot \quad \cdot \quad \cdot \quad \cdot \quad \cdot \quad \cdot \quad \cdot \quad \cdot \quad \cdot \quad \cdot$$

$$a_{1n} w_1 + a_{2n} w_2 + \cdots + a_{mn} w_m \qquad\qquad\qquad + w_{m+n} = c_n$$

with: all variables nonnegative

Solving for the slack variables w_{m+j} $(j = 1, 2, \ldots, n)$ in this program, we find

$$w_{m+j} = c_j - \sum_{i=1}^{m} a_{ij} w_i$$

Substituting this result into (2), and noting that

$$z_2 = \sum_{i=1}^{m} b_i w_i$$

we obtain (1).

5.11   Prove the *complementary slackness principle* (Theorem 5.2).

For optimal solutions $\mathbf{X}^*$ and $\mathbf{W}^*$ of programs (5.1) and (5.2), respectively, relation (1) of Problem 5.10 becomes

$$\sum_{j=1}^{n} x_j^* w_{m+j}^* + \sum_{i=1}^{m} w_i^* x_{n+i}^* = 0$$

the right-hand side being 0 because of Theorem 5.1. As each variable in the above equation is non-negative, the individual summands must vanish; that is,

$$x_j^* w_{m+j}^* = 0 \quad (j = 1, 2, \ldots, n) \qquad \text{and} \qquad w_i^* x_{n+i}^* = 0 \quad (i = 1, 2, \ldots, m)$$

On the left is the product of the jth component of $\mathbf{X}^*$ with the jth slack variable of program (5.2); if either term is positive, the other must be zero. On the right is the product of the ith component of $\mathbf{W}^*$ with the ith surplus variable of program (5.1); if either term is positive, the other must be zero.

5.12 Use the results of Problem 5.3 to verify the complementary slackness principle.

Considering the optimal tableau for the primal program (Tableau 2), we find that the first two slack variables, x_3 and x_4, are positive ($x_3 = 6$ and $x_4 = 2$); hence the first two dual variables, w_1 and w_2, should be zero. They are. We also find for the third dual variable, $w_3 = 1$. Since it is positive, the third slack variable in the primal, x_5, should be zero too. It is.

Next consider the optimal tableau for the dual program (Tableau 4′). The second surplus variable, w_5, is positive; hence the second primal variable, x_2, should be zero. It is. In addition, the first primal variable, x_1, is positive; so the first surplus variable in the dual system, w_4, should be zero too. It is.

Supplementary Problems

In Problems 5.13 through 5.17, determine the duals of the given programs.

5.13

$$\text{minimize:} \quad z = 12x_1 + 26x_2 + 80x_3$$
$$\text{subject to:} \quad 2x_1 + 6x_2 + 5x_3 \geq 4$$
$$4x_1 + 2x_2 + x_3 \geq 10$$
$$x_1 + x_2 + 2x_3 \geq 6$$
$$\text{with:} \quad \text{all variables nonnegative}$$

5.14

$$\text{minimize:} \quad z = 3x_1 + 2x_2 + x_3 + 2x_4 + 3x_5$$
$$\text{subject to:} \quad 2x_1 + 5x_2 + x_4 + x_5 \geq 6$$
$$4x_2 - 2x_3 + 2x_4 + 3x_5 \geq 5$$
$$x_1 - 6x_2 + 3x_3 + 7x_4 + 5x_5 \leq 7$$
$$\text{with:} \quad \text{all variables nonnegative}$$

5.15

$$\text{maximize:} \quad z = 6x_1 - x_2 + 3x_3$$
$$\text{subject to:} \quad 7x_1 + 11x_2 + 3x_3 \leq 25$$
$$2x_1 + 8x_2 + 6x_3 \leq 30$$
$$6x_1 + x_2 + 7x_3 \leq 35$$
$$\text{with:} \quad \text{all variables nonnegative}$$

5.16

$$\text{maximize:} \quad z = 10x_1 + 15x_2 + 20x_3 + 25x_4$$
$$\text{subject to:} \quad 8x_1 + 6x_2 - x_3 + x_4 \geq 16$$
$$3x_1 + 2x_3 - x_4 = 20$$
$$\text{with:} \quad \text{all variables nonnegative}$$

5.17
$$\text{minimize:} \quad z = x_1 + 2x_2 + x_3$$
$$\text{subject to:} \quad x_2 + x_3 = 1$$
$$3x_1 + x_2 + 3x_3 = 4$$
$$\text{with:} \quad \text{all variables nonnegative}$$

5.18 Show that the program given in Problem 5.13 has the same optimal value as its dual by solving both programs directly.

5.19 Find the optimal solution to the program given in Problem 5.14 by solving its dual.

5.20 Determine the symmetric dual of the program given in Problem 4.3.　Solve the dual directly and thereby verify that if either a primal or its symmetric dual has feasible solutions but no optimum, then the other has no feasible solution.

5.21 By finding the unsymmetric dual of the program

$$\text{minimize:} \quad z = -x_1 - x_2$$
$$\text{subject to:} \quad x_1 - x_2 = 5$$
$$x_1 - x_2 = -5$$
$$\text{with:} \quad \text{all variables nonnegative}$$

show that it is possible for both a primal and its dual to have no feasible solutions.

5.22 Use the results of Problem 5.4 to verify the complementary slackness principle.

5.23 Verify (5.7) and (5.8) for the program given in Problem 5.17.

5.24 Prove that if X_0 and W_0 are feasible solutions of programs (5.1) and (5.2), respectively, such that $C^T X_0 = B^T W_0$, then X_0 and W_0 are optimal solutions to their respective programs.

Chapter 6

Integer Programming: Branch-and-Bound Algorithm

FIRST APPROXIMATION

An integer program is a linear program with the added requirement that all variables be integers (see Chapter 1). Therefore, a *first approximation* to the solution of any integer program may be obtained by ignoring the integer requirement and solving the resulting linear program by one of the techniques already presented. If the optimal solution to the linear program happens to be integral, then this solution is also the optimal solution to the original integer program (see Problem 6.3). Otherwise—and this is the usual situation—one may round the components of the first approximation to the nearest feasible integers and obtain a *second approximation*. This procedure is often carried out, especially when the first approximation involves large numbers, but it can be inaccurate when the numbers are small (see Problem 6.5).

BRANCHING

If the first approximation contains a variable that is not integral, say x_j^*, then $i_1 < x_j^* < i_2$, where i_1 and i_2 are consecutive, nonnegative integers. Two new integer programs are then created by augmenting the original integer program with either the constraint $x_j \leq i_1$ or the constraint $x_j \geq i_2$. This process, called *branching*, has the effect of shrinking the feasible region in a way that eliminates from further consideration the current nonintegral solution for x_j but still preserves all possible integral solutions to the original problem. (See Problem 6.8.)

Example 6.1 As a first approximation to the integer program

$$\text{maximize:} \quad z = 10x_1 + x_2$$
$$\text{subject to:} \quad 2x_1 + 5x_2 \leq 11 \qquad\qquad (6.1)$$
$$\text{with:} \quad x_1 \text{ and } x_2 \text{ nonnegative and integral}$$

we consider the associated linear program obtained by deleting the integer requirement. By graphing, the solution is readily found to be $x_1^* = 5.5$, $x_2^* = 0$, with $z^* = 55$. Since $5 < x_1^* < 6$, branching creates the two new integer programs

$$\text{maximize:} \quad z = 10x_1 + x_2$$
$$\text{subject to:} \quad 2x_1 + 5x_2 \leq 11$$
$$x_1 \qquad \leq 5 \qquad\qquad (6.2)$$
$$\text{with:} \quad x_1 \text{ and } x_2 \text{ nonnegative and integral}$$

$$\text{maximize:} \quad z = 10x_1 + x_2$$
$$\text{subject to:} \quad 2x_1 + 5x_2 \leq 11$$
$$x_1 \qquad \geq 6 \qquad\qquad (6.3)$$
$$\text{with:} \quad x_1 \text{ and } x_2 \text{ nonnegative and integral}$$

For the two integer programs created by the branching process, first approximations are obtained by again ignoring the integer requirements and solving the resulting linear programs. If either first approximation is still nonintegral, then the integer program which gave rise to that first approximation becomes a candidate for further branching.

Example 6.2 Using graphical methods, we find that program (6.2) has the first approximation $x_1^* = 5$, $x_2^* = 0.2$, with $z^* = 50.2$, while program (6.3) has no feasible solution. Thus, program (6.2) is a candidate for further branching. Since $0 < x_2^* < 1$, we augment (6.2) with either $x_2 \leq 0$ or $x_2 \geq 1$, and obtain the two new programs

$$\text{maximize:} \quad z = 10x_1 + x_2$$
$$\text{subject to:} \quad 2x_1 + 5x_2 \leq 11$$
$$x_1 \qquad \leq 5 \qquad\qquad (6.4)$$
$$x_2 \leq 0$$
$$\text{with:} \quad x_1 \text{ and } x_2 \text{ nonnegative and integral}$$

(in which $x_2 = 0$ is forced) and

$$\text{maximize:} \quad z = 10x_1 + x_2$$
$$\text{subject to:} \quad 2x_1 + 5x_2 \leq 11$$
$$x_1 \qquad \leq 5 \qquad\qquad (6.5)$$
$$x_2 \geq 1$$
$$\text{with:} \quad x_1 \text{ and } x_2 \text{ nonnegative and integral}$$

With the integer requirements ignored, the solution to program (6.4) is $x_1^* = 5$, $x_2^* = 0$, with $z^* = 50$, while the solution to program (6.5) is $x_1^* = 3$, $x_2^* = 1$, with $z^* = 31$. Since both these first approximations are integral, no further branching is required.

BOUNDING

Assume that the objective function is to be *maximized.* Branching continues until an integral first approximation (which is thus an integral solution) is obtained. The value of the objective for this first integral solution becomes a lower bound for the problem, and all programs whose first approximations, integral or not, yield values of the objective function smaller than the lower bound are discarded.

Example 6.3 Program (6.4) possesses an integral solution with $z^* = 50$; hence 50 becomes a lower bound for the problem. Program (6.5) has a solution with $z^* = 31$. Since 31 is less than the lower bound 50, program (6.5) is eliminated from further consideration, *and would have been so eliminated even if its first approximation had been nonintegral.*

Branching continues from those programs having nonintegral first approximations that give values of the objective function greater than the lower bound. If, in the process, a new integral solution is uncovered having a value of the objective function greater than the current lower bound, then this value of the objective function becomes the new lower bound. The program that yielded the old lower bound is eliminated, as are all programs whose first approximations give values of the objective function smaller than the new lower bound. The branching process continues until there are no programs with nonintegral first approximations remaining under consideration. At this point, the current lower-bound solution is the optimal solution to the original integer program.

If the objective function is to be *minimized*, the procedure remains the same, except that upper bounds are used. Thus, the value of the first integral solution becomes an upper bound for the problem, and programs are eliminated when their first approximate z-values are greater than the current upper bound.

COMPUTATIONAL CONSIDERATIONS

One always branches from that program which appears most nearly optimal. When there are a number of candidates for further branching, one chooses that having the largest z-value, if the objective function is to be maximized, or that having the smallest z-value, if the objective function is to be minimized.

Additional constraints are added one at a time. If a first approximation involves more than one nonintegral variable, the new constraints are imposed on that variable which is furthest from being an integer; i.e., that variable whose fractional part is closest to 0.5. In case of a tie, the solver arbitrarily chooses one of the variables.

Finally, it is possible for an integer program or an associated linear program to have more than one optimal solution. In both cases, we adhere to the convention adopted in Chapter 1, arbitrarily designating one of the solutions as the optimal one and disregarding the rest.

Solved Problems

6.1   Draw a schematic diagram (tree) depicting the results of Examples 6.1 through 6.3.

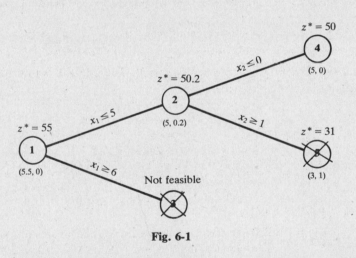

Fig. 6-1

See Fig. 6-1. The original integer program, here (6.1), is designated by a circled 1, and all other programs formed through branching are designated in the order of their creation by circled successive integers. Thus, programs (6.2) through (6.5) are designated by circled 2 through 5, respectively. The first approximate solution to each program is written by the circle designating the program. Each circle (program) is then connected by a line to that circle (program) which generated it via the branching process. The new constraint that defined the branch is written above the line. Finally, a large cross is drawn through a circle if the corresponding program has been eliminated from further consideration. Hence, branch 3 was eliminated because it was not feasible; branch 5 was eliminated by bounding in Example 6.3. Since there are no nonintegral branches left to consider, the schematic diagram indicates that program 1 is solved with $x_1^* = 5$, $x_2^* = 0$, and $z^* = 50$.

6.2

$$\text{maximize:} \quad z = 3x_1 + 4x_2$$

$$\text{subject to:} \quad 2x_1 + x_2 \leq 6$$

$$2x_1 + 3x_2 \leq 9$$

$$\text{with:} \quad x_1, x_2 \text{ nonnegative and integral}$$

Neglecting the integer requirement, we obtain $x_1^* = 2.25$, $x_2^* = 1.5$, with $z^* = 12.75$, as the solution to the associated linear program. Since x_2^* is further from an integral value than x_1^*, we use it to generate the branches $x_2 \leq 1$ and $x_2 \geq 2$.

Program 2

maximize: $z = 3x_1 + 4x_2$

subject to: $2x_1 + x_2 \leq 6$

$2x_1 + 3x_2 \leq 9$

$x_2 \leq 1$

with: x_1, x_2 nonnegative
and integral

Program 3

maximize: $z = 3x_1 + 4x_2$

subject to: $2x_1 + x_2 \leq 6$

$2x_1 + 3x_2 \leq 9$

$x_2 \geq 2$

with: x_1, x_2 nonnegative
and integral

The first approximation to Program 2 is $x_1^* = 2.5$, $x_2^* = 1$, with $z^* = 11.5$; the first approximation to Program 3 is $x_1^* = 1.5$, $x_2^* = 2$, with $z^* = 12.5$. These results are shown in Fig. 6-2. Since Programs 2 and 3 both have nonintegral first approximations, we could branch from either one; we choose Program 3 because it has the larger (more nearly optimal) value of the objective function. Here $1 < x_1^* < 2$, so the new programs are

Program 4

maximize: $z = 3x_1 + 4x_2$

subject to: $2x_1 + x_2 \leq 6$

$2x_1 + 3x_2 \leq 9$

$x_2 \geq 2$

$x_1 \leq 1$

with: x_1, x_2 nonnegative
and integral

Program 5

maximize: $z = 3x_1 + 4x_2$

subject to: $2x_1 + x_2 \leq 6$

$2x_1 + 3x_2 \leq 9$

$x_2 \geq 2$

$x_1 \geq 2$

with: x_1, x_2 nonnegative
and integral

There is no solution to Program 5 (it is infeasible), while the solution to Program 4 with the integer constraints ignored is $x_1^* = 1$, $x_2^* = 7/3$, with $z^* = 12.33$. See Fig. 6-2. The branching can continue from either Program 2 or Program 4; we choose Program 4 since it has the greater z-value.

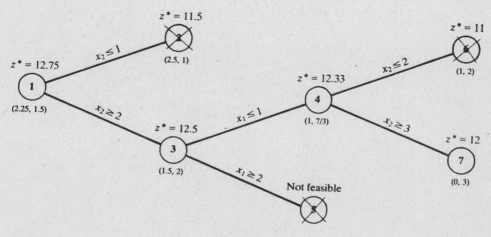

Fig. 6-2

Here $2 < x_2^* < 3$, so the new programs are

<table>
<tr><td>

Program 6

maximize: $z = 3x_1 + 4x_2$

subject to: $2x_1 + x_2 \le 6$

$2x_1 + 3x_2 \le 9$

$x_2 \ge 2$

$x_1 \qquad \le 1$

$x_2 \le 2$

with: x_1, x_2 nonnegative
and integral

</td><td>

Program 7

maximize: $z = 3x_1 + 4x_2$

subject to: $2x_1 + x_2 \le 6$

$2x_1 + 3x_2 \le 9$

$x_2 \ge 2$

$x_1 \qquad \le 1$

$x_2 \ge 3$

with: x_1, x_2 nonnegative
and integral

</td></tr>
</table>

The solution to Program 6 with the integer constraints ignored is $x_1^* = 1$, $x_2^* = 2$, with $z^* = 11$. Since this is an integral solution, $z = 11$ becomes a lower bound for the problem; any program yielding a z-value smaller than 11 will henceforth be eliminated. The first approximation to Problem 7 is $x_1^* = 0$, $x_2^* = 3$, with $z^* = 12$. Since this is an integral solution with a z-value greater than the current lower bound, $z = 12$ becomes the new lower bound, and the program that generated the old lower bound, Program 6, is eliminated from further consideration, as is Program 2. Figure 6-2 now shows no branches left to consider other than the one corresponding to the current lower bound. Consequently, this branch gives the optimal solution to Program 1: $x_1^* = 0$, $x_2^* = 3$, with $z^* = 12$.

6.3   Solve Problem 1.9.

Dropping the integer requirements from program (*1*) of Problem 1.9, we solve the associated linear program first, to find (see Problem 5.4): $x_1^* = 2$, $x_2^* = 18$, $x_3^* = 0$, $x_4^* = 20$, $x_5^* = 0$, $x_6^* = 5$, with $z^* = 45$. This is the first approximation. Since it is integral, however, it is also the optimal solution to the original integer program.

6.4   Solve Problem 1.6.

Ignoring the integer requirements in program (*4*) of Problem 1.6, we obtain $x_1^* = x_2^* = 0$, $x_3^* = 1666.67$, $x_4^* = 5000$, with $z^* = 55\,000$, as the first approximation. Since x_3^* is not integral, we branch to two new programs, and solve each with the integer constraints ignored. The results are indicated in Fig. 6-3. Program 3 possesses an integral solution with a z-value greater than the z-value of Program 2. Consequently, we eliminate Program 2 and accept the solution to Program 3 as the optimal one: $x_1^* = 1$, $x_2^* = 0$, $x_3^* = 1667$, $x_4^* = 4999$, with $z^* = \$55\,000$.

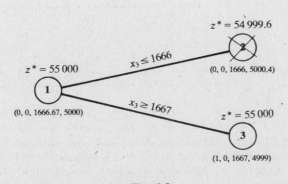

Fig. 6-3

6.5   Discuss the errors involved in rounding the first approximations to the original programs in Problems 6.2 and 6.4 to integers and then taking these answers as the optimal ones.

The first approximation in Problem 6.2 was $x_1^* = 2.25$, $x_2^* = 1.5$. We wish to round to the closest integer point *in the feasible region*. Now, of the four integer points surrounding the first approximation, only one, (2, 1), is found to lie in the feasible region. Thus we take $x_1^* = 2$, $x_2^* = 1$, with a corresponding $z^* = 10$, as the proposed optimal solution. The true optimal solution was found as $z^* = 12$; thus the rounded solution deviates from the true solution by more than 16 percent.

The first approximation in Problem 6.4 was $x_1^* = x_2^* = 0$, $x_3^* = 1666.67$, $x_4^* = 5000$. Rounding x_3^* down, to remain feasible, we obtain $x_1^* = x_2^* = 0$, $x_3^* = 1666$, $x_4^* = 5000$ as the estimated coordinates of the optimal solution. The corresponding z-value, $54\,996$, deviates from the true solution, $z^* = \$55\,000$, by less than 0.008 percent.

6.6
$$\text{minimize:} \quad z = x_1 + x_2$$

$$\text{subject to:} \quad 2x_1 + 2x_2 \geq 5$$

$$12x_1 + 5x_2 \leq 30$$

$$\text{with:} \quad x_1 \text{ and } x_2 \text{ nonnegative and integral}$$

A first approximation to this program is $x_1^* = 2.5$, $x_2^* = 0$, with $z^* = 2.5$. Rounding x_1^* up, thereby remaining feasible, we have $x_1^* = 3$, $x_2^* = 0$, with $z^* = 3$, as an estimate of the optimal solution to the original program. Observe, however, that for integral values of the variables, the objective function must itself be integral. The z-value for the first approximation, $z^* = 2.5$, provides a lower bound for the optimal objective; consequently, the optimal objective cannot be smaller than 3. Since we have an estimate which attains the value 3, the estimate must be optimal; i.e., $x_1^* = 3$, $x_2^* = 0$, with $z^* = 3$.

6.7   Solve the *knapsack problem* formulated in Problem 1.8.

The simplex method could be used to find the first approximation for program (3) of Problem 1.8. A more efficient procedure is the following:

The critical factor in determining whether an item is taken is not its weight or value per se but the ratio of the two, its value per pound. We denote this factor as *desirability*, adjoin it to the data, and construct Table 6-1, where the items are listed in order of decreasing desirability. To obtain the optimal solution to the knapsack problem with the integer constraints ignored, we simply take as much of each item as possible (without exceeding the 60-lb weight limit), beginning with the most desirable. It follows from Table 6-1 that the first approximation consists in all of item 2 (the most desirable one), all of item 5 (the next most desirable item), and 30 lb of item 3: $x_1^* = 0$, $x_2^* = 1$, $x_3^* = 30/35$, $x_4^* = 0$, $x_5^* = 1$, with $z^* = 135$.

Table 6-1

Item	Weight, lb	Value	Desirability, value/lb
2	23	60	2.61
5	7	15	2.14
3	35	70	2.00
1	52	100	1.92
4	15	15	1.00

Since this first approximation is nonintegral, we branch by augmenting the original constraints with either $x_3 \leq 0$ or $x_3 \geq 1$. Before doing so, however, we note that since x_3 is required to be nonnegative, the constraint $x_3 \leq 0$ can be tightened to $x_3 = 0$; and since at most one of an item will be taken, the constraint $x_3 \geq 1$ can be tightened to $x_3 = 1$. This is indicated in the tree diagram, Fig. 6-4.

Dropping the integer requirements, we determine the optimal solutions to both Programs 2 and 3 in Fig. 6-4, using Table 6-1 to find the best mix consistent with the constraints. For Program 2, we obtain $x_1^* = 30/52$, $x_2^* = 1$, $x_3^* = 0$, $x_4^* = 0$, $x_5^* = 1$, with $z^* = 132.69$; and for Program 3, $x_1^* = 0$, $x_2^* = 1$, $x_3^* = 1$, $x_4^* = 0$, $x_5^* = 2/7$, with $z^* = 134.28$.

Continuing the branch-and-bound process, we complete Fig. 6-4. The first integral solution is obtained in Program 8, with $z^* = 90$. A second integral solution is obtained in Program 10, with $z^* =$

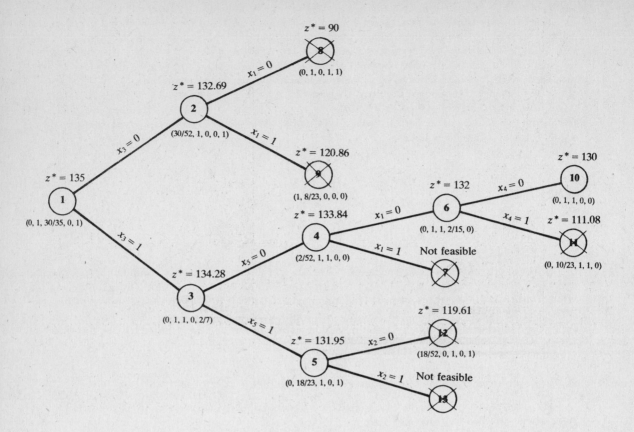

Fig. 6-4

130. Since this second z-value is larger than the first, we eliminate Program 8, as well as Programs 9 and 11. Program 5, however, possesses a z-value greater than the current lower bound, so that we must still branch from it. The resulting Program 12 has a z-value smaller than 130, while Program 13 is infeasible; hence they too are eliminated. We remain with only Program 10; therefore, its solution—take only items 2 and 3, for a total value of 130—is the optimal solution.

Much of the branch-and-bound process might have been avoided. We know in advance that either $x_3 = 0$ or $x_3 = 1$ in the optimal solution. If $x_3 = 0$, then Program 2 coincides with the original program, and the z-value 132.69 obtained when the integer requirements are dropped (thereby expanding the feasible region) must be greater than, or at least equal to, the true optimum. Similarly, if $x_3 = 1$, we see from Program 3 that the true optimum cannot exceed 134.28. Whichever the case, we are assured that the true optimum is less than 135. But, for integral values of the variables, z is integral; in fact, it is a multiple of 5, since the values of the items are multiples of 5. Therefore, the true optimum is at most 130. Now, rounding the first approximate solution to Program 3 gives $x_1^* = 0$, $x_2^* = 1$, $x_3^* = 1$, $x_4^* = 0$, $x_5^* = 0$, with $z^* = 130$. Consequently, this solution is optimal.

6.8   Discuss the geometrical significance of making the first branch in Problem 6.2.

The feasible region for Problem 6.2 with the integer requirements ignored is the shaded region in Fig. 6-5(a); the feasible region for Problem 6.2 as given is the set of all integer points (marked with crosses) belonging to the shaded region. The first approximation is the circled extreme point.

As a result of branching, the feasible region for Program 2, with the integer constraints ignored, is Region I in Fig. 6-5(b), whereas Region II in the same figure represents the feasible region for Program 3 with the integer requirements neglected. Observe that Regions I and II together contain all the feasible integer points of Fig. 6-5(a), and only those integer points. Hence, if the original integer program has an optimal solution (as it does, in this case), that solution will be optimal for one of the two new integer

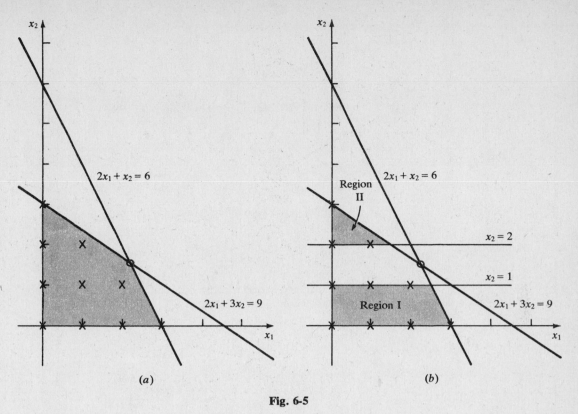

(a)   (b)

Fig. 6-5

programs.   Conversely, *if the two new integer programs have optimal solutions, one of these solutions (the one with the larger z-value, in the case of a maximization problem) will be optimal for the original integer program.*   The validity of the bounding technique follows from the parenthetical remark just made.

Supplementary Problems

Solve the following problems by use of the branch-and-bound algorithm.

6.9

maximize: $z = x_1 + 2x_2 + x_3$

subject to: $2x_1 + 3x_2 + 3x_3 \leq 11$

with: all variables nonnegative and integral

6.10

maximize: $z = x_1 + 2x_2 + 3x_3 + x_4$

subject to: $3x_1 + 2x_2 + \; x_3 + 4x_4 \leq 10$

$5x_1 + 3x_2 + 2x_3 + 5x_4 \leq \; 5$

with: all variables nonnegative and integral

6.11

maximize: $z = 2x_1 + 10x_2 + x_3$

subject to: $5x_1 + 2x_2 + x_3 \leq 15$

$2x_1 + x_2 + 7x_3 \leq 20$

$x_1 + 3x_2 + 2x_3 \leq 25$

with: all variables nonnegative and integral

6.12

minimize: $z = 10x_1 + 2x_2 + 11x_3$

subject to: $2x_1 + 7x_2 + x_3 = 4$

$5x_1 + 8x_2 - 2x_3 = 17$

with: all variables nonnegative and integral

6.13   Problem 1.20.

6.14   Solve Problem 6.7 by applying the branch-and-bound algorithm directly to program (*3*) of Problem 1.8 and compare this procedure with the approach taken in Problem 6.7.

Chapter 7

Integer Programming: Cut Algorithms

At each stage of branching in the branch-and-bound algorithm the current feasible region (for the current program with integer restrictions ignored) is *cut* into two smaller regions (one of them may be empty) by the imposition of two new constraints derived from the first approximation to the current program. This splitting is such that the optimal solution to the current program must show up as the optimal solution to one of the two new programs (Problem 6.8). The cut algorithms of the present chapter operate essentially in like fashion, the only difference being that a single new constraint is added at each stage, whereby the feasible region is diminished without being split.

THE GOMORY ALGORITHM

The new constraints are determined by the following three-step procedure. (See Problem 7.5.)

STEP 1   In the current final simplex tableau, select one (any one) of the nonintegral variables and, *without assigning zero values to the nonbasic variables*, consider the constraint equation represented by the row of the selected variable.

Example 7.1   The simplex tableau

	x_1	x_2	x_3	x_4	x_5	
x_3	$-1/2$	0	1	$-7/3$	1/2	11/2
x_2	1/2	1	0	-1	1/4	1
	4	0	0	1	3/4	25/2

gives the optimal solution (i.e., the current first approximation) as $x_3^* = 11/2$, $x_2^* = 1$, with each of the nonbasic variables x_1^*, x_4^*, and x_5^* set equal to zero. The noninteger assignment for x_3^* came from the first row of the tableau, which represents the constraint

$$-\tfrac{1}{2}x_1 + x_3 - \tfrac{7}{3}x_4 + \tfrac{1}{2}x_5 = \tfrac{11}{2} \tag{7.1}$$

STEP 2   Rewrite each fractional coefficient and constant in the constraint equation obtained from Step 1 as the sum of an integer and a *positive* fraction between 0 and 1. Then rewrite the equation so that the left-hand side contains only terms with fractional coefficients (and a fractional constant), while the right-hand side contains only terms with integral coefficients (and an integral constant).

Example 7.2   Equation (7.1) becomes

$$(-1 + \tfrac{1}{2})x_1 + x_3 + (-3 + \tfrac{2}{3})x_4 + (0 + \tfrac{1}{2})x_5 = 5 + \tfrac{1}{2}$$

or

$$\tfrac{1}{2}x_1 + \tfrac{2}{3}x_4 + \tfrac{1}{2}x_5 - \tfrac{1}{2} = 5 + x_1 - x_3 + 3x_4 \tag{7.2}$$

STEP 3   Require the left-hand side of the rewritten equation to be nonnegative. The resulting inequality is the new constraint.

Example 7.3 From (7.2),

$$\tfrac{1}{2}x_1 + \tfrac{2}{3}x_4 + \tfrac{1}{2}x_5 - \tfrac{1}{2} \geq 0 \qquad \text{or} \qquad \tfrac{1}{2}x_1 + \tfrac{2}{3}x_4 + \tfrac{1}{2}x_5 \geq \tfrac{1}{2}$$

is the new constraint.

COMPUTATIONAL CONSIDERATIONS

Computing time is saved by appending the new constraint inequality obtained from Step 3 to the constraint equations described in the current final simplex tableau rather than to the algebraically equivalent constraints given in the original program. (See Problem 7.1.)

The Gomory cut algorithm may not converge; that is, an integral solution may not be obtained regardless of the number of iterations. Generally, however, if the algorithm does converge, it converges reasonably quickly. For this reason, an upper limit on the number of iterations to be attempted is often established before the computation is initiated. If the integral solution is not obtained within this bound, the algorithm is abandoned.

There are no theoretical reasons for choosing between the Gomory and branch-and-bound algorithms. The branch-and-bound algorithm is the newer of the two procedures, and appears to be favored slightly among practitioners.

Solved Problems

7.1

$$\text{maximize:} \quad z = 2x_1 + x_2$$
$$\text{subject to:} \quad 2x_1 + 5x_2 \leq 17$$
$$3x_1 + 2x_2 \leq 10 \tag{1}$$
$$\text{with:} \quad x_1 \text{ and } x_2 \text{ nonnegative and integral}$$

Ignoring the integer requirements and applying the simplex method to the resulting linear program, we obtain Tableau 1 as the optimal tableau after one iteration.

	x_1	x_2	x_3	x_4	
x_3	0	11/3	1	-2/3	31/3
x_1	1	2/3	0	1/3	10/3
	0	1/3	0	2/3	20/3

Tableau 1

	x_1	x_2	x_3	x_4	x_5	
x_3	0	0	1	-5/2	11/6	17/2
x_1	1	0	0	0	1/3	3
x_2	0	1	0	1/2	-1/2	1/2
	0	0	0	1/2	1/6	13/2

Tableau 2

The first approximation to program (1), therefore, is $x_1^* = 10/3$, $x_3^* = 31/3$, $x_2^* = x_4^* = 0$. Both x_1^* and x_3^* are nonintegral. Arbitrarily selecting x_1^*, we consider the constraint represented by the second row of Tableau 1, the row defining x_1^*; namely,

$$x_1 + \tfrac{2}{3}x_2 + \tfrac{1}{3}x_4 = \tfrac{10}{3}$$

Writing each fraction as the sum of an integer and a fraction between 0 and 1, we have

$$x_1 + (0 + \tfrac{2}{3})x_2 + (0 + \tfrac{1}{3})x_4 = 3 + \tfrac{1}{3} \qquad \text{or} \qquad \tfrac{2}{3}x_2 + \tfrac{1}{3}x_4 - \tfrac{1}{3} = 3 - x_1$$

Requiring the left-hand side of this equation to be nonnegative, we obtain

$$\tfrac{2}{3}x_2 + \tfrac{1}{3}x_4 - \tfrac{1}{3} \geq 0 \qquad \text{or} \qquad 2x_2 + x_4 \geq 1$$

as the new constraint. Rewriting the constraints of the original program (1) in the forms suggested by Tableau 1 and adding the new constraint, we generate the new program maximize: $z = 2x_1 + x_2 + 0x_3 + 0x_4$

subject to: $\frac{11}{3}x_2 + x_3 - \frac{2}{3}x_4 = \frac{31}{3}$

$x_1 + \frac{2}{3}x_2 \qquad + \frac{1}{3}x_4 = \frac{10}{3}$ $\qquad\qquad$ (2)

$2x_2 \qquad + x_4 \geq 1$

with: all variables nonnegative and integral

A surplus variable, x_5, and an artificial variable, x_6, are introduced into the inequality constraint of (2), and then the two-phase method is applied, with x_1, x_3, and x_6 as the initial set of basic variables.   The optimal Tableau 2 is obtained after only one iteration.   The first approximation to program (2) is thus $x_1^* = 3$, $x_2^* = 1/2$, $x_3^* = 17/2$, $x_4^* = x_5^* = 0$.   Choosing x_2^* to generate the new constraint, we obtain from the third row of Tableau 2

$$\tfrac{1}{2}x_4 + \tfrac{1}{2}x_5 - \tfrac{1}{2} \geq 0 \qquad \text{or} \qquad x_4 + x_5 \geq 1$$

This, combined with the constraints of program (2) in the forms suggested by Tableau 2, gives the new integer program

maximize: $z = 2x_1 + x_2 + 0x_3 + 0x_4 + 0x_5$

subject to: $x_3 - \frac{5}{2}x_4 + \frac{11}{6}x_5 = \frac{17}{2}$

$x_1 \qquad\qquad + \frac{1}{3}x_5 = 3$ $\qquad\qquad$ (3)

$x_2 \qquad + \frac{1}{2}x_4 - \frac{1}{2}x_5 = \frac{1}{2}$

$x_4 + \quad x_5 \geq 1$

with: all variables nonnegative and integral

Ignoring the integer constraint and applying the two-phase method to program (3), with x_1, x_2, x_3, and x_7 (artificial) as the initial basic set, we obtain the optimal Tableau 3.

	x_1	x_2	x_3	x_4	x_5	x_6	
x_3	0	0	1	$-13/3$	0	11/6	20/3
x_1	1	0	0	$-1/3$	0	1/3	8/3
x_2	0	1	0	1	0	$-1/2$	1
x_5	0	0	0	1	1	-1	1
	0	0	0	1/3	0	1/6	19/3

Tableau 3

A new iteration of the process is started from $x_1^* = 8/3$ in Tableau 3.   This results in a program whose solution is integral, with $x_1^* = 3$, $x_2^* = 0$, and $z^* = 6$.   This solution is then the optimal solution to integer program (1).

7.2   Discuss the geometrical significance of the first added constraint in Problem 7.1.

Initially, the feasible region consists of all points in the first quadrant having integral coordinates that satisfy

$$2x_1 + 5x_2 \leq 17 \qquad \text{and} \qquad 3x_1 + 2x_2 \leq 10$$

These are the points marked by crosses in Fig. 7-1(a).

The constraint added to the original program (1) was $2x_2 + x_4 \geq 1$; it led to program (2).   Solving the second constraint equation of program (2) for x_4 and substituting the result into the new constraint, we have

$$2x_2 + (10 - 3x_1 - 2x_2) \geq 1 \qquad \text{or} \qquad x_1 \leq 3$$

The effect of imposing $x_1 \leq 3$ is indicated in Fig. 7-1(b): a small piece containing the current first approximation is sliced off the feasible region.   No integer point, however, is lost.

7.3   Solve Problem 1.12.

The first approximation to this integer program (see Problem 4.14 with the variables relabeled) is $x^*_{12} = 700$, $x^*_{13} = 500$, $x^*_{21} = 1000$, $x^*_{11} = x^*_{22} = x^*_{23} = 0$, with $z^* = 27\,600\,\cancel{c}$. Since this first approximation is integral, it is also the optimal solution to the integer program.   Under this optimal schedule, 700 boxes will be shipped from factory 1 to retailer 2, 500 boxes from factory 1 to retailer 3, and 1000 boxes from factory 2 to retailer 1.   The total shipping cost is $276.

7.4   Solve Problem 1.5.

Program (4) of Problem 1.5, brought into standard form, is

$$\text{minimize:} \quad z = 20x_1 + 22x_2 + 18x_3 + 0x_4 + 0x_5 + 0x_6 + 0x_7 + 0x_8 + Mx_9 + Mx_{10}$$

$$
\begin{aligned}
\text{subject to:} \quad & 4x_1 + 6x_2 + x_3 - x_4 & & + x_9 & = 54 \\
& 4x_1 + 4x_2 + 6x_3 & - x_5 & \quad + x_{10} & = 65 \\
& x_1 & + x_6 & & = 7 \\
& x_2 & + x_7 & & = 7 \\
& x_3 & + x_8 & & = 7
\end{aligned}
\qquad (1)
$$

with: all variables nonnegative and integral

Ignoring the integer restrictions and solving this program by the two-phase method, we obtain Tableau 1 after three iterations.   The first approximation to program (1) is thus $x^*_1 = 1.75$, $x^*_2 = 7$, $x^*_3 = 5$, with $z^* = 279$.

	x_1	x_2	x_3	x_4	x_5	x_6	x_7	x_8	
x_1	1	0	0	-0.3	0.05	0	-1.6	0	1.75
x_3	0	0	1	0.2	-0.2	0	0.4	0	5
x_6	0	0	0	0.3	-0.05	1	1.6	0	5.25
x_2	0	1	0	0	0	0	1	0	7
x_8	0	0	0	-0.2	0.2	0	-0.4	1	2
	0	0	0	2.4	2.6	0	2.8	0	-279

Tableau 1

Now, this first approximation may be rounded to the feasible integral solution $x_1 = 2$, $x_2 = 7$, $x_3 = 5$, with $z = 284$.   It follows that the desired minimum cannot exceed 284.   On the other hand, referring to the original program (4) of Problem 1.5, we see that for integral values of the variables z is an *even* integer; hence, in view of the lower bound $z^* = 279$ provided by the first approximation, the minimal z cannot be less than 280.   Therefore, the minimal z can only be 280, 282, or 284, and we are guaranteed that the error committed in taking $(2, 7, 5)^T$ as the optimal solution is at worst

$$\frac{284 - 280}{280} = 1.43\%$$

(Starting from Tableau 1, one finds after six iterations of the Gomory algorithm that $(2, 7, 5)^T$ is in fact the optimal solution.)

7.5   Develop the Gomory cut algorithm.

Consider the optimal tableau that results from applying the simplex method to an integer program with the integer requirements ignored, and assume that one of the basic variables, x_b, is nonin-

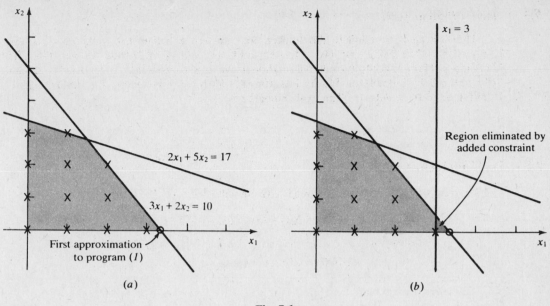

Fig. 7-1

tegral. The constraint equation corresponding to the tableau row that determined x_b must have the form

$$x_b + \sum y_j x_j = y_0 \qquad\qquad (1)$$

where the sum is over all nonbasic variables. The y-terms are the coefficients and the constant term appearing in the tableau row determining x_b. Since x_b is obtained from (1) by setting the nonbasic variables equal to zero, it follows that y_0 is also nonintegral.

Write each y-term in (1) as the sum of an integer and a nonnegative fraction less than 1:

$$y_j = i_j + f_j \qquad \text{and} \qquad y_0 = i_0 + f_0$$

Some of the f_j may be zero, but f_0 is guaranteed to be positive. Equation (1) becomes

$$x_b + \sum (i_j + f_j)x_j = i_0 + f_0$$

or

$$x_b + \sum i_j x_j - i_0 = f_0 - \sum f_j x_j \qquad\qquad (2)$$

If each x-variable is required to be integral, then the left-hand side of (2) is integral, which forces the right-hand side also to be integral. But, since each f_j and x_j is nonnegative, so too is $\Sigma f_j x_j$. The right-hand side of (2) then is an integer which is smaller than a positive fraction less than 1; that is, a nonpositive integer.

$$f_0 - \sum f_j x_j \le 0 \qquad \text{or} \qquad \sum f_j x_j - f_0 \ge 0$$

This is the new constraint in the Gomory algorithm.

7.6   Develop another cut algorithm.

Consider (1) of Problem 7.5. If each nonbasic variable x_j is zero, then $x_b = y_0$ is nonintegral. If x_b is to become integer-valued, then at least one of the nonbasic x_j must be made different from zero. Since all variables are required to be nonnegative and integral, it follows that at least one nonbasic variable must be made greater than or equal to 1. This in turn implies that the sum of all the nonbasic variables must be made greater than or equal to 1. If this condition is used as the new constraint to be adjoined to the original integer program, we have the cut algorithm first suggested by Danzig.

7.7   Use the cut algorithm developed in Problem 7.6 to solve

$$\text{maximize:} \quad z = 3x_1 + 4x_2$$

$$\text{subject to:} \quad 2x_1 + x_2 \le 6$$

$$2x_1 + 3x_2 \le 9$$

$$\text{with:} \quad x_1 \text{ and } x_2 \text{ nonnegative and integral}$$

Introducing slack variables x_3 and x_4 and then solving the resulting program, with the integer requirements ignored, by the simplex method, we obtain Tableau 1.

	x_1	x_2	x_3	x_4	
x_1	1	0	0.75	−0.25	2.25
x_2	0	1	−0.5	0.5	1.5
	0	0	0.25	1.25	12.75

Tableau 1

The first approximation is, therefore, $x_1^* = 2.25$, $x_2^* = 1.5$, which is not integral. The nonbasic variables are x_3 and x_4, so the new constraint is $x_3 + x_4 \ge 1$. Appending this constraint to Tableau 1, after the introduction of surplus variable x_5 and artificial variable x_6, and solving the resulting program by the two-phase method, we generate Tableau 2.

	x_1	x_2	x_3	x_4	x_5	
x_1	1	0	0	−1	0.75	1.5
x_2	0	1	0	1	−0.5	2
x_3	0	0	1	1	−1	1
	0	0	0	1	0.25	12.5

Tableau 2

It follows from Tableau 2 that $x_1^* = 1.5$, $x_2^* = 2$, $x_3^* = 1$, with x_4 and x_5 nonbasic. Since this solution is nonintegral, we take $x_4 + x_5 \ge 1$ as the new constraint. Adjoining this constraint to Tableau 2, after the introduction of surplus variable x_6 and artificial variable x_7, and solving the resulting program by the two-phase method, we generate Tableau 3.

	x_1	x_2	x_3	x_4	x_5	x_6	
x_1	1	0	0	−1.75	0	0.75	0.75
x_2	0	1	0	1.5	0	−0.5	2.5
x_3	0	0	1	2	0	−1	2
x_5	0	0	0	1	1	−1	1
	0	0	0	0.75	0	0.25	12.25

Tableau 3

From Tableau 3, the current optimal solution is nonintegral, with nonbasic variables x_4 and x_6. The new constraint is thus $x_4 + x_6 \ge 1$. Adjoining it to Tableau 3 and solving the resulting program by the two-phase method, we obtain $x_1^* = 0$, $x_2^* = 3$, with $z^* = 12$. Since this solution is integral, it is the optimal solution to the original integer program.

Supplementary Problems

7.8   Use the Gormory algorithm to

$$\text{maximize:} \quad z = x_1 + 9x_2 + x_3$$

$$\text{subject to:} \quad x_1 + 2x_2 + 3x_3 \leq 9$$

$$3x_1 + 2x_2 + 2x_3 \leq 15$$

$$\text{with:} \quad \text{all variables nonnegative and integral}$$

7.9   Solve Problem 1.3 by the Gomory algorithm.

7.10   Solve Problem 6.9 by the Gomory algorithm.

7.11   Solve Problem 6.10 by the Gomory algorithm.

7.12   Solve Problem 6.11 by the Gomory algorithm.

7.13   Solve Problem 6.9 by the cut algorithm of Problem 7.6.

Chapter 8

Integer Programming: The Transportation Algorithm

STANDARD FORM

A *transportation problem* involves m *sources*, each of which has available a_i $(i = 1, 2, \ldots, m)$ units of a homogeneous product, and n *destinations*, each of which requires b_j $(j = 1, 2, \ldots, n)$ units of this product. The numbers a_i and b_j are positive integers. The cost c_{ij} of transporting one unit of product from the ith source to the jth destination is given for each i and j. The objective is to develop an integral transportation schedule (the product may not be fractionalized) that meets all demands from current inventory at a minimum total shipping cost.

It is assumed that total supply and total demand are equal; that is,

$$\sum_{i=1}^{m} a_i = \sum_{j=1}^{n} b_j \tag{8.1}$$

Equation (8.1) is guaranteed by creating either a fictitious destination with a demand equal to the surplus if total demand is less than total supply, or a fictitious source with a supply equal to the shortage if total demand exceeds total supply (see Problem 8.1).

Let x_{ij} represent the (unknown) number of units to be shipped from source i to destination j. Then the standard mathematical model for this problem is:

$$\text{minimize:} \quad z = \sum_{i=1}^{m} \sum_{j=1}^{n} c_{ij} x_{ij}$$

$$\text{subject to:} \quad \sum_{j=1}^{n} x_{ij} = a_i \quad (i = 1, \ldots, m) \tag{8.2}$$

$$\sum_{i=1}^{m} x_{ij} = b_j \quad (j = 1, \ldots, n)$$

$$\text{with:} \quad \text{all } x_{ij} \text{ nonnegative and integral}$$

THE TRANSPORTATION ALGORITHM

The first approximation to system (8.2) is always integral (see Problem 7.3), and therefore is always the optimal solution. Rather than determining this first approximation by a direct application of the simplex method, we find it more efficient to work with Tableau 8-1. All entries are self-explanatory, with the exception of the terms u_i and v_j, which will be explained shortly. The *transportation algorithm* is the simplex method specialized to the format of Tableau 8-1; as usual, it involves

(i) finding an initial, basic feasible solution;

(ii) testing the solution for optimality;

(iii) improving the solution when it is not optimal; and

(iv) repeating steps (ii) and (iii) until the optimal solution is obtained.

Destinations

	1	2	3	$\cdots$	n	Supply	u_i
1	c_{11} x_{11}	c_{12} x_{12}	c_{13} x_{13}	$\cdots$	c_{1n} x_{1n}	a_1	u_1
2	c_{21} x_{21}	c_{22} x_{22}	c_{23} x_{23}	$\cdots$	c_{2n} x_{2n}	a_2	u_2
....	....	....	....	$\cdots$	....	....	....
m	c_{m1} x_{m1}	c_{m2} x_{m2}	c_{m3} x_{m3}	$\cdots$	c_{mn} x_{mn}	a_m	u_m
Demand	b_1	b_2	b_3	$\cdots$	b_n		
v_j	v_1	v_2	v_3	$\cdots$	v_n		

Tableau 8-1

AN INITIAL BASIC SOLUTION

Northwest corner rule. Beginning with the $(1, 1)$ cell in Tableau 8-1 (the northwest corner), allocate to x_{11} as many units as possible without violating the constraints. This will be the smaller of a_1 and b_1. Thereafter, continue by moving one cell to the right, if some supply remains, or, if not, one cell down. At each step, allocate as much as possible to the cell (variable) under consideration without violating the constraints: the sum of the ith-row allocations cannot exceed a_i, the sum of the jth-column allocations cannot exceed b_j, and no allocation can be negative. The allocation may be zero. See Problem 8.3.

Vogel's method. For each row and each column having some supply or some demand remaining, calculate its *difference*, which is the nonnegative difference between the two smallest shipping costs c_{ij} associated with unassigned variables in that row or column. Consider the row or column having the largest difference; in case of a tie, arbitrarily choose one. In this row or column, locate that unassigned variable (cell) having the smallest unit shipping cost and allocate to it as many units as possible without violating the constraints. Recalculate the new differences and repeat the above procedure until all demands are satisfied. See Problems 8.5 and 8.6.

Variables that are assigned values by either one of these starting procedures become the basic variables in the initial solution. The unassigned variables are nonbasic and, therefore, zero. We adopt the convention of not entering the nonbasic variables in Tableau 8-1—they are understood to be zero—and of indicating basic-variable allocations in boldface type.

The northwest corner rule is the simpler of the two rules to apply. However, Vogel's method, which takes into account the unit shipping costs, usually results in a closer-to-optimal starting solution (see Problem 8.5).

TEST FOR OPTIMALITY

Assign one (any one) of the u_i or v_j in Tableau 8-1 the value zero and calculate the remaining u_i and v_j so that for each *basic variable* $u_i + v_j = c_{ij}$. Then, for each *nonbasic variable*, calculate the quantity $c_{ij} - u_i - v_j$. If all these latter quantities are nonnegative, the current solution is optimal; otherwise, the current solution is not optimal. See Problems 8.4 and 8.8.

IMPROVING THE SOLUTION

Definition: A *loop* is a sequence of cells in Tableau 8-1 such that: (i) each pair of consecutive cells lie in either the same row or the same column; (ii) no three consecutive cells lie in the same row or column; (iii) the first and last cells of the sequence lie in the same row or column; (iv) no cell appears more than once in the sequence.

Example 8.1 The sequences $\{(1,2), (1,4), (2,4), (2,6), (4,6), (4,2)\}$ and $\{(1,3), (1,6), (3,6), (3,1), (2,1), (2,2), (4,2), (4,4), (2,4), (2,3)\}$ illustrated in Figs. 8-1 and 8-2, respectively, are loops. Note that a row or column can have more than two cells in the loop (as the second row of Fig. 8-2), but no more than two can be consecutive.

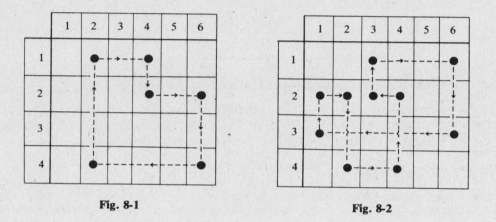

Fig. 8-1   Fig. 8-2

Consider the nonbasic variable corresponding to the most negative of the quantities $c_{ij} - u_i - v_j$ calculated in the test for optimality; it is made the incoming variable. Construct a loop consisting exclusively of this incoming variable (cell) and current basic variables (cells). Then allocate to the incoming cell as many units as possible such that, after appropriate adjustments have been made to the other cells in the loop, the supply and demand constraints are not violated, all allocations remain nonnegative, and one of the old basic variables has been reduced to zero (whereupon it ceases to be basic). See Problem 8.4.

DEGENERACY

In view of condition (8.1), only $n + m - 1$ of the constraint equations in system (8.2) are independent. Then, by Problems 3.13 and 3.14, a *nondegenerate* basic feasible solution will be characterized by positive values for exactly $n + m - 1$ basic variables. If the process of improving the current basic solution results in two or more current basic variables being reduced to zero simultaneously, only one is allowed to become nonbasic (solver's choice, although the variable with the largest unit shipping cost is preferred). The other variable(s) remains (remain) basic, but with a zero allocation, thereby rendering the new basic solution degenerate.

The northwest corner rule always generates an initial basic solution (Problem 8.2); but it may fail to provide $n + m - 1$ *positive* values (Problem 8.3), thus yielding a degenerate solution. If Vogel's method is used, and does not yield that same number of positive values, additional variables with zero allocations must be designated as basic (see Problem 8.6). The choice is arbitrary, to a point: *basic variables cannot form loops*, and preference is usually given to variables with the lowest associated shipping costs.

Improving a degenerate solution may result in replacing one basic variable having a zero value by another such. (This occurs at the first improvement in Problem 8.4.) Although the two degenerate solutions are effectively the same—only the designation of the basic variables has changed, not their values—the additional iteration is necessary for the transportation algorithm to proceed.

Solved Problems

8.1 A car rental company is faced with an allocation problem resulting from rental agreements that allow cars to be returned to locations other than those at which they were originally rented.   At the present time, there are two locations (sources) with 15 and 13 surplus cars, respectively, and four locations (destinations) requiring 9, 6, 7, and 9 cars, respectively.   Unit transportation costs (in dollars) between the locations are as follows:

	Dest. 1	Dest. 2	Dest. 3	Dest. 4
Source 1	45	17	21	30
Source 2	14	18	19	31

Set up the initial transportation tableau (Tableau 8-1) for the minimum-cost schedule.

Since the total demand $(9 + 6 + 7 + 9 = 31)$ exceeds the total supply $(15 + 13 = 28)$, a dummy source is created having a supply equal to the 3-unit shortage.   In reality, shipments from this fictitious source are never made, so the associated shipping costs are taken as zero.   Positive allocations from this source to a distination represent cars that cannot be delivered due to a shortage of supply; they are shortages a destination will experience under an optimal shipping schedule.

For this problem, Tableau 8-1 becomes Tableau 1A.   The x_{ij}, u_i, and v_j are not entered, since they are unknown at the moment.

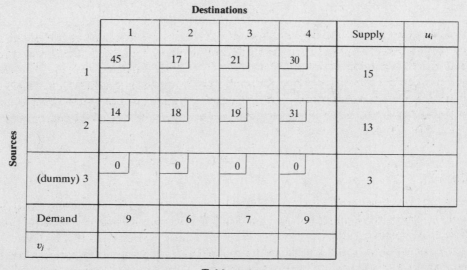

Tableau 1A

8.2 For an $m \times n$ transportation tableau, show that the northwest corner rule evaluates $n + m - 1$ of the variables.

Observe that after treating the $(1, 1)$ cell, the rule is applied *in the same form* to a subtableau, the new northwest corner being either the original $(1, 2)$ cell or the original $(2, 1)$ cell.   Suppose then (mathematical induction) that the result holds for the subtableau, which is either $m \times (n - 1)$ or $(m - 1) \times n$.   In either case, $n + m - 2$ variables are evaluated in the subtableau, so that

$$(n + m - 2) + 1 = n + m - 1$$

variables are evaluated in the tableau.   Since the result obviously holds when $n = m = 1$, the proof by induction is complete.

8.3 Use the northwest corner rule to obtain an initial allocation to Tableau 1A.

We begin with x_{11} and assign it the minimum of $a_1 = 15$ and $b_1 = 9$. Thus, $x_{11} = 9$, leaving six surplus cars at the first source. We next move one cell to the right and assign $x_{12} = 6$. These two allocations together exhaust the supply at the first source, so we move one cell down and consider x_{22}. Observe, however, that the demand at the second destination has been satisfied by the x_{12} allocation. Since we cannot deliver additional cars to it without exceeding its demand, we must assign $x_{22} = 0$ and then move one cell to the right. Continuing in this manner, we obtain the degenerate solution (fewer than $4 + 3 - 1 = 6$ *positive* entries) depicted in Tableau 1B.

	1	2	3	4	Supply	u_i
1	45 **9**	17 **6**	21	30	15	
2	14	18 **0**	19 **7**	31 **6**	13	
(dummy) 3	0	0	0	0 **3**	3	
Demand	9	6	7	9		
v_j						

Tableau 1B

8.4 Solve the transportation problem described in Problem 8.1.

To determine whether the initial allocation found in Tableau 1B is optimal, we first calculate the terms u_i and v_j with respect to the basic-variable cells of the tableau. Arbitrarily choosing $u_2 = 0$ (since the second row contains more basic variables than any other row or column, this choice will simplify the computations), we find:

$(2, 2)$ cell: $u_2 + v_2 = c_{22}$, $0 + v_2 = 18$, or $v_2 = 18$

$(2, 3)$ cell: $u_2 + v_3 = c_{23}$, $0 + v_3 = 19$, or $v_3 = 19$

$(2, 4)$ cell: $u_2 + v_4 = c_{24}$, $0 + v_4 = 31$, or $v_4 = 31$

$(1, 2)$ cell: $u_1 + v_2 = c_{12}$, $u_1 + 18 = 17$, or $u_1 = -1$

$(1, 1)$ cell: $u_1 + v_1 = c_{11}$, $-1 + v_1 = 45$, or $v_1 = 46$

$(3, 4)$ cell: $u_3 + v_4 = c_{34}$, $u_3 + 31 = 0$, or $u_3 = -31$

These values are shown in Tableau 1C. Next we calculate the quantities $c_{ij} - u_i - v_j$ for each nonbasic-variable cell of Tableau 1B.

$(1, 3)$ cell: $c_{13} - u_1 - v_3 = 21 - (-1) - 19 = 3$

$(1, 4)$ cell: $c_{14} - u_1 - v_4 = 30 - (-1) - 31 = 0$

$(2, 1)$ cell: $c_{21} - u_2 - v_1 = 14 - 0 - 46 = -32$

$(3, 1)$ cell: $c_{31} - u_3 - v_1 = 0 - (-31) - 46 = -15$

$(3, 2)$ cell: $c_{32} - u_3 - v_2 = 0 - (-31) - 18 = 13$

$(3, 3)$ cell: $c_{33} - u_3 - v_3 = 0 - (-31) - 19 = 12$

These results also are recorded in Tableau 1C, in parentheses.

Since at least one of these $(c_{ij} - u_i - v_j)$-values is negative, the current solution is not optimal, and a better solution can be obtained by increasing the allocation to the variable (cell) having the largest

	1	2	3	4	Supply	u_i
1	45 9	*17 6	21 (3)	30 (0)	15	−1
2	14 (−32) +	18 0	19 7	31 6	13	0
(dummy) 3	0 (−15)	0 (13)	0 (12)	0 3	3	−31
Demand	9	6	7	9		
v_j	46	18	19	31		

Tableau 1C

negative entry, here the (2, 1) cell of Tableau 1C. We do so by placing a boldface plus sign (signaling an increase) in the (2, 1) cell and identifying a loop containing, besides this cell, only basic-variable cells. Such a loop is shown by the heavy lines in Tableau 1C. We now increase the allocation to the (2, 1) cell as much as possible, simultaneously adjusting the other cell allocations in the loop so as not to violate the supply, demand, or nonnegativity constraints. Any positive allocation to the (2, 1) cell would force x_{22} to become negative. To avoid this, but still make x_{21} basic, we assign $x_{21} = 0$ and remove x_{22} from our set of basic variables. The new basic solution, also degenerate, is given in Tableau 1D.

	1	2	3	4	Supply	u_i
1	45 9	17 6	21	30	15	
2	14 0	18	19 7	31 6	13	
(dummy) 3	0	0	0	0 3	3	
Demand	9	6	7	9		
v_j						

Tableau 1D

We now check whether this solution is optimal. Working directly on Tableau 1D, we first calculate the new u_i and v_j with respect to the new basic variables, and then compute $c_{ij} - u_i - v_j$ for each nonbasic-variable cell. Again we arbitrarily choose $u_2 = 0$, since the second row contains more basic variables than any other row or column. These results are shown in parentheses in Tableau 1E. Since two entries are negative, the current solution is not optimal, and a better solution can be obtained by increasing the allocation to the (1, 4) cell. The loop whereby this is accomplished is indicated by heavy lines in Tableau 1E; it consists of the cells (1, 4), (2, 4), (2, 1), and (1, 1). Any amount added to cell (1, 4) must be simultaneously subtracted from cells (1, 1) and (2, 4) and then added to cell (2, 1), so as not to violate the supply-demand constraints. Therefore, no more than six cars can be added to cell (1, 4) without forcing x_{24} negative. Consequently, we reassign $x_{14} = 4$, make the appropriate adjustments in the loop, and remove x_{24} as a basic variable. The new, nondegenerate basic solution is shown in Tableau 1F.

	1	2	3	4	Supply	u_i
1	45	17 **6**	21 (−29)	30 (−32)	15	31
	9 ════════════════ +					
2	14	18 (32)	19 **7**	31	13	0
	0 ════════════════ 6					
(dummy) 3	0 (17)	0 (45)	0 (12)	0 **3**	3	−31
Demand	9	6	7	9		
v_j	14	−14	19	31		

Tableau 1E

	1	2	3	4	Supply	u_i
1	45 **3**	17 **6**	21	30 **6**	15	
2	14 **6**	18	19 **7**	31	13	
(dummy) 3	0	0	0	0 **3**	3	
Demand	9	6	7	9		
v_j						

Tableau 1F

	1	2	3	4	Supply	u_i
1	45 (29)	17 **6**	21 **3**	30 **6**	15	0
2	14 **9**	18 (3)	19 **4**	31 (3)	13	−2
(dummy) 3	0 (14)	0 (13)	0 (9)	0 **3**	3	−30
Demand	9	6	7	9		
v_j	16	17	21	30		

Tableau 1H

After one further optimality test (negative) and consequent change of basis, we obtain Tableau 1H, which also shows the results of the optimality test of the new basic solution. It is seen that each $c_{ij} - u_i - v_j$ is nonnegative; hence the new solution is optimal. That is, $x_{12}^* = 6$, $x_{13}^* = 3$, $x_{14}^* = 6$, $x_{21}^* = 9$, $x_{23}^* = 4$, $x_{34}^* = 3$, with all other variables nonbasic and, therefore, zero. Furthermore,

$$z^* = 6(17) + 3(21) + 6(30) + 9(14) + 4(19) + 3(0) = \$547$$

The fact that some positive allocation comes from the dummy source indicates that not all demands can be met under this optimal schedule. In particular, destination 4 will receive three fewer cars than it needs.

8.5 Use Vogel's method to determine an initial basic solution to the transportation problem described in Problem 8.1.

The two smallest costs in row 1 of Tableau 1A are 17 and 21; their difference is 4. The two smallest costs in row 2 are 14 and 18; their difference is also 4. The two smallest costs in row 3 are both 0; so their difference is 0. Repeating this analysis on the columns, we generate the differences shown beside Tableau 5A. Since the largest of these differences, indicated by a †, occurs in column 4, we locate the variable (cell) in this column having the lowest unit shipping cost and allocate to it as many units as possible. Thus $x_{34} = 3$, exhausting the supply of source 3 and *eliminating row 3 from further consideration*.

	1	2	3	4	Supply	u_i	DIFFERENCES
1	45	17	21	30	15		4
2	14	18	19	31	13		4
(dummy) 3	0	0	0	0 3	3		0
Demand	9	6	7	9			
v_j							
DIFFERENCES	14	17	19	30†			

Tableau 5A

We now compute the differences for each row and column anew, without reference to the elements in row 3. The results are shown beside Tableau 5B, where the entry X for the second difference in row 3 means simply that this row has been eliminated. The largest difference appears in column 1, and the variable in this column having the smallest cost is x_{21} (since row 3 is no longer under consideration). We assign $x_{21} = 9$, thereby satisfying the demand of destination 1. Accordingly, column 1 will not be involved in the ensuing calculations.

With row 3 and column 1 eliminated, the new differences are shown beside Tableau 5C, where, again, an X indicates that a computation was not required. The largest difference occurs in row 1, and the variable in this row having the lowest unit cost is x_{12}. Note that even if c_{11} had been less than 17, x_{11} would not have been selected here, since it falls in a column that has been eliminated. We set $x_{12} = 6$, thereby meeting the demand of destination 2 and removing column 2 from further calculations.

With row 3 and columns 1 and 2 no longer considered, the new differences are shown beside Tableau 5D. The largest difference occurs in row 2, and the smallest cost in that row and in columns

	1	2	3	4	Supply	u_i	DIFFERENCES	
1	45	17	21	30	15		4	4
2	14 **9**	18	19	31	13		4	4
(dummy) 3	0	0	0	0 **3**	3		0	X
Demand	9	6	7	9				
v_j								
DIFFERENCES	14 31†	17 1	19 2	30† 1				

Tableau 5B

	1	2	3	4	Supply	u_i	DIFFERENCES		
1	45	17 **6**	21	30	15		4	4	4†
2	14 **9**	18	19	31	13		4	4	1
(dummy) 3	0	0	0	0 **3**	3		0	X	X
Demand	9	6	7	9					
v_j									
DIFFERENCES	14 31† X	17 1 1	19 2 2	30† 1 1					

Tableau 5C

still under consideration is 19. Consequently, we assign $x_{23} = 4$, which with the earlier assignment $x_{21} = 9$ exhausts the supply of source 2 and removes row 2 from further consideration.

With rows 2 and 3 eliminated, we no longer can calculate differences for the remaining columns. This is a signal that the remaining allocations are uniquely determined. Here we must set $x_{13} = 3$ and $x_{14} = 6$ if we are to meet all demands without exceeding supplies. The result is the allocation shown in Tableau 1H, which was determined in Problem 8.4 to be optimal.

	1	2	3	4	Supply	u_i	DIFFERENCES			
1	45	17	21	30	15		4	4	4†	9
		6								
2	14	18	19	31	13		4	4	1	12†
	9		**4**							
(dummy) 3	0	0	0	0	3		0	X	X	X
				3						
Demand	9	6	7	9						
v_j										

DIFFERENCES				
	14	17	19	30†
	31†	1	2	1
	X	1	2	1
	X	X	2	1

Tableau 5D

8.6   Use the transportation algorithm to solve Problem 1.12.

Since total supply equals total demand, no fictitious source or destination need be created, and the transportation tableau becomes Tableau 6A.   Applying Vogel's method and using the same notation as adopted in Problem 8.5, we arrive at Tableau 6B after the second set of differences have been calculated.   There is a two-way tie for the largest difference.   A good procedure is to scan each candidate, here row 1 (with column 3 eliminated) and column 1, for that variable with the lowest unit cost.   Again there is a tie, so we arbitrarily select x_{12}.   Setting $x_{12} = 700$ satisfies the entire demand of destination 2 and, along with the previous allocation to x_{13}, exhausts the supply of source 1.   With columns 2 and 3 and row 1 eliminated, the remaining allocation, $x_{21} = 1000$, is uniquely determined, and Vogel's method thus leads to Tableau 6C.   This solution, however, is not complete, as only three of the necessary $3 + 2 - 1 = 4$ basic variables have been identified.   We arbitrarily select $x_{23} = 0$ as the fourth basic variable, since it is the unassigned variable with the lowest unit cost and since its inclusion as a basic variable does not generate a loop with the previously defined basic variables.   The result is the basic solution, necessarily degenerate, given in Tableau 6D.

	1	2	3	Supply	u_i
1	14	13	11	1200	
2	13	13	12	1000	
Demand	1000	700	500		
v_j					

Tableau 6A

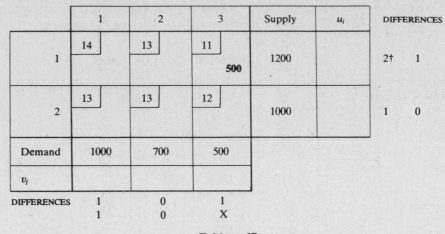

	1	2	3	Supply	u_i	DIFFERENCES	
1	14	13	11	1200		2†	1
			500				
2	13	13	12	1000		1	0
Demand	1000	700	500				
v_j							
DIFFERENCES	1	0	1				
	1	0	X				

Tableau 6B

	1	2	3	Supply	u_i	DIFFERENCES	
1	14	13	11	1200		2†	1†
		700	500				
2	13	13	12	1000		1	0
	1000						
Demand	1000	700	500				
v_j							
DIFFERENCES	1	0	1				
	1	0	X				

Tableau 6C

	1	2	3	Supply	u_i
1	14	13	11	1200	0
	(2)	700 ▬ 500			
2	13	13	12	1000	1
	1000	(−1) +	0		
Demand	1000	700	500		
v_j	12	13	11		

Tableau 6D

We now test this solution for optimality, working directly on Tableau 6D; it is not optimal. Improving it, we obtain the allocation shown in Tableau 6E, which is optimal. Thus, $x_{12}^* = 700$, $x_{13}^* = 500$, $x_{21}^* = 1000$, $x_{11}^* = x_{22}^* = x_{23}^* = 0$, with

$$z^* = 700(13) + 500(11) + 1000(13) = 27\,600\text{¢} = \$276$$

Note that this optimal allocation is identical to the initial allocation; only the designation of the basic variables has changed.

	1	2	3	Supply	u_i
1	14 (1)	13 **700**	11 **500**	1200	0
2	13 **1000**	13 **0**	12 (1)	1000	0
Demand	1000	700	500		
v_j	13	13	11		

Tableau 6E

8.7 Find the unsymmetric dual to system (8.2) with the integer requirements ignored.

The primal constraints may be written as the $(m + n) \times mn$ system

$$
\begin{aligned}
x_{11} + \cdots + x_{1n} &= a_1 \\
x_{21} + \cdots + x_{2n} &= a_2 \\
&\cdots\cdots\cdots\cdots\cdots\cdots\cdots\cdots\cdots\cdots\cdots\cdots\cdots\cdots \\
x_{m1} + \cdots + x_{mn} &= a_m \\
x_{11} \qquad\quad + x_{21} \qquad\quad + x_{m1} &= b_1 \\
x_{12} \qquad\quad + x_{22} \qquad\quad + x_{m2} &= b_2 \\
&\cdots\cdots\cdots\cdots\cdots\cdots\cdots\cdots\cdots\cdots\cdots\cdots\cdots\cdots \\
x_{1n} \qquad\quad + x_{2n} \qquad\quad + x_{mn} &= b_n
\end{aligned}
\tag{1}
$$

It is seen that each column of the coefficient matrix $\mathbf{A}$ contains exactly two 1's; specifically, column $(i - 1)n + j$ has a 1 in row i and a 1 in row $m + j$. Then, the $[(i - 1)n + j]$th dual constraint, as given in (5.4), involves only the ith and $(m + j)$th dual variables. Denoting the dual variables by $u_1, u_2, \ldots, u_m, v_1, v_2, \ldots, v_n$, this constraint is simply

$$u_i + v_j \le c_{(i-1)n+j} \quad (= c_{ij})$$

and the complete dual program is expressible as

$$
\begin{aligned}
\text{maximize:} \quad & z = \sum_{i=1}^{m} a_i u_i + \sum_{j=1}^{n} b_j v_j \\
\text{subject to:} \quad & u_i + v_j \le c_{ij} \quad (i = 1, 2, \ldots, m; \ j = 1, 2, \ldots, n)
\end{aligned}
\tag{2}
$$

Program (2) has matrix form (5.4) with

$$\mathbf{B} \equiv [a_1, \ldots, a_m, b_1, \ldots, b_n]^T \qquad \mathbf{C} \equiv [c_{11}, c_{12}, \ldots, c_{1n}, c_{21}, \ldots, c_{2n}, \ldots, c_{m1}, \ldots, c_{mn}]$$

and $\mathbf{W} = [\mathbf{U}^T, \mathbf{V}^T]^T$.

8.8   Use the result of Problem 8.7 to validate the optimality test in the transportation algorithm.

Let $\mathbf{X} = [x_{11}, x_{12}, \ldots, x_{1n}, \ldots, x_{m1}, \ldots, x_{mn}]^T$ be any feasible solution to the primal program, (8.2), and $\mathbf{W}$ be any feasible solution to the dual program, (2) of Problem 8.7 in matrix form. It follows from Problem 5.9 that

$$\mathbf{C}^T \mathbf{X} \geq \mathbf{B}^T \mathbf{W} \qquad \text{or} \qquad \sum_{i=1}^{m} \sum_{j=1}^{n} c_{ij} x_{ij} \geq \sum_{i=1}^{m} a_i u_i + \sum_{j=1}^{n} b_j v_j \qquad (1)$$

and it is easy to show (compare Problem 5.24) that if (1) holds with equality, $\mathbf{X}$ and $\mathbf{W}$ are optimal solutions to their respective programs.

Now, suppose that the transportation algorithm has produced a tableau for which numbers u_i^* and v_j^* can be computed which have the following properties: (a) for each cell (i, j) containing a basic variable x_{ij}^* (whether positive or zero), $u_i^* + v_j^* = c_{ij}$; (b) for each cell (i, j) containing a nonbasic variable, $x_{ij}^* = 0$, $u_i^* + v_j^* \leq c_{ij}$. Then $\mathbf{X}^*$ is a feasible solution to the primal program and $\mathbf{W}^*$ is a feasible solution to the dual program. Moreover, using the primal constraint equations, we have

$$\sum_{i=1}^{m} a_i u_i^* = \sum_{i=1}^{m} \left(\sum_{j=1}^{n} x_{ij}^* \right) u_i^* = \sum_{i=1}^{m} \sum_{j=1}^{n} u_i^* x_{ij}^* \qquad \text{and} \qquad \sum_{j=1}^{n} b_j v_j^* = \sum_{j=1}^{n} \left(\sum_{i=1}^{m} x_{ij}^* \right) v_j^* = \sum_{i=1}^{m} \sum_{j=1}^{n} v_j^* x_{ij}^*$$

Consequently,

$$\sum_{i=1}^{m} a_i v_i^* + \sum_{j=1}^{n} b_j v_j^* = \sum_{i=1}^{m} \sum_{j=1}^{n} (u_i^* + v_j^*) x_{ij}^* = \sum_{i=1}^{m} \sum_{j=1}^{n} c_{ij} x_{ij}^* \qquad (2)$$

the last equality following from properties (a) and (b) above. But (2) is just (1) for $\mathbf{X}^*$ and $\mathbf{W}^*$, holding with equality. Hence, $\mathbf{X}^*$ is optimal for the transportation problem (and $\mathbf{W}^*$ is optimal for the dual problem).

Supplementary Problems

8.9   Set up a transportation tableau for Problem 1.21 and then use the transportation algorithm to determine an optimal production schedule.

8.10   Use the transportation algorithm to solve Problem 1.23.

8.11   A regional airline can buy its jet fuel from any one of three vendors. The airline's needs for the upcoming month at each of the three airports it serves are 100 000 gal at airport 1, 180 000 gal at airport 2, and 350 000 gal at airport 3. Each vendor can supply fuel to each airport at a price (in cents per gallon) given by the following schedule:

	Airport 1	Airport 2	Airport 3
Vendor 1	92	89	90
Vendor 2	91	91	95
Vendor 3	87	90	92

Each vendor, however, is limited in the total number of gallons it can provide during any one month. These capacities are 320 000 gal for vendor 1, 270 000 gal for vendor 2, and 190 000 gal for vendor 3. Determine a purchasing policy that will supply the airline's requirements at each airport at minimum total cost.

8.12   A baking firm can produce a specialty bread in either of its two plants, as follows:

Plant	Production Capacity, loaves	Production Cost, ¢/loaf
A	2500	23
B	2100	25

Four restaurant chains are willing to purchase this bread; their demands and the prices they are willing to pay are as follows:

Chain	Maximum Demand, loaves	Price Offered, ¢/loaf
1	1800	39
2	2300	37
3	550	40
4	1750	36

The cost (in cents) of shipping a loaf from a plant to a restaurant chain is given in the following table:

	Chain 1	Chain 2	Chain 3	Chain 4
Plant A	6	8	11	9
Plant B	12	6	8	5

Determine a delivery schedule for the baking firm that will *maximize* its total profit from this bread.

8.13   Two drug companies have inventories of 1.1 and 0.9 million doses of a particular flu vaccine, and an epidemic of the flu seems imminent in three cities. Since the flu could be fatal to senior citizens, it is imperative that they be vaccinated first; others will be vaccinated on a first-come-first-served basis while the vaccine supply lasts. The amounts of vaccine (in millions of doses) each city estimates it could administer are as follows:

	City 1	City 2	City 3
To Elders	0.325	0.260	0.195
To Others	0.750	0.800	0.650

The shipping costs (in cents per dose) between drug companies and cities are as follows:

	City 1	City 2	City 3
Company 1	3	3	6
Company 2	1	4	7

Determine a minimum-cost shipping schedule which will provide each city with at least enough vaccine to care for its senior citizens. (*Hint*: Divide each city into two destinations, senior citizens and others. Create a dummy source. Make the shipping costs from the dummy to the senior-citizen destinations prohibitively high, effectively guaranteeing no shipments along those links.)

8.14   Prove that if the costs in any row or any column of a transportation tableau are uniformly reduced by the same number (positive or negative), then the resultant problem has the same optimal solution as the original problem.

Chapter 9

Integer Programming: Scheduling Models

PRODUCTION PROBLEMS

Production problems involve a single product which is to be manufactured over a number of successive time periods to meet prespecified demands. Once manufactured, units of the product can be either shipped or stored. Both production costs and storage costs are known. The objective is to determine a production schedule which will meet all future demands at minimum total cost (which is total production cost plus total storage cost, as total shipping cost is presumed fixed). (See Problem 9.1.)

Production problems may be converted into transportation problems by considering the time periods during which production can take place as sources, and the time periods in which units will be shipped as destinations. The production capacities are taken to be the supplies. Therefore, x_{ij} denotes the number of units to be produced during time period i for shipment during time period j, and c_{ij} is the unit production cost during time period i plus the cost of storing a unit of product from time period i until time period j. Since units cannot be shipped prior to being produced, c_{ij} is made prohibitively large for $i > j$ to force the corresponding x_{ij} to be zero.

TRANSSHIPMENT PROBLEMS

A *transshipment problem*, like a transportation problem, involves sources, having supplies, and destinations, having demands. In addition, however, it also involves *junctions*, through which goods can be shipped. Such junctions may be distinct from sources and destinations, or a source or destination may also function as a junction. Unit shipping costs are given between all directly accessible locations, and the objective is to develop a transportation schedule that will meet all demands at minimum total cost. (See Problems 9.2 and 9.3.)

Transshipment problems may be converted into transportation problems by making every junction both a source and a destination. As in the transportation algorithm, total supply is presumed equal to total demand; if this is not true initially, a fictitious source or destination is added. Thus, the total number of units in the system is given either by the sum of the supplies or by the sum of the demands. Each junction is assigned a supply equal to its original supply (or zero, if the junction did not originally coincide with a source) plus the total number of units in the system; and it is assigned a demand equal to its original demand (or zero, if the junction did not originally coincide with a destination) plus the total number of units in the system. These assignments allow for the possibility that all units may pass through a given junction. The cost of transporting 1 unit from a junction (considered as a source) to itself (considered as a destination) is zero. Those units that do not pass through a junction under the optimal schedule will appear as allocations from the junction to itself.

ASSIGNMENT PROBLEMS

Assignment problems involve scheduling workers to jobs on a *one-to-one* basis (more generally, they involve *permutations* of a set of objects). The number of workers is presumed equal to the number of jobs—a condition that can be guaranteed by creating either fictitious workers or jobs, as needed—and the time c_{ij} required by the ith worker to complete the jth job (or, the value of the the ith

84

object in the jth position) is known. The objective is to schedule every worker to a job so that all jobs are completed in the minimum total time (or, to find the permutation that has the greatest total value). (See Problem 9.4.)

Assignment problems can be converted into transportation problems by considering the workers as sources and the jobs as destinations, where all supplies and demands are equal to 1. A solution procedure more efficient than the general transportation algorithm is the *Hungarian method*, which uses only the cost matrix, Tableau 9-1, as input. There are four steps:

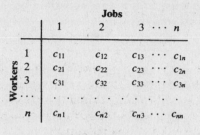

Jobs

		1	2	3 $\cdots$	n
Workers	1	c_{11}	c_{12}	$c_{13}\cdots$	c_{1n}
	2	c_{21}	c_{22}	$c_{23}\cdots$	c_{2n}
	3	c_{31}	c_{32}	$c_{33}\cdots$	c_{3n}
	$\cdots$				
	n	c_{n1}	c_{n2}	$c_{n3}\cdots$	c_{nn}

Tableau 9-1

STEP 1 In each row of Tableau 9-1, locate the smallest element and subtract it from every element in that row. Repeat this procedure for each column (the column minimum is determined after the row subtractions). The revised cost matrix will have at least one zero in every row and column.

STEP 2 Determine whether there exists a feasible assignment involving only zero costs in the revised cost matrix. In other words, find if the revised matrix has n zero entries no two of which are in the same row or column. If such an assignment exists, it is optimal. If no such exists, go to Step 3.

STEP 3 Cover all zeros in the revised cost matrix with as few horizontal and vertical lines as possible. Each horizontal line must pass through an entire row, each vertical line must pass through an entire column; the total number of lines in this minimal covering will be smaller than n. Locate the smallest number in the cost matrix not covered by a line. Subtract this number from every element not covered by a line and add it to every element covered by two lines.

STEP 4 Return to Step 2.

See Problem 9.5. According to a basic result in graph theory, the number of lines required in Step 3 will be precisely equal to the largest number of zeros in the revised matrix such that no two of them are in the same row or column.

THE TRAVELING SALESMAN PROBLEM

This problem involves an individual who must leave a base location, visit $n-1$ other locations (each once and only once), and then return to the base. The cost of traveling between each pair of locations, c_{ij}, is given with c_{ij} not necessarily equal to c_{ji}. The objective is to schedule a minimum-cost itinerary. Since what is important is the *circuit* executed by the salesman, it is purely a matter of convenience which of the n locations is designated the base.

An assignment problem may be associated with each traveling salesman problem, as follows. Arbitrarily label the locations involved in the traveling salesman problem with the integers $1, 2, \ldots, n$. Consider a set of n "workers" and a set of n "jobs." The cost of an assignment, c_{ij}, is the cost of traveling directly from location i to location j. It is clear that every feasible solution to the traveling salesman problem corresponds to a feasible solution to the associated assignment problem. However, the assignment problem will possess feasible solutions (corresponding to noncyclic permutations) which do not represent a feasible solution of the traveling salesman problem. The optimal solution of the associated assignment problem serves as a *first approximation* to the solution of the traveling salesman problem. We apply the Hungarian method to the cost matrix of the assignment problem (which is the same as the matrix of the salesman problem), and if the result corresponds to a feasible itinerary, that itinerary must be optimal. If not, a variant of the branch-and-bound method (Chapter 6) may be used to create two new assignment problems which between them contain the optimal solution of the traveling salesman problem.

Branching is on the matrix element c_{pq}, where $p \to q$ is any one of the assignments in the current first approximation (which, by hypothesis, does not reflect a feasible itinerary). One new cost matrix is obtained by replacing c_{pq} by a prohibitively large number; the other new matrix is obtained by replacing c_{qp} (the transposed element), as well as all elements in the pth row or qth column except c_{pq} itself, by a prohibitively large number.

Branch-and-bound procedures are computationally impractical for large problems involving hundreds of locations, so a number of "near-optimal" algorithms have been devised for such situations. (See Problem 9.7.) The objection to near-optimal procedures is that, although they are quite good generally, they can, in particular instances, generate very poor approximations to the optimal solution. (See Problem 9.9.)

Solved Problems

9.1 An industrial firm must plan for each of the four seasons over the next year. The company's production capacities and the expected demands (all in units) are as follows:

	Spring	Summer	Fall	Winter
Demand	250	100	400	500
Regular Capacity	200	300	350	. . .
Overtime Capacity	100	50	100	150

Regular production costs for the firm are $7.00 per unit; the unit cost of overtime varies seasonally, being $8.00 in spring and fall, $9.00 in summer, and $10.00 in winter.

The company has 200 units of inventory on January 1, but, as it plans to discontinue the product at the end of the year, it wants no inventory after the winter season. Units produced on regular shifts are not available for shipment during the season of production; generally, they are sold during the following season. Those that are not are added to inventory and carried forward at a cost of $0.70 per unit per season. In contrast, units produced on overtime shifts must be shipped in the same season as produced. Determine a production schedule that meets all demands at minimum total cost.

Time periods during which production can take place are: the overtime shifts for the four seasons, and the regular shifts for the first three seasons. Each of these seven periods becomes a source, and to them we add an eighth source, initial inventory, since it too can supply goods. The total supply is 1450 units. Time periods in which products will be required are the four seasons; these become the destinations, with a total demand of 1250 units. Since total supply exceeds total demand, a fictitious destination must be created, with a demand equal to the 200-unit excess.

Positive allocations from a source to the fictitious destination represent units that could be produced by the source but will not be, because they are not needed.   Since all units in initial inventory already *have been* produced, a positive allocation from initial inventory to the dummy must be avoided.   This is done by assigning a prohibitively large number ($10 000) as the associated unit cost.   All other costs associated with the dummy are, as usual, taken to be zero.

Other allocations which must be avoided are also assigned prohibitively large costs.   These include shipments from regular shifts to the current season or to earlier seasons, and shipments from overtime shifts to any but the current season.   Costs associated with the initial inventory are future carrying costs only, since production costs and past carrying charges have already been incurred and cannot be minimized.   The remaining cost entries are simply the production costs plus the storage charges.

Applying the transportation algorithm to this problem, we obtain Tableau 1 as the optimal tableau.   It follows that the spring demand will be met by using all 200 units from inventory and 50 units from overtime production in the spring.   The summer demand is met from the regular spring shift. The fall demand is met by 300 units from the regular summer shift plus 100 units from overtime production in the fall.   The winter demand is satisfied by using 100 units made in the spring on a regular shift and stored, plus 350 units from the regular fall production and 50 units produced in the winter on an overtime shift.

	Spring	Summer	Fall	Winter	dummy	Supply	u_i
Regular (Spring)	10 000 (9993.60)	7.00 **100**	7.70 (0)	8.40 **100**	0 (1.60)	200	8.40
Regular (Summer)	10 000 (9994.30)	10 000 (9993.70)	7.00 **300**	7.70 **0**	0 (2.30)	300	7.70
Regular (Fall)	10 000 (9995)	10 000 (9994.40)	10 000 (9993.70)	7.00 **350**	0 (3)	350	7
Initial Inventory	0 **200**	0.70 (0.10)	1.40 (0.10)	2.10 (0.10)	10 000 (10 008)	200	2
Overtime (Spring)	8.00 **50**	10 000 (9991.40)	10 000 (9990.70)	10 000 (9990)	0 **50**	100	10
Overtime (Summer)	10 000 (9992)	9.00 (0.40)	10 000 (9990.70)	10 000 (9990)	0 **50**	50	10
Overtime (Fall)	10 000 (9993.30)	10 000 (9992.70)	8.00 **100**	10 000 (9991.30)	0 (1.30)	100	8.70
Overtime (Winter)	10 000 (9992)	10 000 (9991.40)	10 000 (9990.70)	10.00 **50**	0 **100**	150	10
Demand	250	100	400	500	200		
v_j	−2	−1.40	−0.70	0	−10		

Tableau 1

9.2   A corporation must transport 70 units of a product from location 1 to locations 2 and 3, in the amounts of 45 and 25 units, respectively.   Air freight charges c_{ij} (in dollars per unit) between locations served by the air carrier are given in Table 9-1, where dotted lines signify that service is not available.   Determine a shipping schedule that allocates the required number of goods to each destination at a minimum total freight cost.   No shipment need be flown directly; shipments through intermediate points are allowed.

Table 9-1

i \ j	1	2	3	4
1	$\cdots$	38	56	34
2	38	$\cdots$	27	$\cdots$
3	56	27	$\cdots$	19
4	34	$\cdots$	19	$\cdots$

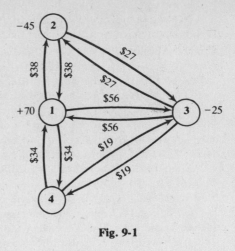

Fig. 9-1

This problem is depicted schematically by Fig. 9-1, wherein supplies are indicated by positive, and demands by negative, numbers. Notice that, despite the symmetry of Table 9-1, the freight rates are not proportional to distance. Location 4 is a pure junction. Locations 2 and 3 serve as both destinations and junctions (goods can be shipped from location 1 to location 3 through location 2, and from 1 to 2 through 3), while location 1 serves as both a source and a junction. Since it could never be optimal to ship goods from location 1 and have them return at some later time, only to be shipped out again, the problem can be simplified by not allowing shipments *to* location 1, thereby restricting it to being solely a source.

For application of the transportation algorithm, we increase the supply and demand of every junction—locations 2, 3, and 4—by the total number of units in the system, 70 units. Also, we define $c_{24} = c_{42} \equiv$ \$10 000, to force zero shipments over the nonexistent routes $2 \rightarrow 4$ and $4 \rightarrow 2$, and define $c_{22} = c_{33} = c_{44} \equiv$ 0. The transportation algorithm produces the optimal Tableau 2. Thus, 45 units will be shipped from location 1 directly to location 2, satisfying its demand, while the remaining 25 units will be shipped from location 1 to location 4, whereupon they will be forwarded to location 3. Note that $x_{22}^* = x_{33}^* = 70$, indicating that (all) 70 units avoid passing *through* these locations. Similarly, $x_{44}^* = 45$, signifying that 45 of the 70 units are not shipped through location 4.

Destinations

Sources		2	3	4	Supply	u_i
	1	38 **45**	56 (3)	34 **25**	70	0
	2	0 **70**	27 (12)	10 000 (10 004)	70	-38
	3	27 (42)	0 **70**	19 (38)	70	-53
	4	10 000 (9996)	19 **25**	0 **45**	70	-34
	Demand	115	95	70		
	v_j	38	53	34		

Tableau 2

9.3   For the data of Fig. 9-2, determine a shipping schedule that meets all demands at a minimum total cost.

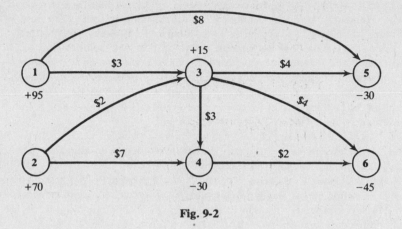

Fig. 9-2

Locations 1 and 2 are sources, while locations 5 and 6 are destinations.   Location 3 is both a source and a junction, whereas location 4 serves both as a destination and a junction.   Because total supply is 180 units but total demand is only 105 units, location 7 is created as a dummy destination with a demand of $180 - 105 = 75$ units.   Since every junction is made both a source and a destination, by adding 180 units to both its supply and its demand, the transportation tableau will involve sources 1, 2, 3, 4, and destinations 3, 4, 5, 6, 7.   Besides the costs given in Fig. 9-2, we have zero as the cost from a junction (as a source) to itself (as a destination), zero as the cost from any source to the dummy, and an excessive amount ($10 000) as the cost over any nonexistent link (e.g., $1 \rightarrow 6$).

Tableau 3 is the optimal transportation tableau.   Location 3 receives 20 units from location 1 and 70 units from location 2, whereupon it redistributes these units along with its own initial supply of 15 units to locations 4, 5, and 6.   After all demands have been satisfied, location 1 will remain with 75 units, indicated in Tableau 3 by the allocation from location 1 to the dummy.   The allocations $x_{33}^* = 90$ and $x_{44}^* = 180$ are book entries signifying the numbers of units that do not pass through junctions 3 and 4, respectively.

		Destinations						
		3	4	5	6	(dummy) 7	Supply	u_i
Sources	1	3 **20**	10 000 (9994)	8 (1)	10 000 (9993)	0 **75**	95	3
	2	2 **70**	7 (2)	10 000 (9994)	10 000 (9994)	0 (1)	70	2
	3	0 **90**	3 **30**	4 **30**	4 **45**	0 (3)	195	0
	4	10 000 (10 003)	0 **180**	10 000 (9999)	2 (1)	0 (6)	180	−3
	Demand	180	210	30	45	75		
	v_j	0	3	4	4	−3		

Tableau 3

9.4 Solve Problem 1.13 by the Hungarian method.

Table 1-1 of Problem 1.13 is expanded to make the number of events equal to the number of swimmers; the result is Tableau 4A. As usual, costs (times) associated with the dummies, events 5 and 6, are taken to be zero. The rationale here is that events 5 and 6 do not exist, so they can be completed in zero time; swimmers assigned to these events will be the ones not entered in the four-swimmer relay.

The Hungarian method is initiated by subtracting 0 from every row of Tableau 4A and then subtracting 65, 69, 63, 55, 0, and 0 from columns 1 through 6, respectively; this generates Tableau 4B. Since this matrix does not contain a zero-cost feasible solution, we cover the existing zeros by as few horizontal and vertical lines as possible. One such covering is that shown in Tableau 4B; another, equally good, is obtained by replacing the line through row 3 by a line through column 4. The smallest uncovered element is 1, appearing in the $(2, 2)$ position. Subtracting 1 from every uncovered element in Tableau 4B and adding 1 to every element covered by two lines—the $(1, 5)$, $(1, 6)$, $(3, 5)$, $(3, 6)$, $(5, 5)$, and $(5, 6)$ elements—we arrive at Tableau 4C.

Tableau 4C also does not contain a feasible zero-cost assignment. Repeating Step 3 of the Hungarian method, we determine that 1 is again the smallest uncovered element. Subtracting it from each uncovered element and adding it to every element covered by two lines, we obtain Tableau 4D, which does contain a feasible zero-cost assignment, as indicated by the starred entries. Thus, an optimal allocation is swimmer 1 to event 1 (backstroke), swimmer 2 to event 3 (butterfly), swimmer 3 to event 4 (freestyle), and swimmer 5 to event 2 (breaststroke); swimmers 4 and 6 are not entered in the medley. The minimum total time (in seconds) is calculated from Tableau 4A as

$$z^* = c_{11} + c_{23} + c_{34} + c_{52} = 65 + 65 + 55 + 69 = 254 \text{ s}$$

This solution, however, is not the only optimal one. An equally optimal assignment can be obtained from Tableau 4D: assign swimmer 1 to event 3 and swimmer 2 to event 1, leaving the other assignments unchanged.

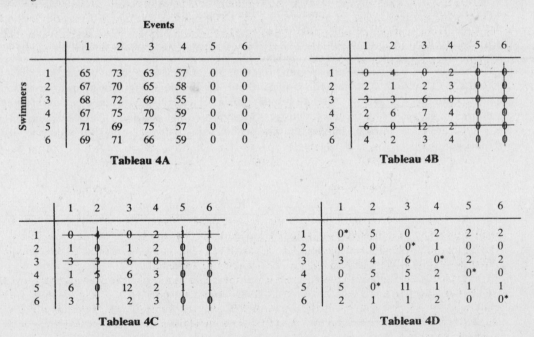

Events

Tableau 4A

Swimmers	1	2	3	4	5	6
1	65	73	63	57	0	0
2	67	70	65	58	0	0
3	68	72	69	55	0	0
4	67	75	70	59	0	0
5	71	69	75	57	0	0
6	69	71	66	59	0	0

Tableau 4B

	1	2	3	4	5	6
1	0	4	0	2	0	0
2	2	1	2	3	0	0
3	3	3	6	0	0	0
4	2	6	7	4	0	0
5	6	0	12	2	0	0
6	4	2	3	4	0	0

Tableau 4C

	1	2	3	4	5	6
1	0	4	0	2	1	1
2	1	0	1	2	0	0
3	3	3	6	0	1	1
4	1	5	6	3	0	0
5	6	0	12	2	1	1
6	3	1	2	3	0	0

Tableau 4D

	1	2	3	4	5	6
1	0*	5	0	2	2	2
2	0	0	0*	1	0	0
3	3	4	6	0*	2	2
4	0	5	5	2	0*	0
5	5	0*	11	1	1	1
6	2	1	1	2	0	0*

9.5 Verify the Hungarian method.

As a consequence of Problem 8.14 (remember that the assignment problem is a special transportation problem), Step 1 of the Hungarian method does not alter the optimal assignment, but simply provides a cost matrix with smaller entries. Since each element in this new cost matrix is nonnegative, a zero-cost assignment, if feasible, must be optimal. Thus Step 2 of the method. If no zero-cost feasible solution exists, then the zeros in the current cost matrix are not well distributed.

Step 3 is a procedure for redistributing and, perhaps, introducing additional zeros. The operations involving c, the smallest (positive) cost not covered by a line in the current matrix, replace the current matrix by a new nonnegative matrix such that (i) the element c itself is replaced by a zero, (ii) those old zeros covered by a single line are retained, and (iii) the rest of the old zeros are replaced by c.   But since these operations are equivalent to subtracting $c/2$ from each uncovered row and each uncovered column, and adding $c/2$ to each covered row and each covered column, Problem 8.14 once more guarantees that the optimal assignment is unaltered.

9.6   Xanadu National Airlines offers an excursion at one low price that allows a person to cover its entire service route.   The ticket, which is valid for two weeks from the date of purchase, carries the following restriction: No city on the route can be revisited except the city of origin, which can be the last stop on the excursion.   A foreign tourist, presently in city 1 (the capital), wishes to see provincial cities 2, 3, and 4, before returning to the capital; she decides to travel on the airlines.   Flight times (in minutes) between the cities of interest are given in the table below, where dotted entries signify that service between corresponding locations is not available.   Determine an acceptable itinerary which will minimize her total flight time.

Cities	1	2	3	4
1	$\cdots$	65	53	37
2	65	$\cdots$	95	$\cdots$
3	53	95	$\cdots$	81
4	37	$\cdots$	81	$\cdots$

	1	2	3	4
1	10 000	65	53	37*
2	65	10 000	95*	10 000
3	53	95*	10 000	81
4	37*	10 000	81	10 000

Tableau 6A

We begin by replacing each dotted entry in the timetable by an exorbitant number of prohibit assignments to those links under an optimal itinerary.   The result is Tableau 6A.   Applying the Hungarian method to this tableau, we obtain (on the second application of Step 2) the assignment indicated by the starred elements; namely, $1 \to 4$, $4 \to 1$, $2 \to 3$, $3 \to 2$.   This is *not* a valid itinerary, for it returns the tourist to city 1 immediately after her first stop in city 4.

	1	2	3	4
1	10 000	65*	53	10 000
2	65	10 000	95*	10 000
3	53	95	10 000	81*
4	37*	10 000	81	10 000

Tableau 6B

	1	2	3	4
1	10 000	10 000	10 000	37*
2	65*	10 000	95	10 000
3	53	95*	10 000	10 000
4	10 000	10 000	81*	10 000

Tableau 6C

We now branch on the starred element $c_{14} = 37$ of Tableau 6A.   The first branch is effected by replacing c_{14} by a prohibitively large number, as shown in Tableau 6B.   The second branch is effected by replacing c_{41}, the transposed element, as well as all elements in the fourth row or first column except c_{14} itself, by a prohibitively large number.   This is done in Tableau 6C.

Applying the Hungarian method to each of these two new cost matrices separately, we obtain valid itineraries   for   both: $1 \to 2$, $2 \to 3$, $3 \to 4$, $4 \to 1$, with   a   cost   of   278 min,   for   Tableau   6B; and $1 \to 4$, $4 \to 3$, $3 \to 2$, $2 \to 1$, with a cost of 278 min, for Tableau 6C.   Both solutions are optimal. Indeed, whenever the cost matrix is symmetric, an optimal circuit remains optimal when described in the opposite sense.

9.7   Develop a "near-optimal"algorithm for the traveling salesman problem.

We develop the *nearest-neighbor method*, based on the principle of sequentially selecting the cheapest remaining link such that its inclusion does not complete a circuit too soon.

STEP 1   Locate the smallest element in the cost matrix (break ties arbitrarily), circle it, and include the corresponding link in the itinerary.

STEP 2 If the newly circled element is c_{pq}, replace all other elements in the pth row and all other elements in the qth column, as well as the transposed element c_{qp}, by a prohibitively large number.

STEP 3 Locate the smallest uncircled element in the latest cost matrix. Tentatively adjoin its corresponding link to the (incomplete) itinerary. If the resulting itinerary is not infeasible, circle the designated cost and go to Step 5.

STEP 4 If the resulting itinerary is infeasible, remove the latest link from the itinerary and replace its corresponding cost by a prohibitively large number. Go to Step 3.

STEP 5 Determine whether the itinerary is complete. If so, accept it as the near-optimal one. If not, go to Step 2.

Step 2 ensures that a location, once left, will not be left again, and that a location, once entered, will not be entered again. Hence, the tentative itinerary of Step 3 will be feasible, unless it contains a circuit of fewer than n links.

9.8 Use the nearest-neighbor method (Problem 9.7) to find a near-optimal, traveling salesman itinerary, if the cost matrix is given by Tableau 8A.

	1	2	3	4	5
1	$\cdots$	35	80	105	165
2	35	$\cdots$	45	20	80
3	80	45	$\cdots$	30	75
4	105	20	30	$\cdots$	60
5	165	80	75	60	$\cdots$

Tableau 8A

	1	2	3	4	5
1	1000	35	80	105	165
2	35	1000	45	20	80
3	80	45	1000	30	75
4	105	20	30	1000	60
5	165	80	75	60	1000

Tableau 8B

We first replace the dotted entries in the cost matrix with a prohibitively large number (1000), thereby obtaining Tableau 8B. The smallest entry in this tableau is either c_{24} or c_{42}. Arbitrarily choosing c_{24}, we circle it, indicating that we have accepted link $2 \rightarrow 4$ as part of the final itinerary. We then replace all other elements in the second row and all other elements in the fourth column, as well as the transposed element c_{42}, by 1000. The result is Tableau 8C.

The smallest uncircled element in Tableau 8C is $c_{43} = 30$. Adjoining link $4 \rightarrow 3$ to the current incomplete itinerary, we have the (still incomplete) itinerary $2 \rightarrow 4$, $4 \rightarrow 3$, which is not infeasible. Consequently, we circle c_{43} and replace all other elements in the fourth row and all other elements in the third column of Tableau 8C, as well as the transposed element c_{34}, by 1000. The result is Tableau 8D.

	1	2	3	4	5
1	1000	35	80	1000	165
2	1000	1000	1000	⑳	1000
3	80	45	1000	1000	75
4	105	1000	30	1000	60
5	165	80	75	1000	1000

Tableau 8C

	1	2	3	4	5
1	1000	35	1000	1000	165
2	1000	1000	1000	⑳	1000
3	80	45	1000	1000	75
4	1000	1000	㉚	1000	1000
5	165	80	1000	1000	1000

Tableau 8D

The smallest uncircled element in Tableau 8D is $c_{12} = 35$. Adjoining link $1 \rightarrow 2$ to the current incomplete itinerary, we generate the itinerary $1 \rightarrow 2$, $2 \rightarrow 4$, $4 \rightarrow 3$, which is not infeasible. Consequently, we circle c_{12} and replace all other elements in the first row and all other elements in the second column of Tableau 8D, as well as the transposed element c_{21}, by 1000. The result is Tableau 8E.

Continuing with the algorithm, we generate sequentially Tableaux 8F and 8G. The itinerary indicated by the circled elements in Tableau 8G—namely, $1 \rightarrow 2$, $2 \rightarrow 4$, $4 \rightarrow 3$, $3 \rightarrow 5$, $5 \rightarrow 1$—is complete and is, therefore, the near-optimal one. Its total cost is

$$z = 35 + 20 + 75 + 30 + 165 = 325$$

See also Problem 9.17.

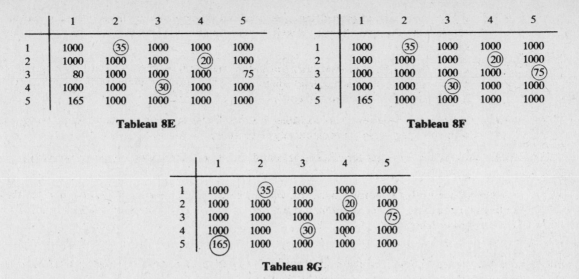

	1	2	3	4	5
1	1000	(35)	1000	1000	1000
2	1000	1000	1000	(20)	1000
3	80	1000	1000	1000	75
4	1000	1000	(30)	1000	1000
5	165	1000	1000	1000	1000

Tableau 8E

	1	2	3	4	5
1	1000	(35)	1000	1000	1000
2	1000	1000	1000	(20)	1000
3	1000	1000	1000	1000	(75)
4	1000	1000	(30)	1000	1000
5	165	1000	1000	1000	1000

Tableau 8F

	1	2	3	4	5
1	1000	(35)	1000	1000	1000
2	1000	1000	1000	(20)	1000
3	1000	1000	1000	1000	(75)
4	1000	1000	(30)	1000	1000
5	(165)	1000	1000	1000	1000

Tableau 8G

9.9 Apply the nearest-neighbor method to Problem 9.6.

The smallest entry in Tableau 6A, an initial cost matrix for this problem, is either c_{14} or c_{41}. We arbitrarily circle c_{14} and then replace all other elements in the first row, all other elements in the fourth column, and c_{41}, by a prohibitively large number. The result is Tableau 9A.

	1	2	3	4
1	10 000	10 000	10 000	(37)
2	65	10 000	95	10 000
3	53	95	10 000	10 000
4	10 000	10 000	81	10 000

Tableau 9A

	1	2	3	4
1	10 000	10 000	10 000	(37)
2	10 000	10 000	95	10 000
3	(53)	10 000	10 000	10 000
4	10 000	10 000	81	10 000

Tableau 9B

Applying the nearest-neighbor algorithm to Tableau 9A, we obtain Tableau 9B with the partially completed itinerary $3 \to 1$, $1 \to 4$. The smallest entry in Tableau 9B is $c_{43} = 81$. Adjoining link $4 \to 3$ to the current itinerary yields $4 \to 3$, $3 \to 1$, $1 \to 4$, which is not feasible, since it is a circuit that omits city 2. Accordingly, we do not accept $4 \to 3$ as part of the final itinerary, and we replace its cost, c_{43}, with a large number. The result is Tableau 9C.

	1	2	3	4
1	10 000	10 000	10 000	(37)
2	10 000	10 000	95	10 000
3	(53)	10 000	10 000	10 000
4	10 000	10 000	10 000	10 000

Tableau 9C

	1	2	3	4
1	10 000	10 000	10 000	(37)
2	10 000	10 000	(95)	10 000
3	(53)	10 000	10 000	10 000
4	10 000	(10 000)	10 000	10 000

Tableau 9D

Continuing with the algorithm, we obtain after two more iterations Tableau 9D. The near-optimal solution suggested by the circled cost elements is $1 \to 4$, $4 \to 2$, $2 \to 3$, $3 \to 1$, with

$$z = 37 + 10\,000 + 95 + 53 = 10\,185$$

This value of the objective function is prohibitively high; in this case, the "near-optimal" solution is actually far from optimal.

Supplementary Problems

9.10   A manufacturer receives an order from a large city for six doubledecker buses, to be delivered two at a time over the next three months.   Production data for the manufacturer are shown in Table 9-2.

Table 9-2

	Months		
	1	2	3
Regular Production Capacity, units	1	2	3
Overtime Production Capacity, units	2	2	2
Regular Production Cost, $1000/unit	35	43	40
Overtime Production Cost, $1000/unit	39	47	45

Buses can be delivered to the city at the end of the same month in which they are assembled, or they can be stored by the manufacturer, at a cost of $3000 per bus per month, for shipment during a later month.   The manufacturer has no current inventory of these doubledecker buses and desires none after the completion of this contract.   Determine a production schedule that will meet the city's demands at minimum cost to the manufacturer.

9.11   A drug company estimates demand (in millions of doses) for one of its vaccines as follows: October, 7.1; November, 13.2; December, 12.8; January, 7.7; and February, 2.1.   There is relatively little demand for the vaccine during the other months, and company policy for supplying these demands is to have 1 million doses in inventory at the end of February.   The vaccine takes four weeks to produce, so no doses are available for shipping during the month they are produced.   Once the vaccine is ready, however, it can either be shipped immediately to customers or carried forward as inventory at a cost of 10¢ per dose per month.   Traditionally, the company produces the vaccine only between August and December inclusively.   Any vaccine remaining in inventory from the previous year is destroyed on September 1.

The company's production capacities (in millions of doses) and the anticipated production costs (in cents per dose) for each month of the upcoming production cycle are as follows:

	August	September	October	November	December
Capacity	12.5	11.0	9.5	8.1	5.5
Cost	63	68	75	52	48

Determine a production schedule that meets all demands at minimum total cost.

9.12   Determine a minimum-cost shipping schedule for the transshipment problem depicted in Fig. 9-3.

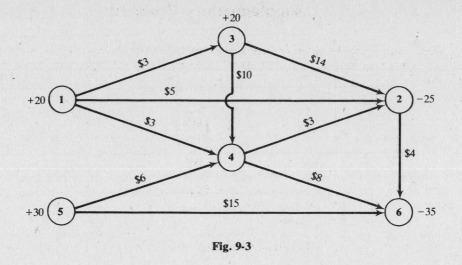

Fig. 9-3

9.13 An automobile manufacturer has orders from locations 5, 6, and 7 for 75, 60, and 80 units, respectively, of a particular model. The production process consists in making the body either at location 1 or 2; shipping the body either to location 3 or 4, where it is assembled onto the rest of the car; and then shipping the entire unit to the waiting customer. Production costs per body are $533 at location 1 and $550 at location 2. Assembly costs at locations 3 and 4 are $2256 and $2239, respectively. Transportation costs (in dollars) between locations are as follows:

Locations	3	4		Locations	5	6	7
1	45	59		3	72	65	79
2	65	52		4	81	74	63

Production capacities at locations 1 and 2 are 150 and 170 bodies, respectively; locations 3 and 4 can assemble all the bodies forwarded to them. Determine a production and shipping schedule that will meet all demands at minimum cost. (*Hint*: Set up as a transshipment problem.)

9.14 A rent-a-car company has an excess of cars in some cities and a shortage in others. In particular, cities 1 and 2 have surpluses of 15 and 12 cars, respectively, while cities 3, 4, and 5 need 7, 18, and 9 additional cars, respectively. Cars can be shipped directly between locations, or they can be shipped through intermediate cities where the company has agencies. If shipping costs (in dollars per car) are as given in Tableau 14, determine a minimum-cost shipping schedule for the rent-a-car company.

Cities	1	2	3	4	5
1	· · ·	7	12	25	65
2	7	· · ·	22	25	75
3	12	22	· · ·	17	28
4	25	25	17	· · ·	15
5	65	75	28	15	· · ·

Tableau 14

9.15 A fast-food chain wants to build four stores in the Chicago area. In the past, the chain has used six different construction companies, and, having been satisfied with each, has invited each to bid on each job. The final bids (in thousands of dollars) were as shown in Table 9-3.

Table 9-3

	Construction Companies					
	1	2	3	4	5	6
Store 1	85.3	88	87.5	82.4	89.1	86.7
Store 2	78.9	77.4	77.4	76.5	79.3	78.3
Store 3	82	81.3	82.4	80.6	83.5	81.7
Store 4	84.3	84.6	86.2	83.3	84.4	85.5

Since the fast-food chain wants to have each of the new stores ready as quickly as possible, it will award at most one job to a construction company. What assignment results in minimum total cost to the fast-food chain?

9.16   Solve Problem 1.23.

9.17   Find an exact solution to Problem 9.8 and compare it with the near-optimal itinerary obtained therein.

9.18   The following tableau is the (unsymmetric) cost matrix for travel among a particular set of locations. Determine a minimum-cost, traveling salesman itinerary.

Cities	1	2	3	4	5
1	$\cdots$	1	8	3	4
2	1	$\cdots$	8	2	3
3	1	3	$\cdots$	5	1
4	2	5	6	$\cdots$	5
5	5	3	7	6	$\cdots$

9.19   Use the nearest-neighbor method to find a near-optimal itinerary for Problem 9.18.

9.20   Show that the branching process for the traveling salesman problem creates two new problems, in one of which link $p \to q$ must be taken and in the other of which link $p \to q$ must not be taken.

9.21   Show by means of an example that an optimal itinerary for the traveling salesman problem may not still be optimal when the constraint that each location be visited *only once* is dropped.

Chapter 10

Nonlinear Programming: Single-Variable Optimization

THE PROBLEM

A one-variable, unconstrained, nonlinear program has the form

$$\text{optimize:} \quad z = f(x) \qquad (10.1)$$

where $f(x)$ is a (nonlinear) function of the single variable x, and the search for the optimum (maximum or minimum) is conducted over the infinite interval $(-\infty, \infty)$. If the search is restricted to a finite subinterval $[a, b]$, then the problem becomes

$$\text{optimize:} \quad z = f(x)$$
$$\text{subject to:} \quad a \leq x \leq b \qquad (10.2)$$

which is a one-variable, constrained program.

LOCAL AND GLOBAL OPTIMA

An objective function $f(x)$ has a *local* (or *relative*) *minimum* at x_0 if there exists a (small) interval centered at x_0 such that $f(x) \geq f(x_0)$ for all x in this interval at which the function is defined. If $f(x) \geq f(x_0)$ for all x at which the function is defined, then the minimum at x_0 (besides being local) is a *global* (or *absolute*) minimum. Local and global maxima are defined similarly, in terms of the reversed inequality.

Example 10.1 The function graphed in Fig. 10-1 is defined only on $[a, b]$. It has relative minima at a, x_2, and x_4; relative maxima at x_1, x_3, and b; a global minimum at x_2; and global maxima at x_1 and b.

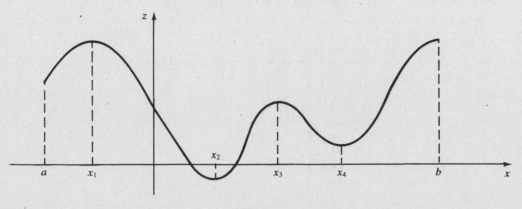

Fig. 10-1

Program (10.1) seeks a global optimum; program (10.2) does too, insofar as it seeks the best of the local optima over $[a, b]$. It is possible that the objective function assumes even better values outside $[a, b]$, but these are not of interest.

RESULTS FROM CALCULUS

Theorem 10.1: If $f(x)$ is continuous on the closed and bounded interval $[a, b]$, then $f(x)$ has global optima (both a maximum and a minimum) on this interval.

Theorem 10.2: If $f(x)$ has a local optimum at x_0 and if $f(x)$ is differentiable on a small interval centered at x_0, then $f'(x_0) = 0$.

Theorem 10.3: If $f(x)$ is twice-differentiable on a small interval centered at x_0, and if $f'(x_0) = 0$ and $f''(x_0) > 0$, then $f(x)$ has a local minimum at x_0. If instead $f'(x_0) = 0$ and $f''(x_0) < 0$, then $f(x)$ has a local maximum at x_0.

It follows from the first two theorems that if $f(x)$ is continuous on $[a, b]$, then local and global optima for program (10.2) will occur among points where $f'(x)$ does not exist, or among points where $f'(x) = 0$ (generally called *stationary* or *critical points*), or among the endpoints $x = a$ and $x = b$. (See Problems 10.1 through 10.3.)

Since program (10.1) is not restricted to a closed and bounded interval, there are no endpoints to consider. Instead, the values of the objective function at the stationary points and at points where $f'(x)$ does not exist are compared to the limiting values of $f(x)$ as $x \to \pm\infty$. It may be that neither limit exists (consider $f(x) = \sin x$). But if either limit does exist—and we accept $\pm\infty$ as a "limit" here—and yields the best value of $f(x)$ (the largest for a maximization program or the smallest for a minimization program), then a global optimum for $f(x)$ does not exist. If the best value occurs at one of the finite points, then this best value is the global optimum. (See Problem 10.4.)

SEQUENTIAL-SEARCH TECHNIQUES

In practice, locating optima by calculus is seldom fruitful: either the objective function is not known analytically, so that differentiation is impossible, or the stationary points cannot be obtained algebraically. (See Problem 10.5.) In such cases, numerical methods are used to approximate the location of (some) local optima to within an acceptable tolerance.

Sequential-search techniques start with a finite interval in which the objective function is presumed *unimodal*; that is, the interval is presumed to include one and only one point at which $f(x)$ has a local maximum or minimum. The techniques then systematically shrink the interval around the local optimum until the optimum is confined to within acceptable limits; this shrinking is effected by sequentially evaluating the objective function at selected points and then using the unimodal property to eliminate portions of the current interval.

Example 10.2 Figure 10-2 exhibits the values of the objective function at the points x_1 and x_2. If a local minimum is known to be the only extremum in $[a, b]$, then this minimum must be to the left of x_2; for $f(x)$ has begun to increase by that point, and, by the unimodal property, must continue to increase to the right of it. Hence, the subinterval $(x_2, b]$ can be discarded.

If a local maximum is the sole extremum in $[a, b]$, then it must be located to the right of x_1, and the subinterval $[a, x_1)$ can be discarded.

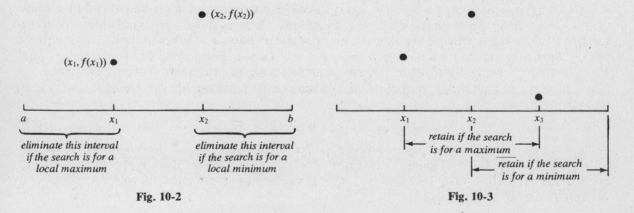

Fig. 10-2   **Fig. 10-3**

Specific sequential searches are considered in the three sections that follow.

THREE-POINT INTERVAL SEARCH

The interval under consideration is divided into quarters and the objective function evaluated at the three equally spaced interior points. The interior point yielding the best value of the objective is determined (in case of a tie, arbitrarily choose one point), and the subinterval centered at this point and made up of two quarters of the current interval replaces the current interval. Including ties, there are 10 possible sampling patterns; one of them is illustrated in Fig. 10-3. (See Problems 10.6 and 10.7.)

The three-point interval search is the most efficient *equally spaced* search procedure in terms of achieving a prescribed tolerance with a minimum number of functional evaluations. It is also one of the easiest sequential searches to code for the computer.

FIBONACCI SEARCH

The *Fibonacci sequence*, $\{F_n\} = \{1, 1, 2, 3, 5, 8, 13, 21, 34, 55, \ldots\}$, forms the basis of the most efficient sequential-search technique. Each number in the sequence is obtained by adding together the two preceding numbers; exceptions are the first two numbers, F_0 and F_1, which are both 1.

The Fibonacci search is initialized by determining the smallest Fibonacci number that satisfies $F_N \epsilon \geq b - a$, where ϵ is a prescribed tolerance and $[a, b]$ is the original interval of interest. Set $\epsilon' \equiv (b - a)/F_N$. The first two points in the search are located $F_{N-1}\epsilon'$ units in from the endpoints of $[a, b]$, where F_{N-1} is the Fibonacci number preceding F_N. Successive points in the search are considered one at a time and are positioned $F_j\epsilon'$ ($j = N - 2, N - 3, \ldots, 2$) units in from the *newest* endpoint of the current interval. (See Problem 10.8.) Observe that with the Fibonacci procedure we can state in advance the number of functional evaluations that will be required to achieve a certain accuracy; moreover, that number is independent of the particular unimodal function.

GOLDEN-MEAN SEARCH

A search nearly as efficient as the Fibonacci search is based on the number $(\sqrt{5} - 1)/2 = 0.6180\cdots$, known as the *golden mean*. The first two points of the search are located $(0.6180)(b - a)$ units in from the endpoints of the initial interval $[a, b]$. Successive points are considered one at a time and are positioned $0.6180 L_i$ units in from the *newest* endpoint of the current interval, where L_i denotes the length of this interval. (See Problem 10.9.)

CONVEX FUNCTIONS

Search procedures are guaranteed to approximate global optima on a search interval only when the objective function is unimodal there. In practice, one usually does not know whether a particular objective function is unimodal over a specified interval. When a search procedure is applied in such a situation, there is no assurance it will uncover the desired global optimum. (See Problem 10.11.) Exceptions include programs that have convex or concave objective functions.

A function $f(x)$ is *convex* on an interval $\mathscr{I}$ (finite or infinite) if for any two points x_1 and x_2 in $\mathscr{I}$ and for all $0 \leq \alpha \leq 1$,

$$f(\alpha x_1 + (1 - \alpha)x_2) \leq \alpha f(x_1) + (1 - \alpha)f(x_2) \qquad (10.3)$$

If (10.3) holds with the inequality reversed, then $f(x)$ is *concave*. Thus, the negative of a convex function is concave, and conversely. The graph of a convex function is shown in Fig. 10-4; a defining geometrical property is that the curve lies on or above any of its tangents. Convex functions and concave functions are unimodal.

Theorem 10.4:   If $f(x)$ is twice-differentiable on $\mathscr{I}$, then $f(x)$ is convex on $\mathscr{I}$ if and only if $f''(x) \geq 0$ for all x in $\mathscr{I}$.   It is concave if and only if $f''(x) \leq 0$ for all x in $\mathscr{I}$.

Theorem 10.5:   If $f(x)$ is convex on $\mathscr{I}$, then any local minimum on $\mathscr{I}$ is a global minimum on $\mathscr{I}$.   If $f(x)$ is concave on $\mathscr{I}$, then any local maximum on $\mathscr{I}$ is a global maximum on $\mathscr{I}$.

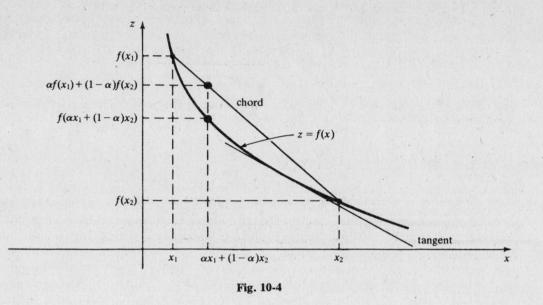

Fig. 10-4

If (10.3) holds with strict inequality except at $\alpha = 0$ and $\alpha = 1$, the function is *strictly convex*.   Such a function has a strictly positive second derivative, and any local (and therefore global) minimum is unique.   Analogous results hold for *strictly concave* functions.

Solved Problems

10.1   Maximize: $z = x(5\pi - x)$ on $[0, 20]$.

Here $f(x) = x(5\pi - x)$ is continuous, and $f'(x) = 5\pi - 2x$.   With the derivative defined everywhere, the global maximum on $[0, 20]$ occurs at an endpoint $x = 0$ or $x = 20$, or at a stationary point, where $f'(x) = 0$.   We find $x = 5\pi/2$ as the only stationary point in $[0, 20]$.   Evaluating the objective function at each of these points, we obtain the table

x	0	$5\pi/2$	20
$f(x)$	0	61.69	-85.84

from which we conclude that $x^* = 5\pi/2$, with $z^* = 61.69$.

10.2   Maximize: $z = |x^2 - 8|$ on $[-4, 4]$.

Here

$$f(x) = |x^2 - 8| = \begin{cases} x^2 - 8 & x \leq -\sqrt{8} \\ 8 - x^2 & -\sqrt{8} \leq x \leq \sqrt{8} \\ x^2 - 8 & \sqrt{8} \leq x \end{cases}$$

is a continuous function, with

$$f'(x) = \begin{cases} 2x & x < -\sqrt{8} \\ -2x & -\sqrt{8} < x < \sqrt{8} \\ 2x & \sqrt{8} < x \end{cases}$$

The derivative does not exist at $x = \pm\sqrt{8}$, and it is zero at $x = 0$; all three points are in $[-4, 4]$. Evaluating the objective function at each of these points, and at the endpoints $x = \pm 4$, we generate the table

x	-4	$-\sqrt{8}$	0	$\sqrt{8}$	4
$f(x)$	8	0	8	0	8

from which we conclude that the global maximum on $[-4, 4]$ is $z^* = 8$, which is assumed at the three points $x^* = \pm 4$ and $x^* = 0$.

10.3 Minimize: $z = f(x)$ on $[0, 1]$, where

$$f(x) = \begin{cases} 1 & x = 0 \\ x & 0 < x \le 1 \end{cases}$$

Theorem 10.1 does not apply if the function is discontinuous on the interval of interest, as it is here. In fact, no local or global minimum exists for this problem, since the function assumes arbitrarily small positive values but not the value zero.

10.4 Maximize: $z = xe^{-x^2}$.

Here

$$f'(x) = e^{-x^2} - 2x^2 e^{-x^2} = e^{-x^2}(1 - 2x^2)$$

which is defined for all x and which vanishes only at $x = \pm 1/\sqrt{2}$. Since x is unrestricted, the values of the objective function at the stationary points,

$$f(\pm 1/\sqrt{2}) = \pm \frac{1}{\sqrt{2}} e^{-1/2} = \pm 0.429$$

must be compared to the limiting values of $f(x)$ as $x \to \pm\infty$, which are both 0 in this case. Recording these results,

x	$x \to -\infty$	$-1/\sqrt{2}$	$1/\sqrt{2}$	$x \to \infty$
$f(x)$	0	-0.429	0.429	0

we see that a global maximum exists at $x^* = 1/\sqrt{2}$ and is $z^* = 0.429$.

10.5 Minimize: $z = x \sin 4x$ on $[0, 3]$.

Here $f'(x) = \sin 4x + 4x \cos 4x$, which is defined everywhere. The equation for the stationary points, ·

$$\sin 4x + 4x \cos 4x = 0$$

cannot be solved algebraically, so that we are unable precisely to identify the stationary points in $[0, 3]$. However, in the case of simple functions like this one, a good deal can be learned from a rough graph (Fig. 10-5). It is seen that the stationary points alternate with the zeros of $f(x)$ (Rolle's theorem), which are the zeros of $\sin 4x$. The global minimum of $f(x)$ on $[0, 3]$ must be attained in the subinterval $[7\pi/8, 3]$, i.e.,

$$2.75 \le x^* \le 3$$

because that is the region in which the negative values of $\sin 4x$ are multiplied by the largest positive values of x.   Making the evaluations

$$f(7\pi/8) = \frac{7\pi}{8}(-1) = -2.75$$

$$f(3) = 3 \sin 12 = -1.61$$

we conclude that the global minimum is attained at the second local minimum of $f(x)$, the one *near* $x = 7\pi/8$, and not at the endpoint $x = 3$.

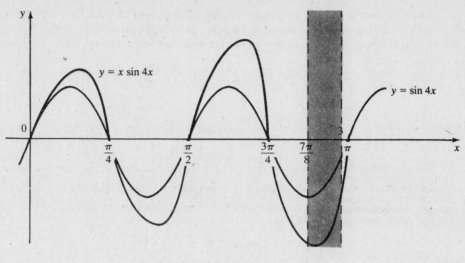

Fig. 10-5

10.6   Use the three-point interval search to approximate the location of the global minimum of $f(x) = x \sin 4x$ on $[0, 3]$ to within $\epsilon = 0.01$.

As a result of the graphical analysis done in Problem 10.5, we restrict attention to the subinterval $[7\pi/8, 3]$.   The global minimum occurs in this subinterval and the function is unimodal there.

First iteration.   Dividing $[7\pi/8, 3]$ into quarters, we take $x_1 = 2.8117$, $x_2 = 2.8744$, and $x_3 = 2.9372$ as the three interior points and calculate

$$f(x_1) = x_1 \sin 4x_1 = 2.8117 \sin 4(2.8117) = -2.7234$$

$$f(x_2) = x_2 \sin 4x_2 = 2.8744 \sin 4(2.8744) = -2.5197$$

$$f(x_3) = x_3 \sin 4x_3 = 2.9372 \sin 4(2.9372) = -2.1426$$

Here, x_1 is the interior point yielding the smallest value of $f(x)$; so we take the subinterval centered at x_1, namely $[7\pi/8, 2.8744]$, as the new interval of interest.

Second iteration.   Dividing $[7\pi/8, 2.8744]$ into quarters, we have $x_4 = 2.7803$, $x_1 = 2.8117$, and $x_5 = 2.8430$ as the three interior points of this new interval.   Thus

$$f(x_4) = x_4 \sin 4x_4 = 2.7803 \sin 4(2.7803) = -2.7584$$

$$f(x_1) = -2.7234 \quad \text{(as before)}$$

$$f(x_5) = x_5 \sin 4x_5 = 2.8430 \sin 4(2.8430) = -2.6439$$

Of these interior points, x_4 yields the smallest value of $f(x)$; so we take the subinterval centered at it, $[7\pi/8, 2.8117]$, as the new interval of interest.

Third iteration.   We divide $[7\pi/8, 2.8117]$ into quarters, with $x_6 = 2.7646$, $x_4 = 2.7803$, and $x_7 = 2.7960$ as the three interior points.   Then

$$f(x_6) = x_6 \sin 4x_6 = 2.7646 \sin 4(2.7646) = -2.7591$$

$$f(x_4) = -2.7584 \quad \text{(as before)}$$

$$f(x_7) = x_7 \sin 4x_7 = 2.7960 \sin 4(2.7960) = -2.7465$$

Here, x_6 is the interior point yielding the smallest value of the objective function; so the new interval of interest is the one centered at it, namely $[7\pi/8, 2.7803]$.

Fourth iteration. We divide $[7\pi/8, 2.7803]$ into quarters, with $x_8 = 2.7567$, $x_6 = 2.7646$, and $x_9 = 2.7724$ as the three new interior points. Now

$$f(x_8) = x_8 \sin 4x_8 = 2.7567 \sin 4(2.7567) = -2.7554$$
$$f(x_6) = -2.7591 \quad \text{(as before)}$$
$$f(x_9) = x_9 \sin 4x_9 = 2.7724 \sin 4(2.7724) = -2.7602$$

Since x_9 is the interior point with the smallest value of $f(x)$, we take the subinterval centered at x_9, namely $[2.7646, 2.7803]$, as the new interval of interest. The midpoint of this interval, however, is within the prescribed tolerance, $\epsilon = 0.01$, of all other points in the interval; we therefore accept it as the location of the minimum. That is,

$$x^* = x_9 = 2.7724 \qquad \text{with} \qquad z^* = f(x_9) = -2.7602$$

10.7 Use the three-point interval search to approximate the location of the maximum of $f(x) = x(5\pi - x)$ on $[0, 20]$ to within $\epsilon = 1$.

Since $f''(x) = -2 < 0$ everywhere, it follows from Theorem 10.4 that $f(x)$ is concave, hence unimodal, on $[0, 20]$. Therefore, the three-point interval search is guaranteed to converge to the global maximum.

First iteration. Dividing $[0, 20]$ into quarters, we have $x_1 = 5$, $x_2 = 10$, and $x_3 = 15$ as the three interior points. Therefore

$$f(x_1) = x_1(5\pi - x_1) = 5(5\pi - 5) = 53.54$$
$$f(x_2) = x_2(5\pi - x_2) = 10(5\pi - 10) = 57.08$$
$$f(x_3) = x_3(5\pi - x_3) = 15(5\pi - 15) = 10.62$$

Since x_2 is the interior point generating the greatest value of the objective function, we take the interval $[5, 15]$, centered at x_2, as the new interval of interest.

Second iteration. We divide $[5, 15]$ into quarters, with $x_4 = 7.5$, $x_2 = 10$, and $x_5 = 12.5$ as the three interior points. So

$$f(x_4) = x_4(5\pi - x_4) = (7.5)(5\pi - 7.5) = 61.56$$
$$f(x_2) = 57.08 \quad \text{(as before)}$$
$$f(x_5) = x_5(5\pi - x_5) = (12.5)(5\pi - 12.5) = 40.10$$

As x_4 is the interior point yielding the largest value of $f(x)$, we take the interval $[5, 10]$, centered at x_4, as the new interval of interest.

Third iteration. We divide $[5, 10]$ into quarters, with $x_6 = 6.25$, $x_4 = 7.5$, and $x_7 = 8.75$ as the new interior points. So

$$f(x_6) = (6.25)(5\pi - 6.25) = 59.11$$
$$f(x_4) = 61.56 \quad \text{(as before)}$$
$$f(x_7) = (8.75)(5\pi - 8.75) = 60.88$$

As x_4 yields the largest value of $f(x)$, we take the interval $[6.25, 8.75]$, centered at x_4, as the new interval of interest.

Fourth iteration. Dividing $[6.25, 8.75]$ into quarters, we generate $x_8 = 6.875$, $x_4 = 7.5$, and $x_9 = 8.125$ as the new interior points. Thus

$$f(x_8) = (6.875)(5\pi - 6.875) = 60.73$$
$$f(x_4) = 61.56 \quad \text{(as before)}$$
$$f(x_9) = (8.125)(5\pi - 8.125) = 61.61$$

Now x_9 is the interior point yielding the largest value of the objective function, so we take the subinterval centered at x_9, namely $[7.5, 8.75]$, as the new interval for consideration. The midpoint of this interval, however, is within the prescribed tolerance, $\epsilon = 1$, of all other points in the interval; hence we take

$$x^* = x_9 = 8.125 \qquad \text{with} \qquad z^* = f(x_9) = 61.61$$

10.8   Redo Problem 10.7 using the Fibonacci search.

Initial points.   The first Fibonacci number such that $F_N(1) \geq 20 - 0$ is $F_7 = 21$.   We set $N = 7$,

$$\epsilon' = \frac{b-a}{F_N} = \frac{20-0}{21} = 0.9524$$

and then position the first two points in the search

$$F_6\epsilon' = 13(0.9524) = 12.38 \text{ units}$$

in from each endpoint.   Consequently,

$$x_1 = 0 + 12.38 = 12.38 \qquad x_2 = 20 - 12.38 = 7.62$$

$$f(x_1) = (12.38)(5\pi - 12.38) = 41.20$$

$$f(x_2) = (7.62)(5\pi - 7.62) = 61.63$$

which are plotted in Fig. 10-6(a).   Using the unimodal property, we conclude that the maximum must occur to the left of 12.38, and we reduce the interval of interest to $[0, 12.38]$.

First iteration.   The next-lower Fibonacci number (F_6 was the last one used) is $F_5 = 8$; so the next point in the search is positioned

$$F_5\epsilon' = 8(0.9524) = 7.619 \text{ units}$$

in from the newest endpoint, 12.38.   Thus

$$x_3 = 12.38 - 7.619 = 4.761$$

$$f(x_3) = (4.761)(5\pi - 4.761) = 52.12$$

Adding this point to the retained portion of Fig. 10-6(a), we generate Fig. 10-6(b), from which we conclude that the maximum must occur in the new interval of interest $[4.761, 12.38]$.

Second iteration.   The next-lower Fibonacci number now is $F_4 = 5$.   Thus

$$x_4 = 4.761 + F_4\epsilon' = 4.761 + 5(0.9524) = 9.523$$

$$f(x_4) = (9.523)(5\pi - 9.523) = 58.90$$

Adding this point to the retained portion of Fig. 10-6(b), we obtain Fig. 10-6(c), from which we conclude that the new interval of interest is $[4.761, 9.523]$.

Third iteration.   The next-lower Fibonacci number now is $F_3 = 3$.   Hence

$$x_5 = 9.523 - 3(0.9524) = 6.666$$

$$f(x_5) = (6.666)(5\pi - 6.666) = 60.27$$

Adding this point to the retained portion of Fig. 10-6(c), we obtain Fig. 10-6(d), and it follows from the unimodal property that the new interval of interest is $[6.666, 9.523]$.

Fourth iteration.   The next-lower Fibonacci number now is $F_2 = 2$.   Hence

$$x_6 = 6.666 + 2(0.9524) = 8.571$$

$$f(x_6) = (8.571)(5\pi - 8.571) = 61.17$$

Adding this point to the retained portion of Fig. 10-6(d), we obtain Fig. 10-6(e), from which we conclude that $[6.666, 8.571]$ is the new interval of interest.   The midpoint of this interval, however, is within $\epsilon = 1$ (in fact, within $\epsilon' = 0.9524$) of every other point of the interval.   (Theoretically, the midpoint should coincide with x_2; the small apparent discrepancy arises from roundoff.)   We therefore accept x_2 as the location of the maximum, i.e.,

$$x^* = x_2 = 7.62 \qquad \text{with} \qquad z^* = f(x_2) = 61.63$$

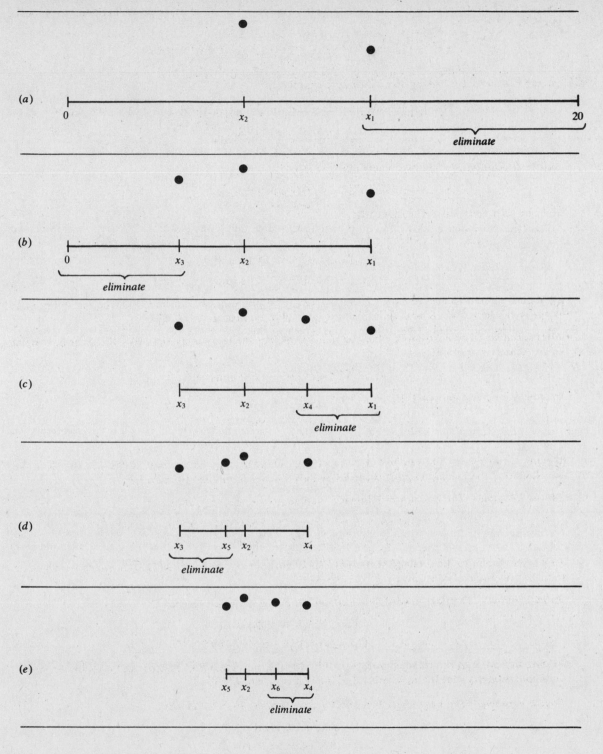

Fig. 10-6

10.9 Redo Problem 10.7 using the golden-mean search.

    Initial points. The length of the initial interval is $L_1 = 20$, so the first two points in the search are positioned

$$(0.6180)(20) = 12.36 \text{ units}$$

in from each endpoint. Thus

$$x_1 = 0 + 12.36 = 12.36 \qquad x_2 = 20 - 12.36 = 7.64$$
$$f(x_1) = (12.36)(5\pi - 12.36) = 41.38$$
$$f(x_2) = (7.64)(5\pi - 7.64) = 61.64$$

The points $(x_1, f(x_1))$ and $(x_2, f(x_2))$ are very close to the points shown in Fig. 10-6(a). It follows from the unimodal property that the maximum must occur to the left of 12.36; hence we retain [0, 12.36] as the new interval of interest.

First iteration. The new interval has length $L_2 = 12.36$, so the next point in the search is positioned $0.6180 L_2$ units in from the newest endpoint. Therefore,

$$x_3 = 12.36 - (0.6180)(12.36) = 4.722$$
$$f(x_3) = (4.722)(5\pi - 4.722) = 51.88$$

When this new point is added, Fig. 10-6(b) applies, and we determine [4.722, 12.36] as the new interval of interest.

Second iteration. $L_3 = 12.36 - 4.722 = 7.638$; thus

$$x_4 = 4.722 + (0.6180)(7.638) = 9.442$$
$$f(x_4) = (9.442)(5\pi - 9.442) = 59.16$$

Now the pattern is that of Fig. 10-6(c), from which we conclude that [4.722, 9.442] is the new interval of interest.

Third iteration. $L_4 = 9.442 - 4.722 = 4.720$; thus

$$x_5 = 9.442 - (0.6180)(4.720) = 6.525$$
$$f(x_5) = (6.525)(5\pi - 6.525) = 59.92$$

Now the pattern is that of Fig. 10-6(d), from which we conclude that [6.525, 9.442] is the new interval of interest.

Fourth iteration. $L_5 = 9.442 - 6.525 = 2.917$; hence

$$x_6 = 6.525 + (0.6180)(2.917) = 8.328$$
$$f(x_6) = (8.328)(5\pi - 8.328) = 61.46$$

With this new point, we reach the pattern of Fig. 10-6(e), and find [6.525, 8.328] as the new interval of interest. Notice that this new interval is of length less than $2\epsilon = 2$, but that the included sample point, x_2, is not within ϵ of *all* other points in the interval. Therefore, another iteration is required.

Fifth iteration. $L_6 = 8.328 - 6.525 = 1.803$; therefore

$$x_7 = 8.328 - (0.6180)(1.803) = 7.214$$
$$f(x_7) = (7.214)(5\pi - 7.214) = 61.28$$

This new point determines $[x_7, x_6] = [7.214, 8.328]$ as the new interval of interest. Now, however, the interior point $x_2 = 7.64$ is within $\epsilon = 1$ of all other points in the interval; so we take it as the location of the maximum. That is,

$$x^* = x_2 = 7.64 \qquad \text{with} \qquad z^* = f(x_2) = 61.64$$

10.10 Compare the efficiencies of the three search methods in locating the maximum of $x(5\pi - x)$ on [0, 20].

Each method succeeded in approximating the location of the maximum, $x^* = 5\pi/2 = 7.854$, to within $\epsilon = 1$, as required. The Fibonacci search was the most efficient (see Problem 10.8), achieving the desired accuracy with six functional evaluations. The three-point interval search (see Problem 10.7) and the golden-mean search (see Problem 10.9) required nine and seven functional evaluations, respectively.

10.11 Redo Problem 10.6 without first constricting the interval $[0, 3]$ to a subinterval on which the function is unimodal. Discuss the result.

Applying the three-point interval search to $f(x) = x \sin 4x$ on $[0, 3]$ directly, we generate sequentially the entries in Table 10-1. It follows that

$$x^* \approx 1.231 \qquad \text{with} \qquad z^* \approx f(x^*) = -1.20354$$

Table 10-1

Current Interval	Interior Points			$f(x) = x \sin 4x$		
	a	b	c	$f(a)$	$f(b)$	$f(c)$
$[0, 3]$	0.75	1.5	2.25	0.1058	−0.4191	0.9273
$[0.75, 2.25]$	1.125	1.5	1.875	−1.100	−0.4191	1.759
$[0.75, 1.5]$	0.9375	1.125	1.313	−0.5358	−1.100	−1.126
$[1.125, 1.5]$	1.219	1.313	1.406	−1.203	−1.126	−0.8611
$[1.125, 1.313]$	1.172	1.219	1.266	−1.172	−1.203	−1.189
$[1.172, 1.266]$	1.196	1.219	1.243	−1.193	−1.203	−1.201
$[1.196, 1.243]$	1.208	1.219	1.231	−1.199	−1.20272	−1.20354
$[1.219, 1.243]$	1.225	1.231	1.237	−1.20350	−1.20354	−1.2028
$[1.225, 1.237]$						

It is apparent from Fig. 10-5 that the search procedure has converged to the local minimum near $3\pi/8$, and not to the global minimum on $[0, 3]$ that was found in Problem 10.6. A similar result would have occurred had we applied the Fibonacci search or golden-mean search to the entire interval $[0, 3]$.

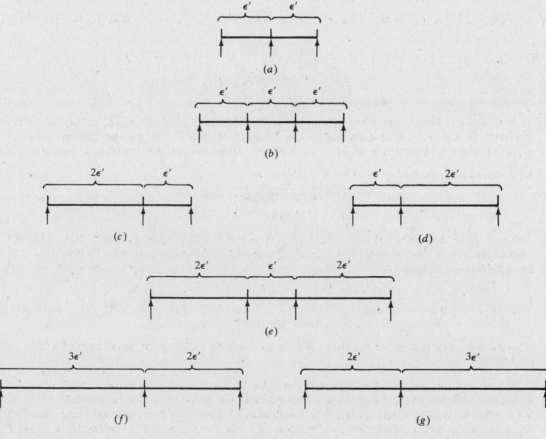

Fig. 10-7

10.12 Derive the Fibonacci search algorithm.

If the last interval under consideration, $\mathscr{I}_{N-1}$, is to be as large as possible yet contain an approximation to a local optimum good to within ϵ', then the search points used to generate this interval must be positioned as shown by the arrows in Fig. 10-7(a). The midpoint of this interval is the final approximation. Now, $\mathscr{I}_{N-1}$ is itself obtained from a larger interval, $\mathscr{I}_{N-2}$, by elimination of a portion of the larger interval, based on the unimodal property. To imply Fig. 10-7(a) *for an arbitrary unimodal function*, $\mathscr{I}_{N-2}$ must have the symmetrical form exhibited in Fig. 10-7(b), where again the arrows indicate the locations of search points or endpoints of the original interval. Either the left-hand one-third or the right-hand one-third of Fig. 10-7(b) is eliminated to yield Fig. 10-7(a). Figure 10-7(b), however, is itself the result of adding one search point. Before this point was added, $\mathscr{I}_{N-2}$ must have had the form of Fig. 10-7(c) or that of Fig. 10-7(d).

Either possibility for $\mathscr{I}_{N-2}$ is obtained from a larger interval, $\mathscr{I}_{N-3}$, by elimination of a portion of this larger interval, based on the unimodal property. To imply Fig. 10-7(c) or 10-7(d), $\mathscr{I}_{N-3}$ had to have the form exhibited in Fig. 10-7(e). Either the left-hand subinterval or the right-hand subinterval of Fig. 10-7(e) is eliminated to generate $\mathscr{I}_{N-2}$. Figure 10-7(e), however, is the result of adding one search point. Before this point was added, $\mathscr{I}_{N-3}$ must have had the form of Fig. 10-7(f) or that of Fig. 10-7(g).

Continuing in this manner and denoting the length of $\mathscr{I}_j$ by L_j, we find that $L_{N-1} = 2\epsilon'$, $L_{N-2} = 3\epsilon'$, $L_{N-3} = 5\epsilon'$, $L_{N-4} = 8\epsilon'$, $L_{N-5} = 13\epsilon'$, and so on. Since the coefficients are part of the Fibonacci sequence, we have

$$L_{N-1} = F_2\epsilon' \qquad L_{N-2} = F_3\epsilon' \qquad \cdots \qquad L_2 = F_{N-1}\epsilon' \qquad L_1 = F_N\epsilon' \qquad (1)$$

But N is chosen such that $F_N\epsilon' = b - a$. Therefore, L_1 is the initial interval, and we have generated (in reverse order) the steps of the Fibonacci search.

10.13 Derive the golden-mean search algorithm.

From (1) of Problem 10.12, $L_1 = F_N\epsilon'$ and $L_2 = F_{N-1}\epsilon'$. Then, if N is large, Problem 10.26 gives

$$\frac{L_2}{L_1} = \frac{F_{N-1}}{F_N} \approx \lim_{N \to \infty} \frac{F_{N-1}}{F_N} = 0.6180 \cdots$$

so that $L_2 \approx 0.6180 L_1$. Identical reasoning shows that, provided N is large enough, the same approximation is valid for any two successive intervals in the Fibonacci search, i.e., $L_i \approx 0.6180 L_{i-1}$, which is the defining equation for the golden-mean search.

Supplementary Problems

10.14 Find all local and global optima for $f(x) = x^3 - 6x^2 + 9x + 6$ on (a) $[0, 3]$, (b) $[1, 4]$, (c) $[-1, 5]$.

10.15 Find all local and global optima for $f(x) = x^4 - 4x^3 + 6x^2 - 4x + 1$ on (a) $[0, 3]$, (b) $[0, 2]$, (c) $[0, \infty)$.

10.16 Find all local and global optima for $f(x) = x + x^{-1}$ on (a) $(0, \infty)$, (b) $(-\infty, 0)$, (c) $[5, 10]$. (*Hint*: In parts (a) and (b), $x = 0$ is handled like an infinite endpoint.)

10.17 Show that $f(x) = x^3 - 6x^2 + 9x + 6$ is strictly concave on $(-\infty, 2)$ and strictly convex on $(2, \infty)$.

10.18 Determine intervals on which $f(x) = x + 4x^{-1}$ is concave or convex.

10.19 Use the three-point interval search to approximate to within $\epsilon = 0.1$ the location of the global minimum on $(0, 2]$ of the function of Problem 10.18. (*Hint*: Proceed as if the interval were $[0, 2]$.)

10.20 Approximate the location of the global maximum on $[0, \pi]$ of $f(x) = x^2 \sin x$, using a three-point search of the unrestricted interval with five functional evaluations (i.e., five search points). How good is this approximation?

10.21 Redo Problem 10.19 with a Fibonacci search.

10.22 Redo Problem 10.20 with a Fibonacci search. (*Hint*: A total of five search points requires that the first two be placed $F_5 \epsilon'$ in from the endpoints of the original interval. Thus $N = 6$ for determining ϵ'.)

10.23 Redo Problem 10.19 with a golden-mean search.

10.24 Redo Problem 10.20 with a golden-mean search.

10.25 Show that the nth term of the Fibonacci sequence is

$$F_n = \frac{1}{\sqrt{5}} \left[\left(\frac{1 + \sqrt{5}}{2} \right)^{n+1} - \left(\frac{1 - \sqrt{5}}{2} \right)^{n+1} \right]$$

(*Hint*: Verify that the given expression satisfies the appropriate recursion relation and initial conditions.)

10.26 From Problem 10.25, derive

$$\lim_{N \to \infty} \frac{F_{N-1}}{F_N} = \left(\frac{1 + \sqrt{5}}{2} \right)^{-1} = 0.6180 \cdots$$

Chapter 11

Nonlinear Programming: Multivariable Optimization without Constraints

The present chapter will very largely consist in a generalization of the results of Chapter 10 to the case of more than one variable. However, only the analog to (10.1),

$$\text{optimize:} \quad z = f(\mathbf{X}) \quad \text{where} \quad \mathbf{X} \equiv [x_1, x_2, \dots, x_n]^T \tag{11.1}$$

will be treated, and not the analog to (10.2). Moreover, we shall always suppose the optimization in (11.1) to be a maximization; all results will apply to a minimization program if $f(\mathbf{X})$ is replaced by $-f(\mathbf{X})$. See Problems 11.2 and 11.3.

LOCAL AND GLOBAL MAXIMA

Definition: An ϵ-neighborhood ($\epsilon > 0$) around $\hat{\mathbf{X}}$ is the set of all vectors $\mathbf{X}$ such that

$$(\mathbf{X} - \hat{\mathbf{X}})^T(\mathbf{X} - \hat{\mathbf{X}}) \equiv (x_1 - \hat{x}_1)^2 + (x_2 - \hat{x}_2)^2 + \cdots + (x_n - \hat{x}_n)^2 \le \epsilon^2$$

In geometrical terms, an ϵ-neighborhood around $\hat{\mathbf{X}}$ is the interior and boundary of an n-dimensional sphere of radius ϵ centered at $\hat{\mathbf{X}}$.

An objective function $f(\mathbf{X})$ has a *local maximum* at $\hat{\mathbf{X}}$ if there exists an ϵ-neighborhood around $\hat{\mathbf{X}}$ such that $f(\mathbf{X}) \le f(\hat{\mathbf{X}})$ for all $\mathbf{X}$ in this ϵ-neighborhood at which the function is defined. If the condition is met for every positive ϵ (no matter how large), then $f(\mathbf{X})$ has a *global maximum* at $\hat{\mathbf{X}}$.

GRADIENT VECTOR AND HESSIAN MATRIX

The *gradient vector* ∇f associated with a function $f(x_1, x_2, \dots, x_n)$ having first partial derivatives is defined by

$$\nabla f \equiv \left[\frac{\partial f}{\partial x_1}, \frac{\partial f}{\partial x_2}, \dots, \frac{\partial f}{\partial x_n} \right]^T$$

The notation $\nabla f|_{\hat{\mathbf{x}}}$ signifies the value of the gradient at $\hat{\mathbf{X}}$. For small displacements from $\hat{\mathbf{X}}$ in various directions, the direction of maximum increase in $f(\mathbf{X})$ is the direction of the vector $\nabla f|_{\hat{\mathbf{x}}}$. (See Problem 11.7.)

Example 11.1 For $f(x_1, x_2, x_3) = 3x_1^2 x_2 - x_2^2 x_3^3$, with $\hat{\mathbf{X}} = [1, 2, 3]^T$,

$$\nabla f = \begin{bmatrix} 6x_1 x_2 \\ 3x_1^2 - 2x_2 x_3^3 \\ -3x_2^2 x_3^2 \end{bmatrix} \quad \text{whence} \quad \nabla f|_{\hat{\mathbf{x}}} = \begin{bmatrix} 6(1)(2) \\ 3(1)^2 - 2(2)(3)^3 \\ -3(2)^2(3)^2 \end{bmatrix} = \begin{bmatrix} 12 \\ -105 \\ -108 \end{bmatrix}$$

Therefore, at $[1, 2, 3]^T$, the function increases most rapidly in the direction of $[12, -105, -108]^T$.

The *Hessian matrix* associated with a function $f(x_1, x_2, \dots, x_n)$ that has second partial derivatives is

$$\mathbf{H}_f \equiv \left[\frac{\partial^2 f}{\partial x_i \, \partial x_j} \right] \quad (i, j = 1, 2, \dots, n)$$

The notation $\mathbf{H}_f|_{\hat{\mathbf{x}}}$ signifies the value of the Hessian matrix at $\hat{\mathbf{X}}$. In preparation for Theorems 11.4 and 11.5 below, we shall need the following:

Definition: An $n \times n$ symmetric matrix $\mathbf{A}$ (one such that $\mathbf{A} = \mathbf{A}^T$) is *negative definite* (*negative semi-definite*) if $\mathbf{X}^T \mathbf{A} \mathbf{X}$ is negative (nonpositive) for every n-dimensional vector $\mathbf{X} \neq \mathbf{0}$.

Theorem 11.1: Let $\mathbf{A} \equiv [a_{ij}]$ be an $n \times n$ symmetric matrix, and define the determinants

$$A_1 \equiv |a_{11}| \qquad A_2 \equiv - \begin{vmatrix} a_{11} & a_{12} \\ a_{21} & a_{22} \end{vmatrix} \qquad A_3 \equiv + \begin{vmatrix} a_{11} & a_{12} & a_{13} \\ a_{21} & a_{22} & a_{23} \\ a_{31} & a_{32} & a_{33} \end{vmatrix} \qquad \cdots \qquad A_n \equiv (-1)^{n-1} \det \mathbf{A}$$

Then $\mathbf{A}$ is negative definite if and only if $A_1, A_2, \ldots, A_n$ are all negative; $\mathbf{A}$ is negative semi-definite if and only if $A_1, A_2, \ldots, A_r$ $(r < n)$ are all negative and the remaining A's are all zero.

Example 11.2 For the function of Example 11.1,

$$\mathbf{H}_f = \begin{bmatrix} 6x_2 & 6x_1 & 0 \\ 6x_1 & -2x_3^3 & -6x_2 x_3^2 \\ 0 & -6x_2 x_3^2 & -6x_2^2 x_3 \end{bmatrix} \qquad \text{whence} \qquad \mathbf{H}_f|_{\hat{\mathbf{x}}} = \begin{bmatrix} 12 & 6 & 0 \\ 6 & -54 & -108 \\ 0 & -108 & -72 \end{bmatrix}$$

For $\mathbf{H}_f|_{\hat{\mathbf{x}}}$, $A_1 = 12 > 0$, so that $\mathbf{H}_f$ is not negative definite, or even negative semi-definite, at $\hat{\mathbf{X}}$.

RESULTS FROM CALCULUS

Theorem 11.2: If $f(\mathbf{X})$ is continuous on a closed and bounded region, then $f(\mathbf{X})$ has a global maximum (and also a global minimum) on that region.

Theorem 11.3: If $f(\mathbf{X})$ has a local maximum (or a local minimum) at $\mathbf{X}^*$ and if ∇f exists on some ϵ-neighborhood around $\mathbf{X}^*$, then $\nabla f|_{\mathbf{X}^*} = \mathbf{0}$.

Theorem 11.4: If $f(\mathbf{X})$ has second partial derivatives on an ϵ-neighborhood around $\mathbf{X}^*$, and if $\nabla f|_{\mathbf{X}^*} = \mathbf{0}$ and $\mathbf{H}_f|_{\mathbf{X}^*}$ is negative definite, then $f(\mathbf{X})$ has a local maximum at $\mathbf{X}^*$.

It follows from Theorems 11.2 and 11.3 that a continuous $f(\mathbf{X})$ assumes its global maximum among those points at which ∇f does not exist or among those points at which $\nabla f = \mathbf{0}$ (*stationary points*)—unless the function assumes even larger values as $\mathbf{X}^T \mathbf{X} \to \infty$. In the latter case, no global maximum exists. (See Problem 11.1.)

Analytical solutions based on calculus are even harder to obtain for multivariable programs than for single-variable programs, and so, once again, numerical methods are used to approximate (local) maxima to within prescribed tolerances.

THE METHOD OF STEEPEST ASCENT

Choose an initial vector $\mathbf{X}_0$, making use of any prior information about where the desired global maximum might be found. Then determine vectors $\mathbf{X}_1, \mathbf{X}_2, \mathbf{X}_3, \ldots$ by the iterative relation

$$\mathbf{X}_{k+1} = \mathbf{X}_k + \lambda_k^* \nabla f|_{\mathbf{X}_k} \tag{11.2}$$

Here λ_k^* is a positive scalar which maximizes $f(\mathbf{X}_k + \lambda \nabla f|_{\mathbf{X}_k})$; this single-variable program is solved by the methods of Chapter 10. It is best if λ_k^* represents a global maximum; however, a local maximum will do. The iterative process terminates if and when the difference between the values of the objective function at two successive $\mathbf{X}$-vectors is smaller than a prescribed tolerance. The last-computed $\mathbf{X}$-vector becomes the final approximation to $\mathbf{X}^*$. (See Problems 11.4 and 11.5.)

THE NEWTON-RAPHSON METHOD

Choose an initial vector $\mathbf{X}_0$, as in the method of steepest ascent.   Vectors $\mathbf{X}_1, \mathbf{X}_2, \mathbf{X}_3, \ldots$ then are determined iteratively by

$$\mathbf{X}_{k+1} = \mathbf{X}_k - (\mathbf{H}_f|_{\mathbf{X}_k})^{-1} \nabla f|_{\mathbf{X}_k} \qquad (11.3)$$

The stopping rule is the same as for the method of steepest ascent.   (See Problems 11.8 and 11.9.)

The Newton-Raphson method will converge to a local maximum if $\mathbf{H}_f$ is negative definite on some ϵ-neighborhood around the maximum and if $\mathbf{X}_0$ lies in that ϵ-neighborhood.

Remark 1:   If $\mathbf{H}_f$ is negative definite, $\mathbf{H}_f^{-1}$ exists and is negative definite.

If $\mathbf{X}_0$ is not chosen correctly, the method may converge to a local *minimum* (see Problem 11.10) or it may not converge at all (see Problem 11.9).   In either case, the iterative process is terminated and then begun anew with a better initial approximation.

THE FLETCHER-POWELL METHOD

This method, an eight-step algorithm, is begun by choosing an initial vector $\hat{\mathbf{X}}$ and prescribing a tolerance ϵ, and by setting an $n \times n$ matrix $\mathbf{G}$ equal to the identity matrix.   Both $\hat{\mathbf{X}}$ and $\mathbf{G}$ are continually updated until successive values of the objective function differ by less than ϵ, whereupon the last value of $\hat{\mathbf{X}}$ is taken as $\mathbf{X}^*$.

STEP 1   Evaluate $\alpha = f(\hat{\mathbf{X}})$ and $\mathbf{B} = \nabla f|_{\hat{\mathbf{X}}}$.

STEP 2   Determine λ^* such that $f(\hat{\mathbf{X}} + \lambda \mathbf{GB})$ is maximized when $\lambda = \lambda^*$.   Set $\mathbf{D} = \lambda^* \mathbf{GB}$.

STEP 3   Designate $\hat{\mathbf{X}} + \mathbf{D}$ as the updated value of $\hat{\mathbf{X}}$.

STEP 4   Calculate $\beta = f(\hat{\mathbf{X}})$ for the updated value of $\hat{\mathbf{X}}$.   If $\beta - \alpha < \epsilon$, go to Step 5; if not, go to Step 6.

STEP 5   Set $\mathbf{X}^* = \hat{\mathbf{X}}$, $f(\mathbf{X}^*) = \beta$, and stop.

STEP 6   Evaluate $\mathbf{C} = \nabla f|_{\hat{\mathbf{X}}}$ for the updated vector $\hat{\mathbf{X}}$, and set $\mathbf{Y} = \mathbf{B} - \mathbf{C}$.

STEP 7   Calculate the $n \times n$ matrices

$$\mathbf{L} = \left(\frac{1}{\mathbf{D}^T \mathbf{Y}}\right) \mathbf{D} \mathbf{D}^T \qquad \text{and} \qquad \mathbf{M} = \left(\frac{-1}{\mathbf{Y}^T \mathbf{G} \mathbf{Y}}\right) \mathbf{G} \mathbf{Y} \mathbf{Y}^T \mathbf{G}$$

STEP 8   Designate $\mathbf{G} + \mathbf{L} + \mathbf{M}$ as the updated value of $\mathbf{G}$.   Set α equal to the current value of β, $\mathbf{B}$ equal to the current value of $\mathbf{C}$, and return to Step 2.

HOOKE-JEEVES' PATTERN SEARCH

This method is a direct-search algorithm that utilizes *exploratory moves*, which determine an appropriate direction, and *pattern moves*, which accelerate the search.   The method is begun by choosing an initial vector, $\mathbf{B} \equiv [b_1, b_2, \ldots, b_n]^T$, and a step size, h.

STEP 1   Exploratory moves around $\mathbf{B}$ are made by perturbing the components of $\mathbf{B}$, in sequence, by $\pm h$ units.   If either perturbation improves (i.e., increases) the value of the objective function beyond the current value, the initial value being $f(\mathbf{B})$, the perturbed value of that component is retained; otherwise the original value of the component is kept.   After each component has been tested in turn, the resulting vector is denoted by $\mathbf{C}$.   If $\mathbf{C} = \mathbf{B}$, go to Step 2; otherwise go to Step 3.

STEP 2 $\mathbf{B}$ is the location of the maximum to within a tolerance of h.   Either h is reduced and Step 1 repeated, or the search is terminated with $\mathbf{X}^* = \mathbf{B}$.

STEP 3   Make a pattern move to a temporary vector $\mathbf{T} = 2\mathbf{C} - \mathbf{B}$.   (**T** is reached by moving from **B** to **C** and continuing for an equal distance in the same direction.)

STEP 4   Make exploratory moves around **T** similar to the ones around **B** described in Step 1. Call the resulting vector **S**.   If $\mathbf{S} = \mathbf{T}$, go to Step 5; otherwise go to Step 6.

STEP 5   Set $\mathbf{B} = \mathbf{C}$ and return to Step 1.

STEP 6   Set $\mathbf{B} = \mathbf{C}$, $\mathbf{C} = \mathbf{S}$, and return to Step 3.

A MODIFIED PATTERN SEARCH

Hooke-Jeeves' pattern search terminates when no perturbation of any one component of **B** leads to an improvement in the objective function.   Occasionally this termination is premature, in that perturbations of two or more of the components simultaneously may lead to an improvement in the objective function.   Simultaneous perturbations can be included in the method by modifying Step 2 as follows:

STEP 2'   Conduct an exhaustive search over the surface of the hypercube centered at **B** by considering all possible perturbations of the components of **B** by kh units, where $k = -1, 0, 1$.   For a vector of n components, there are $3^n - 1$ perturbations to consider.   As soon as an improvement is realized, terminate the exhaustive search, set the improved vector equal to **B**, and return to Step 1.   If no improvement is realized, **B** is the location of the maximum to within a tolerance of h.   Either h is reduced and Step 1 repeated, or the search is terminated with $\mathbf{X}^* = \mathbf{B}$.

CHOICE OF AN INITIAL APPROXIMATION

Each numerical method starts with a first approximation to the desired global maximum.   At times, such an approximation is apparent from physical or geometrical aspects of the problem.   (See Problem 11.12.)   In other cases, a random number generator is used to provide different values for **X**.   Then $f(\mathbf{X})$ is calculated for each randomly chosen **X**, and that **X** which yields the best value of the objective function is taken as the initial approximation.   Even this random sampling procedure implies an initial guess of the location of the maximum, in that the random numbers must be normalized so as to lie in some fixed interval.   (See Problem 11.4.)

CONCAVE FUNCTIONS

There is no guarantee that a numerical method will uncover a global maximum.   It may converge to merely a local maximum or, worse yet, may not converge at all.   Exceptions include programs having concave objective functions.

A function $f(\mathbf{X})$ is *convex* on a convex region $\mathcal{R}$ (see Chapter 3) if for any two vectors $\mathbf{X}_1$ and $\mathbf{X}_2$ in $\mathcal{R}$ and for all $0 \le \alpha \le 1$,

$$f(\alpha \mathbf{X}_1 + (1 - \alpha)\mathbf{X}_2) \le \alpha f(\mathbf{X}_1) + (1 - \alpha)f(\mathbf{X}_2) \qquad (11.4)$$

[compare (*10.3*)].   A function is *concave* on $\mathcal{R}$ if and only if its negative is convex on $\mathcal{R}$.   The convex region $\mathcal{R}$ may be finite or infinite.

Theorem 11.5:   If $f(\mathbf{X})$ has second partial derivatives on $\mathcal{R}$, then $f(\mathbf{X})$ is concave on $\mathcal{R}$ if and only if its Hessian matrix $\mathbf{H}_f$ is negative semi-definite for all **X** in $\mathcal{R}$.

Theorem 11.6:   If $f(\mathbf{X})$ is concave on $\mathcal{R}$, then any local maximum on $\mathcal{R}$ is a global maximum on $\mathcal{R}$.

These two theorems imply that, if $\mathbf{H}_f$ is negative semi-definite everywhere, then any local maximum yields a solution to program (*11.1*).   If $\mathbf{H}_f$ is negative definite everywhere, then $f(\mathbf{X})$ is *strictly concave* (everywhere), and the solution to program (*11.1*) is unique.

Solved Problems

11.1   Maximize: $z = x_1(x_2 - 1) + x_3(x_3^2 - 3)$.

Here $f(x_1, x_2, x_3) = x_1(x_2 - 1) + x_3(x_3^2 - 3)$. The gradient vector, $\nabla f = [x_2 - 1, x_1, 3x_3^2 - 3]^T$, exists everywhere and is zero only at

$$\mathbf{X}_1 = [0, 1, 1]^T \qquad \text{and} \qquad \mathbf{X}_2 = [0, 1, -1]^T$$

We have $f(\mathbf{X}_1) = -2$ and $f(\mathbf{X}_2) = 2$. But $f(x_1, x_2, x_3)$ becomes arbitrarily large as x_3 (for instance) does so; hence no global maximum exists. The vector $\mathbf{X}_2$ is only the site of a local maximum.

11.2   Minimize: $z = (x_1 - \sqrt{5})^2 + (x_2 - \pi)^2 + 10$.

Multiplying this objective function by -1, we obtain the equivalent maximization program

$$\text{maximize:} \quad z = -(x_1 - \sqrt{5})^2 - (x_2 - \pi)^2 - 10$$

for which $\nabla z = -2[x_1 - \sqrt{5}, x_2 - \pi]^T$. Thus there is a single stationary point, $x_1 = \sqrt{5}$, $x_2 = \pi$, at which $z = -10$. Now, as $x_1^2 + x_2^2 \to \infty$, z becomes arbitrarily small; consequently, $z^* = -10$ is the global maximum, and $z^* = +10$ is the global minimum for the original minimization program. The minimum is, of course, also assumed at $x_1^* = \sqrt{5} \approx 2.2361$, $x_2^* = \pi \approx 3.1416$.

11.3   Minimize: $z = \sin x_1 x_2 - \cos(x_1 - x_2)$.

Multiplying the objective function by -1, we obtain the equivalent maximization program

$$\text{maximize:} \quad z = -\sin x_1 x_2 + \cos(x_1 - x_2)$$

Here $f(x_1, x_2) = -\sin x_1 x_2 + \cos(x_1 - x_2)$ and

$$\nabla f = \begin{bmatrix} -x_2 \cos x_1 x_2 - \sin(x_1 - x_2) \\ -x_1 \cos x_1 x_2 + \sin(x_1 - x_2) \end{bmatrix}$$

which exists everywhere. Stationary points therefore satisfy

$$\begin{aligned} -x_2 \cos x_1 x_2 - \sin(x_1 - x_2) &= 0 \\ -x_1 \cos x_1 x_2 + \sin(x_1 - x_2) &= 0 \end{aligned} \qquad (1)$$

Although a *complete* solution to system (1) cannot be obtained algebraically, it is possible to find a partial solution that suffices for the present program. Observe first of all that, for all x_1 and x_2,

$$|f(x_1, x_2)| \le |\sin x_1 x_2| + |\cos(x_1 - x_2)| \le 1 + 1 = 2$$

Hence, if a stationary point can be found at which $f(x_1, x_2) = 2$, that point is necessarily the site of a global maximum. Now, it is clear that (1) will be satisfied if $\cos x_1 x_2$ and $\sin(x_1 - x_2)$ separately vanish, i.e., if

$$x_1 x_2 = \left(k + \frac{1}{2}\right)\pi \qquad \text{and} \qquad x_1 - x_2 = n\pi$$

where k and n are integers. Trying $k = 1$ and $n = 0$, we find that

$$f\left(\sqrt{\frac{3\pi}{2}}, \sqrt{\frac{3\pi}{2}}\right) = -\sin\frac{3\pi}{2} + \cos 0 = 2$$

and our search is over. The original minimization program then has the solution $z^* = -2$, attained at $x_1^* = x_2^* = \sqrt{3\pi/2}$ (and elsewhere).

11.4   Use the method of steepest ascent to

$$\text{minimize:} \quad z = (x_1 - \sqrt{5})^2 + (x_2 - \pi)^2 + 10$$

Going over to the equivalent program

$$\text{maximize:} \quad z = -(x_1 - \sqrt{5})^2 - (x_2 - \pi)^2 - 10 \qquad (1)$$

we require a starting approximate solution, which we obtain by a random sampling of the objective function over the region $-10 \le x_1, x_2 \le 10$. The sample points and corresponding z-values are shown in the table below. The maximum z-entry is -36.58, occurring at $\mathbf{X}_0 = [6.597, 5.891]^T$, which we take as the initial approximation to $\mathbf{X}^*$. The gradient of the objective function for program (1) is

$$\nabla f = \begin{bmatrix} -2(x_1 - \sqrt{5}) \\ -2(x_2 - \pi) \end{bmatrix}$$

x_1	-8.537	-0.9198	9.201	9.250	6.597	8.411	8.202	-9.173	-9.337	-5.794
x_2	-1.099	-8.005	-2.524	7.546	5.891	-9.945	-5.709	-6.914	8.163	-0.0210
z	-144.0	-144.2	-90.61	-78.59	-36.58	-219.4	-123.9	-241.3	-169.2	-84.48

First iteration.

$$\mathbf{X}_0 + \lambda \, \nabla f|_{\mathbf{x}_0} = \begin{bmatrix} 6.597 \\ 5.891 \end{bmatrix} + \lambda \begin{bmatrix} -2(6.597 - \sqrt{5}) \\ -2(5.891 - \pi) \end{bmatrix} = \begin{bmatrix} 6.597 - 8.722\lambda \\ 5.891 - 5.499\lambda \end{bmatrix}$$

$$f(\mathbf{X}_0 + \lambda \nabla f|_{\mathbf{x}_0}) = -(6.597 - 8.722\lambda - \sqrt{5})^2 - (5.891 - 5.499\lambda - \pi)^2 - 10$$
$$= -106.3\lambda^2 + 106.3\lambda - 36.58$$

Using the analytical methods described in Chapter 10, we determine that this function of λ assumes a (global) maximum at $\lambda_0^* = 0.5$. Thus,

$$\mathbf{X}_1 = \mathbf{X}_0 + \lambda_0^* \, \nabla f|_{\mathbf{x}_0} = \begin{bmatrix} 6.597 - 8.722(0.5) \\ 5.891 - 5.499(0.5) \end{bmatrix} = \begin{bmatrix} 2.236 \\ 3.142 \end{bmatrix}$$

with $f(\mathbf{X}_1) = -10.00$. Since the difference between $f(\mathbf{X}_0) = -36.58$ and $f(\mathbf{X}_1) = -10.00$ is significant, we continue iterating.

Second iteration.

$$\mathbf{X}_1 + \lambda \, \nabla f|_{\mathbf{x}_1} = \begin{bmatrix} 2.236 \\ 3.142 \end{bmatrix} + \lambda \begin{bmatrix} -2(2.236 - \sqrt{5}) \\ -2(3.142 - \pi) \end{bmatrix} = \begin{bmatrix} 2.236 + 0.0001\lambda \\ 3.142 - 0.0008\lambda \end{bmatrix}$$

$$f(\mathbf{X}_1 + \lambda \, \nabla f|_{\mathbf{x}_1}) = -(2.236 + 0.0001\lambda - \sqrt{5})^2 - (3.142 - 0.0008\lambda - \pi)^2 - 10$$
$$= -(6.500\lambda^2 - 6.382\lambda + 10^8)10^{-7}$$

Using the analytical methods described in Chapter 10, we find that this function of λ has a (global) maximum at $\lambda_1^* = 0.4909$. Thus,

$$\mathbf{X}_2 = \mathbf{X}_1 + \lambda_1^* \, \nabla f|_{\mathbf{x}_1} = \begin{bmatrix} 2.236 + 0.0001(0.4909) \\ 3.142 - 0.0008(0.4909) \end{bmatrix} = \begin{bmatrix} 2.236 \\ 3.142 \end{bmatrix}$$

Since $\mathbf{X}_1 = \mathbf{X}_2$ (to four significant figures), we accept $\mathbf{X}^* = [2.236, 3.142]^T$, with $z^* = -10.00$, as the solution to program (1). The solution to the original minimization program is then $\mathbf{X}^* = [2.236, 3.142]^T$, with $z^* = +10.00$. Compare this with the results obtained in Problem 11.2.

11.5   Use the method of steepest ascent to

$$\text{maximize:} \quad z = -\sin x_1 x_2 + \cos (x_1 - x_2)$$

to within a tolerance of 0.05.

Here

$$\nabla f = \begin{bmatrix} -x_2 \cos x_1 x_2 - \sin (x_1 - x_2) \\ -x_1 \cos x_1 x_2 + \sin (x_1 - x_2) \end{bmatrix}$$

From a random number search of the region $-1 \le x_1, x_2 \le 1$, we get $\mathbf{X}_0 = [-0.7548, 0.5303]^T$, with $f(\mathbf{X}_0) = 0.6715$.

First iteration.

$$\nabla f|_{\mathbf{x}_0} = \begin{bmatrix} -0.5303 \cos\left[(-0.7548)(0.5303)\right] - \sin\left(-0.7548 - 0.5303\right) \\ 0.7548 \cos\left[(-0.7548)(0.5303)\right] + \sin\left(-0.7548 - 0.5303\right) \end{bmatrix} = \begin{bmatrix} 0.4711 \\ -0.2643 \end{bmatrix}$$

$$\mathbf{X}_0 + \lambda \nabla f|_{\mathbf{x}_0} = \begin{bmatrix} -0.7548 \\ 0.5303 \end{bmatrix} + \lambda \begin{bmatrix} 0.4711 \\ -0.2643 \end{bmatrix} = \begin{bmatrix} -0.7548 + 0.4711\lambda \\ 0.5303 - 0.2643\lambda \end{bmatrix}$$

$$\begin{aligned} f(\mathbf{X}_0 + \lambda \nabla f|_{\mathbf{x}_0}) &= -\sin\left[(-0.7548 + 0.4711\lambda)(0.5303 - 0.2643\lambda)\right] \\ &\quad + \cos\left[(-0.7548 + 0.4711\lambda) - (0.5303 - 0.2643\lambda)\right] \\ &= -\sin\left(-0.4003 + 0.4493\lambda - 0.1245\lambda^2\right) + \cos\left(-1.285 + 0.7354\lambda\right) \end{aligned}$$

Using the golden-mean search on $[0, 8]$, we determine that this function of λ has a maximum at $\lambda_0^* \approx 1.7$. Thus,

$$\mathbf{X}_1 = \mathbf{X}_0 + \lambda_0^* \nabla f|_{\mathbf{x}_0} = \begin{bmatrix} -0.7548 + 0.4711(1.7) \\ 0.5303 - 0.2643(1.7) \end{bmatrix} = \begin{bmatrix} 0.04607 \\ 0.08099 \end{bmatrix}$$

with $f(\mathbf{X}_1) = 0.9957$. Since

$$f(\mathbf{X}_1) - f(\mathbf{X}_0) = 0.9957 - 0.6715 = 0.3242 > 0.05$$

we continue iterating.

Second iteration.

$$\begin{aligned} \nabla f|_{\mathbf{x}_1} &= \begin{bmatrix} -0.08099 \cos\left[(0.04607)(0.08099)\right] - \sin\left(0.04607 - 0.08099\right) \\ -0.04607 \cos\left[(0.04607)(0.08099)\right] + \sin\left(0.04607 - 0.08099\right) \end{bmatrix} \\ &= \begin{bmatrix} -0.04608 \\ -0.08098 \end{bmatrix} \end{aligned}$$

$$\mathbf{X}_1 + \lambda \nabla f|_{\mathbf{x}_1} = \begin{bmatrix} 0.04607 - 0.04608\lambda \\ 0.08099 - 0.08098\lambda \end{bmatrix}$$

$$\begin{aligned} f(\mathbf{X}_1 + \lambda \nabla f|_{\mathbf{x}_1}) &= -\sin\left[(0.04607 - 0.04608\lambda)(0.08099 - 0.08098\lambda)\right] \\ &\quad + \cos\left[(0.04607 - 0.04608\lambda) - (0.08099 - 0.08098\lambda)\right] \\ &= -\sin\left(0.003731 - 0.007463\lambda + 0.003732\lambda^2\right) + \cos\left(-0.03492 + 0.03490\lambda\right) \end{aligned}$$

Using the golden-mean search on $[0, 8]$, we determine that this function of λ has a maximum at $\lambda_1^* \approx 1$. Thus,

$$\mathbf{X}_2 = \mathbf{X}_1 + \lambda_1^* \nabla f|_{\mathbf{x}_1} = \begin{bmatrix} 0.04607 - 0.04608(1) \\ 0.08099 - 0.08098(1) \end{bmatrix} = \begin{bmatrix} 0.0000 \\ 0.0000 \end{bmatrix}$$

with $f(\mathbf{X}_2) = 1.000$. Since

$$f(\mathbf{X}_2) - f(\mathbf{X}_1) = 1.000 - 0.9957 = 0.0043 < 0.05$$

we take $\mathbf{X}^* = \mathbf{X}_2$ and $z^* = 1.000$.

11.6   Is the maximum found in Problem 11.5 a global maximum?

For the objective function $f(x_1, x_2) = -\sin x_1 x_2 + \cos (x_1 - x_2)$, the Hessian matrix is *not* negative semi-definite everywhere. Indeed,

$$\frac{\partial^2 f}{\partial x_1^2} = x_2^2 \sin x_1 x_2 - \cos (x_1 - x_2)$$

and the right-hand side is positive for $x_1 = x_2 = \sqrt{\pi/2}$. Thus $f(x_1, x_2)$ is not concave everywhere, and the question remains open. Referring to Problem 11.3, we see that the global maximum actually is $z^* = 2$, so that $z^* = 1.000$ must be only a local maximum.

11.7   Derive the method of steepest ascent.

For any fixed vector $\hat{\mathbf{X}}$ and any unit vector $\mathbf{U}$, the *directional derivative*,

$$D_U f(\hat{\mathbf{X}}) \equiv \nabla f|_{\hat{\mathbf{x}}} \cdot \mathbf{U}$$

gives the rate of change of $f(\mathbf{X})$ at $\hat{\mathbf{X}}$ in the direction of $\mathbf{U}$. Since

$$\nabla f \cdot \mathbf{U} = |\nabla f| \, |\mathbf{U}| \cos \theta = |\nabla f| \cos \theta$$

the greatest *increase* in $f(\mathbf{X})$ occurs when $\theta = 0$, i.e., when $\mathbf{U}$ is in the same direction as ∇f. Therefore, any (small) movement from $\hat{\mathbf{X}}$ in the direction of $\nabla f|_{\hat{\mathbf{x}}}$ will, initially, increase the function over $f(\hat{\mathbf{X}})$ as rapidly as possible. The vector $\lambda \, \nabla f|_{\hat{\mathbf{x}}}$ represents a displacement of this kind. The best value of λ is the one that maximizes $f(\hat{\mathbf{X}} + \lambda \, \nabla f|_{\hat{\mathbf{x}}})$, the value of function after the displacement.

11.8 Use the Newton-Raphson method to

$$\text{maximize:} \quad z = -(x_1 - \sqrt{5})^2 - (x_2 - \pi)^2 - 10$$

to within a tolerance of 0.05.

From Problem 11.4 we take the initial approximation $\mathbf{X}_0 = [6.597, 5.891]^T$, with $f(\mathbf{X}_0) = -36.58$. The gradient vector, Hessian matrix, and inverse Hessian matrix for this objective function are, respectively,

$$\nabla f = \begin{bmatrix} -2(x_1 - \sqrt{5}) \\ -2(x_2 - \pi) \end{bmatrix} \qquad \mathbf{H}_f = \begin{bmatrix} -2 & 0 \\ 0 & -2 \end{bmatrix} \qquad \mathbf{H}_f^{-1} = \begin{bmatrix} -0.5 & 0 \\ 0 & -0.5 \end{bmatrix}$$

for all x_1 and x_2.

First iteration.

$$\nabla f|_{\mathbf{x}_0} = \begin{bmatrix} -2(6.597 - \sqrt{5}) \\ -2(5.891 - \pi) \end{bmatrix} = \begin{bmatrix} -8.722 \\ -5.499 \end{bmatrix}$$

$$\mathbf{X}_1 = \mathbf{X}_0 - (\mathbf{H}_f|_{\mathbf{x}_0})^{-1} \nabla f|_{\mathbf{x}_0}$$

$$= \begin{bmatrix} 6.597 \\ 5.891 \end{bmatrix} - \begin{bmatrix} -0.5 & 0 \\ 0 & -0.5 \end{bmatrix} \begin{bmatrix} -8.722 \\ -5.499 \end{bmatrix} = \begin{bmatrix} 2.236 \\ 3.142 \end{bmatrix}$$

with $f(\mathbf{X}_1) = -10.00$. Since

$$f(\mathbf{X}_1) - f(\mathbf{X}_0) = -10.00 - (-36.58) = 26.58 > 0.05$$

we continue iterating.

Second iteration.

$$\nabla f|_{\mathbf{x}_1} = \begin{bmatrix} -2(2.236 - \sqrt{5}) \\ -2(3.142 - \pi) \end{bmatrix} = \begin{bmatrix} -0.0001 \\ 0.0008 \end{bmatrix}$$

$$\mathbf{X}_2 = \mathbf{X}_1 - (\mathbf{H}_f|_{\mathbf{x}_1})^{-1} \nabla f|_{\mathbf{x}_1}$$

$$= \begin{bmatrix} 2.236 \\ 3.142 \end{bmatrix} - \begin{bmatrix} -0.5 & 0 \\ 0 & -0.5 \end{bmatrix} \begin{bmatrix} -0.0001 \\ 0.0008 \end{bmatrix} = \begin{bmatrix} 2.236 \\ 3.142 \end{bmatrix}$$

with $f(\mathbf{X}_2) = -10.00$. Since $f(\mathbf{X}_2) - f(\mathbf{X}_1) = 0 < 0.05$, we take $\mathbf{X}^* = \mathbf{X}_2 = [2.236, 3.142]^T$, with $z^* = f(\mathbf{X}_2) = -10.00$.

11.9 Use the Newton-Raphson method to

$$\text{maximize:} \quad z = -\sin x_1 x_2 + \cos (x_1 - x_2)$$

to within a tolerance of 0.05.

The gradient vector and Hessian matrix for this objective function are

$$\nabla f = \begin{bmatrix} -x_2 \cos x_1 x_2 - \sin (x_1 - x_2) \\ -x_1 \cos x_1 x_2 + \sin (x_1 - x_2) \end{bmatrix} \tag{1}$$

$$\mathbf{H}_f = \begin{bmatrix} x_2^2 \sin x_1 x_2 - \cos (x_1 - x_2) & -\cos x_1 x_2 + x_1 x_2 \sin x_1 x_2 + \cos (x_1 - x_2) \\ -\cos x_1 x_2 + x_1 x_2 \sin x_1 x_2 + \cos (x_1 - x_2) & x_1^2 \sin x_1 x_2 - \cos (x_1 - x_2) \end{bmatrix} \tag{2}$$

From Problem 11.5 we appropriate the initial approximation $\mathbf{X}_0 = [-0.7548, 0.5303]^T$.

First iteration. Substituting the components of X_0 into (*1*) and (*2*), we obtain

$$\nabla f|_{x_0} = \begin{bmatrix} 0.4711 \\ -0.2643 \end{bmatrix} \qquad H_f|_{x_0} = \begin{bmatrix} -0.3914 & -0.4832 \\ -0.4832 & -0.5038 \end{bmatrix} \qquad (H_f|_{x_0})^{-1} = \begin{bmatrix} 13.88 & -13.31 \\ -13.31 & 10.78 \end{bmatrix}$$

Then

$$X_1 = X_0 - (H_f|_{x_0})^{-1}\nabla f|_{x_0}$$

$$= \begin{bmatrix} -0.7548 \\ 0.5303 \end{bmatrix} - \begin{bmatrix} 13.88 & -13.31 \\ -13.31 & 10.78 \end{bmatrix}\begin{bmatrix} 0.4711 \\ -0.2643 \end{bmatrix} = \begin{bmatrix} -10.81 \\ 9.650 \end{bmatrix}$$

Observe that X_1 is not close to X_0, which suggests that the numerical scheme is not converging. In this case, Theorem 11.1 shows that $H_f|_{x_0}$ is not negative definite; hence X_0 was not chosen sufficiently close to a maximum to guarantee convergence of the Newton-Raphson method. Therefore, rather than continuing to iterate, it is wiser to begin the method anew with a better approximation to a maximum.

An improved initial approximation can be obtained in two ways. First, we could use a random number generator to provide additional values for X until a better approximation is found. Second, we could use the method of steepest ascent for one iteration with the current X_0, and then use the resulting vector to start the Newton-Raphson method. Adopting the second approach, we obtain from Problem 11.5 the improved starting vector

$$X_0 = \begin{bmatrix} 0.04607 \\ 0.08099 \end{bmatrix} \qquad \text{with} \qquad f(X_0) = 0.9957$$

(New) first iteration. Substituting $x_1 = 0.04607$ and $x_2 = 0.08099$ into (*1*) and (*2*), we obtain

$$\nabla f|_{x_0} = \begin{bmatrix} -0.04608 \\ -0.08098 \end{bmatrix} \qquad H_f|_{x_0} = \begin{bmatrix} -0.9994 & -0.0005888 \\ -0.0005888 & -0.9994 \end{bmatrix} \qquad (H_f|_{x_0})^{-1} = \begin{bmatrix} -1.001 & 0.0005895 \\ 0.0005895 & -1.001 \end{bmatrix}$$

Then

$$X_1 = X_0 - (H_f|_{x_0})^{-1}\nabla f|_{x_0}$$

$$= \begin{bmatrix} 0.04607 \\ 0.08099 \end{bmatrix} - \begin{bmatrix} -1.001 & 0.0005895 \\ 0.0005895 & -1.001 \end{bmatrix}\begin{bmatrix} -0.04608 \\ -0.08098 \end{bmatrix} = \begin{bmatrix} 0 \\ 0 \end{bmatrix}$$

with $f(X_1) = 1$. Since

$$f(X_1) - f(X_0) = 1.0000 - 0.9957 = 0.0043 < 0.05$$

we take $X^* = X_1 = [0, 0]^T$ and $z^* = f(X_1) = 1$.

11.10 Use the Newton-Raphson method to

$$\text{maximize:} \quad z = -\sin x_1 x_2 + \cos (x_1 - x_2)$$

to within a tolerance of 0.05, starting with $X_0 = [4.8, 1.6]^T$.

The gradient vector and Hessian matrix for this objective function are given by (*1*) and (*2*) of Problem 11.9.

First iteration.

$$\nabla f|_{x_0} = \begin{bmatrix} -1.6 \cos [(4.8)(1.6)] - \sin (4.8 - 1.6) \\ -4.8 \cos [(4.8)(1.6)] + \sin (4.8 - 1.6) \end{bmatrix} = \begin{bmatrix} -0.2186 \\ -0.8893 \end{bmatrix}$$

$$H_f|_{x_0} = \begin{bmatrix} 3.520 & 6.393 \\ 6.393 & 23.69 \end{bmatrix} \qquad (H_f|_{x_0})^{-1} = \begin{bmatrix} 0.5572 & -0.1504 \\ -0.1504 & 0.08279 \end{bmatrix}$$

Then

$$X_1 = X_0 - (H_f|_{x_0})^{-1}\nabla f|_{x_0}$$

$$= \begin{bmatrix} 4.8 \\ 1.6 \end{bmatrix} - \begin{bmatrix} 0.5572 & -0.1504 \\ -0.1504 & 0.08279 \end{bmatrix}\begin{bmatrix} -0.2186 \\ -0.8893 \end{bmatrix} = \begin{bmatrix} 4.788 \\ 1.641 \end{bmatrix}$$

with $f(X_1) = -2.000$. Now, $f(X_0) = -1.983$; so even though X_1 is close to X_0, we have

$$f(X_1) < f(X_0)$$

and the iterations are tending toward a minimum rather than a maximum. (Notice that $\mathbf{H}_f|_{\mathbf{x}_0}$ is not negative definite; in fact, it is *positive definite*.)   A different value for $\mathbf{X}_0$ must be used, similar to the one determined in Problem 11.5, if the Newton-Raphson method is to succeed.

11.11 Solve Problem 1.14 to within 0.25 km by the Fletcher-Powell method.

Problem 1.14 is equivalent to a maximization program with objective function

$$f(\mathbf{X}) = -\sqrt{x_1^2 + x_2^2} - \sqrt{(x_1 - 300)^2 + (x_2 - 400)^2} - \sqrt{(x_1 - 700)^2 + (x_2 - 300)^2} \tag{1}$$

and gradient vector

$$\nabla f = \begin{bmatrix} -\dfrac{x_1}{\sqrt{x_1^2 + x_2^2}} - \dfrac{x_1 - 300}{\sqrt{(x_1 - 300)^2 + (x_2 - 400)^2}} - \dfrac{x_1 - 700}{\sqrt{(x_1 - 700)^2 + (x_2 - 300)^2}} \\ -\dfrac{x_2}{\sqrt{x_1^2 + x_2^2}} - \dfrac{x_2 - 400}{\sqrt{(x_1 - 300)^2 + (x_2 - 400)^2}} - \dfrac{x_2 - 300}{\sqrt{(x_1 - 700)^2 + (x_2 - 300)^2}} \end{bmatrix} \tag{2}$$

To initialize the Fletcher-Powell method, we set $\epsilon = 0.25$ and

$$\mathbf{G} = \begin{bmatrix} 1 & 0 \\ 0 & 1 \end{bmatrix}$$

and choose $\hat{\mathbf{X}} = [400, 200]^T$, which from Fig. 1-4 appears to be a good approximation to the optimal location of the refinery.

STEP 1

$$\alpha = f(\hat{\mathbf{X}}) = f(400, 200)$$
$$= -\sqrt{(400)^2 + (200)^2} - \sqrt{(100)^2 + (-200)^2} - \sqrt{(-300)^2 + (-100)^2} = -987.05$$

$$\mathbf{B} = \nabla f|_{\hat{\mathbf{x}}} = \begin{bmatrix} -0.39296 \\ 0.76344 \end{bmatrix}$$

STEP 2

$$f(\hat{\mathbf{X}} + \lambda \mathbf{GB}) = f\left(\begin{bmatrix} 400 \\ 200 \end{bmatrix} + \lambda \begin{bmatrix} 1 & 0 \\ 0 & 1 \end{bmatrix} \begin{bmatrix} -0.39296 \\ 0.76344 \end{bmatrix} \right) = f\left(\begin{bmatrix} 400 - 0.39296\lambda \\ 200 + 0.76344\lambda \end{bmatrix} \right)$$
$$= -\sqrt{(400 - 0.39296\lambda)^2 + (200 + 0.76344\lambda)^2}$$
$$- \sqrt{(100 - 0.39296\lambda)^2 + (-200 + 0.76344\lambda)^2}$$
$$- \sqrt{(-300 - 0.39296\lambda)^2 + (-100 + 0.76344\lambda)^2}$$

Making a three-point interval search of $[0, 425]$, we determine $\lambda^* \approx 212.5$.   Therefore,

$$\mathbf{D} = \lambda^* \mathbf{GB} = (212.5) \begin{bmatrix} 1 & 0 \\ 0 & 1 \end{bmatrix} \begin{bmatrix} -0.39296 \\ 0.76344 \end{bmatrix} = \begin{bmatrix} -83.504 \\ 162.23 \end{bmatrix}$$

STEP 3

$$\hat{\mathbf{X}} + \mathbf{D} = \begin{bmatrix} 400 \\ 200 \end{bmatrix} + \begin{bmatrix} -83.504 \\ 162.23 \end{bmatrix} = \begin{bmatrix} 316.50 \\ 362.23 \end{bmatrix}$$

which we take as the updated $\hat{\mathbf{X}}$: $\hat{\mathbf{X}} = [316.50, 362.23]^T$.

STEP 4

$$\beta = f(\hat{\mathbf{X}}) = f(316.50, 362.23) = -910.76$$

$$\beta - \alpha = -910.76 - (-987.05) = 76.29 > 0.25$$

STEP 6

$$\mathbf{C} = \nabla f|_{\hat{\mathbf{x}}} = \begin{bmatrix} -0.071207 \\ 0.0031594 \end{bmatrix} \qquad \mathbf{Y} = \mathbf{B} - \mathbf{C} = \begin{bmatrix} -0.39296 \\ 0.76344 \end{bmatrix} - \begin{bmatrix} -0.071207 \\ 0.0031594 \end{bmatrix} = \begin{bmatrix} -0.32175 \\ 0.76028 \end{bmatrix}$$

STEP 7

$$\mathbf{D}^T\mathbf{Y} = [-83.504, 162.23]\begin{bmatrix} -0.32175 \\ 0.76028 \end{bmatrix} = 150.21$$

$$\mathbf{L} = \frac{1}{150.21}\mathbf{D}\mathbf{D}^T = \frac{1}{150.21}\begin{bmatrix} -83.504 \\ 162.23 \end{bmatrix}[-83.504, 162.23]$$

$$= \frac{1}{150.21}\begin{bmatrix} 6972.9 & -13\,547 \\ -13\,547 & 26\,319 \end{bmatrix} = \begin{bmatrix} 46.421 & -90.187 \\ -90.187 & 175.21 \end{bmatrix}$$

$$\mathbf{Y}^T\mathbf{GY} = [-0.32175, 0.76028]\begin{bmatrix} 1 & 0 \\ 0 & 1 \end{bmatrix}\begin{bmatrix} -0.32175 \\ 0.76028 \end{bmatrix} = 0.68155$$

$$\mathbf{M} = \frac{-1}{0.68155}\mathbf{GYY}^T\mathbf{G}$$

$$= \frac{-1}{0.68155}\begin{bmatrix} 1 & 0 \\ 0 & 1 \end{bmatrix}\begin{bmatrix} -0.32175 \\ 0.76028 \end{bmatrix}[-0.32175, 0.76028]\begin{bmatrix} 1 & 0 \\ 0 & 1 \end{bmatrix}$$

$$= \frac{-1}{0.68155}\begin{bmatrix} 0.10352 & -0.24462 \\ -0.24462 & 0.57803 \end{bmatrix} = \begin{bmatrix} -0.15189 & 0.35892 \\ 0.35892 & -0.84811 \end{bmatrix}$$

STEP 8

$$\mathbf{G}+\mathbf{L}+\mathbf{M} = \begin{bmatrix} 1 & 0 \\ 0 & 1 \end{bmatrix}+\begin{bmatrix} 46.421 & -90.187 \\ -90.187 & 175.21 \end{bmatrix}+\begin{bmatrix} -0.15189 & 0.35892 \\ 0.35892 & -0.84811 \end{bmatrix} = \begin{bmatrix} 47.269 & -89.828 \\ -89.828 & 175.36 \end{bmatrix}$$

which we take as the updated **G**. We also update $\alpha = -910.76$ and

$$\mathbf{B} = \begin{bmatrix} -0.071207 \\ 0.0031594 \end{bmatrix}$$

STEP 2

$$f(\hat{\mathbf{X}}+\lambda\mathbf{GB}) = f\left(\begin{bmatrix} 316.50 \\ 362.23 \end{bmatrix}+\lambda\begin{bmatrix} 47.269 & -89.828 \\ -89.828 & 175.36 \end{bmatrix}\begin{bmatrix} -0.071207 \\ 0.0031594 \end{bmatrix}\right)$$

$$= f\left(\begin{bmatrix} 316.50 - 3.6497\lambda \\ 362.23 + 6.9504\lambda \end{bmatrix}\right)$$

$$= -\sqrt{(316.50 - 3.6497\lambda)^2 + (362.23 + 6.9504\lambda)^2}$$
$$-\sqrt{(16.50 - 3.6497\lambda)^2 + (-37.77 + 6.9504\lambda)^2}$$
$$-\sqrt{(-383.50 - 3.6497\lambda)^2 + (62.23 + 6.9504\lambda)^2}$$

Making a three-point interval search of [0, 10], we determine $\lambda^* \approx 1.25$. Therefore,

$$\mathbf{D} = \lambda^*\mathbf{GB} = (1.25)\begin{bmatrix} 47.269 & -89.828 \\ -89.828 & 175.36 \end{bmatrix}\begin{bmatrix} -0.071207 \\ 0.0031594 \end{bmatrix} = \begin{bmatrix} -4.5621 \\ 8.6880 \end{bmatrix}$$

STEP 3

$$\hat{\mathbf{X}}+\mathbf{D} = \begin{bmatrix} 316.50 \\ 362.23 \end{bmatrix}+\begin{bmatrix} -4.5621 \\ 8.6880 \end{bmatrix} = \begin{bmatrix} 311.94 \\ 370.92 \end{bmatrix}$$

which we take as the updated $\hat{\mathbf{X}}$.

STEP 4

$$\beta = f(\hat{\mathbf{X}}) = f(311.94, 370.92) = -910.58$$

$$\beta - \alpha = -910.58 - (-910.76) = 0.18 < 0.25$$

STEP 5

$$\mathbf{X}^* = \hat{\mathbf{X}} = \begin{bmatrix} 311.94 \\ 370.92 \end{bmatrix} \qquad \text{and} \qquad f(\mathbf{X}^*) = \beta = -910.58$$

Thus Problem 1.14 is solved by $x_1^* = 311.94$ km, $x_2^* = 370.92$ km, with $z^* = +910.58$ km.

11.12 Show that the maximum located by the Fletcher-Powell method in Problem 11.11 is in fact the desired global maximum.

In view of Theorem 11.6, it suffices to show that $f(\mathbf{X})$, as given by (1) of Problem 11.11, is concave everywhere.   Indeed, we need only show that the function

$$g(\mathbf{X}) = -\sqrt{x_1^2 + x_2^2}$$

is concave everywhere, since $f(\mathbf{X})$ is the sum of three functions of this type, and the sum of concave functions is a concave function.   Now,

$$\mathbf{H}_g = \frac{1}{(x_1^2 + x_2^2)^{3/2}} \begin{bmatrix} -x_2^2 & x_1 x_2 \\ x_1 x_2 & -x_1^2 \end{bmatrix}$$

which, by Theorem 11.1, is negative semi-definite everywhere.   Thus, by Theorem 11.5, $g(\mathbf{X})$ is concave everywhere.

11.13 Derive the Newton-Raphson method.

Suppose that an approximation, $\mathbf{X}_k$, to a stationary point of $f(\mathbf{X})$ has been determined; we wish to find a nearby point, $\mathbf{X}_{k+1}$, that furnishes an even better approximation.   Expanding the *vector* ∇f in a Taylor series about $\mathbf{X}_k$, we have

$$\nabla f|_{\mathbf{x}_{k+1}} = \nabla f|_{\mathbf{x}_k} + \mathbf{H}_f|_{\mathbf{x}_k}(\mathbf{X}_{k+1} - \mathbf{X}_k) + \cdots \tag{1}$$

[The reader should verify that the ith row of (1) is the ordinary multivariable Taylor series for $\partial f / \partial x_i$.]   Thus $\nabla f|_{\mathbf{x}_{k+1}}$ will vanish, to the second order in small quantities, if

$$\mathbf{H}_f|_{\mathbf{x}_k}(\mathbf{X}_{k+1} - \mathbf{X}_k) = -\nabla f|_{\mathbf{x}_k} \qquad \text{or} \qquad \mathbf{X}_{k+1} - \mathbf{X}_k = -(\mathbf{H}_f|_{\mathbf{x}_k})^{-1} \nabla f|_{\mathbf{x}_k}$$

which is precisely the Newton-Raphson formula.

11.14 Use the modified Hooke-Jeeves' pattern search to

$$\text{maximize:} \quad z = 3x_1 + 2x_2 + x_3 - 0.02(x_1^4 + x_2^4 + x_3^4 - 325)^2 - 0.02(x_1 x_2)^2$$

We arbitrarily begin with $h = 1$ and $\mathbf{B} = [0, 0, 0]^T$.   Then $f(\mathbf{B}) = -2112.5$.

STEP 1

$$f(0 + 1, 0, 0) = -2096.52 \quad \text{(an improvement)}$$
$$f(1, 0 + 1, 0) = -2081.60 \quad \text{(an improvement)}$$
$$f(1, 1, 0 + 1) = -2067.70 \quad \text{(an improvement)}$$

Set $\mathbf{C} = [1, 1, 1]^T$, with $f(\mathbf{C}) = -2067.70$.

STEP 3

$$\mathbf{T} = 2[1, 1, 1]^T - [0, 0, 0]^T = [2, 2, 2]^T$$

STEP 4

$$f(2 + 1, 2, 2) = -884.60 \quad \text{(an improvement over } -2067.70)$$
$$f(3, 2 + 1, 2) = -416.80 \quad \text{(an improvement)}$$
$$f(3, 3, 2 + 1) = -118.10 \quad \text{(an improvement)}$$

Set $\mathbf{S} = [3, 3, 3]^T$.

STEP 6   Set $\mathbf{B} = [1, 1, 1]^T$ and $\mathbf{C} = [3, 3, 3]^T$, with $f(\mathbf{C}) = -118.10$.

STEP 3

$$\mathbf{T} = 2[3, 3, 3]^T - [1, 1, 1]^T = [5, 5, 5]^T$$

STEP 4

$$f(5+1, 5, 5) = -98\,641.8 \quad \text{(not an improvement over } -118.10)$$
$$f(5-1, 5, 5) = -27\,876.2 \quad \text{(not an improvement)}$$
$$f(5, 5+1, 5) = -98\,642.8 \quad \text{(not an improvement)}$$
$$f(5, 5-1, 5) = -27\,875.2 \quad \text{(not an improvement)}$$
$$f(5, 5, 5+1) = -98\,638.3 \quad \text{(not an improvement)}$$
$$f(5, 5, 5-1) = -27\,867.7 \quad \text{(not an improvement)}$$

Set $\mathbf{S} = [5, 5, 5]^T$.

STEP 5   Set $\mathbf{B} = [3, 3, 3]^T$, with $f(\mathbf{B}) = -118.10$.

STEP 1

$$f(3+1, 3, 3) = -154.86 \quad \text{(not an improvement)}$$
$$f(3-1, 3, 3) = -417.90 \quad \text{(not an improvement)}$$
$$f(3, 3+1, 3) = -155.86 \quad \text{(not an improvement)}$$
$$f(3, 3-1, 3) = -416.90 \quad \text{(not an improvement)}$$
$$f(3, 3, 3+1) = -155.60 \quad \text{(not an improvement)}$$
$$f(3, 3, 3-1) = -416.80 \quad \text{(not an improvement)}$$

Set $\mathbf{C} = [3, 3, 3]^T$.

STEP 2'   We sequentially evaluate the objective at all points obtained from $\mathbf{B}$ by perturbing one or more of the components of $\mathbf{B}$ by either 1 or -1. There are 26 possible perturbations, excluding the null perturbation. Functional evaluations cease if and when one yields a value larger than $f(\mathbf{B}) = -118.10$. As shown in Table 11-1, this occurs at $[2, 2, 4]^T$. Therefore, we update $\mathbf{B} = [2, 2, 4]^T$, with $f(\mathbf{B}) = -13.70$.

Table 11-1

x_1	x_2	x_3	$f(x_1, x_2, x_3)$
2	2	2	-1522.90
2	2	3	-886.20
2	2	4	-13.70
2	3	2	
...	...	...	
4	4	3	
4	4	4	

STEP 1

$$f(2+1, 2, 4) = 0.60 \quad \text{(an improvement)}$$
$$f(3, 2+1, 4) = -155.6 \quad \text{(not an improvement)}$$
$$f(3, 2-1, 4) = 11.44 \quad \text{(an improvement)}$$
$$f(3, 1, 4+1) = -2902.66 \quad \text{(not an improvement)}$$
$$f(3, 1, 4-1) = -511.06 \quad \text{(not an improvement)}$$

Set $\mathbf{C} = [3, 1, 4]^T$, with $f(\mathbf{C}) = 11.44$.

STEP 3

$$\mathbf{T} = 2[3, 1, 4]^T - [2, 2, 4]^T = [4, 0, 4]^T$$

STEP 4

$f(4 + 1, 0, 4) = -6163.72$ (not an improvement over 11.44)

$f(4 - 1, 0, 4) = 10.12$ (not an improvement)

$f(4, 0 + 1, 4) = -689.32$ (not an improvement)

$f(4, 0 - 1, 4) = -693.20$ (not an improvement)

$f(4, 0, 4 + 1) = -6165.72$ (not an improvement)

$f(4, 0, 4 - 1) = 12.12$ (an improvement)

Set $\mathbf{S} = [4, 0, 3]^T$.

STEP 6   Set $\mathbf{B} = [3, 1, 4]^T$ and $\mathbf{C} = [4, 0, 3]^T$, with $f(\mathbf{C}) = 12.12$.

STEP 3

$$\mathbf{T} = 2[4, 0, 3]^T - [3, 1, 4]^T = [5, -1, 2]^T$$

STEP 4

$f(5 + 1, -1, 2) = -19\,505.6$ (not an improvement over 12.12)

$f(5 - 1, -1, 2) = -42.40$ (not an improvement)

$f(5, -1 + 1, 2) = -1980.12$ (not an improvement)

$f(5, -1 - 1, 2) = -2193.48$ (not an improvement)

$f(5, -1, 2 + 1) = -2902.98$ (not an improvement)

$f(5, -1, 2 - 1) = -1810.58$ (not an improvement)

Set $\mathbf{S} = [5, -1, 2]^T$.

STEP 5   Set $\mathbf{B} = [4, 0, 3]^T$, with $f(\mathbf{B}) = 12.12$.

Table 11-2

x_1	x_2	x_3	$f(x_1, x_2, x_3)$
3	0	2	-1028.68
3	0	3	-519.38
3	0	4	10.12
3	1	2	-1017.76
3	1	3	-511.06
3	1	4	11.44
3	2	2	-884.60
3	2	3	-416.90
3	2	4	0.60
4	0	2	-42.18
4	0	3	12.12
4	0	4	-683.38
4	1	2	-38.40
4	1	4	-689.20
4	2	2	-10.66
4	2	3	2.04
4	2	4	-805.46
5	0	2	-1980.12
5	0	3	-2885.22
5	0	4	-6163.72
5	1	2	-1991.28
5	1	3	-2898.98
5	1	4	-6184.48
5	2	2	-2185.48
5	2	3	-3132.18
5	2	4	-6522.68

STEP 1   Exploratory moves around **B** yield $f(4, 1, 3) = 13.30$, an improvement. Set $\mathbf{C} = [4, 1, 3]^T$, with $f(\mathbf{C}) = 13.30$.

STEP 3

$$\mathbf{T} = 2[4, 1, 3]^T - [4, 0, 3]^T = [4, 2, 3]^T$$

STEP 4   Exploratory moves around **T** do not yield any improvements. Set $\mathbf{S} = [4, 2, 3]^T$.

STEP 5   Set $\mathbf{B} = [4, 1, 3]^T$, with $f(\mathbf{B}) = 13.30$.

STEP 1   Exploratory moves around **B** do not yield any improvements. Set $\mathbf{C} = [4, 1, 3]^T$, with $f(\mathbf{C}) = 13.30$.

STEP 2'   As shown in Table 11-2, none of the 26 perturbations of **B** yields an improvement in the current value of the objective function, $f(\mathbf{B}) = 13.30$. Therefore, $\mathbf{B} = [4, 1, 3]^T$ is the best integral solution (because $h = 1$, and we started at the integer point $x_1 = x_2 = x_3 = 0$) to the given program.

     To improve this approximation, we reduce h sequentially to 0.1, 0.01, and 0.001, beginning the algorithm anew each time with the latest **B**. The results are exhibited in Table 11-3. We take $x_1^* = 3.825$, $x_2^* = 2.447$, and $x_3^* = 2.946$, with $z^* = 17.56$, as the optimal solution.

Table 11-3

| h | Final Vector | | | |
	x_1	x_2	x_3	z
1	4	1	3	13.30
0.1	3.9	1.4	3.1	16.88
0.01	3.89	2.40	2.82	17.54
0.001	3.825	2.447	2.946	17.56

Supplementary Problems

     Solve Problems 11.15 through 11.23 numerically, using either a random number generator or a reasonable guess to provide an initial approximation. Wherever possible, also solve analytically.

11.15   maximize: $z = -(2x_1 - 5)^2 - (x_2 - 3)^2 - (5x_3 - 2)^2$

11.16   minimize: $z = |x_1| + \sqrt{(x_1 - 1)^2 + x_2^2}$

11.17   minimize: $z = \dfrac{8x_1 + 4x_2 - x_1x_2}{(x_1x_2)^2}$

11.18   minimize: $z = -\sin x_1 \sin x_2 \sin (x_1 + x_2)$

11.19   maximize: $z = (x_1^2 + 2x_2^2)e^{-(x_1^2 + x_2^2)}$

11.20   maximize: $z = -(x_1 - x_2)^2 - (x_3 - 1)^2 - 1 - 0.02(x_1^5 + x_2^5 + x_3^5 - 16)^2$

11.21   maximize: $z = -(x_1 - \sqrt{5})^2 - (x_2 - \pi)^2 - 10$

with: x_1 and x_2 integers

(*Hint*:   See Problem 11.12.)

11.22   Minimize the *Rosenbrock function*, $z = (1 - x_1)^2 + 100(x_2 - x_1^2)^2$.

11.23   Census figures for a midwestern town are as follows:

Year	1930	1940	1950	1960	1970
Population	4953	7389	11 023	16 445	24 532

Based on these data, an estimate for the population in 1980 is required.

(1)   Assume that the population growth is exponential and follows a curve of the form $N = Ae^{mt}$, where N denotes the population and t denotes time.

(2)   At any given census year T, there may be a discrepancy between the actual value of N given by the data and the theoretical value $N = Ae^{mT}$.   Designate this error as e_T; e.g.,

$$e_{1930} = 4953 - Ae^{m(1930)}$$

(3)   Determine the constants A and m so that

$$e_{1930}^2 + e_{1940}^2 + e_{1950}^2 + e_{1960}^2 + e_{1970}^2$$

is minimized.

(4)   Using these constants, evaluate the theoretical exponential curve (often called the *least-squares exponential curve*) at $t = 1980$ and take that number to be the estimated population for 1980.

11.24   Show that the quadratic function

$$f(x_1, x_2, \ldots, x_n) = \sum_{i=1}^{n} \sum_{j=1}^{n} a_{ij} x_i x_j$$

with symmetric coefficient matrix $\mathbf{A}$, is concave if and only if $\mathbf{A}$ is negative semi-definite.

Chapter 12

Nonlinear Programming: Multivariable Optimization with Constraints

STANDARD FORMS

With $\mathbf{X} \equiv [x_1, x_2, \ldots, x_n]^T$, standard form for nonlinear programs containing only *equality* constraints is

$$\begin{aligned} \text{maximize:} \quad & z = f(\mathbf{X}) \\ \text{subject to:} \quad & g_1(\mathbf{X}) = 0 \\ & g_2(\mathbf{X}) = 0 \\ & \ldots\ldots\ldots \\ & g_m(\mathbf{X}) = 0 \end{aligned} \qquad (12.1)$$

$$\text{with:} \quad m < n \quad \text{(fewer constraints than variables)}$$

As in Chapter 11, minimization programs are converted into maximization programs by multiplying the objective function by -1.

Standard form for nonlinear programs containing only *inequality* constraints is either

$$\begin{aligned} \text{maximize:} \quad & z = f(\mathbf{X}) \\ \text{subject to:} \quad & g_1(\mathbf{X}) \le 0 \\ & g_2(\mathbf{X}) \le 0 \\ & \ldots\ldots\ldots \\ & g_p(\mathbf{X}) \le 0 \end{aligned} \qquad (12.2)$$

or

$$\begin{aligned} \text{maximize:} \quad & z = f(\mathbf{X}) \\ \text{subject to:} \quad & g_1(\mathbf{X}) \le 0 \\ & g_2(\mathbf{X}) \le 0 \\ & \ldots\ldots\ldots \\ & g_m(\mathbf{X}) \le 0 \end{aligned} \qquad (12.3)$$

$$\text{with:} \quad \mathbf{X} \ge \mathbf{0}$$

The two forms are equivalent: (12.2) goes over into (12.3) (with $m = p$) under the substitution $\mathbf{X} = \mathbf{U} - \mathbf{V}$, with $\mathbf{U} \ge \mathbf{0}$ and $\mathbf{V} \ge \mathbf{0}$; on the other hand, (12.3) is just (12.2) in the special case $p = m + n$ and $g_{m+i}(\mathbf{X}) = -x_i$ $(i = 1, 2, \ldots, n)$. Form (12.3) is appropriate when the solution procedure requires nonnegative variables. In (12.1), (12.2), or (12.3), f is a nonlinear function, but some or all of the g's may be linear.

Nonlinear programs not in standard form are solved either by putting them in such form (see Problems 12.7, 12.10, and 12.11) or by suitably modifying the solution procedures given below for programs in standard form (see Problems 12.8, 12.9, and 12.12).

LAGRANGE MULTIPLIERS

To solve program (12.1), first form the *Lagrangian function*

$$L(x_1, x_2, \ldots, x_n, \lambda_1, \lambda_2, \ldots, \lambda_m) \equiv f(\mathbf{X}) - \sum_{i=1}^{m} \lambda_i g_i(\mathbf{X}) \tag{12.4}$$

where λ_i $(i = 1, 2, \ldots, m)$ are (unknown) constants called *Lagrange multipliers*. Then solve the system of $n + m$ equations

$$\frac{\partial L}{\partial x_j} = 0 \qquad (j = 1, 2, \ldots, n)$$

$$\frac{\partial L}{\partial \lambda_i} = 0 \qquad (i = 1, 2, \ldots, m) \tag{12.5}$$

Theorem 12.1: *If a solution to program (12.1) exists*, it is contained among the solutions to system (12.5), provided $f(\mathbf{X})$ and $g_i(\mathbf{X})$ $(i = 1, 2, \ldots, m)$ all have continuous first partial derivatives and the $m \times n$ *Jacobian matrix*,

$$\mathbf{J} \equiv \left[\frac{\partial g_i}{\partial x_j} \right]$$

has rank m at $\mathbf{X} = \mathbf{X}^*$.

(See Problems 12.1 through 12.5.) The method of Lagrange multipliers is equivalent to using the constraint equations to eliminate certain of the x-variables from the objective function and then solving an unconstrained maximization problem in the remaining x-variables.

NEWTON-RAPHSON METHOD

Since $L(x_1, x_2, \ldots, x_n, \lambda_1, \lambda_2, \ldots, \lambda_m) \equiv L(\mathbf{Z})$ is nonlinear, it is usually impossible to solve (12.5) analytically. However, since the solutions to (12.5) are the stationary points of $L(\mathbf{Z})$, and since (Theorem 11.3) the maxima and minima of $L(\mathbf{Z})$ occur among these stationary points, it should be possible to use the Newton-Raphson method (Chapter 11) to approximate the "right" extremum of $L(\mathbf{Z})$; that is, the one that corresponds to the optimal solution of (12.1). The iterative formula applicable here is

$$\mathbf{Z}_{k+1} = \mathbf{Z}_k - (\mathbf{H}_L|_{\mathbf{Z}_k})^{-1} \nabla L|_{\mathbf{Z}_k} \tag{12.6}$$

(See Problem 12.3.)

This approach is of limited value because, as in Chapter 11, it is very difficult to determine an adequate $\mathbf{Z}_0$. For an incorrect $\mathbf{Z}_0$, the Newton-Raphson method may diverge or may converge to the "wrong" extremum of $L(\mathbf{Z})$. It is also possible (see Problems 12.1 and 12.4) for the method to converge when no optimal solution exists.

PENALTY FUNCTIONS

An alternative approach to solving program (12.1) involves the unconstrained program

$$\text{maximize:} \quad \hat{z} = f(\mathbf{X}) - \sum_{i=1}^{m} p_i g_i^2(\mathbf{X}) \tag{12.7}$$

where $p_i > 0$ are constants (still to be chosen) called *penalty weights*. The solution to program (12.7) is the solution to program (12.1) when each $g_i(\mathbf{X}) = 0$. For large values of the p_i, the solution to (12.7) will have each $g_i(\mathbf{X})$ near zero to avoid adverse effects on the objective function from the terms $p_i g_i^2(\mathbf{X})$; and as each $p_i \to \infty$, each $g_i(\mathbf{X}) \to 0$. (See Problem 12.6.)

In practice, this process cannot be accomplished analytically except in rare cases. Instead, program (*12.7*) is solved repeatedly by the modified pattern search described in Chapter 11, each time with either a new set of increased penalty weights or a decreased step size. Each pattern search with a specified set of penalty weights and a given step size is one phase of the solution procedure. The starting vector for a particular phase is the final vector from the phase immediately preceding it. Penalty weights for the first phase are chosen small, often $1/50 = 0.02$; the first step size generally is taken as 1.

Convergence of this procedure is affected by the rates at which the penalty weights are increased and the step size is decreased. Decisions governing these rates are more a matter of art than of science. (See Problem 12.7.)

KUHN-TUCKER CONDITIONS

To solve program (*12.3*), first rewrite the nonnegativity conditions as $-x_1 \le 0$, $-x_2 \le 0$, ..., $-x_n \le 0$, so that the constraint set is $m + n$ inequality requirements each with a less than or equals sign. Next add slack variables $x_{n+1}^2, x_{n+2}^2, \ldots, x_{2n+m}^2$, respectively, to the left-hand sides of the constraints, thereby converting each inequality into an equality. Here the slack variables are added as squared terms to guarantee their nonnegativity. Then form the Lagrangian function

$$L \equiv f(\mathbf{X}) - \sum_{i=1}^{m} \lambda_i [g_i(\mathbf{X}) + x_{n+i}^2] - \sum_{i=m+1}^{m+n} \lambda_i [-x_i + x_{n+i}^2] \qquad (12.8)$$

where $\lambda_1, \lambda_2, \ldots, \lambda_{m+n}$ are Lagrange multipliers. Finally solve the system

$$\frac{\partial L}{\partial x_j} = 0 \qquad (j = 1, 2, \ldots, 2n + m) \qquad (12.9)$$

$$\frac{\partial L}{\partial \lambda_i} = 0 \qquad (i = 1, 2, \ldots, m + n) \qquad (12.10)$$

$$\lambda_i \ge 0 \qquad (i = 1, 2, \ldots, m + n) \qquad (12.11)$$

Equations (*12.9*) through (*12.11*) constitute the *Kuhn-Tucker conditions* for program (*12.2*) or (*12.3*). The first two sets, (*12.9*) and (*12.10*), follow directly from Lagrange multiplier theory; set (*12.11*) is known as the *constraint qualification*. Among the solutions to the Kuhn-Tucker conditions will be the solution to program (*12.3*) if $f(\mathbf{X})$ and each $g_i(\mathbf{X})$ have continuous first partial derivatives. (See Problem 12.10.)

METHOD OF FEASIBLE DIRECTIONS

This is a five-step algorithm for solving program (*12.2*). The method is applicable only when the feasible region has an interior, and then it will converge to the global maximum only if the initial approximation is "near" the solution (see Problems 12.13 and 12.14). The feasible region will have no interior if two of the inequality constraints have arisen from the conversion of an equality constraint (see Problem 12.11).

STEP 1   Determine an initial, feasible approximation to the solution, designating it **B**.

STEP 2   Solve the following linear program for the variables $d_1, d_2, \ldots, d_{n+1}$:

maximize: $z = d_{n+1}$

subject to: $-\dfrac{\partial f}{\partial x_1}\bigg|_{\cdot \mathbf{B}} d_1 - \dfrac{\partial f}{\partial x_2}\bigg|_{\mathbf{B}} d_2 - \cdots - \dfrac{\partial f}{\partial x_n}\bigg|_{\mathbf{B}} d_n + \quad d_{n+1} \leq \quad 0$

$\dfrac{\partial g_1}{\partial x_1}\bigg|_{\cdot \mathbf{B}} d_1 + \dfrac{\partial g_1}{\partial x_2}\bigg|_{\mathbf{B}} d_2 + \cdots + \dfrac{\partial g_1}{\partial x_n}\bigg|_{\mathbf{B}} d_n + k_1 d_{n+1} \leq -g_1(\mathbf{B})$

$\dfrac{\partial g_2}{\partial x_1}\bigg|_{\mathbf{B}} d_1 + \dfrac{\partial g_2}{\partial x_2}\bigg|_{\mathbf{B}} d_2 + \cdots + \dfrac{\partial g_2}{\partial x_n}\bigg|_{\mathbf{B}} d_n + k_2 d_{n+1} \leq -g_2(\mathbf{B})$ (12.12)

. . . .

$\dfrac{\partial g_p}{\partial x_1}\bigg|_{\mathbf{B}} d_1 + \dfrac{\partial g_p}{\partial x_2}\bigg|_{\mathbf{B}} d_2 + \cdots + \dfrac{\partial g_p}{\partial x_n}\bigg|_{\mathbf{B}} d_n + k_p d_{n+1} \leq -g_p(\mathbf{B})$

with: $d_j \leq 1 \quad (j = 1, 2, \ldots, n+1)$

Here k_i $(i = 1, 2, \ldots, p)$ is 0 if $g_i(\mathbf{X})$ is linear and 1 if $g_i(\mathbf{X})$ is nonlinear.

STEP 3   If $d_{n+1} = 0$, then $\mathbf{X}^* = \mathbf{B}$; if not, go to Step 4.

STEP 4   Set $\mathbf{D} = [d_1, d_2, \ldots, d_n]^T$.   Determine a nonnegative value for λ that maximizes $f(\mathbf{B} + \lambda \mathbf{D})$ while keeping $\mathbf{B} + \lambda \mathbf{D}$ feasible; designate this value as λ^*.

STEP 5   Set $\mathbf{B} = \mathbf{B} + \lambda^* \mathbf{D}$ and return to Step 2.

(See Problems 12.13 through 12.15.)

Solved Problems

12.1

maximize: $z = 2x_1 + x_1 x_2 + 3x_2$

subject to: $x_1^2 + x_2 = 3$

It is apparent that for any large negative x_1 there is a large negative x_2 such that the constraint equation is satisfied.   But then $z \approx x_1 x_2 \to \infty$.   There is no global maximum.

12.2

minimize: $z = x_1 + x_2 + x_3$

subject to: $x_1^2 + x_2 = 3$

$x_1 + 3x_2 + 2x_3 = 7$

The given program is equivalent to the unconstrained minimization of

$$z = \tfrac{1}{2}(x_1^2 + x_1 + 4)$$

which obviously has a solution.   We may therefore apply the method of Lagrange multipliers to the original program standardized as

maximize: $z = -x_1 - x_2 - x_3$

subject to: $x_1^2 + x_2 - 3 = 0$ (1)

$x_1 + 3x_2 + 2x_3 - 7 = 0$

Here, $f(x_1, x_2, x_3) = -x_1 - x_2 - x_3$, $n = 3$ (variables), $m = 2$ (constraints),

$$g_1(x_1, x_2, x_3) = x_1^2 + x_2 - 3 \qquad g_2(x_1, x_2, x_3) = x_1 + 3x_2 + 2x_3 - 7$$

The Lagrangian function is then

$$L = (-x_1 - x_2 - x_3) - \lambda_1(x_1^2 + x_2 - 3) - \lambda_2(x_1 + 3x_2 + 2x_3 - 7)$$

and system (12.5) becomes

$$\frac{\partial L}{\partial x_1} = -1 - 2x_1\lambda_1 - \lambda_2 = 0 \tag{2}$$

$$\frac{\partial L}{\partial x_2} = -1 - \lambda_1 - 3\lambda_2 = 0 \tag{3}$$

$$\frac{\partial L}{\partial x_3} = -1 - 2\lambda_2 = 0 \tag{4}$$

$$\frac{\partial L}{\partial \lambda_1} = -(x_1^2 + x_2 - 3) = 0 \tag{5}$$

$$\frac{\partial L}{\partial \lambda_2} = -(x_1 + 3x_2 + 2x_3 - 7) = 0 \tag{6}$$

Successively solving (4) for λ_2, (3) for λ_1, (2) for x_1, (5) for x_2, and (6) for x_3, we obtain the unique solution $\lambda_2 = -0.5$, $\lambda_1 = 0.5$, $x_1 = -0.5$, $x_2 = 2.75$, and $x_3 = -0.375$, with

$$z = -x_1 - x_2 - x_3 = -(-0.5) - 2.75 - (-0.375) = -1.875$$

Since the first partial derivatives of $f(x_1, x_2, x_3)$, $g_1(x_1, x_2, x_3)$, and $g_2(x_1, x_2, x_3)$ are all continuous, and since

$$\mathbf{J} = \begin{bmatrix} \dfrac{\partial g_1}{\partial x_1} & \dfrac{\partial g_1}{\partial x_2} & \dfrac{\partial g_1}{\partial x_3} \\ \dfrac{\partial g_2}{\partial x_1} & \dfrac{\partial g_2}{\partial x_2} & \dfrac{\partial g_2}{\partial x_3} \end{bmatrix} = \begin{bmatrix} 2x_1 & 1 & 0 \\ 1 & 3 & 2 \end{bmatrix}$$

is of rank 2 everywhere (the last two columns are linearly independent everywhere), either $x_1 = -0.5$, $x_2 = 2.75$, $x_3 = -0.375$ is the optimal solution to program (1) or no optimal solution exists. Checking feasible points in the region around $(-0.5, 2.75, -0.375)$, we find that this point is indeed the location of a (global) maximum for program (1). Therefore, it is also the location of a global minimum for the original program, with $z^* = -(-1.875) = 1.875$.

$$z^* = -(-1.875) = 1.875$$

12.3   maximize: $z = \sin(x_1 x_2 + x_3)$

subject to: $-x_1 x_2^3 + x_1^2 x_3^2 = 5$

As in Problem 12.2, it is possible to establish in advance that an optimal solution exists. Indeed, by inspection, the point $x_1 = 2\sqrt{5}/\pi$, $x_2 = 0$, $x_3 = \pi/2$ satisfies the constraint equation and makes $z = 1$; therefore it must represent a global maximum.

Let us apply the method of Lagrange multipliers to this problem. The Lagrangian function here is

$$L = \sin(x_1 x_2 + x_3) - \lambda_1 (x_1^2 x_3^2 - x_1 x_2^3 - 5)$$

so that the Lagrangian equations are

$$\frac{\partial L}{\partial x_1} = x_2 \cos(x_1 x_2 + x_3) - 2\lambda_1 x_1 x_3^2 + \lambda_1 x_2^3 = 0$$

$$\frac{\partial L}{\partial x_2} = x_1 \cos(x_1 x_2 + x_3) + 3\lambda_1 x_1 x_2^2 = 0$$

$$\frac{\partial L}{\partial x_3} = \cos(x_1 x_2 + x_3) - 2\lambda_1 x_1^2 x_3 = 0$$

$$\frac{\partial L}{\partial \lambda_1} = -(x_1^2 x_3^2 - x_1 x_2^3 - 5) = 0$$

As these equations cannot be solved algebraically, we go over to the Newton-Raphson approach. The gradient vector and Hessian matrix of the Lagrangian function are

$$\nabla L = \begin{bmatrix} x_2 \cos(x_1 x_2 + x_3) - 2\lambda_1 x_1 x_3^2 + \lambda_1 x_2^3 \\ x_1 \cos(x_1 x_2 + x_3) + 3\lambda_1 x_1 x_2^2 \\ \cos(x_1 x_2 + x_3) - 2\lambda_1 x_1^2 x_3 \\ -(x_1^2 x_3^2 - x_1 x_2^3 - 5) \end{bmatrix}$$

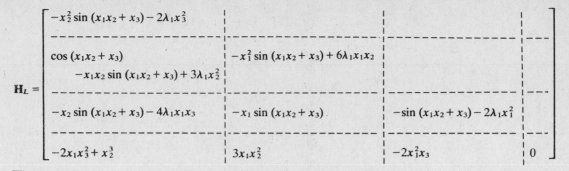

(The superdiagonal entries of the symmetric matrix have been omitted to save space.) Arbitrarily taking

$$\mathbf{Z}_0 = [-1, 1, 2.5, 1]^T$$

we calculate as follows (rounding all computations to four significant figures).

First iteration.

$$\nabla L|_{\mathbf{z}_0} = \begin{bmatrix} 13.57 \\ -3.071 \\ -4.929 \\ -2.25 \end{bmatrix} \qquad \mathbf{H}_L|_{\mathbf{z}_0} = \begin{bmatrix} -13.50 & 4.068 & 9.003 & 13.5 \\ 4.068 & -6.997 & 0.9975 & -3 \\ 9.003 & 0.9975 & -2.998 & -5 \\ 13.5 & -3 & -5 & 0 \end{bmatrix}$$

$$(\mathbf{H}_L|_{\mathbf{z}_0})^{-1} = \begin{bmatrix} 0.05737 & 0.03845 & 0.1318 & 0.03194 \\ 0.03845 & -0.08206 & 0.1531 & -0.03889 \\ 0.1318 & 0.1531 & 0.2641 & -0.09044 \\ 0.03194 & -0.03889 & -0.09044 & 0.1040 \end{bmatrix}$$

Hence

$$\mathbf{Z}_1 = \mathbf{Z}_0 - (\mathbf{H}_L|_{\mathbf{z}_0})^{-1} \nabla L|_{\mathbf{z}_0} = [-0.9388, 0.8931, 2.279, 0.2353]^T$$

Second iteration.

$$\nabla L|_{\mathbf{z}_1} = \begin{bmatrix} 2.579 \\ -0.6503 \\ -0.8158 \\ -0.2479 \end{bmatrix} \qquad \mathbf{H}_L|_{\mathbf{z}_1} = \begin{bmatrix} -3.236 & 1.524 & 1.128 & 10.47 \\ 1.524 & -2.058 & 0.9309 & -2.247 \\ 1.128 & 0.9309 & -1.406 & -4.018 \\ 10.47 & -2.247 & -4.018 & 0 \end{bmatrix}$$

$$(\mathbf{H}_L|_{\mathbf{z}_1})^{-1} = \begin{bmatrix} 0.8072 & 1.224 & 1.418 & 0.01391 \\ 1.224 & 1.574 & 2.309 & -0.09969 \\ 1.418 & 2.309 & 2.404 & -0.1569 \\ 0.01391 & -0.09969 & -0.1569 & 0.03573 \end{bmatrix}$$

Hence

$$\mathbf{Z}_2 = \mathbf{Z}_1 - (\mathbf{H}_L|_{\mathbf{z}_1})^{-1} \nabla L|_{\mathbf{z}_1} = [-1.064, 0.6190, 2.046, 0.01545]^T$$

Continuing in this manner, we obtain successively

$$\mathbf{Z}_3 = [-1.053, 0.5067, 2.099, 0.001369]^T$$
$$\mathbf{Z}_4 = [-1.053, 0.4982, 2.095, 0.000009]^T$$
$$\mathbf{Z}_5 = [-1.053, 0.4981, 2.095, 0]^T$$

As the components of $\mathbf{Z}$ have stabilized to three significant figures, we take $x_1^* = -1.05$, $x_2^* = 0.498$, $x_3^* = 2.10$, and $\lambda_1 = 0$, with

$$z^* = \sin(x_1^* x_2^* + x_3^*) = 1.00$$

Observe that the Newton-Raphson method has converged to a different global maximum from the one originally identified.

12.4   Disregarding Problem 12.1, use the Newton-Raphson method to

$$\text{maximize:} \quad z = 2x_1 + x_1x_2 + 3x_2$$

$$\text{subject to:} \quad x_1^2 + x_2 = 3$$

Here, $L = (2x_1 + x_1x_2 + 3x_2) - \lambda_1(x_1^2 + x_2 - 3)$.   Therefore,

$$\nabla L = \begin{bmatrix} 2 + x_2 - 2\lambda_1 x_1 \\ x_1 + 3 - \lambda_1 \\ -x_1^2 - x_2 + 3 \end{bmatrix} \qquad H_L = \begin{bmatrix} -2\lambda_1 & 1 & -2x_1 \\ 1 & 0 & -1 \\ -2x_1 & -1 & 0 \end{bmatrix}$$

Arbitrarily taking $Z_0 = [1, 1, 1]^T$, we calculate:

First iteration.

$$\nabla L|_{z_0} = \begin{bmatrix} 1 \\ 3 \\ 1 \end{bmatrix} \qquad H_L|_{z_0} = \begin{bmatrix} -2 & 1 & -2 \\ 1 & 0 & -1 \\ -2 & -1 & 0 \end{bmatrix} \qquad (H_L|_{z_0})^{-1} = \frac{1}{6}\begin{bmatrix} -1 & 2 & -1 \\ 2 & -4 & -4 \\ -1 & -4 & -1 \end{bmatrix}$$

and

$$Z_1 = Z_0 - (H_L|_{z_0})^{-1}\nabla L|_{z_0} = [1/3, 10/3, 10/3]^T$$

Second iteration.

$$\nabla L|_{z_1} = \begin{bmatrix} 28/9 \\ 0 \\ -4/9 \end{bmatrix} \qquad H_L|_{z_1} = \frac{1}{3}\begin{bmatrix} -20 & 3 & -2 \\ 3 & 0 & -3 \\ -2 & -3 & 0 \end{bmatrix} \qquad (H_L|_{z_1})^{-1} = \frac{1}{72}\begin{bmatrix} -9 & 6 & -9 \\ 6 & -4 & -66 \\ -9 & -66 & -9 \end{bmatrix}$$

and

$$Z_2 = Z_1 - (H_L|_{z_1})^{-1}\nabla L|_{z_1} = [2/3, 8/3, 11/3]^T$$

Continuing for two more iterations, we obtain

$$Z_3 = [0.6333, 2.6, 3.633]^T$$
$$Z_4 = [0.6330, 2.599, 3.633]^T$$

As the components of Z have stabilized to three significant figures, we take $x_1^* = 0.633$, $x_2^* = 2.60$, and $\lambda_1^* = 3.63$, with

$$z^* = 2x_1^* + x_1^* x_2^* + 3x_2^* = 10.7$$

By expressing z as a (cubic) function of x_1 alone, we can easily see that in this particular case the Newton-Raphson method has converged on a local maximum.

12.5   Give a geometrical argument for the method of Lagrange multipliers in three dimensions.

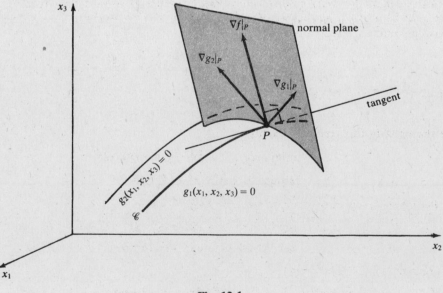

Fig. 12-1

Refer to Fig. 12-1.   The problem is to maximize a function $f(x_1, x_2, x_3)$ along the space curve $\mathscr{C}$ in which the two surfaces

$$g_1(x_1, x_2, x_3) = 0 \qquad \text{and} \qquad g_2(x_1, x_2, x_3) = 0$$

intersect.   Let P be the point of $\mathscr{C}$ at which the maximum is attained.   From Problem 11.7, we know that the gradient of f must have a zero projection on the tangent to $\mathscr{C}$ at P; otherwise a small displacement along the curve would produce an even larger functional value.   Thus $\nabla f|_P$ must lie in the normal plane to the curve at P.   But then this vector is expressible as a linear combination of the two surface normals at P, $\nabla g_1|_P$ and $\nabla g_2|_P$; that is,

$$\nabla f|_P = \lambda_1 \nabla g_1|_P + \lambda_2 \nabla g_2|_P \qquad \text{or} \qquad \nabla L|_P = \mathbf{0} \qquad (1)$$

where $L \equiv f - \lambda_1 g_1 - \lambda_2 g_2$.

The three scalar equations represented by (1) are the first three Lagrangian equations (12.5); the remaining two Lagrangian equations merely restate the requirement that P actually lie on $\mathscr{C}$.

12.6   Use the penalty function approach to

$$\text{maximize:} \quad z = -4 - 3(1 - x_1)^2 - (1 - x_2)^2$$

$$\text{subject to:} \quad 3x_1 + x_2 = 5$$

Here (12.7) becomes

$$\text{maximize:} \quad \hat{z} = -4 - 3(1 - x_1)^2 - (1 - x_2)^2 - p_1(3x_1 + x_2 - 5)^2$$

This unconstrained maximization program in the two variables x_1 and x_2 is sufficiently simple that it may be solved analytically.   Setting $\nabla \hat{z} = \mathbf{0}$, we obtain

$$(1 + 3p_1)x_1 + \qquad p_1 x_2 = 1 + 5p_1$$
$$3p_1 x_1 + (1 + p_1)x_2 = 1 + 5p_1$$

Solving these equations for x_1 and x_2 in terms of p_1, we obtain

$$x_1 = x_2 = \frac{1 + 5p_1}{1 + 4p_1} = \frac{(1/p_1) + 5}{(1/p_1) + 4}$$

Since the Hessian matrix

$$\mathbf{H}_{\hat{z}} = \begin{bmatrix} -6 - 18p_1 & -6p_1 \\ -6p_1 & -2 - 2p_1 \end{bmatrix}$$

is negative definite for every positive value of p_1, $\hat{z}$ is a strictly concave function, and its sole stationary point must be a global maximum.   Therefore, letting $p_1 \to +\infty$ we obtain the optimal solution to the original program:

$$x_1 \to \frac{5}{4} = x_1^* \qquad x_2 \to \frac{5}{4} = x_2^*$$

with $z^* = -4 - 3(1 - x_1^*)^2 - (1 - x_2^*)^2 = -4.25$.

12.7   Use the penalty function approach to

$$\text{minimize:} \quad z = (x_1 - x_2)^2 + (x_3 - 1)^2 + 1$$

$$\text{subject to:} \quad x_1^5 + x_2^5 + x_3^5 = 16$$

Putting this program in standard form, we have

$$\text{maximize:} \quad z = -(x_1 - x_2)^2 - (x_3 - 1)^2 - 1$$

$$\text{subject to:} \quad x_1^5 + x_2^5 + x_3^5 - 16 = 0 \qquad (1)$$

For program (1), (12.7) becomes

$$\text{maximize:} \quad \hat{z} = -(x_1 - x_2)^2 - (x_3 - 1)^2 - 1 - p_1(x_1^5 + x_2^5 + x_3^5 - 16)^2 \qquad (2)$$

Phase 1. We set $p_1 = 0.02$ in (2) and consider the program

$$\text{maximize:} \quad \hat{z} = -(x_1 - x_2)^2 - (x_3 - 1)^2 - 1 - 0.02(x_1^5 + x_2^5 + x_3^5 - 16)^2 \tag{3}$$

Arbitrarily selecting $[0, 0, 0]^T$ as our initial vector, and setting $h = 1$, we apply the modified pattern search (Chapter 11) to program (3). The result after 78 functional evaluations is $[1, 1, 1]^T$, with

$$f(1, 1, 1) = -1 \qquad \text{and} \qquad g_1(1, 1, 1) = -13$$

Phase 2. Since $g_1(1, 1, 1) = -13 \neq 0$, the constraint in program (1) is not satisfied. To improve this situation, we increase p_1 in (2) to 0.2 and consider the program

$$\text{maximize:} \quad \hat{z} = -(x_1 - x_2)^2 - (x_3 - 1)^2 - 1 - 0.2(x_1^5 + x_2^5 + x_3^5 - 16)^2 \tag{4}$$

Taking $[1, 1, 1]^T$ from Phase 1 as the initial approximation, we apply the modified pattern search to (4), still keeping $h = 1$. The result remains $[1, 1, 1]^T$, indicating that the constraint cannot be satisfied in integers.

Phase 3. Since increasing p_1 did not improve the current solution, we return to program (3), reduce h to 0.1, and make a new pattern search, again with $[1, 1, 1]^T$ as initial approximation. The result is $[1.5, 1.5, 1]^T$, with

$$f(1.5, 1.5, 1) = -1 \qquad \text{and} \qquad g_1(1.5, 1.5, 1) = 0.1875$$

Table 12-1

Phase	p_1	h	Final Vector X			$f(X)$	$g_1(X)$
			x_1	x_2	x_3		
1	0.02	1	1	1	1	−1	−13
2	0.2	1	1	1	1	−1	−13
3	0.02	0.1	1.5	1.5	1	−1	0.1875
4	0.2	0.1	1.5	1.5	1	−1	0.1875
5	0.02	0.01	1.49	1.5	1	−1.000	−0.0623
6	0.2	0.01	1.49	1.5	1.01	−1.000	−0.0113
7	0.2	0.001	1.496	1.496	1.002	−1.000	−0.0039
8	2	0.001	1.496	1.496	1.003	−1.000	0.0012
9	20	0.001	1.496	1.496	1.003	−1.000	0.0012

Continuing in this manner, we complete Table 12-1. Using the results of Phase 9, we conclude that $x_1^* = 1.496$, $x_2^* = 1.496$, $x_3^* = 1.003$, with $z^* = +1.000$, approximates the optimal solution to the original minimization program.

By inspection, the exact solution is

$$x_1^* = x_2^* = \left(\frac{15}{2}\right)^{1/5} = 1.4963 \qquad x_3^* = 1$$

with $z^* = 1$. Thus the penalty function approach has yielded a result good to four significant figures.

12.8

$$\text{maximize:} \quad z = -x_1^6 x_2^2 - x_1^4 x_3^2 - 1$$

$$\text{subject to:} \quad x_1 + 2x_2 + 3x_3 - 4 = 0$$

$$x_1 x_3 - 19 = 0$$

$$\text{with:} \quad \text{all variables integral}$$

The penalty function method is applicable to this integer program, provided that the pattern search starts from an integral first approximation, say $[0, 0, 0]^T$, and employs $h = 1$ throughout. Using it, we generate Table 12-2 and find $x_1^* = 1$, $x_2^* = -27$, $x_3^* = 19$, with $z^* = -1091$.

Table 12-2

Phase	p_1	p_2	h	x_1	x_2	x_3	$f(\mathbf{X})$	$g_1(\mathbf{X})$	$g_2(\mathbf{X})$
				Final Vector $\mathbf{X}$					
1	0.02	0.02	1	4	0	0	−1	0	−19
2	0.02	0.2	1	4	0	0	−1	0	19
3	0.02	2	1	1	−1	12	−146	31	−7
4	0.2	20	1	1	−11	17	−411	26	−2
5	2	200	1	1	−24	19	−938	6	0
6	20	200	1	1	−27	19	−1091	0	0

12.9   Describe how the penalty function approach can be modified to solve program (12.1) if nonnegativity conditions are added.

Require the initial approximation to have only nonnegative components.   Then restrict exploratory moves to vectors satisfying the nonnegativity conditions.   This can best be accomplished by penalizing the objective function whenever the nonnegativity conditions are violated.   That is, $f(\mathbf{X})$ is evaluated as a prohibitively large negative number, perhaps -1×10^{30}, whenever any component of the perturbed vector $\mathbf{X}$ is negative.

12.10   Solve the following program by use of the Kuhn-Tucker conditions:

$$\text{minimize:} \quad z = x_1^2 + 5x_2^2 + 10x_3^2 - 4x_1x_2 + 6x_1x_3 - 12x_2x_3 - 2x_1 + 10x_2 + 5x_3$$

$$\text{subject to:} \quad x_1 + 2x_2 + x_3 \geq 4$$

$$\text{with:} \quad \text{all variables nonnegative}$$

First transforming into system (12.3) and then introducing squared slack variables, we obtain

$$\text{maximize:} \quad z = -x_1^2 - 5x_2^2 - 10x_3^2 + 4x_1x_2 - 6x_1x_3 + 12x_2x_3 + 2x_1 - 10x_2 - 5x_3$$

$$\text{subject to:} \quad -x_1 - 2x_2 - x_3 + 4 + x_4^2 \qquad\qquad = 0$$
$$-x_1 \qquad\qquad\quad + x_5^2 \qquad\qquad = 0$$
$$- x_2 \qquad\qquad\quad + x_6^2 \quad = 0$$
$$- x_3 \qquad\qquad\qquad\quad + x_7^2 = 0$$

For this program, the Lagrangian function is

$$L = -x_1^2 - 5x_2^2 - 10x_3^2 + 4x_1x_2 - 6x_1x_3 + 12x_2x_3 + 2x_1 - 10x_2 - 5x_3$$
$$- \lambda_1(-x_1 - 2x_2 - x_3 + 4 + x_4^2) - \lambda_2(-x_1 + x_5^2) - \lambda_3(-x_2 + x_6^2) - \lambda_4(-x_3 + x_7^2)$$

Taking the derivatives indicated in (12.9) and (12.10), we have

$$\frac{\partial L}{\partial x_1} = -2x_1 + 4x_2 - 6x_3 + 2 + \lambda_1 + \lambda_2 = 0 \tag{1}$$

$$\frac{\partial L}{\partial x_2} = -10x_2 + 4x_1 + 12x_3 - 10 + 2\lambda_1 + \lambda_3 = 0 \tag{2}$$

$$\frac{\partial L}{\partial x_3} = -20x_3 - 6x_1 + 12x_2 - 5 + \lambda_1 + \lambda_4 = 0 \tag{3}$$

$$\frac{\partial L}{\partial x_4} = -2\lambda_1 x_4 = 0 \tag{4}$$

$$\frac{\partial L}{\partial x_5} = -2\lambda_2 x_5 = 0 \tag{5}$$

$$\frac{\partial L}{\partial x_6} = -2\lambda_3 x_6 = 0 \tag{6}$$

$$\frac{\partial L}{\partial x_7} = -2\lambda_4 x_7 = 0 \qquad (7)$$

$$\frac{\partial L}{\partial \lambda_1} = x_1 + 2x_2 + x_3 - x_4^2 - 4 = 0 \qquad (8)$$

$$\frac{\partial L}{\partial \lambda_2} = x_1 - x_5^2 = 0 \qquad (9)$$

$$\frac{\partial L}{\partial \lambda_3} = x_2 - x_6^2 = 0 \qquad (10)$$

$$\frac{\partial L}{\partial \lambda_4} = x_3 - x_7^2 = 0 \qquad (11)$$

These equations can be simplified. Set

$$s_1 \equiv x_4^2 \qquad (12)$$

Equations (4) through (7) imply respectively that either λ_1 or x_4, either λ_2 or x_5, either λ_3 or x_6, and either λ_4 or x_7, equals zero. But, by (9) through (12), x_4, x_5, x_6, and x_7 are zero if and only if s_1, x_1, x_2, and x_3 are respectively zero. Thus, (4) through (7) and (9) through (12) are equivalent to the system

$$
\begin{aligned}
\lambda_1 s_1 &= 0 \\
\lambda_2 x_1 &= 0 \\
\lambda_3 x_2 &= 0 \\
\lambda_4 x_3 &= 0
\end{aligned}
\qquad (13)
$$

There are 16 solutions to this system.

One of these solutions is $s_1 = \lambda_2 = \lambda_3 = x_3 = 0$. Substituting these values into (8), (1), (2), and (3), and simplifying, we get the linear system

$$
\begin{aligned}
x_1 + 2x_2 &&&&= 4 \\
-2x_1 + 4x_2 + \lambda_1 &&&&= -2 \\
4x_1 - 10x_2 + 2\lambda_1 &&&&= 10 \\
-6x_1 + 12x_2 + \lambda_1 + \lambda_4 &&&&= 5
\end{aligned}
$$

which has the unique solution $x_1 = 2.941$, $x_2 = 0.5294$, $\lambda_1 = 1.764$, and $\lambda_4 = 14.53$. These results are listed in row 10 of Table 12-3. (Boldface entries in the table correspond to solutions of (13).)

A second solution of (13) is $s_1 = x_1 = x_2 = x_3 = 0$. Substituting these values into (8), (1), (2), and (3), and simplifying, we get the linear system

$$
\begin{aligned}
0 &= 4 \\
\lambda_1 + \lambda_2 &= -2 \\
2\lambda_1 + \lambda_3 &= 10 \\
\lambda_1 + \lambda_4 &= 5
\end{aligned}
$$

which has no solution, as indicated in row 16 of Table 12-3. The other 14 possibilities are handled similarly, and the results are also listed in Table 12-3.

The only row in Table 12-3 having nonnegative entries for all variables, as required by the Kuhn-Tucker conditions, is row 10. Now, since $z = f(\mathbf{X})$ and

$$g_1(\mathbf{X}) = -x_1 - 2x_2 - x_3 + 4$$

have continuous first partial derivatives, *one* of the solutions to the Kuhn-Tucker conditions must reflect the optimal solution of the maximization program. But the Kuhn-Tucker conditions here have a unique solution! Consequently, $x_1^* = 2.941$, $x_2^* = 0.5294$, $x_3^* = 0$, giving $z^* = 3.235$ for the original minimization program.

Table 12-3

λ_1	λ_2	λ_3	λ_4	x_1	x_2	x_3	s_1
0	0	0	0	11.5	-3	-5.5	-4
0	0	0	11	-5	-3	0	-15
0	0	6	0	17.5	0	-5.5	-4
0	0	6	11	1	0	0	-3
0	-1.643	0	0	0	-4.643	-3.036	-16.32
0	2	0	17	0	-1	0	-2
0	-3.5	13	0	0	0	-0.25	-4.25
0	-2	10	5	0	0	0	-4
0.3809	0	0	0	14.36	-2.238	-5.881	0
1.764	0	0	14.53	2.941	0.5294	0	0
-3.2	0	18.8	0	6.3	0	-2.3	0
6	0	-8	11	4	0	0	0
6.623	-8.738	0	0	0	1.507	0.9855	0
15	-25	0	-34	0	2	0	0
85	-63	-208	0	0	0	4	0
...	...	...	...	0	0	0	0

12.11 Transform the following program into system (*12.3*):

$$\text{minimize:} \quad z = 12x_1^2 + 2.8x_2^2 + 55.2x_3^2 - 5.6x_1x_2$$
$$-5.6x_2x_1 + 23x_1x_3 + 23x_3x_1 - 12x_2x_3 - 12x_3x_2$$

$$\text{subject to:} \quad x_1 + x_2 + x_3 = 10\,000 \qquad (1)$$
$$9x_1 + 7x_2 + 10x_3 \geq 80\,000 \qquad (2)$$

with: all variables nonnegative

Multiplying the objective function by -1, we obtain:

$$\text{maximize:} \quad z = -12x_1^2 - 2.8x_2^2 - 55.2x_3^2 + 5.6x_1x_2$$
$$+5.6x_2x_1 - 23x_1x_3 - 23x_3x_1 + 12x_2x_3 + 12x_3x_2 \qquad (3)$$

The equality constraint is equivalent to the *two* inequalities

$$x_1 + x_2 + x_3 \leq 10\,000 \qquad \text{and} \qquad -x_1 - x_2 - x_3 \leq -10\,000$$

Hence the complete set of constraints can be given as

$$x_1 + x_2 + x_3 - 10\,000 \leq 0$$
$$-x_1 - x_2 - x_3 + 10\,000 \leq 0 \qquad (4)$$
$$-9x_1 - 7x_2 - 10x_3 + 80\,000 \leq 0$$

Expressions (*3*) and (*4*), augmented by nonnegativity conditions on the variables, represent standard form for this problem.

The problem now can be solved by utilizing the Kuhn-Tucker conditions (see Problem 12.33). Another solution procedure is given in Problem 12.12.

12.12 How may the penalty function approach be used to solve Problem 12.11?

The second constraint, (2) of Problem 12.11, can be converted into an equality by subtracting a surplus variable, x_4, from its left-hand side. Then the system composed of (3), (1), and (2) can be solved by the penalty function approach as modified in Problem 12.9.

12.13 Use the method of feasible directions to

$$\text{maximize:} \quad z = x_1 + x_2$$

$$\text{subject to:} \quad x_2x_1 - 2x_2 \le 3$$

$$3x_1 + 2x_2 \le 24$$

$$\text{with:} \quad \text{all variables nonnegative}$$

Put into standard form (12.2), the program is

$$\text{maximize:} \quad z = x_1 + x_2$$

$$\text{subject to:} \quad x_2x_1 - 2x_2 - 3 \le 0$$

$$3x_1 + 2x_2 - 24 \le 0 \qquad (1)$$

$$-x_1 \le 0$$

$$-x_2 \le 0$$

Here, $f(\mathbf{X}) = x_1 + x_2$, $g_1(\mathbf{X}) = x_2x_1 - 2x_2 - 3$, $g_2(\mathbf{X}) = 3x_1 + 2x_2 - 24$, $g_3(\mathbf{X}) = -x_1$, and $g_4(\mathbf{X}) = -x_2$;

$$\frac{\partial f}{\partial x_1} = 1 \qquad\qquad \frac{\partial f}{\partial x_2} = 1$$

$$\frac{\partial g_1}{\partial x_1} = x_2 \qquad\qquad \frac{\partial g_1}{\partial x_2} = x_1 - 2$$

$$\frac{\partial g_2}{\partial x_1} = 3 \qquad\qquad \frac{\partial g_2}{\partial x_2} = 2$$

$$\frac{\partial g_3}{\partial x_1} = -1 \qquad\qquad \frac{\partial g_3}{\partial x_2} = 0$$

$$\frac{\partial g_4}{\partial x_1} = 0 \qquad\qquad \frac{\partial g_4}{\partial x_2} = -1$$

Furthermore, $g_1(\mathbf{X})$ is nonlinear, while $g_2(\mathbf{X})$, $g_3(\mathbf{X})$, and $g_4(\mathbf{X})$ are all linear; therefore, $k_1 = 1$ and $k_2 = k_3 = k_4 = 0$ in program (12.12).

STEP 1 We arbitrarily initialize **B** as $[1, 1]^T$, which is feasible.

STEP 2 With this **B**, program (12.12) becomes

$$\text{maximize:} \quad z = d_3$$

$$\text{subject to:} \quad -d_1 - d_2 + d_3 \le 0$$

$$d_1 - d_2 + d_3 \le 4$$

$$3d_1 + 2d_2 \qquad \le 19$$

$$-d_1 \qquad\qquad \le 1$$

$$-d_2 \qquad \le 1$$

$$\text{with:} \quad d_1 \qquad\qquad \le 1$$

$$d_2 \qquad \le 1$$

$$d_3 \le 1$$

Its solution is $d_1 = 1$, $d_2 = 0$, $d_3 = 1$.

STEP 3 $d_3 = 1 \neq 0$.

STEP 4 $\mathbf{D} = [1, 0]^T$, hence

$$f\left(\begin{bmatrix} 1 \\ 1 \end{bmatrix} + \lambda \begin{bmatrix} 1 \\ 0 \end{bmatrix}\right) = f(1 + \lambda, 1) = 2 + \lambda$$

which becomes arbitrarily large as λ tends to ∞. To keep $[1 + \lambda, 1]^T$ feasible, however, λ can be no greater than 4 if the first constraint in program (*1*) is to be satisfied, and no greater than 19/3 if the second constraint is to be satisfied. Thus, $\lambda^* = 4$.

STEP 5

$$\mathbf{B} = \begin{bmatrix} 1 \\ 1 \end{bmatrix} + 4 \begin{bmatrix} 1 \\ 0 \end{bmatrix} = \begin{bmatrix} 5 \\ 1 \end{bmatrix}$$

STEP 2   With this updated **B**, program (*12.12*) becomes

$$\begin{aligned}
\text{maximize:} \quad & z = d_3 \\
\text{subject to:} \quad & -d_1 - d_2 + d_3 \leq 0 \\
& d_1 + 3d_2 + d_3 \leq 0 \\
& 3d_1 + 2d_2 \qquad \leq 7 \\
& -d_1 \qquad\qquad \leq 5 \\
& \quad\; - d_2 \qquad \leq 1 \\
\text{with:} \quad & d_1 \qquad\qquad \leq 1 \\
& \quad\; d_2 \qquad\qquad \leq 1 \\
& \quad\qquad d_3 \leq 1
\end{aligned}$$

Its solution is $d_1 = 1$, $d_2 = -1/2$, $d_3 = 1/2$.

STEP 3 $d_3 = 1/2 \neq 0$.

STEP 4 $\mathbf{D} = [1, -\tfrac{1}{2}]^T$, so

$$f\left(\begin{bmatrix} 5 \\ 1 \end{bmatrix} + \lambda \begin{bmatrix} 1 \\ -\tfrac{1}{2} \end{bmatrix}\right) = f(5 + \lambda, 1 - \tfrac{1}{2}\lambda) = 6 + \tfrac{1}{2}\lambda$$

which becomes arbitrarily large as λ tends to ∞. To keep $[5 + \lambda, 1 - \tfrac{1}{2}\lambda]^T$ feasible, however, λ can be no greater than 3.5 if the second constraint in program (*1*) is to be satisfied, and no greater than 2 if the nonnegativity constraint on x_2 is to be satisfied. (The other two constraints in program (*1*) are satisfied for any nonnegative choice of λ.) Thus, $\lambda^* = 2$.

STEP 5

$$\mathbf{B} = \begin{bmatrix} 5 \\ 1 \end{bmatrix} + 2 \begin{bmatrix} 1 \\ -\tfrac{1}{2} \end{bmatrix} = \begin{bmatrix} 7 \\ 0 \end{bmatrix}$$

Table 12-4

x_1	x_2	d_1	d_2	d_3	λ^*
1	1	1	0	1	4
5	1	1	$-\tfrac{1}{2}$	$\tfrac{1}{2}$	2
7	0	1	0	1	1
8	0	$-\tfrac{2}{3}$	1	$\tfrac{1}{3}$	0.531373
7.64575	0.531373	0	0	0	$\cdots$

Continuing in this manner, we complete Table 12-4. It follows that $x_1^* = 7.64575$, $x_2^* = 0.531373$, with

$$z^* = f(x_1^*, x_2^*) = 7.64575 + 0.531373 = 8.17712$$

12.14 Show that the solution found in Problem 12.13 is not optimal.

The second constraint of the original program may be written as

$$z \le 12 - \frac{x_1}{2}$$

which shows that if $x_1 > 0$, then $z < 12$. On the other hand, if $x_1 = 0$, then $z = x_2 \le 12$. It follows that the global maximum is $z^* = 12$, assumed at $x_1^* = 0$, $x_2^* = 12$. The solution obtained in Problem 12.13 is only a locally constrained maximum; the method of feasible directions would have located the global maximum had **B** initially been chosen closer to $[0, 12]^T$.

12.15 Interpret graphically the method of feasible directions.

The method of feasible directions produces a direction **D** along which one can move from **B**, the current best approximation to **X***, so as to achieve a better value of the objective function. Such a move is possible only if $d_{n+1} \ne 0$, and then λ^* represents the maximal step size that can be taken. Figure 12-2 illustrates the solution procedure for the calculations in Problem 12.13.

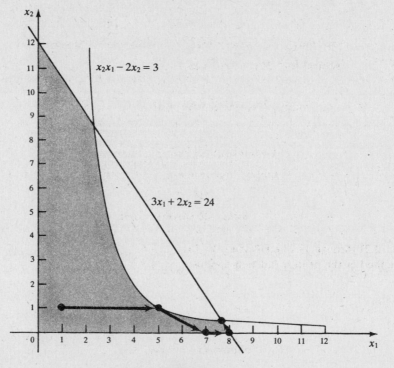

Fig. 12-2

Supplementary Problems

Put programs 12.16 through 12.20 in standard form.

12.16

maximize: $z = x_1^4 e^{-0.01(x_1 x_2)^2}$

subject to: $2x_1^2 + x_2^2 = 10$

12.17

minimize: $z = (x_1 - 1)^2 + x_2^2$

subject to: $x_1^2 + x_2^2 = 4$

12.18

maximize: $z = 6x_1 - 2x_1^2 + 2x_1 x_2 - 2x_2^2$

subject to: $x_1 + x_2 \leq 2$

with: all variables nonnegative

12.19

minimize: $z = 24x_1^2 + 14x_2^2 + 46x_3^2 - 28x_1 x_2 - 24x_1 x_3 + 34x_2 x_3$

subject to: $11x_1 + 9x_2 + 12x_3 \geq 1000$

$x_2 + x_3 = 40$

with: all variables nonnegative

12.20

maximize: $z = 3x_1 x_3 + 4x_2 x_3$

subject to: $x_2^2 + x_3^2 = 4$

$x_1 x_3 = 3$

with: all variables nonnegative

Solve Problems 12.21 through 12.23 analytically by Lagrange multipliers and then numerically by either the Newton-Raphson method or the penalty function approach.

12.21   Problem 12.17.

12.22

minimize: $z = x_1 x_2 + x_3$

subject to: $x_1^2 + x_2^2 + x_3^2 = 1$

12.23

maximize: $z = x_1^2 + x_2 x_3$

subject to: $4x_1^2 + x_2^2 = 16$

$2x_2 + 3x_3 = 25$

12.24   Find the point on the parabola $y^2 = 4x$ that is closest to the point $(1, 0)$.

12.25   Use Lagrange multipliers to solve Problem 12.20 without the nonnegativity conditions. Based on the result, solve the problem with the nonnegativity conditions.

12.26   Solve Problem 12.16.

12.27

$$\text{minimize:} \quad z = x_1^2 + x_2^2 + x_3^2$$
$$\text{subject to:} \quad x_1 x_2 x_3 = 3$$
$$x_1 + x_2 - x_3 = 3$$

12.28   Solve Problem 12.27 with the additional constraint that all variables be integral.

12.29

$$\text{maximize:} \quad z = x_1^2 + 2x_2^2 + x_3^2 + x_1 x_2 + x_1 x_3$$
$$\text{subject to:} \quad x_1^2 + x_2^2 + x_3^2 = 25$$
$$8x_1 + 14x_2 + 7x_3 = 56$$
$$\text{with:} \quad \text{all variables nonnegative}$$

12.30

$$\text{minimize:} \quad z = x_1^6 x_2^2 + x_1^4 x_3^2 + 1$$
$$\text{subject to:} \quad x_1 + 2x_2 + 3x_3 = 4$$
$$x_1 x_3 = 19$$

12.31   Solve Problem 12.18.

12.32   Solve Problem 12.19.

12.33   Use the Kuhn-Tucker conditions to solve the program given in Problem 12.11.

Solve Problems 12.34 and 12.35 by the penalty function approach.

12.34

$$\text{minimize:} \quad z = (x_1 - 2)^2 + (x_2 - 1)^2$$
$$\text{subject to:} \quad x_1 - 2x_2 = -1$$
$$x_1^2 + 4x_2^2 \leq 4$$

12.35

$$\text{maximize:} \quad z = \ln(1 + x_1) + 2\ln(1 + x_2)$$
$$\text{subject to:} \quad x_1 + x_2 \leq 2$$
$$\text{with:} \quad \text{all variables nonnegative}$$

(*Hint*: Simplify the problem by maximizing e^z and establishing beforehand that the constraint must hold with equality.)

Use the method of feasible directions to solve Problems 12.36 and 12.37.

12.36

$$\text{minimize:} \quad z = (x_1 - 2)^2 + (x_2 - 2)^2$$
$$\text{subject to:} \quad x_1 + 2x_2 \leq 3$$
$$8x_1 + 5x_2 \geq 10$$
$$\text{with:} \quad x_1 \text{ and } x_2 \text{ nonnegative}$$

12.37

$$\text{maximize:} \quad z = x_1 + 3x_2$$
$$\text{subject to:} \quad x_1 x_2 \geq 3$$
$$x_1^2 + x_2^2 \leq 9$$
$$\text{with:} \quad x_1 \text{ and } x_2 \text{ nonnegative}$$

Chapter 13

Quadratic Programming

STANDARD FORM

The general maximization quadratic program has the matrix form

$$\text{maximize:} \quad z = \mathbf{X}^T \mathbf{C} \mathbf{X} + \mathbf{D}^T \mathbf{X}$$

$$\text{subject to:} \quad \mathbf{A} \mathbf{X} \leq \mathbf{B} \tag{13.1}$$

$$\text{with:} \quad \mathbf{X} \geq \mathbf{0}$$

in which the symmetric matrix $\mathbf{C}$ is negative semi-definite (see Chapter 11).

The condition on $\mathbf{C}$, which was not imposed in the original definition of a quadratic program (Chapter 1), makes z a concave function (by Problem 11.24), thereby guaranteeing that any local maximum over the convex feasible region will be a global maximum over that region. The nonnegativity requirements, also absent from Chapter 1, are imposed to aid solution procedures. If not originally present, they can always be effected in the usual way—by expressing the variables as differences of nonnegative variables. Notice, however, that this substitution will convert an originally negative definite matrix into one that is only negative semi-definite.

Minimization quadratic programs are solved by converting them into maximization programs in standard form. (See Problem 13.1.)

A KUHN-TUCKER SYSTEM

It follows from applying the Kuhn-Tucker conditions (see Chapter 12) to program (13.1) that the optimal solution to this program, if it exists, must satisfy the new matrix equation

$$\hat{\mathbf{A}} \mathbf{Y} = \hat{\mathbf{B}} \tag{13.2}$$

where

$$\hat{\mathbf{A}} \equiv \begin{bmatrix} \mathbf{A} & \mathbf{I}_1 & \mathbf{0}_1 & \mathbf{0}_2 \\ -2\mathbf{C} & \mathbf{0}_3 & -\mathbf{I}_2 & \mathbf{A}^T \end{bmatrix} \qquad \hat{\mathbf{B}} \equiv \begin{bmatrix} \mathbf{B} \\ \mathbf{D} \end{bmatrix} \qquad \mathbf{Y} \equiv \begin{bmatrix} \mathbf{X} \\ \mathbf{S} \\ \mathbf{U} \\ \mathbf{V} \end{bmatrix}.$$

If $\mathbf{A}$ is of order $m \times n$ [i.e., if (13.1) involves m inequalities in the n variables $x_1, x_2, \ldots, x_n$], then $\mathbf{I}_1$ and $\mathbf{I}_2$ are identity matrices of orders $m \times m$ and $n \times n$, respectively; $\mathbf{0}_1$, $\mathbf{0}_2$, and $\mathbf{0}_3$ are zero matrices of orders $m \times n$, $m \times m$, and $n \times m$, respectively; $\mathbf{S}$ is an m-dimensional vector of slack variables; and $\mathbf{U}$ and $\mathbf{V}$ are vectors of Lagrange multipliers, having n and m components, respectively (see Problem 13.8).

The Kuhn-Tucker conditions also require the optimal solution of (13.1) to satisfy the equation

$$\mathbf{U}^T \mathbf{X} + \mathbf{V}^T \mathbf{S} = 0 \qquad \text{or} \qquad \tilde{\mathbf{Y}}^T \mathbf{Y} = 0 \tag{13.3}$$

where

$$\tilde{\mathbf{Y}} \equiv \begin{bmatrix} \mathbf{U} \\ \mathbf{V} \\ \mathbf{X} \\ \mathbf{S} \end{bmatrix}.$$

Last, the Kuhn-Tucker conditions require that all variables be nonnegative; that is, $\mathbf{Y} \geq \mathbf{0}$.

THE METHOD OF FRANK AND WOLFE

This method is an eight-step algorithm for solving (13.2) and (13.3) based on the simplex method, which automatically keeps all variables nonnegative. New vectors $\mathbf{P}$ and $\mathbf{Y}_c$ (the current $\mathbf{Y}$-vector) are determined and then systematically updated until $\mathbf{Y}_c$ contains the optimal solution.

To employ the simplex method, one must have $\hat{\mathbf{B}}$ nonnegative. Therefore, if any component of $\hat{\mathbf{B}}$ is negative, the corresponding constraint equation must first be multiplied by -1.

STEP 1   Determine a basic feasible solution to (13.2) and designate it as both $\mathbf{Y}_c$ and $\mathbf{P}$. Such a solution can be found by adding an artificial variable to each constraint equation and then applying the two-phase method to *minimize M* times the sum of these artificial variables, where M denotes a very large, positive penalty cost. If an initial solution free of artificial variables cannot be obtained, then the original quadratic program has no solution.

STEP 2   Evaluate $\theta \equiv \tilde{\mathbf{P}}^T \mathbf{Y}_c$. If $\theta = 0$, then $\mathbf{X}^*$ is the first n components of $\mathbf{Y}_c$, and the program is solved. If $\theta \neq 0$, go to Step 3.

STEP 3   Use as the current objective

$$\text{maximize:} \quad z = -\tilde{\mathbf{P}}^T \mathbf{Y}$$

Apply *one* iteration of the simplex method to this objective coupled with the current set of basic variables and the constraint tableau that defined those variables. Designate the new solution as the updated $\mathbf{Y}_c$.

STEP 4   Evaluate $\theta_c \equiv \tilde{\mathbf{Y}}_c^T \mathbf{Y}_c$. If $\theta_c = 0$, then $\mathbf{X}^*$ is the first n components of $\mathbf{Y}_c$, and the program is solved. If $\theta_c \neq 0$, go to Step 5.

STEP 5   Evaluate $\tilde{\mathbf{P}}^T \mathbf{Y}_c$. If $\tilde{\mathbf{P}}^T \mathbf{Y}_c \leq \frac{1}{2}\theta$, go to Step 6. If not, return to Step 3 and perform another iteration of the simplex method.

STEP 6   Evaluate

$$\alpha \equiv \frac{\tilde{\mathbf{P}}^T (\mathbf{P} - \mathbf{Y}_c)}{(\tilde{\mathbf{P}} - \tilde{\mathbf{Y}}_c)^T (\mathbf{P} - \mathbf{Y}_c)}$$

If $\alpha \geq 1$, go to Step 7; if $\alpha < 1$, go to Step 8.

STEP 7   Set $\theta = \theta_c$, $\mathbf{P} = \mathbf{Y}_c$, and return to Step 3.

STEP 8   Calculate the vector $\mathbf{P} - \alpha(\mathbf{P} - \mathbf{Y}_c)$. Designate this vector as the updated $\mathbf{P}$ and return to Step 2.

AN APPLICATION TO PORTFOLIO ANALYSIS

A fixed sum of money, F, is to be spread among n different investments, each of which has a known history of returns. The portfolio problem is to determine how much money should be allocated to each investment so that the total expected return is greater than or equal to some lowest, acceptable amount, L, and so that the total variability in future payments is minimized.

Let x_i ($i = 1, 2, \ldots, n$) designate the amount of funds to be allocated to investment i, and let x_{ik} denote the return per dollar invested from investment i during the kth time period in the past ($k = 1, 2, \ldots, p$). If the past history of payments is indicative of future performance, the expected future return per dollar from investment i is

$$E_i = \frac{\sum_{k=1}^{p} x_{ik}}{p} \tag{13.4}$$

and the expected return from all investments combined is

$$E = E_1 x_1 + E_2 x_2 + \cdots + E_n x_n \tag{13.5}$$

As the measure of total variability in future payments, based on past returns, we choose the quantity

$$z = \frac{\sum_{k=1}^{p} (x_{1k}x_1 + x_{2k}x_2 + \cdots + x_{nk}x_n - E)^2}{p} \tag{13.6}$$

i.e., the average over the p past time periods of the squared deviation between the total return from an allocation $(x_1, x_2, \ldots, x_n)$ and the expected value of that total return. [In statistical terminology, the quantity (13.6) would be called the *variance* of the total return, and would be designated σ^2.] By substituting (13.5) into (13.6) and rearranging, we may simplify as follows:

$$z = \frac{1}{p} \sum_{k=1}^{p} [(x_{1k} - E_1)x_1 + (x_{2k} - E_2)x_2 + \cdots + (x_{nk} - E_n)x_n]^2$$

$$= \frac{1}{p} \sum_{k=1}^{p} \sum_{i=1}^{n} \sum_{j=1}^{n} (x_{ik} - E_i)(x_{jk} - E_j)x_i x_j \tag{13.7}$$

$$= \sum_{i=1}^{n} \sum_{j=1}^{n} \sigma_{ij}^2 x_i x_j$$

in which the *covariances* σ_{ij}^2 are given by

$$\sigma_{ij}^2 = \frac{1}{p} \sum_{k=1}^{p} (x_{ik} - E_i)(x_{jk} - E_j) = \frac{1}{p} \sum_{k=1}^{p} x_{ik}x_{jk} - \frac{1}{p^2} \left(\sum_{k=1}^{p} x_{ik} \right) \left(\sum_{k=1}^{p} x_{jk} \right) \tag{13.8}$$

From (13.6) it is apparent that z, as a sum of squares, is nonnegative for all values of $x_1, x_2, \ldots, x_n$. This means that the symmetric matrix $\mathbf{C} \equiv [\sigma_{ij}^2]$ in (13.7), the *covariance matrix*, is positive semi-definite.

The portfolio problem may thus be modeled by the quadratic program

$$\text{minimize:} \quad z = \sum_{i=1}^{n} \sum_{j=1}^{n} \sigma_{ij}^2 x_i x_j = \mathbf{X}^T \mathbf{C} \mathbf{X}$$

$$\text{subject to:} \quad x_1 + x_2 + \cdots + x_n = F \tag{13.9}$$

$$E_1 x_1 + E_2 x_2 + \cdots + E_n x_n \geq L$$

$$\text{with:} \quad \text{all variables nonnegative}$$

Program (13.9) will be infeasible if L is set too high.

Solved Problems

13.1 Put the following program in standard form:

$$\text{minimize:} \quad z = x_1^2 + 5x_2^2 + 10x_3^2 - 4x_1x_2 + 6x_1x_3 - 12x_2x_3 - 2x_1 + 10x_2 + 5x_3$$

$$\text{subject to:} \quad x_1 + 2x_2 + x_3 \geq 4$$

$$\text{with:} \quad \text{all variables nonnegative}$$

As was shown in Problem 12.10, this program is equivalent to

$$\text{maximize:} \quad z = -x_1^2 - 5x_2^2 - 10x_3^2 + 4x_1x_2 - 6x_1x_3 + 12x_2x_3 + 2x_1 - 10x_2 - 5x_3$$

$$\text{subject to:} \quad -x_1 - 2x_2 - x_3 \leq -4$$

$$\text{with:} \quad \text{all variables nonnegative}$$

or, in matrix form,

$$\text{maximize:} \quad z = [x_1, x_2, x_3] \begin{bmatrix} -1 & 2 & -3 \\ 2 & -5 & 6 \\ -3 & 6 & -10 \end{bmatrix} \begin{bmatrix} x_1 \\ x_2 \\ x_3 \end{bmatrix} + [2, -10, -5] \begin{bmatrix} x_1 \\ x_2 \\ x_3 \end{bmatrix}$$

$$\text{subject to:} \quad [-1, -2, -1] \begin{bmatrix} x_1 \\ x_2 \\ x_3 \end{bmatrix} \le -4 \tag{1}$$

$$\text{with:} \quad \mathbf{X} \ge \mathbf{0}$$

Program (1) is in standard form, (13.1), with

$$\mathbf{A} \equiv [-1, -2, -1] \qquad \mathbf{B} \equiv [-4] \qquad \mathbf{C} \equiv \begin{bmatrix} -1 & 2 & -3 \\ 2 & -5 & 6 \\ -3 & 6 & -10 \end{bmatrix} \qquad \mathbf{D} \equiv \begin{bmatrix} 2 \\ -10 \\ -5 \end{bmatrix} \tag{2}$$

Matrix $\mathbf{C}$ is negative semi-definite, as required; in fact, it is negative definite (see Theorem 11.1).

13.2 Determine the Kuhn-Tucker system for the standardized program of Problem 13.1.

For the matrices defined in (2) of Problem 13.1, (13.2) becomes

$$\begin{bmatrix} -1 & -2 & -1 & 1 & 0 & 0 & 0 & 0 \\ 2 & -4 & 6 & 0 & -1 & 0 & 0 & -1 \\ -4 & 10 & -12 & 0 & 0 & -1 & 0 & -2 \\ 6 & -12 & 20 & 0 & 0 & 0 & -1 & -2 \end{bmatrix} \begin{bmatrix} x_1 \\ x_2 \\ x_3 \\ s_1 \\ u_1 \\ u_2 \\ u_3 \\ v_1 \end{bmatrix} = \begin{bmatrix} -4 \\ 2 \\ -10 \\ -5 \end{bmatrix} \tag{1}$$

and (13.3) becomes

$$[u_1, u_2, u_3, v_1, x_1, x_2, x_3, s_1] \begin{bmatrix} x_1 \\ x_2 \\ x_3 \\ s_1 \\ u_1 \\ u_2 \\ u_3 \\ v_1 \end{bmatrix} = 0 \tag{2}$$

Equations (1) and (2), along with the condition that all variables be nonnegative, constitute the Kuhn-Tucker system.

13.3 Solve the program given in Problem 13.1.

The optimal solution to this program is embedded in the solution to the associated Kuhn-Tucker system; that system was obtained in Problem 13.2. We solve the Kuhn-Tucker system by the method of Frank and Wolfe.

As a preliminary step, we check whether $\hat{\mathbf{B}}$ is nonnegative. Since this is not the case, we multiply the first, third, and fourth constraint equations in (1) of Problem 13.2 by -1, obtaining

$$\begin{array}{rrrrrrrr} x_1 + & 2x_2 + & x_3 - s_1 & & & & & = 4 \\ 2x_1 - & 4x_2 + & 6x_3 & -u_1 & & & - v_1 & = 2 \\ 4x_1 - & 10x_2 + & 12x_3 & & +u_2 & & +2v_1 & = 10 \\ -6x_1 + & 12x_2 - & 20x_3 & & & +u_3 & + v_1 & = 5 \end{array}$$

STEP 1 To generate a basic feasible solution to the above set of equations, we could introduce an artificial variable in each equation and then minimize M times the sum of those artificial variables. Alternatively, we note that u_2 and u_3 can be used as basic variables to solve the last two equations ($u_2 = 10$ and $u_3 = 5$), so that artificial variables w_1 and w_2 need be added only to the first two equations, respectively. Doing so and then minimizing $Mw_1 + Mw_2$ by the two-phase method, we generate Tableaux 1, 2, and 3. (All calculations are rounded to four significant figures; pivot elements are starred.) An initial solution is read from Tableau 3 as

$$[0, 1.375, 1.25, 0, 0, 8.75, 13.5, 0]^T$$

which we designate as both the initial **P** and Y_c.

		x_1	x_2	x_3	s_1	u_1	u_2	u_3	v_1	w_1	w_2	
		0	0	0	0	0	0	0	0	M	M	
w_1	M	1	2	1	−1	0	0	0	0	1	0	4
w_2	M	2	−4	6*	0	−1	0	0	−1	0	1	2
u_2	0	4	−10	12	0	0	1	0	2	0	0	10
u_3	0	−6	12	−20	0	0	0	1	1	0	0	5
$(c_j - z_j)$:		0	0	0	0	0	0	0	0	0	0	0
		−3	2	−7	1	1	0	0	1	0	0	−6

Tableau 1

	x_1	x_2	x_3	s_1	u_1	u_2	u_3	v_1	w_1	
w_1	0.6667	2.667*	0	−1	0.1667	0	0	0.1667	0	3.667
x_3	0.3333	−0.6667	1	0	−0.1667	0	0	−0.1667	0	0.3333
u_2	0	−2	0	0	2	1	0	4	1	6
u_3	0.6660	−1.334	0	0	−3.334	0	1	−2.334	0	11.67
	0	0	0	0	0	0	0	0	0	0
	−0.6669	−2.667	0	1	−0.1669	0	0	−0.1669	0	−3.667

Tableau 2

	x_1	x_2	x_3	s_1	u_1	u_2	u_3	v_1	
x_2	0.2500	1	0	−0.3750	0.06250	0	0	0.06250	1.375
x_3	0.5000	0	1	−0.2500	−0.1250	0	0	−0.1250	1.250
u_2	0.5000	0	0	−0.7500	2.125	1	0	4.125	8.750
u_3	0.9995	0	0	−0.5003	−3.251	0	1	−2.251	13.50
	0	0	0	0	0	0	0	0	0

Tableau 3

STEP 2

$$\theta = \tilde{P}^T Y_c = [0, 8.75, 13.5, 0, 0, 1.375, 1.25, 0] \begin{bmatrix} 0 \\ 1.375 \\ 1.25 \\ 0 \\ 0 \\ 8.75 \\ 13.5 \\ 0 \end{bmatrix} = 57.81 \neq 0$$

STEP 3   The new objective is to *maximize*

$$z = -\bar{\mathbf{P}}^T \mathbf{Y} = -[0, 8.75, 13.5, 0, 0, 1.375, 1.25, 0] \begin{bmatrix} x_1 \\ x_2 \\ x_3 \\ s_1 \\ u_1 \\ u_2 \\ u_3 \\ v_1 \end{bmatrix}$$

$$= -0x_1 - 8.75x_2 - 13.5x_3 - 0s_1 - 0u_1 - 1.375u_2 - 1.25u_3 - 0v_1$$

Combining this objective function with both the constraint equations and basic variables given in Tableau 3, we generate Tableau 4. One iteration of the simplex method yields Tableau 5, from which we read the solution

$$[2.5, 0.75, 0, 0, 0, 7.5, 11, 0]^T$$

This vector becomes the updated $\mathbf{Y}_c$.

STEP 4

$$\theta_c = \bar{\mathbf{Y}}_c^T \mathbf{Y}_c = [0, 7.5, 11, 0, 2.5, 0.75, 0, 0] \begin{bmatrix} 2.5 \\ 0.75 \\ 0 \\ 0 \\ 0 \\ 7.5 \\ 11 \\ 0 \end{bmatrix} = 11.25 \neq 0$$

		x_1 0	x_2 −8.75	x_3 −13.50	s_1 0	u_1 0	u_2 −1.375	u_3 −1.250	v_1 0	
x_2	−8.75	0.2500	1	0	−0.3750	0.06250	0	0	0.06250	1.375
x_3	−13.50	0.5000*	0	1	−0.2500	−0.1250	0	0	−0.1250	1.250
u_2	−1.375	0.5000	0	0	−0.7500	2.125	1	0	4.125	8.750
u_3	−1.250	0.9995	0	0	−0.5003	−3.251	0	1	−2.251	13.50
$(z_j - c_j)$:		−10.87	0	0	8.313	2.283	0	0	−1.718	−57.81

Tableau 4

	x_1	x_2	x_3	s_1	u_1	u_2	u_3	v_1	
x_2	0	1	−0.5000	−0.2500	0.1250	0	0	0.1250	0.7500
x_1	1	0	2.000	−0.5000	−0.2500	0	0	−0.2500	2.500
u_2	0	0	−1.000	−0.5000	2.250	1	0	4.250*	7.500
u_3	0	0	−1.999	0.0006	−3.001	0	1	−2.001	11.00
	0	0	21.74	2.878	−0.4345	0	0	−4.436	−30.64

Tableau 5

	x_1	x_2	x_3	s_1	u_1	u_2	u_3	v_1	
x_2	0	1	−0.4706	−0.2353	0.05883	−0.02941	0	0	0.5294
x_1	1	0	1.941	−0.5294	−0.1177	0.05883	0	0	2.941
v_1	0	0	−0.2353	−0.1176	0.5294	0.2353	0	1	1.765
u_3	0	0	−2.470	−0.2347	−1.942	0.4708	1	0	14.53
	0	0	20.70	2.356	1.914	1.044	0	0	−22.81

Tableau 6

STEP 5

$$\tilde{\mathbf{P}}^T \mathbf{Y}_c = [0, 8.75, 13.5, 0, 0, 1.375, 1.25, 0] \begin{bmatrix} 2.5 \\ 0.75 \\ 0 \\ 0 \\ 0 \\ 0 \\ 7.5 \\ 11 \\ 0 \end{bmatrix} = 30.63$$

which is *not* less than or equal to

$$\tfrac{1}{2}\theta = \tfrac{1}{2}(57.81) = 28.91$$

STEP 3 Since **P** has not been updated, the objective remains unchanged and the tableau of interest remains Tableau 5. Applying one iteration of the simplex method to this tableau, we obtain Tableau 6. The solution defined by Tableau 6 becomes the updated $\mathbf{Y}_c$, namely

$$\mathbf{Y}_c = [2.941, 0.5294, 0, 0, 0, 0, 14.53, 1.765]^T$$

STEP 4

$$\theta_c = \tilde{\mathbf{Y}}_c^T \mathbf{Y}_c = [0, 0, 14.53, 1.765, 2.941, 0.5294, 0, 0] \begin{bmatrix} 2.941 \\ 0.5294 \\ 0 \\ 0 \\ 0 \\ 0 \\ 14.53 \\ 1.765 \end{bmatrix} = 0$$

Therefore, the first three components of $\mathbf{Y}_c$ constitute the optimal solution to the original minimization program; that is, $x_1^* = 2.941$, $x_2^* = 0.5294$, and $x_3^* = 0$, with $z^* = 3.235$. Compare with the solution found in Problem 12.10.

13.4 Determine the covariance matrix for the data in Table 13-1, which are returns (in cents) per dollar invested.

Table 13-1

	Years					
	1	2	3	4	5	6
Investment 1	0	20	0	20	0	20
Investment 2	0	0	30	0	0	30

To apply (*13.8*), it is convenient to retabulate the data as in Table 13-2.

Table 13-2

k	x_{1k}	x_{2k}	x_{1k}^2	x_{2k}^2	$x_{1k}x_{2k}$
1	0	0	0	0	0
2	20	0	400	0	0
3	0	30	0	900	0
4	20	0	400	0	0
5	0	0	0	0	0
6	20	30	400	900	600
TOTALS	60	60	1200	1800	600

Then,

$$\sigma_{11}^2 = \frac{1200}{6} - \frac{(60)^2}{36} = 100 \qquad \sigma_{22}^2 = \frac{1800}{6} - \frac{(60)^2}{36} = 200$$

$$\sigma_{12}^2 = \sigma_{21}^2 = \frac{600}{6} - \frac{(60)^2}{36} = 0$$

and the covariance matrix is

$$C = \begin{bmatrix} 100 & 0 \\ 0 & 200 \end{bmatrix}$$

13.5 Determine the covariance matrix for the data in Table 13-3, which are returns (in cents) per dollar invested.

Table 13-3

	Years				
	1	2	3	4	5
Investment 1	10	4	12	13	6
Investment 2	6	9	6	5	9
Investment 3	17	1	11	19	2

Proceed as in Problem 13.4.

Table 13-4

k	x_{1k}	x_{2k}	x_{3k}	x_{1k}^2	x_{2k}^2	x_{3k}^2	$x_{1k}x_{2k}$	$x_{1k}x_{3k}$	$x_{2k}x_{3k}$
1	10	6	17	100	36	289	60	170	102
2	4	9	1	16	81	1	36	4	9
3	12	6	11	144	36	121	72	132	66
4	13	5	19	169	25	361	65	247	95
5	6	9	2	36	81	4	54	12	18
TOTALS	45	35	50	465	259	776	287	565	290

From Table 13-4,

$$\sigma_{11}^2 = \frac{465}{5} - \frac{(45)^2}{25} = 12 \qquad \sigma_{12}^2 = \sigma_{21}^2 = \frac{287}{5} - \frac{(45)(35)}{25} = -5.6$$

$$\sigma_{22}^2 = \frac{259}{5} - \frac{(35)^2}{25} = 2.8 \qquad \sigma_{13}^2 = \sigma_{31}^2 = \frac{565}{5} - \frac{(45)(50)}{25} = 23$$

$$\sigma_{33}^2 = \frac{776}{5} - \frac{(50)^2}{25} = 55.2 \qquad \sigma_{23}^2 = \sigma_{32}^2 = \frac{290}{5} - \frac{(35)(50)}{25} = -12$$

and so

$$C = \begin{bmatrix} 12 & -5.6 & 23 \\ -5.6 & 2.8 & -12 \\ 23 & -12 & 55.2 \end{bmatrix}$$

13.6 An individual with \$10 000 to invest has identified three mutual funds as attractive opportunities. Over the last 5 years, dividend payments (in cents per dollar invested) have been as shown in Table 13-3, and the individual assumes that these payments are indicative of what can be expected in the future. This particular individual has two requirements: (1) the combined expected yearly return from his investments must be no less than $800 (the amount $10 000 would earn at 8 percent interest) and (2) the variance in future, yearly, dividend payments should be as small as possible. How much should this individual invest in each fund to achieve these requirements?

There are $p = 5$ time periods for which data are provided; from (13.4) or Table 13-4,

$$E_1 = \frac{45}{5} = 9 \, \text{¢/\$} \qquad E_2 = \frac{35}{5} = 7 \, \text{¢/\$} \qquad E_3 = \frac{50}{5} = 10 \, \text{¢/\$}$$

Here $F = \$10\,000$ and $L = \$800 = 80\,000\text{¢}$, so that the constraints in (13.9) become

$$x_1 + x_2 + x_3 = 10\,000$$
$$9x_1 + 7x_2 + 10x_3 \geq 80\,000 \tag{1}$$

Using the covariances calculated in Problem 13.5, we have for the objective:

$$\text{minimize:} \quad z = 12x_1^2 + 2.8x_2^2 + 55.2x_3^2 - 5.6x_1x_2$$
$$+ 23x_1x_3 - 5.6x_2x_1 - 12x_2x_3 + 23x_3x_1 - 12x_3x_2 \tag{2}$$

The system (1) and (2), augmented by nonnegativity conditions on each variable, constitutes a quadratic program which was put in standard form in Problem 12.11. Its solution, either by the method of Frank and Wolfe or from the Kuhn-Tucker conditions directly (Problem 12.33), is $x_1^* = x_2^* = \$5000$, $x_3^* = 0$. Consequently, the individual should divide funds evenly between the first two opportunities and not invest at all in the third.

13.7 A financial adviser must recommend a portfolio consisting of two investments to a client having $15 000 to invest. One investment returns 20 percent every other year, while the second investment returns 30 percent every third year. Determine the best investment mix for the portfolio if the client's only stipulation is that the combined, yearly, expected return vary as little as possible.

The relevant data for each investment are presented in Table 13-1. For these data,

$$E_1 = E_2 = \frac{60}{6} = 10 \, \text{¢/\$}$$

so that the total expected return is

$$E = E_1x_1 + E_2x_2 = 10(x_1 + x_2) = 10(15\,000) = 150\,000\text{¢}$$

regardless of the investment mix. Therefore, the sole constraint for the problem is

$$x_1 + x_2 = 15\,000 \tag{1}$$

In terms of the covariances calculated in Problem 13.4, the objective is to

$$\text{minimize:} \quad z = 100x_1^2 + 200x_2^2 \tag{2}$$

and we have the additional conditions

$$x_1, x_2 \geq 0 \tag{3}$$

The quadratic program (1), (2), (3) is easily solved (graphically or from the Kuhn-Tucker conditions), yielding $x_1^* = \$10\,000$, $x_2^* = \$5000$, with $z^* = 1.5 \times 10^{10}$ (in units of ¢^{2}).

13.8 Verify that the Kuhn-Tucker conditions for the program described in Problem 13.1 have the forms (13.2) and (13.3).

The Kuhn-Tucker conditions for this program were derived in Problem 12.10; in particular, in (8), (1) through (3), and (13). Setting $s_1 = x_4^2$, $v_1 = \lambda_1$, $u_1 = \lambda_2$, $u_2 = \lambda_3$, $u_3 = \lambda_4$, and rearranging, we can write these equations as

$$-x_1 - \ 2x_2 - \ x_3 + s_1 \qquad\qquad\qquad = -4$$
$$2x_1 - \ 4x_2 + \ 6x_3 \qquad - u_1 \qquad\quad - \ v_1 = \ \ 2$$
$$-4x_1 + 10x_2 - 12x_3 \qquad\qquad - u_2 \quad - 2v_1 = -10$$
$$6x_1 - 12x_2 + 20x_3 \qquad\qquad\qquad - u_3 - \ v_1 = \ -5$$

and

$$v_1 s_1 = 0$$
$$u_1 x_1 = 0$$
$$u_2 x_2 = 0$$
$$u_3 x_3 = 0$$

The first set of four equations is precisely (13.2), as shown by (1) of Problem 13.2.   The second set of four equations may be combined into the single equation

$$v_1 s_1 + u_1 x_1 + u_2 x_2 + u_3 x_3 = 0$$

which has the form (13.3), as shown by (2) of Problem 13.2.   Note that solving this one equation is equivalent to solving the four equations from which it came, since all the variables are required to be nonnegative.

Supplementary Problems

13.9   Put the following program in standard form:

$$\text{minimize:} \quad z = 24x_1^2 + 14x_2^2 + 46x_3^2 - 28x_1 x_2 - 24x_1 x_3 + 34x_2 x_3$$
$$\text{subject to:} \quad 11x_1 + 9x_2 + 12x_3 \ge 1000$$
$$x_2 + \ \ x_3 = \ \ \ 40$$

with: all variables nonnegative

13.10   Determine the Kuhn-Tucker system for the standardized program of Problem 13.9.

Use the method of Frank and Wolfe to solve Problems 13.11, 13.12, and 13.13.   Check your answer to Problem 13.12 by the graphical method.

13.11   Problem 13.9.

13.12
$$\text{maximize:} \quad z = -x_1^2 - 2x_2^2 + 2x_1 + 4x_2$$
$$\text{subject to:} \quad 2x_1 + \ x_2 \le 8$$
$$x_1 + 2x_2 \ge 2$$

with: x_1 and x_2 nonnegative

13.13
$$\text{maximize:} \quad z = 10x_1^2 + 20x_2^2 + 30x_3^2 + 10x_1 x_2 - 8x_1 x_3 - 6x_2 x_3 + x_1 + 2x_2 - x_3$$
$$\text{subject to:} \quad x_1 + 2x_2 + x_3 \le 10$$

with: all variables nonnegative

13.14 A corporation requires 6 million dollars to finance a new manufacturing process, and three different banks have agreed to supply all or part of this amount. Although each bank insists that the loan plus interest charges be repaid over 6 years, the repayment schedules differ from bank to bank, as shown in Table 13-5.

Table 13-5

	Percent of Principal To Be Repaid Each Year					
	Year 1	Year 2	Year 3	Year 4	Year 5	Year 6
Bank 1	0	0	30	40	50	55
Bank 2	5	15	25	35	40	45
Bank 3	40	40	0	35	15	15

The corporation feels it is advantageous to borrow in such a manner that the total yearly payments on the loan are as nearly equal as possible, yet it does not wish to pay more than 4 million dollars in total interest charges. Set up a mathematical program that will determine the amount of money to be borrowed from each bank, such that the corporation's objectives are realized.

13.15 By a known result in matrix algebra, the quadratic program *with equality constraints*,

$$\text{optimize:} \quad z = \mathbf{X}^T \mathbf{Q} \mathbf{X} + \mathbf{D}^T \mathbf{X}$$

$$\text{subject to:} \quad \mathbf{A} \mathbf{X} = \mathbf{B}$$

may be solved in closed form, provided $\mathbf{Q}$ is definite (negative definite for a maximization or positive definite for a minimization) and the rows of $\mathbf{A}$ are linearly independent. Explicitly,

$$z^* = \frac{\det \begin{bmatrix} \mathbf{A}\mathbf{Q}^{-1}\mathbf{A}^T & -(\mathbf{B} + \frac{1}{2}\mathbf{A}\mathbf{Q}^{-1}\mathbf{D}) \\ (\mathbf{B} + \frac{1}{2}\mathbf{A}\mathbf{Q}^{-1}\mathbf{D})^T & \mathbf{0}_{1\times 1} \end{bmatrix}}{\det \mathbf{A}\mathbf{Q}^{-1}\mathbf{A}^T} - \frac{1}{4}\mathbf{D}^T\mathbf{Q}^{-1}\mathbf{D}$$

with a more complicated expression for $\mathbf{X}^*$. Use this result to check the value of z^* in Problem 13.7.

13.16 Rework Problem 12.6, in the form

$$\text{maximize:} \quad 8 + z = -3x_1^2 - x_2^2 + 6x_1 - 2x_2$$

$$\text{subject to:} \quad 3x_1 + x_2 = 5$$

by use of Problem 13.15.

Chapter 14

Deterministic Dynamic Programming

MULTISTAGE DECISION PROCESSES

A *multistage decision process* is a process that can be separated into a number of sequential steps, or *stages*, which may be completed in one or more ways. The options for completing the stages are called *decisions*. A *policy* is a sequence of decisions, one for each stage of the process.

The condition of the process at a given stage is called the *state* at that stage; each decision effects a transition from the current state to a state associated with the next stage. A multistage decision process is *finite* if there are only a finite number of stages in the process and a finite number of states associated with each stage.

Many multistage decision processes have returns (costs or benefits) associated with each decision, and these returns may vary with both the stage and state of the process. The objective in analyzing such processes is to determine an *optimal policy*, one that results in the best total return.

Example 14.1 In Problem 1.15, the process of determining how much to invest in each opportunity in order to maximize the total return is a three-stage decision process. Consideration of opportunity i constitutes stage i ($i = 1, 2, 3$). The state of the process at stage i is the amount of funds still available for investment at stage i. For stage 1, the beginning of the process, there are 4 units of money available; hence the state is 4. For stages 2 and 3, the states can be 0, 1, 2, 3, or 4, depending on the allocations (decisions) at previous stages. The decision at stage i is represented by the variable x_i; the possible values of x_i are the integers from 0 to the state at stage i, inclusive.

An optimal policy for the process is determined in Problem 14.1.

A multistage decision process is *deterministic* if the outcome of each decision (in particular, the state produced by the decision) is known exactly. This chapter covers only those multistage processes which are both finite and deterministic. Finite, stochastic processes are discussed in Chapter 18; infinite processes are introduced in Chapter 20.

A MATHEMATICAL PROGRAM

The mathematical program

$$\text{optimize:} \quad z = f_1(x_1) + f_2(x_2) + \cdots + f_n(x_n)$$

$$\text{subject to:} \quad x_1 + x_2 + \cdots + x_n \le b \tag{14.1}$$

$$\text{with:} \quad \text{all variables nonnegative and integral}$$

in which $f_1(x_1), f_2(x_2), \ldots, f_n(x_n)$ are known (nonlinear) functions of a single variable and b is a known nonnegative integer, models an important class of multistage decision processes. Here the number of stages is n. Stage 1 involves the specification of decision variable x_1, with a resulting contribution $f_1(x_1)$ to the total return; etc. The states are $0, 1, 2, \ldots, b$, representing possible values for the number of units available for allocation. All stages after the first have these same states associated with them; stage 1 has the single state b.

Example 14.2 Program (*14.1*), with $n = 3$ and $b = 4$, models Problem 1.15.

DYNAMIC PROGRAMMING

Dynamic programming is an approach for optimizing multistage decision processes. It is based on Bellman's

Principle of optimality. An optimal policy has the property that, regardless of the decisions taken to enter a particular state in a particular stage, the remaining decisions must constitute an optimal policy for leaving that state.

To implement this principle, begin with the last stage of an n-stage process and determine for each state the *best policy for leaving that state and completing the process*, assuming that all preceding stages have been completed. Then move backwards through the process, stage by stage. At each stage, determine the best policy for leaving each state and completing the process, assuming that all preceding stages have been completed and making use of the results already obtained for the succeeding stage. In doing so, the entries of Table 14-1 will be calculated, where

$u \equiv$ the state variable, whose values specify the states

$m_j(u) \equiv$ optimum return from completing the process beginning at stage j in state u

$d_j(u) \equiv$ decision taken at stage j that achieves $m_j(u)$

Table 14-1

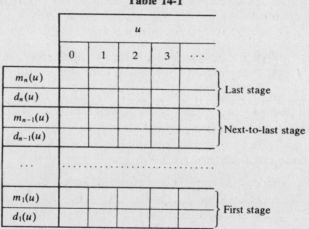

The entries corresponding to the last stage of the process, $m_n(u)$ and $d_n(u)$, are generally straightforward to compute. (See Problems 14.1 and 14.3.) The remaining entries are obtained recursively; that is, the entries for the jth stage ($j = 1, 2, \ldots, n-1$) are determined as functions of the entries for the $(j+1)$st stage. The recursion formula is problem dependent, and must be obtained anew for each different type of multistage process. (See Problems 14.5 and 14.8.)

For simplicity, Table 14-1 has been drawn as though each stage had the same set of states. While this can always be brought about artificially (by suitably penalizing the return functions m_j), it is often more natural to use different state variables, each with its own range of values, for the different stages. Such use, of course, in no way alters the application of the principle of optimality. (See Problems 14.19 and 14.20.)

The dynamic programming approach is particularly well suited to those processes modeled by system (*14.1*)—processes in which each decision pays off separately, independent of previous decisions. For system (*14.1*), the values of $m_n(u)$ for $u = 0, 1, \ldots, b$ are given by the formula

$$m_n(u) = \operatorname*{optimum}_{0 \leq x \leq u} \{f_n(x)\} \tag{14.2}$$

The recursion formula is (see Problem 14.1)

$$m_j(u) = \operatorname*{optimum}_{0 \leq x \leq u} \{f_j(x) + m_{j+1}(u - x)\} \tag{14.3}$$

for $j = n - 1, n - 2, \ldots, 1$. In ($14.2$), the decision variable x [which is denoted x_n in (14.1)] runs through integral values, as does x ($\equiv x_j$) in (14.3). That value of x which yields the optimum in (14.2) is taken as $d_n(u)$, and that value of x which yields the optimum in (14.3) is taken as $d_j(u)$. If more than one value of x yields either optimum, arbitrarily choose one as the optimal decision. The optimal solution to program (14.1) is $z^* = m_1(b)$, the optimal return from completing the process beginning at stage 1 with b units available for allocation. With z^* determined, the optimal decisions $x_1^*, x_2^*, \ldots, x_n^*$ are found sequentially from

$$
\begin{aligned}
x_1^* &= d_1(b) \\
x_2^* &= d_2(b - x_1^*) \\
x_3^* &= d_3(b - x_1^* - x_2^*) \\
&\cdots\cdots\cdots\cdots\cdots\cdots\cdots\cdots\cdots\cdots \\
x_n^* &= d_n(b - x_1^* - x_2^* - \cdots - x_{n-1}^*)
\end{aligned}
\tag{14.4}
$$

DYNAMIC PROGRAMMING WITH DISCOUNTING

If money earns interest at the rate i per period, an amount $P(n)$ due n periods in the future has the *present* (or *discounted*) *value*

$$
P(0) = \alpha^n P(n) \qquad \text{where} \qquad \alpha \equiv \frac{1}{1+i}
\tag{14.5}
$$

Discounting, the replacement of all dollar sums in the future by their present values, is often incorporated in those multistage decision processes in which the stages represent time periods and the objective is to optimize a monetary quantity. In the solution by dynamic programming, the recurrence formula for $m_j(u)$, the best return beginning in stage j and state u, involves terms of the form $m_{j+c}(y)$, the best return beginning in stage $j + c$ (c time periods after stage j) and state y. [See, for example, (14.3).] If $m_{j+c}(y)$ is multiplied by α^c, where α is the above-defined *discount factor*, then $m_{j+c}(y)$ is discounted to its present value at the beginning of stage j. It follows that $m_1(u)$ will be discounted to the beginning of stage 1, which is the start of the process. (See Problem 14.10.)

Solved Problems

14.1 Determine an optimal policy for Problem 1.15 (see Example 14.1).

We begin by considering the last stage of the process, stage 3, under the assumption that all previous stages, stages 1 and 2, have been completed. That is, allocations to investments 1 and 2 have been made (although, at this time, we do not know what they are), and we are to complete the process by allocating units of money to investment 3. Since we do not know how many units were allocated to the first two investments, we do not know how many units are available for investment 3; we must therefore consider all possibilities. There will be either 0, 1, 2, 3, or 4 units available.

No matter how many units of money are available at stage 3, it is clear from the definition of $f_3(x)$ in Table 1-2 that the best way to complete the process is to allocate all the available units to investment 3. The same conclusion follows from applying (14.2). Thus,

$$m_3(4) = \max\{f_3(0), f_3(1), f_3(2), f_3(3), f_3(4)\}$$
$$= \max\{0, 1, 4, 5, 8\} = 8 \quad \text{with} \quad d_3(4) = 4$$
$$m_3(3) = \max\{f_3(0), f_3(1), f_3(2), f_3(3)\}$$
$$= \max\{0, 1, 4, 5\} = 5 \quad \text{with} \quad d_3(3) = 3$$
$$m_3(2) = \max\{f_3(0), f_3(1), f_3(2)\}$$
$$= \max\{0, 1, 4\} = 4 \quad \text{with} \quad d_3(2) = 2$$
$$m_3(1) = \max\{f_3(0), f_3(1)\} = \max\{0, 1\} = 1 \quad \text{with} \quad d_3(1) = 1$$
$$m_3(0) = \max\{f_3(0)\} = \max\{0\} = 0 \quad \text{with} \quad d_3(0) = 0$$

These results give us the first two rows in the tabular solution, Table 14-2.

Table 14-2

	u				
	0	1	2	3	4
$m_3(u)$	0	1	4	5	8
$d_3(u)$	0	1	2	3	4
$m_2(u)$	0	1	4	6	8
$d_2(u)$	0	1	0	3	0
$m_1(u)$	$\cdots$	$\cdots$	$\cdots$	$\cdots$	9
$d_1(u)$	$\cdots$	$\cdots$	$\cdots$	$\cdots$	2

Having completed stage 3, we next consider stage 2 under the assumption that stage 1 has been completed (although, at this time, we do not know how). Since we do not know how many units were allocated to investment 1, we do not know how many units are available for investment 2; we must therefore consider all possibilities.

One possibility is that 4 units are available at stage 2, which presupposes that no units were allocated to investment 1. Now, all or some of these 4 units can be allocated to investment 2, with the remainder available for stage 3. If x of these 4 units are allocated to investment 2, the return is $f_2(x)$, and the remaining $4 - x$ units are available for stage 3. But we have already found the best continuation from stage 3 when $4 - x$ units are at hand; namely, $m_3(4 - x)$. The total return, therefore, is $f_2(x) + m_3(4 - x)$; and the value of x $(x = 0, 1, 2, 3, 4)$ that maximizes this total return represents the optimal decision at stage 2 with 4 units available. Formula (*14.3*), with $j = 2$ and $u = 4$, simply formalizes this conclusion.

$$m_2(4) = \max\{f_2(0) + m_3(4 - 0), f_2(1) + m_3(4 - 1), f_2(2) + m_3(4 - 2), f_2(3) + m_3(4 - 3), f_2(4) + m_3(4 - 4)\}$$
$$= \max\{0 + 8, 1 + 5, 3 + 4, 6 + 1, 7 + 0\} = 8 \quad \text{with} \quad d_2(4) = 0.$$

Similarly treating the other possibilities at stage 2, we obtain:

$$m_2(3) = \max\{f_2(0) + m_3(3 - 0), f_2(1) + m_3(3 - 1), f_2(2) + m_3(3 - 2), f_2(3) + m_3(3 - 3)\}$$
$$= \max\{0 + 5, 1 + 4, 3 + 1, 6 + 0\} = 6 \quad \text{with} \quad d_2(3) = 3$$
$$m_2(2) = \max\{f_2(0) + m_3(2 - 0), f_2(1) + m_3(2 - 1), f_2(2) + m_3(2 - 2)\}$$
$$= \max\{0 + 4, 1 + 1, 3 + 0\} = 4 \quad \text{with} \quad d_2(2) = 0$$
$$m_2(1) = \max\{f_2(0) + m_3(1 - 0), f_2(1) + m_3(1 - 1)\}$$
$$= \max\{0 + 1, 1 + 0\} = 1 \quad \text{with} \quad d_2(1) = 1 \quad \text{(breaking the tie arbitrarily)}$$
$$m_2(0) = \max\{f_2(0) + m_3(0 - 0)\} = \max\{0 + 0\} = 0 \quad \text{with} \quad d_2(0) = 0$$

Collecting the calculations for stage 2, we obtain the third and fourth rows of Table 14-2.

Having completed stage 2, we now turn to stage 1. There is only one state associated with this stage, $u = 4$.

$$m_1(4) = \max \{f_1(0) + m_2(4-0),\ f_1(1) + m_2(4-1),\ f_1(2) + m_2(4-2),\ f_1(3) + m_2(4-3),\ f_1(4) + m_2(4-4)\}$$

$$= \max \{0+8,\ 2+6,\ 5+4,\ 6+1,\ 7+0\} = 9 \qquad \text{with} \quad d_1(4) = 2$$

With these data we complete Table 14-2.

The maximum return that can be realized from this three-stage investment program beginning with 4 units is $m_1(4) = 9$ units. To achieve this return, allocate $d_1(4) = 2$ units to investment 1, leaving $4 - 2 = 2$ units for stage 2. But $d_2(2) = 0$, indicating that no units should be expended at this stage if only 2 units are available. Thus, 2 units remain for stage 3. Since $d_3(2) = 2$, both units should be allocated to investment 3. These conclusions are formalized by equations (14.4). The optimal policy, therefore, is to allocate 2 units to investment 1, 0 units to investment 2, and 2 units to investment 3.

14.2 An independent trucker has $8\,m^3$ of available space on a truck scheduled to depart for New York City. A distributor with large quantities of three different appliances, all destined for New York City, has offered the trucker the following fees to transport as many items as the truck can accommodate:

Appliance	Fee, $/item	Volume, m^3/item
I	11	1
II	32	3
III	58	5

How many items of each appliance should the trucker accept to maximize shipping fees without exceeding the truck's available capacity?

This problem can be viewed as a three-stage process, involving allocations of space to appliances I, II, and III, respectively. It can be modeled by program (14.1), with $n = 3$, $b = 8$, if x_j $(j = 1, 2, 3)$ is defined as the *number of cubic meters of appliance j* to be shipped, and if $f_j(x_j)$, the return from allocating x_j to stage j, is defined by Table 14-3. The state at a given stage is the number of cubic meters of space still unoccupied.

Table 14-3

f \ x	0	1	2	3	4	5	6	7	8
$f_1(x)$	0	11	22	33	44	55	66	77	88
$f_2(x)$	0	0	0	32	32	32	64	64	64
$f_3(x)$	0	0	0	0	0	58	58	58	58

The first row of Table 14-3 is straightforward, since each additional cubic meter allocated to appliance I brings an additional $11 return. To generate the second row of the table, note that each appliance II occupies $3\,m^3$, so that until at least $3\,m^3$ of space is available, no item of this type can be shipped and no return realized. If 3, 4, or $5\,m^3$ is allocated to appliance II, only one item can be accommodated, for a net return of $32. If 6, 7 or $8\,m^3$ is allocated, then two items can be shipped, for a net return of $64. A similar analysis holds for appliance III. No return is realized until at least $5\,m^3$ is allocated to it; and if 5, 6, 7, or $8\,m^3$ is allocated, then only one appliance III can be shipped, for a net return of $58.

The model, program (14.1), is solved by use of (14.2) and (14.3), exactly as in Problem 14.1. The results are exhibited in Table 14-4; all ties were broken by choosing the *smallest* maximizing x as $d_j(u)$. Table 14-4 shows that the best total return the trucker can obtain, starting stage 1 with $8\,m^3$ of available space, is $m_1(8) = \$91$.   To achieve this, 3 m^3 $[d_1(8) = 3]$ must be allocated to appliance I, leaving 5 m^3 for the following stages.   No volume should be allocated to appliance II $[d_2(5) = 0]$, leaving 5 m^3 for stage 3, all of which should be assigned to appliance III $[d_3(5) = 5]$.   In terms of items, the trucker should take three items of appliance I and one item of appliance III.

Table 14-4

	u								
	0	1	2	3	4	5	6	7	8
$m_3(u)$	0	0	0	0	0	58	58	58	58
$d_3(u)$	0	0	0	0	0	5	5	5	5
$m_2(u)$	0	0	0	32	32	58	64	64	90
$d_2(u)$	0	0	0	3	3	0	6	6	3
$m_1(u)$	...	...	...	...	...	...	...	...	91
$d_1(u)$	...	...	...	...	...	...	...	...	3

14.3   Convert the following program into system (*14.1*):

$$\text{maximize:} \quad z = 11y_1 + 32y_2 + 58y_3$$

$$\text{subject to:} \quad y_1 + 3y_2 + 5y_3 \leq 8 \tag{1}$$

$$\text{with:} \quad \text{all variables nonnegative and integral}$$

This program is a mathematical model for Problem 14.2 if we designate y_j $(j = 1, 2, 3)$ as the *number of items* (in contrast to the number of cubic meters) of appliance j to be shipped.   The linear constraint models the volume limitation, the coefficient of y_j being the volume per item of appliance j.   As was shown in Problem 14.2, a mathematical model for this program in the form of (*14.1*)—which has *unit coefficients* in the inequality constraint—is obtained if new variables x_j are defined to denote the number of cubic meters of each appliance to be shipped.   We then have

$$\text{maximize:} \quad z = f_1(x_1) + f_2(x_2) + f_3(x_3)$$

$$\text{subject to:} \quad x_1 + x_2 + x_3 \leq 8 \tag{2}$$

$$\text{with:} \quad \text{all variables nonnegative and integral}$$

where the return functions $f_j(x)$ are defined by Table 14-3.

Observe that (*1*) is *not* taken into the form (*14.1*) by the linear transformation

$$x_1 = y_1 \qquad x_2 = 3y_2 \qquad x_3 = 5y_3$$

Although this transformation produces the desired type of objective function and the desired type of inequality constraint, it maps the set of nonnegative integer points (y_1, y_2, y_3) into a *subset* of the nonnegative integer points (x_1, x_2, x_3).   One needs precisely the functions $f_j(x)$ defined in Problem 14.2 to make possible the expansion of this subset into the whole set.

14.4   Convert the following program into system (*14.1*):

$$\text{maximize:} \quad z = g_1(y_1) + g_2(y_2) + g_3(y_3) + g_4(y_4)$$

$$\text{subject to:} \quad 2y_1 + y_2 + 6y_3 + 3y_4 \leq 9$$

$$\text{with:} \quad \text{all variables nonnegative and integral}$$

where the $g_j(y)$ $(j = 1, 2, 3, 4)$ are defined in Table 14-5.

Table 14-5

y \ g	0	1	2	3	4	5	6	7	8	9
$g_1(y)$	0	4	8	11	14	17	19	21	22	23
$g_2(y)$	0	2	4	6	8	10	12	14	16	18
$g_3(y)$	0	1	2	3	6	8	11	15	20	26
$g_4(y)$	0	1	7	9	14	16	21	23	25	27

Mimicking the approach used in Problem 14.3, we think of y_j as the *number of items of product j* to be shipped in a certain truck. Table 14-5 then represents a schedule of shipping fees, while the linear constraint models the limitation on the total volume that can be accommodated, 9 units. The coefficient of y_j in this constraint is interpreted as the volume occupied by one item of product j (see Table 14-6).

Table 14-6

Product	1	2	3	4
Volume/Item	2	1	6	3

We now designate new variables x_j $(j = 1, 2, 3, 4)$ as the *number of units of volume of product j* to be shipped. Program (*1*) is equivalent to the following program of the form (*14.1*):

$$\text{maximize:} \quad z = f_1(x_1) + f_2(x_2) + f_3(x_3) + f_4(x_4)$$

$$\text{subject to:} \quad x_1 + x_2 + x_3 + x_4 \le 9 \tag{2}$$

$$\text{with:} \quad \text{all variables nonnegative and integral}$$

where $f_j(x_j)$ denotes the return from allocating x_j units of volume to product j. These functions are derived from Tables 14-5 and 14-6; for example,

$$f_4(7) = \text{return from shipping 7 units of volume of product 4}$$
$$= \text{return from shipping 2 items of product 4, since each}$$
$$\text{item of product 4 requires 3 units of volume}$$
$$= g_4(2) = 7$$

Continuing in this fashion, we complete Table 14-7.

Table 14-7

x \ f	0	1	2	3	4	5	6	7	8	9
$f_1(x)$	0	0	4	4	8	8	11	11	14	14
$f_2(x)$	0	2	4	6	8	10	12	14	16	18
$f_3(x)$	0	0	0	0	0	0	1	1	1	1
$f_4(x)$	0	0	0	1	1	1	7	7	7	9

14.5 *Establish a recursion formula analogous to* (*14.3*) *for the following problem.* A small firm can manufacture up to four computers weekly, and has agreed to deliver in each of the next 4 weeks three, two, four, and two computers, respectively. Production costs are a function of the number of computers manufactured, and are given (in thousands of dollars) as follows:

Units Produced, x	0	1	2	3	4
Cost, $f(x)$	4	13	19	27	32

Computers can be delivered to customers at the end of the same week in which they are manufactured, or they can be stored for future delivery at a cost of $4000 per week. Because of limited warehouse facilities, the company can store no more than three computers at a time. Current inventory is zero, and the firm desires no inventory at the end of week 4. How many computers should the firm manufacture in each of the next 4 weeks to meet all demands at a minimum total cost?

As shown in Chapter 9, production problems of this sort are modeled as transportation problems. Such models do not have the form (14.1); hence (14.3) is not applicable. Production problems are, however, multistage decision processes that can be solved by dynamic programming.

The present production problem is a four-stage process, with stage j representing the jth week ($j = 1, 2, 3, 4$). The state u at stage j is the number of computers in inventory at the beginning of week j. Let

$m_j(u) \equiv$ the minimum cost of completing the production schedule beginning at stage j in state u

$d_j(u) \equiv$ the production schedule for stage j that achieves $m_j(u)$

$\quad D_j \equiv$ the demand in stage j

$I_j(u) \equiv$ the inventory cost charged against stage j when the state is u

$f_j(x) \equiv$ the cost of producing x computers in stage j

Consider the case where the company enters stage j with u computers in inventory. The company may produce any number of computers up to its capacity during this stage, provided the sum of its production level and its inventory level is at least as large as the demand D_j. Any amount in excess of D_j is stored in inventory for the next stage. In particular, if x computers are produced in stage j, a production cost $f_j(x)$ is incurred. The u units in stock generate a storage cost of $I_j(u)$, for a total cost in period j of $f_j(x) + I_j(u)$. This leaves $u + x - D_j$ units in inventory for stage $j + 1$, and the minimum cost for completing the process at that point is $m_{j+1}(u + x - D_j)$. Hence the total cost for completing the process beginning at stage j with a production schedule of x units is $f_j(x) + I_j(u) + m_{j+1}(u + x - D_j)$. The best decision for stage j with u units in stock is to produce that amount x which minimizes this cost. Accordingly, for $j = 1, 2, 3$,

$$m_j(u) = \min_x \{f_j(x) + I_j(u) + m_{j+1}(u + x - D_j)\}$$

$$= I_j(u) + \min_x \{f_j(x) + m_{j+1}(u + x - D_j)\} \tag{1}$$

wherein x runs through the values $0, 1, 2, 3, 4$. To guarantee that

$$0 \le u + x - D_j \le 3 \quad \text{(storage capacity)}$$

we set $m_{j+1}(u)$ equal to a prohibitively large penalty cost, M, whenever $u < 0$ or $u > 3$.

For the problem at hand, both the inventory costs and the production costs are independent of the stage, and are given respectively by $I_j(u) = 4u$ (thousand-dollar units) and $f_j(x) = f(x)$, as defined in the production cost table. The demands are $D_1 = 3$, $D_2 = 2$, $D_3 = 4$, and $D_4 = 2$. Relation (1) simplifies to

$$m_j(u) = 4u + \min_{x=0,1,2,3,4} \{f(x) + m_{j+1}(u + x - D_j)\} \tag{2}$$

14.6   Solve the problem formulated in Problem 14.5.

There are either zero, one, two, or three computers in stock at the beginning of week 4. Since no inventory is desired at the end of week 4, the optimal decision at stage 4 is to produce only that portion of the fourth week's demand, $D_4 = 2$, that cannot be met from inventory. Difficulty arises only if the incoming inventory is three computers, which exceeds the demand. To prevent this situation in the final policy, we assign it a very high penalty cost to completion, 1000 (thousand-dollar units). The cost to completion for all other states is the holding cost of the current inventory plus the production cost of the shortfall between demand and inventory. Thus,

$$m_4(3) = 1000$$

$$m_4(2) = \text{storage cost of two computers and production cost of zero computers}$$
$$= 4(2) + 4 = 12 \quad \text{with} \quad d_4(2) = 0$$

$$m_4(1) = \text{storage cost of one computer and production cost of one computer}$$
$$= 4(1) + 13 = 17 \quad \text{with} \quad d_4(1) = 1$$

$$m_4(0) = \text{storage cost of zero computers and production cost of two computers}$$
$$= 4(0) + 19 = 19 \quad \text{with} \quad d_4(0) = 2$$

Collecting these results, we have the first two rows of Table 14-8. The remaining entries are obtained by stepwise application of (2) of Problem 14.5, for $j = 3, 2, 1$. Again, $M = 1000$ is used to rule out impossible inventory states.

Table 14-8

	\multicolumn{4}{c}{u}			
	0	1	2	3
$m_4(u)$	19	17	12	1000
$d_4(u)$	2	1	0	$\cdots$
$m_3(u)$	51	50	46	44
$d_3(u)$	4	3	2	1
$m_2(u)$	70	68	63	66
$d_2(u)$	2	1	0	0
$m_1(u)$	97	$\cdots$	$\cdots$	$\cdots$
$d_1(u)$	3	$\cdots$	$\cdots$	$\cdots$

It follows from Table 14-8 that the minimum production cost for completing the entire process beginning at stage 1 with 0 units in inventory is

$$m_1(0) = \$97\,000$$

To achieve this, the company must produce $d_1(0) = 3$ computers in the first week, all of which are shipped immediately to customers. The company then enters week 2 with an inventory of zero, and must produce $d_2(0) = 2$ computers, which again just meets demand. The optimal production level for stage 3 with zero computers in inventory is $d_3(0) = 4$, thereby exactly meeting demand; and the optimal production level for stage 4 with zero computers in storage is $d_4(0) = 2$. Thus, the optimal policy is to produce exactly the number of computers needed to satisfy the demand and never to have any in inventory.

14.7   A manufacturer has an order from a railroad for 12 diesels to be delivered three per year for the next 4 years. Production data are displayed in Table 14-9. Diesels can be delivered at the end of the same year in which they are produced, or they can be stored by the manufacturer, at a cost of $30 000 per diesel per year, for shipment during a later year. Currently the manufacturer has one diesel in stock and would like to build this inventory to three at the end of four years. Determine a production schedule which will meet all requirements at a minimum total cost.

Table 14-9

	Years			
	1	2	3	4
Production Capacity (regular shift)	1	2	3	4
Production Capacity (overtime shift)	2	2	3	2
Cost per Diesel (regular shift)	$350 000	$370 000	$395 000	$420 000
Cost per Diesel (overtime shift)	$375 000	$400 000	$430 000	$465 000

We solve this problem by dynamic programming, using the notation and recursion formula (1) developed in Problem 14.5. There are four stages (years) to consider, with the decisions being the specifications of the production levels for the stages. The production capacity at each stage is the sum of the capacities for the regular and overtime shifts for that year. Setting $f_j(x) = M$, a very large penalty cost, if a level x cannot be met in stage j, we reformulate the production data as Table 14-10, with all costs given in thousand-dollar units.

Table 14-10

x / f	0	1	2	3	4	5	6
$f_1(x)$	0	350	725	1100	M	M	M
$f_2(x)$	0	370	740	1140	1540	M	M
$f_3(x)$	0	395	790	1185	1615	2045	2475
$f_4(x)$	0	420	840	1260	1680	2145	2610

A final inventory of three diesels is most easily ensured by increasing the demand in the last stage by three. Thus, $D_1 = D_2 = D_3 = 3$, while $D_4 = 6$. The maximum possible inventory at any stage is five diesels, achieved at the end of stage 3 under conditions of maximum production at all stages. Consequently, we take the states to be $u = 0, 1, 2, 3, 4, 5$, and define $I_j(u) \equiv 30u$ (independent of j). Also we set $m_{j+1}(u) = M$ $(j = 1, 2, 3)$ whenever $u > 5$ or $u < 0$.

Stage 4 If u diesels are in stock at the beginning of this stage, there is a holding charge of $30u$ thousand dollars. Then the minimum-cost decision for completing the process is to manufacture

$$d_4(u) = D_4 - u = 6 - u$$

diesels at a cost of $f_4(6 - u)$. The minimum cost to completion is

$$m_4(u) = 30u + f_4(6 - u)$$

These are the entries in the first two rows of Table 14-11.

The remainder of Table 14-11 is obtained from the recursion formula, (1) of Problem 14.5, in which the minimization is over $x = 0, \ldots, 6$. Ties for $d_2(2)$, $d_2(1)$, and $d_2(0)$ were broken by choosing the smallest minimizing x in each case. It is seen that the minimum total cost to complete the process is $m_1(1) = \$5\,680\,000$. To achieve this cost, a production run of two diesels is required for stage 1 [$d_1(1) = 2$], leaving nothing in storage; a production run of three diesels is required for stage 2 [$d_2(0) = 3$], leaving nothing in storage; a production run of five diesels is necessary for stage 3 [$d_3(0) = 5$], leaving two diesels in inventory; and a production run of four diesels is required for the last stage [$d_4(2) = 4$].

Table 14-11

	u					
	0	1	2	3	4	5
$m_4(u)$	2610	2175	1740	1350	960	570
$d_4(u)$	6	5	4	3	2	1
$m_3(u)$	3785	3385	2985	2620	2255	1890
$d_3(u)$	5	4	3	2	1	0
$m_2(u)$	4925	4555	4185	3815	3475	3135
$d_2(u)$	3	2	2	2	1	0
$m_1(u)$	$\cdots$	5680	$\cdots$	$\cdots$	$\cdots$	$\cdots$
$d_1(u)$	$\cdots$	2	$\cdots$	$\cdots$	$\cdots$	$\cdots$

14.8 *Establish a recursion formula for solving the following problem by dynamic programming.* A vending machine company currently operates a 2-year-old machine at a certain location. Table 14-12 gives estimates of upkeep, replacement cost, and income (all in dollars) for any machine at this location, as functions of the age of the machine.

Table 14-12

	Age, u					
	0	1	2	3	4	5
Income, $I(u)$	10 000	9500	9200	8500	7300	6100
Maintenance, $M(u)$	100	400	800	2000	2800	3300
Replacement, $R(u)$	$\cdots$	3500	4200	4900	5800	5900

As a matter of policy, no machine is ever kept past its sixth anniversary and replacements are only with new machines. Determine a replacement policy that will maximize the total profit from this one location over the next 4 years.

This equipment replacement problem is a four-stage process, with each stage representing a year in the time period under consideration. The states at a given stage are the possible ages of the machine entering that stage, i.e., $u = 1, \ldots, 5$. At each stage, the decision variable has only two values, which may be denoted KEEP (retain the current machine) and BUY (replace the current machine with a new machine). Define

$m_j(u) \equiv$ the maximum profit to be achieved beginning at stage j in state u

$d_j(u) \equiv$ the decision at stage j that achieves $m_j(u)$

and let the functions $I(u)$, $M(u)$, and $R(u)$ be defined by Table 14-12. If the company enters stage j with a u-year-old machine and decides to KEEP the machine, it will cost the firm $M(u)$ to maintain the machine, for a yearly profit of $I(u) - M(u)$. The firm will then enter the next stage with a $(u + 1)$-year-old machine, and the best profit it can achieve with it (and its possible successors) is $m_{j+1}(u + 1)$. Thus, the overall profit to completion is

$$I(u) - M(u) + m_{j+1}(u + 1) \qquad (1)$$

If instead the company decides to sell the u-year-old machine at stage j and to BUY a new machine, it incurs a replacement cost of $R(u)$. The new machine is 0 years old, so it will generate income $I(0)$ and cost $M(0)$ to maintain. The yearly profit would be $I(0) - M(0) - R(u)$. The firm then enters the next stage with a 1-year-old machine, and the best subsequent profit it can achieve is $m_{j+1}(1)$. In this case, the overall profit to completion is

$$I(0) - M(0) - R(u) + m_{j+1}(1) \tag{2}$$

The optimal decision at stage j produces the larger of the quantities (1) and (2); that is,

$$m_j(u) = \max\{I(u) - M(u) + m_{j+1}(u+1),\ I(0) - M(0) - R(u) + m_{j+1}(1)\} \tag{3}$$

14.9   Solve the problem formulated in Problem 14.8.

We observe that, beginning stage 1 with a 2-year-old machine, it is impossible to enter stage j ($j = 1, \ldots, 4$) with a machine older than $j + 1$ or of age j. Therefore, we will set $m_j(u) = -M$, a very large negative return, whenever $u > j + 1$ or $u = j$.

Stage 4   Formula (3) of Problem 14.8 also holds for $j = 4$ if we define $m_5(u) \equiv 0$. Thus,

$$m_4(5) = \max\{I(5) - M(5),\ I(0) - M(0) - R(5)\}$$
$$= \max\{6100 - 3300,\ 10\,000 - 100 - 5900\} = 4000 \qquad \text{with} \quad d_4(5) = \text{BUY}$$

$$m_4(4) = -M$$

$$m_4(3) = \max\{I(3) - M(3),\ I(0) - M(0) - R(3)\}$$
$$= \max\{8500 - 2000,\ 10\,000 - 100 - 4900\} = 6500 \qquad \text{with} \quad d_4(3) = \text{KEEP}$$

$$m_4(2) = \max\{I(2) - M(2),\ I(0) - M(0) - R(2)\}$$
$$= \max\{9200 - 800,\ 10\,000 - 100 - 4200\} = 8400 \qquad \text{with} \quad d_4(2) = \text{KEEP}$$

$$m_4(1) = \max\{I(1) - M(1),\ I(0) - M(0) - R(1)\}$$
$$= \max\{9500 - 400,\ 10\,000 - 100 - 3500\} = 9100 \qquad \text{with} \quad d_4(1) = \text{KEEP}$$

These results constitute the first two rows of Table 14-13.

Table 14-13

	u				
	1	2	3	4	5
$m_4(u)$	9100	8400	6500	$-M$	4000
$d_4(u)$	KEEP	KEEP	KEEP	$\cdots$	BUY
$m_3(u)$	17 500	14 900	$-M$	13 200	$-M$
$d_3(u)$	KEEP	KEEP	$\cdots$	BUY	$\cdots$
$m_2(u)$	24 000	$-M$	22 500	$-M$	$-M$
$d_2(u)$	KEEP	$\cdots$	BUY	$\cdots$	$\cdots$
$m_1(u)$	$\cdots$	30 900	$\cdots$	$\cdots$	$\cdots$
$d_1(u)$	$\cdots$	KEEP	$\cdots$	$\cdots$	$\cdots$

The remaining entries in Table 14-13 are obtained by sequential application of the recursion formula for $j = 3, 2, 1$, with returns from impossible states penalized as previously stipulated. It follows from Table 14-13 that the company can achieve a maximum total profit of \$30 900 over the next 4 years, beginning with a 2-year-old machine. To do so, it should keep the current machine for one more year, then buy a new machine and keep it for the remainder of the time period.

14.10 Solve the problem described in Problem 14.8 if the objective is to maximize the total *discounted* profit over the next 4 years under an effective interest rate of 10 percent per annum.

Without discounting, the recursion formula for the optimal profit is (3) of Problem 14.8. In terms of present values for stage j, the formula becomes

$$m_j(u) = \max \{I(u) - M(u) + \alpha m_{j+1}(u+1), \; I(0) - M(0) - R(u) + \alpha m_{j+1}(1)\} \qquad (1)$$

Here

$$\alpha = \frac{1}{1 + 0.10} = 0.90909091$$

We solve (1) by the same procedure as employed in Problem 14.9. The solution is presented in Table 14-14. Comparing with Table 14-13, we see that *in this case* discounting has not changed the optimal policy—it is still KEEP, BUY, KEEP, KEEP—but has reduced the optimal profit to $26 777.

Table 14-14

	u				
	1	2	3	4	5
$m_4(u)$	9100	8400	6500	$-M$	4000
$d_4(u)$	KEEP	KEEP	KEEP	$\cdots$	BUY
$m_3(u)$	16 736	14 309	$-M$	12 373	$-M$
$d_3(u)$	KEEP	KEEP	$\cdots$	BUY	$\cdots$
$m_2(u)$	22 108	$-M$	20 215	$-M$	$-M$
$d_2(u)$	KEEP	$\cdots$	BUY	$\cdots$	$\cdots$
$m_1(u)$	$\cdots$	26 777	$\cdots$	$\cdots$	$\cdots$
$d_1(u)$	$\cdots$	KEEP	$\cdots$	$\cdots$	$\cdots$

Supplementary Problems

14.11 David Jeremy, a certified public accountant, has offers from three different clients for his services. Each client would like Mr. Jeremy to work for him on a full-time basis; however, each client is willing to employ Mr. Jeremy for as many days of the week as he is prepared to give, for the fees shown in Table 14-15. How many days should Mr. Jeremy devote to each client to maximize his weekly income?

Table 14-15

Number of Days	Client 1, $	Client 2, $	Client 3, $
0	0	0	0
1	100	125	150
2	250	250	300
3	400	375	400
4	525	500	550
5	600	625	650

14.12　Redo Problem 14.11 under the additional constraint that Mr. Jeremy work at least 1 day per week for each client. (*Hint*: Penalize the possibility of working 0 days for any client.)

14.13　A cargo barge capable of transporting up to 10 tons of material has requests from four companies to carry their merchandise from St. Louis to New Orleans. Each company can supply as much merchandise as the barge captain is willing to accept. The merchandise must be shipped in unit amounts; Table 14-16 gives the shipping fees.

Table 14-16

Company	Weight of Merchandise, tons/item	Shipping Fee, $/item
I	1	10
II	2	25
III	3	45
IV	4	60

How many items of each company's merchandise should the barge captain accept to maximize the total shipping fees without exceeding the barge's capacity?

14.14　Use dynamic programming to solve Problem 1.16, under the additional constraint that games be produced in whole numbers. (*Hint*: Count time in half-hour units.)

14.15

$$\text{maximize:}\quad z = 5x_1^2 + 5x_2^3 + 3x_3$$

$$\text{subject to:}\quad 3x_1 + 4x_2 + x_3 \le 11$$

$$\text{with:}\quad \text{all variables nonnegative and integral}$$

14.16　Use dynamic programming to solve Problem 1.8.

14.17　Use dynamic programming to solve Problem 9.10.

14.18　Obtain a recursion formula for, and then solve, the problem described in Problem 14.8, if, in addition to either keeping the current machine or buying a new model, the company may also purchase a used machine younger than its current model. Take the cost of replacing a u-year-old machine by an x-year-old machine to be the difference between the costs of their replacement by a new machine. For example, the cost of replacing a 3-year-old machine by a 1-year-old machine is $4900 - $3500 = $1400.

14.19　*Establish a recursion formula for, and then solve, the following problem.* A small construction company currently has a 1-year-old dump truck. Estimates of its upkeep, replacement costs, and the revenues it can be expected to generate, together with similar data for new trucks that may be purchased in the future, are given in Table 14-17; all amounts are in units of $1000. Trucks are never kept more than 3 years, and replacements are only with new models. Determine a maximum-profit replacement policy for this company over the next 5 years.

Table 14-17

	Age	Revenue	Upkeep	Replacement
Current Model	1	20	8	18
	2	17	11	25
	3	...	...	35
New Model	0	21	1	6
	1	20	8	19
	2	17	11	26
	3	...	...	36
Next Year's Model	0	21	1	6
	1	17	7	18
	2	15	12	26
	3	...	...	36
Model Two Years Hence	0	22	2	7
	1	19	8	19
	2	17	12	24
	3	...	...	37
Model Three Years Hence	0	24	3	6
	1	18	4	12
	2	15	11	27
	3	...	...	37
Model Four Years Hence	0	25	3	6
	1	19	5	13
	2	14	10	27
	3	...	...	38

14.20 Solve the 3×3 assignment problem, with cost matrix

		Jobs	
	1	**2**	**3**
Workers 1	c_{11}	c_{12}	c_{13}
2	c_{21}	c_{22}	c_{23}
3	c_{31}	c_{32}	c_{33}

(see Chapter 9), by dynamic programming. For larger matrices, would this approach rival the Hungarian method?

14.21 Solve Problem 14.7 with discounting, if the effective interest rate is 7 percent per annum.

14.22 Solve Problem 14.18 with discounting, if the effective interest rate is 8 percent per annum.

Chapter 15

Network Analysis

NETWORKS

A *network* is a set of points, called *nodes*, and a set of curves, called *branches* (or *arcs* or *links*), that connect certain pairs of nodes. Only those networks will be considered here in which a given pair of nodes is joined by at most one branch. We denote nodes by uppercase letters and branches by the nodes they connect.

Example 15.1 Figure 15-1 is a network consisting of five nodes, labeled A through E, and six branches defined by the curves AB, AC, AD, BC, CD, and DE.

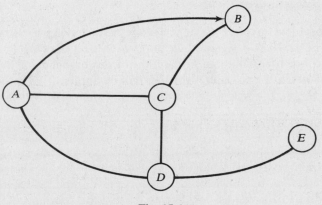

Fig. 15-1

A branch is *oriented* if it has a direction associated with it. Schematically, directions are indicated by arrows. The arrow on branch AB in Fig. 15-1 signifies that this branch is directed from A to B. Any movement along this branch must originate at A and terminate at B; movement from B to A is not permitted.

Two branches are *connected* if they have a common node. In Fig. 15-1, branches AB and AC are connected, but branches AB and CD are not connected. A *path* is a sequence of connected branches such that in the alternation of nodes and branches no node is repeated. A network is *connected* if for each pair of nodes in the network there exists at least one path joining the pair. If the path is unique for each pair of nodes, the connected network is called a *tree*. Equivalently, a tree is a connected network having one more node than branch.

Example 15.2 In Fig. 15-1, $\{ED, DA, AB\}$ is a path, but the sequence of connected branches $\{CA, AD, DC, CB\}$ is not a path, as node C occurs in it twice. The network is connected, and remains connected even if branches DA and AB are deleted. If, however, DE were deleted, the network would not be connected, since there would not be a path linking D with E. Because D and C are joined by three paths, the network is not a tree.

169

MINIMUM-SPAN PROBLEMS

A minimum-span problem involves a set of nodes and a set of *proposed* branches, none of them oriented. Each proposed branch has a nonnegative cost associated with it. The objective is to construct a connected network that contains all the nodes and is such that the sum of the costs associated with those branches actually used is a minimum. We shall suppose that there are enough proposed branches to ensure the existence of a solution.

It is not hard to see that a minimum-span problem is always solved by a tree. (If two nodes in a connected network are joined by two paths, one of these paths must contain a branch whose removal does not disconnect the network. Removing such a branch can only lower the total cost.) A minimal spanning tree may be found by initially selecting any one node and determining which branch incident on the selected node has the smallest cost. This branch is accepted as part of the final network. The network is then completed iteratively. At each stage of the iterative process, attention is focused on those nodes already linked together. All branches linking these nodes to unconnected nodes are considered, and the cheapest such branch identified. Ties are broken arbitrarily. This branch is accepted as part of the final network. The iterative process terminates when all nodes have been linked. (See Problems 15.1 and 15.2.)

If the costs are all distinct (this can always be brought about by infinitesimal changes), it can be proved that the minimal spanning tree is unique and is produced by the above algorithm for any choice of the starting node.

SHORTEST-ROUTE PROBLEMS

A shortest-route problem involves a connected network having a nonnegative cost associated with each branch. One node is designated as the *source*, and another node is designated as the *sink*. (These terms do not here imply an orientation of the branches of the network; they merely suggest the direction in which the solution algorithm will be applied.) The objective is to determine a path joining the source and the sink such that the sum of the costs associated with the branches in the path is a minimum.

Cheapest-path problems are solved by the following algorithm, in the application of which all ties are to be broken arbitrarily.

STEP 1   Construct a master list by tabulating under each node, in ascending order of cost, the branches incident on it. Each branch under a given node is written with that node as its first node. Omit from the list any branch having the source as its second node or having the sink as its first node.

STEP 2   Star the source and assign it the value 0. Locate the cheapest branch incident on the source and circle it. Star the second node of this branch and assign this node a value equal to the cost of the branch. Delete from the master list all other branches that have the newly starred node as second node.

STEP 3   If the newly starred node is the sink, go to Step 5. If not, go to Step 4.

STEP 4   Consider all starred nodes having uncircled branches under them in the current master list. For each one, add the value assigned to the node to the cost of the cheapest uncircled branch under it. Denote the smallest of these sums as M, and circle that branch whose cost contributed to M. Star the second node of this branch and assign it the value M. Delete from the master list all other branches having this newly starred node as second node. Go to Step 3.

STEP 5 z^* is the value assigned to the sink. A minimum-cost path is obtained recursively, beginning with the sink, by including in the path each circled branch whose second node belongs to the path.

(See Problems 15.3 and 15.4.) From the operation of Step 4, we can see that the set of circled branches produced by the algorithm constitutes a subtree of the original network, having the property that the unique distance (cost) in the subtree between the source and another node is equal to the shortest distance between these two nodes in the original network. In general, however, the subtree will not span the network.

MAXIMAL-FLOW PROBLEMS

The objective in a maximal-flow problem is to develop a shipping schedule that maximizes the amount of material sent between two points. The point of origin is called the *source*; the destination is called the *sink*. Various shipping lanes exist which link the source and sink directly or via intermediate locations called *junctions*. It is assumed that junctions cannot store material; that is, any material arriving at a junction is shipped immediately to another location.

A maximal-flow problem can be modeled by a network. The source, sink, and junctions are represented by nodes, while the branches represent the conduits through which material is transported. Associated with each node N and each branch NM emanating from N is a nonnegative number, or *capacity*, representing the maximum amount of material that can be shipped through NM from N.

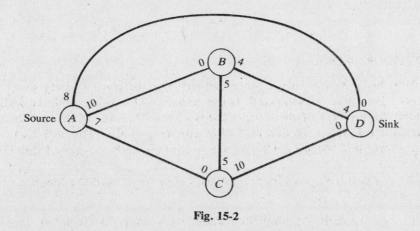

Fig. 15-2

EXAMPLE 15.3 Figure 15-2 is a network having A as the source, D as the sink, and B and C as junctions. The capacities of each branch for flows in the two directions are indicated near the ends of the branch. Note that 7 units can be shipped from A to C along AC, but 0 units can be shipped in the opposite direction; this asymmetry allows us, if we wish, to define an orientation of AC. In contrast, flows along BC can move in either direction, with a capacity of 5 units either way.

Maximal-flow problems are solved by the following algorithm:

STEP 1 Find a path from source to sink that can accommodate a positive flow of material. If none exists, go to Step 5.

STEP 2 Determine the maximum flow that can be shipped along this path and denote it by k.

STEP 3 Decrease the direct capacity (i.e., the capacity in the direction of flow of the k units) of each branch of this path by k and *increase* the reverse capacity by k. Add k units to the amount delivered to the sink.

STEP 4 Go to Step 1.

STEP 5 The maximal flow is the amount of material delivered to the sink. The optimal shipping schedule is determined by comparing the original network with the final network. Any reduction in capacity signifies a shipment.

(See Problems 15.6 and 15.7.)

FINDING A POSITIVE-FLOW PATH

The difficult aspect of the maximal-flow algorithm is Step 1—identifying a path from source to sink with positive flow capacity.   To discover such a path, first connect to the source all nodes that can be reached by a single branch having positive flow capacity in the forward direction (the direction out of the source).   Connect these nodes to all *new* nodes that can be reached by single branches having positive forward capacities.   Continue this process until either the sink is reached—in which case an appropriate path has been identified—or no new nodes can be reached from existing ones and the sink has not been reached—in which case no appropriate path exists.   (See Problem 15.5.)

Solved Problems

15.1   Solve the minimum-span problem for the network given in Fig. 15-3.   The numbers on the branches represent the costs of including the branches in the final network.

We arbitrarily choose *A* as our starting node and consider all branches incident on it; they are *AE*, *AB*, *AD*, and *AC*, with costs 10, 2, 1, and 4, respectively.   Since *AD* is the cheapest, we add this branch to the solution, as shown in Fig. 15-4(*a*).   Nodes *A* and *D* are now connected.

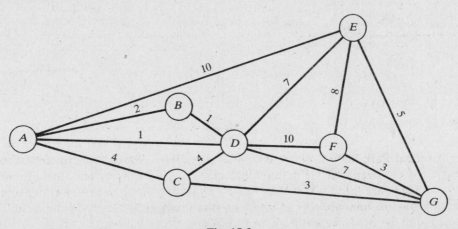

Fig. 15-3

We next consider all branches incident on either *A* or *D* that connect to other nodes.   Such branches are *AE*, *AB*, *AC*, *DB*, *DE*, *DF*, *DG*, and *DC*, with costs 10, 2, 4, 1, 7, 10, 7, and 4, respectively.   Since *DB* is the cheapest to include, we adjoin it to Fig. 15-4(*a*) and obtain Fig. 15-4(*b*).   The connected nodes are now *A*, *B*, and *D*.

We next consider all branches incident on *A*, *B*, or *D* that connect to other nodes.   These are *AE*, *AC*, *DE*, *DF*, *DG*, and *DC*, with costs 10, 4, 7, 10, 7, and 4.   The cheapest branch of interest is either *AC* or *DC*.   We arbitrarily select *DC* and adjoin it to Fig. 15-4(*b*) to obtain Fig. 15-4(*c*).

Continuing in this manner, we obtain sequentially Figs. 15-4(*d*) through 15-4(*f*).   Figure 15-4(*f*) contains all the nodes; hence it is a minimal-span network.   The minimum cost for connecting the network is

$$z^* = 1 + 1 + 4 + 3 + 3 + 5 = 17$$

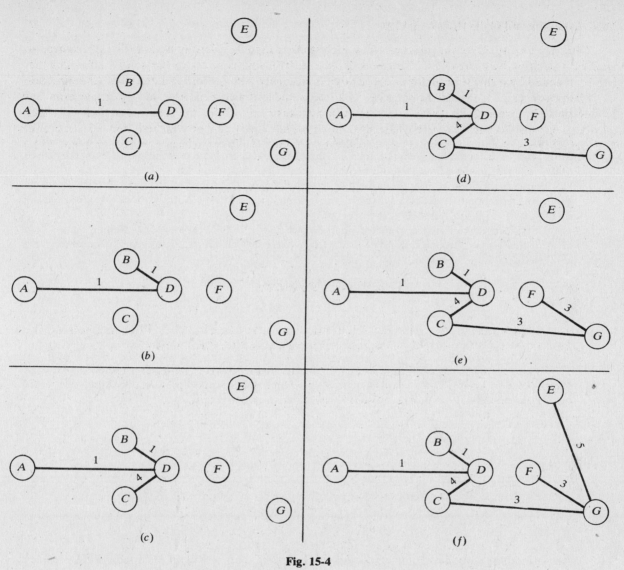

Fig. 15-4

15.2 The National Park Service plans to develop a wilderness area for tourism. Four locations in the area are designated for automobile access. These sites, and the distances (in miles) between them, are listed in Table 15-1. To inflict the least harm on the environment, the Park Service wants to minimize the miles of roadway required to provide the desired accessibility. Determine how roads should be built to achieve this objective.

Table 15-1

	Park Entrance	Wild Falls	Majestic Rock	Sunset Point	The Meadow
Park Entrance	· · ·	7.1	19.5	19.1	25.7
Wild Falls	7.1	· · ·	8.3	16.2	13.2
Majestic Rock	19.5	8.3	· · ·	18.1	5.2
Sunset Point	19.1	16.2	18.1	· · ·	17.2
The Meadow	25.7	13.2	5.2	17.2	· · ·

This is a minimum-span problem. The nodes are the four locations to be developed and the park entrance, while the proposed branches are the possible roadways linking the sites. The costs are the mileages. The complete network is shown in Fig. 15-5, where each site is represented by the first letter of its name.

We arbitrarily select Park Entrance as the initial node. The costs of the branches incident on this node are listed in the first row of Table 15-1. Since the lowest cost is 7.1, we add the branch from Park Entrance to Wild Falls to the network.

We next consider all branches joining either Park Entrance or Wild Falls to a new site. These are the branches from Park Entrance to Majestic Rock, Sunset Point, and The Meadow, as well as those from Wild Falls to the same three sites. Of these, the cheapest branch is the one from Wild Falls to Majestic Rock; so we adjoin it to the network.

We next consider all branches to either Sunset Point or The Meadow from either Park Entrance, Wild Falls, or Majestic Rock. Of these, the branch from Majestic Rock to The Meadow has the smallest cost; so it too is added to the network.

At this stage, the only unconnected site is Sunset Point. The cheapest branch linking Sunset Point to any other site is the one from Wild Falls. Adjoining this branch to the network, we arrive at Fig. 15-6, having a minimal cost of

$$z^* = 7.1 + 8.3 + 5.2 + 16.2 = 36.8 \text{ mi}$$

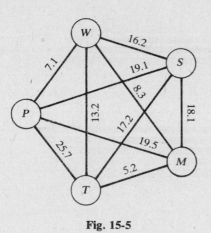

Fig. 15-5

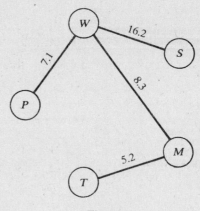

Fig. 15-6

15.3 An individual who lives in Ridgewood, New Jersey, and works in Whippany, New Jersey, seeks a car route that will minimize the morning driving time. This person has recorded driving times (in minutes) along major highways between different intermediate cities; these data are shown in Table 15-2. A blank entry signifies that no major highway directly links the corresponding points. Determine the best commuting route for this individual.

Table 15-2

	Ridgewood	Clifton	Orange	Troy Hills	Parsippany	Whippany
Ridgewood	· · ·	18	· · ·	32	· · ·	· · ·
Clifton	18	· · ·	12	28	· · ·	· · ·
Orange	· · ·	12	· · ·	17	· · ·	32
Troy Hills	32	28	17	· · ·	4	17
Parsippany	· · ·	· · ·	· · ·	4	· · ·	11
Whippany	· · ·	· · ·	32	17	11	· · ·

This situation may be modeled as a shortest-route problem. The nodes are the cities, the branches are the connecting highways, and the costs associated with the branches are the travel times. The source is Ridgewood, and the sink is Whippany.

STEP 1 The master list is shown in Fig. 15-7(*a*), with each city represented by the first letter in its name. Branches *CR* and *TR* are absent under *C* and *T*, respectively; these appear, as *RC* and *RT*, under the source only. Similarly, no branches are listed with the sink as first node.

STEP 2 We star the source node, *R*, and assign it the value 0. The cheapest branch leaving *R* is *RC*; so we star *C* and assign it the value 18, the cost of *RC*. We circle branch *RC* and then delete from Fig. 15-7(*a*) all other branches whose second node is *C*, i.e., *OC* and *TC*. The new master list is Fig. 15-7(*b*).

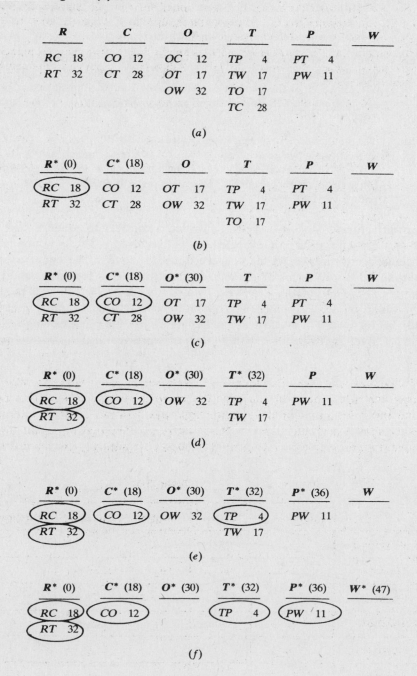

R	C	O	T	P	W
RC 18	CO 12	OC 12	TP 4	PT 4	
RT 32	CT 28	OT 17	TW 17	PW 11	
		OW 32	TO 17		
			TC 28		

(*a*)

R* (0)	C* (18)	O	T	P	W
RC 18	CO 12	OT 17	TP 4	PT 4	
RT 32	CT 28	OW 32	TW 17	PW 11	
			TO 17		

(*b*)

R* (0)	C* (18)	O* (30)	T	P	W
RC 18	CO 12	OT 17	TP 4	PT 4	
RT 32	CT 28	OW 32	TW 17	PW 11	

(*c*)

R* (0)	C* (18)	O* (30)	T* (32)	P	W
RC 18	CO 12	OW 32	TP 4	PW 11	
RT 32			TW 17		

(*d*)

R* (0)	C* (18)	O* (30)	T* (32)	P* (36)	W
RC 18	CO 12	OW 32	TP 4	PW 11	
RT 32			TW 17		

(*e*)

R* (0)	C* (18)	O* (30)	T* (32)	P* (36)	W* (47)
RC 18	CO 12		TP 4	PW 11	
RT 32					

(*f*)

Fig. 15-7

STEP 4 The starred nodes are R and C. The sums of interest are $0 + 32 = 32$ under R, obtained by adding the value of R to the cost of RT, and $18 + 12 = 30$ under C, obtained by adding the value of C to the cost of CO. Since 30 is the smaller sum, we circle CO, star O, assign O the value 30, and delete from Fig. 15-7(b) all other branches having O as second node, i.e., TO. The result is Fig. 15-7(c).

STEP 4 The starred nodes are R, C, and O. The sums of interest are $0 + 32 = 32$ under R, $18 + 28 = 46$ under C, and $30 + 17 = 47$ under O. The smallest sum is 32; hence we circle RT, star T, assign T the value 32, and delete from Fig. 15-7(c) all other branches with second node T. The result is Fig. 15-7(d).

STEP 4 The only starred nodes having uncircled branches under them in the current master list, Fig. 15-7(d), are O and T. For these nodes, the sums of interest are $30 + 32 = 62$ and $32 + 4 = 36$, respectively. Therefore, we circle TP, star P, assign P the value 36, and delete all other branches with second node P, of which there are none. The new master list is Fig. 15-7(e).

STEP 4 The only starred nodes having uncircled branches under them in the new master list are O, T, and P. The sums of interest are, respectively, $30 + 32 = 62$, $32 + 17 = 49$, and $36 + 11 = 47$. Since 47 is the smallest, we circle PW, star W (the sink), assign W the value 47, and delete from Fig. 15-7(e) all other branches having W as second node. The result is Fig. 15-7(f).

STEP 5 The minimum driving time from Ridgewood to Whippany is $z^* = 47$ min. To identify the optimal path, we search Fig. 15-7(f) for a circled branch having W as second node; it is PW. Next we search for a circled branch having P as second node; it is TP. Then we search for a circled branch having T as second node; it is RT. Since R is the source, the desired path is $\{RT, TP, PW\}$.

15.4 A manufacturing concern has been awarded a contract to produce casings. The contract is for 4 years and it is not expected to be renewed. The production process requires a specialized machine which the concern does not have. The concern can buy the machine, maintain it for the 4 years of the contract, and then sell it for scrap value; or it can replace the machine at the end of any given year by a new model. New models require less maintenance than older ones. Estimated net operating cost (purchase price plus maintenance minus trade-in) for buying a machine in the beginning of year i and trading it in at the beginning of year j is given in Table 15-3, with all figures expressed in thousand-dollar units.

Table 15-3

i \ j	1	2	3	4	5
1	$\cdots$	12	19	33	49
2	$\cdots$	$\cdots$	14	23	38
3	$\cdots$	$\cdots$	$\cdots$	16	26
4	$\cdots$	$\cdots$	$\cdots$	$\cdots$	13

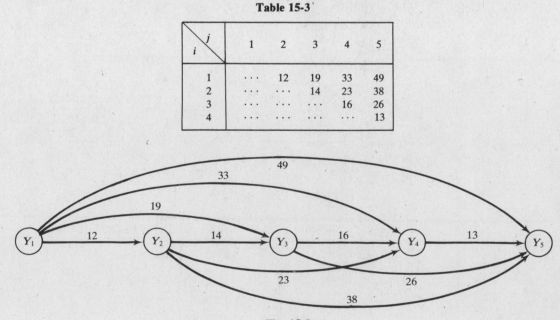

Fig. 15-8

Determine a replacement policy that will minimize the total operating cost for the machine over the life of the contract.

This problem can be solved by dynamic programming; alternatively, it can be modeled as a shortest-route problem on an *oriented* network.   We let nodes $Y_1, \ldots, Y_4$ represent the beginnings of the years of the contract, and Y_5 the beginning of the fifth year.   An oriented branch from Y_i to Y_j signifies purchase of a machine at the beginning of year i and trade-in or scrapping of the machine at the beginning of year j.   The cost associated with each branch is the net operating cost.   The network is shown in Fig. 15-8.

The master list for this oriented network is given in Fig. 15-9(a).   Applying the cheapest-path algorithm to it, we obtain successively Figs. 15-9(b) through 15-9(e).   From Fig. 15-9(e).

$$z^* = 45 \text{ (thousand dollars)}$$

The optimal path is found as $\{Y_1 Y_3, Y_3 Y_5\}$.   This path represents the policy of buying a machine at the beginning of year 1, trading it in for a new machine at the beginning of year 3, and finally scrapping the 2-year-old machine at the beginning of year 5.

Y_1	Y_2	Y_3	Y_4	Y_5
Y_1Y_2 12	Y_2Y_3 14	Y_3Y_4 16	Y_4Y_5 13	
Y_1Y_3 19	Y_2Y_4 23	Y_3Y_5 26		
Y_1Y_4 23	Y_2Y_5 38			
Y_1Y_5 49				

(a)

Y_1^* (0)	Y_2^* (12)	Y_3	Y_4	Y_5
⟨Y_1Y_2 12⟩	Y_2Y_3 14	Y_3Y_4 16	Y_4Y_5 13	
Y_1Y_3 19	Y_2Y_4 23	Y_3Y_5 26		
Y_1Y_4 33	Y_2Y_5 38			
Y_1Y_5 49				

(b)

Y_1^* (0)	Y_2^* (12)	Y_3^* (19)	Y_4	Y_5
⟨Y_1Y_2 12⟩	Y_2Y_4 23	Y_3Y_4 16	Y_4Y_5 13	
⟨Y_1Y_3 19⟩	Y_2Y_5 38	Y_3Y_5 26		
Y_1Y_4 33				
Y_1Y_5 49				

(c)

Y_1^* (0)	Y_2^* (12)	Y_3^* (19)	Y_4^* (33)	Y_5
⟨Y_1Y_2 12⟩	Y_2Y_5 38	Y_3Y_5 26	Y_4Y_5 13	
⟨Y_1Y_3 19⟩				
⟨Y_1Y_4 33⟩				
Y_1Y_5 49				

(d)

Y_1^* (0)	Y_2^* (12)	Y_3^* (19)	Y_4^* (33)	Y_5^* (45)
⟨Y_1Y_2 12⟩		⟨Y_3Y_5 26⟩		
⟨Y_1Y_3 19⟩				
⟨Y_1Y_4 33⟩				

(e)

Fig. 15-9

15.5 In Fig. 15-10, identify a path from source A to sink G that can accommodate positive flow.

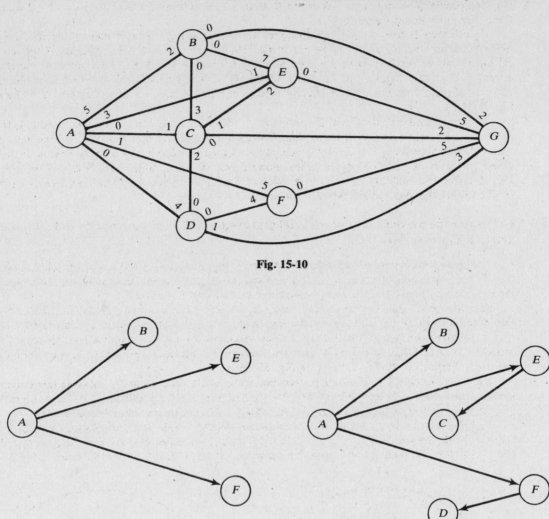

Fig. 15-10

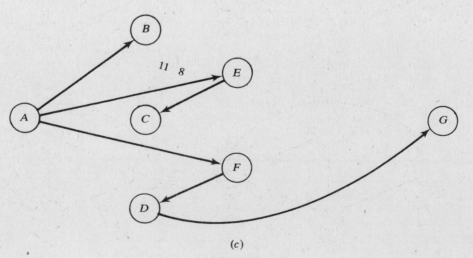

Fig. 15-11

We begin with the source and find all nodes that can be reached directly from A along branches allowing positive flow out of A. They are B, E, and F, as indicated in Fig. 15-11(a). Next we consider these three new nodes successively.

Focusing on B first, we identify all nodes *not shown* in Fig. 15-11(a) that can be reached from B along branches allowing positive flow out of B. There are none such. Focusing on E, we see that A, B, and C can be reached along branches allowing positive flow out of E; but since A and B already appear in Fig. 15-11(a), only C is added. From F, nodes A and D can be reached along branches allowing positive flow; but since A already appears in Fig. 15-11(a), we add only node D. The result is Fig. 15-11(b).

We now consider nodes C and D successively. Focusing on C first, we determine that A, B, E, and D all can be reached directly from C along branches with positive flow out of C. Since each of these nodes already appears in Fig. 15-11(b), we make no adjustments to it and consider next node D. From D, we can reach A and G along branches allowing positive flow. Since only G is new, we adjoin it to Fig. 15-11(b), obtaining Fig. 15-11(c). It follows from this last figure that $\{AF, FD, DG\}$ is a path from source to sink that can accommodate a positive flow (of 1 unit).

15.6 Determine the maximal flow of material that can be sent from source A to sink D through the network shown in Fig. 15-2.

One path from source to sink is the branch AD linking these two nodes directly. It can accommodate 8 units. Shipping this amount, we deliver 8 units to D, decrease the capacity of AD by 8, and increase the capacity of DA by 8. The resulting network is shown in Fig. 15-12(a).

Another path from source to sink that can accommodate positive flow is $\{AC, CB, BD\}$. The maximum amount of material that can be sent along this path is 4 units, the capacity of BD. Making such a shipment, we increase the supply at D by 4 units to $8 + 4 = 12$. Simultaneously, we decrease the capacities of AC, CB, and BD by 4 units and increase by this same amount the capacities of CA, BC, and DB. Figure 15-12(a) then becomes Fig. 15-12(b).

Path $\{AC, CD\}$ in Fig. 15-12(b) can accommodate 3 units from A to D. Making this shipment, we increase the supply at D by 3 units to $12 + 3 = 15$, and decrease the capacities of AC and CD by 3. We also increase by 3 units the capacities of CA and DC. The new network is Fig. 15-12(c).

Path $\{AB, BC, CD\}$ in Fig. 15-12(c) can accommodate 7 units from source to sink. Making this shipment, we increase the supply at D to $15 + 7 = 22$ units, and decrease the capacities of AB, BC, and CD by 7. We also increase by 7 units the capacities of BA, CB, and DC. The result is Fig. 15-12(d).

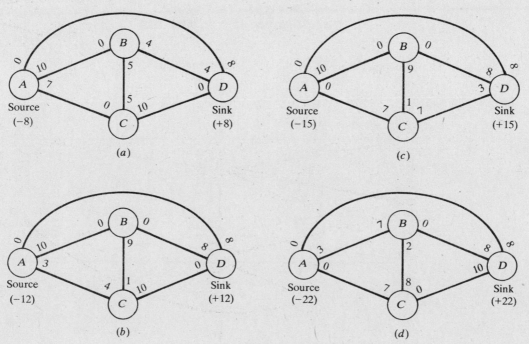

Fig. 15-12

There is no path from source to sink in Fig. 15-12(d) that permits positive flow. Therefore, the maximum amount of material that can be sent from A to D is 22 units. To determine the optimal shipping schedule, we compare Fig. 15-12(d) with Fig. 15-2. We note the following reductions in capacity: 7 units from A to B, 8 units from A to D, 7 units from A to C, 4 units from B to D, 3 units from B to C, and 10 units from C to D. These reductions, considered as shipments, constitute the optimal shipping schedule.

15.7 Explain the significance of increasing the reverse capacities, as stipulated in Step 3 of the maximal-flow algorithm.

Increasing these capacities allows for flows in the reverse directions at a later stage in the algorithm. Such potential flows are necessary to correct a previously designated flow which proves to be unoptimal.

An example is given by Problem 15.6. In the second iteration, it was determined that path $\{AC, CB, BD\}$ could accommodate a direct flow of 4 units. Using this path, however, is not optimal; it was found that the optimal schedule ships 3 units from B to C and *nothing* from C to B. Nonetheless, shipping 4 units from C to B and then increasing the capacity from B to C by 4 units allowed one to correct this error later in the algorithm. Indeed, the last step in the iterative solution called for a shipment of 7 units along $\{AB, BC, CD\}$. But this shipment could not have been made had the capacity of BC not been increased from its original value of 5. Effectively, this 7-unit flow from B to C corrects the previous nonoptimal flow of 4 units from C to B, leaving a net flow of 3 units along BC in the direction of C.

Supplementary Problems

15.8 Solve the minimum-span problem for the network shown in Fig. 15-13.

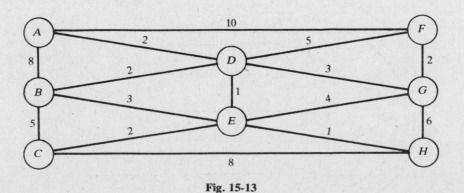

Fig. 15-13

15.9 Solve the minimum-span problem for the network shown in Fig. 15-14.

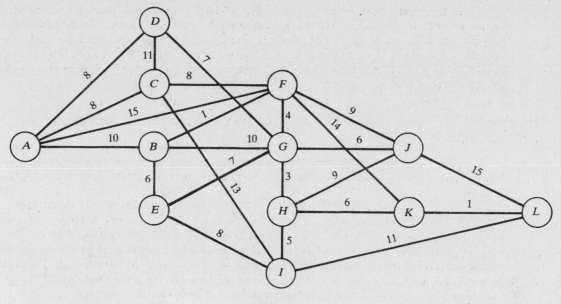

Fig. 15-14

15.10 Find the minimum-cost path connecting A and L in the network of Fig. 15-14.

15.11 Determine the maximum amount of material that can be shipped from H to A through the network shown in Fig. 15-13, assuming that the numbers on the branches represent the flow capacities in both directions.

15.12 Determine the maximum amount of material that can be shipped from A to K through the network shown in Fig. 15-14, assuming that the numbers on the branches represent the flow capacities in both directions.

15.13 Solve the maximal-flow problem for the network shown in Fig. 15-15 if A is the source and J is the sink.

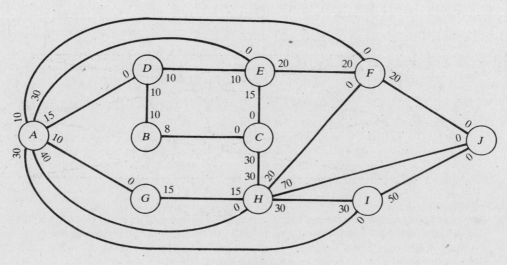

Fig. 15-15

15.14   Resolve Problem 15.11 if, in addition to H, node D is a source.

15.15   A shipping company must move 50 units of a product from Los Angeles to New York.   Table 15-4 gives transportation costs (in dollars per unit) between the company's various depots; blank entries in the table signify that shipments cannot be made directly between corresponding depots.   Find the cheapest shipping schedule.   Solve first as a shortest-route problem, then, as a check, solve as a transshipment problem.

Table 15-4

	Los Angeles	San Francisco	Phoenix	Laramie	St. Louis	Chicago	New York
Los Angeles	...	7	8	...	39	...	95
San Francisco	7	...	22	17	...	36	85
Phoenix	8	22	...	14	25	27	...
Laramie	...	17	14	...	31	19	...
St. Louis	39	...	25	31	...	14	20
Chicago	...	36	27	19	14	...	13
New York	95	85	...	...	20	13	...

15.16   A construction firm has collected data on dump trucks, as shown in Table 15-5 (dollar amounts).

Table 15-5

	Age in Years				
	0–1	1–2	2–3	3–4	4–5
Maintenance Cost	7000	7500	9700	7700	9000
Lost Revenue for Down Time	500	800	1200	800	1000
Year-End Trade-In Value	16 000	6000	9000	3500	2500

No dump truck is kept more than 5 years.   Determine a replacement policy for a dump truck currently 2 years old, that will minimize the total operating cost over the next 9 years.   Assume that new trucks cost $21 000 and only new trucks are purchased as replacements.   Solve first as a shortest-route problem, then check your solution with dynamic programming.   (*Hint*: Take Y_0 as the beginning of the period.   Then Y_1 through Y_9 are the beginnings of the next 9 years, and Y_{-2} represents the day the current truck was purchased. Y_{-1} is not needed.)

15.17   A *cut* through a network having a source and a sink is any set of oriented branches that contains at least one branch from every path from source to sink.   The *cut value* is the sum of the flow capacities in the specified directions of the branches comprising the cut.   For the network of Fig. 15-16, which of the three indicated sets of branches are cuts, and what are the cut values?

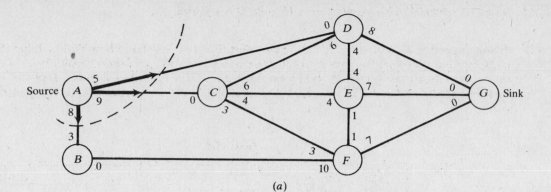

(a)

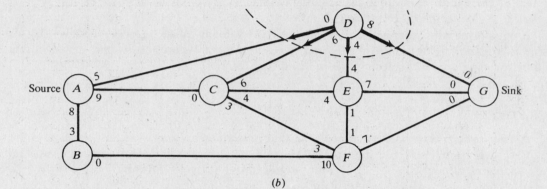

(b)

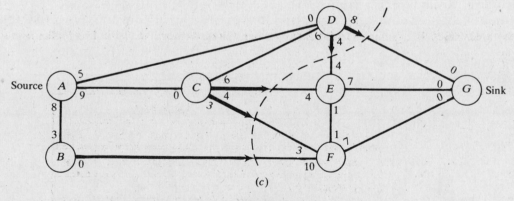

(c)

Fig. 15-16

15.18 The *max-flow, min-cut theorem* states that for any network with a single source and a single sink the maximum flow through the network equals the minimum cut value in the network. Using this theorem and the results of Problem 15.17, determine an upper bound on the *flow* through the network of Fig. 15-16.

15.19 Find a cut through Fig. 15-10 that has value 1. Using the max-flow, min-cut theorem and the result of Problem 15.5, conclude that the maximum flow through the network is 1 unit.

Chapter 16

Game Theory

GAMES

A *game* is a competitive situation among *N* persons or groups, called *players*, that is conducted under a prescribed set of rules with known payoffs. The rules define the elementary activities, or *moves*, of the game. Different players may be allowed different moves, but each player knows the moves available to the other players.

If one player wins what another player loses, the game is called a *zero-sum* game. A *two-person* game is a game having only two players. Two-person, zero-sum games, also called *matrix games*, will be the only type of games considered in this chapter.

STRATEGIES

A *pure strategy* is a predetermined plan that prescribes for a player the sequence of moves and countermoves he will make during a complete game. In a matrix game, either player has a finite set of pure strategies, although their number may be enormous. Player I (II) knows player II's (I's) set, but he does not know for sure which element of the set II (I) has picked at the commencement of a given play of the game. Thus, a complete characterization of the game is provided by its *payoff matrix*, Table 16-1, which gives the amount g_{ij} won by player I from player II when I plays his ith pure strategy, A_i, and II plays his jth pure strategy, B_j. (The matrix of payoffs to player II is the negative of the above matrix.)

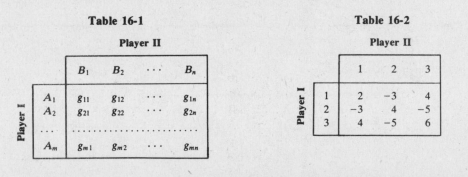

Table 16-1

Player II

	B_1	B_2	$\cdots$	B_n
A_1	g_{11}	g_{12}	$\cdots$	g_{1n}
A_2	g_{21}	g_{22}	$\cdots$	g_{2n}
$\cdots$	$\cdots$	$\cdots$	$\cdots$	$\cdots$
A_m	g_{m1}	g_{m2}	$\cdots$	g_{mn}

Player I

Table 16-2

Player II

	1	2	3
1	2	-3	4
2	-3	4	-5
3	4	-5	6

Player I

Example 16.1 Consider the game in which two players simultaneously reveal 1, 2, or 3 fingers each. If the sum of the revealed fingers is even, player II pays to player I the sum in dollars; if the sum is odd, player I pays to player II the sum in dollars.

For this very simple two-person, zero-sum game, the pure strategies can be identified with the individual moves. (This could not be done for, say, ticktacktoe, in which a single pure strategy might run: "If he moves first to the center, I will move to the upper right-hand corner; if he then moves to the lower right-hand corner, I will . . . .") Furthermore, both players have the same set of pure strategies, {1, 2, 3}. The payoff matrix is given in Table 16-2.

The objective in game theory is to determine a "best" strategy for a given player under the assumption that the opponent is rational and will make intelligent countermoves. Consequently, if one player always chooses the same pure strategy or chooses pure strategies in a fixed order, his opponent will in time recognize the pattern and will move to defeat it, if possible. Generally, therefore, the most effective strategy is a *mixed strategy*, defined by a probability distribution over the set of pure strategies. For the game of Table 16-1, a mixed strategy for player I will be specified by a probability vector

$$\mathbf{X} \equiv [x_1, x_2, \ldots, x_m]^T$$

where x_i $(i = 1, \ldots, m)$ is the proportion of time (i.e., the relative frequency or probability) that A_i is chosen. Similarly, a mixed strategy for player II will be designated by

$$\mathbf{Y} \equiv [y_1, y_2, \ldots, y_n]^T$$

where y_j $(j = 1, \ldots, n)$ is the probability that B_j is chosen. As probabilities, the x_i and y_j are nonnegative, with

$$\sum_{i=1}^{m} x_i = \sum_{j=1}^{n} y_j = 1$$

Example 16.2 In the game of Example 16.1, if player I always shows 3 fingers, player II can defeat that pure strategy by always showing 2 fingers. If player I adopts the set sequence of pure strategies 3, 3, 2, 3, 3, 2, 3, 3, 2, ..., player II can defeat it with the sequence 2, 2, 3, 2, 2, 3, 2, 2, 3, ...

If player I adopts the mixed strategy $\mathbf{X} = [1/6, 1/3, 1/2]^T$, then player I plans to show 1 finger one-sixth of the time, 2 fingers one-third of the time, and 3 fingers one-half of the time. To implement the strategy, player I could roll one die before each play. If the die showed a 1 (having probability 1/6), he would show 1 finger; if the die showed a 2 or 3 (having probability 2/6 = 1/3), he would show 2 fingers; if the die showed 4, 5, or 6 (having probability 3/6 = 1/2), he would show 3 fingers.

STABLE GAMES

Suppose that the players of the game defined by Table 16-1 are restricted to using pure strategies. Write:

$$m_I \equiv \text{maximum value of the minimum gain to player I}$$
$$\equiv \underset{i=1,\ldots,m}{\text{maximum}} \left(\underset{j=1,\ldots,n}{\text{minimum}} \{g_{ij}\} \right) \tag{16.1}$$

$$m_{II} \equiv \text{minimum value of the maximum loss to player II}$$
$$\equiv \underset{j=1,\ldots,n}{\text{minimum}} \left(\underset{i=1,\ldots,m}{\text{maximum}} \{g_{ij}\} \right) \tag{16.2}$$

If player I plays the row that yields the maximum in (16.1)—the *maximin strategy*—he is assured of winning an amount m_I *at worst*; whereas, by playing another row, he could win less than m_I. (Equivalently, under the maximin strategy, player I loses $-m_I$ *at worst*.) Analogously, if player II plays the column that yields the minimum in (16.2)—the *minimax strategy*—his assured loss (which is I's gain) will be m_{II} *at worst*. We shall say that these two strategies satisfy the *minimax criterion*.

Now, by their definitions,

$$m_I \leq m_{II} \tag{16.3}$$

for any matrix game. If $m_I = m_{II}$, then player I would only worsen his position by departing from the maximin strategy, and player II would only worsen his position by departing from the minimax strategy. Such a game is *stable*, and the strategies prescribed by the minimax criterion are *optimal* for the two players. Furthermore, both players can agree as to what a play of the game is worth (to player I); namely,

$$G^* = m_I = m_{II}$$

The number G^* is called the *value* of the game; it is the amount paid by player II to player I when both players have used their optimal strategies.

In summary: Every stable game has a unique value, and an optimal (pure) strategy for either player. (Note that the optimal strategies need not be unique.)

UNSTABLE GAMES

When the inequality holds in (*16.3*), the game is *unstable*, and the pure strategies dictated by the minimax criterion are no longer optimal. The fundamental result in the theory of matrix games is that, when *mixed* strategies are admitted, unstable games also have a solution—i.e., optimal strategies and a value—provided that the random payoff is replaced by its *expected value*.

Under mixed strategies (defined by the probability vectors $\mathbf{X}$ for player I and $\mathbf{Y}$ for player II, the payoff from II to I is a random variable having expected value

$$E(\mathbf{X}, \mathbf{Y}) \equiv \sum_{i=1}^{m} \sum_{j=1}^{n} g_{ij} x_i y_j \tag{16.4}$$

Analogous to (*16.1*) and (*16.2*), write:

$$M_I \equiv \text{maximum value of minimum expected gain to player I}$$

$$\equiv \max_{\mathbf{X}} (\min_{\mathbf{Y}} E(\mathbf{X}, \mathbf{Y})) \tag{16.5}$$

$$M_{II} \equiv \text{minimum value of maximum expected loss to player II}$$

$$\equiv \min_{\mathbf{Y}} (\max_{\mathbf{X}} E(\mathbf{X}, \mathbf{Y})) \tag{16.6}$$

in which $\mathbf{X}$ and $\mathbf{Y}$ run through all m-dimensional and all n-dimensional probability vectors, respectively. Then we have the

Minimax theorem: For any game matrix, there exist optimal strategies $\mathbf{X}^*$ and $\mathbf{Y}^*$ such that

$$E(\mathbf{X}^*, \mathbf{Y}^*) = M_I = M_{II} = G^*$$

In other words, any matrix game has a value. Observe that stable games are also covered by the minimax theorem, since a pure strategy is a special mixed strategy that has a single nonzero component (equal to 1).

SOLUTION BY LINEAR PROGRAMMING

The optimal strategies guaranteed by the minimax theorem, as well as the value of the game, can be calculated via linear programming. The optimal strategy for player II is incorporated in the solution of the following linear program:

$$\text{maximize:} \quad z = -y_{n+1}$$

$$\text{subject to:} \quad g_{11}y_1 + g_{12}y_2 + \cdots + g_{1n}y_n - y_{n+1} \leq 0$$

$$g_{21}y_1 + g_{22}y_2 + \cdots + g_{2n}y_n - y_{n+1} \leq 0$$

$$\cdots\cdots\cdots\cdots\cdots\cdots\cdots\cdots\cdots\cdots\cdots \tag{16.7}$$

$$g_{m1}y_1 + g_{m2}y_2 + \cdots + g_{mn}y_n - y_{n+1} \leq 0$$

$$y_1 + y_2 + \cdots + y_n = 1$$

$$\text{with:} \quad y_1, y_2, \ldots, y_n \text{ nonnegative}$$

Here $G^* = y_{n+1}^*$ and $\mathbf{Y}^* = [y_1^*, y_2^*, \ldots, y_n^*]^T$. By initially increasing each g_{ij} by the same positive amount (this leaves unchanged the nature of the game), we can force $g_{ij} \geq 0$. Then the expected gain to player I is also nonnegative. Since this quantity is represented by y_{n+1} in program (*16.7*), it follows that all variables can be restricted to nonnegative values under such circumstances. Equivalently, y_{n+1} can be replaced by the difference of two, new, nonnegative variables. The optimal strategy for player I is the probability vector whose components are the solution to the dual of program (*16.7*). (See Problem 16.9.)

Whenever a player has only two pure strategies, the optimal strategy for that player can be determined graphically. (See Problem 16.10.) If both players have exactly two pure strategies, then the optimal strategies are

$$x_1^* = \frac{g_{22} - g_{21}}{g_{11} + g_{22} - g_{12} - g_{21}} \qquad x_2^* = \frac{g_{11} - g_{12}}{g_{11} + g_{22} - g_{12} - g_{21}} \qquad (16.8)$$

$$y_1^* = \frac{g_{22} - g_{12}}{g_{11} + g_{22} - g_{12} - g_{21}} \qquad y_2^* = \frac{g_{11} - g_{21}}{g_{11} + g_{22} - g_{12} - g_{21}} \qquad (16.9)$$

with

$$G^* = \frac{g_{11}g_{22} - g_{12}g_{21}}{g_{11} + g_{22} - g_{12} - g_{21}} \qquad (16.10)$$

(See Problem 16.7.)

DOMINANCE

A pure strategy P is *dominated* by a pure strategy Q if, for each pure strategy of the opponent's, the payoff associated with P is no better than the payoff associated with Q. Since a dominated pure strategy can never be part of an optimal strategy, the corresponding row or column of the game matrix may be deleted *a priori*.

Solved Problems

16.1 *Construct a payoff matrix for the following game.* Each of two supermarket chains proposes to build a store in a rural region that is served by three towns. The distances between towns are shown in Fig. 16-1. Approximately 45 percent of the region's population live near town A, 35 percent live near town B, and 20 percent live near town C. Because chain I is larger and has developed a better reputation than chain II, chain I will control a majority of the business whenever their situations are comparable. Both chains are aware of the other's interest in the region and both have completed marketing surveys that give identical projections. If both chains locate in the same town or equidistant from a town, chain I will control 65 percent of the business in that town. If chain I is closer to a town than chain II, chain I will control 90 percent of that town's business. If chain I is farther from a town than chain II, it will still draw 40 percent of that town's business. The remaining business under all circumstances will go to chain II. Furthermore, both chains know that it is the policy of chain I not to locate in towns that are too small, and town C falls into this category.

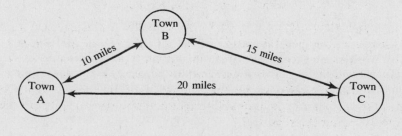

Fig. 16-1

There are two players of this game, chain I and chain II. Player I has two pure strategies: A_1 (locate in town A) and A_2 (locate in town B); Player II has three pure strategies: B_1 (locate in town A), B_2 (locate in town B), and B_3 (locate in town C). We take the payoffs to chain I to be the percentages of business in the region that will fall to chain I, according to the marketing surveys. Since each percentage point increase or decrease represents an identical decrease or increase, respectively, for chain II, this is a two-person, zero-sum game.

If both chains locate in the same town, then player I will receive 65 percent of the business from the entire region. Thus, $g_{11} = g_{22} = 65$. If chain I locates in town A while chain II locates in town B, then player I is closer to town A than player II, but player II is closer to both towns B and C than player I. Consequently, player I will capture

$$(0.90)(0.45) + (0.40)(0.35) + (0.40)(0.20) = 0.625$$

or 62.5 percent of the region's business. Therefore, $g_{12} = 62.5$. If chain I locates in town B and chain II locates in town C, then player I is closer to towns A and B, while player II is closer to town C. Consequently, player I will have

$$(0.90)(0.45) + (0.90)(0.35) + (0.40)(0.20) = 0.80$$

or 80 percent of the region's business. Therefore, $g_{23} = 80$. Similarly, $g_{13} = 80$ and $g_{21} = 67.5$. These results are collected in Table 16-3, which is the payoff matrix for this game.

Table 16-3

Player II

		B_1	B_2	B_3
Player I	A_1	65	62.5	80
	A_2	67.5	65	80

16.2 *Construct a payoff matrix for the following game.* A barrel contains equal numbers of red and green marbles. Player I randomly selects one marble and inspects it for color without showing it to player II. If the marble is red, player I says, "I have a red marble," and demands \$1 from player II. If the marble is green, either player I says, "The marble is green," and pays player II \$1, or player I bluffs by saying, "The marble is red," and demands \$1 from player II. Whenever player I demands \$1, player II either can pay or can challenge player I's claim that the selected marble is red. Once challenged, player I must show the marble to player II. If it is indeed red, player II pays player I \$2; if it is not red, player I pays player II \$2.

Player I has only two pure strategies; namely,

A_1: To claim the marble's actual color.

A_2: To claim the marble red whether or not it is red.

[Note that I's pure strategies are not identical with his *moves*, which are (i) to claim red and (ii) to claim green.] Player II also has just two pure strategies; these are

B_1: To believe player I.

B_2: To believe if the claim is green and to challenge if the claim is red.

Since each person wins what the other loses, this is a two-person, zero-sum game.

In this game, the payoffs associated with the *pure* strategies are random variables; we replace them by their expected values. Thus, g_{11} is the expected gain to player I if player I claims the true color of the chosen marble and player II believes. Since half the time the marble is red and half the time it is green,

$$g_{11} = \tfrac{1}{2}(1) + \tfrac{1}{2}(-1) = 0$$

The payoff g_{12} is the expected gain to player I when player I claims the true color of the marble and player II challenges if red is claimed.   Since the marble has probability 1/2 of being either color, half the time there will be no challenge, and half the time player II will challenge and lose.   Therefore,

$$g_{12} = \tfrac{1}{2}(-1) + \tfrac{1}{2}(2) = \tfrac{1}{2}$$

Similarly,

$$g_{21} = 1 \qquad g_{22} = \tfrac{1}{2}(-2) + \tfrac{1}{2}(2) = 0$$

These results are collected in Table 16-4, which is the payoff matrix for the game.

Table 16-4

Player II

		B_1	B_2
	A_1	0	1/2
Player I	A_2	1	0

16.3   Determine whether any pure strategies in the game of Table 16-3 can be discarded through dominance.

Player I can discard A_1 (locating in town A), since the payoffs from this strategy are always less than or equal to the corresponding payoffs from A_2.   Player II can discard both B_1 and B_3 as inferior to B_2 (note that the payoffs to player II are the negatives of those given in Table 16-3 for player I).   With the first row and the first and third columns deleted, the payoff matrix consists of a single entry.   Thus A_2 and B_2 are optimal strategies.   Both supermarket chains should locate in town B.   Chain I will control 65 percent of the region's business, with the remaining 35 percent going to chain II.

16.4   Let **G'** denote the game matrix obtained from matrix **G** by eliminating dominated rows and columns.   Show that **G** is stable if and only if **G'** is stable.

It suffices to consider the case in which the first row of **G** is dominated by the second row.   If g_{1p} and g_{2q} are the two row minima (indicated by circles below),

$$\begin{bmatrix} g_{11} & g_{12} & \cdots & \boxed{g_{1p}} & \cdots & g_{1q} & \cdots & g_{1n} \\ g_{21} & g_{22} & \cdots & g_{2p} & \cdots & \boxed{g_{2q}} & \cdots & g_{2n} \\ \cdots & \cdots & \cdots & \cdots & \cdots & \cdots & \cdots & \cdots \end{bmatrix}$$

then $g_{1p} \leq g_{1q}$.   Also, $g_{1q} \leq g_{2q}$ (by dominance).   Hence,

$$g_{1p} \leq g_{2q}$$

This means that the maximum of the row minima in **G** is the same as the maximum of the row minima in **G'**, i.e., $m_I = m'_I$.

Further, if row 1 contains a column maximum of **G**—say, g_{1s}—it follows from dominance that $g_{2s} = g_{1s}$ is also a column maximum.   Consequently, the minimum of the column maxima in **G** is the same as the minimum of the column maxima in **G'**, i.e., $m_{II} = m'_{II}$.   We conclude that

$$m_I = m_{II} \qquad \text{if and only if} \qquad m'_I = m'_{II}$$

16.5   Is the game of Table 16-3 stable?

Yes, by Problems 16.3 and 16.4.

16.6   Is the game of Table 16-4 stable?

Here, $m_I = 0 < 1/2 = m_{II}$; the game is unstable.

16.7 Find the optimal strategies for both players of the game of Table 16-4.

As determined in Problem 16.6, the game is unstable and hence not solvable in pure strategies. Since this game involves exactly two pure strategies for each player, the optimal (mixed) strategies are given by (16.8) and (16.9) as

$$x_1^* = \frac{0-1}{0+0-(1/2)-1} = \frac{2}{3} \qquad x_2^* = 1 - x_1^* = \frac{1}{3}$$

$$y_1^* = \frac{0-(1/2)}{0+0-(1/2)-1} = \frac{1}{3} \qquad y_2^* = 1 - y_1^* = \frac{2}{3}$$

Accordingly, player II should believe player I one-third of the time, while challenging player I the other two-thirds of the time if player I claims a red marble. Player I should claim the true color of the marble two-thirds of the time, while bluffing the other third of the time if the marble is green. The net result will be, by (16.10), an expected gain of

$$G^* = \frac{(0)(0) - (1/2)(1)}{0+0-(1/2)-1} = \frac{1}{3} \text{ dollar}$$

to player I each time the game is played. The expected payoff to player II is the negative of this amount.

16.8 Find optimal strategies for both players of the game defined by the payoffs given in Table 16-5.

Table 16-5

Player II

		B_1	B_2	B_3	B_4	B_5
Player I	A_1	3	−2	−4	0	6
	A_2	−4	2	−1	7	−8
	A_3	2	−5	−4	1	−1
	A_4	0	−3	−2	−1	−1

Table 16-6

Player II

		B_1	B_2	B_3	B_5
Player I	A_1	3	−2	−4	6
	A_2	−4	2	−1	−8
	A_4	0	−3	−2	−1

Pure strategy B_4 is dominated by B_3 (and by B_2), so it can be eliminated. Once it is, then A_3 is dominated by A_1; hence A_3 also can be discarded. The resulting payoff matrix is Table 16-6, for which

$$m_I = -3 < -1 = m_{II}$$

As the game is not stable, the optimal strategies for both players are mixed strategies incorporated in the solution of program (16.7). For the payoffs in Table 16-6, this program becomes

$$\text{maximize:} \quad z = -y_6$$

$$\begin{aligned}
\text{subject to:} \quad & 3y_1 - 2y_2 - 4y_3 + 6y_5 - y_6 \le 0 \\
& -4y_1 + 2y_2 - y_3 - 8y_5 - y_6 \le 0 \\
& -3y_2 - 2y_3 - y_5 - y_6 \le 0 \\
& y_1 + y_2 + y_3 + y_5 = 1
\end{aligned} \qquad (1)$$

with: y_1, y_2, y_3, and y_5 nonnegative

Since y_6 is unrestricted, we set $y_6 \equiv y_7 - y_8$, where both y_7 and y_8 are nonnegative variables (see Chapter 2). The initial simplex tableau is Tableau 1, with slack variables y_9, y_{10}, and y_{11}, and artificial variable y_{12}. Five iterations of the simplex algorithm yield Tableau 6. It follows that the optimal strategy for player II (with $y_4^* = 0$ because B_4 is not used) is

$$\mathbf{Y}^* = [y_1^*, y_2^*, y_3^*, y_4^*, y_5^*]^T = [0, 7/60, 7/10, 0, 11/60]^T$$

The optimal strategy for player I (with $x_3^* = 0$ because A_3 is not used) is given in terms of the dual solution (see Chapter 5) as

$$\mathbf{X}^* = [x_1^*, x_2^*, x_3^*, x_4^*]^T = [1/15, 1/5, 0, 11/15]^T$$

The value of the game is

$$G^* = y_6^* = y_7^* - y_8^* = 0 - \frac{29}{15} = -\frac{29}{15}$$

that is, player I can expect to lose 29/15 units to player II at each play, provided both players use their optimal strategies.

		y_1	y_2	y_3	y_5	y_7	y_8	y_9	y_{10}	y_{11}	y_{12}	
		0	0	0	0	-1	1	0	0	0	$-M$	
y_9	0	3	-2	-4	6	-1	1	1	0	0	0	0
y_{10}	0	-4	2	-1	-8	-1	1	0	1	0	0	0
y_{11}	0	0	-3	-2	-1	-1	1	0	0	1	0	0
y_{12}	$-M$	1	1	1	1	0	0	0	0	0	1	1
$(z_j - c_j)$:		0	0	0	0	1	-1	0	0	0	0	0
		-1	-1	-1	-1	0	0	0	0	0	0	-1

Tableau 1

	y_1	y_2	y_3	y_5	y_7	y_8	y_9	y_{10}	y_{11}	
y_5	7/12	0	0	1	0	0	1/15	$-1/20$	$-1/60$	11/60
y_2	$-1/12$	1	0	0	0	0	4/15	3/20	$-17/20$	7/60
y_8	4/3	0	0	0	-1	1	1/15	1/5	11/15	29/15
y_3	1/2	0	1	0	0	0	$-1/5$	$-1/10$	3/10	7/10
	4/3	0	0	0	0	0	1/15	1/5	11/15	29/15

Tableau 6

16.9 (a) Derive a linear program for the optimal strategy for player I in the matrix game defined by Table 16-1. (b) Show that this program is the symmetric dual of (16.7), the program for player II's optimal strategy.

(a) Let $\mathbf{X}^*$ denote the maximizing $\mathbf{X}$ in (16.5). Then (16.5) is equivalent to the following two conditions:

(i) $E(\mathbf{X}^*, \mathbf{Y}) \geq M_I$ for all probability vectors $\mathbf{Y}$.

(ii) If $x_{m+1} > M_I$, there is no probability vector $\mathbf{X}$ that satisfies

$$E(\mathbf{X}, \mathbf{Y}) \geq x_{m+1}$$

for all probability vectors $\mathbf{Y}$.

Condition (i) says that player I is guaranteed an expected return of at least M_I if he plays $\mathbf{X}^*$; condition (ii) says that no other strategy gives player I a larger minimum expected return. From (i) and (ii), it follows that the program

$$\text{maximize:} \quad z = x_{m+1}$$
$$\text{subject to:} \quad E(\mathbf{X}, \mathbf{Y}) \geq x_{m+1} \quad (\mathbf{Y} \text{ arbitrary})$$

(1)

in the variables $x_1, \ldots, x_m, x_{m+1}$ has the solution $[x_1^*, \ldots, x_m^*, M_I]^T$. However,

$$E(\mathbf{X}, \mathbf{Y}) \equiv \sum_{j=1}^{n} \left(\sum_{i=1}^{m} g_{ij} x_i \right) y_j \geq x_{m+1} \quad \left(y_j \geq 0, \quad \sum y_j = 1 \right)$$

(2)

if and only if

$$\sum_{i=1}^{m} g_{ij} x_i \geq x_{m+1} \quad (j = 1, 2, \ldots, n)$$

(3)

Indeed, relation (2) is just the convex combination (Chapter 3), with weights y_j, of relations (3). Consequently, program (1) may be rewritten as

$$\text{minimize:} \quad z = -x_{m+1}$$

$$\text{subject to:} \quad g_{11}x_1 + g_{21}x_2 + \cdots + g_{m1}x_m - x_{m+1} \ge 0$$

$$g_{12}x_1 + g_{22}x_2 + \cdots + g_{m2}x_m - x_{m+1} \ge 0$$

$$\cdots\cdots\cdots\cdots\cdots\cdots\cdots\cdots\cdots\cdots\cdots$$

$$g_{1n}x_1 + g_{2n}x_2 + \cdots + g_{mn}x_m - x_{m+1} \ge 0 \tag{4}$$

$$x_1 + x_2 + \cdots + x_m = 1$$

$$\text{with:} \quad x_1, x_2, \ldots, x_m \text{ nonnegative}$$

where we have changed the maximization to a minimization and have included the restrictions on the probabilities x_i.

(b) In program (4) above, replace x_{m+1} by $x_{m+1} - x_{m+2}$, where the new x_{m+1} and x_{m+2} are nonnegative variables.   Also, replace the equality constraint by

$$-x_1 - x_2 - \cdots - x_m \ge -1$$
$$x_1 + x_2 + \cdots + x_m \ge 1$$

Make the analogous replacements in program (16.7).   Then program (4) falls into form (5.1) and program (16.7) falls into form (5.2), wherein

$$\mathbf{X} \equiv [x_1, x_2, \ldots, x_{m+1}, x_{m+2}]^T \qquad \mathbf{W} \equiv [y_1, y_2, \ldots, y_{n+1}, y_{n+2}]^T$$

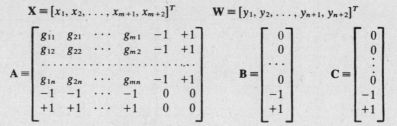

16.10 Use a graphical method to determine an optimal strategy for player I in the game defined by Table 16-7.

Table 16-7

		Player II		
		B_1	B_2	B_3
Player I	A_1	2	−3	−4
	A_2	−6	−1	1

For this game, program (4) of Problem 16.9(a) becomes

$$\text{minimize:} \quad z = -x_3$$

$$\text{subject to:} \quad 2x_1 - 6x_2 - x_3 \ge 0$$

$$-3x_1 - x_2 - x_3 \ge 0 \tag{1}$$

$$-4x_1 + x_2 - x_3 \ge 0$$

$$x_1 + x_2 = 1$$

$$\text{with:} \quad x_1 \text{ and } x_2 \text{ nonnegative}$$

Before this program can be solved graphically, it must be reduced to a system involving just two variables.

The equality constraint can be rewritten as

$$x_2 = 1 - x_1 \tag{2}$$

Then the nonnegativity of x_2 is guaranteed by requiring

$$x_1 \le 1 \tag{3}$$

Substituting (2) into the constraints of system (1), replacing the nonnegativity condition on x_2 by the new constraint (3), and going over to a maximization program, we obtain:

$$\text{maximize:} \quad z = x_3$$

$$\text{subject to:} \quad \begin{aligned} 8x_1 - x_3 &\geq 6 \\ -2x_1 - x_3 &\geq 1 \\ 5x_1 + x_3 &\leq 1 \\ x_1 &\leq 1 \end{aligned} \qquad (4)$$

$$\text{with:} \quad x_1 \geq 0$$

The graphical solution to program (4) is shown in Fig. 16-2.

$$x_1^* = 1/2 \qquad x_2^* = 1 - x_1^* = 1/2$$

The value of the game is $z^* = x_3^* = -2$.

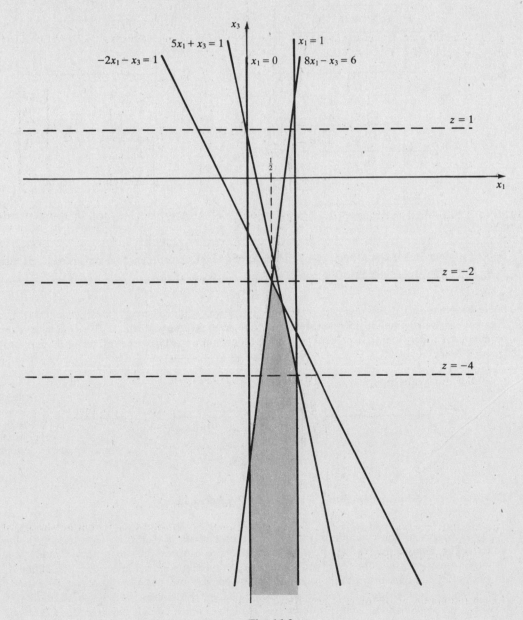

Fig. 16-2

Supplementary Problems

16.11 Determine whether each matrix game, as defined below by the payoffs to the row player, is stable. Then find both optimal strategies and the value of the game.

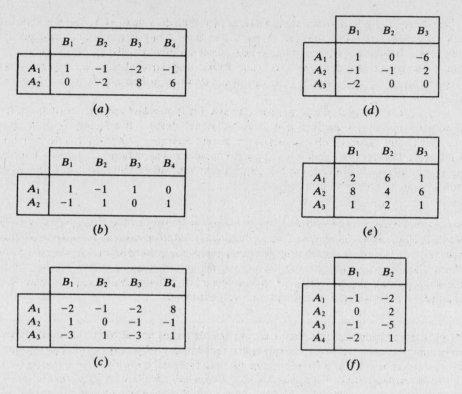

	B_1	B_2	B_3	B_4
A_1	1	-1	-2	-1
A_2	0	-2	8	6

(a)

	B_1	B_2	B_3
A_1	1	0	-6
A_2	-1	-1	2
A_3	-2	0	0

(d)

	B_1	B_2	B_3	B_4
A_1	1	-1	1	0
A_2	-1	1	0	1

(b)

	B_1	B_2	B_3
A_1	2	6	1
A_2	8	4	6
A_3	1	2	1

(e)

	B_1	B_2	B_3	B_4
A_1	-2	-1	-2	8
A_2	1	0	-1	-1
A_3	-3	1	-3	1

(c)

	B_1	B_2
A_1	-1	-2
A_2	0	2
A_3	-1	-5
A_4	-2	1

(f)

16.12 Solve Problem 16.1 if chain I controls 70 percent of a town's business whenever both chains locate in the same town or are equidistant from a town.

16.13 Solve Problem 16.1 if the region is served by four towns situated along a straight highway as shown in Fig. 16-3. Approximately 15 percent of the population live near town A, 30 percent near town B, 20 percent near town C, and 35 percent near town D; each town is large enough for both chains to consider locating in it.

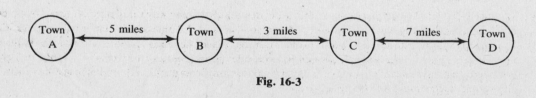

Fig. 16-3

16.14 Devise a method for implementing strategy **X*** of Problem 16.8.

16.15 Army A wishes to truck supplies to a border outpost which is expecting an attack by army B within hours. The nearest supply depot is connected to the outpost by two separate roads, one running through forests and the other over flatlands. A supply convoy moves faster over the flatlands route but enjoys better camouflage on the forest route. The convoy must take one route or the other.

Army B anticipates a supply effort along one of the routes, and plans to hinder it with air strikes. It has available a single squadron of airplanes, which cannot be divided. If army B sends its airplanes above the forest route and finds army A there, army B will have time for four strikes against the convoy. If army B sends its planes above the flatlands route and army A is using that route, army B will have time for three strikes. If army B sends its planes over the wrong route, valuable time is lost. Once it realizes its error and locates the convoy on the other route, army B will have time for two strikes on the flatlands route, but time for only one strike on the forest route (because of the added difficulty in finding the convoy through the trees). Determine the optimal strategies of the two armies.

16.16 A Blue Army and a Red Army are contesting two airfields, valued at 20 and 8 million dollars, which are both under the control of the Red Army. The Blue Army is charged with attacking either or both airfields and inflicting maximum damage (measured in dollars) to the facilities. It is the task of the Red Army to minimize this damage. To achieve their respective objectives, each army can assign its full force to one of the two airfields or it can divide its force in half and cover both airfields with reduced capacity.

A facility will experience 25 percent damage if it is attacked and defended at full force, but only 10 percent damage if it is attacked and defended at half force. If a facility is attacked at full force but defended at half force, it will experience 50 percent damage. Any facility attacked either at half force or full force but not defended will experience complete destruction. A facility that is not attacked, or one that is attacked at half force but defended at full force, will experience no damage. Determine optimal strategies for both armies.

16.17 Two ranchers have brought a dispute over a 6-yard-wide strip of land that separates their properties to a referee. Both claim the strip as entirely their own. Both ranchers are aware that the referee will ask each party to submit a confidential proposal for settling the dispute fairly and will then accept that proposal which gives the most. If both proposals give equally or not at all, the referee will split the difference, setting the boundary in the middle of the 6-yard width. Determine the ranchers' best proposals, if proposals are restricted to integral amounts.

16.18 Cigarette bootleggers use two routes for moving cigarettes out of North Carolina, Interstate 95 or back roads. Both routes are known to the police, but because of personnel limitations they can patrol only one of these routes sufficiently at any one time—a fact well known to the bootleggers.

Police estimate that the average load of contraband traveling on Interstate 95 is worth $1000 to the bootlegger if it reaches New York. The back roads limit the size of vehicles somewhat, so the average load of contraband traveling this route is worth only $800 if it reaches its destination. Any contraband discovered by the police is confiscated and the bootlegger is fined. For cigarettes traveling I-95, the loss to the bootlegger averages $700; the loss on cargo traveling the back roads averages $600. Furthermore, the police estimate that they intercept only 40 percent of the contraband traffic traveling I-95 when they are patrolling the highway, and 25 percent of the traffic traveling the back roads when they patrol there. Determine an optimal patrol strategy for the police if its objective is to minimize the bootleggers' gains.

16.19 With one day left before elections, both candidates for Governor have targeted the same three cities as crucial and potentially worth a last visit. Since no visit is useful unless sufficient advance work has been completed by the candidate's staff, plans must be made by each candidate prior to knowing the opposition's choice. Polls commissioned by both sides show identical projections. Table 16-8 gives the estimated gain (in thousands of votes) for candidate I resulting from each combination of last-day visits. Which city should each candidate choose to visit?

Table 16-8

Candidate II

	To City 1	To City 2	To City 3
To City 1	12	−9	14
To City 2	−8	7	12
To City 3	11	−10	10

Candidate I

16.20 A game is *fair* if $G^* = 0$. A game is *symmetric* if both players have the same number of pure strategies and if, for all i and j, the gain to player I from his ith pure strategy and II's jth pure strategy is equal to the gain to player II from *his* ith pure strategy and I's jth pure strategy. Prove that any symmetric game is fair.

16.21 In a well-known gambling game, player I holds a red ace and a black deuce, while player II holds a red deuce and a black three. Simultaneously, both players show one card of their choice. If the two cards match in color, player I wins; otherwise player II wins. The payoffs are determined by the following formula: If player I shows the ace, the players exchange the difference (in dollars) of the amounts shown on the two cards (ace counts as one); if player I shows the deuce, the players exchange the sum (in dollars) of the amounts shown on the two cards. Player I, noting that he can win either $1 or $5 or lose either $2 or $4, reasons that the game is fair. Is it?

Chapter 17

Decision Theory

DECISION PROCESSES

A *decision process* is a process requiring either a single or sequential set of decisions for its completion. Each allowable decision has a gain or loss associated with it which is codetermined by *external* circumstances surrounding the process, a feature which distinguishes these processes from the processes treated in Chapter 14. The set of possible circumstances, known as the *states of nature*, and a probability distribution governing the occurrence of each state are presumed known. Both the set of allowable decisions and the set of states of nature will be assumed finite (an assumption not made in the more elaborate theory).

We denote the allowable decisions by $D_1, D_2, \ldots, D_m$; the states of nature by $S_1, S_2, \ldots, S_n$; and the return associated with decision D_i and state S_j by g_{ij} $(i = 1, 2, \ldots, m; j = 1, 2, \ldots, n)$. A process requiring the implementation of just one decision is defined completely by Table 17-1. This payoff table is known as a *gain matrix* whenever the entries g_{ij} are in terms of gains to the decision maker. Losses are then represented as negative gains.

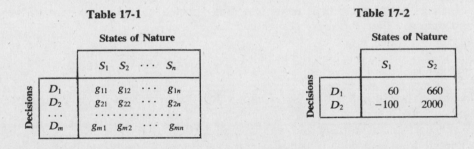

Table 17-1

States of Nature

Decisions	S_1	S_2	$\cdots$	S_n
D_1	g_{11}	g_{12}	$\cdots$	g_{1n}
D_2	g_{21}	g_{22}	$\cdots$	g_{2n}
$\cdots$				
D_m	g_{m1}	g_{m2}	$\cdots$	g_{mn}

Table 17-2

States of Nature

Decisions	S_1	S_2
D_1	60	660
D_2	-100	2000

Example 17.1 A major energy company offers a landowner \$60 000 for the exploration rights to natural gas on a certain site and the option for future development. The option, if exercised, is worth an additional \$600 000 to the landowner, but this will occur only if natural gas is discovered during the exploration phase. The landowner, believing that the energy company's interest is a good indication that gas is present, is tempted to develop the field herself. To do so, she must contract with local outfits with expertise in exploration and development. The initial cost is \$100 000, which is lost if no gas is found. If gas is discovered, however, the landowner estimates a net profit of 2 million dollars.

The decisions for the landowner are D_1 (to accept the energy company's offer) and D_2 (to explore and develop on her own). The states of nature are S_1 (there is no gas on the land) and S_2 (there is gas on the land). The gains (in thousands of dollars) to the landowner for each combination of events are given in Table 17-2.

It remains to specify or estimate the probabilities attached to the two states of nature, $P(S_1)$ and $P(S_2)$.

Although Table 17-1 is identical in form to Table 16-1, there are significant differences between decision processes and matrix games. In a decision process, only the decision maker is capable of making rational decisions; nature is not. The actual state of nature in existence at any given time is a random event, but the underlying probability distribution cannot be considered a "mixed strategy," designed to inflict losses on the decision maker. Furthermore, we generally rule out any randomness in the decision maker's choice; he or she is restricted to one or another "pure strategy" $D_1, \ldots, D_m$. Because of these differences, optimal game strategies tend, for decision processes, to be too conservative.

NAIVE DECISION CRITERIA

The *minimax* (or *pessimistic*) *criterion* is to select the decision that minimizes the maximum possible loss to the decision maker. In terms of a gain matrix, it is the decision that maximizes the minimum possible gain. The *optimistic criterion* is to choose the decision that maximizes the possible gain. The *middle-of-the road criterion* is to select that decision for which the average of the maximum and minimum gains is greatest. (See Problems 17.1 and 17.2.) As none of these three criteria is based on the *probable* state of nature, they are considered inferior to other criteria that are so based. Two probabilistic criteria will now be given.

A PRIORI CRITERION

The *a priori* (or *Bayes'*) *criterion* is to select the decision that maximizes the expected gain. (See Problems 17.3 and 17.4.)

A POSTERIORI CRITERION

If an imperfect experiment can be conducted that provides information on the true state of nature, then data from this experiment may be combined with the initial probabilities of the various states to yield an updated probability distribution. Designate the outcome of the experiment by θ and assume that the reliability of the experiment is given by the conditional probabilities $P(\theta \mid S_1)$, $P(\theta \mid S_2), \ldots, P(\theta \mid S_n)$. The updated (or *a posteriori*) probabilities of the states—$P(S_1 \mid \theta)$, $P(S_2 \mid \theta), \ldots, P(S_n \mid \theta)$—are determined from Bayes' theorem (Problem 17.5). The *a posteriori* criterion is to select the decision that maximizes the expected gain with respect to the updated probability distribution. (See Problems 17.6 and 17.7.)

DECISION TREES

A *decision tree* is an oriented tree (see Chapter 15) that represents a decision process. The nodes designate points in time where (i) one or another decision must be made by the decision maker, or (ii) the decision maker is faced with one or another state of nature, or (iii) the process terminates. Directed out of a node (i) is a branch for each possible decision; directed out of a node (ii) is a branch for each possible state of nature. Under each branch the probability of the corresponding event is written, when defined. (See Problems 17.3 and 17.6.)

Decision trees are useful in determining optimal decisions for complicated processes. The technique is to begin with the terminal nodes and sequentially to move backwards through the network, calculating the expected gains at the intermediate nodes. Each gain is written above its corresponding node. A recommended decision is one that leads to a maximum expected gain. Decisions that turn out to be nonrecommended have their corresponding branches crossed out. (See Problems 17.8 and 17.9.)

UTILITY

The *utility* of a payoff is its numerical value to a decision maker. Since no decision criterion is applicable unless all payoffs are quantified in identical units, the first step in analyzing any decision process is to determine the utility of all nonnumeric payoffs. (See Problem 17.12.)

A common utility is monetary worth, whereby each payoff (e.g., a new house) is replaced in the gain matrix by its dollar value. Monetary worth, however, is not always appropriate. A payoff of 2 million dollars is twice that of 1 million dollars, yet the former may not be worth twice the latter to a decision maker. The first million may be more valuable than the second million. In cases where dollars do not reflect the true worth of one payoff relative to another payoff, or where dollars are not a convenient quantification unit, other utilities must be used.

LOTTERIES

A *lottery* $\mathcal{L}(A, B; p)$ is a random event having two outcomes, A and B, occurring with probabilities p and $1 - p$, respectively.

VON NEUMANN UTILITIES

The following four-step procedure is used to determine *von Neumann utilities* for a finite number of payoffs.

STEP 1   List the payoffs in decreasing order of desirability: $e_1, e_2, \ldots, e_p$. Here, e_i is at least as desirable as e_j if $i < j$.

STEP 2   Arbitrarily assign finite numerical values $u(e_1)$ and $u(e_p)$ to payoffs e_1 and e_p, respectively, such that $u(e_1) > u(e_p)$.

STEP 3   For each payoff e_j ranked between e_1 and e_p in desirability, determine an *equivalence probability* p_j having the property that the decision maker is indifferent between obtaining e_j with certainty and participating in the lottery $\mathcal{L}(e_1, e_p; p_j)$.

STEP 4   Let $u(e_j) \equiv p_j u(e_1) + (1 - p_j) u(e_p)$ be the utility of payoff e_j.

Step 3 is highly subjective.   The value of p_j for each payoff e_j $(j = 2, 3, \ldots, p - 1)$ is an individual determination that may change drastically from one person to another or even for the same person at two different times.   The resulting utilities, therefore, quantify the relative worths of payoffs to a particular decision maker at a particular moment.   However, for a rational individual, it may always be expected that the *order* of the p's, and therefore of the u's, will be the same as the order of the e's.   (See Problems 17.10 and 17.12.)

A utility is *normalized* if $u(e_1) = 1$ and $u(e_p) = 0$, making the utilities identical to the equivalence probabilities.

Solved Problems

17.1   Determine recommended decisions under each naive criterion for the process described in Example 17.1.

The gain matrix for this process is Table 17-2.   The minimum gain for decision D_1 is 60, while that for D_2 is -100.   Since max $\{60, -100\} = 60$ is the gain associated with D_1, D_1 is the recommended decision under the minimax criterion.

The largest entry in the matrix is 2000, the gain associated with D_2.   Therefore D_2 is the recommended decision under the optimistic criterion.

The averages of the maximum and minimum gains for D_1 and D_2 are, respectively,

$$\frac{660 + 60}{2} = 360 \qquad \text{and} \qquad \frac{2000 + (-100)}{2} = 950$$

Since max $\{360, 950\} = 950$ is associated with D_2, D_2 is the recommended decision under the middle-of-the-road criterion.

17.2   *Determine recommended decisions under each naive criterion for the following decision process.*   A dress buyer for a large department store must place orders with a dress manufacturer 9 months before the dresses are needed.   One decision is as to the number of knee-length dresses to stock. The ultimate gain to the department store depends both on this decision and on the fashion prevailing 9 months later. The buyer's estimates of the gains (in thousands of dollars) are given in Table 17-3.

Table 17-3

	S_1: Knee lengths are high fashion	S_2: Knee lengths are acceptable	S_3: Knee lengths are not acceptable
D_1: Order none	−50	0	80
D_2: Order a little	−10	30	35
D_3: Order moderately	60	45	−30
D_4: Order a lot	80	40	−45

The minimum gains for decisions D_1 through D_4 are, respectively, −50, −10, −30, and −45. Since the maximum of these four amounts is −10, a gain associated with D_2, D_2 is the recommended decision under the minimax criterion.

The maximum gain is 80, associated with both D_1 and D_4. Hence, either D_1 or D_4 is the recommended decision under the optimistic criterion.

The averages of the maximum and minimum gains for D_1 through D_4, respectively, are 15, 12.5, 15, and 17.5. Since the maximum of these averages is associated with D_4, D_4 is the recommended decision under the middle-of-the-road criterion.

17.3 Determine the recommended decision under the *a priori* criterion for the process of Example 17.1, if the landowner estimates the probability of finding gas as 0.6.

With $P(S_2) = 0.6$, it follows that $P(S_1) = 1 - 0.6 = 0.4$. Using the data in Table 17-2, we calculate the expected gain from D_1 as

$$E(G_1) = (60)(0.4) + (660)(0.6) = 420$$

and the expected gain from D_2 as

$$E(G_2) = (-100)(0.4) + (2000)(0.6) = 1160$$

Since the maximum of these two amounts, 1160, is associated with D_2, D_2 is the recommended decision under the *a priori* criterion.

This decision process is represented by the decision tree in Fig. 17-1. The expected gain of the process, 1160 at node B, is carried back from node D.

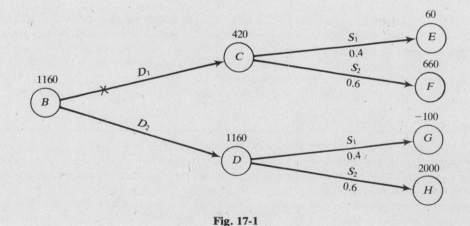

Fig. 17-1

17.4 Determine the recommended decision under the *a priori* criterion for the decision process described in Problem 17.2, if the buyer estimates $P(S_1) = 0.25$, $P(S_2) = 0.40$, and $P(S_3) = 0.35$.

Using the data from Table 17-3, we calculate the expected gains for decisions D_1 through D_4, respectively, as

$$E(G_1) = (-50)(0.25) + (0)(0.40) + (80)(0.35) = 15.5$$
$$E(G_2) = (-10)(0.25) + (30)(0.40) + (35)(0.35) = 21.75$$
$$E(G_3) = (60)(0.25) + (45)(0.40) + (-30)(0.35) = 22.5$$
$$E(G_4) = (80)(0.25) + (40)(0.40) + (-45)(0.35) = 20.25$$

Since the maximum of these expected gains, 22.5, is associated with D_3, D_3 is the recommended decision under the *a priori* criterion.

This process is represented by the decision tree in Fig. 17-2.

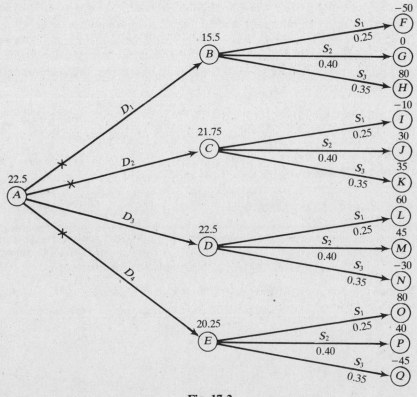

Fig. 17-2

17.5 State and prove Bayes' theorem.

Consider a sample space $\mathscr{S}$ consisting of all possible outcomes of a conceptual experiment (e.g., predicting the state of nature at a particular time). If A and B are two events (subsets) of $\mathscr{S}$, then the conditional probability of A given that B has occurred and the conditional probability of B given that A has occurred are defined by

$$P(A \cap B) = P(B) P(A \mid B) = P(A) P(B \mid A) \tag{1}$$

where $A \cap B$ is the intersection of A and B. Solving (1), we obtain

$$P(B \mid A) = \frac{P(A \mid B)\, P(B)}{P(A)} \tag{2}$$

in which it is assumed that $P(A) > 0$. Equation (2) is the simple form of Bayes' theorem.

The more usual form is obtained by introducing a set of mutually exclusive events, $\{H_1, H_2, \ldots, H_s\}$, whose union is $\mathcal{S}$. Then

$$P(A) = P(A \cap H_1) + P(A \cap H_2) + \cdots + P(A \cap H_s)$$
$$= P(A \mid H_1)\, P(H_1) + P(A \mid H_2)\, P(H_2) + \cdots + P(A \mid H_s)\, P(H_s) \tag{3}$$

Substituting (3) into (2) and choosing $B = H_i$, we have

$$P(H_i \mid A) = \frac{P(A \mid H_i)\, P(H_i)}{\displaystyle\sum_{j=1}^{s} P(A \mid H_j)\, P(H_j)} \tag{4}$$

Loosely speaking, Bayes' theorem, (4), evaluates the probability of the "cause" H_i given the "effect" A.

17.6 The landowner in Example 17.1 has soundings taken on the site where natural gas is suspected, at a cost of \$30 000. The soundings indicate that gas is not present, but the test is not a perfect one. The company conducting the soundings concedes that 30 percent of the time the test will indicate no gas when gas in fact exists. When gas does not exist, the test is accurate 90 percent of the time. Using these data, update the landowner's initial estimate that the probability of finding gas is 0.6 and then determine the recommended decision under the *a posteriori* criterion.

Initially, $P(S_2) = 0.6$, $P(S_1) = 0.4$. Let θ_1 designate the event that soundings indicate no gas. Then the reliability of the test is given by the conditional probabilities $P(\theta_1 \mid S_1) = 0.90$ and $P(\theta_1 \mid S_2) = 0.30$. Bayes' theorem, (4) of Problem 17.4, gives the updated probabilities as

$$P(S_1 \mid \theta_1) = \frac{P(\theta_1 \mid S_1)\, P(S_1)}{P(\theta_1 \mid S_1)\, P(S_1) + P(\theta_1 \mid S_2)\, P(S_2)} = \frac{(0.90)(0.4)}{(0.90)(0.4) + (0.30)(0.6)} = \frac{2}{3}$$

$$P(S_2 \mid \theta_1) = 1 - P(S_1 \mid \theta_1) = \frac{1}{3}$$

The *a posteriori* gain matrix is obtained from Table 17-2 by subtracting 30 (thousand dollars) from each entry, thereby reflecting the cost of the test. The expected gains (in thousands of dollars) for decisions D_1 and D_2, respectively, in terms of the updated probabilities are

$$E(G_1 \mid \theta_1) = (60 - 30)(\tfrac{2}{3}) + (660 - 30)(\tfrac{1}{3}) = 230$$

$$E(G_2 \mid \theta_1) = (-100 - 30)(\tfrac{2}{3}) + (2000 - 30)(\tfrac{1}{3}) = 570$$

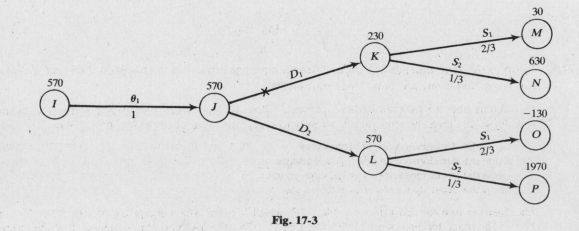

Fig. 17-3

Since the maximum expected gain is associated with D_2, D_2 is the recommended decision under the *a posteriori* criterion.

Figure 17-3 is the decision tree for this process. The probability that the soundings indicate no gas, $P(\theta_1)$, is unity, since the result of the experiment is known.

17.7 Solve Problem 17.6 if the soundings had indicated that gas was present.

Designate the event that soundings indicate gas by θ_2. From the data of Problem 17.6,

$$P(\theta_2 \mid S_1) = 0.10 \qquad P(\theta_2 \mid S_2) = 0.70$$

The initial probabilities are $P(S_1) = 0.4$, $P(S_2) = 0.6$; therefore, the updated probability distribution is

$$P(S_1 \mid \theta_2) = \frac{P(\theta_2 \mid S_1) P(S_1)}{P(\theta_2 \mid S_1) P(S_1) + P(\theta_2 \mid S_2) P(S_2)} = \frac{(0.10)(0.4)}{(0.10)(0.4) + (0.70)(0.6)} = 0.087$$

$$P(S_2 \mid \theta_2) = 1 - P(S_1 \mid \theta_2) = 0.913$$

Again each entry in the original gain matrix, Table 17-2, must be reduced by 30 (thousand dollars) to reflect the cost of the test. Then the expected gains (in thousands of dollars) for decisions D_1 and D_2 with respect to the latest probability distribution are

$$E(G_1 \mid \theta_2) = (60 - 30)(0.087) + (660 - 30)(0.913) = 577.8$$

$$E(G_2 \mid \theta_2) = (-100 - 30)(0.087) + (2000 - 30)(0.913) = 1787.3$$

Since the maximum expected gain is associated with D_2, D_2 is the recommended decision under the *a posteriori* criterion.

Figure 17-4 is the decision tree for this process. The probability that the soundings indicate gas is present, $P(\theta_2)$, is unity, since the result of the experiment is known.

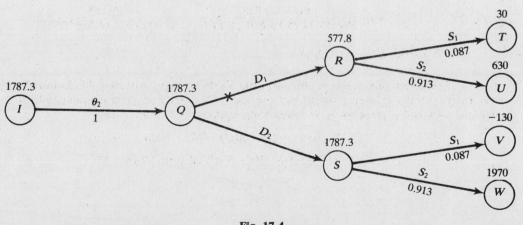

Fig. 17-4

17.8 What is the recommended decision if the soundings discussed in Problems 17.6 and 17.7 have not been taken but are only being considered.

This is now a two-stage decision process. First the landowner must decide whether to conduct soundings, and then she must decide whether to accept the energy company's offer. Write

$D_I \equiv$ the decision to conduct soundings
$D_{II} \equiv$ the decision not to conduct soundings
$\theta_1 \equiv$ the event that soundings indicate no gas
$\theta_2 \equiv$ the event that soundings indicate gas

The decision tree for this process is Fig. 17-5, which is essentially a composite of Figs. 17-1, 17-3, and 17-4. The main differences are in $P(\theta_1)$ and $P(\theta_2)$. These probabilities are no longer 1, as they were in

Figs. 17-3 and 17-4, because the result of the soundings is unknown. The states S_1 and S_2 are, however, a disjoint, exhaustive set of outcomes; hence, from (3) of Problem 17.5 and the data provided in Problems 17.6 and 17.7,

$$P(\theta_1) = P(\theta_1 \mid S_1)\,P(S_1) + P(\theta_1 \mid S_2)\,P(S_2) = (0.90)(0.4) + (0.30)(0.6) = 0.54$$

$$P(\theta_2) = P(\theta_2 \mid S_1)\,P(S_1) + P(\theta_2 \mid S_2)\,P(S_2) = (0.10)(0.4) + (0.70)(0.6) = 0.46$$

With these probabilities, the expected gain at node I is

$$(570)(0.54) + (1787.3)(0.46) = 1130$$

Since node B has a larger expected gain than node I, D_I is recommended over D_{II}. The recommended decisions, therefore, are not to conduct soundings and not to accept the offer of the energy company. Instead the landowner should begin exploring the land on her own immediately.

Observe that the recommended decision is D_2 regardless of whether soundings are taken and regardless of the outcome of the soundings if they are conducted. Thus, the soundings have no effect on the final decision and represent only an expense. This is reflected in the fact that the difference between the expected gains at nodes B and I in Fig. 17-5 is precisely the cost of the test.

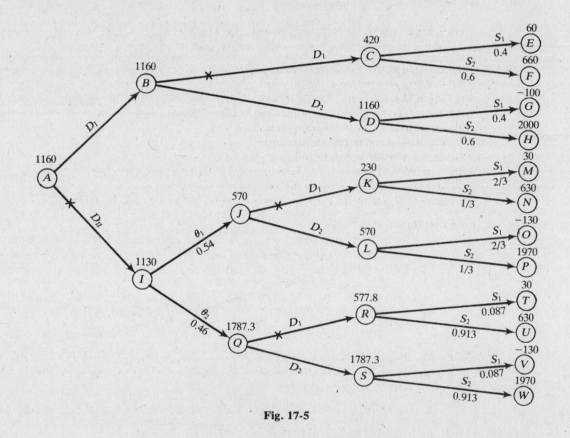

Fig. 17-5

17.9　A city is considering replacing its fleet of municipally owned, gasoline-powered automobiles by electric cars. The manufacturer of the electric cars claims that the city will experience significant savings over the life of the fleet if it converts, but the city has its doubts. If the manufacturer is correct, the city will save 1 million dollars. If the new technology is faulty, as some critics suggest, the conversion will cost the city $450 000. A third possibility is that neither situation will occur and the city will break even with the conversion. According to a recently completed consultant's report, the respective probabilities of these three events are 0.25, 0.45, and 0.30.

The city has before it a pilot program that if implemented would indicate the potential cost or savings in a conversion to electric cars. The program involves renting three electric cars for 3 months and running them under normal conditions. The cost to the city of this pilot program would be $50 000. The city's consultant believes that the results of the pilot program would be significant but not conclusive; she submits Table 17-4, a compilation of probabilities based on the experience of other cities, to support her contention. What actions should the city take if it wants to maximize expected savings?

Table 17-4

A pilot program will indicate

		Savings	No Change	A Loss
Given that a conversion	Saves Money	0.6	0.3	0.1
	Breaks Even	0.4	0.4	0.2
	Loses Money	0.1	0.5	0.4

This is a two-stage process. First the city must decide whether to conduct the pilot program, and then it must decide whether to convert its fleet to electric cars. Set

$D_I \equiv$ the decision not to conduct the pilot program
$D_{II} \equiv$ the decision to conduct the pilot program
$\theta_1 \equiv$ the event that the pilot program indicates a savings
$\theta_2 \equiv$ the event that the pilot program indicates neither a savings nor a loss
$\theta_3 \equiv$ the event that the pilot program indicates a loss
$D_1 \equiv$ the decision to convert to electric cars
$D_2 \equiv$ the decision not to convert to electric cars
$S_1 \equiv$ the state that electric cars are cheaper to run than gasoline models
$S_2 \equiv$ the state that electric cars cost the same to run as gasoline models
$S_3 \equiv$ the state that electric cars are more expensive to run than gasoline models

The gain matrix (in thousands of dollars) is

	S_1	S_2	S_3
D_1	1000	0	−450
D_2	0	0	0

The initial probability distribution for the states has $P(S_1) = 0.25$, $P(S_2) = 0.30$, and $P(S_3) = 0.45$.

If the pilot program is not conducted, the initial probability distribution is not updated, and the expected gains for D_1 and D_2 are, respectively,

$$E(G_1) = (1000)(0.25) + (0)(0.30) + (-450)(0.45) = 47.5$$

$$E(G_2) = (0)(0.25) + (0)(0.30) + (0)(0.45) = 0$$

Since the maximum expected gain is associated with D_1, D_1 is the recommended decision under the *a priori* criterion.

If the pilot program is conducted, all entries in the gain matrix must be reduced by 50 to reflect the cost of the test. It follows from Table 17-4 that

$$P(\theta_1 | S_1) = 0.6 \qquad P(\theta_1 | S_2) = 0.4 \qquad P(\theta_1 | S_3) = 0.1$$

$$P(\theta_2 | S_1) = 0.3 \qquad P(\theta_2 | S_2) = 0.4 \qquad P(\theta_2 | S_3) = 0.5$$

$$P(\theta_3 | S_1) = 0.1 \qquad P(\theta_3 | S_2) = 0.2 \qquad P(\theta_3 | S_3) = 0.4$$

Using Bayes' theorem, (4) of Problem 17.5, we obtain

$$P(S_1 \mid \theta_1) = \frac{(0.6)(0.25)}{(0.6)(0.25) + (0.4)(0.30) + (0.1)(0.45)} = 0.4762 \qquad (1)$$

$$P(S_2 \mid \theta_1) = \frac{(0.4)(0.30)}{(0.6)(0.25) + (0.4)(0.30) + (0.1)(0.45)} = 0.3810 \qquad (2)$$

$$P(S_3 \mid \theta_1) = \frac{(0.1)(0.45)}{(0.6)(0.25) + (0.4)(0.30) + (0.1)(0.45)} = 0.1429 \qquad (3)$$

$$P(S_1 \mid \theta_2) = \frac{(0.3)(0.25)}{(0.3)(0.25) + (0.4)(0.30) + (0.5)(0.45)} = 0.1786 \qquad (4)$$

$$P(S_2 \mid \theta_2) = \frac{(0.4)(0.30)}{(0.3)(0.25) + (0.4)(0.30) + (0.5)(0.45)} = 0.2857 \qquad (5)$$

$$P(S_3 \mid \theta_2) = \frac{(0.5)(0.45)}{(0.3)(0.25) + (0.4)(0.30) + (0.5)(0.45)} = 0.5357 \qquad (6)$$

$$P(S_1 \mid \theta_3) = \frac{(0.1)(0.25)}{(0.1)(0.25) + (0.2)(0.30) + (0.4)(0.45)} = 0.0943 \qquad (7)$$

$$P(S_2 \mid \theta_3) = \frac{(0.2)(0.30)}{(0.1)(0.25) + (0.2)(0.30) + (0.4)(0.45)} = 0.2264 \qquad (8)$$

$$P(S_3 \mid \theta_3) = \frac{(0.4)(0.45)}{(0.1)(0.25) + (0.2)(0.30) + (0.4)(0.45)} = 0.6792 \qquad (9)$$

To within roundoff errors, each set of three probabilities sums to 1.

If the result of the pilot program is θ_1, the updated probabilities are given by (1) through (3), and the expected gains for decisions D_1 and D_2 are, respectively,

$$E(G_1 \mid \theta_1) = (950)(0.4762) + (-50)(0.3810) + (-500)(0.1429) = 361.9 \qquad E(G_2 \mid \theta_1) = -50$$

The recommended decision under the *a posteriori* criterion is D_1.

If the result of the pilot program is θ_2, the updated probabilities are given by (4) through (6), and the expected gains for decisions D_1 and D_2 are, respectively,

$$E(G_1 \mid \theta_2) = (950)(0.1786) + (-50)(0.2857) + (-500)(0.5357) = -112.5 \qquad E(G_2 \mid \theta_2) = -50$$

The recommended decision under the *a posteriori* criterion is D_2.

If the result of the pilot program is θ_3, the updated probabilities are given by (7) through (9), and the expected gains for D_1 and D_2 are, respectively,

$$E(G_1 \mid \theta_3) = (950)(0.0943) + (-50)(0.2264) + (-500)(0.6792) = -261.3 \qquad E(G_2 \mid \theta_3) = -50$$

The recommended decision under the *a posteriori* criterion is D_2.

The decision tree for this process is Fig. 17-6, wherein the results obtained so far appear on the unlettered nodes and the branches leading to and from those nodes. The expected gains at nodes B, E, F, and G are the gains associated with the succeeding nodes if the recommended decisions are taken.

It follows from (3) of Problem 17.5 that

$$P(\theta_1) = P(\theta_1 \mid S_1) P(S_1) + P(\theta_1 \mid S_2) P(S_2) + P(\theta_1 \mid S_3) P(S_3)$$
$$= (0.6)(0.25) + (0.4)(0.30) + (0.1)(0.45) = 0.315$$

$$P(\theta_2) = P(\theta_2 \mid S_1) P(S_1) + P(\theta_2 \mid S_2) P(S_2) + P(\theta_2 \mid S_3) P(S_3)$$
$$= (0.3)(0.25) + (0.4)(0.30) + (0.5)(0.45) = 0.420$$

$$P(\theta_3) = P(\theta_3 \mid S_1) P(S_1) + P(\theta_3 \mid S_2) P(S_2) + P(\theta_3 \mid S_3) P(S_3)$$
$$= (0.1)(0.25) + (0.2)(0.30) + (0.4)(0.45) = 0.265$$

Then the expected gain at node C is

$$(361.9)(0.315) + (-50)(0.420) + (-50)(0.265) = 79.75$$

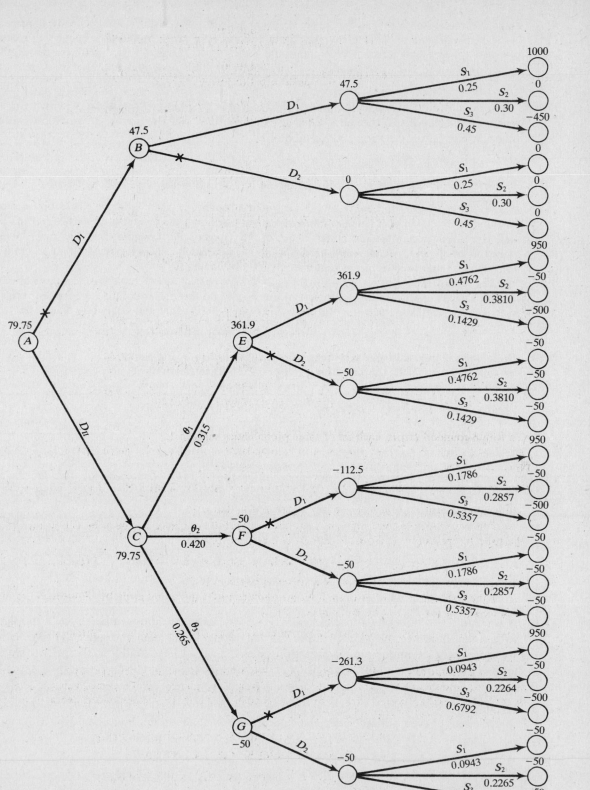

Fig. 17-6

Since this value is greater than the expected gain at node B, the decision leading to node C, namely D_{II}, is the recommended one. The city should conduct the pilot program and then convert to electrically powered vehicles only if the pilot program has indicated a savings. This solution to the problem is represented in Fig. 17-6 by the subtree made up of all paths from node A that are not blocked by a cross.

17.10 Devise a situation in which the gains listed in Table 17-2 do not realistically reflect the actual worth of the payoffs to the landowner in Example 17.1. Show how the von Neumann utility function can be used to correct the inequities.

The payoffs in descending order of preference are

$$e_1 = \$2\,000\,000 \qquad e_2 = \$660\,000 \qquad e_3 = \$60\,000 \qquad e_4 = -\$100\,000$$

If \$100 000 represents the entire life savings of the landowner, then losing it would be catastrophic. Avoiding such a loss might be more important to the landowner than winning \$2 000 000, yet this preference is not reflected in the raw dollar figures of the payoffs. Furthermore, \$660 000 might be enough money to satisfy all the landowner's earthly wants. Two million dollars is obviously better; but it might not be three times as valuable, as suggested by the raw numbers.

The landowner might set the utility of e_1 at 100 and that of e_4 at -1000 to reflect the fear of losing her life savings. After much introspection, she might find that she is indifferent between receiving e_2 with certainty and participating in the lottery $\mathcal{L}(e_1, e_4; 0.999)$. Then the utility of e_2 would be

$$u(e_2) = (0.999)u(e_1) + (1 - 0.999)u(e_4) = (0.999)(100) + (0.001)(-1000) = 98.9$$

The landowner might also find that she is indifferent between receiving e_3 with certainty and participating in the lottery $\mathcal{L}(e_1, e_4; 0.95)$. Then the utility of e_3 is

$$u(e_3) = (0.95)u(e_1) + (1 - 0.95)u(e_4) = (0.95)(100) + (0.05)(-1000) = 45$$

The gain matrix for the decision process in terms of these utilities is Table 17-5.

Table 17-5

	S_1	S_2
D_1	45	98.9
D_2	-1000	100

17.11 Determine the recommended decision under the *a priori* criterion for the landowner in Example 17.1, if the gain matrix is given by the utilities in Table 17-5 and if the landowner estimates the probability of gas being present as 0.6.

With $P(S_1) = 0.4$ and $P(S_2) = 0.6$, the expected gains for D_1 and D_2 are, respectively,

$$E(G_1) = (45)(0.4) + (98.9)(0.6) = 77.34 \qquad E(G_2) = (-1000)(0.4) + (100)(0.6) = -340$$

The recommended decision is D_1. Contrast this result with the result of Problem 17.3.

17.12 A woman has a ticket to a football game on a day for which the weather bureau predicts rain with a likelihood of 40 percent. She can stay home and watch the game on television, the preferable choice under rainy conditions, or she can go to the stadium, the preferable choice under dry conditions. Which decision should she make?

Designate the decision to go to the stadium by D_1 and the decision to stay home by D_2. The states of nature are S_1 (it will rain) and S_2 (it will not rain), with $P(S_1) = 0.4$, $P(S_2) = 0.6$. The four possible combinations of events, listed in descending order of desirability to the woman, are

e_1: Goes to the stadium and it does not rain.
e_2: Stays home and it rains.
e_3: Stays home and it does not rain.
e_4: Goes to the stadium and it rains.

The individual quantifies her levels of satisfaction for e_1 and e_4 at 100 and 0, respectively. After careful consideration, she feels that she would be indifferent to having e_2 occur with certainty or participating in the lottery $\mathcal{L}(e_1, e_4; 0.85)$. She sets the equivalence probability for e_3 at $p_3 = 0.5$. Therefore,

$$u(e_2) = (0.85)(100) + (0.15)(0) = 85 \qquad u(e_3) = (0.5)(100) + (0.5)(0) = 50$$

The gain matrix in terms of utilities for this process becomes

	S_1	S_2
D_1	0	100
D_2	85	50

The expected gains for decisions D_1 and D_2 are, respectively,

$$E(G_1) = (0)(0.4) + (100)(0.6) = 60$$
$$E(G_2) = (85)(0.4) + (50)(0.6) = 64$$

Since $E(G_2)$ is greater than $E(G_1)$, the recommended decision under the *a priori* criterion is D_2; the woman should stay home.

17.13 Solve Problem 17.4 if the department store's utility for money is given by Fig. 17-7.

Since the monetary amounts in Table 17-3 do not reflect the relative worth to the store of the various payoffs, we replace each amount by its utility, obtaining Table 17-6.

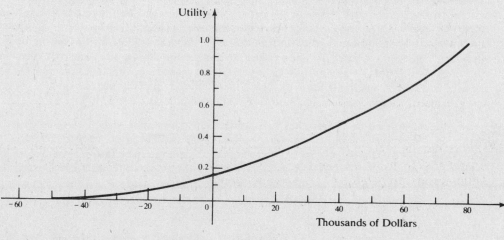

Fig. 17-7

With $P(S_1) = 0.25$, $P(S_2) = 0.4$, $P(S_3) = 0.35$, the expected gains are

$$E(G_1) = (0)(0.25) + (0.15)(0.4) + (1)(0.35) = 0.410$$
$$E(G_2) = (0.09)(0.25) + (0.38)(0.4) + (0.43)(0.35) = 0.325$$
$$E(G_2) = (0.72)(0.25) + (0.53)(0.4) + (0.02)(0.35) = 0.399$$
$$E(G_4) = (1)(0.25) + (0.48)(0.4) + (0)(0.35) = 0.442$$

The recommended decision under the *a priori* criterion is now D_4.

Table 17-6

	S_1	S_2	S_3
D_1	0	0.15	1
D_2	0.09	0.38	0.43
D_3	0.72	0.53	0.02
D_4	1	0.48	0

17.14 The *certainty equivalent* of a decision with monetary payoffs is a dollar amount C having a utility equal to the expected utility of that decision. Determine the certainty equivalents for each of the decisions in Problem 17.13.

The expected utility for D_1 was determined in Problem 17.13 to be 0.410. Using Fig. 17-7, we estimate $u(33\,000) = 0.410$; hence $C_1 = \$33\,000$.

Similarly, we estimate the certainty equivalents of D_2, D_3, and D_4 as $C_2 = \$24\,000$, $C_3 = \$32\,000$, and $C_4 = \$36\,000$, respectively.

17.15 The *risk premium* for a decision with monetary payoffs is the amount R by which the expected dollar gain from that decision exceeds the certainty equivalent of the decision. Determine the risk premiums for each of the decisions in Problem 17.13.

The expected dollar gains for D_1 through D_4 were obtained in Problem 17.4 as $15 500$, $21 750$, $22 500$, and $20 250$, respectively. Taking the differences between these amounts and their corresponding certainty equivalents as determined in Problem 17.14, we find that

$$R_1 = 15\,500 - 33\,000 = -\$17\,500$$
$$R_2 = 21\,750 - 24\,000 = -\$2250$$
$$R_3 = 22\,500 - 32\,000 = -\$9500$$
$$R_4 = 20\,250 - 36\,000 = -\$15\,750$$

Supplementary Problems

17.16 *Determine recommended decisions under each naive criterion for the following decision process.* In the fall, a farmer is offered $50 000 for his orange crop, which will be harvested in the beginning of the following year. If the farmer accepts the offer, the money is his, regardless of the quality or quantity of the harvest. If the farmer does not accept the offer, he must sell his oranges on the open market after they are harvested. Under normal growing conditions, the farmer can anticipate receiving $70 000 on the open market for his harvest. If he experiences a frost, however, then much of his harvest will be ruined, and he can anticipate receiving only $15 000 on the open market.

17.17 A manufacturer must decide whether to extend credit to a retailer wishing to open an account with the firm. Past experience with new accounts shows that 50 percent are poor risks, 30 percent are average risks, and 20 percent are good risks. If credit is extended, the manufacturer can expect to lose $30 000 with a poor risk, make $25 000 with an average risk, and make $50 000 with a good risk. If credit is not extended, the manufacturer neither makes nor loses money, since no business is transacted with the retailer. Determine the recommended decision under the *a priori* criterion.

17.18 A corporation is considering a new production process that, if efficient, will save the corporation $350 000 a year for the next 5 years. If it is not efficient, the amount of lost sales plus the expense of converting to the new process and then reconverting to the old will come to $925 000. Determine the recommended decision under the *a priori* criterion if the company feels that the new process has an 80 percent chance of being efficient.

17.19 Determine the recommended decision under the *a priori* criterion for the process of Problem 17.16 if, in the past, the farmer has lost much of his harvest to frost one out of every 7 years.

17.20 Assume that prior to making a decision, the manufacturer described in Problem 17.17 pays $1000 for a credit rating report on the retailer. The report rates the retailer as a poor risk, but the manufacturer knows that the rating procedure is not totally reliable. The credit bureau concedes that it will rate an average risk as a poor risk 30 percent of the time, and it will rate a good risk as a poor risk 5 percent of the time. It will rate a poor risk correctly 90 percent of the time. Based on these data, determine the recommended decision for the manufacturer under the *a posteriori* criterion.

17.21 The corporation of Problem 17.18 has a third option available to it; namely, to integrate one stand-alone phase of the new process into its current process and test its efficiency before deciding whether to convert. The cost of testing the stand-alone phase is $125 000, of which $75 000 is recoverable if the new process is adopted. If the stand-alone phase is not efficient, then an additional $25 000 in sales is lost during the test.

If the entire new process is efficient, then the stand-alone phase should operate efficiently with probability 0.99. If the entire new process is not efficient, the stand-alone phase could still operate efficiently, and the company estimates this would happen with probability 0.6. Construct a decision tree for the entire decision process and determine the recommended actions.

17.22 The president of a firm in a highly competitive industry believes that an employee of the company is providing confidential information to the competition. She is 90 percent certain that this informer is the treasurer of the firm, whose contacts have been extremely valuable in obtaining financing for the company. If she fires him and he is the informer, the company gains $100 000. If he is fired but is not the informer, the company loses his expertise and still has an informer on the staff, for a net loss to the company of $500 000. If the president does not fire the treasurer, the company loses $300 000 whether or not he is the informer, since in either case the informer is still with the company.

Before deciding the fate of the treasurer, the president could order lie detector tests. To avoid possible lawsuits, such tests would have to be administered to all company employees, at a total cost of $30 000. Another problem is that lie detector tests are not definitive. If a person is lying, the test will reveal it 90 percent of the time; but if a person is not lying, the test will indicate it only 70 percent of the time. What actions should the president take?

17.23 A food processor is considering the introduction of a new line of instant lunches. On a national basis, the company estimates a net profit of 50 million dollars if the product is highly successful, a net profit of 20 million dollars if it is moderately successful, and a loss of 14 million dollars if it is not successful. If the company does not introduce the line, its research and development costs totaling 3 million dollars must be written off as a loss. Current estimates place the probability of high success at 0.1 and the probability of moderate success at 0.4.

Prior to introducing it on a national level, the company could test market the line on a regional basis. The cost of such a test would be one million dollars. Although the test results would be significant, they would not be conclusive; the reliability of such a test is given by the conditional probabilities in Table 17-7. What should be the processor's decisions?

Test results will indicate

	High Success	Moderate Success	No Success
Highly Successful	0.6	0.4	0
Moderately Successful	0.2	0.6	0.2
Not Successful	0.1	0.3	0.6

(Given that a product is)

17.24 Determine the maximum amount of money the city in Problem 17.9 should be willing to pay for the pilot program. (*Hint*: The *value* of a test is the difference between the expected gain of the process if the test is conducted *at no cost* and the expected gain of the process if no testing is conducted.)

17.25 Determine the maximum amount of money that the president in Problem 17.22 should be willing to pay for lie detector tests. Construct a tree for the process.

17.26 Solve Problem 17.23 if the processor's utility for money is given by Fig. 17-8.

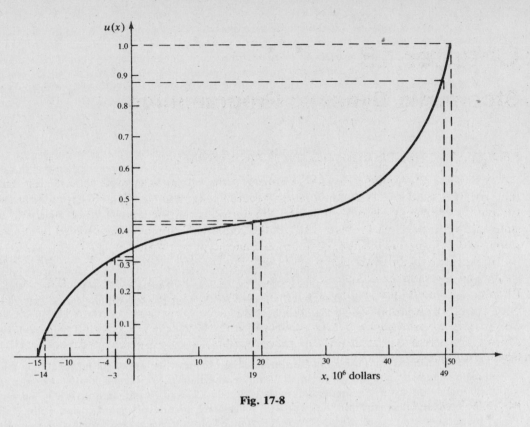

Fig. 17-8

17.27 Derive utilities for the dollar outcomes $e_1 = \$5000$, $e_2 = \$4000$, $e_3 = \$3000$, $e_4 = \$2000$, and $e_5 = \$1000$ if $u(e_1) = 100$, $u(e_5) = -50$, and the equivalence probabilities are $p_2 = 0.9$, $p_3 = 0.7$, and $p_4 = 0.2$.

17.28 Determine the certainty equivalent and the risk premium for the recommended decisions in Problem 17.26

17.29 A decision maker is *risk-seeking* with respect to a decision process over a specified range of payoffs if his or her utility function $u(x)$ is strictly convex (i.e., $u''(x) > 0$) over that range. The decision maker is *risk-averse* if $u(x)$ is strictly concave (i.e., $u''(x) < 0$) over that range. If $u(x)$ is a straight line (i.e., $u''(x) = 0$) on that range, the decision maker is *risk-indifferent* there. Determine the risk attitudes of the processor in Problem 17.26.

17.30 From the definitions of concave and convex functions given in Chapter 11 and the fact that utility functions increase monotonically, show that risk premiums are positive for a risk-averse decision maker and negative for a risk-seeking decision maker.

17.31 A *regret matrix* is a gain matrix in which the elements of each column have been diminished by the largest element of that column.   Give the regret matrix corresponding to Table 17-3.

17.32 Solve Problems 17.1 and 17.3 using the regret matrix instead of Table 17-2. Thereby verify that recommended decisions with a regret matrix need not be the same as those with a gain matrix under naive criteria, but the two matrices always yield the same recommended decision under the *a priori* criterion.

Chapter 18

Stochastic Dynamic Programming

STOCHASTIC MULTISTAGE DECISION PROCESSES

A multistage decision process is *stochastic* if the return associated with at least one decision in the process is random. This randomness generally enters in one of two ways: either the states (see Chapter 14) are uniquely determined by the decisions but the returns associated with one or more states are uncertain (see Problem 18.1) or the returns are uniquely determined by the states but the states arising from one or more decisions are uncertain (see Problem 18.2).

If the probability distributions governing the random events are known and if the number of stages and the number of states are finite, then the dynamic programming approach introduced in Chapter 14 is useful for optimizing a stochastic multistage decision process. The general procedure is to optimize the expected value of the return. (For an exception, see Problem 18.3.) In those cases where the randomness occurs exclusively in the returns associated with the states and not in the states arising from the decisions, this procedure has the effect of transforming a stochastic process into a deterministic one.

POLICY TABLES

For processes in which randomness exists in the states associated with the decisions, a policy—in particular, an optimal policy—may be exhibited as a *policy table*, similar to Table 18-1. Here, $d_j(a_k)$ $(j = 1, 2, \ldots, n; \; k = 1, 2, \ldots, r)$ denotes the decision at stage j if the process finds itself in state a_k. (See Problem 18.3.)

Table 18-1

States

Stages		a_1	a_2	$\cdots$	a_r
	1	$d_1(a_1)$	$d_1(a_2)$	$\cdots$	$d_1(a_r)$
	2	$d_2(a_1)$	$d_2(a_2)$	$\cdots$	$d_2(a_r)$
	$\cdots$				
	n	$d_n(a_1)$	$d_n(a_2)$	$\cdots$	$d_n(a_r)$

Solved Problems

18.1 Eight bushels of oranges are to be distributed among three stores. The demand for oranges at each store is random, according to the probability distributions shown in Table 18-2. The profit per sold bushel at stores 1, 2, and 3 is $18, $20, and $21, respectively. Determine the number of bushels (constrained to be an integer) that should be allocated to each store to maximize expected total profit.

This is a three-stage decision process, with stage j representing a delivery of oranges to store j. The states for each stage are $u = 0, 1, \ldots, 8$, representing the numbers of bushels available for delivery

Table 18-2

	Demand Probabilities		
Bushels	Store 1	Store 2	Store 3
0	0.1	0	0.1
1	0.2	0.2	0.3
2	0.3	0.6	0.2
3	0.2	0	0.2
4	0.1	0.2	0
5	0.1	0	0.2

to a store.   There is no randomness in the state resulting from any decision—if 2 bushels are allocated to a store, then that store will stock 2 bushels—but there is randomness in the return from any state.   With 2 bushels in stock, a store may sell either 0, 1, or 2 bushels, with each possibility generating a different profit.   Consequently, we maximize *expected* total profit rather than total profit.   We define

$f_j(x) \equiv$ the expected profit from allocating x bushels to store j

$m_j(u) \equiv$ the maximum expected total profit beginning at stage j in state u

$d_j(u) \equiv$ the decision taken at stage j that achieves $m_j(u)$

The values of the payoff functions (in dollars) are exhibited in Table 18-3.   A typical calculation—say, that of $f_1(3)$—follows: With 3 bushels allocated to it, store 1 makes a profit of \$0 if 0 bushels are sold; \$18 if 1; \$36 if 2; \$54 if 3.   The respective probabilities of the first three of these events are, from Table 18-2, 0.1, 0.2, and 0.3.   The probability of the fourth event is the probability that the demand will equal or exceed 3 bushels, $0.2 + 0.1 + 0.1 = 0.4$.   Thus,

$$f_1(3) = (0)(0.1) + (18)(0.2) + (36)(0.3) + (54)(0.4) = 36$$

In terms of these $f_j(x)$, we have a formally deterministic problem that is covered by the model

Table 18-3

f \ x	0	1	2	3	4	5	6	7	8
$f_1(x)$	0	16.20	28.80	36.00	39.60	41.40	41.40	41.40	41.40
$f_2(x)$	0	20.00	36.00	40.00	44.00	44.00	44.00	44.00	44.00
$f_3(x)$	0	18.90	31.50	39.90	44.10	48.30	48.30	48.30	

Table 18-4

	u								
	0	1	2	3	4	5	6	7	8
$m_3(u)$	0	18.90	31.50	39.90	44.10	48.30	48.30	48.30	48.30
$d_3(u)$	0	1	2	3	4	5	5	5	5
$m_2(u)$	0	20.00	38.90	54.90	67.50	75.90	80.10	84.30	88.30
$d_2(u)$	0	1	1	2	2	2	2	2	3
$m_1(u)$	...	...	...	...	...	...	...	...	111.90
$d_1(u)$	...	...	...	...	...	...	...	...	3

(14.1). Applying the techniques of Chapter 14, we generate Table 18-4. The optimal policy is to allocate 3 bushels of oranges to store 1, 2 bushels to store 2, and 3 bushels to store 3, for an expected total profit of $111.90.

18.2 A person has 3 (thousand-dollar) units of money available for investment in a business opportunity that matures in 1 year. The opportunity is risky in that the return is either double or nothing. Based on past performance, the likelihood of doubling one's money is 0.6, while the chance of losing an investment is 0.4. Determine an investment strategy for the next 4 years that will maximize expected total holdings at the end of that period, if money earned one year can be reinvested in a later year and if investments are restricted to unit amounts.

This is a four-stage process, with each stage representing a year. The states are the amounts available for investment: $u_4 = 0, 1, \ldots, 24$ (the last obtained by investing all available funds each year and having the investment double each time) for stage 4; $u_3 = 0, 1, \ldots, 12$ for stage 3; $u_2 = 0, 1, \ldots, 6$ for stage 2; $u_1 = 3$ for stage 1. Randomness here occurs in the state induced by a particular decision. For example, if one has 3 units (i.e., the present state is 3) and decides to invest 2 units, then the succeeding state is either 5 or 1, depending on whether the invested amount is doubled or is lost. Write

$m_j(u_j) \equiv$ the maximum expected holdings at the end of the process, starting in state u_j at stage j

$d_j(u_j) \equiv$ the amount invested at stage j that achieves $m_j(u_j)$

If one enters stage j with u_j units, then x units ($x = 0, 1, \ldots, u_j$) may be invested, leaving $u_j - x$ units in reserve. If the invested amount doubles, there will be

$$2x + (u_j - x) = u_j + x$$

units available for the next stage; if the invested units are lost, then only the reserve of $(u_j - x)$ units will be available for the next stage. The best return from that point is either $m_{j+1}(u_j + x)$ or $m_{j+1}(u_j - x)$, the expected value of this best return being

$$0.6\, m_{j+1}(u_j + x) + 0.4\, m_{j+1}(u_j - x)$$

The optimal choice for x is that amount which maximizes the above expression:

$$m_j(u_j) = \underset{x=0, 1, \ldots, u_j}{\text{maximum}} [0.6\, m_{j+1}(u_j + x) + 0.4\, m_{j+1}(u_j - x)] \tag{1}$$

Equation *(1)*, the recursion formula for the process, holds for $j = 1, 2, 3$; it also holds for $j = 4$, under the end condition $m_5(u) \equiv u$. It is obvious that since m_5 is a linear, increasing function, so are $m_4, \ldots, m_1$. Indeed, carrying out the maximization in *(1)*, we readily obtain

$$m_4(u_4) = 1.2 u_4 \qquad m_3(u_3) = (1.2)^2 u_3 \qquad m_2(u_2) = (1.2)^3 u_2 \qquad m_1(u_1) = (1.2)^4 u_1$$

with $d_j(u_j) = u_j$ $(j = 4, 3, 2, 1)$. Thus the optimal expected holdings is

$$m_1(3) = (1.2)^4(3) = 6.2208 \text{ units}$$

obtained by investing all available units each year of the process. Note that such an optimal policy results in either 48 units or 0 units at the end of 4 years, depending on whether all investments double or one investment is completely lost. Nonetheless, the *expected* return under that policy is

$$(48)(0.6)^4 + (0)[1 - (0.6)^4] = 6.2208 \text{ units}$$

where $(0.6)^4$ is the probability that all four investments are successful and $1 - (0.6)^4$ is the probability that at least one investment fails.

18.3 Solve Problem 18.2 if the objective is to maximize the probability of accumulating holdings of at least 5 (thousand-dollar) units after 4 years.

This problem deals not with the *expected value* of the return but rather with the *probability* that the return is of a certain size. For example, if the investor adopts the policy of investing all available units at each stage, then, as was shown in Problem 18.2, the probability that he or she ends up with 5 or more units is $(0.6)^4 = 0.1296$. The question is: can that value be bettered by another choice of policy?

The states and stages are as defined in Problem 18.2. Write

$E \equiv$ the event of finishing the process with 5 or more units

$m_j(u_j) \equiv$ the probability of E given that the state at stage j is u_j and an optimal policy is followed from stage j onwards

$d_j(u_j) \equiv$ the amount invested at stage j that achieves $m_j(u_j)$

If x units $(x = 0, 1, \ldots, u_j)$ are invested at stage j, then, as in Problem 18.2,

$$P(u_{j+1} = u_j + x) = 0.6 \qquad P(u_{j+1} = u_j - x) = 0.4$$

By the rules of conditional probabilities [(3) of Problem 17.5, with $H_1 \equiv$ "double" and $H_2 \equiv$ "nothing"], the expression

$$0.6 m_{j+1}(u_j + x) + 0.4 m_{j+1}(u_j - x)$$

represents the probability of E given u_j, the decision x, and an optimal continuation from stage $j + 1$. Hence,

$$m_j(u_j) = \max_{x=0,1,\ldots,u_j} [0.6 m_{j+1}(u_j + x) + 0.4 m_{j+1}(u_j - x)] \tag{1}$$

for $j = 1, 2, 3$. Formally, this is identical to the difference equation obtained in Problem 18.2; however, a new end condition applies.

Conditioning on the outcome of the final investment decision, we have

$$m_4(u_4) = \max_{x=0,1,\ldots,u_4} [0.6 P(u_4 + x \geq 5) + 0.4 P(u_4 - x \geq 5)]$$

$$\equiv \max_x [F + G] \tag{2}$$

With the aid of Fig. 18-1, we carry out the maximization in (2), obtaining

$$m_4(u_4) = \begin{cases} 0 & u_4 = 0, 1, 2 \\ 0.6 & u_4 = 3, 4 \\ 1 & u_4 = 5, 6, \ldots, 24 \end{cases} \quad \text{with} \quad d_4(u_4) = \begin{cases} 0 & u_4 = 0, 1, 2 \\ 2 & u_4 = 3 \\ 1 & u_4 = 4 \\ 0 & u_4 = 5, 6, \ldots, 24 \end{cases} \tag{3}$$

where the *smallest* optimal investment $d_4(u_4)$ has been indicated.

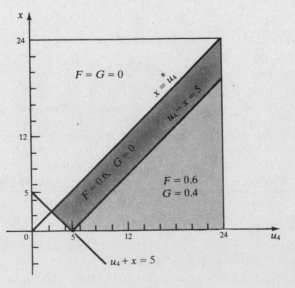

Fig. 18-1

Table 18-5 presents the solution of (1) subject to the end condition (3). Again, only the smallest $d_j(u_j)$ is listed in the event of a tie. It is seen that the maximum probability for accumulating at least 5 units of money in 4 years is 0.7056. A policy table, of the form of Table 18-1, for realizing this maximum probability may be composed by extracting rows 8, 4, 6, and 2 of Table 18-5. Either table shows that under this particular optimal policy the investor finishes with 0, 1, or 5 units, the probability of the last event being 0.7056. Alternative optimal policies exist which allow the investor to accumulate more than 5 units, but always with a probability of 0.7056 for 5 or more units.

Table 18-5

	0	1	2	3	4	5	6	$\cdots$	12	$\cdots$	24
$m_4(u_4)$	0	0	0	0.6	0.6	1	1	$\cdots$	1	$\cdots$	1
$d_4(u_4)$	0	0	0	2	1	0	0	$\cdots$	0	$\cdots$	0
$m_3(u_3)$	0	0	0.36	0.6	0.84	1	1	$\cdots$	1		
$d_3(u_3)$	0	0	1	0	1	0	0	$\cdots$	0		
$m_2(u_2)$	0	0.216	0.504	0.648	0.84	1	1				
$d_2(u_2)$	0	1	2	1	0	0	0				
$m_1(u_1)$	$\cdots$	$\cdots$	$\cdots$	0.7056							
$d_1(u_1)$	$\cdots$	$\cdots$	$\cdots$	1							

18.4　The manufacturer of a space shuttle for NASA has the capability to produce at most two shuttles each year. It takes a full year to manufacture a shuttle, but since orders are not placed by NASA until July, for delivery in December, the manufacturer must set the production schedule prior to knowing the exact demand. This demand will be for either one shuttle, with probability 0.6, or two shuttles, with probability 0.4. Any shuttle ordered but not delivered incurs a penalty cost of 1.5 million dollars and must be delivered the following year, taking priority over any new orders in the future. Production costs are a function of the number of shuttles made, with the cost of one shuttle set at 10 million dollars and the cost of two shuttles set at 19 million dollars. Overproduction can be stored for future delivery, at a cost of 1.1 million dollars per shuttle per year, and is limited by company policy to a maximum of 1 shuttle. Determine a production schedule for the next 3 years that will minimize expected total cost, if the current inventory is zero shuttles.

We view this as a four-stage process, with stages 1, 2, and 3 representing the next 3 years in the planning horizon, respectively, and stage 4 representing the delayed production of those shuttles ordered in year 3 but not delivered. The states are the possible inventories at the beginning of a stage: they range from a low of −2 (signifying two shuttles ordered but not delivered) to a high of 1. We set

$u \equiv$ the number of shuttles in inventory $(u = -2, -1, 0, 1)$

$m_j(u) \equiv$ the minimum expected cost for completing the process beginning at stage j in state u

$d_j(u) \equiv$ the production in stage j that achieves $m_j(u)$

$D \equiv$ the yearly demand $[P(D = 1) = 0.6,\ P(D = 2) = 0.4]$

$f(x) \equiv$ the cost of producing x shuttles in 1 year

If the firm enters stage j $(j = 1, 2, 3)$ with $u = 0, 1$ shuttles in inventory and decides to produce x additional shuttles $(x = 0, 1, 2)$ in that stage, it incurs a carrying charge of $1.1u$ on its inventory and a production cost $f(x)$ for the new shuttles, for a yearly expenditure of

$$f(x) + 1.1u \qquad (1)$$

The total number of shuttles available for delivery at the end of the year is $u + x$, which leaves $u + x - D$ shuttles in inventory for the following stage. The minimum cost of completing the process from that point is $m_{j+1}(u + x - D)$. Since $D = 1$ with probability 0.6 and $D = 2$ with probability 0.4, the minimum expected cost to completion beginning with stage $j + 1$ is

$$0.6 m_{j+1}(u + x - 1) + 0.4 m_{j+1}(u + x - 2) \qquad (2)$$

Therefore, the minimum expected cost to completion from stage j is the minimum, with respect to x, of the sum of (1) and (2):

$$m_j(u) = 1.1u + \min_{x = 0, 1, 2} [f(x) + 0.6 m_{j+1}(u + x - 1) + 0.4 m_{j+1}(u + x - 2)] \qquad (3)$$

for $u = 0, 1$ and $j = 1, 2, 3$. Here we agree that $m_j(3) \equiv +M$ for all j.

If the firm enters stage j with $u = -2$ or $u = -1$, then it had a shortfall of $-u$ shuttles from the previous stage and is subject to a penalty cost of $-1.5u$. A decision to produce x shuttles, where x must be at least as great as $-u$ to satisfy the previous shortfall, results in a production cost of $f(x)$. The resulting cost to the company in stage j is

$$f(x) - 1.5u \qquad (4)$$

Continuing the analysis as in the case $u = 0, 1$, we obtain the recursion formula

$$m_j(u) = -1.5u + \min_{x = -u, \dots, 2} [f(x) + 0.6 m_{j+1}(u + x - 1) + 0.4 m_{j+1}(u + x - 2)] \qquad (5)$$

for $u = -2, -1$ and $j = 1, 2, 3$. We can replace (3) and (5) by the single relation

$$m_j(u) = g(u) + \min_{x = -u, \dots, 2} [f(x) + 0.6 m_{j+1}(u + x - 1) + 0.4 m_{j+1}(u + x - 2)] \qquad (6)$$

for $u = -2, \dots, 1$ and $j = 1, 2, 3$, provided we define

$$g(u) \equiv \begin{cases} 1.1u & u \ge 0 \\ -1.5u & u < 0 \end{cases} \qquad \text{and} \qquad f(-1) \equiv +M$$

The stepwise solution of (6), extended to $j = 4$ with the end condition $m_5(u) \equiv 0$, is given in Table 18-6. The minimum expected cost is 42.24 million dollars, achieved by the optimal policy shown in Table 18-7.

Table 18-6

	u			
	-2	-1	0	1
$m_4(u)$	22	11.5	0	1.1
$d_4(u)$	2	1	0	0
$m_3(u)$	37.7	25.1	14.6	5.7
$d_3(u)$	2	2	1	0
$m_2(u)$	52.14	39.3	28.26	19.9
$d_2(u)$	2	2	2	0
$m_1(u)$	$\cdots$	$\cdots$	42.24	$\cdots$
$d_1(u)$	$\cdots$	$\cdots$	2	$\cdots$

Table 18-7

Inventory levels

		-2	-1	0	1
Years	1	$\cdots$	$\cdots$	2	$\cdots$
	2	2	2	2	0
	3	2	2	1	0
	4	2	1	0	0

18.5 A Presidential nominee has reduced the field of possible Vice Presidential running mates to three people. Each of these candidates has been rated on a scale from 1 (lowest) to 10 (highest); person 1 received 10 points, person 2 received 8 points, and person 3 received 5 points. The probability of person i $(i = 1, 2, 3)$ accepting the jth $(j = 1, 2, 3)$ offer to run for Vice President (assuming the first $j - 1$ offers, to other people, were declined) is denoted by p_{ij}, where

$$p_{11} = 0.5 \qquad p_{12} = 0.2 \qquad p_{13} = 0$$
$$p_{21} = 0.9 \qquad p_{22} = 0.5 \qquad p_{23} = 0.2$$
$$p_{31} = 1 \qquad p_{32} = 0.8 \qquad p_{33} = 0.4$$

In what order should the three potential running mates be offered the Vice Presidential nomination if the Presidential nominee wants to maximize the expected number of points?

It is assumed that no person is asked more than once, and that each time a candidate declines, another is asked, until either one candidate accepts or all have declined. We then have a three-stage process, with stage j representing the jth position in the asking order. We take the states to be the *sets of people still unasked*. Stage 1 then has the single state

$$U_{11} = \{1, 2, 3\}$$

stage 2 has the three states

$$U_{21} = \{1, 2\} \qquad U_{22} = \{1, 3\} \qquad U_{23} = \{2, 3\}$$

and stage 3 has the three states

$$U_{31} = \{1\} \qquad U_{32} = \{2\} \qquad U_{33} = \{3\}$$

We set

$m_j(U_{jk}) \equiv$ the maximum expected number of points achievable starting at stage j in state U_{jk}, given that there was no acceptance in previous stages

$d_j(U_{jk}) \equiv$ the person to ask in stage j in order to achieve $m_j(U_{jk})$

$V_i \equiv$ the point-value of person i

For this problem, the recursion formula is

$$m_j(U_{jk}) = \max_{i \in U_{jk}} \left[V_i p_{ij} + (1 - p_{ij}) m_{j+1}(U_{jk} - \{i\}) \right] \tag{1}$$

that is, if in stage j person i is asked and accepts, the payoff is V_i; whereas, if that individual declines, the best continuation is from the state consisting of the remaining unasked persons. Formula (1) holds for $j = 1, 2, 3$ if we define $m_4(U) \equiv 0$. It is seen that the present problem is a stochastic version of Problem 14.20.

Stage 3

$$m_3(U_{31}) = 10(0) = 0 \quad \text{with} \quad d_3(U_{31}) = 1$$
$$m_3(U_{32}) = 8(0.2) = 1.6 \quad \text{with} \quad d_3(U_{32}) = 2$$
$$m_3(U_{33}) = 5(0.4) = 2.0 \quad \text{with} \quad d_3(U_{33}) = 3$$

Stage 2

$$m_2(U_{21}) = \max \{10(0.2) + (1 - 0.2)m_3(U_{32}), \, 8(0.5) + (1 - 0.5)m_3(U_{31})\}$$
$$= \max \{2 + (0.8)(1.6), \, 4 + (0.5)(0)\} = 4 \quad \text{with} \quad d_2(U_{21}) = 2$$
$$m_2(U_{22}) = \max \{10(0.2) + (1 - 0.2)m_3(U_{33}), \, 5(0.8) + (1 - 0.8)m_3(U_{31})\}$$
$$= \max \{2 + (0.8)(2.0), \, 4 + (0.2)(0)\} = 4 \quad \text{with} \quad d_2(U_{22}) = 3$$
$$m_2(U_{23}) = \max \{8(0.5) + (1 - 0.5)m_3(U_{33}), \, 5(0.8) + (1 - 0.8)m_3(U_{32})\}$$
$$= \max \{4 + (0.5)(2), \, 4 + (0.2)(1.6)\} = 5 \quad \text{with} \quad d_2(U_{23}) = 2$$

Stage 1

$$m_1(U_{11}) = \max \{10(0.5) + (1 - 0.5)m_2(U_{23}), 8(0.9) + (1 - 0.9)m_2(U_{22}), 5(1) + (1 - 1)m_2(U_{21})\}$$
$$= \max \{5 + (0.5)(5), 7.2 + (0.1)(4), 5 + 0(4)\}$$
$$= 7.6 \quad \text{with} \quad d_1(U_{11}) = 2$$

The optimal policy is to ask person 2 first; if that person declines, then to ask person 3 $[d_2(U_{22}) = 3]$; and if that person declines, then to ask person 1. The expected number of points from such a policy is 7.6.

Supplementary Problems

18.6 Solve Problem 18.1 with the additional consideration that any unsold oranges spoil, resulting in a loss of $15 per bushel.

18.7 A person has $2000 available for investment and two opportunities, A and B. Both opportunities are risky; the possible yearly returns per each $1000 invested and the probabilities of realizing these returns are given in Table 18-8.

Table 18-8

	Return, $	Probability
A	3000	0.4
	0	0.6
B	2000	0.2
	1000	0.8

Determine an investment strategy for the next 3 years that will maximize expected final holdings, if the person is restricted to either one $1000 investment or a zero investment each year.

18.8 Solve Problem 18.7 if the objective is to maximize the probability of accumulating at least $5000 after 3 years.

18.9 An oil company has 8 units of money available for exploration of three sites. If oil is present at a site, the probability of finding it is a function of the funds allocated for exploring the site, as detailed in Table 18-9.

Table 18-9

	Units Allocated								
	0	1	2	3	4	5	6	7	8
Site 1	0	0	0.1	0.2	0.3	0.5	0.7	0.9	1
Site 2	0	0.1	0.2	0.3	0.4	0.6	0.7	0.8	1
Site 3	0	0.1	0.1	0.2	0.3	0.5	0.8	0.9	1

The probabilities that oil exists at the sites are 0.4, 0.3, and 0.2, respectively. How much money should be allocated to exploration of each site to maximize the probability of discovering oil?

18.10 A department manager has 4 weeks to complete a project that requires 10 units of work. The department has six people who can be assigned to the project each week. The costs (in thousand-dollar units) and the work that can be accomplished depend on the number of people assigned to the project each week, as follows:

People Assigned	0	1	2	3	4	5	6
Work Units Completed	0	2	4	6	7	9	10
Cost	0	1	2	4	8	16	32

Once assignments are made for the week, the Vice President for Operations may transfer people to jobs outside of the department. This happens often enough that the department manager must take the possibility into account in allocating personnel. Although the vice president never pulls everyone from a project, there is a 20 percent chance of losing one person whenever two or more are assigned to the same project, and a 10 percent chance of losing two people if three or more are assigned to a project. Any person transferred from the department for the week is not charged against the department, and returns to the department at the end of the week. Determine an optimal policy for assigning people to this one project over the next 4 weeks that will minimize expected total cost to the department yet guarantee that the project will be completed on time.

18.11 A manufacturing firm has placed an order for a new production facility that will be installed in 4 years. Until that time, it must use the current facility, which includes a particularly troublesome machine. Each year a decision is made whether to keep the existing machine in the facility or to replace it with a new model. The cost data for such machines are as follows: (1) A u-year-old machine costs $(500 + 10u^2)$ dollars to operate for one year. (2) An operable u-year-old machine has a salvage value of $(200 - 30u)$ dollars; an inoperable machine has no salvage value. (3) The cost of a new machine j years in the future is $(300 + 100j)$ dollars. (4) The probability that a machine will experience a catastrophic failure which is beyond repair is 0.75, regardless of the age of the machine. It is assumed that a catastrophe can occur only at the very end of the year.

   Determine an optimal replacement policy for this piece of equipment over the next 4 years if the current machine is 1 year old.

18.12 A computer firm has the capability to manufacture as many as four computers each week. The demand for computers is variable, being governed by the probability distributions given in Table 18-10.

Table 18-10

Demand

		0	1	2	3	4	5
Weeks	1	0	0.1	0.2	0.5	0.2	0
	2	0	0.1	0.1	0.2	0.5	0.1
	3	0.1	0.2	0.4	0.2	0.1	0

Production costs are a function of the number of computers manufactured and are given (in thousands of dollars) as follows:

Units Produced	0	1	2	3	4
Cost	0	18	30	42	56

Computers can be delivered to customers at the end of the week of manufacture, or they can be stored for future delivery at a cost of $4000 per computer per week. Orders that are not filled during the week they are placed incur a penalty cost of $2000 per computer per week and must be filled as soon as possible during the following weeks. How many computers should the firm produce in the next 3 weeks to minimize expected total cost of satisfying demand, if the current inventory is zero?

18.13 An electronic system consists of three components in series. The components function independently of one another, and each component must function if the system as a whole is to function. The *reliability* of the system (the probability that it will function) can be improved by installing several parallel units in one or more of the components. The probability that a component will function depends on the number of parallel units installed, according to Table 18-11.

Table 18-11

	Units in Parallel				
	1	2	3	4	5
Component 1	0.40	0.64	0.78	0.87	0.92
Component 2	0.50	0.75	0.88	0.94	0.97
Component 3	0.60	0.84	0.94	0.97	0.99

The cost for each unit is $100 for component 1, $200 for component 2, and $300 for component 3. Determine how many units of each component should be designed into the system to maximize the reliability, if the cost of the components is not to exceed $1000. (*Hint*: This problem is deterministic, despite the fact that the return is a probability. Choose as the objective function the logarithm of the reliability, and take as the state at stage j the number of hundred-dollar cost units that may be spent for units of component j.)

18.14 A contractor needs three different components to complete a project by its due date. Three sub-contractors are available to manufacture each of these components. The probability that a sub-contractor will deliver an ordered component by the due date is listed in Table 18-12.

Table 18-12

	Component 1	Component 2	Component 3
Subcontractor 1	0.83	0.92	0.91
Subcontractor 2	0.89	0.83	0.85
Subcontractor 3	0.91	0.93	0.93

Determine an optimal assignment policy that will maximize the probability of all components being delivered by the due date, if no subcontractor can be awarded more than one job. (*Hint*: Maximize the logarithm of the probability, proceeding as in Problem 14.20.)

18.15 *Determine a recursion formula for the following problem.* A physician wishes to raise a patient's level of a particular antibody at least 6 units over a 4-day period by prescribing pills for the patient to take each evening. The actual amount of antibody absorbed by the patient, which is a function of the number of pills taken, is limited to a maximum of 3 units per day. The absorption rates, along with the probabilities that the patient will experience a reaction severe enough to keep him from work the following day, are given in Table 18-13. Determine a dosage schedule for the patient that will achieve the prescribed level of antibody with the minimum expected number of workdays lost.

Table 18-13

Daily Dosage of Pills	0	1	2	3	4	5	6	7
Units of Antibody Absorbed	0	0.9	1.7	2.4	2.9	3.0	3.0	3.0
Probability of Missing Work the Next Day	0	0.05	0.15	0.30	0.50	0.70	0.95	1

18.16 *Determine a recursion formula for the following problem.* A contractor has two projects that must be completed in 5 days. Project 1 still requires 16 units of work and project 2 needs 23 units of work. The contractor employs five crews full-time, at a cost of $1000 per day per crew, and, at any time, can subcontract work to outside crews at a cost of $1500 per day per crew. The units of work accomplished on each project are a function of the number of crews assigned to the project, as shown in Table 18-14. Crew schedules are set each evening for the next day, and always include assignments for all five of the contractor's own crews. However, 10 percent of the time, one of the contractor's crews will call in sick the following day, in which event that crew is not paid for the day. Subcontracted crews are never sick. Project 1 has priority; so that if a crew calls in sick, project 1 is still guaranteed its assignment of contractor's crews, *unless* that assignment was five. In that case, project 1 receives only four contractor's crews. No more than six crews are ever assigned to a single project on any day, and once a crew arrives at a project it stays there for the entire day. How may the contractor complete both projects in the prescribed time at minimum expected cost?

Table 18-14

Number of Crews Assigned	0	1	2	3	4	5	6
Work Completed, Project 1	0	1	1.9	2.7	3.5	4.2	5.0
Work Completed, Project 2	0	1	1.9	2.8	3.7	4.5	5.2

18.17 *Obtain the recursion formula for the following problem.* A Presidential candidate for a major-party nomination needs 100 electoral votes to clinch the nomination. There are five winner-take-all primaries remaining, and the candidate has 10 units of money available to spend on them. The probability of winning a primary is a function of the money spent on it, as shown in Table 18-15.

Table 18-15

	Units of Money Spent							
	0	1	2	3	4	5	6	7
Primary 1	0.10	0.15	0.25	0.38	0.44	0.48	0.54	0.60
Primary 2	0.15	0.21	0.27	0.40	0.45	0.51	0.56	0.61
Primary 3	0.05	0.12	0.17	0.22	0.27	0.31	0.35	0.38
Primary 4	0.20	0.25	0.31	0.38	0.45	0.52	0.59	0.67
Primary 5	0.17	0.22	0.29	0.30	0.38	0.44	0.51	0.55

The probability of winning any primary does not increase if more than 7 units of money are allocated to it. There are 89 votes at stake in primary 1, 69 votes in primary 2, 52 votes in primary 3, 38 votes in primary 4, and 21 votes in primary 5. Determine a policy for maximizing the candidate's chances of winning at least 100 votes.

Chapter 19

Finite Markov Chains

MARKOV PROCESSES

A *Markov process* consists of a set of objects and a set of states such that

   (i)   at any given time each object must be in a state (distinct objects need not be in distinct states);

   (ii) the probability that an object moves from one state to another state (which may be the same as the first state) in one time period depends only on those two states.

The integral numbers of time periods past the moment when the process is started represent the stages of the process, which may be finite or infinite. If the number of states is finite or countably infinite, the Markov process is a *Markov chain*. A finite Markov chain is one having a finite number of states.

We denote the probability of moving from state i to state j in one time period by p_{ij}. For an N-state Markov chain (where N is a fixed positive integer), the $N \times N$ matrix $\mathbf{P} = [p_{ij}]$ is the *stochastic* or *transition matrix* associated with the process. Necessarily, the elements of each row of $\mathbf{P}$ sum to unity. Furthermore,

Theorem 19.1: Every stochastic matrix has 1 as an eigenvalue (possibly multiple), and none of the eigenvalues exceeds 1 in absolute value.

(See Problems 19.14 and 19.32.) Because of the way $\mathbf{P}$ is defined, it proves convenient in this chapter to indicate N-dimensional vectors as row vectors, with matrices operating on them from the right. According to Theorem 19.1, there exists a vector $\mathbf{X} \neq \mathbf{0}$ such that

$$\mathbf{XP} = \mathbf{X}$$

This left eigenvector is called a *fixed point* of $\mathbf{P}$.

Example 19.1 Census data divide households into economically stable and economically depressed populations. Over a 10-year period the probability of a stable household remaining stable is 0.92, while the probability of a stable household becoming depressed is 0.08. The probability of a depressed household becoming stable is 0.03, while the probability of a depressed household remaining depressed is 0.97.

If we designate economic stability as state 1 and economic depression as state 2, then we can model this process with a two-state Markov chain, having the transition matrix

$$\mathbf{P} = \begin{bmatrix} 0.92 & 0.08 \\ 0.03 & 0.97 \end{bmatrix}$$

POWERS OF STOCHASTIC MATRICES

Denote the nth power of a matrix $\mathbf{P}$ by $\mathbf{P}^n \equiv [p_{ij}^{(n)}]$. If $\mathbf{P}$ is stochastic, then $p_{ij}^{(n)}$ represents the probability that an object moves from state i to state j in n time periods. (See Problem 19.12.) It follows that $\mathbf{P}^n$ is also a stochastic matrix.

Denote the proportion of objects in state i at the end of the nth time period by $x_i^{(n)}$, and designate

$$\mathbf{X}^{(n)} \equiv [x_1^{(n)}, x_2^{(n)}, \ldots, x_N^{(n)}]$$

the *distribution vector* for the end of the nth time period. Accordingly,

$$\mathbf{X}^{(0)} = [x_1^{(0)}, x_2^{(0)}, \ldots, x_N^{(0)}]$$

represents the proportion of objects in each state at the beginning of the process. $\mathbf{X}^{(n)}$ is related to $\mathbf{X}^{(0)}$ by the equation

$$\mathbf{X}^{(n)} = \mathbf{X}^{(0)}\mathbf{P}^n \tag{19.1}$$

(See Problems 19.6 and 19.7.)   In writing (19.1), we implicitly identify the probability p_{ij} with the proportion of objects in state i that make the transition to state j in one time period.

ERGODIC MATRICES

A stochastic matrix $\mathbf{P}$ is *ergodic* if $\lim_{n\to\infty}\mathbf{P}^n$ exists; that is, if each $p_{ij}^{(n)}$ has a limit as $n \to \infty$.   We denote the limit matrix, necessarily a stochastic matrix, by $\mathbf{L}$.   The components of $\mathbf{X}^{(\infty)}$, defined by the equation

$$\mathbf{X}^{(\infty)} = \mathbf{X}^{(0)}\mathbf{L} \tag{19.2}$$

are the *limiting state distributions* and represent the approximate proportions of objects in the various states of a Markov chain after a large number of time periods.   (See Problems 19.6, 19.8, and 19.9.)

Theorem 19.2:   A stochastic matrix is ergodic if and only if the only eigenvalue λ of magnitude 1 is 1 itself and, if $\lambda = 1$ has multiplicity k, there exist k linearly independent (left) eigenvectors associated with this eigenvalue.

(See Problem 19.5.)

Theorem 19.3:   If *every* eigenvalue of a matrix $\mathbf{P}$ yields linearly independent (left) eigenvectors in number equal to its multiplicity, then there exists a nonsingular matrix $\mathbf{M}$, whose rows are left eigenvectors of $\mathbf{P}$, such that $\mathbf{D} \equiv \mathbf{MPM}^{-1}$ is a diagonal matrix.   The diagonal elements of $\mathbf{D}$ are the eigenvalues of $\mathbf{P}$, repeated according to multiplicity.

(See Problem 19.33.)   We adopt the convention of positioning the eigenvectors corresponding to $\lambda = 1$ above all other eigenvectors in $\mathbf{M}$.   Then, for a diagonalizable, ergodic, $N \times N$ matrix $\mathbf{P}$ with $\lambda = 1$ of multiplicity k, the limit matrix $\mathbf{L}$ may be calculated as

$$\mathbf{L} = \mathbf{M}^{-1}(\lim_{n\to\infty}\mathbf{D}^n)\mathbf{M} = \mathbf{M}^{-1}\begin{bmatrix} 1 & & & & & & \\ & 1 & & & & & \\ & & \ddots & & & & \\ & & & \ddots & & & \\ & & & & 1 & & \\ & & & & & 0 & \\ & & & & & & \ddots \\ & & & & & & & 0 \end{bmatrix}\mathbf{M} \tag{19.3}$$

The diagonal matrix on the right has k 1's and $(N - k)$ 0's on the main diagonal.   (See Problem 19.5.)

REGULAR MATRICES

A stochastic matrix is *regular* if one of its powers contains only positive elements.   (See Problems 19.3 and 19.4.)

Theorem 19.4:   If a stochastic matrix is regular, then 1 is an eigenvalue of multiplicity one, and all other eigenvalues λ_i satisfy $|\lambda_i| < 1$.

Theorem 19.5:   A regular matrix is ergodic.

If $\mathbf{P}$ is regular, with limit matrix $\mathbf{L}$, then the rows of $\mathbf{L}$ are identical with one another, each being the unique left eigenvector of $\mathbf{P}$ associated with the eigenvalue $\lambda = 1$ and having the sum of its components equal to unity. (See Problem 19.13.) Denote this eigenvector by $\mathbf{E}_1$. It follows directly from (19.2) that if $\mathbf{P}$ is regular, then, regardless of the initial distribution $\mathbf{X}^{(0)}$,

$$\mathbf{X}^{(\infty)} = \mathbf{E}_1 \tag{19.4}$$

(See Problems 19.6, 19.7, and 19.11.)

Solved Problems

19.1 *Formulate the following process as a Markov chain.* The manufacturer of Hi-Glo toothpaste currently controls 60 percent of the market in a particular city. Data from the previous year show that 88 percent of Hi-Glo's customers remained loyal to Hi-Glo, while 12 percent of Hi-Glo's customers switched to rival brands. In addition, 85 percent of the competition's customers remained loyal to the competition, while the other 15 percent switched to Hi-Glo. Assuming that these trends continue, determine Hi-Glo's share of the market (*a*) in 5 years and (*b*) over the long run.

We take state 1 to be consumption of Hi-Glo toothpaste and state 2 to be consumption of a rival brand. Then p_{11}, the probability that a Hi-Glo consumer remains loyal to Hi-Glo, is 0.88; p_{12}, the probability that a Hi-Glo consumer switches to another brand, is 0.12; p_{21}, the probability that the consumer of another brand switches to Hi-Glo, is 0.15; and p_{22}, the probability that the consumer of another brand remains loyal to the competition, is 0.85. The stochastic matrix defined by these transition probabilities is

$$\mathbf{P} = \begin{bmatrix} 0.88 & 0.12 \\ 0.15 & 0.85 \end{bmatrix}$$

The initial probability distribution vector is $\mathbf{X}^{(0)} = [0.60, 0.40]$, where the components $x_1^{(0)} = 0.60$ and $x_2^{(0)} = 0.40$ represent the proportions of people initially in states 1 and 2, respectively.

19.2 *Formulate the following process as a Markov chain.* The training program for production supervisors at a particular company consists of two phases. Phase 1, which involves 3 weeks of classroom work, is followed by phase 2, which is a 3-week apprenticeship program under the direction of working supervisors. From past experience, the company expects only 60 percent of those beginning classroom training to be graduated into the apprenticeship phase, with the remaining 40 percent dropped completely from the training program. Of those who make it to the apprenticeship phase, 70 percent are graduated as supervisors, 10 percent are asked to repeat the second phase, and 20 percent are dropped completely from the program. How many supervisors can the company expect from its current training program if it has 45 people in the classroom phase and 21 people in the apprenticeship phase?

We consider one time period to be 3 weeks and define states 1 through 4 as the conditions of being dropped, a classroom trainee, an apprentice, and a supervisor, respectively. If we assume that discharged individuals never reenter the training program and that supervisors remain supervisors, then the transition probabilities are given by the stochastic matrix

$$\mathbf{P} = \begin{bmatrix} 1 & 0 & 0 & 0 \\ 0.4 & 0 & 0.6 & 0 \\ 0.2 & 0 & 0.1 & 0.7 \\ 0 & 0 & 0 & 1 \end{bmatrix}$$

There are $45 + 21 = 66$ people in the training program currently, so the initial probability vector is

$$\mathbf{X}^{(0)} = [0, 45/66, 21/66, 0]$$

19.3   Is the stochastic matrix

$$P = \begin{bmatrix} 0.88 & 0.12 \\ 0.15 & 0.85 \end{bmatrix}$$

regular?   ergodic?   Calculate $L = \lim_{n \to \infty} P^n$, if it exists.

Since each entry of the first power of **P** (**P** itself) is positive, **P** is regular and, therefore, ergodic. Hence the limit exists.   The left eigenvector corresponding to $\lambda = 1$ is given by

$$[x_1, x_2] \begin{bmatrix} 0.88 & 0.12 \\ 0.15 & 0.85 \end{bmatrix} = [x_1, x_2] \qquad \text{or} \qquad 0.12 x_1 - 0.15 x_2 = 0$$

Adjoining the condition $x_1 + x_2 = 1$ and solving, we obtain

$$E_1 = [x_1, x_2] = [5/9, 4/9]$$

It follows that

$$L = \lim_{n \to \infty} P^n = \begin{bmatrix} 5/9 & 4/9 \\ 5/9 & 4/9 \end{bmatrix}$$

19.4   Is the stochastic matrix

$$P = \begin{bmatrix} 0 & 1 \\ 0.4 & 0.6 \end{bmatrix}$$

regular?   ergodic?   Calculate $L = \lim_{n \to \infty} P^n$, if it exists.

Since each entry of

$$P^2 = \begin{bmatrix} 0.40 & 0.60 \\ 0.24 & 0.76 \end{bmatrix}$$

is positive, **P** itself is regular and, therefore, ergodic; hence **L** exists.   Solving

$$[x_1, x_2] \begin{bmatrix} 0 & 1 \\ 0.4 & 0.6 \end{bmatrix} = [x_1, x_2] \qquad \text{or} \qquad x_1 - 0.4 x_2 = 0$$

together with $x_1 + x_2 = 1$, we find $E_1 = [2/7, 5/7]$ and

$$L = \begin{bmatrix} 2/7 & 5/7 \\ 2/7 & 5/7 \end{bmatrix}$$

19.5   Is the stochastic matrix

$$P = \begin{bmatrix} 1 & 0 & 0 & 0 \\ 0.4 & 0 & 0.6 & 0 \\ 0.2 & 0 & 0.1 & 0.7 \\ 0 & 0 & 0 & 1 \end{bmatrix}$$

regular?   ergodic?   Calculate $L = \lim_{n \to \infty} P^n$, if it exists.

Rather than raise **P** to successively higher powers to ascertain whether it is regular, let us instead determine its eigenvalues by solving the characteristic equation:

$$\begin{vmatrix} 1-\lambda & 0 & 0 & 0 \\ 0.4 & -\lambda & 0.6 & 0 \\ 0.2 & 0 & 0.1-\lambda & 0.7 \\ 0 & 0 & 0 & 1-\lambda \end{vmatrix} = (1-\lambda)(-\lambda)(0.1-\lambda)(1-\lambda) = 0$$

Thus, $\lambda_1 = 1$ (double root), $\lambda_2 = 0.1$, $\lambda_3 = 0$. By Theorem 19.4, $\mathbf{P}$ is not regular. However, by Theorem 19.2, $\mathbf{P}$ is ergodic, since it possesses the two linearly independent left eigenvectors

$$[1, 0, 0, 0] \qquad \text{and} \qquad [0, 0, 0, 1]$$

corresponding to $\lambda_1 = 1$. As an easy calculation shows, the left eigenvectors

$$[-2, 0, 9, -7] \qquad \text{and} \qquad [4, 5, -30, 21]$$

respectively correspond to λ_2 and λ_3.

Theorem 19.3 now tells us that $\mathbf{P}$ is diagonalizable, with

$$\mathbf{M} = \begin{bmatrix} 1 & 0 & 0 & 0 \\ 0 & 0 & 0 & 1 \\ -2 & 0 & 9 & -7 \\ 4 & 5 & -30 & 21 \end{bmatrix} \qquad \text{and} \qquad \mathbf{D} = \begin{bmatrix} 1 & 0 & 0 & 0 \\ 0 & 1 & 0 & 0 \\ 0 & 0 & 0.1 & 0 \\ 0 & 0 & 0 & 0 \end{bmatrix}$$

Calculating

$$\mathbf{M}^{-1} = \begin{bmatrix} 1 & 0 & 0 & 0 \\ 8/15 & 7/15 & 10/15 & 3/15 \\ 2/9 & 7/9 & 1/9 & 0 \\ 0 & 1 & 0 & 0 \end{bmatrix}$$

we obtain from (*19.3*)

$$\mathbf{L} = \begin{bmatrix} 1 & 0 & 0 & 0 \\ 8/15 & 7/15 & 10/15 & 3/15 \\ 2/9 & 7/9 & 1/9 & 0 \\ 0 & 1 & 0 & 0 \end{bmatrix} \begin{bmatrix} 1 & 0 & 0 & 0 \\ 0 & 1 & 0 & 0 \\ 0 & 0 & 0 & 0 \\ 0 & 0 & 0 & 0 \end{bmatrix} \begin{bmatrix} 1 & 0 & 0 & 0 \\ 0 & 0 & 0 & 1 \\ -2 & 0 & 9 & -7 \\ 4 & 5 & -30 & 21 \end{bmatrix} = \begin{bmatrix} 1 & 0 & 0 & 0 \\ 8/15 & 0 & 0 & 7/15 \\ 2/9 & 0 & 0 & 7/9 \\ 0 & 0 & 0 & 1 \end{bmatrix}$$

19.6 Solve the problem formulated in Problem 19.1.

(*a*)
$$\mathbf{X}^{(5)} = \mathbf{X}^{(0)}\mathbf{P}^5 = [0.60, 0.40] \begin{bmatrix} 0.6477 & 0.3523 \\ 0.4404 & 0.5596 \end{bmatrix} = [0.5648, 0.4352]$$

After 5 years, Hi-Glo's share of the market will have declined to 56.48 percent.

(*b*) It follows from the results of Problem 19.3 that $\mathbf{P}$ is ergodic, with limit matrix $\mathbf{L}$. Hence,

$$\mathbf{X}^{(\infty)} = \mathbf{X}^{(0)}\mathbf{L} = [0.60, 0.40] \begin{bmatrix} 5/9 & 4/9 \\ 5/9 & 4/9 \end{bmatrix} = [5/9, 4/9] = \mathbf{E}_1$$

Over the long run, Hi-Glo's share of the market will stabilize at 5/9, or approximately 55.56 percent.

19.7 Solve the problem formulated in Problem 19.1, if Hi-Glo currently controls 90 percent of the market.

(*a*)
$$\mathbf{X}^{(5)} = \mathbf{X}^{(0)}\mathbf{P}^5 = [0.90, 0.10] \begin{bmatrix} 0.6477 & 0.3523 \\ 0.4404 & 0.5596 \end{bmatrix} = [0.6270, 0.3730]$$

After 5 years, Hi-Glo will control approximately 63 percent of the market.

(*b*) Since $\mathbf{P}$ is regular, the limiting distribution remains the left eigenvector of $\mathbf{P}$ associated with $\lambda = 1$,

$$\mathbf{X}^{(\infty)} = \mathbf{E}_1 = [5/9, 4/9]$$

19.8 Solve the problem formulated in Problem 19.2.

Using (*19.2*) and the results of Problems 19.2 and 19.5, we have

$$\mathbf{X}^{(\infty)} = \mathbf{X}^{(0)}\mathbf{L} = [0, 45/66, 21/66, 0] \begin{bmatrix} 1 & 0 & 0 & 0 \\ 8/15 & 0 & 0 & 7/15 \\ 2/9 & 0 & 0 & 7/9 \\ 0 & 0 & 0 & 1 \end{bmatrix} = [0.4343, 0, 0, 0.5657]$$

Therefore, eventually, 43.43 percent of those currently in training (or about 29 people) will be dropped from the program, and 56.57 percent (or about 37 people) will become supervisors.

19.9 Solve the problem formulated in Problem 19.2, if all 66 people are currently in the classroom phase of the training program.

Now $\mathbf{X}^{(0)} = [0, 1, 0, 0]$, and so

$$\mathbf{X}^{(\infty)} = \mathbf{X}^{(0)}\mathbf{L} = [0, 1, 0, 0]\begin{bmatrix} 1 & 0 & 0 & 0 \\ 8/15 & 0 & 0 & 7/15 \\ 2/9 & 0 & 0 & 7/9 \\ 0 & 0 & 0 & 1 \end{bmatrix} = [8/15, 0, 0, 7/15]$$

Therefore, 8/15 of the 66 people in training (or about 35 people) will ultimately be dropped from the program, with the remaining 31 people eventually becoming supervisors. Comparing this result with the result of Problem 19.8, we see that the limiting distributions are influenced by the initial distributions, the usual situation whenever a stochastic matrix is ergodic but not regular.

19.10 Construct the *state-transition diagram* for the Markov chain of Problem 19.2.

A state-transition diagram is an oriented network (see Chapter 15) in which the nodes represent states and the arcs represent possible transitions. Labeling the states as in Problem 19.2, we have the state-transition diagram shown in Fig. 19-1. The number on each arc is the probability of the transition.

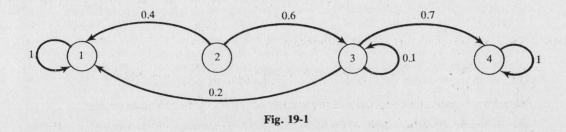

Fig. 19-1

19.11 A sewing machine operator works solely on one phase of the production process for a particular design of clothing. This phase requires exactly half an hour per garment to complete. Every 30 min a messenger arrives at the operator's table to collect all garments the operator has completed and to deliver new garments for the operator to sew. The number of new garments that the messenger carries is uncertain: 30 percent of the time the messenger has no garments for the operator; 50 percent of the time the messenger has only one garment to leave; 20 percent of the time the messenger has two garments for the operator. However, the messenger is instructed never to leave the operator with more than three unfinished garments altogether. (Unfinished garments that cannot be left with the operator, as a result of this policy, are taken to another operator for processing.) Determine the percentage of time that the operator is idle, assuming that any unfinished garments on the operator's table at the end of a work shift remain there for processing by the operator on the next business day.

We can model this process as a three-state Markov chain by letting the states be the number of unfinished garments on the operator's table *just before the messenger arrives*. We designate the states as 1, 2, and 3, respectively, representing 0, 1, and 2 unfinished garments; the stages are the half-hour interarrival intervals.

If the operator has one unfinished garment at the beginning of a stage (just before the messenger arrives) and if the messenger leaves one garment (with probability 0.5), then one garment will be completed by the beginning of the next stage, leaving the operator again with one unfinished garment; hence, $p_{22} = 0.5$. If the operator has two unfinished garments at the beginning of a stage and if the messenger arrives with either 1 or 2 new garments (with probability $0.5 + 0.2 = 0.7$), then the messenger will leave only one garment, and at the beginning of the next period the operator will have two unfinished garments remaining, since one will have been processed during the period. Therefore, $p_{33} = 0.7$. Considering all other possibilities in the same fashion, we generate the stochastic matrix

$$\mathbf{P} = \begin{bmatrix} 0.8 & 0.2 & 0 \\ 0.3 & 0.5 & 0.2 \\ 0 & 0.3 & 0.7 \end{bmatrix}$$

All the elements of $\mathbf{P}^2$ are positive, so $\mathbf{P}$ is regular. The left eigenvector associated with $\lambda_1 = 1$ and having component-sum unity is found to be

$$\mathbf{E}_1 = \begin{bmatrix} \dfrac{9}{19}, & \dfrac{6}{19}, & \dfrac{4}{19} \end{bmatrix}$$

Since $\mathbf{P}$ is regular, this vector is also $\mathbf{X}^{(\infty)}$. Over the long run, the operator starts a stage in state 1 (no unfinished garments remaining) 9/19 of the time. The messenger then arrives and, with probability 0.3, leaves no new garments for processing, thereby rendering the operator idle. Thus the operator is idle

$$\frac{9}{19}(0.3) = 0.1421$$

or approximately 14 percent of the time.

19.12 Verify that, for the stochastic matrix defined in Example 19.1, $p_{ij}^{(2)}$ represents the probability of moving from state i to state j in two time periods.

There are two ways for a stable household to remain stable after 20 years, as shown in Fig. 19-2(a): either it remains stable throughout the first 10 years and throughout the second 10 years or it becomes depressed after 10 years and then reverts to stability after another 10 years. The probability that a stable household will remain stable over one time period is 0.92; hence the probability that it will remain stable over two time periods is (0.92)(0.92). The probability that a stable household will become depressed in 10 years is 0.08, and the probability that a depressed household will become stable over the next 10 years is 0.03; so the probability of both events happening to the same household is (0.08)(0.03). Thus, the probability that a stable household will be stable after two time periods is

$$(0.92)(0.92) + (0.08)(0.03)$$

which is exactly the $(1, 1)$-element of $\mathbf{P}^2$.

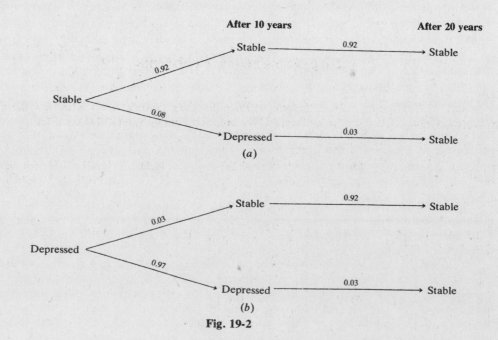

Fig. 19-2

Figure 19-2(b) depicts the ways a depressed household can become stable over two time periods. The probability that it becomes stable over the first time period and then remains stable over the next time period is $(0.03)(0.92)$. The probability that it remains depressed over the first time period and then becomes stable over the next time period is $(0.97)(0.03)$. Thus, the probability that either one of these two situations occurs is

$$(0.03)(0.92) + (0.97)(0.03)$$

which is exactly the $(2, 1)$-element of $\mathbf{P}^2$. The other two cases are handled similarly.

19.13 Prove that if $\mathbf{P}$ is regular, then all the rows of $\mathbf{L} = \lim_{n \to \infty} \mathbf{P}^n$ are identical.

Given $\mathbf{L} = \lim_{n \to \infty} \mathbf{P}^n$, it is also true that $\mathbf{L} = \lim_{n \to \infty} \mathbf{P}^{n-1}$. Consequently,

$$\mathbf{L} = \lim_{n \to \infty} \mathbf{P}^n = \lim_{n \to \infty} (\mathbf{P}^{n-1}\mathbf{P}) = (\lim_{n \to \infty} \mathbf{P}^{n-1})\mathbf{P} = \mathbf{LP}$$

which implies that every row of $\mathbf{L}$ is a left eigenvector of $\mathbf{P}$ corresponding to $\lambda = 1$.

Now, $\mathbf{P}$ being regular, all such eigenvectors are scalar multiples of a single vector. On the other hand, $\mathbf{L}$ being stochastic, each of its rows sums to unity. It follows that all rows are identical.

19.14 Prove that if λ is an eigenvalue of a stochastic matrix $\mathbf{P}$, then $|\lambda| \le 1$.

Let $\mathbf{E} \equiv [e_1, e_2, \ldots, e_N]^T$ be a *right* eigenvector belonging to λ. Then $\mathbf{PE} = \lambda \mathbf{E}$, and considering the jth component of both sides of this equality, we conclude that

$$\sum_{k=1}^{N} p_{jk}e_k = \lambda e_j \tag{1}$$

Let e_i be that component of $\mathbf{E}$ having the greatest magnitude; i.e.,

$$|e_i| = \max \{|e_1|, |e_2|, \ldots, |e_N|\} \tag{2}$$

By definition, $\mathbf{E} \ne \mathbf{0}$, so that $|e_i| > 0$. It follows from (1), with j set equal to i, and (2) that

$$|\lambda| \, |e_i| = |\lambda e_i| = \left| \sum_{k=1}^{N} p_{ik}e_k \right| \le \sum_{k=1}^{N} p_{ik}|e_k| \le |e_i| \sum_{k=1}^{N} p_{ik} = |e_i|$$

and the result $|\lambda| \le 1$ follows immediately.

Supplementary Problems

In Problems 19.15 through 19.21, determine whether the given matrices are stochastic. If so, determine whether they are regular or ergodic, or neither. Calculate their limiting values, if these exist.

19.15 $\begin{bmatrix} 1 & 0 \\ 0.21 & 0.79 \end{bmatrix}$

19.18 $\begin{bmatrix} 0 & 0 & 1 \\ 0.5 & 0.3 & 0.2 \\ 1 & 0 & 0 \end{bmatrix}$

19.21 $\begin{bmatrix} 1 & 0 & 0 \\ 0.21 & 0.79 & 0 \\ 0.17 & 0.35 & 0.48 \end{bmatrix}$

19.16 $\begin{bmatrix} 0.5 & 0.3 & 0.2 \\ 0.5 & 0.5 & 0 \\ 0 & 0 & 0 \end{bmatrix}$

19.19 $\begin{bmatrix} 1 & 0 & 0 & 0 \\ 0 & 0.5 & 0 & 0.5 \\ 0 & 0 & 1 & 0 \\ 0 & 0.3 & 0 & 0.7 \end{bmatrix}$

19.17 $\begin{bmatrix} 1 & 0 & 0 \\ 0 & -1 & 0 \\ 0 & 0 & -1 \end{bmatrix}$

19.20 $\begin{bmatrix} 0.1 & 0.8 & 0.1 \\ 0.9 & 0 & 0.1 \\ 0.2 & 0.2 & 0.6 \end{bmatrix}$

19.22 Find the proportion of households that ultimately are classified as economically stable, if the data in Example 19.1 remain valid over the long run.

19.23 A recently completed survey of subscribers to a travel magazine shows that 65 percent of them have at least one airline credit card. When compared with a similar survey taken 5 years ago, the data indicate that 40 percent of those individuals who did not have an airline credit card subsequently obtained one, while 10 percent of those who carried such cards 5 years ago no longer do so. Assuming that these trends continue into the future, determine the proportion of subscribers who will own airline credit cards (*a*) in 10 years, and (*b*) over the long run.

19.24 An airline with a 7:15 A.M. commuter flight between New York City and Washington, D.C., does not want the flight to depart late 2 days in a row. If the flight leaves late one day, the airline makes a special effort the next day to have the flight leave on time, and succeeds 90 percent of the time. If the flight was not late in leaving the previous day, the airline makes no special arrangements, and the flight departs as scheduled 60 percent of the time. What percentage of the time is the flight late in departing?

19.25 Grapes in the Sonoma Valley are classified as either superior, average, or poor. Following a superior harvest, the probabilities of having a superior, average, and poor harvest the next year are 0, 0.8, and 0.2, respectively. Following an average harvest, the probabilities of a superior, average, and poor harvest are 0.2, 0.6, and 0.2. Following a poor harvest, the probabilities of a superior, average, and poor harvest are 0.1, 0.8, and 0.1. Determine the probabilities of a superior harvest for each of the next 5 years, if the most recent harvest was average.

19.26 The geriatric ward of a hospital lists its patients as bedridden or ambulatory. Historical data indicate that over a 1-week period, 30 percent of all ambulatory patients are discharged, 40 percent remain ambulatory, and 30 percent are remanded to complete bed rest. During the same period, 50 percent of all bedridden patients become ambulatory, 20 percent remain bedridden, and 30 percent die. Currently the hospital has 100 patients in its geriatric ward, with 30 bedridden and 70 ambulatory. Determine the status of these patients (*a*) after 2 weeks, and (*b*) over the long run. (The status of a discharged patient does not change if the patient dies.)

19.27 The owners of a large block of rental apartments in Chicago is considering as its operating agent a real estate management firm with an excellent record in Boston. Based on ratings of good, average, and poor for the condition of buildings in Boston under the firm's control, it has been documented that 50 percent of all buildings that begin a year in good condition remain in good condition at the end of the year, with the other 50 percent deteriorating to average condition. Of all buildings that begin a year in average condition, 30 percent remain in average condition at the end of the year and 70 percent are upgraded to good condition. Of all buildings that begin a year in poor condition, 90 percent remain in poor condition after 1 year, while the other 10 percent are upgraded to good condition. Assuming that these trends will prevail for Chicago also if the firm is hired, determine the condition of apartments under the firm's management that can be expected over the long run.

19.28 A state in a Markov chain is *absorbing* if no objects can leave the state once they enter it. Find all absorbing states for the Markov chains defined by the matrices given in (*a*) Problem 19.15, (*b*) Problem 19.18, (*c*) Problem 19.19, and (*d*) Problem 19.21.

19.29 Prove that the stochastic matrix for a Markov chain that has at least one absorbing state cannot be regular.

19.30 From the definition of matrix multiplication, verify that the product of two stochastic matrices of the same order is itself stochastic.

19.31   Show that $U = [1, 1, 1, \ldots, 1]$ is a left eigenvector of P^T, the transpose of an arbitrary stochastic matrix **P**.

19.32   Using the result of Problem 19.31, prove that every stochastic matrix **P** has $\lambda = 1$ as an eigenvalue.

19.33   Prove Theorem 19.3.

19.34   Show by example that the converse to Theorem 19.4 is not valid.

Chapter 20

Unbounded Horizons

OPTIMAL POLICIES UNDER STATIONARITY

A decision process with an *unbounded horizon* is one that has infinitely many stages. Although such situations rarely occur in practice, they are convenient models for analyzing processes that have no obvious terminal point. The following condition is generally assumed for such processes.

Assumption of stationarity. The decisions, returns, and states associated with the process are the same in every stage.

For processes that conform to this assumption, optimal policies depend only on the states and not on the stages. Whatever decision is optimal for state u in stage 1 will also be optimal for state u in stage 100, since all the underlying conditions remain invariant. We shall use the notation $d^*(u)$ to indicate the decision that is optimal whenever the process is in state u.

The stationarity assumption is restrictive in that it does not allow interest rates, costs, charges, or any other quantity to change as the process continues into the future. An optimal policy, therefore, remains optimal only so long as the stationarity assumption remains valid.

DISCOUNTING

Since monies spent or received in the (distant) future are not equal in value to funds of the same denomination spent or received in the present, discounting is often used to offset time differences [see (14.5)]. We denote the present value of the optimal return (or optimal expected return, in the case of a stochastic process) with an unbounded horizon for a decision process beginning in state u by $m(u)$. An equation for $m(u)$ is called a *functional equation* for the process.

DETERMINISTIC PROCESSES WITH DISCOUNTING

The functional equation for deterministic processes is most easily found by deriving the recurrence formula for the process, using a dynamic programming approach with discounting over a *finite* number of stages, and then suppressing all subscripts that refer to the stages.

Example 20.1 From (1) of Problem 14.10 we obtain

$$m(u) = \max \{I(u) - M(u) + \alpha m(u+1), I(0) - M(0) - R(u) + \alpha m(1)\}$$

as the functional equation for the equipment replacement process with an unbounded horizon.

The following **five-step algorithm** is used to solve functional equations for $m(u)$ and to determine the optimal policy.

STEP 1   Arbitrarily choose an initial policy and denote the decision for each state u by $\hat{d}(u)$. Designate this policy as the current one.

STEP 2   Under the current policy, calculate, for each value of u, the total discounted return from the process beginning in state u. Designate the calculated values as the function PV(u).

STEP 3   Replace the m-function by the PV-function *in the right-hand side* of the functional equation, thereby obtaining $\hat{m}(u)$, the left-hand side of the new equation, and $d(u)$, the decision yielding $\hat{m}(u)$.

234

STEP 4   If $d(u) = \hat{d}(u)$ for each state u, the current policy is optimal; i.e. $d^*(u) = \hat{d}(u)$ and $m(u) = \hat{m}(u) = PV(u)$.   If not, go to Step 5.

STEP 5   Set $\hat{d}(u) = d(u)$ for each state u, thereby establishing an updated current policy, and return to Step 2.

(See Problem 20.3.)

MARKOV CHAINS WITH DISCOUNTING

Some decision processes can be modeled as Markov chains once a policy has been established. In such cases, the transition probabilities generally depend on both the states and the policy.   (See Problems 20.5 and 20.6.)   Set

$d_i \equiv$ a feasible decision when the process is in state i $(i = 1, 2, \ldots, N)$

$C(i, d_i) \equiv$ the (expected) cost or gain from implementing decision d_i, the process being in state i

$p_{ij}(d_i) \equiv$ the transition probability of moving from state i to state j if decision d_i is implemented in state i

The cost $C(i, d_i)$ is incurred each time the process finds itself in state i and d_i is implemented.   For given i and d_i, this cost may, or may not, be a random variable.   If it is, we understand $C(i, d_i)$ to denote the expected value of the random variable.

The functional equation for an N-state Markov chain with discount factor α is

$$m(i) = \underset{d_i}{\text{optimum}} \left\{ C(i, d_i) + \alpha \sum_{j=1}^{N} p_{ij}(d_i) m(j) \right\} \qquad (20.1)$$

The optimization is over all decisions d_i possible when the process is in state i.   Equation (20.1) can be solved for $m(i)$ by the same algorithm given for deterministic processes with discounting, with one modification.   The (expected) present values $PV(i)$ required in Step 2 cannot be calculated independently for each state i but are obtained by solving the simultaneous set of equations

$$PV(i) = C(i, \hat{d}_i) + \alpha \sum_{j=1}^{N} p_{ij}(\hat{d}_i) PV(j) \qquad (i = 1, 2, \ldots, N) \qquad (20.2)$$

Here $\hat{d}_i$ is the decision associated with state i under the current policy.   The form of (20.2) is, of course, the basis for the form of (20.1).

It should be mentioned that present values for deterministic processes, too, may be calculated from equations similar to (20.2).   These equations may be obtained formally by writing $PV(u)$ instead of $m(u)$ in the functional equation and optimizing over the single value $d_i = \hat{d}_i$.   (See Problem 20.4.)

EXPECTED RETURN PER PERIOD

In situations where the stationarity assumption is known to hold for a short but still uncertain length of time—or where the discount factor is close to 1, thereby resulting in exceedingly large present values for an unbounded horizon—expected return (either gain or cost) per period (stage) may be a more appropriate measure than present value for determining optimal policies.

We assume that the process in question can be modeled by a Markov chain whenever a policy is established, and that the limiting state distribution,

$$\mathbf{X}^{(\infty)} = [x_1^{(\infty)}, x_2^{(\infty)}, \ldots, x_N^{(\infty)}]$$

is independent of the initial state distribution, $\mathbf{X}^{(0)}$.   This latter condition is satisfied not only if the transition matrix $\mathbf{P}$ is regular, but also for a large class of nonregular ergodic matrices, those which have the rows of $\mathbf{L} = \lim_{n \to \infty} \mathbf{P}^n$ identical to one another.

Definition: The *expected return per period* is

$$R \equiv C(1, d_1)x_1^{(\infty)} + C(2, d_2)x_2^{(\infty)} + \cdots + C(N, d_N)x_N^{(\infty)}$$

where $C(i, d_i)$ is the expected cost or gain from implementing decision d_i while the process is in state i $(i = 1, 2, \ldots, N)$.

The expected return per period depends on the policy in effect. A policy is optimal if it results in the optimal value for R. (See Problem 20.7.)

Since R involves the components of $\mathbf{X}^{(\infty)}$, it represents the average return per period with the process in its steady-state pattern. Furthermore, since $\mathbf{X}^{(\infty)}$ is assumed independent of $\mathbf{X}^{(0)}$, R too is independent of the initial state of the process. The initial state does, however, influence the early history of the process. Denote the expected (undiscounted) worth of the process over n periods beginning in state i by $w_n(i)$. Then $w_i \equiv w_n(i) - nR$ represents the discrepancy over n periods between the expected total return given that the process began in state i and the expected total return had steady-state conditions initially prevailed. Since steady-state conditions will prevail eventually, regardless of the initial state, w_i must converge to a fixed number as n increases. (See Problem 20.10.) Consequently, w_i is effectively a constant for large values of n.

The values of w_i for each state i and large n can be used to generate the following **six-step algorithm** for determining optimal policies.

STEP 1 Arbitrarily choose an initial policy and denote the decision for each state i by $\hat{d}_i$. Designate this policy as the current one.

STEP 2 Determine the transition matrix $\mathbf{P} = [p_{ij}(\hat{d}_i)]$ corresponding to the current policy, and the returns $C(i, \hat{d}_i)$ associated with the decisions.

STEP 3 Solve the following set of equations for R and w_i $(i = 2, 3, \ldots, N)$, with w_1 taken as zero:

$$w_i + R = C(i, \hat{d}_i) + \sum_{j=1}^{N} p_{ij}(\hat{d}_i)w_j \qquad (i = 1, 2, \ldots, N) \tag{20.3}$$

STEP 4 For each state i $(i = 1, 2, \ldots, N)$, determine decision $\bar{d}_i$ that yields the

$$\underset{d_i}{\text{optimum}} \left\{ C(i, d_i) + \sum_{j=1}^{N} p_{ij}(d_i)w_j \right\} \tag{20.4}$$

where the optimum is taken over all decisions d_i possible in that state.

STEP 5 If $\bar{d}_i = \hat{d}_i$ for all i, then the current policy is optimal, with $R = R^*$ given in Step 3. If not, go to Step 6.

STEP 6 Set $\hat{d}_i = \bar{d}_i$ for each i, thereby establishing an updated current policy, and return to Step 2.

(See Problems 20.8 through 20.12.)

Solved Problems

20.1 Determine PV(u) for each state u, with an unbounded horizon, for the equipment replacement process of Problems 14.8 and 14.10, under the following policy:

State, u	1	2	3	4	5	6
Decision, $d(u)$	BUY	BUY	BUY	BUY	BUY	BUY

Take the effective interest rate to be 10 percent per annum and the cost of replacing a 6-year-old machine to be $R(6) = \$7000$.

The state u at any stage ranges from 1 to 6, since, with an unbounded horizon, it is possible to enter a stage with a 6-year-old machine (which, however, must then be immediately replaced). The discount factor is

$$\alpha = \frac{1}{1 + 0.10} = 0.909091$$

To calculate PV(1), note that, when the process begins with a 1-year-old machine, the current policy requires that the machine be replaced, at a cost of $3500 (see Table 14-12). A new machine is installed which generates an income of $10 000 and a maintenance cost of $100. The net revenue for the year is

$$10\,000 - 100 - 3500 = \$6400$$

One then enters the second year of the process with a 1-year-old machine which, according to the current policy, must also be replaced. The net revenue for the second year is also $6400, but since it is realized 1 year later it must be discounted by α. The net revenue for every year thereafter continues to be $6400, but each amount must be discounted appropriately to yield its present value. As a result, the present value of the total revenue from the process beginning with a 1-year-old machine is

$$\text{PV}(1) = 6400 + 6400\alpha + 6400\alpha^2 + 6400\alpha^3 + \cdots = \frac{6400}{1 - \alpha} = \$70\,400$$

To calculate PV(2), the present value of the total revenue beginning with a 2-year-old machine, note that the current policy requires that the 2-year-old machine be replaced immediately with a new model. The replacement cost is $4200. A new machine, once installed, generates an income of $10 000 and a maintenance cost of $100. The net revenue for the first year is

$$10\,000 - 100 - 4200 = \$5700$$

From the second year on, the financial conditions are identical to those considered in determining PV(1). Thus,

$$\text{PV}(2) = 5700 + 6400\alpha + 6400\alpha^2 + 6400\alpha^3 + \cdots = 5700 + \frac{6400\alpha}{1 - \alpha} = \$69\,700$$

Similarly,

$$\text{PV}(3) = (10\,000 - 100 - 4900) + 6400\alpha + 6400\alpha^2 + 6400\alpha^3 + \cdots = 5000 + \frac{6400\alpha}{1 - \alpha} = \$69\,000$$

$$\text{PV}(4) = (10\,000 - 100 - 5800) + 6400\alpha + 6400\alpha^2 + 6400\alpha^3 + \cdots = 4100 + \frac{6400\alpha}{1 - \alpha} = \$68\,100$$

$$\text{PV}(5) = (10\,000 - 100 - 5900) + 6400\alpha + 6400\alpha^2 + 6400\alpha^3 + \cdots = 4000 + \frac{6400\alpha}{1 - \alpha} = \$68\,000$$

$$\text{PV}(6) = (10\,000 - 100 - 7000) + 6400\alpha + 6400\alpha^2 + 6400\alpha^3 + \cdots = 2900 + \frac{6400\alpha}{1 - \alpha} = \$66\,900$$

20.2   Rework Problem 20.1 if the current policy is

State, u	1	2	3	4	5	6
Decision, $d(u)$	KEEP	KEEP	BUY	BUY	BUY	BUY

To calculate PV(1), the total discounted revenue beginning with a 1-year-old machine, note that the current policy requires that the 1-year-old machine be kept. From Table 14-12, such a machine will generate a yearly income of $9500 and a maintenance cost of $400, for a net revenue of $9100. The machine becomes 2 years old at the beginning of the second stage, and again the current policy calls for it to be kept. A 2-year-old machine generates a net revenue of

$$9200 - 800 = \$8400$$

but since this occurs in the second stage of the process, the amount must be discounted by α. The company then enters stage 3 with a 3-year-old machine which, according to the current policy, must be replaced. The replacement cost is $4900. A new machine, once installed, generates an income of $10 000 and a maintenance cost of $100; hence net revenue for the third stage is

$$10\,000 - 100 - 4900 = \$5000$$

which must be discounted by α^2. The company then enters stage 4 with a 1-year-old machine which, according to the current policy, must be kept. Therefore,

$$PV(1) = 9100 + 8400\alpha + 5000\alpha^2 + 9100\alpha^3 + 8400\alpha^4 + 5000\alpha^5 + \cdots$$

$$= (9100 + 8400\alpha + 5000\alpha^2)(1 + \alpha^3 + \alpha^6 + \cdots) = \frac{9100 + 8400\alpha + 5000\alpha^2}{1 - \alpha^3} = \$83\,916$$

To calculate PV(2), the total discounted revenue beginning the process with a 2-year-old machine, note that the current policy requires the 2-year-old machine to be kept. Such a machine will generate a net revenue of

$$9200 - 800 = \$8400$$

The machine enters stage 2 of the process as a 3-year-old model, and the current policy calls for it to be replaced. The replacement cost is $4900, which, when coupled with the income and maintenance cost generated by the new replacement, yields a net yearly revenue of

$$10\,000 - 100 - 4900 = \$5000$$

Since this amount is received in the second stage of the process, it must be discounted by α. The company enters the third stage with a 1-year-old machine. The situation is now identical to that which produced PV(1), but it occurs two stages later. Consequently,

$$PV(2) = 8400 + 5000\alpha + \alpha^2 PV(1) = \$82\,298$$

Similarly,

$$PV(3) = (10\,000 - 100 - 4900) + \alpha PV(1) = \$81\,287$$

$$PV(4) = (10\,000 - 100 - 5800) + \alpha PV(1) = \$80\,387$$

$$PV(5) = (10\,000 - 100 - 5900) + \alpha PV(1) = \$80\,287$$

$$PV(6) = (10\,000 - 100 - 7000) + \alpha PV(1) = \$79\,187$$

20.3 Solve Problem 14.10 with an unbounded horizon.

The functional equation for this process was determined in Example 20.1 to be

$$m(u) = \max\{I(u) - M(u) + \alpha m(u+1),\ I(0) - M(0) - R(u) + \alpha m(1)\}$$

To guarantee that 6-year-old machines are sold under the optimal policy, we set $I(6) = 0$, $M(6) = 10^9$, and PV(7) = 0. Using the data of Problems 14.8 and 20.1, we solve (1) by the five-step algorithm.

STEP 1 We arbitrarily choose as the initial policy

u	1	2	3	4	5	6
$d(u)$	BUY	BUY	BUY	BUY	BUY	BUY

STEP 2 Using the results of Problem 20.1, we have for this policy

$$PV(1) = \$70\,400 \qquad PV(2) = \$69\,700 \qquad PV(3) = \$69\,000$$

$$PV(4) = \$68\,100 \qquad PV(5) = \$68\,000 \qquad PV(6) = \$66\,900$$

STEP 3 Replacing $m(u)$ with PV(u) in the right-hand side of (1), we obtain

$$\hat{m}(1) = \max \{I(1) - M(1) + \alpha\, PV(2),\ I(0) - M(0) - R(1) + \alpha\, PV(1)\}$$

$$= \max \{9500 - 400 + (0.909091)(69\,700),\ 10\,000 - 100 - 3500 + (0.909091)(70\,400)\}$$

$$= \max \{72\,464,\ 70\,400\} = \$72\,464 \qquad \text{with} \quad d(1) = \text{KEEP}$$

$$\hat{m}(2) = \max \{I(2) - M(2) + \alpha\, PV(3),\ I(0) - M(0) - R(2) + \alpha\, PV(1)\}$$

$$= \max \{9200 - 800 + (0.909091)(69\,000),\ 10\,000 - 100 - 4200 + (0.909091)(70\,400)\}$$

$$= \max \{71\,127,\ 69\,700\} = \$71\,127 \qquad \text{with} \quad d(2) = \text{KEEP}$$

and

$$\hat{m}(3) = \max \{68\,409,\ 69\,000\} = \$69\,000 \qquad \text{with} \quad d(3) = \text{BUY}$$

$$\hat{m}(4) = \max \{66\,318,\ 68\,100\} = \$68\,100 \qquad \text{with} \quad d(4) = \text{BUY}$$

$$\hat{m}(5) = \max \{63\,618,\ 68\,000\} = \$68\,000 \qquad \text{with} \quad d(5) = \text{BUY}$$

$$\hat{m}(6) = \max \{-10^9,\ 66\,900\} = \$66\,900 \qquad \text{with} \quad d(6) = \text{BUY}$$

Collecting these results into a table we have

u	1	2	3	4	5	6
$d(u)$	KEEP	KEEP	BUY	BUY	BUY	BUY

STEPS 4 AND 5   Since this new policy differs from the current one, we take the new policy as the updated current policy and return to Step 2.

STEP 2   Using the results of Problem 20.2, we have for the updated current policy

$$PV(1) = \$83\,916 \qquad PV(2) = \$82\,298 \qquad PV(3) = \$81\,287$$

$$PV(4) = \$80\,387 \qquad PV(5) = \$80\,287 \qquad PV(6) = \$79\,187$$

STEP 3

$$\hat{m}(1) = \max \{I(1) - M(1) + \alpha\, PV(2),\ I(0) - M(0) - R(1) + \alpha\, PV(1)\}$$

$$= \max \{83\,916,\ 82\,687\} = \$83\,916 \qquad \text{with} \quad d(1) = \text{KEEP}$$

$$\hat{m}(2) = \max \{82\,297,\ 81\,987\} = \$82\,297 \qquad \text{with} \quad d(2) = \text{KEEP}$$

$$\hat{m}(3) = \max \{79\,579,\ 81\,287\} = \$81\,287 \qquad \text{with} \quad d(3) = \text{BUY}$$

$$\hat{m}(4) = \max \{77\,488,\ 80\,387\} = \$80\,387 \qquad \text{with} \quad d(4) = \text{BUY}$$

$$\hat{m}(5) = \max \{74\,788,\ 80\,287\} = \$80\,287 \qquad \text{with} \quad d(5) = \text{BUY}$$

$$\hat{m}(6) = \max \{-10^9,\ 79\,187\} = \$79\,187 \qquad \text{with} \quad d(6) = \text{BUY}$$

Collecting these results into a table, we have

u	1	2	3	4	5	6
$d(u)$	KEEP	KEEP	BUY	BUY	BUY	BUY

STEP 4   Since this new policy is identical to the current policy, it is the optimal one.   One- and two-year-old machines should be kept; older machines should be replaced by new models. As the process starts with a 2-year-old machine, the company's total discounted profit under an optimal policy is $m(2) = PV(2) = \$82\,297$ (to within roundoff error).

20.4   Use the functional-equation approach to recalculate the present values found in Problem 20.2.

The procedure is to replace $m(u)$ by $PV(u)$ in both sides of the functional equation and then, for each state, to optimize over the single decision dictated by the current policy.   The functional equation for this problem is given in Example 20.1 as

$$m(u) = \max\{I(u) - M(u) + \alpha m(u+1),\ I(0) - M(0) - R(u) + \alpha m(1)\} \tag{1}$$

and the policy under consideration is

u	1	2	3	4	5	6
$d(u)$	KEEP	KEEP	BUY	BUY	BUY	BUY

Maximizing over a KEEP decision means choosing the first of the two terms in (1); maximizing over BUY means choosing the second term. Thus, the current policy yields the set of equations:

$$PV(1) = I(1) - M(1) + \alpha\,PV(2)$$
$$PV(2) = I(2) - M(2) + \alpha\,PV(3)$$
$$PV(3) = I(0) - M(0) - R(3) + \alpha\,PV(1)$$
$$PV(4) = I(0) - M(0) - R(4) + \alpha\,PV(1) \tag{2}$$
$$PV(5) = I(0) - M(0) - R(5) + \alpha\,PV(1)$$
$$PV(6) = I(0) - M(0) - R(6) + \alpha\,PV(1)$$

The last four equations of (2) are identical to the equations used to determine PV(3), ..., PV(6) in Problem 20.2. Combining the second and third equations of (2), we obtain

$$PV(2) = I(2) - M(2) + \alpha[I(0) - M(0) - R(3)] + \alpha^2 PV(1) \tag{3}$$

which is identical to the equation for PV(2) in Problem 20.2. Finally, combining the first equation of (2) with (3), we get

$$PV(1) = \frac{I(1) - M(1) + \alpha[I(2) - M(2)] + \alpha^2[I(0) - M(0) - R(3)]}{1 - \alpha^3}$$

which is exactly the expression for PV(1) found in Problem 20.2.

20.5 Solve Problem 18.4 with discounting and an unbounded horizon, if the effective interest rate is 8 percent per annum.

Given a production policy, this problem can be modeled as a Markov chain. As determined in Problem 18.4, the states for each stage are the possible inventories at the beginning of a year—namely, $-2, -1, 0,$ or 1 space shuttles—with negative inventory representing unfulfilled orders from the previous year. The possible decisions are the production levels for new shuttles. These levels are limited to 2, for state -2; 1 or 2, for state -1; 0, 1, or 2, for state 0; 0 or 1, for state 1. The transition probabilities and costs (in millions of dollars) associated with each state and each decision are listed in Table 20-1. For instance, to determine line 3 of the table, the line corresponding to an inventory of -1 shuttles and the decision to produce two shuttles during the current year, note that once the back order of one shuttle has been fulfilled there will remain one shuttle to satisfy new demand. If this demand is one (which will occur with probability 0.6), then the state at the beginning of the next period will be 0; hence, $p_{-1,0}(2) = 0.6$. If the new demand is for two shuttles (which will occur with probability 0.4), then the state at the beginning of the next period will be -1; hence $p_{-1,-1}(2) = 0.4$. Since no other states can be reached from state -1 with a decision to produce 2 shuttles, all other transition probabilities are 0. An initial state of -1 signifies that one shuttle was not delivered as needed the previous year, and so a penalty cost of 1.5 million dollars is assessed. This cost, coupled with a production cost of 19 million dollars for manufacturing two new shuttles, results in a yearly cost of 20.5 million dollars. Observe that the yearly cost is strictly determined by the state and decision; it is independent of the random demand.

For $i = 0.08$, the discount factor is

$$\alpha = \frac{1}{1 + 0.08} = 0.92592593$$

The functional equation is (20.1), where the optimization is a minimization and where i and j range over $-2, \ldots, 1$ (not over $1, \ldots, 4$). We solve for the optimal policy using the five-step algorithm.

Table 20-1

	State, i	Decision, d_i	Transition Probabilities, $p_{ij}(d_i)$				Penalty Cost	Production Cost	Storage Cost	Yearly Cost, $C(i, d_i)$
			$j=-2$	$j=-1$	$j=0$	$j=1$				
1	-2	2	0.4	0.6	0	0	3.0	19	0	22
2	-1	1	0.4	0.6	0	0	1.5	10	0	11.5
3	-1	2	0	0.4	0.6	0	1.5	19	0	20.5
4	0	0	0.4	0.6	0	0	0	0	0	0
5	0	1	0	0.4	0.6	0	0	10	0	10
6	0	2	0	0	0.4	0.6	0	19	0	19
7	1	0	0	0.4	0.6	0	0	0	1.1	1.1
8	1	1	0	0	0.4	0.6	0	10	1.1	11.1

STEP 1 We arbitrarily choose as an initial policy

i	-2	-1	0	1
$\hat{d}_i$	2	2	2	0

STEP 2 For the data in lines 1, 3, 6, and 7 of Table 20-1, the data corresponding to the current policy, (*20.2*) gives

$$PV(-2) = 22 \;\;+ (0.92592593)[(0.4)PV(-2) + (0.6)PV(-1) + \;\;(0)PV(0) + \;\;(0)PV(1)]$$
$$PV(-1) = 20.5 + (0.92592593)[\;\;(0)PV(-2) + (0.4)PV(-1) + (0.6)PV(0) + \;\;(0)PV(1)]$$
$$PV(0) = 19 \;\;\; + (0.92592593)[\;\;(0)PV(-2) + \;\;(0)PV(-1) + (0.4)PV(0) + (0.6)PV(1)]$$
$$PV(1) = \;\;1.1 + (0.92592593)[\;\;(0)PV(-2) + (0.4)PV(-1) + (0.6)PV(0) + \;\;(0)PV(1)]$$

which is equivalent to the system

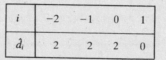

$$(0.62962963)PV(-2) - (0.55555556)PV(-1) \qquad\qquad\qquad = 22$$
$$(0.62962963)PV(-1) - (0.55555556)PV(0) \qquad\qquad = 20.5$$
$$(0.62962963)PV(0) - (0.55555556)PV(1) = 19$$
$$- (0.37037037)PV(-1) - (0.55555556)PV(0) + \qquad\qquad PV(1) = \;\;1.1$$

Solving,

$$PV(-2) = 210.57768 \qquad PV(-1) = 199.05471 \qquad PV(0) = 188.69533 \qquad PV(1) = 179.65471$$

STEP 3 Using these present values and the data from Table 20-1, we carry out the calculations exhibited in Table 20-2. For each state i, the smallest calculated value is $\hat{m}(i)$. Thus, the new policy is

i	-2	-1	0	1
d_i	2	2	1	0

STEPS 4 AND 5 Since this new policy differs from the previous one, we designate this new policy as the current one and return to Step 2.

STEP 2 For the data in lines 1, 3, 5, and 7 of Table 20-1, the data corresponding to the latest policy, (*20.2*) gives

Table 20-2

State, i	Decision, $\hat{d}_i$	Expected Discounted Cost, $C(i, \hat{d}_i) + \alpha \sum\limits_{j=-2}^{1} p_{ij}(\hat{d}_i)\mathrm{PV}(j)$	
−2	2	$22 + (0.92592593)[(0.4)(210.57768) + (0.6)(199.05471)$ $+ (0)(188.69533) + (0)(179.65471)]$	= 210.578
−1	1	$11.5 + (0.92592593)[(0.4)(210.57768) + (0.6)(199.05471)$ $+ (0)(188.69533) + (0)(179.65471)]$	= 200.078
−1	2	$20.5 + (0.92592593)[(0)(210.57768) + (0.4)(199.05471)$ $+ (0.6)(188.69533) + (0)(179.65471)]$	= 199.055
0	0	$0 + (0.92592593)[(0.4)(210.57768) + (0.6)(199.05471)$ $+ (0)(188.69533) + (0)(179.65471)]$	= 188.578
0	1	$10 + (0.92592593)[(0)(210.57768) + (0.4)(199.05471)$ $+ (0.6)(188.69533) + (0)(179.65471)]$	= 188.555
0	2	$19 + (0.92592593)[(0)(210.57768) + (0)(199.05471)$ $+ (0.4)(188.69533) + (0.6)(179.65471)]$	= 188.695
1	0	$1.1 + (0.92592593)[(0)(210.57768) + (0.4)(199.05471)$ $+ (0.6)(188.69533) + (0)(179.65471)]$	= 179.655
1	1	$11.1 + (0.92592593)[(0)(210.57768) + (0)(199.05471)$ $+ (0.4)(188.69533) + (0.6)(179.65471)]$	= 180.795

$$\mathrm{PV}(-2) = 22 \ \ + (0.92592593)[(0.4)\mathrm{PV}(-2) + (0.6)\mathrm{PV}(-1) + \ \ (0)\mathrm{PV}(0) + (0)\mathrm{PV}(1)]$$
$$\mathrm{PV}(-1) = 20.5 + (0.92592593)[\ \ (0)\mathrm{PV}(-2) + (0.4)\mathrm{PV}(-1) + (0.6)\mathrm{PV}(0) + (0)\mathrm{PV}(1)]$$
$$\mathrm{PV}(0) \ = 10 \ \ + (0.92592593)[\ \ (0)\mathrm{PV}(-2) + (0.4)\mathrm{PV}(-1) + (0.6)\mathrm{PV}(0) + (0)\mathrm{PV}(1)]$$
$$\mathrm{PV}(1) \ = \ \ 1.1 + (0.92592593)[\ \ (0)\mathrm{PV}(-2) + (0.4)\mathrm{PV}(-1) + (0.6)\mathrm{PV}(0) + (0)\mathrm{PV}(1)]$$

which is equivalent to the system

$$(0.62962963)\mathrm{PV}(-2) - (0.55555556)\mathrm{PV}(-1) \qquad\qquad\qquad = 22$$
$$(0.62962963)\mathrm{PV}(-1) - (0.55555556)\mathrm{PV}(0) \qquad\qquad = 20.5$$
$$- (0.37037037)\mathrm{PV}(-1) + (0.44444444)\mathrm{PV}(0) \qquad\qquad = 10$$
$$- (0.37037037)\mathrm{PV}(-1) - (0.55555556)\mathrm{PV}(0) + \mathrm{PV}(1) = \ \ 1.1$$

Solving,

$$\mathrm{PV}(-2) = 209.64706 \qquad \mathrm{PV}(-1) = 198 \qquad \mathrm{PV}(0) = 187.5 \qquad \mathrm{PV}(1) = 178.6$$

Table 20-3

State, i	Decision, d_i	Expected Discounted Cost, $C(i, d_i) + \alpha \sum\limits_{j=-2}^{1} p_{ij}(d_i)\mathrm{PV}(j)$	
−2	2	$22 \ \ + (0.92592593)[(0.4)(209.64706) + (0.6)(198) + (0)(187.5) \ \ + (0)(178.6)]$	= 209.647
−1	1	$11.5 + (0.92592593)[(0.4)(209.64706) + (0.6)(198) + (0)(187.5) \ \ + (0)(178.6)]$	= 199.147
−1	2	$20.5 + (0.92592593)[(0)(209.64706) \ \ + (0.4)(198) + (0.6)(187.5) + (0)(178.6)]$	= 198.000
0	0	$0 \ \ + (0.92592593)[(0.4)(209.64706) + (0.6)(198) + (0)(187.5) \ \ + (0)(178.6)]$	= 187.647
0	1	$10 \ \ + (0.92592593)[(0)(209.64706) \ \ + (0.4)(198) + (0.6)(187.5) + (0)(178.6)]$	= 187.500
0	2	$19 \ \ + (0.92592593)[(0)(209.64706) \ \ + (0)(198) \ \ + (0.4)(187.5) + (0.6)(178.6)]$	= 187.667
1	0	$1.1 + (0.92592593)[(0)(209.64706) \ \ + (0.4)(198) + (0.6)(187.5) + (0)(178.6)]$	= 178.600
1	1	$11.1 + (0.92592593)[(0)(209.64706) \ \ + (0)(198) \ \ + (0.4)(187.5) + (0.6)(178.6)]$	= 179.767

STEP 3   Using these present values and the data from Table 20-1, we carry out the calculations shown
in Table 20-3.   The new policy is seen to be

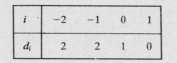

i	-2	-1	0	1
d_i	2	2	1	0

STEP 4   Since this new policy is identical to the current policy, it is the optimal one.   Under this policy
and starting with zero inventory, the shuttle manufacturer's expected discounted cost is

$$m(0) = PV(0) = 187.5 \text{ million dollars}$$

20.6   A farmer raises corn for sale on the open market and for feed for the farm's own livestock.
The corn yield is variable from year to year, being governed by the following probability
distribution:

Yield, units	10	11	12	13	14
Probability	0.10	0.20	0.30	0.25	0.15

The farmer requires 10 units of corn over the winter for the farm's livestock and has facilities
to store as much as 12 units.   Any corn stored but not used as feed during the winter can be
re-stored or sold the following fall.

Each winter a feed distributor is willing to pay a premium price for the farmer's corn
according to the rate scale below, if the farmer guarantees delivery after the following fall's
harvest:

Units of Corn Contracted	0	1	2	3	4
Total Price, $	0	400	900	1400	2000

If the farmer contracts too much of a future harvest to the feed distributor, leaving less than
10 units for the farm's own needs, then the shortfall must be made up by purchasing corn on
the spot market at \$700 per unit.   Any corn held at the end of the harvest for which storage
facilities are unavailable is sold on the spot market for \$300 per unit.   The farmer limits
transactions on the spot market to those that are absolutely necessary.   How much corn
should the farmer contract to the feed distributor each year if the farmer wishes to maximize
expected discounted profit over the foreseeable future, with an effective interest rate of 7
percent?

 We take the beginning of a stage to be the end of a harvest, after any previous contract has been
honored and any transactions on the spot market have been completed in preparation for the upcoming
winter.   At such time, the farmer has either 10, 11, or 12 units of corn in storage, so we designate these
levels as states 1, 2, and 3, respectively.   The decision facing the farmer is as to the number of units of
corn from next year's harvest to contract to the distributor.   The transition probabilities and expected
yearly gains associated with each state and each decision are listed in Table 20-4.   For instance, to
calculate line 4 of Table 20-4, which corresponds to a current storage level of 10 units and a decision to
contract 3 units of next year's harvest, note that there are four ways for the farmer to remain in state 1
after 1 year: after the 10 stored units have been consumed over the winter, the farmer could (i) harvest
10 and buy 3, (ii) harvest 11 and buy 2, (iii) harvest 12 and buy 1, (iv) harvest 13.   Thus,

$$p_{11} = 0.10 + 0.20 + 0.30 + 0.25 = 0.85$$

The only way for the farmer to begin one stage with 10 units and the next stage with 11 units, given that livestock consume 10 units and 3 units must be delivered to the distributor, is for the harvest to yield 14 units; hence, $p_{12} = 0.15$. There is no way (without unnecessary spot market transactions) to move from an inventory of 10 units to one of 12 units; $p_{13} = 0$.

For none of the five possible yields is any corn left for sale on the spot market. The income from spot market sales, therefore, will be 0. Since 3, 2, or 1 units are bought on the spot market according as the harvest is 10, 11, or 12 units, the expected spot market cost is

$$(0.10)(2100) + (0.20)(1400) + (0.30)(700) = \$700$$

Note that, in contrast to Problem 20.5, the net income for the stage is not strictly determined by the state and the decision; instead, it also depends on the random harvest.

The discount factor is

$$\alpha = \frac{1}{1 + 0.07} = 0.934579$$

Technically, since all costs and incomes occur at the end of the period, they should be discounted by α before being used. If we assume that this has already been done—for example, that the spot market cost is really \$749, which when discounted by α becomes \$700—then the dollar figures in Table 20-3 are automatically discounted appropriately.

The functional equation is (20.1), with the optimization a maximization. We determine the optimal policy by using the five-step algorithm.

Table 20-4

	State, i	Decision, d_i	Transition Probabilities, $p_{ij}(d_i)$			Contracted Income, CI	Expected Spot Market Income, SI	Expected Spot Market Cost, SC	Expected Yearly Income, CI + SI − SC = $C(i, d_i)$
			$j = 1$	$j = 2$	$j = 3$				
1	1	0	0.10	0.20	0.70	0	165	0	165
2	1	1	0.30	0.30	0.40	400	45	70	375
3	1	2	0.60	0.25	0.15	900	0	280	620
4	1	3	0.85	0.15	0	1400	0	700	700
5	1	4	1	0	0	2000	0	1295	705
6	2	0	0	0.10	0.90	0	375	0	375
7	2	1	0.10	0.20	0.70	400	165	0	565
8	2	2	0.30	0.30	0.40	900	45	70	875
9	2	3	0.60	0.25	0.15	1400	0	280	1120
10	2	4	0.85	0.15	0	2000	0	700	1300
11	3	0	0	0	1	0	645	0	645
12	3	1	0	0.10	0.90	400	375	0	775
13	3	2	0.10	0.20	0.70	900	165	0	1065
14	3	3	0.30	0.30	0.40	1400	45	70	1375
15	3	4	0.60	0.25	0.15	2000	0	280	1720

STEP 1   We arbitrarily choose as the initial policy

i	1	2	3
d_i	3	4	4

STEP 2   For the data in lines 4, 10, and 15 of Table 20-4, the data corresponding to the current policy, (20.2) gives

$$PV(1) = 700 + (0.934579)[(0.85)PV(1) + (0.15)PV(2) + (0)PV(3)]$$
$$PV(2) = 1300 + (0.934579)[(0.85)PV(1) + (0.15)PV(2) + (0)PV(3)]$$
$$PV(3) = 1720 + (0.934579)[(0.60)PV(1) + (0.25)PV(2) + (0.15)PV(3)]$$

which is equivalent to the system

$$(0.205607)PV(1) - (0.140187)PV(2) = 700$$
$$-(0.794393)PV(1) + (0.859813)PV(2) = 1300$$
$$-(0.560748)PV(1) - (0.233645)PV(2) + (0.859813)PV(3) = 1720$$

The solution to this set of equations is

$$PV(1) = \$11\,986 \qquad PV(2) = \$12\,586 \qquad PV(3) = \$13\,238$$

Table 20-5

State, i	Decision, $\hat{d}_i$	Expected Discounted Profit, $C(i, \hat{d}_i) + \alpha \sum_{j=1}^{3} p_{ij}(\hat{d}_i)PV(j)$
1	0	$165 + (0.934579)[(0.10)(11\,986) + (0.20)(12\,586) + (0.70)(13\,238)] = 12\,298$
1	1	$375 + (0.934579)[(0.30)(11\,986) + (0.30)(12\,586) + (0.40)(13\,238)] = 12\,213$
1	2	$620 + (0.934579)[(0.60)(11\,986) + (0.25)(12\,586) + (0.15)(13\,238)] = 12\,138$
1	3	$700 + (0.934579)[(0.85)(11\,986) + (0.15)(12\,586) + (0)(13\,238)] = 11\,986$
1	4	$705 + (0.934579)[(1)(11\,986) + (0)(12\,586) + (0)(13\,238)] = 11\,907$
2	0	$375 + (0.934579)[(0)(11\,986) + (0.10)(12\,586) + (0.90)(13\,238)] = 12\,686$
2	1	$565 + (0.934579)[(0.10)(11\,986) + (0.20)(12\,586) + (0.70)(13\,238)] = 12\,698$
2	2	$875 + (0.934579)[(0.30)(11\,986) + (0.30)(12\,586) + (0.40)(13\,238)] = 12\,713$
2	3	$1120 + (0.934579)[(0.60)(11\,986) + (0.25)(12\,586) + (0.15)(13\,238)] = 12\,638$
2	4	$1300 + (0.934579)[(0.85)(11\,986) + (0.15)(12\,586) + (0)(13\,238)] = 12\,586$
3	0	$645 + (0.934579)[(0)(11\,986) + (0)(12\,586) + (1)(13\,238)] = 13\,017$
3	1	$775 + (0.934579)[(0)(11\,986) + (0.10)(12\,586) + (0.90)(13\,238)] = 13\,086$
3	2	$1065 + (0.934579)[(0.10)(11\,986) + (0.20)(12\,586) + (0.70)(13\,238)] = 13\,198$
3	3	$1375 + (0.934579)[(0.30)(11\,986) + (0.30)(12\,586) + (0.40)(13\,238)] = 13\,213$
3	4	$1720 + (0.934579)[(0.60)(11\,986) + (0.25)(12\,586) + (0.15)(13\,238)] = 13\,238$

Table 20-6

State, i	Decision, d_i	Expected Discounted Profit, $C(i, d_i) + \alpha \sum_{j=1}^{3} p_{ij}(d_i)PV(j)$
1	0	$165 + (0.934579)[(0.10)(14\,253) + (0.20)(14\,714) + (0.70)(15\,294)] = 14\,253$
1	1	$375 + (0.934579)[(0.30)(14\,253) + (0.30)(14\,714) + (0.40)(15\,294)] = 14\,214$
1	2	$620 + (0.934579)[(0.60)(14\,253) + (0.25)(14\,714) + (0.15)(15\,294)] = 14\,194$
1	3	$700 + (0.934579)[(0.85)(14\,253) + (0.15)(14\,714) + (0)(15\,294)] = 14\,085$
1	4	$705 + (0.934579)[(1)(14\,253) + (0)(14\,714) + (0)(15\,294)] = 14\,026$
2	0	$375 + (0.934579)[(0)(14\,253) + (0.10)(14\,714) + (0.90)(15\,294)] = 14\,614$
2	1	$565 + (0.934579)[(0.10)(14\,253) + (0.20)(14\,714) + (0.70)(15\,294)] = 14\,653$
2	2	$875 + (0.934579)[(0.30)(14\,253) + (0.30)(14\,714) + (0.40)(15\,294)] = 14\,714$
2	3	$1120 + (0.934579)[(0.60)(14\,253) + (0.25)(14\,714) + (0.15)(15\,294)] = 14\,694$
2	4	$1300 + (0.934579)[(0.85)(14\,253) + (0.15)(14\,714) + (0)(15\,294)] = 14\,685$
3	0	$645 + (0.934579)[(0)(14\,253) + (0)(14\,714) + (1)(15\,294)] = 14\,938$
3	1	$775 + (0.934579)[(0)(14\,253) + (0.10)(14\,714) + (0.90)(15\,294)] = 15\,014$
3	2	$1065 + (0.934579)[(0.10)(14\,253) + (0.20)(14\,714) + (0.70)(15\,294)] = 15\,153$
3	3	$1375 + (0.934579)[(0.30)(14\,253) + (0.30)(14\,714) + (0.40)(15\,294)] = 15\,214$
3	4	$1720 + (0.934579)[(0.60)(14\,253) + (0.25)(14\,714) + (0.15)(15\,294)] = 15\,294$

STEP 3   Using these present values and the data from Table 20-4, we carry out the calculations exhibited in Table 20-5.   For each state i, the largest calculated value is $\hat{m}(i)$.   Thus, the new policy is

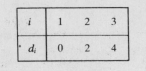

STEPS 4 AND 5   Since this new policy differs from the previous one, we designate this new policy as the current one and return to Step 2.

STEP 2   For the data in lines 1, 8, and 15 of Table 20-4, the data corresponding to the latest policy, (*20.2*) gives

$$PV(1) = \ \ \ 165 + (0.934579)[(0.10)PV(1) + (0.20)PV(2) + (0.70)PV(3)]$$
$$PV(2) = \ \ \ 875 + (0.934579)[(0.30)PV(1) + (0.30)PV(2) + (0.40)PV(3)]$$
$$PV(3) = 1720 + (0.934579)[(0.60)PV(1) + (0.25)PV(2) + (0.15)PV(3)]$$

which is equivalent to the system

$$(0.906542)PV(1) - (0.186916)PV(2) - (0.654206)PV(3) = \ \ \ 165$$
$$-(0.280374)PV(1) + (0.719626)PV(2) - (0.373832)PV(3) = \ \ \ 875$$
$$-(0.560748)PV(1) - (0.233645)PV(2) + (0.859813)PV(3) = 1720$$

The solution to this set of equations is

$$PV(1) = \$14\,253 \qquad PV(2) = \$14\,714 \qquad PV(3) = \$15\,294$$

STEP 3   Using these present values and the data from Table 20-4, we carry out the calculations exhibited in Table 20-6.   The new policy is seen to be

i	1	2	3
d_i	0	2	4

STEP 4   Since this latest policy is identical to the current policy, it is the optimal one.   If the farmer enters a stage with an inventory of 10 units of corn, no contract should be signed; if the inventory is 11 units, a contract for 2 units should be signed; and if the inventory is 12 units, a contract for 4 units should be signed.

20.7   A supermarket chain rates its weekly profits from each store as either high or low.   Whenever profits from a particular store are high one week, the store manager has the option of either continuing the current promotional campaign or introducing a new one.   If the current campaign is retained, the profits for the following week will reach a high of $8000 with probability 0.5 and a low of $4000 with probability 0.5.   With a new promotional campaign, profits the following week will reach a high of $7000 with probability 0.8 and a low of $4000 with probability 0.2.   Whenever profits for a particular week are low, the store manager must introduce a new promotional campaign, which will result the following week in a high profit of $6000 with probability 0.4 and a low profit of $3000 with probability 0.6.   Determine a promotional policy for a given store that ultimately will maximize the expected weekly profits.

We take the beginning of a stage to be the end of a business week, after all profits have been determined but before a decision on the following week's promotional campaign is made.   The possible states for each stage are those of high and low profits, which we designate as states 1 and 2, respectively.   The possible decisions are to keep the current campaign and to introduce a new one; these decisions we designate as 1 and 2, respectively.   Both decisions are feasible for state 1, but only decision 2 is permitted in state 2.   The transition probabilities and expected profits depend on both the state and the decision; they are compiled in Table 20-7.

Table 20-7

	State, i	Decision, d_i	Transition Probabilities, $p_{ij}(d_i)$		High Profit, Π_1	Low Profit, Π_2	Expected Weekly Profit, $C(i, d_i) = \sum\limits_{j=1}^{2} p_{ij}\Pi_j$
			$j = 1$	$j = 2$			
1	1	1	0.5	0.5	8000	4000	$(0.5)(8000) + (0.5)(4000) = 6000$
2	1	2	0.8	0.2	7000	4000	$(0.8)(7000) + (0.2)(4000) = 6400$
3	2	2	0.4	0.6	6000	3000	$(0.4)(6000) + (0.6)(3000) = 4200$

There are only two possible policies for this process:

i	1	2
$d_{(1)i}$	1	2

and

i	1	2
$d_{(2)i}$	2	2

The transition matrix for the first policy is obtained from lines 1 and 3 of Table 20-7 as

$$\mathbf{P}_{(1)} = \begin{bmatrix} 0.5 & 0.5 \\ 0.4 & 0.6 \end{bmatrix}$$

The limiting matrix for $\mathbf{P}_{(1)}$ is

$$\mathbf{L}_{(1)} = \lim_{n \to \infty} \mathbf{P}_{(1)}^n = \begin{bmatrix} 4/9 & 5/9 \\ 4/9 & 5/9 \end{bmatrix}$$

Consequently, $\mathbf{X}_{(1)}^{(\infty)} = [4/9, 5/9]$, regardless of the initial state of the process, and the expected return per week is, in the steady state,

$$R_{(1)} = C(1, 1)x_{(1)1}^{(\infty)} + C(2, 2)x_{(1)2}^{(\infty)} = (6000)(\tfrac{4}{9}) + (4200)(\tfrac{5}{9}) = \$5000$$

The transition matrix for the second policy is obtained from lines 2 and 3 of Table 20-7 as

$$\mathbf{P}_{(2)} = \begin{bmatrix} 0.8 & 0.2 \\ 0.4 & 0.6 \end{bmatrix}$$

The limiting matrix for this transition matrix is

$$\mathbf{L}_{(2)} = \lim_{n \to \infty} \mathbf{P}_{(2)}^n = \begin{bmatrix} 2/3 & 1/3 \\ 2/3 & 1/3 \end{bmatrix}$$

Hence, $\mathbf{X}_{(2)}^{(\infty)} = [2/3, 1/3]$, and the expected return per week is, in the steady state,

$$R_{(2)} = C(1, 2)x_{(2)1}^{(\infty)} + C(2, 2)x_{(2)2}^{(\infty)} = (6400)(\tfrac{2}{3}) + (4200)(\tfrac{1}{3}) = \$5666.67$$

The expected return per week for policy 2 is better than that for policy 1; hence policy 2 is the optimal one.   The store manager should introduce a new promotional campaign each week.

20.8   Solve Problem 20.7 by the six-step algorithm.

STEP 1   As the initial policy $\{\hat{d}_i\}$, arbitrarily choose the policy $\{d_{(1)i}\}$ of Problem 20.7.

STEP 2   The transition matrix and expected weekly profits associated with this policy are obtained from lines 1 and 3 of Table 20-7 as

$$\mathbf{P} = \begin{bmatrix} 0.5 & 0.5 \\ 0.4 & 0.6 \end{bmatrix} \qquad C(1, 1) = 6000 \qquad C(2, 2) = 4200$$

STEP 3   With these data, system (*20.3*) becomes

$$w_1 + R = 6000 + (0.5)w_1 + (0.5)w_2$$
$$w_2 + R = 4200 + (0.4)w_1 + (0.6)w_2$$

Setting $w_1 = 0$ and solving, we obtain $R = 5000$, $w_2 = -2000$.

Table 20-8

State, i	Decision, d_i	$C(i, d_i) + \sum_{j=1}^{2} p_{ij}(d_i)w_j$
1	1	$6000 + (0.5)(0) + (0.5)(-2000) = 5000$
1	2	$6400 + (0.8)(0) + (0.2)(-2000) = 6000$
2	2	$4200 + (0.4)(0) + (0.6)(-2000) = 3000$

STEP 4   Using these values for w_1 and w_2, along with data from Table 20-7, we carry out the maximization indicated in (*20.4*).   See Table 20-8, which shows the new policy to be

i	1	2
$\bar{d}_i$	2	2

STEPS 5 AND 6   Since this latest policy is different from the current one, we designate this new policy as the updated current policy and return to Step 2.

STEP 2   The transition matrix and expected profits for this new policy are obtained from lines 2 and 3 of Table 20-7 as

$$\mathbf{P} = \begin{bmatrix} 0.8 & 0.2 \\ 0.4 & 0.6 \end{bmatrix} \qquad C(1, 2) = 6400 \qquad C(2, 2) = 4200$$

STEP 3   With these data, (*20.3*) becomes

$$w_1 + R = 6400 + (0.8)w_1 + (0.2)w_2$$
$$w_2 + R = 4200 + (0.4)w_1 + (0.6)w_2$$

Setting $w_1 = 0$ and solving, we obtain $R = 5666.67$, $w_2 = -3666.67$.

Table 20-9

State, i	Decision, d_i	$C(i, d_i) + \sum_{j=1}^{2} p_{ij}(d_i)w_j$
1	1	$6000 + (0.5)(0) + (0.5)(-3666.67) = 4166.67$
1	2	$6400 + (0.8)(0) + (0.2)(-3666.67) = 5666.67$
2	2	$4200 + (0.4)(0) + (0.6)(-3666.67) = 2000.00$

STEP 4   Using these values for w_1 and w_2, along with data from Table 20-7, we generate Table 20-9.   The new policy is seen to be

i	1	2
$\bar{d}_i$	2	2

STEP 5 Since this latest policy is identical to the current policy, it is the optimal policy. The steady-state, expected return per week for this policy is given in the last iteration of Step 3 as $R = \$5666.67$.

20.9 Solve Problem 20.6 if the objective is to maximize the expected profit per year (in the steady state).

STEP 1 We arbitrarily choose as the initial policy

i	1	2	3
$\hat{d}_i$	0	2	4

STEP 2 Using the data in lines 1, 8, and 15 of Table 20-4, the data corresponding to the current policy, we find

$$\mathbf{P} = \begin{bmatrix} 0.10 & 0.20 & 0.70 \\ 0.30 & 0.30 & 0.40 \\ 0.60 & 0.25 & 0.15 \end{bmatrix} \qquad C(1,0) = 165 \qquad C(2,2) = 875 \qquad C(3,4) = 1720$$

STEP 3 With these data, (*20.3*) becomes

$$w_1 + R = \ \ 165 + (0.10)w_1 + (0.20)w_2 + (0.70)w_3$$
$$w_2 + R = \ \ 875 + (0.30)w_1 + (0.30)w_2 + (0.40)w_3$$
$$w_3 + R = 1720 + (0.60)w_1 + (0.25)w_2 + (0.15w_3)$$

Setting $w_1 = 0$ and solving for the remaining variables, we find $R = 967.340$, $w_2 = 449.645$, and $w_3 = 1017.73$.

STEP 4 Using these values for w_1, w_2, and w_3, along with data from Table 20-4, we generate Table 20-10. The new policy is found as

$\hat{i}$	1	2	3
$\bar{d}_i$	0	2	4

Table 20-10

State, i	Decision, d_i	$C(i, d_i) + \sum\limits_{j=1}^{3} p_{ij}(d_i)w_j$
1	0	$165 + (0.10)(0) + (0.20)(449.645) + (0.70)(1017.73) = \ \ 967.34$
1	1	$375 + (0.30)(0) + (0.30)(449.645) + (0.40)(1017.73) = \ \ 916.99$
1	2	$620 + (0.60)(0) + (0.25)(449.645) + (0.15)(1017.73) = \ \ 885.07$
1	3	$700 + (0.85)(0) + (0.15)(449.645) + \ \ \ \ \ (0)(1017.73) = \ \ 767.45$
1	4	$705 + \ \ \ \ (1)(0) + \ \ \ \ \ (0)(449.645) + \ \ \ \ \ (0)(1017.73) = \ \ 705.00$
2	0	$375 + \ \ \ \ (0)(0) + (0.10)(449.645) + (0.90)(1017.73) = 1335.92$
2	1	$565 + (0.10)(0) + (0.20)(449.645) + (0.70)(1017.73) = 1367.34$
2	2	$875 + (0.30)(0) + (0.30)(449.645) + (0.40)(1017.73) = 1416.99$
2	3	$1120 + (0.60)(0) + (0.25)(449.645) + (0.15)(1017.73) = 1385.07$
2	4	$1300 + (0.85)(0) + (0.15)(449.645) + \ \ \ \ \ (0)(1017.73) = 1367.45$
3	0	$645 + \ \ \ \ (0)(0) + \ \ \ \ \ (0)(449.645) + \ \ \ \ \ (1)(1017.73) = 1662.73$
3	1	$775 + \ \ \ \ (0)(0) + (0.10)(449.645) + (0.90)(1017.73) = 1735.92$
3	2	$1065 + (0.10)(0) + (0.20)(449.645) + (0.70)(1017.73) = 1867.34$
3	3	$1375 + (0.30)(0) + (0.30)(449.645) + (0.40)(1017.73) = 1916.99$
3	4	$1720 + (0.60)(0) + (0.25)(449.645) + (0.15)(1017.73) = 1985.07$

STEP 5 Since this latest policy is identical to the current policy, it is the optimal policy, with an expected profit per year given in Step 3 as $R = \$967.34$. By coincidence, this optimal policy is identical to the one obtained in Problem 20.6, where expected discounted profit was maximized. In general, different objectives result in different optimal policies.

20.10 Using the data of Problem 20.7, determine w_1 for the first n weeks ($n = 1, 2, 3, \ldots$), under the policy $\{d_{(1)i}\}$.

As shown in Problem 20.7 the transition matrix for the given policy is

$$\mathbf{P} = \mathbf{P}_{(1)} = \begin{bmatrix} 0.5 & 0.5 \\ 0.4 & 0.6 \end{bmatrix}$$

Successive powers of $\mathbf{P}$ are

$$\mathbf{P}^2 = \begin{bmatrix} 0.45 & 0.55 \\ 0.44 & 0.56 \end{bmatrix} \qquad \mathbf{P}^3 = \begin{bmatrix} 0.445 & 0.555 \\ 0.444 & 0.556 \end{bmatrix} \qquad \mathbf{P}^4 = \begin{bmatrix} 0.4445 & 0.5555 \\ 0.4444 & 0.5556 \end{bmatrix}$$

$$\mathbf{P}^5 = \begin{bmatrix} 0.44445 & 0.55555 \\ 0.44444 & 0.55556 \end{bmatrix} \qquad \cdots$$

which converge to

$$\mathbf{L} = \begin{bmatrix} 4/9 & 5/9 \\ 4/9 & 5/9 \end{bmatrix}$$

The expected return per week is, in the steady state,

$$R = (6000)(\tfrac{4}{9}) + (4200)(\tfrac{5}{9}) = \$5000$$

If the process begins in state 1, then $\mathbf{X}^{(0)} = [1, 0]$, and it follows from (19.1) that

$$\mathbf{X}^{(n)} = \mathbf{X}^{(0)}\mathbf{P}^n = [1, 0]\begin{bmatrix} p_{11}^{(n)} & p_{12}^{(n)} \\ p_{21}^{(n)} & p_{22}^{(n)} \end{bmatrix} = [p_{11}^{(n)}, p_{12}^{(n)}]$$

for $n = 0, 1, 2, \ldots$, where we define $p_{11}^{(0)} \equiv 1$, $p_{12}^{(0)} \equiv 0$. The expected return for the nth week ($n = 1, 2, 3, \ldots$) is

$$C(1, 1)x_1^{(n-1)} + C(2, 2)x_2^{(n-1)} = 6000p_{11}^{(n-1)} + 4200p_{12}^{(n-1)}$$

Since the expected return for the first n weeks is the expected return for the first $n - 1$ weeks plus the expected return for the nth week, we have, for $n = 1, 2, 3, \ldots$,

$$w_n(1) = w_{n-1}(1) + 6000p_{11}^{(n-1)} + 4200p_{12}^{(n-1)} \tag{1}$$

where $w_0(1) \equiv 0$. From (1) we generate Table 20-11. The last column of the table shows that w_1 converges to $1111\tfrac{1}{9}$. To two-decimal accuracy, $w_1 = 1111.11$ for all n greater than 5.

Table 20-11

n	$p_{11}^{(n-1)}$	$p_{12}^{(n-1)}$	$6000p_{11}^{(n-1)} + 4200p_{12}^{(n-1)}$	$w_{n-1}(1)$	$w_n(1)$	nR	$w_1 = w_n(1) - nR$
1	1	0	6000	0	6 000	5 000	1000
2	0.5	0.5	5100	6 000	11 100	10 000	1100
3	0.45	0.55	5010	11 100	16 110	15 000	1110
4	0.445	0.555	5001	16 110	21 111	20 000	1111
5	0.4445	0.5555	5000.1	21 111	26 111.1	25 000	1111.1
6	0.44445	0.55555	5000.01	26 111.1	31 111.11	30 000	1111.11
7	0.444445	0.555555	5000.001	31 111.11	36 111.111	35 000	1111.111
8	0.4444445	0.5555555	5000.0001	36 111.111	41 111.1111	40 000	1111.1111

20.11 Derive *(20.3)*.

Let $\mathbf{P} \equiv [p_{ij}(\hat{d}_i)]$ be the transition matrix for a Markov decision process with an unbounded horizon, under the policy $\{\hat{d}_i\}$. The undiscounted expected worth of the process over n periods, if the process starts in state i, is the expected return from the first period, $C(i, \hat{d}_i)$, plus the expected return from the remaining $n - 1$ periods:

$$w_n(i) = C(i, \hat{d}_i) + \sum_{j=1}^{N} p_{ij}(\hat{d}_i) w_{n-1}(j) \tag{1}$$

Subtract

$$nR \equiv R + \sum_{j=1}^{N} (n-1)R p_{ij}(\hat{d}_i)$$

from *(1)* to obtain

$$w_n(i) - nR = C(i, \hat{d}_i) + \sum_{j=1}^{N} p_{ij}(\hat{d}_i) w_{n-1}(j) - R - \sum_{j=1}^{N} (n-1)R p_{ij}(\hat{d}_i)$$

or

$$[w_n(i) - nR] + R = C(i, \hat{d}_i) + \sum_{j=1}^{N} p_{ij}(\hat{d}_i)[w_{n-1}(j) - (n-1)R] \tag{2}$$

Since $w_i = w_n(i) - nR$ and since

$$w_j = w_n(j) - nR \approx w_{n-1}(j) - (n-1)R$$

if n is large (see Problem 20.10), *(2)* is equivalent to *(20.3)* for all i $(i = 1, 2, \ldots, N)$.

20.12 Show that if $w_1^*, w_2^*, \ldots, w_N^*, R^*$ is a solution to system *(20.3)*, so too is $w_1^* + k, w_2^* + k, \ldots, w_N^* + k, R^*$, for any constant k.

$$[(w_i^* + k) + R^*] - \left[C(i, \hat{d}_i) + \sum_{j=1}^{N} p_{ij}(\hat{d}_i)(w_j^* + k) \right] = [(w_i^* + k) + R^*] - \left[C(i, \hat{d}_i) + \sum_{j=1}^{N} p_{ij}(\hat{d}_i)w_j^* + k \right]$$

$$= [w_i^* + R^*] - \left[C(i, \hat{d}_i) + \sum_{j=1}^{N} p_{ij}(\hat{d}_i)w_j^* \right]$$

$$= 0$$

The choice $k = -w_1^*$ justifies setting w_1 equal to zero in Step 3 of the six-step algorithm.

The fact that the w_i, and hence the $w_n(i)$, are determined only up to an additive constant k is of no economic significance to the objective at hand, being equivalent merely to an additional, fixed payoff of k dollars to the decision maker before the process begins. This can have no effect on the optimal policy [notice that the optimization in *(20.4)* is not affected by the replacement $w_j \to w_j + k$], nor any effect on the optimal return per period in the steady state (the k dollars being spread over infinitely many periods).

Supplementary Problems

20.13 The profit P (in dollars) that a chicken farmer receives from each chicken sent to market is given by the formula

$$P = 1 - (0.9)^{N^2}$$

where N denotes the age of the fowl in weeks. Chickens are sent to market once a week, at the end of the week, and their places are immediately taken by newborn birds from the farm's incubators. There is no market for chickens less than 1 week old. Show that it is unprofitable for the farmer to keep chickens more than 5 weeks, and then determine the best age to market them, if the farmer's objective is to maximize total discounted profit at an effective interest rate of 9 percent *per annum*.

20.14 A large corporation budgets 2 units of money each year for a Goodwill Fund that is distributed by the president of the corporation in the form of grants (in unit amounts) to organizations. Since large grants bring more goodwill to the corporation than do small ones, the president need not distribute these funds each year, but may retain unit amounts for 1 or more years to accumulate sufficient funds for the awarding of larger grants. Corporation policy, however, never allows the balance in the Goodwill Fund to exceed 5 units, for at that level the fund begins to attract demands on it from other segments of the company. Determine a policy for awarding grants that will maximize the total discounted value of goodwill, at an effective interest rate of 6 percent per annum, if the returns from various grants are as follows:

Amount of Grant, units	0	1	2	3	4	5
Cash Value of Goodwill, units	0	1	2.1	3.3	4.5	5.6

20.15 A machine costs \$7000 new and, as a matter of policy, is never kept more than 2 years. At the beginning of each year, a decision must be reached whether to KEEP the current machine (if it is not too old), BUY a new machine, or LEASE a new machine. A lease is nominally in effect for 2 years, but it may be broken after 1 year with the payment of a \$700 penalty cost. The operating cost, salvage value, and leasing cost for a machine depend on its age, as shown in Table 20-12.

Table 20-12

	Age		
	0	1	2
Operating Cost	\$500	1000	$\cdots$
Salvage Value	$\cdots$	4500	4000
Leasing Cost	1700	1600	$\cdots$

Leased machines have no salvage value, since they are owned by the leasing company. Determine an equipment replacement policy that will minimize the total discounted cost with an unbounded horizon, at an effective interest rate of $7\frac{1}{2}$ percent per annum.

20.16 Prove that system (20.2) uniquely determines $PV(1), PV(2), \ldots, PV(N)$.

20.17 Determine $PV(i)$ for each state i of the unbounded process described in Problem 20.6, under the policy

i	1	2	3
d_i	0	1	2

20.18 Apply one iteration of the five-step algorithm to Problem 20.6, using the initial policy given in Problem 20.17. What is the resulting updated policy?

20.19 A machine that produces plastic milk bottles is characterized at the end of each shift as being in either good operating condition (state 1), acceptable operating condition (state 2), or poor operating condition (state 3); the rating is based on the percentage of unusable bottles made by it during the shift. Between shifts, the machine can be adjusted at a cost of \$50, in which case it starts the next shift in state 1. The probability that a machine will remain in state i from the beginning to the end of a shift is given in the following table:

i	1	2	3
p_{ii}	0.8	0.5	1

If a machine does not remain in a given state, it deteriorates to the next higher state. Expected costs for unusable bottles for an entire shift is a function of the state of the machine at the beginning of the shift:

State	1	2	3
Expected Cost	$10	$40	$100

Determine an optimal policy for adjusting machines that will minimize expected discounted cost for an unbounded horizon, given that $\alpha = 0.95$.

20.20 An auto parts store orders and receives a certain model of muffler each Saturday night, for sale the following week. If mufflers are ordered, the transportation cost to the store is $30, regardless of the number; if no mufflers are ordered, there is no delivery charge. Space limitations restrict the store's inventory of this muffler to a maximum of 4. The carrying charge for an unsold muffler is $9 per week.

The demand for the muffler is random, with the following probability distribution:

Weekly Demand	0	1	2	3
Probability	0.3	0.4	0.2	0.1

A sale, with its unrealized profit of $23 per muffler, is lost whenever a customer wants a muffler and the store has none in stock. Determine an optimal reordering policy for the store that will minimize expected discounted cost for an unbounded horizon, if $\alpha = 0.98$.

20.21 Apply one iteration of the six-step algorithm toward maximizing the expected profit per year of the process described in Problem 20.6, using the initial policy given in Problem 20.17. What is the updated policy?

20.22 Solve Problem 20.20 if the objective is to minimize expected cost per week.

20.23 Ratings for a national television show are published weekly and are used to set advertising rates for the succeeding week according to the following schedule:

Rating, points	15	16	17	18	19
Advertising Rate, units	10	11	12	14	16

Any show rated under 15 points is dropped from the network and replaced by a new series which initially can expect to gain a rating of 17. No show ever garners more than 19 points.

Each week management either can do nothing for a show (at no cost) or can give it additional promotion (at a cost of 0.7 unit). The probability distributions for the succeeding week's rating, corresponding to the two options, are given in Tables 20-13 and 20-14, respectively.

Table 20-13

Last Rating	15	16	17	18	19
Probability of Retaining Rating	0.4	0.5	0.6	0.8	0.9
Probability of Losing 1 Point	0.6	0.4	0.2	0.2	0.1
Probability of Losing 2 points	0	0.1	0.2	0	0

Table 20-14

Last Rating	15	16	17	18	19
Probability of Gaining 1 Point	0.1	0.3	0.2	0.1	0
Probability of Retaining Rating	0.6	0.6	0.7	0.8	0.9
Probability of Losing 1 Point	0.3	0.1	0.1	0.1	0.1

Determine a decision policy for management that will maximize the expected return per week from television shows under its control.

Chapter 21

Markovian Birth-Death Processes

POPULATION GROWTH PROCESSES

A *population* is a set of objects having a common characteristic. Examples include individuals affected with measles, automobiles waiting at a toll plaza, and inventory in a warehouse. A large number of decision processes are concerned with analyzing and controlling the growth of a population.

We designate the number of members in a given population at time t by $N(t)$. The *states* of a growth process are the various values $N(t)$ can assume; these are generally the nonnegative integers. The probability that $N(t)$ equals a specific nonnegative integer n is denoted by $p_n(t)$.

A *birth* occurs whenever a new member joins the population; a *death* occurs whenever a member leaves the population. A *pure birth process* is one that experiences only births, no deaths; a *pure death process* is one that experiences only deaths, no births.

Example 21.1 A college advertises for candidates for the position of Academic Dean, with a closing date for receiving applications specified. If no processing of applications is undertaken until the closing date and if no applications are withdrawn by the candidates themselves, then the process of receiving applications is a pure birth process up to the closing date. If no applications are accepted after the closing date, then the process of reducing the pool of applications under active consideration through evaluation and elimination is a pure death process. If applications are processed during the same period they are received, the process is a birth-death process. In all cases, the population is the set of completed applications under active consideration.

Definition: A function $f(t)$ is $o(\Delta t)$, read "little oh of Δt," if

$$\lim_{\Delta t \to 0} \frac{f(\Delta t)}{\Delta t} = 0$$

Such a function tends to zero at a faster rate than the first power of its argument. If $f(t)$ and $g(t)$ are each $o(\Delta t)$, so are $f(t) + g(t)$ and $f(t)g(t)$.

Example 21.2 The function $f(t) = t^3$ is $o(\Delta t)$, since

$$\lim_{\Delta t \to 0} \frac{(\Delta t)^3}{\Delta t} = \lim_{\Delta t \to 0} (\Delta t)^2 = 0$$

But $\sin t \neq o(\Delta t)$, because

$$\lim_{\Delta t \to 0} \frac{\sin (\Delta t)}{\Delta t} = 1 \neq 0$$

GENERALIZED MARKOVIAN
BIRTH-DEATH PROCESSES

A population growth process is a Markov process (see Chapter 19) if the transition probabilities for moving from one state to another depend only on the current state and not on any of the past history experienced by the process in reaching the current state. More formally, a generalized Markovian birth-death process satisfies the following criteria:

The probability distributions governing the numbers of births and deaths in a specific time interval depend on the length of the interval but not on its starting point.

255

The probability of exactly one birth in a time interval of length Δt, given a population of n members at the beginning of the interval, is $\lambda_n \Delta t + o(\Delta t)$, where λ_n is a constant, possibly different for different values of n.

The probability of exactly one death in a time interval of length Δt, given a population of n members at the beginning of the interval, is $\mu_n \Delta t + o(\Delta t)$, where μ_n is a constant, possibly different for different values of n.

The probability of more than one birth and the probability of more than one death in a time interval of length Δt are both $o(\Delta t)$.

These criteria imply, in the limit as Δt approaches zero, the *Kolmogorov equations* for the state probabilities:

$$\frac{dp_n(t)}{dt} = -(\lambda_n + \mu_n)p_n(t) + \mu_{n+1}p_{n+1}(t) + \lambda_{n-1}p_{n-1}(t) \qquad (n = 1, 2, \ldots)$$

$$\frac{dp_0(t)}{dt} = -\lambda_0 p_0(t) + \mu_1 p_1(t) \qquad\qquad (21.1)$$

(See Problem 21.6.)

LINEAR MARKOVIAN BIRTH PROCESSES

A *linear* Markovian birth process is a Markovian pure birth process in which the probability of a birth in a small time interval is proportional to both the current number of members in the population and the length of the interval. That is, for all n, $\mu_n = 0$ and $\lambda_n = n\lambda$. The constant of proportionality λ is the *birth rate* or *arrival rate*. The solution to (21.1), for an initial population of one member, is

$$p_n(t) = \begin{cases} (1 - e^{-\lambda t})^{n-1} e^{-\lambda t} & (n = 1, 2, \ldots) \\ 0 & (n = 0) \end{cases} \qquad (21.2)$$

The expected size of the population at time t is $E[N(t)] = e^{\lambda t}$. If the population is initialized with $N(0)$ members, then its expected size at time t is

$$E[N(t)] = N(0)e^{\lambda t} \qquad (21.3)$$

(See Problem 21.1.)

LINEAR MARKOVIAN DEATH PROCESSES

A *linear* Markovian death process is a Markovian pure death process in which the probability of a death in a small time interval is proportional to both the current size of the population and the length of the interval. That is, for all n, $\lambda_n = 0$ and $\mu_n = n\mu$. The constant of proportionality μ is the *death rate*. The solution to (21.1), for an initial population of $N(0)$, is

$$p_n(t) = \begin{cases} \binom{N(0)}{n} e^{-n\mu t}(1 - e^{-\mu t})^{N(0)-n} & [n \leq N(0)] \\ 0 & [n > N(0)] \end{cases} \qquad (21.4)$$

The expected size of the population at time t is

$$E[N(t)] = N(0)e^{-\mu t} \qquad (21.5)$$

(See Problem 21.3.)

LINEAR MARKOVIAN BIRTH-DEATH PROCESSES

A *linear* Markovian birth-death process is a Markovian birth-death process in which, for all n, $\lambda_n = n\lambda$ and $\mu_n = n\mu$. The solution to (21.1), for an initial population of one member, is

$$p_n(t) = \begin{cases} [1 - r(t)][1 - s(t)][s(t)]^{n-1} & (n = 1, 2, \ldots) \\ r(t) & (n = 0) \end{cases} \tag{21.6}$$

where

$$r(t) \equiv \frac{\mu[e^{(\lambda-\mu)t} - 1]}{\lambda e^{(\lambda-\mu)t} - \mu} \qquad \text{and} \qquad s(t) \equiv \frac{\lambda[e^{(\lambda-\mu)t} - 1]}{\lambda e^{(\lambda-\mu)t} - \mu}$$

The expected size of the population at time t is $E[N(t)] = e^{(\lambda-\mu)t}$. If the population is initialized at $N(0)$ members, then its expected size at time t is

$$E[N(t)] = N(0)e^{(\lambda-\mu)t} \tag{21.7}$$

(See Problem 21.5.)

It is clear that the linear birth-death process includes the linear birth process and the linear death process as the special cases $\mu = 0$ and $\lambda = 0$, respectively. Another important property, which is suggested by (21.7), is contained in the following remark [see Problem 21.9(b)].

Remark:　A linear Markovian birth-death process with parameters λ and μ and an initial population $N(0)$ is equivalent to the sum of $N(0)$ concurrent but independent processes, each with parameters λ and μ and an initial population 1.

Example 21.3　Find the state probabilities $p_n^{(2)}(t)$ for the linear Markovian birth process beginning with a population of 2.

The two independent subprocesses each have the state probabilities given by (21.2). The overall process will be in state n if the first subprocess is in state 0 and the second is in state n, or if the first is in state 1 and the second is in state $n - 1$, or .... Thus,

$$p_n^{(2)}(t) = p_0(t)p_n(t) + p_1(t)p_{n-1}(t) + \cdots + p_n(t)p_0(t) \tag{21.8}$$

Using (21.2) in (21.8), we find

$$p_n^{(2)}(t) = \begin{cases} (n - 1)(1 - e^{-\lambda t})^{n-2}e^{-2\lambda t} & (n = 2, 3, \ldots) \\ 0 & (n = 0, 1) \end{cases}$$

POISSON BIRTH PROCESSES

A *Poisson birth process* is a Markovian pure birth process in which the probability of a birth in any small time interval is independent of the size of the population. That is, for all n, $\lambda_n = \lambda$ and $\mu_n = 0$. In such a process, new arrivals to the population are not created by current members; rather, they enter the population from without, as did the completed applications in Example 21.1. New members can enter the population even when the current state is 0, a marked difference from the linear Markovian birth situation.

The solution to (21.1), for an initial population of 0, is

$$p_n(t) = \frac{(\lambda t)^n}{n!} e^{-\lambda t} \qquad (n = 0, 1, 2, \ldots) \tag{21.9}$$

If the population is initialized at $N(0)$ members, the solution to (21.1) is

$$p_n(t) = \begin{cases} \dfrac{(\lambda t)^{n-N(0)}e^{-\lambda t}}{[n - N(0)]!} & [n \geq N(0)] \\ 0 & [n < N(0)] \end{cases} \tag{21.10}$$

The expected size of the population at time t is

$$E[N(t)] = N(0) + \lambda t \tag{21.11}$$

(See Problem 21.2.)

***Definition*:** A discrete random variable N has a *Poisson distribution*, with parameter $\alpha \geq 0$, if

$$P(N = n) = \frac{\alpha^n}{n!} e^{-\alpha} \qquad (n = 0, 1, 2, \ldots) \qquad (21.12)$$

The expected value of N is $E(N) = \alpha$.

***Definition*:** A continuous random variable T has an *exponential distribution*, with parameter $\beta \geq 0$, if

$$P(T \leq t) = 1 - e^{-\beta t} \qquad (t \geq 0) \qquad (21.13)$$

The expected value of T is $E(T) = 1/\beta$.

We may summarize (*21.9*) and (*21.10*) by saying that, in a Poisson birth process with birth rate λ, $N(t) - N(0)$ has a Poisson distribution, with parameter λt. Furthermore, in such a process, the *interarrival time*, which is the time between successive births, has an exponential distribution, with expected value $1/\lambda$. (See Problem 21.8.) Conversely,

***Theorem 21.1*:** If the interarrival time is exponentially distributed, with expected value $1/\beta$, then the number of arrivals is a Poisson birth process, with birth rate $\lambda = \beta$.

POISSON DEATH PROCESSES

A *Poisson death process* is a Markovian pure death process in which the probability of a death in any small time interval is independent of the size of the population. That is, for all n, $\lambda_n = 0$ and $\mu_n = \mu$. The solution to (*21.1*), for an initial population $N(0)$, is

$$p_n(t) = \begin{cases} 0 & [n > N(0)] \\ \dfrac{(\mu t)^{N(0)-n} e^{-\mu t}}{[N(0) - n]!} & [1 \leq n \leq N(0)] \\ 1 - \displaystyle\sum_{n=1}^{N(0)} p_n(t) & (n = 0) \end{cases} \qquad (21.14)$$

(See Problem 21.4.)

POISSON BIRTH-DEATH PROCESSES

A Poisson birth-death process is a Markovian birth-death process in which both the probability of a birth and the probability of a death in any small time interval are independent of the size of the population. That is, for all n, $\lambda_n = \lambda$ and $\mu_n = \mu$. Such processes form the basis of queueing theory and are developed in Chapter 23.

Solved Problems

21.1   A linear Markovian birth process initialized at one member experiences an average hourly birth rate $\lambda = 2$.   Determine the probability of having a population larger than 3 after 1 h, and the expected size of the population at that time.

With $\lambda = 2$ new births per member per hour and with $t = 1$ h, (21.2) gives

$$p_0(1) = 0 \qquad\qquad p_2(1) = (1 - e^{-2})^1 e^{-2} = 0.117$$
$$p_1(1) = (1 - e^{-2})^0 e^{-2} = 0.135 \qquad p_3(1) = (1 - e^{-2})^2 e^{-2} = 0.101$$

The probability of having more than three members in the population after 1 h is then

$$1 - (0 + 0.135 + 0.117 + 0.101) = 0.647$$

The expected size of the population at that time is given by (21.3) as

$$E[N(1)] = 1e^{2(1)} = 7.389 \text{ members}$$

21.2   Solve Problem 21.1 if the process is a Poisson birth process.

With $N(0) = 1$, $t = 1$ h, and $\lambda = 2$ births per hour, (21.10) gives

$$p_0(1) = 0 \qquad\qquad p_2(1) = \frac{2^1}{1!} e^{-2} = 0.271$$

$$p_1(1) = \frac{2^0}{0!} e^{-2} = 0.135 \qquad p_3(1) = \frac{2^2}{2!} e^{-2} = 0.271$$

The probability of having more than three members in the population after 1 h is then

$$1 - (0 + 0.135 + 0.271 + 0.271) = 0.323$$

The expected size of the population at that time is given by Eq. (21.11) as

$$E[N(1)] = 1 + 2(1) = 3 \text{ members}$$

21.3   A linear Markovian death process initialized at 10 members experiences an average weekly death rate $\mu = 0.6$.   Determine the probability of having a population of at least eight members after 3 days, and the expected size of the population at that time.

With $N(0) = 10$, $t = (3/7)$ week, and $\mu = 0.6$ deaths per member per week, (21.4) gives

$$p_8(3/7) = \binom{10}{8} e^{-8(0.6)(3/7)} (1 - e^{-(0.6)(3/7)})^{10-8} = 45(0.1278)(1 - 0.7733)^2 = 0.296$$

$$p_9(3/7) = \binom{10}{9} e^{-9(0.6)(3/7)} (1 - e^{-(0.6)(3/7)})^{10-9} = 10(0.0988)(1 - 0.7733)^1 = 0.224$$

$$p_{10}(3/7) = \binom{10}{10} e^{-10(0.6)(3/7)} (1 - e^{-(0.6)(3/7)})^{10-10} = 1(0.0764)(1 - 0.7733)^0 = 0.076$$

The probability of having eight or more members in the population after 3 days is therefore

$$0.296 + 0.224 + 0.076 = 0.596$$

The expected size of the population at that time is given by (21.5) as

$$E[N(3/7)] = 10e^{-(0.6)(3/7)} = 7.73 \text{ members}$$

21.4   Solve Problem 21.3 if the process is a Poisson death process.

With $N(0) = 10$, $t = (3/7)$ week, and $\mu = 0.6$ deaths per week, (21.14) gives

$$p_{10}(3/7) = \frac{[(0.6)(3/7)]^{10-10}}{(10-10)!} \, e^{-(0.6)(3/7)} = 0.7733$$

$$p_9(3/7) = \frac{[(0.6)(3/7)]^{10-9}}{(10-9)!} \, e^{-(0.6)(3/7)} = 0.1988$$

$$p_8(3/7) = \frac{[(0.6)(3/7)]^{10-8}}{(10-8)!} \, e^{-(0.6)(3/7)} = 0.0256$$

The probability of having eight or more members in the population after 3 days is then

$$0.0256 + 0.1988 + 0.7733 = 0.9977$$

To calculate the expected value of $N(3/7)$, the remaining state probabilities for $t = 3/7$ are needed. Equation (21.14) gives these, to four decimals, as

$$p_7(3/7) = 0.0022 \qquad p_6(3/7) = 0.0001 \qquad p_5(3/7) = p_4(3/7) = \cdots = p_0(3/7) = 0$$

Thus,

$$E[N(3/7)] = 10(0.7733) + 9(0.1988) + 8(0.0256) + 7(0.0022) + 6(0.0001) + 5(0) + \cdots + 0(0)$$
$$= 9.74 \text{ members}$$

21.5   A biologist observes the growth of bacteria strands in a culture and finds that both the probability of the birth of a strand and the probability of the death of a strand are proportional to the number of strands in the culture and to elapsed time. On the average, each strand produces a new strand every 7 h and dies after 30 h. How many strands should be expected in a culture after 1 week, if the population is initialized at one strand?

Taking one day as the unit of time, we have $N(0) = 1$,

$$\lambda = \frac{1}{7}(24) = 3.428571429 \text{ births per member per day}$$

and

$$\mu = \frac{1}{30}(24) = 0.8 \text{ deaths per member per day}$$

It follows from (21.7) that the expected size of the population after 7 days is

$$E[N(7)] = 1e^{(3.428571429-0.8)(7)} = 97\,953\,164 \text{ strands}$$

21.6   Derive the Kolmogorov equations, (21.1).

The size of the population at time $t + \Delta t$, $N(t + \Delta t)$, is governed by the size at time t, $N(t)$, together with whatever changes (births and/or deaths) occur in the interval $(t, t + \Delta t]$. Thus, for $n \geq 1$,

$$
\begin{aligned}
P\{N(t + \Delta t) = n\} = {} & P\{N(t) = n \text{ and there are 0 births and 0} \\
& \text{deaths in } (t, t + \Delta t]\} \\
& + \\
& P\{N(t) = n \text{ and there are 1 birth and 1} \\
& \text{death in } (t, t + \Delta t]\} \\
& + \\
& P\{N(t) = n - 1 \text{ and there are 1 birth and 0} \\
& \text{deaths in } (t, t + \Delta t]\} \\
& + \\
& P\{N(t) = n + 1 \text{ and there are 0 births and 1} \\
& \text{death in } (t, t + \Delta t]\} \\
& + \\
& P\{\text{a combination of events involving} \\
& \text{more than 1 birth or more than 1 death} \\
& \text{in } (t, t + \Delta t]\}
\end{aligned}
$$

or

$$p_n(t + \Delta t) = a + b + c + d + e \tag{1}$$

Utilizing the notion of conditional probability (see Problem 17.5), we have

$$a = P\{N(t) = n\} \times P\{0 \text{ births and } 0 \text{ deaths in } \Delta t \mid N(t) = n\}$$

By the fundamental assumptions, the probability of zero births in a time interval of length Δt is, to within $o(\Delta t)$, 1 minus the probability of exactly one birth; given state n at the beginning of the interval, this latter probability equals $\lambda_n \Delta t + o(\Delta t)$. Hence, the probability of zero births is

$$1 - \lambda_n \Delta t + o(\Delta t)$$

and, under the same conditions, the probability of zero deaths is

$$1 - \mu_n \Delta t + o(\Delta t)$$

Moreover, births occur independently from deaths. Therefore,

$$a = p_n(t) \times [1 - \lambda_n \Delta t + o(\Delta t)][1 - \mu_n \Delta t + o(\Delta t)]$$
$$= p_n(t) [1 - (\lambda_n + \mu_n)\Delta t] + o(\Delta t)$$

Reasoning in similar fashion, we obtain

$$b = o(\Delta t)$$
$$c = p_{n-1}(t) (\lambda_{n-1}\Delta t) + o(\Delta t)$$
$$d = p_{n+1}(t) (\mu_{n+1}\Delta t) + o(\Delta t)$$
$$e = o(\Delta t)$$

and (1) becomes

$$p_n(t + \Delta t) = p_n(t) + [-(\lambda_n + \mu_n)p_n(t) + \lambda_{n-1}p_{n-1}(t) + \mu_{n+1}p_{n+1}(t)] \Delta t + o(\Delta t) \tag{2}$$

Transposing $p_n(t)$ to the left-hand side of (2), dividing through by Δt, and letting $\Delta t \to 0$, we obtain the Kolmogorov equations for $n = 1, 2, \ldots$.

The case $n = 0$ requires separate consideration, since no deaths are possible in state 0. Carrying out the analysis as above, we readily obtain the remaining Kolmogorov equation.

21.7 (a) Derive (21.6) and (b) generalize to the case of an arbitrary initial population $N(0)$.

(a) With $\lambda_n = n\lambda$ and $\mu_n = n\mu$, the Kolmogorov equations, (21.1), become

$$\frac{dp_n(t)}{dt} = -n(\lambda + \mu)p_n(t) + (n + 1)\mu p_{n+1}(t) + (n - 1)\lambda p_{n-1}(t) \tag{1}$$

for $n = 1, 2, \ldots$, and

$$\frac{dp_0(t)}{dt} = \mu p_1(t) \tag{2}$$

One way to solve these equations is by replacing them with a single partial differential equation for the *probability generating function*

$$F(z, t) \equiv \sum_{n=0}^{\infty} p_n(t)z^n \tag{3}$$

The procedure is as follows. Multiply (1) by z^n, sum over all n $(n = 1, 2, \ldots)$, and add the result to (2), giving, after rearrangement,

$$\sum_{n=0}^{\infty} \frac{dp_n(t)}{dt} z^n = -(\lambda + \mu) \sum_{n=1}^{\infty} np_n(t)z^n + \mu \sum_{n=0}^{\infty} (n + 1)p_{n+1}(t)z^n + \lambda \sum_{n=1}^{\infty} (n - 1)p_{n-1}(t)z^n \tag{4}$$

But, from differentiation of (3),

$$\sum_{n=0}^{\infty} \frac{dp_n(t)}{dt} z^n = \frac{\partial F(z, t)}{\partial t}$$

$$\sum_{n=1}^{\infty} np_n(t)z^n = z \frac{\partial F(z, t)}{\partial z}$$

$$\sum_{n=0}^{\infty} (n + 1)p_{n+1}(t)z^n = \frac{\partial F(z, t)}{\partial z}$$

$$\sum_{n=1}^{\infty} (n - 1)p_{n-1}(t)z^n = z^2 \frac{\partial F(z, t)}{\partial z}$$

Hence, (4) becomes

$$\frac{\partial F(z, t)}{\partial t} = [-(\lambda + \mu)z + \mu + \lambda z^2] \frac{\partial F(z, t)}{\partial z} \tag{5}$$

Solving this partial differential equation by separation of variables, we find that one solution is

$$e^t \left(\frac{z - 1}{z - \delta}\right)^{1/(\lambda - \mu)} \qquad \text{where} \qquad \delta \equiv \mu/\lambda$$

The general solution to (5) is

$$F(z, t) = g\left[e^t\left(\frac{z - 1}{z - \delta}\right)^{1/(\lambda - \mu)}\right] \tag{6}$$

where g is an arbitrary function of one variable. To determine g, we note that, for an initial population of one member, $p_1(0) = 1$ and $p_n(0) = 0$ $(n \neq 1)$; hence

$$F(z, 0) = \sum_{n=0}^{\infty} p_n(0)z^n = z \tag{7}$$

Applying this initial condition to (6), we obtain

$$z = g\left[\left(\frac{z - 1}{z - \delta}\right)^{1/(\lambda - \mu)}\right] \tag{8}$$

Setting

$$y = \left(\frac{z - 1}{z - \delta}\right)^{1/(\lambda - \mu)}$$

we have, inversely,

$$z = \frac{\delta y^{\lambda - \mu} - 1}{y^{\lambda - \mu} - 1} \tag{9}$$

whereupon (8) may be written as

$$g(y) = \frac{\delta y^{\lambda - \mu} - 1}{y^{\lambda - \mu} - 1} \tag{10}$$

Then (6) becomes

$$F(z, t) = \frac{\delta\left[e^t\left(\frac{z - 1}{z - \delta}\right)^{1/(\lambda - \mu)}\right]^{\lambda - \mu} - 1}{\left[e^t\left(\frac{z - 1}{z - \delta}\right)^{1/(\lambda - \mu)}\right]^{\lambda - \mu} - 1}$$

which simplifies to

$$F(z, t) = \frac{\mu[e^{t(\lambda - \mu)} - 1] + z[-\mu e^{t(\lambda - \mu)} + \lambda]}{[\lambda e^{t(\lambda - \mu)} - \mu] - z\lambda[e^{t(\lambda - \mu)} - 1]} \tag{11}$$

Finally, we need to expand $F(z, t)$ in powers of z, thereby obtaining $p_n(t)$ as the coefficient of z^n. Set

$$r(t) \equiv \frac{\mu[e^{t(\lambda - \mu)} - 1]}{\lambda e^{t(\lambda - \mu)} - \mu} \qquad s(t) \equiv \frac{\lambda[e^{t(\lambda - \mu)} - 1]}{\lambda e^{t(\lambda - \mu)} - \mu} \qquad m(t) \equiv \frac{\lambda - \mu e^{t(\lambda - \mu)}}{\lambda e^{t(\lambda - \mu)} - \mu}$$

Then

$$F(z, t) = \frac{r(t) + zm(t)}{1 - zs(t)} = [r(t) + zm(t)]\left[\frac{1}{1 - zs(t)}\right] \tag{12}$$

In view of the geometric series

$$\frac{1}{1 - x} = \sum_{n=0}^{\infty} x^n \qquad (|x| < 1)$$

(*12*) gives

$$F(z, t) = r(t) + \sum_{n=1}^{\infty} [r(t)s(t) + m(t)][s(t)]^{n-1}z^n$$

It is easily verified algebraically that

$$r(t)s(t) + m(t) = [1 - r(t)][1 - s(t)]$$

Hence,

$$F(z, t) = r(t) + \sum_{n=1}^{\infty} \{[1 - r(t)][1 - s(t)][s(t)]^{n-1}\}z^n \tag{13}$$

The coefficients in (*13*) give (*21.6*).

(*b*) One readily verifies that any power of a solution to (*5*) above is itself a solution.   In particular,

$$\Phi(z, t) = [F(z, t)]^{N(0)}$$

where $F(z, t)$ is given by (*11*) or (*13*), is a solution; and this solution satisfies the initial condition

$$\Phi(z, 0) = [F(z, 0)]^{N(0)} = z^{N(0)}$$

[see (*7*)]. Thus, $\Phi(z, t)$ is the generating function of the state probabilities for a population initialized at $N(0)$ members.   The fact that Φ equals $F^{N(0)}$ implies that the random variable corresponding to Φ [i.e., the population with initial size $N(0)$] is expressible as the sum of $N(0)$ independent random variables, each corresponding to F [i.e., $N(0)$ populations with initial size 1]. This is the additivity property remarked on earlier in this chapter.

21.8 Show that the interarrival time in a Poisson birth process with birth rate λ is exponentially distributed with parameter λ.

Designate the time of the *first* birth by T, a random variable.   The population will still have its initial size, $N(0)$, at time t if and only if $T > t$. Hence, by (*21.10*),

$$P(T \le t) = 1 - P(T > t) = 1 - P[N(t) = N(0)]$$
$$= 1 - p_{N(0)}(t) = 1 - e^{-\lambda t}$$

i.e., T has an exponential distribution, with parameter λ.   Now, the probability distribution governing births in a time interval is independent of the starting point of the interval (the first assumption of a generalized Markovian birth-death process) and independent of the state of the process (the basic Poisson assumption).   Consequently, T also measures the time from *now* until the *next* birth.   In particular, if *now* is *this birth*, T measures the interarrival time.

21.9 A linear Markovian birth process, with birth rate λ, begins with a population $N(0) = 1$.   (*a*) Find the expected time until the population size first equals n ($n = 2, 3, \ldots$).   (*b*) Is the time calculated in (*a*) the same as the time at which the expected size of the population becomes equal to n?

(*a*) The population first reaches n in the infinitesimal time interval $(t, t + dt]$ if and only if the state is $n - 1$ at time t [with probability $p_{n-1}(t)$] *and* there is exactly one birth in $(t, t + dt]$ [with probability $(n - 1)\lambda \, dt + o(dt)$].   Hence, the desired expected value is

$$\int_0^{\infty} tp_{n-1}(t)(n-1)\lambda \, dt = \frac{1}{\lambda} \sum_{j=1}^{n-1} \frac{1}{j}$$

(The calculation is most easily effected by multiplying the Kolmogorov equation for dp_k/dt by t, integrating by parts, using (21.2) with the substitution $z = 1 - e^{-\lambda t}$ to evaluate the integral of $p_k(t)$, and solving the resulting difference equation.) The result has a simple interpretation: The expected time to the first birth is $1/\lambda$. Now the population is 2, with an effective birth rate 2λ; hence, the expected additional time to the next birth is $1/2\lambda$. And so on.

(b) According to (21.3), the expected size of the population equals n when

$$e^{\lambda t} = n \qquad \text{or} \qquad t = \frac{1}{\lambda} \ln n$$

which is not the same as the expected time found in (a). For large n,

$$\sum_{j=1}^{n-1} \frac{1}{j} \approx \ln n + \gamma$$

where $\gamma = 0.5772157 \cdots$ is *Euler's constant*. Hence, the percent difference between the two times becomes very small.

Supplementary Problems

21.10 A linear Markovian birth process initialized at one member experiences an average daily birth rate $\lambda = 0.3$. Determine the probability of having a population larger than five members after 1 week. What is the expected size of the population at that time? What would the expected size of the population be after 1 week if it began with 10 members?

21.11 Solve Problem 21.10 if $\lambda = 0.6$.

21.12 Solve Problem 21.10 if the process is a Poisson birth process.

21.13 A linear Markovian birth process initialized at 15 members has an average hourly birth rate $\lambda = 0.1$. What is the expected size of the population after 3 h?

21.14 A car company judges that, in the range 40 000 to 300 000 cars, sales for a new model follow a linear Markovian birth process. If, on the average, every 50 new cars on the road generates one new buyer each day, how many new models can the company expect to sell 60 days after it sells its 40 000th vehicle?

21.15 An advertisement for salespeople is placed in a newspaper by a department store. Based on previous experience, the store expects applications to arrive according to a Poisson distribution at an average rate of two per day, for as long as the ad runs. How many days should the ad run if the store wants to guarantee with 98 percent certainty that it will receive at least six applications?

21.16 Each Monday morning, 15 min before the scheduled opening of a local bank, patrons line up at the door to transact business. The arrival pattern appears to follow a Poisson distribution, with $\lambda = 40$ customers per hour. Determine the probability that there are fewer than five people in line at opening time, assuming that no patron leaves the line once he or she arrives.

21.17 A linear Markovian death process initialized at five members experiences an average daily death rate $\mu = 0.1$. Determine the probability of having fewer than three members in the population after a week. What is the expected size of the population at that time?

21.18   Solve Problem 21.17 if $\mu = 0.2$.

21.19   Solve Problem 21.17 if the process is a Poisson death process.

21.20   It is the practice on election day to allow anyone to vote who is on line at the time polls are scheduled to close.   At a particular polling place, the time it takes an individual to vote appears to follow an exponential distribution, with an expected value 1.5 min.   What is the probability that it will take more than 12 min to accommodate those waiting to vote at the scheduled closing, if the line numbers eight people?   (*Hint*:   Theorem 21.1 extends to Poisson death processes.)

21.21   A linear Markovian birth-death process initialized at one member has a daily average birth rate $\lambda = 0.05$ and a daily average death rate $\mu = 0.03$.   Determine the probability that the population will be extinct after 4 days.

21.22   Solve Problem 21.21 if both λ and μ are doubled.

21.23   The population growth of an endangered species appears to follow a linear Markovian birth-death process.   On the average, two members of the species produce one offspring every other year.   The average life span of a member of the species is $3\frac{1}{2}$ years.   What is the expected size of the population in 20 years, if the current population numbers 100?

21.24   Derive (*21.9*) by first solving the Kolmogorov equations for $p_0(t)$ and then successively for $p_1(t)$, $p_2(t)$, ...

21.25   Solve Problem 21.9 for a Poisson birth process.   Assume an initial population of zero.

21.26   Two independent Poisson birth processes run concurrently.   Show that the result is a Poisson birth process, with a birth rate that is the sum of the two birth rates.

Chapter 22

Queueing Systems

INTRODUCTION

A queueing process consists in customers arriving at a service facility, then waiting in a line (*queue*) if all servers are busy, eventually receiving service, and finally departing from the facility. A *queueing system* is a set of customers, a set of servers, and an order whereby customers arrive and are processed. Figure 22-1 depicts several queueing systems.

A queueing system is a birth-death process with a population consisting of customers either waiting for service or currently in service. A birth occurs when a customer arrives at the service facility; a death occurs when a customer departs from the facility. The state of the system is the number of customers in the facility.

QUEUE CHARACTERISTICS

Queueing systems are characterized by five components: the arrival pattern of customers, the service pattern, the number of servers, the capacity of the facility to hold customers, and the order in which customers are served.

ARRIVAL PATTERNS

The arrival pattern of customers is usually specified by the *interarrival time*, the time between successive customer arrivals to the service facility. It may be deterministic (i.e., known exactly), or it may be a random variable whose probability distribution is presumed known. It may depend on the number of customers already in the system, or it may be state-independent.

Also of interest is whether customers arrive singly or in batches and whether balking or reneging is permitted. *Balking* occurs when an arriving customer refuses to enter the service facility because the queue is too long. *Reneging* occurs when a customer already in a queue leaves the queue and the facility because the wait is too long. Unless stated to the contrary, the standard assumption will be made that all customers arrive singly and that neither balking nor reneging occurs.

SERVICE PATTERNS

The service pattern is usually specified by the *service time*, the time required by one server to serve one customer. The service time may be deterministic, or it may be a random variable whose probability distribution is presumed known. It may depend on the number of customers already in the facility, or it may be state-independent. Also of interest is whether a customer is attended completely by one server or, as in Fig. 22-1(*d*), the customer requires a sequence of servers. Unless stated to the contrary, the standard assumption will be made that one server can completely serve a customer.

SYSTEM CAPACITY

The *system capacity* is the maximum number of customers, both those in service and those in the queue(s), permitted in the service facility at the same time. Whenever a customer arrives at a facility that is full, the arriving customer is denied entrance to the facility. Such a customer is not allowed to wait

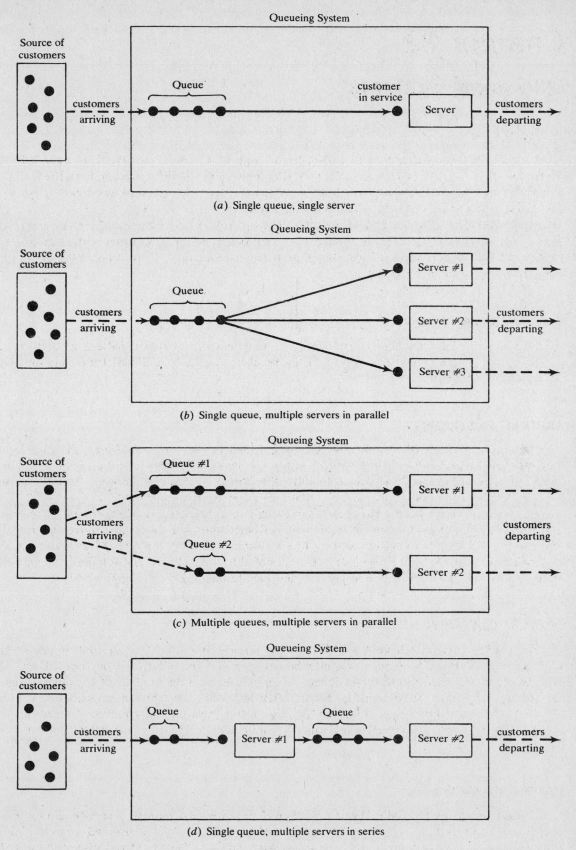

(a) Single queue, single server

(b) Single queue, multiple servers in parallel

(c) Multiple queues, multiple servers in parallel

(d) Single queue, multiple servers in series

Fig. 22-1

outside the facility (since that effectively increases the capacity) but is forced to leave without receiving service. A system that has no limit on the number of customers permitted inside the facility has *infinite capacity*; a system with a limit has *finite capacity*.

QUEUE DISCIPLINES

The *queue discipline* is the order in which customers are served. This can be on a first-in, first-out (FIFO) basis (i.e., service in order of arrival), a last-in, first-out (LIFO) basis (i.e., the customer who arrives last is the next served), a random basis, or a priority basis.

KENDALL'S NOTATION

Kendall's notation for specifying a queue's characteristics is v/w/x/y/z, where v indicates the arrival pattern, w denotes the service pattern, x signifies the number of available servers, y represents the system's capacity, and z designates the queue discipline. Various notations used for three of the components are listed in Table 22-1. If y or z is not specified, it is taken to be ∞ or FIFO, respectively.

Example 22.1 An M/D/2/5/LIFO system has exponentially distributed interarrival times, deterministic service times, two servers, and a limit of five customers allowed into the service facility at any one time, with the last customer to arrive being the next customer to go into service. A D/D/1 system has both deterministic interarrival times and deterministic service times, and only one server. Since system capacity and queue discipline are not specified, they are assumed to be infinite and FIFO, respectively.

Table 22-1

Queue Characteristic	Symbol	Meaning
Interarrival time or Service time	D M E_k G	Deterministic Exponentially distributed Erlang-type-k $(k = 1, 2, \ldots)$ distributed Any other distribution
Queue discipline	FIFO LIFO SIRO PRI GD	First in, first out Last in, first out Service in random order Priority ordering Any other specialized ordering

Solved Problems

22.1 Identify the customers, the servers, and those queue characteristics that are apparent, in a single-lane, automatic car wash establishment.

Customers are the cars entering the establishment for the purpose of being washed. A *server* is the machinery that does the cleaning, and the single lane indicates one or more servers in series.

Generally, car washes operate on a first-come, first-served basis; so the *queue discipline* is FIFO. The *system capacity* is the number of cars that can be safely handled on car wash grounds. If additional cars are allowed to wait on public streets for eventual entrance into the car wash grounds, then the system capacity is infinite.

22.2 Identify the customers, the servers, and those queue characteristics that are apparent, in the billing department of a large store.

Customers are the charges made by patrons of the store, after these charges are received by the billing department but before they are completely processed.   The *servers* are the individuals in the billing department who do the processing.

Invoice processing often follows a LIFO *queue discipline* in that the last charge received by the billing department is placed on the top of the unprocessed pile and is then the first charge taken for processing by an idle server.   Generally, there is no limit to the number of charges that can be forwarded to the billing department; hence the *system capacity* is infinite.

22.3 A new television set arrives for inspection every 3 min and is taken by a quality control engineer on a first-come, first-served basis.   There is only one engineer on duty, and it takes exactly 4 min to inspect each new set.   Determine the average number of sets waiting to be inspected over the first half-hour of a shift, if there are no sets awaiting inspection at the beginning of the shift.

This is a D/D/1 system, with television sets as customers and the engineer as the single server.   The interarrival time is exactly 3 min, while the service time is exactly 4 min.

Table 22-2

Simulated Clock, min	Customer in Service	Queue
0	. . .	. . .
3	#1	. . .
6	#1	#2
7	#2	. . .
9	#2	#3
11	#3	. . .
12	#3	#4
15	#4	#5
18	#4	#5, #6
19	#5	#6
21	#5	#6, #7
23	#6	#7
24	#6	#7, #8
27	#7	#8, #9
30	#7	#8, #9, #10

Table 22-2 charts the history of the system over the first half-hour of operation.   Only those instants at which a change occurs in the state of the system (through a customer arrival or a service completion) are surveyed.   Observe that there are no customers in the queue from time 0 to 6, 7 to 9, and 11 to 12, for a total of 9 min.   There is one customer in the queue from time 6 to 7, 9 to 11, 12 to 18, 19 to 21, and 23 to 24, for a total of 12 min.   Similarly, there are two customers in the queue from time 18 to 19, 21 to 23, and 24 to 30, for a total of 9 min; and three customers in the queue from time 30 to 30, for a total of 0 min.   The average length of the queue, which is the average number of sets waiting to be inspected, over the first half-hour is then

$$\frac{0(9) + 1(12) + 2(9) + 3(0)}{30} = 1 \text{ set}$$

22.4 Buses arrive for cleaning at a central depot in groups of five every hour on the hour.   The buses are serviced in random order, one at a time.   Each bus requires 11 min to service completely, and it leaves the depot as soon as it is clean.   Determine (*a*) the average number of buses in the depot, (*b*) the average number of buses waiting to be cleaned, and (*c*) the average time a bus spends in the depot.

This is a deterministic system, with buses as customers and the cleaning crew as the single server. Arrivals occur once an hour but in batches; the service time is 11 min. A bus is in service while it is being cleaned.

Table 22-3 charts the history of the system over a 1-h period, at the epochs of arrivals and departures. Since service is provided on a random ordering basis, the particular sequence shown is one of many possible sequences for processing buses through the depot. The required statistics, however, are independent of the sequence. Furthermore, since the system renews itself each hour, the statistics that characterize the system over the first hour also are valid over the long run.

Table 22-3

Simulated Clock, min	Customer in Service	Queue
0	#4	#3, #1, #2, #5
11	#1	#3, #2, #5
22	#5	#3, #2
33	#3	#2
44	#2	. . .
55	. . .	. . .

(a) There are five customers in the facility from time 0 to 11, 4 customers from 11 to 22, 3 customers from 22 to 33, 2 customers from 33 to 44, and 1 customer from 44 to 55, each interval being 11 min. In addition, there are no customers in the facility from time 55 to 60, or 5 min. The average number of customers in the facility is then

$$\frac{5(11) + 4(11) + 3(11) + 2(11) + 1(11) + 0(5)}{60} = 2.75 \text{ buses}$$

(b) The average number of customers in the queue, those buses waiting for but not yet in service, is

$$\frac{4(11) + 3(11) + 2(11) + 1(11) + 0(16)}{60} = 1.83 \text{ buses}$$

(c) One bus, bus #4 in Table 22-3, is in the system for 11 min, since it is serviced as soon as it arrives. A second bus, bus #1 in Table 22-3, waits for 11 min before it is serviced, so it is in the system for 22 min. Similarly, the other three buses spend 33, 44, and 55 min, respectively, in system. The average time a bus spends in the depot is therefore

$$\frac{11 + 22 + 33 + 44 + 55}{5} = 33 \text{ min}$$

22.5 Simulate an M/D/2/3 system over the first 45 min of operation, if the mean interarrival time is 3 min and if it takes servers I and II exactly 5 and 7 min, respectively, to serve a customer. Assume that there are no customers in the system at the beginning.

If an exponentially distributed random variable has a mean (expected value) of 3, then the distribution function, (21.13), has 1/3 as its parameter. Using a random number generator to create values (in minutes and seconds) obeying such a distribution, we obtain: 3:54, 2:11, 1:26, 1:25, 0:05, 5:24, 6:09, 0:57, 1:14, 5:57, 1:19, 2:39, 0:52, 8:54, 2:49. We take successive values to be the interarrival times of successive customers. Thus, customer #1 enters the system 3 min and 54 s after the process begins, customer #2 enters the system 2 min and 11 s after customer 1, and so on.

The queueing process is charted in Table 22-4 for the first 45 min of operation, with only those times at which a customer arrives or departs surveyed. Observe that, at time 9:01, customers #2 and #3 are in service, customer #4 is in the queue awaiting service, and customer #5 arrives. Since the system's capacity is 3, customer #5 is denied entrance and never receives service. A similar situation occurs at time 33:32.

Table 22-4

Simulated Clock, min:sec	Customers in Service		Queue
	Server I	Server II	
00:00	...	...	...
3:54	#1	...	
6:05	#1	#2	...
7:31	#1	#2	#3
8:54	#3	#2	...
8:56	#3	#2	#4
9:01	#3	#2	#4 ⟵ #5
13:05	#3	#4	...
13:54	...	#4	...
14:25	#6	#4	...
19:25	...	#4	...
20:05	...	...	...
20:34	#7	...	...
21:31	#7	#8	...
22:45	#7	#8	#9
25:34	#9	#8	...
28:31	#9	...	...
28:42	#9	#10	...
30:01	#9	#10	#11
30:34	#11	#10	...
32:40	#11	#10	#12
33:32	#11	#10	#12 ⟵ #13
35:34	#12	#10	...
35:42	#12	...	...
40:34	...	...	...
42:26	#14	...	...
45:00	#14	...	...

Supplementary Problems

Identify (a) the customers, (b) the server(s), and (c) those queue characteristics that are apparent, for the systems described in Problems 22.6 through 22.13.

22.6   A one-counter cafeteria.

22.7   A barber shop with two barbers, four chairs for waiting, and a local fire ordinance that sets the maximum number of customers in the shop at seven.

22.8   A self-service gasoline station with three pumps.

22.9   Airplanes requesting permission to land at a small airport.

22.10   Automobiles at a toll plaza.

22.11   Work forwarded to a typing pool.

22.12 Combat troops awaiting transportation to a rest and recreation site.

22.13 A municipal judge hearing civil cases in court.

22.14 Patients are scheduled for a certain test at a clinic every 5 min, beginning at 9:00 A.M. The test takes exactly 8 min to complete and is normally administered by a single doctor hired for this purpose. Whenever three or more patients are in the waiting room, a second doctor at the clinic also administers the test, and continues to do so until the waiting room is empty upon his completing a test. At that point, this second doctor takes up his previous duties until his services are required again. (*a*) At what time does the second doctor first begin administering tests and when does he first stop? (*b*) What is the average number of patients in the waiting room from 9:00 to 10:00 A.M.? (*c*) What is the average number of patients in the clinic from 9:00 to 10:00 A.M.?

22.15 Jobs arrive at a work center three at a time, every 15 min. The center is staffed by one employee who takes exactly 6 min to complete each job. Jobs that are not being processed by the employee are stored at the work center and are then taken in random order. Assume that jobs begin arriving as soon as the employee reports for work and that initially there are no jobs awaiting processing from a previous shift. (*a*) What is the average number of jobs in the work center during the first 2 h of the employee's shift? (*b*) How long will the queue be after an 8-h shift?

22.16 An orthodontist schedules patients for a routine checkup every 15 min and limits the total number of patients to 10 a day. It takes 12 min to examine the first patient but, because the dentist tires quickly, each subsequent examination takes 1 min longer than the one before it. Determine the average time that a patient spends in the dentist's office, both waiting and being examined, assuming that each patient arrives precisely when scheduled.

22.17 How many customers are denied entrance to a D/D/1/3 queueing system in the first hour, if customers arrive every 4 min for a service that requires 8 min to provide? Assume that the first customer arrives as soon as the service facility is opened.

Chapter 23

M/M/1 Systems

SYSTEM CHARACTERISTICS

An M/M/1 system is a queueing system having exponentially distributed interarrival times, with parameter λ; exponentially distributed service times, with parameter μ; one server; no limit on the system capacity; and a queue discipline of first come, first served. The constant λ is the *average customer arrival rate*; the constant μ is the *average service rate* of customers. Both are in units of customers per unit time. The expected interarrival time and the expected time to serve one customer are $1/\lambda$ and $1/\mu$, respectively.

Since exponentially distributed interarrival times with mean $1/\lambda$ are equivalent, over a time interval τ, to a Poisson-distributed arrival pattern with mean $\lambda\tau$ (see Theorem 21.1), M/M/1 systems are often referred to as single-server, infinite-capacity, queueing systems having Poisson input and exponential service times.

THE MARKOVIAN MODEL

An M/M/1 system is a Poisson birth-death process (see Chapter 21). The probability, $p_n(t)$, that the system has exactly n customers, either waiting for service or in service, at time t satisfies the Kolmogorov equations, (21.1), with $\lambda_n = \lambda$ and $\mu_n = \mu$, for all n. The complete solution of these equations, while possible, is largely unnecessary. As in Chapter 19, it is the limiting distribution that is of greatest interest.

STEADY-STATE SOLUTIONS

The *steady-state probabilities* for a queueing system are

$$p_n \equiv \lim_{t\to\infty} p_n(t) \qquad (n = 0, 1, 2, \ldots) \tag{23.1}$$

if the limits exist. For an M/M/1 system, we define the *utilization factor* (or *traffic intensity*) as

$$\rho \equiv \frac{\lambda}{\mu} \tag{23.2}$$

i.e., ρ is the expected number of arrivals per mean service time. If $\rho < 1$, then (Problem 23.7) steady-state probabilities exist and are given by

$$p_n = \rho^n (1 - \rho) \tag{23.3}$$

If $\rho > 1$, the arrivals come at a faster rate than the server can accommodate: the expected queue length increases without limit and a steady state does not occur. A similar situation prevails when $\rho = 1$.

MEASURES OF EFFECTIVENESS

For a queueing system in steady state, the measures of greatest interest are:

$L \equiv$ the average number of customers in the system
$L_q \equiv$ the average length of the queue

273

$W \equiv$ the average time a customer spends in the system

$W_q \equiv$ the average time a customer spends (or waits) in the queue

$W(t) \equiv$ the probability that a customer spends more than t units of time in the system

$W_q(t) \equiv$ the probability that a customer spends more than t units of time in the queue

The first four of these measures are related in many queueing systems by

$$W = W_q + \frac{1}{\mu} \tag{23.4}$$

and by *Little's formulas* (Problem 23.10)

$$L = \bar{\lambda} W \tag{23.5}$$

$$L_q = \bar{\lambda} W_q \tag{23.6}$$

The waiting-time formula, (23.4), holds whenever (as in an M/M/1 system) there is a single expected service time, $1/\mu$, for all customers. Little's formulas are valid for quite general systems, provided that $\bar{\lambda}$ denotes the average arrival rate of customers *into* the service facility.

For an M/M/1 system, $\bar{\lambda} = \lambda$, and the six measures are explicitly:

$$L = \frac{\rho}{1 - \rho} \tag{23.7}$$

$$L_q = \frac{\rho^2}{1 - \rho} \tag{23.8}$$

$$W = \frac{1}{\mu - \lambda} \tag{23.9}$$

$$W_q = \frac{\rho}{\mu - \lambda} \tag{23.10}$$

$$W(t) = e^{-t/W} \qquad (t \geq 0) \tag{23.11}$$

$$W_q(t) = \rho e^{-t/W} \qquad (t \geq 0) \tag{23.12}$$

Observe from (23.12) that although the time spent in the system has the exponential distribution (23.11), and the time spent in service is also exponentially distributed, the difference of these two times, which is the time spent in the queue, is *not* exponentially distributed.

Solved Problems

23.1   Show that "most of" the values of an exponentially distributed random variable are smaller than the mean value.

If T has an exponential distribution, with parameter β, the mean value of T is $1/\beta$. From (21.13),

$$P(T \leq 1/\beta) = 1 - e^{-1} \approx 0.632$$

$$P(T \leq 1/2\beta) = 1 - e^{-1/2} \approx 0.393$$

Thus we might say that 63 percent of the values are smaller than the mean, and, of *those* values, some 63 percent are smaller than half the mean.

23.2   Discuss the implications of having both the service times and the interarrival times exponentially distributed.

By Problem 23.1, exponentially distributed service times imply a preponderance of shorter-than-average servicings, combined with a few long ones. This would be the situation, for example, at banks where a majority of customers make simple deposits requiring very little teller time, but a few have more complicated transactions that consume a lot of time. Such distributions do not model satisfactorily situations where the service is essentially identical for each customer, as in work on an assembly line.

Exponentially distributed interarrival times imply a preponderance of interarrival times that are less than the average, with a few that are very long. The net result is that a number of customers arrive in a short period of time, thereby creating a queue, which is followed eventually by a long interval during which no new customer arrives, allowing the server to reduce the size of the queue.

As was shown in Problem 21.8, exponential distributions also possess the Markovian (or *memoryless*) property:

$$P(T \le a + b \mid T > a) = P(T \le b)$$

When T measures interarrival times, the implication is that the time to the next arrival is independent of the time since the last arrival. For service times, the implication is that the time required to complete service on a customer cannot be predicted by knowing (i.e., is independent of) the time the customer has already been in service.

23.3 The men's department of a large store employs one tailor for customer fittings. The number of customers requiring fittings appears to follow a Poisson distribution with mean arrival rate 24 per hour. Customers are fitted on a first-come, first-served basis, and they are always willing to wait for the tailor's service, because alterations are free. The time it takes to fit a customer appears to be exponentially distributed, with a mean of 2 min. (*a*) What is the average number of customers in the fitting room? (*b*) How much time should a customer expect to spend in the fitting room? (*c*) What percentage of the time is the tailor idle? (*d*) What is the probability that a customer will wait more than 10 min for the tailor's service?

This is an M/M/1 system, with $\lambda = 24 \text{ h}^{-1}$,

$$\mu = \tfrac{1}{2} \text{ min}^{-1} = 30 \text{ h}^{-1}$$

and $\rho = 24/30 = 0.8$.

(*a*) From (*23.7*),

$$L = \frac{0.8}{1 - 0.8} = 4 \text{ customers}$$

(*b*) From (*23.9*),

$$W = \frac{1}{30 - 24} = \tfrac{1}{6} \text{ h} = 10 \text{ min}$$

The result also follows from (*23.5*):

$$W = \frac{1}{\lambda} L = \frac{1}{24}(4) = \tfrac{1}{6} \text{ h}$$

(*c*) The tailor is idle if and only if there is no customer in the fitting room. The probability of this event is given by (*23.3*) as

$$p_0 = \rho^0(1 - \rho) = 1(1 - 0.8) = 0.2$$

The tailor is idle 20 percent of the time.

(*d*) From (*23.12*), with $t = 10 \text{ min} = \tfrac{1}{6} \text{ h} = W$,

$$W_q(\tfrac{1}{6}) = (0.8)e^{-1} = 0.2943$$

23.4 For the system of Problem 23.3, determine (*a*) the average wait for the tailor's service experienced by all customers, (*b*) the average wait for the tailor's service experienced by those customers who have to wait at all.

(a) From (23.10),

$$W_q = \frac{\rho}{\mu - \lambda} = \frac{0.8}{30 - 24} = 0.133 \text{ h} = 8 \text{ min}$$

(b) Denote the desired average wait as W_q'. The proportion of arriving customers that have no wait is $1 - \rho$ [this being the probability that an arriving customer finds the system empty—see Problem 23.3(c)]. Hence, the average wait over all arriving customers is given by

$$W_q = (1 - \rho)(0) + \rho W_q'$$

whence

$$W_q' = \frac{1}{\rho} W_q = \frac{1}{\mu - \lambda} = W = 10 \text{ min}$$

23.5 A gourmet delicatessen is operated by one person, the owner. The arrival pattern of customers on Saturdays appears to follow a Poisson distribution, with a mean arrival rate of 10 people per hour. Customers are served on a FIFO basis, and because of the reputation of the store they are willing to wait for service once they arrive. The time it takes to serve a customer is estimated to be exponentially distributed, with an average service time of 4 min. Determine (a) the probability that there is a queue, (b) the average size of the queue, (c) the expected time that a customer must wait in the queue, and (d) the probability that a customer will spend less than 12 min in the store.

This is an M/M/1 system, with

$$\lambda = 10 \text{ h}^{-1} = \tfrac{1}{6} \text{ min}^{-1} \qquad \mu = \tfrac{1}{4} \text{ min}^{-1} \qquad \rho = \frac{1/6}{1/4} = \frac{2}{3}$$

(a) The probability of having a queue is the probability of having two or more customers in the system. By (23.3),

$$p_0 = \rho^0(1 - \rho) = 1(1 - \tfrac{2}{3}) = \tfrac{1}{3} \qquad p_1 = \rho(1 - \rho) = \tfrac{2}{3}(1 - \tfrac{2}{3}) = \tfrac{2}{9}$$

Therefore, the probability of having a queue is

$$1 - p_0 - p_1 = 1 - \frac{1}{3} - \frac{2}{9} = \frac{4}{9}$$

(b) From (23.8),

$$L_q = \frac{(2/3)^2}{1 - (2/3)} = \frac{4}{3} \text{ customers}$$

(c) From (23.10),

$$W_q = \frac{2/3}{(1/4) - (1/6)} = 8 \text{ min}$$

(d) From (23.4) and (23.11),

$$W = 8 + 4 = 12 \text{ min}$$

$$1 - W(12) = 1 - e^{-12/12} = 1 - 0.3679 = 0.6321$$

23.6 Simulate the process described in Problem 23.5.

Two sets of exponentially distributed random numbers, one having parameter 1/6 (interarrival times) and the second having parameter 1/4 (service times), are listed in Table 23-1, with all values converted into minutes and seconds. As expected for exponential distributions, a majority of values in each set (10 out of 16, or 62.5 percent) are smaller than the theoretical means, 6 min for the interarrival times and 4 min for the service times. The sample averages for the times shown in Table 23-1 are 6 min 10 s for the interarrival times and 4 min 12 s for the service times.

Table 23-1

Interarrival Times	Service Times
3:30	0:16
3:30	0:01
6:36	2:37
11:45	10:19
5:32	11:53
4:27	2:57
8:17	1:02
15:24	4:03
3:29	0:59
3:12	0:09
2:01	9:57
13:37	3:44
0:40	7:12
0:12	0:10
2:42	11:51
13:43	0:04

Table 23-2

Simulated Clock	Customer in Service	Queue
00:00	. . .	. . .
3:30	#1 (0:16)	. . .
3:46	. . .	. . .
7:00	#2 (0:01)	. . .
7:01	. . .	. . .
13:36	#3 (2:37)	. . .
16:13	. . .	. . .
25:21	#4 (10:19)	. . .
30:53	#4 (4:47)	#5 (11:53)
35:20	#4 (0:20)	#5 (11:53), #6 (2:57)
35:40	#5 (11:53)	#6 (2:57)
43:37	#5 (3:56)	#6 (2:57), #7 (1:02)
47:33	#6 (2:57)	#7 (1:02)
50:30	#7 (1:02)	. . .
51:32	. . .	. . .
59:01	#8 (4:03)	
62:30	#8 (0:34)	#9 (0:59)
63:04	#9 (0:59)	. . .
64:03	. . .	. . .
65:42	#10 (0:09)	. . .
65:51	. . .	. . .
67:43	#11 (9:57)	. . .
77:40	. . .	. . .
81:20	#12 (3:44)	. . .
82:00	#12 (3:04)	#13 (7:12)
82:12	#12 (2:52)	#13 (7:12), #14 (0:10)
84:54	#12 (0:10)	#13 (7:12), #14 (0:10), #15 (11:51)
85:04	#13 (7:12)	#14 (0:10), #15 (11:15)
92:16	#14 (0:10)	#15 (11:51)
92:26	#15 (11:51)	. . .
98:37	#15 (5:40)	#16 (0:04)

We assign the first interarrival time and the first service time to customer #1, the second interarrival time and the second service time to customer #2, and so on. The queueing process is then charted in Table 23-2, where the simulated clock times listed are those at which a new customer arrives or a current customer is completely served and departs. The times in parentheses are the amounts of service time still required by the corresponding customers.

Observe how the queue builds when a long service time is matched with a succession of short interarrival times, and how it ebbs when a long interarrival time allows the server to accommodate customers currently in the system. This ebb and flow of queue size is characteristic of M/M/1 systems when the mean service time is shorter than the mean interarrival time.

23.7   Derive (23.3), which gives the steady-state probabilities for an M/M/1 system having $\rho < 1$.

Equations (21.1), with $dp_n/dt = 0$ (steady state), $\mu_n = \mu$, and $\lambda_n = \lambda$, become the *balance equations*

$$p_{n+1} = (\rho + 1)p_n - \rho p_{n-1} \qquad (n = 1, 2, \ldots) \tag{1}$$

$$p_1 = \rho p_0 \tag{2}$$

Equation (2) gives p_1 in terms of p_0, and all other steady-state probabilities can also be obtained in terms of p_0 by solving (1) recursively:

$$\textbf{n = 1:} \qquad p_2 = (\rho + 1)p_1 - \rho p_0 = (\rho + 1)(\rho p_0) - \rho p_0 = \rho^2 p_0$$

$$\textbf{n = 2:} \qquad p_3 = (\rho + 1)p_2 - \rho p_1 = (\rho + 1)(\rho^2 p_0) - \rho(\rho p_0) = \rho^3 p_0$$

$$\textbf{n = 3:} \qquad p_4 = (\rho + 1)p_3 - \rho p_2 = (\rho + 1)(\rho^3 p_0) - \rho(\rho^2 p_0) = \rho^4 p_0$$

and, in general,

$$p_n = \rho^n p_0 \tag{3}$$

Since the sum of the probabilities must equal unity and $0 < \rho < 1$,

$$1 = \sum_{n=0}^{\infty} p_n = p_0 \sum_{n=0}^{\infty} \rho^n = p_0 \left(\frac{1}{1-\rho} \right)$$

Therefore, $p_0 = 1 - \rho$, and (3) becomes (23.3).

23.8   Derive (23.7).

Using the definition of expected value and the results of Problem 23.7, we calculate the expected number of customers in an M/M/1 system as

$$L = \sum_{n=0}^{\infty} np_n = \sum_{n=0}^{\infty} n(1-\rho)\rho^n = \rho(1-\rho) \sum_{n=0}^{\infty} n\rho^{n-1} = \rho(1-\rho) \frac{d}{d\rho} \left(\sum_{n=0}^{\infty} \rho^n \right)$$

$$= \rho(1-\rho) \frac{d}{d\rho} \left(\frac{1}{1-\rho} \right) = \rho(1-\rho) \frac{1}{(1-\rho)^2} = \frac{\rho}{1-\rho}$$

23.9   Derive (23.4).

Denote the time a customer spends in the system by T, the time spent in the queue by T_q, and the time spent being served by T_s. All three are random variables, with

$$T = T_q + T_s$$

Therefore,

$$E(T) = E(T_q) + E(T_s) \tag{1}$$

The expected service time is $E(T_s) = 1/\mu$. We are denoting $E(T)$ by W and $E(T_q)$ by W_q, so (1) coincides with (23.4).

23.10 Deduce Little's formulas intuitively.

During the "average customer's" time in the system, W, new customers arrive at an average rate λ; so, at the end of W time units, λW new customers are expected in the system. That is, as the original customer leaves the system, that customer can expect to see λW other customers remaining in the system. Since the queue statistics are independent of time in the steady state, $L = \lambda W$ always.

Equation (23.6) is deduced similarly, by replacing W, L, and the word "system" by W_q, L_q, and the word "queue," respectively, in the preceding paragraph.

23.11 For an M/M/1 system, does $L_q = L - 1$?

No:

$$L = \sum_{n=0}^{\infty} np_n = \sum_{n=1}^{\infty} np_n \qquad L_q = \sum_{n=2}^{\infty} (n-1)p_n = \sum_{n=1}^{\infty} (n-1)p_n$$

and so

$$L - L_q = \sum_{n=1}^{\infty} p_n = 1 - p_0 = \rho$$

23.12 Show that $S_k \equiv T_1 + T_2 + \cdots + T_k$, the sum of k mutually independent, exponentially distributed random variables, each with parameter μ, has the *Erlang type k*, or *gamma*, distribution;

$$P(S_k \le t) = \int_0^t \frac{\mu^k \tau^{k-1}}{(k-1)!} e^{-\mu\tau} \, d\tau \qquad (t \ge 0) \tag{23.13}$$

Interpret the T-variables as the first k interarrival times in a Poisson birth process having initial population zero. Then the population at time t is k or more if and only if $S_k \le t$; that is,

$$P(S_k \le t) = P(N(t) \ge k) = \sum_{n=k}^{\infty} \frac{(\mu t)^n}{n!} e^{-\mu t} \tag{1}$$

where we have made use of (21.9), with λ replaced by μ.

One way to prove the equivalence of (1) and (23.13) is to show that they have the same first derivative (the probability density function for S_k) and the same value at $t = 0$ (which they obviously do). Differentiating (23.13),

$$f_k(t) = \frac{\mu^k t^{k-1}}{(k-1)!} e^{-\mu t}$$

Differentiating (1),

$$f_k(t) = \sum_{n=k}^{\infty} \frac{\mu^n}{n!} (nt^{n-1}e^{-\mu t} - \mu t^n e^{-\mu t})$$

$$= \sum_{n=k}^{\infty} \frac{\mu^n t^{n-1}}{(n-1)!} e^{-\mu t} - \sum_{n=k}^{\infty} \frac{\mu^{n+1} t^n}{n!} e^{-\mu t}$$

$$= \frac{\mu^k t^{k-1}}{(k-1)!} e^{-\mu t}$$

and the proof is complete.

23.13 Derive (23.12).

To obtain the distribution of T_q, the time a customer spends in the queue of an M/M/1 system, use conditional probabilities (Problem 17.5). If an arriving customer finds the system in state 0, then $T_q = 0$; if the customer finds the system in state k $(k = 1, 2, \ldots)$, then, because of the memoryless property (Problem 23.2) of the current service time, $T_q = S_k$ (see Problem 23.12). Consequently, for $t \ge 0$,

$$W_q(t) \equiv P(T_q > t) = 1 - P(T_q \leq t) = 1 - \left[p_0 P(0 \leq t) + \sum_{k=1}^{\infty} p_k P(S_k \leq t) \right]$$

$$= 1 - \left[(1-\rho)(1) + \sum_{k=1}^{\infty} \rho^k (1-\rho) \int_0^t \frac{\mu^k \tau^{k-1}}{(k-1)!} e^{-\mu\tau} d\tau \right]$$

$$= \rho - \rho\mu(1-\rho) \int_0^t \left[\sum_{k=1}^{\infty} \frac{(\mu\rho\tau)^{k-1}}{(k-1)!} \right] e^{-\mu\tau} d\tau = \rho - \rho\mu(1-\rho) \int_0^t e^{\mu\rho\tau} e^{-\mu\tau} d\tau$$

$$= \rho - \rho\mu(1-\rho) \int_0^t e^{-\mu(1-\rho)\tau} d\tau = \rho e^{-\mu(1-\rho)t} = \rho e^{-t/W}$$

Supplementary Problems

23.14 The take-out counter at an ice cream parlor is serviced by one attendant. Customers arrive according to a Poisson process, at a mean arrival rate of 30 per hour. They are served on a FIFO basis, and, because of the quality of the ice cream, they are willing to wait if necessary. The service time per customer appears to be exponentially distributed, with a mean of $1\frac{1}{2}$ min. Determine (a) the average number of customers waiting for service, (b) the amount of time a customer should expect to wait for service, (c) the probability that a customer will have to spend more than 15 min in the queue, and (d) the probability that the server is idle.

23.15 A barber runs a one-man shop. He does not make appointments but attends customers on a first-come, first-served basis. Because of the barber's reputation, customers are willing to wait for service once they arrive; arrivals follow a Poisson pattern, with a mean arrival rate of two per hour. The barber's service time appears to be exponentially distributed, with a mean of 20 min. Determine (a) the expected number of customers in the shop, (b) the expected number of customers waiting for service, (c) the average time a customer spends in the shop, and (d) the probability that a customer will spend more than the average amount of time in the shop.

23.16 The arrival pattern of cars to a single-lane, drive-in window at a bank appears to be a Poisson process, with a mean rate of one per minute. Service times by the teller appear to be exponentially distributed, with a mean of 45 s. Assuming that an arriving car will wait as long as necessary, determine (a) the expected number of cars waiting for service, (b) the average time a car waits for service, (c) the average time a car spends in the system, and (d) the probability that there will be cars waiting in the street if bank grounds can hold a maximum of five automobiles.

23.17 Aircraft request permission to land at a single-runway airport on an average of one every 5 min; the actual distribution appears to be Poisson. Planes are landed on a first-come, first-served basis, with those not able to land immediately due to traffic congestion put in a holding pattern. The time required by the traffic controller to land a plane varies with the experience of the pilot; it is exponentially distributed, with a mean of 3 min. Determine (a) the average number of planes in a holding pattern, (b) the average number of planes that have requested permission to land but are still in motion, (c) the probability that an arriving plane will be on the ground in less than 10 min after first requesting permission to land, and (d) the probability that there are more than three planes in a holding pattern.

23.18 A typist receives work according to a Poisson process, at an average rate of four jobs per hour. Jobs are typed on a first-come, first-served basis, with the average job requiring 12 min of the typist's time; the actual time per job appears to be exponentially distributed about this mean. Determine (a) the probability that an arriving job will be completed in under 45 min, (b) the probability that all jobs will have been completed by the typist at the end of the business day, and (c) the probability that a job will take less than 12 min to complete once the typist begins it.

23.19 As mechanics need parts for automobiles they are servicing in a repair shop, they go to the parts department of the shop and requisition the needed material. Mechanics are accommodated by the single attendant in the parts department on a first-come, first-served basis. Mechanics arrive according to a Poisson process, with a mean rate of 35 per hour, and they wait their turn whenever the parts attendant is busy with someone else. On the average, it takes the parts attendant 1 min to serve a mechanic, with the actual service time exponentially distributed about this mean. What is the expected hourly cost to the repair shop to have its mechanics obtain parts, if a mechanic is paid $12 an hour?

23.20 Buses arrive at a service facility according to a Poisson process, at a mean rate of 10 per day. The facility can service only one bus at a time, the service time being exponentially distributed about a mean of 1/12 day. It costs the bus company $200 a day to operate the service facility and $50 for each day a bus is tied up in the facility. By purchasing newer equipment that will raise the daily operating cost of the service facility to $245, the bus company can decrease the mean service time to 1/15 day. Is such an update economically attractive?

23.21 Jobs arrive at an inspection station according to a Poisson process, at a mean rate of two per hour, and are inspected one at a time on a FIFO basis. The quality control engineer both inspects and makes minor adjustments, if that is all that is required to pass a job through this phase. The total service time per job appears to be exponentially distributed, with a mean of 25 min. Jobs that arrive but cannot be inspected immediately by the engineer must be stored until the engineer is free to take them. Each job requires 10 ft^2 of floor space while it is in storage. How much floor space should be provided, if the objective is to have sufficient storage space within the quality control section 90 percent of the time?

23.22 Determine the effect on L, L_q, and W of doubling both λ and μ in an M/M/1 system.

23.23 Find the conditional probability that there are $n \geq 2$ customers in an M/M/1 system, given that there is a queue.

23.24 Determine the expected number of customers in the queue of an M/M/1 system when there is a queue. (*Hint*: Use the results of Problem 23.23.)

23.25 Derive (*23.8*) without the use of Little's formula, by calculating directly the expected number of customers in the queue.

23.26 Derive the balance equations (see Problem 23.7) directly by using the fact that in the steady state the expected rate of transitions of the system into state n must equal the expected rate of transitions out of state n. (Note that the expected rates of *customers* into and out of state n, $\lambda_n = \lambda$ and $\mu_n = \mu$, are not in general equal.)

23.27 Use the generating function approach suggested in Problem 21.7 to solve the balance equations for an M/M/1 system.

23.28 Without using Problem 23.26, verify that the mean rate of departure from a steady-state M/M/1 system equals the mean rate of arrival into the system.

Chapter 24

Other Systems with Poisson-Type Input and Exponential-Type Service Times

STATE-DEPENDENT PROCESSES

In many queueing situations, the number of customer arrivals does not constitute a strict Poisson process, with constant parameter λ; instead, it seems to follow a Poisson-like process in which λ varies according to the number of customers in the system. It may also be the case that departures from the system do not occur at a constant mean rate μ, as they would for a single server with an exponentially distributed service time; rather, the departures are as though there were a single server having an exponential-like service time distribution for which μ varies according to the state of the system. Such queueing processes can be modeled as generalized Markovian birth-death processes (Chapter 21), for which $\lambda_n \Delta t$ and $\mu_n \Delta t$ give, respectively, the expected numbers of arrivals and departures in a small time interval Δt, if the system is in state n at the beginning of the interval. The steady-state probabilities for these processes are found to satisfy

$$p_n = \frac{\lambda_{n-1}}{\mu_n} p_{n-1} \qquad \text{or} \qquad p_n = \frac{\lambda_{n-1}\lambda_{n-2}\cdots\lambda_0}{\mu_n\mu_{n-1}\cdots\mu_1} p_0 \qquad (24.1)$$

in which p_0 is determined by the condition that the sum of all the probabilities be unity. This sum converges provided the λ's are not too large with respect to the μ's. In particular, the existence of a steady state is assured if

$$\frac{\lambda_{n-1}}{\mu_n} \le \theta < 1$$

for all large n.

LITTLE'S FORMULAS

Little's formulas, (23.5) and (23.6), hold for the above-described processes, where

$$\bar{\lambda} = \sum_{n=0}^{\infty} \lambda_n p_n \qquad (24.2)$$

is the average arrival rate of customers *into* the service facility.

In any queueing system, the expected number of customers in the system is

$$L = \sum_{n=0}^{\infty} n p_n$$

and the expected number of customers in the queue is

$$L_q = \sum_{n=0}^{\infty} [\max\{n - s_n, 0\}] p_n$$

where s_n is the number of servers available in state n. If it is possible to evaluate L and L_q, then, knowing $\bar{\lambda}$, we can at once find W and W_q from Little's formulas.

BALKING AND RENEGING

A balk occurs when a customer *arrives at* but refuses to *enter into* a service facility, because the queue is too long. Designate the probability that an arriving customer will balk when there are n customers already in the system by the *balking function* $b(n)$. The probability that an arriving customer will not balk is then $1 - b(n)$. If the arrival pattern *to* the service facility is state-independent, with mean arrival rate λ, then the expected rate of customers *into* the service facility is

$$\lambda_n = [1 - b(n)]\lambda \qquad (24.3)$$

which is state-dependent. (See Problem 24.4.)

Reneging occurs when a customer leaves the queue after joining it, because the waiting time for service has become too long. The net effect is to increase the rate at which customers are processed through the system. An M/M/1 system with reneging is modeled by a state-dependent process for which

$$\mu_n = \mu + r(n) \qquad (24.4)$$

Here, $r(n)$ is a *reneging function* defined by

$$r(n) \equiv \lim_{\Delta t \to 0} \frac{P\{\text{a customer reneges in a time interval } \Delta t \mid n \text{ customers in the system}\}}{\Delta t}$$

Since no reneging occurs when there is no queue, $r(0) = r(1) = 0$. (See Problem 24.10.)

M/M/s SYSTEMS

An M/M/s system is a queueing process having a Poisson arrival pattern; s servers, with s independent, identically distributed, exponential service times (which do not depend on the state of the system); infinite capacity; and a FIFO queue discipline. The arrival pattern being state-independent, $\lambda_n = \lambda$ for all n. The service times associated with *each server* are also state-independent; but since the number of servers that actually attend customers (i.e., are not idle) *does* depend on the number of customers in the system, the effective time it takes the *system* to process customers through the service facility is state-dependent. In particular, if $1/\mu$ is the mean service time for one server to handle one customer, then the mean rate of service completions when there are n customers in the system is

$$\mu_n = \begin{cases} n\mu & (n = 0, 1, \ldots, s) \\ s\mu & (n = s + 1, s + 2, \ldots) \end{cases}$$

Steady-state conditions prevail whenever

$$\rho \equiv \frac{\lambda}{s\mu} < 1$$

The steady-state probabilities are given by (24.1) as

$$p_0 = \left[\frac{s^s \rho^{s+1}}{s!(1-\rho)} + \sum_{n=0}^{s} \frac{(s\rho)^n}{n!} \right]^{-1} \qquad (24.5)$$

and

$$p_n = \begin{cases} \dfrac{(s\rho)^n}{n!} p_0 & (n = 1, \ldots, s) \\[3mm] \dfrac{s^s \rho^n}{s!} p_0 & (n = s + 1, s + 2, \ldots) \end{cases} \qquad (24.6)$$

(See Problem 24.5.) With p_0 given by (24.5),

$$L_q = \frac{s^s \rho^{s+1} p_0}{s!\,(1-\rho)^2} \tag{24.7}$$

Once L_q is determined, W_q, W, and L are obtained from (23.6), (23.4), and (23.5), respectively, with $\bar{\lambda} = \lambda$. Equation (23.4) applies here, because, regardless of the state of the system, the expected service time for each customer has the fixed value $1/\mu$. Furthermore,

$$W(t) = e^{-\mu t}\left\{1 + \frac{(s\rho)^s p_0[1 - e^{-\mu t(s-1-s\rho)}]}{s!\,(1-\rho)(s-1-s\rho)}\right\} \qquad (t \ge 0) \tag{24.8}$$

$$W_q(t) = \frac{(s\rho)^s p_0}{s!\,(1-\rho)} e^{-s\mu t(1-\rho)} \qquad (t \ge 0) \tag{24.9}$$

(See Problems 24.5 and 24.6.)

M/M/1/K SYSTEMS

An M/M/1/K system can accommodate a maximum of K customers in the service facility at the same time. Customers arriving at the facility when it is full are denied entrance and are not permitted to wait outside the facility for entrance at a later time. If λ designates the mean arrival rate of customers *to* the service facility, then the mean arrival rate *into* the facility when the facility is in state n is

$$\lambda_n = \begin{cases} \lambda & (n = 0, 1, \ldots, K-1) \\ 0 & (n = K, K+1, \ldots) \end{cases}$$

A steady state is always attained, whatever the value of $\rho \equiv \lambda/\mu$, with probabilities given by (24.1) as $p_n = 0$ $(n > K)$ and, for $n = 0, 1, \ldots, K$,

$$p_n = \begin{cases} \dfrac{\rho^n(1-\rho)}{1-\rho^{K+1}} & (\rho \ne 1) \\[3mm] \dfrac{1}{K+1} & (\rho = 1) \end{cases} \tag{24.10}$$

The measures of effectiveness are

$$L = \begin{cases} \dfrac{\rho}{1-\rho} - \dfrac{(K+1)\rho^{K+1}}{1-\rho^{K+1}} & (\rho \ne 1) \\[3mm] \dfrac{K}{2} & (\rho = 1) \end{cases} \tag{24.11}$$

with W, W_q, and L_q obtained from (23.5), (23.4), and (23.6), respectively, wherein

$$\bar{\lambda} = \lambda(1 - p_K) \tag{24.12}$$

(See Problem 24.7.)

M/M/s/K SYSTEMS

An M/M/s/K system is a finite-capacity system with s servers having independent, identically distributed, exponential service times (which do not depend on the state of the system). Since the capacity of the system must be at least as large as the number of servers, $s \le K$. For such a system,

$$\lambda_n = \begin{cases} \lambda & (n = 0, 1, \ldots, K-1) \\ 0 & (n = K, K+1, \ldots) \end{cases} \qquad \mu_n = \begin{cases} n\mu & (n = 0, 1, \ldots, s) \\ s\mu & (n = s+1, s+2, \ldots) \end{cases}$$

Steady-state probabilities exist for all values of $\rho \equiv \lambda/s\mu$, and are given by (24.1) as

$$p_0 = \begin{cases} \left[\dfrac{s^s \rho^{s+1}(1-\rho^{K-s})}{s!\,(1-\rho)} + \displaystyle\sum_{n=0}^{s} \dfrac{(s\rho)^n}{n!} \right]^{-1} & (\rho \neq 1) \\[3ex] \left[\dfrac{s^s}{s!}(K-s) + \displaystyle\sum_{n=0}^{s} \dfrac{s^n}{n!} \right]^{-1} & (\rho = 1) \end{cases} \qquad (24.13)$$

and

$$p_n = \begin{cases} \dfrac{(s\rho)^n}{n!}\,p_0 & (n = 1, 2, \ldots, s) \\[2ex] \dfrac{s^s \rho^n}{s!}\,p_0 & (n = s+1, \ldots, K) \\[2ex] 0 & (n = K+1, K+2, \ldots) \end{cases} \qquad (24.14)$$

The measures of effectiveness are

$$L_q = \frac{s^s \rho^{s+1}}{s!(1-\rho)^2}[1 - \rho^{K-s} - (1-\rho)(K-s)\rho^{K-s}]p_0 \qquad (24.15)$$

with W_q, W, and L obtained from (23.6), (23.4), and (23.5), respectively; $\bar{\lambda}$ is again given by (24.12). (See Problem 24.8.) An M/M/1/K system is a special M/M/s/K system with $s = 1$ (see Problem 24.28).

Solved Problems

24.1 A grocery store has a single checkout counter attended by a cashier who also functions as the bagger when the store is not too busy. Customers arrive at the checkout counter according to a Poisson process, at a mean rate of 30 per hour. The time required for the cashier to total a customer's purchases, bag the groceries, and make change is exponentially distributed, with a mean of 2 min. Whenever there are three or more customers at the counter (including the customer in service), a second employee of the store is instructed to assist the cashier as a bagger. When the two employees work together, the service time for a customer remains exponentially distributed, but with a mean of 1 min. Determine (a) the average number of customers at the checkout counter at the same time, (b) the length of time a customer should expect to spend at the checkout counter, and (c) the length of time a customer should expect to wait on line before having his or her purchases totaled.

Throughout the process the arrival rate remains state-independent at $\lambda_n = \lambda = 30\text{ h}^{-1}$. The service times, however, are state-dependent. When there are fewer than three customers at the counter, the mean service time is 2 min; hence the mean service rate is 30 h^{-1}. When there are three or more customers at the counter, the mean service time is 1 min; hence the mean service rate increases to 60 h^{-1}. Thus

$$\mu_n = \begin{cases} 30\text{ h}^{-1} & (n = 1, 2) \\ 60\text{ h}^{-1} & (n = 3, 4, \ldots) \end{cases}$$

Note that, when a new arrival changes the state of the system from 2 to 3, the customer in service is instantly subject to the new exponential distribution (the "memoryless" property).

It follows from (24.1) that

$$p_1 = \frac{\lambda_0}{\mu_1}p_0 = \frac{30}{30}p_0 = p_0 \qquad\qquad p_2 = \frac{\lambda_1}{\mu_2}p_1 = \frac{30}{30}(p_0) = p_0$$

$$p_3 = \frac{\lambda_2}{\mu_3}p_2 = \frac{30}{60}(p_0) = \tfrac{1}{2}p_0 \qquad\qquad p_4 = \frac{\lambda_3}{\mu_4}p_3 = \frac{30}{60}(\tfrac{1}{2}p_0) = (\tfrac{1}{2})^2 p_0$$

and, in general,

$$p_n = (\tfrac{1}{2})^{n-2} p_0 \qquad (n \geq 2)$$

To find p_0, we solve

$$1 = \sum_{n=0}^{\infty} p_n = p_0 + p_1 + \sum_{n=2}^{\infty} p_n = 2p_0 + \sum_{n=2}^{\infty} (\tfrac{1}{2})^{n-2} p_0$$

$$= 2p_0 + 2p_0 = 4p_0$$

obtaining $p_0 = 1/4$. Therefore,

$$p_n = \begin{cases} \tfrac{1}{4} & (n = 0, 1) \\ (\tfrac{1}{2})^n & (n = 2, 3, \ldots) \end{cases}$$

The generating function for these probabilities is

$$F(z) \equiv \sum_{n=0}^{\infty} p_n z^n = \frac{1}{4} + \frac{1}{4} z + \sum_{n=2}^{\infty} \left(\frac{z}{2}\right)^n = \frac{2 + z + z^2}{8 - 4z}$$

(a)
$$L = \sum_{n=0}^{\infty} n p_n = \frac{dF}{dz}\bigg|_{z=1} = \frac{28}{16} = 1.75 \text{ customers}$$

(b) Since $\bar{\lambda} = \lambda = 30 \text{ h}^{-1}$,

$$W = \frac{L}{\lambda} = \frac{1.75}{30} = 0.05833 \text{ h} = 3.5 \text{ min}$$

(c) Because the bagger and the cashier work together, the number of servers is state-independent at $s_n = 1$. Then, as in Problem 23.11,

$$L_q = \sum_{n=2}^{\infty} (n-1)p_n = L - (1 - p_0) = 1.75 - 0.75 = 1.00 \text{ customer}$$

and

$$W_q = \frac{L_q}{\bar{\lambda}} = \frac{1.00}{30} = 0.0333 \text{ h} = 2 \text{ min}$$

Observe that the average service time *per customer* is

$$W - W_q = 1.5 \text{ min}$$

24.2 Rework Problem 24.1 if the second employee comes in as a separate, equally efficient cashier-bagger, working in parallel with the first. Whenever only two customers remain, the momentarily free employee leaves the checkout counter, to return whenever the state again reaches 3. Would this arrangement be preferable from the customers' point of view?

The λ_n and μ_n are the same as in Problem 24.1; hence, the state probabilities, and along with them L and W, remain unchanged. However, the number of servers is now state-dependent, with

$$s_n = \begin{cases} 1 & (n = 0, 1, 2) \\ 2 & (n = 3, 4, \ldots) \end{cases}$$

and so

$$L_q = 1p_2 + \sum_{n=3}^{\infty} (n-2)p_n = p_2 + \sum_{n=1}^{\infty} (n-2)p_n + p_1$$

$$= p_2 + L - 2(1 - p_0) + p_1 = \tfrac{1}{4} + 1.75 - 2(\tfrac{3}{4}) + \tfrac{1}{4} = 0.75 \text{ customer}$$

$$W_q = \frac{0.75}{30} = 0.025 \text{ h} = 1.5 \text{ min}$$

As compared with the situation in Problem 24.1, customers wait an average of 0.5 min less *for* service and spend an average of 0.5 min more *in* service. Probably they would favor such a tradeoff.

24.3 Derive (24.1).

Setting $dp_n/dt = 0$ (steady-state conditions) in the Kolmogorov equations for a generalized Markovian birth-death process, (21.1), we obtain, after rearrangement,

$$p_{n+1} = \frac{\lambda_n + \mu_n}{\mu_{n+1}} p_n - \frac{\lambda_{n-1}}{\mu_{n+1}} p_{n-1} \qquad (n = 1, 2, \ldots) \tag{1}$$

$$p_1 = \frac{\lambda_0}{\mu_1} p_0 \tag{2}$$

Equation (2) gives p_1 in terms of p_0. Solving (1) iteratively, we also find

$$p_2 = \frac{\lambda_1 + \mu_1}{\mu_2} p_1 - \frac{\lambda_0}{\mu_2} p_0 = \frac{\lambda_1 + \mu_1}{\mu_2} \left(\frac{\lambda_0}{\mu_1} p_0 \right) - \frac{\lambda_0}{\mu_2} p_0 = \frac{\lambda_1 \lambda_0}{\mu_2 \mu_1} p_0$$

$$p_3 = \frac{\lambda_2 + \mu_2}{\mu_3} p_2 - \frac{\lambda_1}{\mu_3} p_1$$

$$= \frac{\lambda_2 + \mu_2}{\mu_3} \left(\frac{\lambda_1 \lambda_0}{\mu_2 \mu_1} p_0 \right) - \frac{\lambda_1}{\mu_3} \left(\frac{\lambda_0}{\mu_1} p_0 \right) = \frac{\lambda_2 \lambda_1 \lambda_0}{\mu_3 \mu_2 \mu_1} p_0$$

and, in general,

$$p_n = \frac{\lambda_{n-1} \lambda_{n-2} \cdots \lambda_0}{\mu_n \mu_{n-1} \cdots \mu_1} p_0 \qquad \text{or} \qquad p_n = \frac{\lambda_{n-1}}{\mu_n} p_{n-1}$$

24.4 The owner of a small but busy newspaper and tobacco store serves customers on an average of one every 30 s, the actual distribution being exponential. Customers arrive according to a Poisson process, at a mean rate of three per minute, and they can wait for service if the owner is busy with another customer. A number of customers choose not to wait and take their business elsewhere. The probability that an arriving customer balks is $n/3$, where n is the number of customers already in the store. How much profit must the shop owner expect to lose from customers who take their business elsewhere, if the average profit per customer is 30¢.

Since the probability of balking is 1 when there are three customers in the store, the store never experiences more than three customers at the same time, and the only feasible states are 0, 1, 2, and 3. We take the balking function to be

$$b(n) = \begin{cases} n/3 & (n = 0, 1, 2, 3) \\ 1 & (n = 4, 5, \ldots) \end{cases}$$

The mean arrival rate of customers *to* the store is $\lambda = 3$, whence, by (24.3), the mean rates *into* the store are

$$\lambda_0 = (1 - \tfrac{0}{3})(3) = 3 \qquad \lambda_1 = (1 - \tfrac{1}{3})(3) = 2 \qquad \lambda_2 = (1 - \tfrac{2}{3})(3) = 1$$

and $\lambda_n = (1 - 1)(3) = 0$ when $n = 3, 4, \ldots$. The service rate is state-independent, with $\mu_n = \mu = 2$ customers per minute. From (24.1),

$$p_1 = \frac{\lambda_0}{\mu_1} p_0 = \tfrac{3}{2} p_0$$

$$p_2 = \frac{\lambda_1}{\mu_2} p_1 = \tfrac{2}{2}(\tfrac{3}{2} p_0) = \tfrac{3}{2} p_0$$

$$p_3 = \frac{\lambda_2}{\mu_3} p_2 = \tfrac{1}{2}(\tfrac{3}{2} p_0) = \tfrac{3}{4} p_0$$

and $p_n = 0$ $(n = 4, 5, \ldots)$. The requirement that the probabilities sum to 1 gives $p_0 = 4/19$. Hence,

$$p_1 = \frac{6}{19} \qquad p_2 = \frac{6}{19} \qquad p_3 = \frac{3}{19} \qquad p_n = 0 \quad (n > 3)$$

The expected rate at which customers balk is

$$\sum_{n=0}^{\infty} (\lambda - \lambda_n)p_n = (3-3)\frac{4}{19} + (3-2)\frac{6}{19} + (3-1)\frac{6}{19} + (3-0)\frac{3}{19} + 0 + 0 + \cdots$$

$$= 1.4211 \text{ customers per minute}$$

so that the expected loss rate is

$$(30\cancel{c})(1.4211) = 42.633 \ \cancel{c}/\text{min} = \$25.58 \text{ per hour}$$

24.5 A small bank has two tellers, who are equally efficient and who are each capable of handling an average of 60 customer transactions per hour, with the actual service times exponentially distributed.   Customers arrive at the bank according to a Poisson process, at a mean rate of 100 per hour.   Determine (a) the probability that there are more than three customers in the bank at the same time, (b) the probability that a given teller is idle, and (c) the probability that a customer spends more than 3 min in the bank.

This is an M/M/2 system, with $\lambda = 100$ and $\mu = 60$.   Since

$$\rho = \frac{100}{2(60)} = \frac{5}{6} < 1$$

steady-state conditions will prevail eventually.   Using (24.5), we calculate

$$\frac{1}{p_0} = \frac{2^2(5/6)^3}{2!\,[1-(5/6)]} + \sum_{n=0}^{2} \frac{(5/3)^n}{n!} = \frac{125}{18} + \frac{1}{0!}\left(\frac{5}{3}\right)^0 + \frac{1}{1!}\left(\frac{5}{3}\right)^1 + \frac{1}{2!}\left(\frac{5}{3}\right)^2 = 11$$

or $p_0 = 1/11 = 0.0909$.   The remaining steady-state probabilities are then determined from (24.6) as

$$p_1 = \frac{(5/3)^1}{1!}\left(\frac{1}{11}\right) = 0.1515$$

$$p_2 = \frac{(5/3)^2}{2!}\left(\frac{1}{11}\right) = 0.1263$$

$$p_3 = \frac{2^2(5/6)^3}{2!}\left(\frac{1}{11}\right) = 0.1052$$

$$p_4 = \rho p_3 = \frac{5}{6}(0.1052) = 0.0877$$

and so on.

(a) $$1 - (p_0 + p_1 + p_2 + p_3) = 1 - (0.0909 + 0.1515 + 0.1263 + 0.1052) = 0.5261$$

(b) A given teller is idle if there are no customers in the bank or if there is one customer in the bank and that customer is being served by the other teller.

$$p_0 + \tfrac{1}{2}p_1 = 0.0909 + \tfrac{1}{2}(0.1515) = 0.1667$$

(c) Using (24.8), we find the probability that a customer will spend more than 3 min, or 1/20 h, in the bank to be

$$W\left(\frac{1}{20}\right) = e^{-60(1/20)}\left\{1 + \frac{(5/3)^2(1/11)[1 - e^{-60(1/20)[2-1-(5/3)]}]}{2![1-(5/6)][2-1-(5/3)]}\right\} = 0.4113$$

24.6 A state department of transportation has three safety investigation teams who are on call continuously and whose job it is to analyze road conditions in the vicinity of each fatal accident on a state road.   The teams are equally efficient; each takes on the average 2 days to investigate and report on an accident, with the actual time apparently exponentially distributed.   The number of fatal accidents on state roads appears to follow a Poisson process, at a mean rate of 300 per year.   Determine L, L_q, W, and W_q for this process and give meaning to each of these quantities.

This is an M/M/3 process, with $\lambda = 300$ accidents per year, $\mu = 365/2 = 182.5$ reports per team per year, and

$$\rho = \frac{300}{3(182.5)} = \frac{40}{73}$$

To evaluate L_q by (24.7), we must first determine p_0.   From (24.5),

$$\frac{1}{p_0} = \frac{3^3(40/73)^4}{3![1-(40/73)]} + \sum_{n=0}^{3} \frac{1}{n!}\left(\frac{300}{182.5}\right)^n$$

$$= 0.89737 + \frac{1}{0!}\left(\frac{300}{182.5}\right)^0 + \frac{1}{1!}\left(\frac{300}{182.5}\right)^1 + \frac{1}{2!}\left(\frac{300}{182.5}\right)^2 + \frac{1}{3!}\left(\frac{300}{182.5}\right)^3 = 5.63263$$

Hence $p_0 = 1/5.63263 = 0.177537$.   Then,

$$L_q = \frac{3^3(40/73)^4(0.177537)}{3!\,[1-(40/73)]^2} = 0.3524$$

On the average, the department has a backlog of 0.3524 accidents.
   Using (23.6), with $\bar{\lambda} = \lambda = 300$, we have

$$W_q = \frac{1}{300}(0.3524) = 0.001175 \text{ year} = 0.429 \text{ day}$$

There elapses, on the average, slightly less than $\frac{1}{2}$ day between a fatal accident and the start of its investigation.
   It follows from (23.4) that

$$W = 0.001175 + \frac{1}{182.5} = 0.006654 \text{ year} = 2.429 \text{ days}$$

On the average, it takes slightly less than $2\frac{1}{2}$ days for the department to complete its work once a fatal accident has occurred.
   Finally, we determine from (23.5) that

$$L = 300(0.006654) = 1.996 \text{ accidents}$$

On the average, the department has nearly two cases under its jurisdiction, awaiting final action.

24.7   A service station on a rural road has a single pump from which to dispense gasoline.   Cars arrive at the station for gasoline according to a Poisson process, at a mean rate of 10 per hour.   The time required to service a car appears to be exponentially distributed, with a mean of 2 min.   The station can accommodate a maximum of four cars, and local traffic laws prohibit cars from waiting on the road.   Determine (a) the average number of cars simultaneously at the station; (b) the average time a customer must wait for service once access to the station is achieved; (c) the average rate at which revenue is lost from customers' taking their business elsewhere when the station is full, if the average sale is \$15.00.

   This is an M/M/1/4 system, with

$$\mu_n = \mu = \tfrac{1}{2} \text{ min}^{-1} = 30 \text{ h}^{-1}$$

The mean arrival rate *to* the station is $\lambda = 10 \text{ h}^{-1}$; so the mean arrival rates *into* the station are

$$\lambda_n = \begin{cases} 10 \text{ h}^{-1} & (n = 0, 1, 2, 3) \\ 0 \text{ h}^{-1} & (n = 4, 5, \dots) \end{cases}$$

The traffic intensity *offered* to the system is $\rho \equiv \lambda/\mu = 1/3$.

(a) From (24.11),

$$L = \frac{1}{2} - \frac{5(1/3)^5}{1-(1/3)^5} = 0.4793 \text{ car}$$

(b) To obtain W_q, we use (23.4), after first determining p_4, $\bar{\lambda}$, and W from (24.10), (24.12), and (23.5), respectively.   Here,

$$p_4 = \frac{(1/3)^4(2/3)}{1-(1/3)^5} = 0.008264$$

Hence $\bar{\lambda} = 10(1 - 0.008264) = 9.917$ h^{-1}, which represents the mean rate at which cars actually enter the station. Then

$$W = \frac{0.4793}{9.917} = 0.04833 \text{ h}$$

$$W_q = 0.04833 - \frac{1}{30} = 0.015 \text{ h} = 54 \text{ s}$$

(c)   Cars are denied entrance to the station at the mean rate

$$\lambda - \bar{\lambda} = 10 - 9.917 = 0.083 \text{ h}^{-1}$$

so that the mean rate of revenue loss is $(15)(0.083) = \$1.25$ per hour.

24.8 A self-service car wash has four stalls in which customers can clean and wax their automobiles and room to accommodate a maximum of three additional cars when all stalls are full. Customers arrive at the car wash according to a Poisson process, at a mean rate of 15 per hour. If there is no room for them on the grounds of the car wash, arriving customers must go elsewhere. The time required to service a car appears to be exponentially distributed, with a mean of 12 min. Determine (a) the average number of cars at the car wash at any given time, and (b) the expected rate at which cars are denied entrance to the car wash.

This is an M/M/4/7 system, with

$$\mu = 5 \text{ h}^{-1} \qquad \lambda = 15 \text{ h}^{-1} \qquad \rho \equiv \frac{15}{4(5)} = \frac{3}{4}$$

(a)   To determine L we use (23.5), after first calculating p_0, L_q, p_7, $\bar{\lambda}$, W_q, and W sequentially. From (24.13),

$$p_0 = \left[\frac{(4^4)(3/4)^5[1 - (3/4)^3]}{4!\,(1/4)} + \sum_{n=0}^{4} \frac{3^n}{n!} \right]^{-1}$$
$$= \left[\frac{2997}{512} + \frac{3^0}{0!} + \frac{3^1}{1!} + \frac{3^2}{2!} + \frac{3^3}{3!} + \frac{3^4}{4!} \right]^{-1} = (22.2285)^{-1} = 0.04499$$

By (24.15),

$$L_q = \frac{(4^4)(3/4)^5}{4!\,(1/4)^2}\,[1 - (3/4)^3 - (1/4)(3)(3/4)^3](0.04499) = 0.4768 \text{ car}$$

Using (24.14), we find that

$$p_7 = \frac{(4)^4(3/4)^7}{4!}\,(0.04499) = 0.06406$$

and, from (24.12),

$$\bar{\lambda} = 15(1 - 0.06406) = 14.04 \text{ h}^{-1}$$

Finally,

$$W_q = \frac{L_q}{\bar{\lambda}} = \frac{0.4768}{14.04} = 0.03396 \text{ h}$$

$$W = W_q + \frac{1}{\mu} = 0.03396 + 0.2 = 0.23396 \text{ h}$$

$$L = \bar{\lambda}W = (14.04)(0.23396) = 3.285 \text{ cars}$$

(b) $$\lambda - \bar{\lambda} = 15 - 14.04 = 0.96 \text{ cars per hour}$$

24.9 Customers arrive at a barber shop at an average rate of five per hour, the actual arrivals being Poisson-distributed. There is one barber on duty at all times and there are four chairs for customers who arrive when the barber is busy. Local fire ordinances limit the total number of customers in the shop at the same time to a maximum of five. Customers who arrive when the shop is full are denied entrance and their business is presumed lost. The barber's service time is exponentially distributed, but the mean changes with the number of customers in the shop. As the shop fills, the barber tries to speed service, but actually becomes less efficient, as shown in the following table:

Number in Shop	1	2	3	4	5
Mean Service Time, min	9	10	12	15	20

Determine (a) the average number of people in the shop at the same time, (b) the expected time a customer must wait for service, and (c) the percentage of time the barber is idle.

This is a finite-capacity system, but it is *not* an M/M/1/5 system, because the service times are state-dependent. Nonetheless, the measures of effectiveness can be calculated directly, once the steady-state probabilities are known. For this system, the mean arrival rate *to* the shop is $\lambda = 5 \text{ h}^{-1} = (1/12) \text{ min}^{-1}$; so the mean arrival rates *into* the shop are, in min^{-1},

$$\lambda_n = \begin{cases} 1/12 & (n = 0, 1, 2, 3, 4) \\ 0 & (n = 5, 6, \ldots) \end{cases}$$

The mean service rates are, in min^{-1}: $\mu_1 = 1/9$, $\mu_2 = 1/10$, $\mu_3 = 1/12$, $\mu_4 = 1/15$, $\mu_5 = 1/20$. The steady-state probabilities are given by (24.1) as

$$p_1 = \frac{\lambda_0}{\mu_1} p_0 = \frac{3}{4} p_0 \qquad\qquad p_4 = \frac{\lambda_3}{\mu_4} p_3 = \frac{25}{32} p_0$$

$$p_2 = \frac{\lambda_1}{\mu_2} p_1 = \frac{5}{8} p_0 \qquad\qquad p_5 = \frac{\lambda_4}{\mu_5} p_4 = \frac{125}{96} p_0$$

$$p_3 = \frac{\lambda_2}{\mu_3} p_2 = \frac{5}{8} p_0 \qquad\qquad p_n = 0 \quad (n > 5)$$

and, normalizing, we find

$$1 = \sum_{n=0}^{\infty} p_n = 5.0833 p_0 \qquad \text{or} \qquad p_0 = 0.1967$$

Hence, $p_1 = 0.1475$, $p_2 = 0.1230$, $p_3 = 0.1230$, $p_4 = 0.1537$, and $p_5 = 0.2561$.

(a) $$L = \sum_{n=1}^{5} n p_n = 1(0.1475) + 2(0.1230) + 3(0.1230) + 4(0.1537) + 5(0.2561) = 2.658 \text{ customers}$$

(b) We use (23.6) to determine W_q, after first calculating $\bar{\lambda}$ and L_q. By (24.2),

$$\bar{\lambda} = \sum_{n=0}^{4} \lambda_n p_n = \frac{1}{12}(1 - p_5) = 0.06199 \text{ min}^{-1}$$

and ($s_n = 1$)

$$L_q = \sum_{n=2}^{5} (n - 1) p_n = (1)(0.1230) + (2)(0.1230) + (3)(0.1537) + (4)(0.2561)$$
$$= 1.8545 \text{ customers}$$

Therefore,

$$W_q = \frac{1.8545}{0.06119} = 30.31 \text{ min}$$

(c) The barber is idle when there are no customers in the shop. This occurs with probability $p_0 = 0.1967$, or just under 20 percent of the time.

24.10 The service station described in Problem 24.7 is popular because it sells gas at a slightly lower price than its competitors. The price, however, is not sufficiently low to compensate for a long wait in line; so customers tend to renege according to the reneging function

$$r(n) = \begin{cases} 0 & \text{h}^{-1} & (n = 0, 1) \\ e^{n/2} \text{ h}^{-1} & (n = 2, 3, 4) \end{cases}$$

Determine (a) the average number of cars in the station at any time, and (b) the expected number of cars that renege each hour.

This system is an M/M/1/4 system with reneging. Alternatively, it can be viewed as an M/M/1 system with reneging, and with forced balking whenever the state of the system reaches 4. In this latter approach, the balking function is

$$b(n) = \begin{cases} 0 & (n = 0, 1, 2, 3) \\ 1 & (n = 4, 5, \ldots) \end{cases}$$

Either way, the mean arrival rate to the station is $\lambda = 10\,\text{h}^{-1}$ and the mean rate of attending to customers is $\mu = 30\,\text{h}^{-1}$, as in Problem 24.7. It follows that the mean arrival rates of customers $into$ the station are

$$\lambda_n = \begin{cases} 10\ \text{h}^{-1} & (n = 0, 1, 2, 3) \\ 0\ \text{h}^{-1} & (n = 4, 5, \ldots) \end{cases}$$

The mean rates for processing customers through the system, either by serving them or having them renege, are

$$\mu_1 = \mu + r(1) = 30 + 0 = 30$$
$$\mu_2 = \mu + r(2) = 30 + 2.718 = 32.718$$
$$\mu_3 = \mu + r(3) = 30 + 4.482 = 34.482$$
$$\mu_4 = \mu + r(4) = 30 + 7.389 = 37.389$$

We use (24.1) to determine the steady-state probabilities, and, from them, calculate the required measures of efficiency directly. Note that (24.10) through (24.12), which presume exponential service times for all customers, do not apply to the present process.

$$p_1 = \frac{\lambda_0}{\mu_1} p_0 = \frac{10}{30} p_0 = (0.3333)p_0$$

$$p_2 = \frac{\lambda_1}{\mu_2} p_1 = \frac{10}{32.718} (0.3333)p_0 = (0.1019)p_0$$

$$p_3 = \frac{\lambda_2}{\mu_3} p_2 = \frac{10}{34.482} (0.1019)p_0 = (0.02955)p_0$$

$$p_4 = \frac{\lambda_3}{\mu_4} p_3 = \frac{10}{37.389} (0.02955)p_0 = (0.007903)p_0$$

and $p_n = 0$ for $n = 5, 6, \ldots$. Normalizing,

$$1 = \sum_{n=0}^{\infty} p_n = (1.473)p_0 \qquad \text{or} \qquad p_0 = 0.6789$$

Consequently, $p_1 = 0.2263$, $p_2 = 0.0692$, $p_3 = 0.0201$, and $p_4 = 0.0054$.

(a)
$$L = \sum_{n=1}^{4} np_n = 1(0.2263) + 2(0.0692) + 3(0.0201) + 4(0.0054) = 0.4466 \text{ car}$$

(b) The expected reneging rate, in cars per hour, as a function of the state of the system is $r(n)$. Therefore, the expected number of cars, N, that renege each hour is

$$N = \sum_{n=0}^{4} r(n)p_n = (0)(0.6789) + (0)(0.2263) + (2.718)(0.0692) + (4.482)(0.0201) + (7.389)(0.0054)$$
$$= 0.3181 \text{ cars per hour}$$

Supplementary Problems

24.11 A bakery is staffed by two clerks, each of them capable of handling an average of 30 customers an hour, with the actual service times exponentially distributed.   Customers arrive at the bakery according to a Poisson process, at a mean rate of 40 per hour.   Determine (a) the fraction of time a given clerk is idle, and (b) the probability that there are more than two customers awaiting service at any given time.

24.12 A suburban train station has five public telephones.   During afternoon rush hours, individuals wanting to place calls arrive at the telephone booths according to a Poisson process, at the rate of 100 per hour.   The average duration of a call is 2 min, the actual duration being exponentially distributed. Determine (a) the expected amount of time an individual must wait for a telephone once having arrived at the booths, (b) the probability that this wait will exceed 1 min, and (c) the number of people expected to be using or waiting for a telephone.

24.13 A small bank has two tellers, one for deposits and one for withdrawals.   The service time for each teller is exponentially distributed, with a mean of 1 min.   Customers arrive at the bank according to a Poisson process, with mean rate 40 per hour; it is assumed (see Problem 21.26) that depositors and withdrawers constitute separate Poisson processes, each with mean rate 20 per hour, and that no customer is both a depositor and a withdrawer.   The bank is thinking of changing the current arrangement to allow each teller to handle both deposits and withdrawals.   The bank would expect that each teller's mean service time would increase to 1.2 min, but it hopes that the new arrangement would prevent long lines in front of one teller while the other teller is idle, a situation that occurs from time to time under the current setup.   Analyze the two arrangements with respect to the average idle time of a teller and the expected number of customers in the bank at any given time.

24.14 A tree surgeon hires an answering service to handle incoming telephone calls.   The answering service is attended by one operator and has the ability to keep two callers on hold if the operator is busy with another caller.   If all three lines are busy (one for the operator and two for keeping customers on hold), a caller receives a busy signal.   Calls are made to the tree surgeon according to a Poisson process, at the mean rate 20 per hour.   Once a connection is made with the operator, the duration of a call is exponentially distributed, with mean length 1 min.   Determine (a) the probability that a caller will receive a busy signal, (b) the probability that a caller will be placed on hold, and (c) the probability that a caller will speak with the operator immediately upon placing a call.

24.15 A takeout Chinese restaurant has space to accommodate at most five customers.   During the winter months, it is noticed that when customers arrive and the restaurant is full, virtually no one waits outside in the subfreezing weather but goes to another establishment.   Customers arrive at the restaurant according to a Poisson process, at a mean rate of 15 per hour.   The restaurant serves customers at the average rate of 15 per hour, with the actual service times exponentially distributed.   The restaurant is staffed only by the owner, who attends to customers on a first-come, first-served basis.   Determine (a) the average number of customers in the restaurant at any given time, (b) the expected time a customer must wait for service, and (c) the expected rate at which revenue is lost by the restaurant due to limited facilities if the average bill is $10.00.

24.16 A bus company directs its buses to its service facility for routine maintenance every 25 000 m.   The service facility is open 24 h each day and is staffed by a single crew capable of working on one bus at a time.   The time it takes to service a bus is exponentially distributed, with a mean of 4 h.   Buses arrive at the facility according to a Poisson process, at a mean rate of 12 per day.   Drivers, however, are instructed not to enter the facility if there are four or more buses already there, but to return to the dispatcher for reassignment.   Determine (a) the expected amount of time a bus spends at the service facility, when it remains there; (b) the expected monetary loss each day to the bus company from its limited service facilities, if the cost of sending a bus to the facility and having it return unserviced is $80.

24.17   The bus company described in Problem 24.16 is thinking of expanding the service staff to two equally efficient crews.   The daily cost of the added crew would be $300.   Is such an expansion advisable?

24.18   A hospital maternity section has five labor rooms.   Maternity patients arrive at the hospital according to a Poisson process, at a mean rate of 12 per day, and are assigned a labor room if one is available; otherwise they are directed to another hospital.   A patient occupies a labor room for 6 h, on the average; the actual time appears to be exponentially distributed about this mean.   Determine (*a*) the average occupancy rate of the labor rooms (i.e., the percentage of labor rooms in use over the long run), and (*b*) the average rate at which maternity patients are directed to other hospitals.

24.19   A store has two clerks, each capable of serving customers at an average rate of 60 per hour; actual service times are exponentially distributed.   The capacity of the store is five customers, with no waiting outside allowed.   Customers come to the store in a Poisson-type process where the average arrival rate depends on the number of people in the store, as follows:

Number in Store	0	1	2	3	4	5
Average Arrival Rate, h^{-1}	100	110	120	140	170	200

Determine (*a*) the expected number of customers in the store together, (*b*) the expected amount of time a customer must wait for service, and (*c*) the expected rate at which customers are lost due to limited facilities.

24.20   A car wash has room for only three waiting cars and has two lanes for washing cars.   Each lane can accommodate one car at a time.   Cars arrive according to a Poisson process, at a mean rate of 20 per hour, but are denied entrance whenever the wash is full.   Washing and cleaning is done manually, and appears to follow an exponential distribution.   Under normal conditions, each lane services a car in an average of 5 min.   However, when two or more cars are waiting for service, the washing procedure is streamlined, reducing the average service time to 4 min.   Determine (*a*) the expected number of cars at the car wash, and (*b*) the expected length of time a car spends at the wash if it is not denied entrance.

24.21   Customers arrive at a small delicatessen according to a Poisson process, at a mean rate of 30 per hour.   The establishment can hold at most four customers; whenever it is full, arriving customers are denied entrance and their business is lost.   The owner of the delicatessen is the only server, and his service time is exponentially distributed so long as there is but one customer in the store, the average service time then being 5 min.   The owner, however, becomes more efficient as the store fills, decreasing his conversations with customers and thereby decreasing the mean service time by 1 min for each customer in line waiting for service.   Determine (*a*) the expected number of people together in the delicatessen (not including the owner), and (*b*) the average service time for the owner.

24.22   Determine the steady-state probabilities for an M/M/1 system with balking, if there is a 20 percent chance of a balk whenever there are one or more customers already in the system.

24.23   Solve Problem 24.21 if the probability of a customer's balking is $1 - (\frac{1}{2})^n$ when the state of the system is $n = 0, 1, 2, 3$.

24.24   Solve Problem 24.15 if customers renege according to the reneging function

$$r(n) = \begin{cases} 0 \ h^{-1} & (n = 0, 1) \\ n^2 \ h^{-1} & (n = 2, 3, 4, 5) \end{cases}$$

24.25   Interpret (24.1), $\mu_n p_n = \lambda_{n-1} p_{n-1}$, in terms of transition rates.

24.26 Show that $L = L_q + s\rho$ for an M/M/s system.

24.27 Derive (24.13) and (24.14).

24.28 Show that the steady-state probabilities for an M/M/s/K system reduce to those of an M/M/1/K system when $s = 1$.

24.29 For an M/M/s/K system, deduce that

$$L = L_q + s - \sum_{n=0}^{s-1} (s - n)p_n$$

24.30 For the queueing process described in Problem 24.8, first determine the steady-state probabilities directly from (24.1) and then use them to calculate L. Compare your answer with the result of Problem 24.8(a).

24.31 An M/M/∞ system is a queueing process having a Poisson arrival pattern, with mean rate λ; a sufficient number of servers to accommodate all customers that enter the system, the servers having independent, identically distributed, exponential service times with parameter μ; and infinite capacity. Such a model often applies to self-service establishments. Show that for an M/M/∞ system the steady-state probabilities constitute a Poisson distribution, with parameter $\rho \equiv \lambda/\mu$. Then determine L, W, W_q, and L_q.

24.32 Students are accepted into a correspondence course in electrical wiring as soon as they register, and then they complete the course at their own pace. The completion times seem to follow an exponential distribution, with a mean of 7 weeks. New enrollments to the course follow a Poisson process, with a mean rate of 50 per week. Determine (a) the number of students that are expected to be concurrently enrolled in the course, and (b) the probability that it will take a student more than 7 weeks to complete the course. (*Hint*: Use the results of Problem 24.31.)

24.33 A *finite-source queueing system* is one that has a limited number of potential customers. This number must be small enough so that it is unreasonable to approximate the population of potential customers by means of an infinite source, as has been done in all previous queueing processes in this book. Consider a source initially consisting of N_0 potential customers. Their actualization times, i.e., the times at which they arrive at the service facility, are N_0 independent, exponentially distributed random variables, each with parameter λ. At the moment of service completion, a customer is returned to the source as a new potential customer. Therefore, whenever the state of the service facility is n, the state of the source is $N_0 - n$, giving

$$\lambda_n = (N_0 - n)\lambda \qquad (n = 0, 1, \ldots, N_0) \tag{1}$$

Moreover, for $s < N_0$ servers with independent, exponentially distributed service times having parameter μ,

$$\mu_n = \begin{cases} n\mu & (n = 1, 2, \ldots, s) \\ s\mu & (n = s + 1, s + 2, \ldots, N_0) \end{cases} \tag{2}$$

Find the steady-state probabilities in terms of $\rho \equiv \lambda/s\mu$, and compare with the infinite-source expressions, (24.5) and (24.6).

24.34 Infer directly from (1) of Problem 24.33 that $\bar{\lambda} = (N_0 - L)\lambda$.

24.35 A company which has seven delicate machines that frequently break down employs two service people with the sole task of repairing them. Each service person can repair a machine in 2 h, on the average, the actual service time being exponentially distributed about this mean. A newly repaired machine runs an average of 12 h before breaking down again; the actual running time is exponentially distributed about this mean.   Determine (*a*) the expected number of machines that are operative at any given time, and (*b*) the percentage of time any given machine will be inoperative.   (*Hint*:   Use the results of Problems 24.33 and 24.34.)

24.36 For a general queueing process, denote by $\hat{S}$ the average number of customers in service (which is the same thing as the average number of *busy* servers) over all periods in which the system is not empty.   Infer from Little's formulas that the mean service time for all customers who are served, $1/\bar{\mu}$, can be expressed as

$$\frac{1}{\bar{\mu}} = \frac{(1 - p_0)\hat{S}}{\bar{\lambda}}$$

Answers to Supplementary Problems

1.16
$$\text{maximize:} \quad z = 28x_1 + 31x_2$$
$$\text{subject to:} \quad 3.5x_1 + 4x_2 \leq 50$$
$$\text{with:} \quad \text{both variables nonnegative}$$

Note: Integer constraints on the variables are not required, since partially completed games can be finished in following weeks.

1.17
$$\text{minimize:} \quad z = 2x_1 + 3x_2 + 5x_3 + 6x_4 + 8x_5 + 8x_6$$
$$\text{subject to:} \quad 20x_1 + 30x_2 + 40x_3 + 40x_4 + 45x_5 + 30x_6 \geq 70$$
$$50x_1 + 30x_2 + 20x_3 + 25x_4 + 50x_5 + 20x_6 \geq 100$$
$$4x_1 + 9x_2 + 11x_3 + 10x_4 + 9x_5 + 10x_6 \geq 20$$
$$\text{with:} \quad \text{all variables nonnegative}$$

Note: Since feed F is no better than feed C, which is cheaper, no feed F will be used in the optimal mix. Thus, the program can be simplified by substituting $x_6 = 0$.

1.18
$$\text{maximize:} \quad z = 6x_1 + 4x_2 + 6x_3 + 8x_4$$
$$\text{subject to:} \quad 3x_1 + 2x_2 + 2x_3 + 4x_4 \leq 480$$
$$x_1 + x_2 + 2x_3 + 3x_4 \leq 400$$
$$2x_1 + x_2 + 2x_3 + x_4 \leq 400$$
$$x_1 \geq 50$$
$$x_2 + x_3 \geq 100$$
$$x_4 \leq 25$$
$$\text{with:} \quad \text{all variables nonnegative}$$

1.19
$$\text{minimize:} \quad z = 1.50x_1 + 0.75x_2 + 2.00x_3 + 1.75x_4 + 0.25x_5$$
$$\text{subject to:} \quad 0.2x_1 - 0.15x_2 + 0.8x_3 - 0.2x_4 - 0.2x_5 \geq 0$$
$$0.3x_1 - 0.1x_3 + 0.9x_4 - 0.1x_5 \geq 0$$
$$-0.05x_1 + 0.15x_2 - 0.05x_3 - 0.05x_4 - 0.05x_5 \geq 0$$
$$x_1 + x_2 + x_3 + x_4 + x_5 \geq 500$$
$$x_1 \leq 200$$
$$x_2 \leq 400$$
$$x_3 \leq 100$$
$$x_4 \leq 50$$
$$x_5 \leq 800$$
$$\text{with:} \quad \text{all variables nonnegative}$$

1.20
$$\text{maximize:} \quad z = 20x_1 + 17x_2 + 15x_3 + 15x_4 + 10x_5 + 8x_6 + 5x_7$$
$$\text{subject to:} \quad 145x_1 + 92x_2 + 70x_3 + 70x_4 + 84x_5 + 14x_6 + 47x_7 \leq 250$$
$$x_i \leq 1 \quad (i = 1, 2, \ldots, 7)$$
$$\text{with:} \quad \text{all variables nonnegative and integral}$$

1.21 The cost of delivering a module from a factory to a manufacturer is the production cost plus the shipping cost.

$$\text{minimize:} \quad z = (1.10 + 0.11)x_{11} + (1.10 + 0.13)x_{12} + \cdots + (1.03 + 0.15)x_{34}$$

$$
\begin{aligned}
\text{subject to:} \quad & x_{11} + x_{12} + x_{13} + x_{14} \le 7\,500 \\
& x_{21} + x_{22} + x_{23} + x_{24} \le 10\,000 \\
& x_{31} + x_{32} + x_{33} + x_{34} \le 8\,100 \\
& x_{11} + x_{21} + x_{31} = 4\,200 \\
& x_{12} + x_{22} + x_{32} = 8\,300 \\
& x_{13} + x_{23} + x_{33} = 6\,300 \\
& x_{14} + x_{24} + x_{34} = 2\,700
\end{aligned}
$$

with: all variables nonnegative and integral

1.22 Since the filler is inexpensive, no more meat will be be used in each product than is required. Let x_1, x_2, and x_3, respectively, designate the poundages of hamburger, picnic patties, and meat loaf to be made.

$$\text{minimize:} \quad (200 - 0.2x_1 - 0.1x_3) + (800 - 0.5x_1 - 0.5x_2 - 0.4x_3) + (150 - 0.2x_2 - 0.3x_3)$$

$$
\begin{aligned}
\text{subject to:} \quad & 0.2x_1 + 0.1x_3 \le 200 \\
& 0.5x_1 + 0.5x_2 + 0.4x_3 \le 800 \\
& 0.2x_2 + 0.3x_3 \le 150
\end{aligned}
$$

with: all variables nonnegative

The objective is equivalent to

$$\text{maximize:} \quad z = 0.7x_1 + 0.7x_2 + 0.8x_3$$

1.23
$$\text{minimize:} \quad z = 145x_{11} + 122x_{12} + 130x_{13} + \cdots + 80x_{54} + 111x_{55}$$

$$\text{subject to:} \quad \sum_{i=1}^{5} x_{ij} = 1 \quad (j = 1, 2, 3, 4, 5)$$

$$\sum_{j=1}^{5} x_{ij} = 1 \quad (i = 1, 2, 3, 4, 5)$$

with: all variables nonnegative and integral

1.24
$$\text{minimize:} \quad z = 210\,000x_1 + 190\,000x_2 + 182\,000x_3$$

$$
\begin{aligned}
\text{subject to:} \quad & 40x_1 + 65x_2 \ge 1500 \\
& 35x_1 + 53x_3 \ge 1100 \\
& x_1 \le 30 \\
& x_2 \le 30 \\
& x_3 \le 30
\end{aligned}
$$

with: all variables nonnegative and integral

1.25
$$\text{maximize:} \quad z = 250x_1 + (600 - x_2)x_2$$

$$
\begin{aligned}
\text{subject to:} \quad & 0.25x_1 + 0.40x_2 \le 500 \\
& 0.75x_1 + 0.60x_2 \le 1200
\end{aligned}
$$

with: both variables nonnegative

1.26 The gravitational potential energy of the system is (for a suitably chosen reference level) proportional to $a + b + c$, and this energy is a minimum at equilibrium.

CHAPTER 2

2.7 Set $x_2 = x_4 - x_5$ and $x_3 = x_6 - x_7$, with each new variable nonnegative. Multiply the first constraint by -1.

$$\mathbf{X} \equiv [x_1, x_4, x_5, x_6, x_7, x_8, x_9]^T \qquad \mathbf{C} \equiv [2, -1, 1, 4, -4, 0, 0]^T$$

$$\mathbf{A} \equiv \begin{bmatrix} -5 & -2 & 2 & 3 & -3 & 1 & 0 \\ 2 & -2 & 2 & 1 & -1 & 0 & 1 \end{bmatrix} \qquad \mathbf{B} \equiv \begin{bmatrix} 7 \\ 8 \end{bmatrix} \qquad \mathbf{X}_0 \equiv \begin{bmatrix} x_8 \\ x_9 \end{bmatrix}$$

2.8

$$\mathbf{X} \equiv [x_1, x_2, x_3, x_4, x_5]^T \qquad \mathbf{C} \equiv [10, 11, 0, 0, 0]^T$$

$$\mathbf{A} \equiv \begin{bmatrix} 1 & 2 & 1 & 0 & 0 \\ 3 & 4 & 0 & 1 & 0 \\ 6 & 1 & 0 & 0 & 1 \end{bmatrix} \qquad \mathbf{B} \equiv \begin{bmatrix} 150 \\ 200 \\ 175 \end{bmatrix} \qquad \mathbf{X}_0 \equiv \begin{bmatrix} x_3 \\ x_4 \\ x_5 \end{bmatrix}$$

2.9

$$\mathbf{X} \equiv [x_1, x_2, x_3, x_4, x_5, x_6, x_7, x_8]^T \qquad \mathbf{C} \equiv [10, 11, 0, 0, 0, -M, -M, -M]^T$$

$$\mathbf{A} = \begin{bmatrix} 1 & 2 & -1 & 0 & 0 & 1 & 0 & 0 \\ 3 & 4 & 0 & -1 & 0 & 0 & 1 & 0 \\ 6 & 1 & 0 & 0 & -1 & 0 & 0 & 1 \end{bmatrix} \qquad \mathbf{B} \equiv \begin{bmatrix} 150 \\ 200 \\ 175 \end{bmatrix} \qquad \mathbf{X}_0 \equiv \begin{bmatrix} x_6 \\ x_7 \\ x_8 \end{bmatrix}$$

2.10

$$\mathbf{X} \equiv [x_1, x_2, x_3, x_4, x_5, x_6, x_7, x_8]^T \qquad \mathbf{C} \equiv [3, 2, 4, 6, 0, 0, M, M]^T$$

$$\mathbf{A} \equiv \begin{bmatrix} 1 & 2 & 1 & 1 & -1 & 0 & 1 & 0 \\ 2 & 1 & 3 & 7 & 0 & -1 & 0 & 1 \end{bmatrix} \qquad \mathbf{B} \equiv \begin{bmatrix} 1000 \\ 1500 \end{bmatrix} \qquad \mathbf{X}_0 \equiv \begin{bmatrix} x_7 \\ x_8 \end{bmatrix}$$

2.11

$$\mathbf{X} \equiv [x_1, x_2, x_3, x_4, x_5]^T \qquad \mathbf{C} \equiv [6, 3, 4, M, M]^T$$

$$\mathbf{A} \equiv \begin{bmatrix} 1 & 6 & 1 & 1 & 0 \\ 2 & 3 & 1 & 0 & 1 \end{bmatrix} \qquad \mathbf{B} \equiv \begin{bmatrix} 10 \\ 15 \end{bmatrix} \qquad \mathbf{X}_0 \equiv \begin{bmatrix} x_4 \\ x_5 \end{bmatrix}$$

2.12 Set $x_4 = x_5 - x_6$, with each new variable nonnegative. Then x_3 and x_5 can be used as part of the initial solution once the second constraint is divided by 2.

$$\mathbf{X} \equiv [x_1, x_2, x_3, x_5, x_6, x_7]^T \qquad \mathbf{C} \equiv [7, 2, 3, 1, -1, -M]^T$$

$$\mathbf{A} \equiv \begin{bmatrix} 2 & 7 & 0 & 0 & 0 & 1 \\ 2.5 & 4 & 0 & 1 & -1 & 0 \\ 1 & 0 & 1 & 0 & 0 & 0 \end{bmatrix} \qquad \mathbf{B} \equiv \begin{bmatrix} 7 \\ 5 \\ 11 \end{bmatrix} \qquad \mathbf{X}_0 \equiv \begin{bmatrix} x_7 \\ x_5 \\ x_3 \end{bmatrix}$$

2.13

$$\mathbf{X} \equiv [x_1, x_2, x_3, x_4, x_5, x_6, x_7, x_8, x_9, x_{10}]^T \qquad \mathbf{C} \equiv [10, 2, -1, 0, 0, 0, 0, M, M, M]^T$$

$$\mathbf{A} \equiv \begin{bmatrix} 1 & 1 & 0 & 1 & 0 & 0 & 0 & 0 & 0 & 0 \\ 1 & 1 & 0 & 0 & -1 & 0 & 0 & 1 & 0 & 0 \\ 0 & 1 & 1 & 0 & 0 & 1 & 0 & 0 & 0 & 0 \\ 0 & 1 & 1 & 0 & 0 & 0 & -1 & 0 & 1 & 0 \\ 1 & 1 & 1 & 0 & 0 & 0 & 0 & 0 & 0 & 1 \end{bmatrix} \qquad \mathbf{B} \equiv \begin{bmatrix} 50 \\ 10 \\ 30 \\ 7 \\ 60 \end{bmatrix} \qquad \mathbf{X}_0 \equiv \begin{bmatrix} x_4 \\ x_8 \\ x_6 \\ x_9 \\ x_{10} \end{bmatrix}$$

CHAPTER 3

3.16 No; $[1, 2]^T$ is not on the line segment between the other two points.

3.17

$$x_1 \begin{bmatrix} 1 \\ 2 \end{bmatrix} + x_2 \begin{bmatrix} 2 \\ 4 \end{bmatrix} + x_3 \begin{bmatrix} 1 \\ 0 \end{bmatrix} + x_4 \begin{bmatrix} 0 \\ -1 \end{bmatrix} + x_5 \begin{bmatrix} 0 \\ 1 \end{bmatrix} = \begin{bmatrix} 3 \\ 6 \end{bmatrix}$$

3.18   (*b*) and (*c*) are basic feasible solutions; (*b*) is degenerate.

3.19

$$x_1 \begin{bmatrix} 1 \\ 2 \\ -1 \end{bmatrix} + x_2 \begin{bmatrix} 2 \\ 1 \\ 1 \end{bmatrix} + x_3 \begin{bmatrix} 1 \\ 0 \\ 1 \end{bmatrix} + x_4 \begin{bmatrix} 3 \\ 3 \\ 0 \end{bmatrix} + x_5 \begin{bmatrix} 1 \\ 0 \\ 0 \end{bmatrix} + x_6 \begin{bmatrix} 0 \\ 1 \\ 0 \end{bmatrix} + x_7 \begin{bmatrix} 0 \\ 0 \\ 1 \end{bmatrix} = \begin{bmatrix} 9 \\ 9 \\ 0 \end{bmatrix}$$

3.20   (*a*), (*c*), and (*d*) are basic feasible, degenerate solutions.

3.21   Let $f(\mathbf{X}) = \mathbf{C}^T\mathbf{X}$ assume its minimum, *m*, at $\mathbf{P}_1$ and $\mathbf{P}_2$. Then, for $\beta_1 \geq 0$, $\beta_2 \geq 0$, $\beta_1 + \beta_2 = 1$,

$$f(\beta_1\mathbf{P}_1 + \beta_2\mathbf{P}_2) = \beta_1 f(\mathbf{P}_1) + \beta_2 f(\mathbf{P}_2) = \beta_1 m + \beta_2 m = m$$

3.22   If the subset were linearly dependent, then the nonzero constants which satisfied (*3.1*) for this subset would also satisfy (*3.1*) for the entire set, with all extra constants taken as zero. This would imply that the set is linearly dependent, which it is not.

3.23   In (*3.1*), take the constant in front of the zero vector to be nonzero and all other constants as zero.

CHAPTER 4

4.9 $x_1^* = \dfrac{5}{3}$, $x_2^* = \dfrac{2}{3}$; $z^* = \dfrac{7}{3}$

4.11 $x_1^* = \dfrac{16}{5}$, $x_2^* = \dfrac{13}{5}$; $z^* = \dfrac{42}{5}$

4.10 $x_1^* = \dfrac{9}{4}$, $x_2^* = \dfrac{3}{2}$; $z^* = \dfrac{51}{4}$

4.12 $x_1^* = 1285.7$, $x_2^* = 1857.1$; $z^* = -3142.8$

4.13   No feasible solution exists.

4.14 $x_1^* = 0$, $x_2^* = 700$, $x_3^* = 500$, $x_4^* = 1000$, $x_5^* = 0$, $x_6^* = 0$; $z^* = 27\,600$. (Not only is this solution degenerate, but the solution includes a zero artificial variable among the basic variables. This may occur when one or more of the constraints is redundant. Here, the last constraint is the sum of the first two constraints minus the sum of the next two.)

4.15 $x_1^* = 23.8095$, $x_2^* = 32.1429$; $z^* = 591.667$.

4.16 $x_1^* = 0$, $x_2^* = 423.077$, $x_3^* = 0$, $x_4^* = 153.846$; $z^* = 1769.23$.

4.17   No maximum exists.

4.18 $x_1^* = 6.66667$, $x_2^* = 0.555556$, $x_3^* = 0$; $z^* = 41.6667$.

4.19 $x_1^* = 30$, $x_2^* = 0$, $x_3^* = 30$; $z^* = 270$.

4.20 $x_1^* = 69\,090.9$ bbl, $x_2^* = 17\,272.7$ bbl, $x_3^* = 2272.73$ bbl, $x_4^* = 2727.27$ bbl; $z^* = \$235\,454$.

4.21 $x_1^* = 0.90909$ oz, $x_2^* = 1.81818$ oz, $x_3^* = x_4^* = x_5^* = x_6^* = 0$; $z^* = 7.27273$¢.

4.22 $x_1^* = 50$, $x_2^* = 0$, $x_3^* = 145$, $x_4^* = 10$; $z^* = \$1250$.

4.23 $x_1^* = 93.75$ gal, $x_2^* = 125$ gal, $x_3^* = 56.25$ gal, $x_4^* = 0$, $x_5^* = 225$ gal; $z^* = \$403.125$.

4.24 $x_1^* = 937.5$ lb, $x_2^* = 562.5$ lb, $x_3^* = 125$ lb; $z^* = 0$ lb.

CHAPTER 5

5.13

$$\text{maximize:} \quad z = 4w_1 + 10w_2 + 6w_3$$

$$\text{subject to:} \quad 2w_1 + 4w_2 + \; w_3 \le 12$$
$$6w_1 + 2w_2 + \; w_3 \le 26$$
$$5w_1 + \; w_2 + 2w_3 \le 80$$

$$\text{with:} \quad \text{all variables nonegative}$$

5.14 Multiply the last constraint in the primal by -1.

$$\text{maximize:} \quad z = 6w_1 + 5w_2 - 7w_3$$

$$\text{subject to:} \quad 2w_1 \qquad - \; w_3 \le 3$$
$$5w_1 + 4w_2 + 6w_3 \le 2$$
$$- 2w_2 - 3w_3 \le 1$$
$$w_1 + 2w_2 - 7w_3 \le 2$$
$$w_1 + 3w_2 - 5w_3 \le 3$$

$$\text{with:} \quad \text{all variables nonnegative}$$

5.15

$$\text{minimize:} \quad z = 25w_1 + 30w_2 + 35w_3$$

$$\text{subject to:} \quad 7w_1 + 2w_2 + 6w_3 \ge 6$$
$$-11w_1 - 8w_2 - \; w_3 \le 1$$
$$3w_1 + 6w_2 + 7w_3 \ge 3$$

$$\text{with:} \quad \text{all variables nonnegative}$$

(The right-hand side of the second constraint has been rendered positive.)

5.16 Introduce surplus variable x_5 in the first constraint.

$$\text{minimize:} \quad z = 16w_1 + 20w_2$$

$$\text{subject to:} \quad 8w_1 + 3w_2 \ge 10$$
$$6w_1 \qquad \ge 15$$
$$-w_1 + 2w_2 \ge 20$$
$$w_1 - \; w_2 \ge 25$$
$$-w_1 \qquad \ge 0$$

(Observe that this program has no feasible solution.)

5.17   maximize: $z = w_1 + 4w_2$

subject to: $3w_2 \le 1$
$$w_1 + \; w_2 \le 2$$
$$w_1 + 3w_2 \le 1$$

5.18 $z^* = 72$ in both cases.

5.19 $x_2^* = 1.25$, $x_1^* = x_3^* = x_4^* = x_5^* = 0$; $z^* = 2.5$.

5.20 Multiply each constraint by -1. Then the symmetric dual is:

$$\text{minimize:} \quad z = -6w_1 - 12w_2 - 4w_3$$

$$\text{subject to:} \quad -6w_1 - 4w_2 - \; w_3 \ge 5$$
$$-w_1 - 3w_2 - 2w_3 \ge 2$$

$$\text{with:} \quad \text{all variables nonnegative}$$

This program has no feasible solution.

5.21

$$\text{maximize:} \quad z = 5w_1 - 5w_2$$
$$\text{subject to:} \quad w_1 + w_2 \le -1$$
$$-w_1 - w_2 \le -1$$

5.22 The second slack variable in the optimal solution to the primal, x_5^*, is positive; hence w_2^* must be zero (as it is, in the last row of Tableau 2).

5.23 $x_1^* = 1/3$, $x_2^* = 0$, $x_3^* = 2/3$; $w_1^* = 0$, $w_2^* = 1/3$.

5.24 From the result of Problem 5.9,

$$\mathbf{B}^T \mathbf{W}_0 = \mathbf{C}^T \mathbf{X}_0 \ge \mathbf{B}^T \mathbf{W} \qquad \text{and} \qquad \mathbf{C}^T \mathbf{X}_0 = \mathbf{B}^T \mathbf{W}_0 \le \mathbf{C}^T \mathbf{X}$$

Therefore, $\mathbf{W}_0$ is optimal and $\mathbf{X}_0$ is optimal.

CHAPTER 6

6.9 $x_1^* = 1$, $x_2^* = 3$, $x_3^* = 0$; $z^* = 7$.

6.10 $x_1^* = x_2^* = x_4^* = 0$, $x_3^* = 2$; $z^* = 6$.

6.11 $x_1^* = 0$, $x_2^* = 7$, $x_3^* = 1$; $z^* = 71$.

6.12 Infeasible.

6.13 Develop sites B, C, D, and F, for a net capacity of 55 ton/wk.

CHAPTER 7

7.8 $x_1^* = 1$, $x_2^* = 4$, $x_3^* = 0$; $z^* = 37$.

7.9 $x_1^* = 3$, $x_2^* = 0$; $z^* = \$360$.

7.10 $x_1^* = 1$, $x_2^* = 3$, $x_3^* = 0$; $z^* = 7$.

7.11 $x_1^* = x_2^* = x_4^* = 0$, $x_3^* = 2$; $z^* = 6$.

7.12 $x_1^* = 0$, $x_2^* = 7$, $x_3^* = 1$; $z^* = 71$.

7.13 $x_1^* = 1$, $x_2^* = 3$, $x_3^* = 0$; $z^* = 7$.

CHAPTER 8

8.9 Transportation cost equals production cost plus shipping cost.

	I	II	III	IV	(dummy) V	Supply	u_i
A	1.21 3200	1.23 200	1.19 (0)	1.29 (0.06)	0 4100	7500	0
B	1.07 1000	1.11 (0.02)	1.05 6300	1.09 2700	0 (0.14)	10 000	−0.14
C	1.17 (0.03)	1.16 8100	1.15 (0.03)	1.18 (0.02)	0 (0.07)	8100	−0.07
Demand	4200	8300	6300	2700	4100		
v_j	1.21	1.23	1.19	1.23	0		

Plant A produces 3200 units for customer I, 200 for customer II, and remains with an unused capacity of 400; plant B produces 1000 units for customer I, 6300 for customer III, and 2700 for customer IV; plant C produces 8100 units for customer II.

8.10

	1	2	3	4	5	Supply	u_i
1	145 (18)	122 (17)	130 (11)	95 0	115 1	1	95
2	80 0	63 (5)	85 (13)	48 1	78 (10)	1	48
3	121 (20)	107 (28)	93 1	69 0	95 (6)	1	69
4	118 (13)	83 1	116 (19)	80 (7)	105 (12)	1	73
5	97 1	75 0	120 (31)	80 (15)	111 (26)	1	65
Demand	1	1	1	1	1		
v_j	32	10	24	0	20		

Lawyer 1 to case 5, lawyer 2 to case 4, lawyer 3 to case 3, lawyer 4 to case 2, and lawyer 5 to case 1.

8.11

	1	2	3	(dummy) 4	Supply	u_i
1	92 (7)	89 (1)	90 **320 000**	0 (3)	320 000	88
2	91 (3)	91 **120 000**	95 (2)	0 **150 000**	270 000	91
3	87 **100 000**	90 **60 000**	92 **30 000**	0 (1)	190 000	90
Demand	100 000	180 000	350 000	150 000		
v_j	−3	0	2	−91		

Vendor 1 to deliver 320 000 gal to airport 3; vendor 2 to deliver 120 000 gal to airport 2 and will remain with 150 000 gal; vendor 3 to deliver 100 000 gal, 60 000 gal, and 30 000 gal, respectively, to airports 1, 2, and 3.

8.12   Maximizing profit is equivalent to minimizing negative profit.

	1	2	3	4	Supply	u_i
A	−10 **1800**	−6 **700**	−6 (1)	−4 (2)	2500	0
B	−2 (8)	−6 (0)	−7 **550**	−6 **1550**	2100	0
(dummy) C	0 (4)	0 **1600**	0 (1)	0 **200**	1800	6
Demand	1800	2300	550	1750		
v_j	−10	−6	−7	−6		

Plant A to supply chains 1 and 2 with 1800 and 700 loaves, respectively; plant B to supply chains 3 and 4 with 550 and 1550 loaves, respectively.

8.13

	City 1 Elders	City 1 Others	City 2 Elders	City 2 Others	City 3 Elders	City 3 Others	Supply	u_i
1	3 (0)	3 **0.175**	3 **0.260**	3 **0.470**	6 **0.195**	6 (3)	1.100	0
2	1 **0.325**	1 **0.575**	4 (3)	4 (3)	7 (3)	7 (6)	0.900	−2
(dummy) 3	100 (100)	0 (0)	100 (100)	0 **0.330**	100 (97)	0 **0.650**	0.980	−3
Demand	0.325	0.750	0.260	0.800	0.195	0.650		
v_j	3	3	3	3	6	3		

8.14 If c is subtracted from each element of the rth row and d from each element of the tth column, then the new objective, z', is related to the old objective, z, by $z' = z - ca_r - db_t$. Thus, $z' - z$ is a constant, and whatever allocation minimizes the one objective also minimizes the other.

CHAPTER 9

9.10

	1	2	3	(dummy) 4	Supply	u_i
Month 1, Regular	35 1	38 (0)	41 (6)	0 (5)	1	−5
Month 1, Overtime	39 1	42 1	45 (6)	0 (1)	2	−1
Month 2, Regular	1000 (960)	43 1	46 (6)	0 1	2	0
Month 2, Overtime	1000 (960)	47 (4)	50 (10)	0 2	2	0
Month 3, Regular	1000 (960)	1000 (957)	40 2	0 1	3	0
Month 3, Overtime	1000 (960)	1000 (957)	45 (5)	0 2	2	0
Demand	2	2	2	6		
v_j	40	43	40	0		

9.11

	Oct.	Nov.	Dec.	Jan.	Feb.	dummy	Supply	u_i
Aug.	73 (0)	83 (0)	93 **4.5**	103 **2.2**	113 **3.1**	0 **2.7**	12.5	0
Sept.	68 **7.1**	78 **3.9**	88 (0)	98 (0)	108 (0)	0 (5)	11.0	−5
Oct.	1000 (935)	75 **9.3**	85 **0.2**	95 (0)	105 (0)	0 (8)	9.5	−8
Nov.	1000 (968)	1000 (958)	52 **8.1**	62 (0)	72 (0)	0 (41)	8.1	−41
Dec.	1000 (982)	1000 (972)	1000 (962)	48 **5.5**	58 (0)	0 (55)	5.5	−55
Demand	7.1	13.2	12.8	7.7	3.1	2.7		
v_j	73	83	93	103	113	0		

9.12

	2	3	4	6	(dummy) 7	Supply	u_i
1	5 **20**	3 (11)	3 (1)	100 (91)	0 (8)	20	2
2	0 **35**	100 (113)	100 (103)	4 **35**	0 (13)	70	−3
3	14 (1)	0 **70**	10 **10**	100 (83)	0 **10**	90	10
4	3 **40**	100 (110)	0 **30**	8 (1)	0 (10)	70	0
5	100 (91)	100 (104)	6 **30**	15 (2)	0 (4)	30	6
Demand	95	70	70	35	10		
v_j	3	−10	0	7	−10		

9.13

	3	4	5	6	7	(dummy) 8	Supply	u_i
1	578 **135**	592 **15**	10 000 (7094)	10 000 (7101)	10 000 (7106)	0 (10)	150	578
2	615 (27)	602 **65**	10 000 (7084)	10 000 (7091)	10 000 (7096)	0 **105**	170	588
3	0 **185**	10 000 (9986)	2328 **75**	2321 **60**	2335 (19)	0 (588)	320	0
4	10 000 (10 014)	0 **240**	2320 (6)	2313 (6)	2302 **80**	0 (602)	320	−14
Demand	320	320	75	60	80	105		
v_j	0	14	2328	2321	2316	−588		

75 units from location 1 through location 3 to location 5; 60 units from location 1 through location 3 to location 6; 15 units from location 1 through location 4 to location 7; 65 units from location 2 through location 4 to location 7.

9.14

	1	2	3	4	5	Supply	u_i
1	0 **34**	7 (7)	12 **7**	25 **8**	65 (25)	49	0
2	7 (7)	0 **34**	22 (10)	25 **12**	75 (35)	46	0
3	12 (24)	22 (34)	0 **34**	17 (4)	28 (0)	34	−12
4	25 (50)	25 (50)	17 (30)	0 **32**	15 **2**	34	−25
5	65 (105)	75 (115)	28 (56)	15 (30)	0 **34**	34	−40
(dummy) 6	0 (40)	0 (40)	0 (28)	0 (15)	0 **7**	7	−40
Demand	34	34	41	52	43		
v_j	0	0	12	25	40		

City 3 receives its seven cars from city 1. City 4 receives a total of 20 cars from cities 1 and 2, keeps 18 of them, and transships two to city 5. City 5 lacks seven cars in the final disposition.

9.15   Store 1 to company 4, store 2 to company 3, store 3 to company 2, and store 4 to company 1; $z^* = \$325\,400$.

9.16   Lawyer 1 to case 5, lawyer 2 to case 4, lawyer 3 to case 3, lawyer 4 to case 2, and lawyer 5 to case 1; $z^* = 436\,\text{h}$.

9.17 $1 \rightarrow 2 \rightarrow 4 \rightarrow 5 \rightarrow 3 \rightarrow 1$, with $z^* = 270$.

9.18 $1 \rightarrow 4 \rightarrow 3 \rightarrow 5 \rightarrow 2 \rightarrow 1$, with $z^* = 14$.

9.21   For the cost matrix

$$\begin{bmatrix} 1000 & 1 & 1 & 1 & 1 \\ 1 & 1000 & 1000 & 1000 & 1 \\ 1 & 1000 & 1000 & 1 & 1000 \\ 1 & 1000 & 1 & 1000 & 1000 \\ 1 & 1 & 1000 & 1000 & 1000 \end{bmatrix}$$

the closed, self-intersecting route $1 \rightarrow 3 \rightarrow 4 \rightarrow 1 \rightarrow 2 \rightarrow 5 \rightarrow 1$ is cheaper than any circuit of length 5.

CHAPTER 10

10.14   (a) Local and global maximum at $x = 1$, boundary (local) and global minimum at $x = 0$, boundary (local) and global minimum at $x = 3$. (b) Boundary (local) and global maximum at $x = 1$, local and global minimum at $x = 3$, boundary (local) and global maximum at $x = 4$. (c) Boundary (local) and global minimum at $x = -1$, local maximum at $x = 1$, local minimum at $x = 3$, boundary (local) and global maximum at $x = 5$.

10.15   (a) Boundary (local) maximum at $x = 0$, local and global minimum at $x = 1$, boundary (local) and global maximum at $x = 3$. (b) Boundary (local) and global maximum at $x = 0$, local and global minimum at $x = 1$, boundary (local) and global maximum at $x = 2$. (c) Boundary (local) maximum at $x = 0$, local and global minimum at $x = 1$. There is no global maximum.

10.16   (a) Local and global minimum at $x = 1$. (b) Local and global maximum at $x = -1$. (c) Boundary (local) and local minimum at $x = 5$, boundary (local) and local maximum at $x = 10$.

10.17 $f''(x) = 6(x - 2)$, which is negative for $x < 2$ and positive for $x > 2$.

10.18   (Strictly) convex on $(0, \infty)$ and (strictly) concave on $(-\infty, 0)$.

10.19 $x^* = 1.9375$, with $z^* = 4.002$.

10.20 $x^* = 3\pi/4 = 2.356$, with $z^* = 3.926$; $\epsilon = \pi/8 = 0.393$.

10.21 $x^* = 1.905$, with $z^* = 4.005$.

10.22 $x^* = 2.175$, with $z^* = 3.893$ and $\epsilon' = 0.242$.

10.23 $x^* = 1.931$, with $z^* = 4.002$.

10.24 $x^* = 2.225$, with $z^* = 3.928$; $\epsilon = 0.283$.

CHAPTER 11

11.15 $x_1^* = 2.5$, $x_2^* = 3$, $x_3^* = 0.4$; $z^* = 0$.

11.16 $z^* = 1$ occurs at many points, one being $x_1^* = x_2^* = 0$.

11.17   There is a local minimum at $x_1 = 12$, $x_2 = 24$, with $z = -0.001157$, but there is no global minimum (the function approaches $-\infty$ as x_1 and x_2 approach zero through negative values).

11.18 $z^* = -0.6495$ occurs at many points, one being $x_1^* = \pi/3$, $x_2^* = \pi/3$.

11.19 $x_1^* = 0$, $x_2^* = \pm 1$; $z^* = 0.7358$.

11.20 $x_1^* = x_2^* = 1.496$, $x_3^* = 1$; $z^* = -1$.

11.21 $x_1^* = 2$, $x_2^* = 3$; $z^* = -10.076$.

11.22 $x_1^* = x_2^* = 1$; $z^* = 0$.

11.23 $A = 1.47 \times 10^{-30}$, $m = 0.04$.   In 1980, $N = 36\,597$.

11.24 $\mathbf{H}_f = 2\mathbf{A}$.

CHAPTER 12

12.16

$$\text{maximize:} \quad z = x_1^4 e^{-0.01(x_1 x_2)^2}$$
$$\text{subject to:} \quad 2x_1^2 + x_2^2 - 10 = 0$$

12.17

$$\text{maximize:} \quad z = -(x_1 - 1)^2 - x_2^2$$
$$\text{subject to:} \quad x_1^2 + x_2^2 - 4 = 0$$

12.18

$$\text{maximize:} \quad z = 6x_1 - 2x_1^2 + 2x_1 x_2 - 2x_2^2$$
$$\text{subject to:} \quad x_1 + x_2 - 2 \le 0$$
$$\text{with:} \quad \text{all variables nonnegative}$$

12.19
$$\text{maximize:} \quad z = -24x_1^2 - 14x_2^2 - 46x_3^2 + 28x_1x_2 + 24x_2x_3 - 34x_2x_3$$
$$\text{subject to:} \quad -11x_1 - 9x_2 - 12x_3 + 1000 \le 0$$
$$x_2 + x_3 - 40 \le 0$$
$$- x_2 - x_3 + 40 \le 0$$

with: all variables nonnegative

12.20
$$\text{maximize:} \quad z = 3x_1x_3 + 4x_2x_3$$
$$\text{subject to:} \quad x_2^2 + x_3^2 - 4 \le 0$$
$$-x_2^2 - x_3^2 + 4 \le 0$$
$$x_1x_3 - 3 \le 0$$
$$- x_1x_3 + 3 \le 0$$

with: all variables nonnegative

12.21 $x_1^* = 2$, $x_2^* = 0$; $z^* = 1$.

12.22 $x_1^* = x_2^* = 0$, $x_3^* = -1$; $z^* = -1$.

12.23 $x_1^* = 0$, $x_2^* = 4$, $x_3^* = 17/3$; $z^* = 68/3$.

12.24 $x_1^* = x_2^* = 0$; $z^* = 1$.

12.25 $x_1^* = \pm 3/\sqrt{2}$, $x_2^* = x_3^* = \pm\sqrt{2}$; $z^* = 17$.   To satisfy the nonnegativity conditions, take the plus sign in each case.

12.26 $x_1^* = \pm\sqrt{5}$, $x_2^* = 0$; $z^* = 25$.

12.27 $z^* = 7.980$ at a number of points, one of which is $x_1^* = x_2^* = 1.911$, $x_3^* = 0.822$.

12.28 $z^* = 11$ at six points, one of which is $x_1^* = 3$, $x_2^* = x_3^* = 1$.

12.29 $x_1^* = 3.512$, $x_2^* = 0.217$, $x_3^* = 3.552$; $z^* = 38.28$.

12.30   No global minimum exists: $z \to 1$ as $x_1 \to 0$, keeping (x_1, x_2, x_3) feasible.

12.31 $x_1^* = 1.5$, $x_2^* = 0.5$; $z^* = 5.5$.

12.32 $x_1^* = 58.18$, $x_2^* = 40$, $x_3^* = 0$; $z^* = 38\,476$.

12.33 $x_1^* = x_2^* = 5000$, $x_3^* = 0$; $z^* = 9 \times 10^7$.

12.34 $x_1^* = 0.823$, $x_2^* = 0.911$; $z^* = 1.393$.   **12.36** $x_1^* = 1.4$, $x_2^* = 0.8$; $z^* = 1.8$.

12.35 $x_1^* = 1/3$, $x_2^* = 5/3$; $z^* = 2.249$.   **12.37** $x_1^* = 1.07$, $x_2^* = 2.80$; $z^* = 9.47$.

CHAPTER 13

13.9

$$\text{maximize:} \quad z = [x_1, x_2, x_3] \begin{bmatrix} -24 & 14 & 12 \\ 14 & -14 & -17 \\ 12 & -17 & -46 \end{bmatrix} \begin{bmatrix} x_1 \\ x_2 \\ x_3 \end{bmatrix} + [0, 0, 0] \begin{bmatrix} x_1 \\ x_2 \\ x_3 \end{bmatrix}$$

$$\text{subject to:} \quad \begin{bmatrix} -11 & -9 & -12 \\ 0 & 1 & 1 \\ 0 & -1 & -1 \end{bmatrix} \begin{bmatrix} x_1 \\ x_2 \\ x_3 \end{bmatrix} \leq \begin{bmatrix} -1000 \\ 40 \\ -40 \end{bmatrix}$$

with: x_1, x_2, and x_3 nonnegative

13.10

$$\hat{A} = \left[\begin{array}{ccc|ccc|ccc|ccc} -11 & -9 & -12 & 1 & 0 & 0 & 0 & 0 & 0 & 0 & 0 & 0 \\ 0 & 1 & 1 & 0 & 1 & 0 & 0 & 0 & 0 & 0 & 0 & 0 \\ 0 & -1 & -1 & 0 & 0 & 1 & 0 & 0 & 0 & 0 & 0 & 0 \\ \hline 48 & -28 & -24 & 0 & 0 & 0 & -1 & 0 & 0 & -11 & 0 & 0 \\ -28 & 28 & 34 & 0 & 0 & 0 & 0 & -1 & 0 & -9 & 1 & -1 \\ -24 & 34 & 92 & 0 & 0 & 0 & 0 & 0 & -1 & -12 & 1 & -1 \end{array} \right] \qquad \hat{B} = \begin{bmatrix} -1000 \\ 40 \\ -40 \\ 0 \\ 0 \\ 0 \end{bmatrix}$$

$$Y = [x_1, x_2, x_3, s_1, s_2, s_3, u_1, u_2, u_3, v_1, v_2, v_3]^T$$

$$\tilde{Y} = [u_1, u_2, u_3, v_1, v_2, v_3, x_1, x_2, x_3, s_1, s_2, s_3]^T$$

13.11 $x_1^* = 58.18$, $x_2^* = 40$, $x_3^* = 0$; $z^* = 38\,476$.

13.12 $x_1^* = 1$, $x_2^* = 1$; $z^* = 3$.

13.13 $x_1^* = 2.5$, $x_2^* = 2.882$, $x_3^* = 1.736$; $z^* = 332.9$.

13.14

$$\text{minimize:} \quad z = [x_1, x_2, x_3] \begin{bmatrix} 486.8 & 302.1 & -209.0 \\ 302.1 & 197.9 & -114.6 \\ -209.0 & -114.6 & 228.5 \end{bmatrix} \begin{bmatrix} x_1 \\ x_2 \\ x_3 \end{bmatrix}$$

$$\text{subject to:} \quad x_1 + x_2 + x_3 = 6\,000\,000$$

$$1.75 x_1 + 1.65 x_2 + 1.45 x_3 \leq 10\,000\,000$$

with: all variables nonnegative

13.15 Show first that the nonnegativity conditions (3) may be dropped. Then,

$$Q \equiv \begin{bmatrix} 100 & 0 \\ 0 & 200 \end{bmatrix} \qquad D \equiv \begin{bmatrix} 0 \\ 0 \end{bmatrix} \qquad A \equiv [1, 1] \qquad B \equiv [15\,000] = 15\,000$$

$$AQ^{-1}A^T = [1, 1] \begin{bmatrix} 1/100 & 0 \\ 0 & 1/200 \end{bmatrix} \begin{bmatrix} 1 \\ 1 \end{bmatrix} = 3/200$$

and

$$z^* = \frac{\begin{vmatrix} 3/200 & -15\,000 \\ 15\,000 & 0 \end{vmatrix}}{3/200} = 1.5 \times 10^{10}$$

13.16

$$8 + z^* = \frac{\begin{vmatrix} -4 & -(5-4) \\ (5-4) & 0 \end{vmatrix}}{-4} - (-4) = 3.75 \qquad \text{or} \qquad z^* = -4.25$$

CHAPTER 14

14.11 $z^* = \$700$; $x_1^* = 3$ days, $x_2^* = 0$, $x_3^* = 2$ days.

14.12 $z^* = \$675$; $x_1^* = 2$ days, $x_2^* = 1$ day, $x_3^* = 2$ days; or $x_1^* = 3$ days, $x_2^* = 1$ day, $x_3^* = 1$ day.

14.13 $z^* = \$150$; $x_1^* = x_2^* = 0$, $x_3^* = 2$, $x_4^* = 1$.

14.14 $z^* = \$398$; $x_1^* = 12$, $x_2^* = 2$.

14.15 $z^* = 51$; $x_1^* = 3$, $x_2^* = 0$, $x_3^* = 2$.

14.16 $z^* = 130$; $x_1^* = 0$, $x_2^* = 1$, $x_3^* = 1$, $x_4^* = 0$, $x_5^* = 0$.

14.17 $x_1^* = 3$, $x_2^* = 1$, $x_3^* = 2$.

14.18 Using the notation of Problem 14.8, we have, for $j = 4, 3, 2, 1$,

$$m_j(u) = \max_{0 \le x \le u} \{I(x) - M(x) - R(u) + R(x) + m_{j+1}(x+1)\}$$

with $m_5 \equiv 0$ and $R(0) = 0$. Then $z^* = \$33\,600$, either by purchasing a 1-year-old machine each year or by purchasing a 1-year-old machine each year for the first 3 years and keeping the last of these machines for the fourth year.

14.19 The state variable for stage j has the values $u = 1, 2, \ldots, j$, which are the possible ages of the truck in use at the beginning of year j. Let

$I_k(u) \equiv$ anticipated income from a u-year-old machine purchased in stage k
$R_k(u) \equiv$ cost of replacing a u-year-old machine purchased in stage k with a new model
$M_k(u) \equiv$ cost of maintaining a u-year-old machine purchased in stage k

and set $I_j(3) = -M$ (a large negative number). Then, for $j = 5, 4, 3, 2, 1$, with $m_6(u) \equiv 0$,

$$m_j(u) = \max \{I_{j-u}(u) - M_{j-u}(u) + m_{j+1}(u+1), I_j(0) - M_j(0) - R_{j-u}(u) + m_{j+1}(1)\}$$

The solution is $z^* = \$26\,000$, with $x_1^* = \text{KEEP}$, $x_2^* = \text{BUY}$, $x_3^* = \text{KEEP}$, $x_4^* = \text{BUY}$, $x_5^* = \text{KEEP}$.

14.20 Let each job correspond to a stage, and specify the state at stage j by the triplet (a_1, a_2, a_3), where a_i $(i = 1, 2, 3)$ is 1 or 0 according as worker i is or is not available for assignment to job j. Then,

$$z^* = \min \{c_{11} + \min \{c_{22} + c_{33}, c_{32} + c_{23}\}, c_{21} + \min \{c_{12} + c_{33}, c_{32} + c_{13}\}, c_{31} + \min \{c_{12} + c_{23}, c_{22} + c_{13}\}\}$$

The Hungarian method is far preferable for larger assignment problems.

14.21 $\$4\,985\,980$; by producing $2, 3, 3, 6$ computers. (Note that discounting has changed the optimal policy.)

14.22 $\$30\,047.62$; same optimal policies as in Problem 14.18.

CHAPTER 15

15.8 $z^* = 13$, for the tree $\{AD, BD, CE, DE, DG, EH, GF\}$.

15.9 $z^* = 55$, for a number of trees including $\{AD, AC, DG, BF, BE, FG, GH, HI, GJ, HK, KL\}$.

15.10 $z^* = 25$, for the path $\{AD, DG, GH, HK, KL\}$ or the path $\{AB, BF, FG, GH, HK, KL\}$.

15.11 $z^* = 14$ units.

15.12 $z^* = 21$ units.

15.13 $z^* = 123$ units.

15.14 $z^* = 17$ units.

15.15 $z^* = \$2400$ (50 units at \$48 each), via Los Angeles to Phoenix to Chicago to New York.

15.16 Initially, either KEEP, KEEP, KEEP or KEEP, BUY, BUY; thereafter, buy a new truck each year.

15.17 (a) 22; (c) 19.

15.18 19 units.

15.19 The cut is $\{BG, EG, CG, FG, DG\}$. Its cut value, 1, represents an upper bound on the flow, and since a flow of 1 unit is feasible (by Problem 15.5), it is the maximal flow.

CHAPTER 16

16.11 (a) B_1 and B_4 are dominated by B_2. Unstable.

$$\mathbf{X}^* = \left[\frac{10}{11}, \frac{1}{11}\right] \qquad \mathbf{Y}^* = \left[0, \frac{10}{11}, \frac{1}{11}, 0\right] \qquad G^* = -\frac{12}{11}$$

(b) B_3 is dominated by B_1, and B_4 is dominated by B_2. Unstable.

$$\mathbf{X}^* = \left[\frac{1}{2}, \frac{1}{2}\right] \qquad \mathbf{Y}^* = \left[\frac{1}{2}, \frac{1}{2}, 0, 0\right] \qquad G^* = 0$$

(c) B_1, B_2, and B_4 are dominated by B_3. Stable, with $G^* = -1$. Row player should use A_2 only; column player should use B_3 only.

(d) Unstable.

$$\mathbf{X}^* = \mathbf{Y}^* = [2/7, 4/7, 1/7] \qquad G^* = -4/7$$

(e) A_3 is dominated by A_2, and B_1 is dominated by B_3.

$$\mathbf{X}^* = [2/7, 5/7, 0] \qquad \mathbf{Y}^* = [0, 5/7, 2/7] \qquad G^* = 32/7$$

(f) A_1, A_3, and A_4 are dominated by A_2. Stable, with $G^* = 0$. Row player should use A_2 only; column player should use B_1 only.

16.12 $\mathbf{X}^* = [1/4, 3/4]$, $\mathbf{Y}^* = [3/4, 1/4, 0]$; $G^* = 68.125$.

16.13 Both chains should locate in town C, with chain I capturing 65 percent of the total business.

16.14 Write "A_1" on one slip of paper, "A_2" on three slips, and "A_4" on eleven slips. Draw a slip (with replacement) before each play.

16.15 Army A uses the forest route with probability 1/4 and the flatlands route with probability 3/4; army B attacks either route with probability 1/2. The value of the game (to army B) is $G^* = 5/2$ strikes.

16.16 Blue Army attacks the 20-million-dollar airfield at full force with probability 4/9 and attacks the other airfield at full force with probability 5/9. Red Army defends the expensive airfield at full force with probability 2/3 and splits its forces between airfields with probability 1/3. $G^* = 6\frac{2}{3}$ million dollars.

16.17 Both should offer 2 yards.

16.18 I-95 with probability 0.53 and the back roads with probability 0.47.

16.19 $\mathbf{X} = [5/12, 7/12, 0]$, $\mathbf{Y}^* = [4/9, 5/9, 0]$.

16.20 From $g_{ij} = -g_{ji}$ ($i, j = 1, 2, \ldots, r$), it follows that $E(\mathbf{X}, \mathbf{Y}) = -E(\mathbf{Y}, \mathbf{X})$ for any two r-dimensional probability vectors. Then,

$$M_I = \max_{\mathbf{X}} \, (\min_{\mathbf{Y}} E(\mathbf{X}, \mathbf{Y})) = \max_{\mathbf{X}} \, (\min_{\mathbf{Y}} - E(\mathbf{Y}, \mathbf{X}))$$

$$= -\min_{\mathbf{X}} \, (\max_{\mathbf{Y}} E(\mathbf{Y}, \mathbf{X})) = -\min_{\mathbf{Y}} \, (\max_{\mathbf{X}} E(\mathbf{X}, \mathbf{Y})) = -M_{II}$$

But $M_I = M_{II}$, by the minimax theorem. Hence,

$$M_I = M_{II} = 0 = G^*$$

16.21 No; $G^* = -\$0.25$.

CHAPTER 17

17.16 To take offer under minimax or middle-of-the-road, not to take offer under optimistic.

17.17 To extend credit.   **17.19** Not to take offer.

17.18 To convert.   **17.20** Not to extend credit.

17.21 See Fig. A-1 (gains in thousands of dollars). To test stand-alone phase, then to convert to new process only if stand-alone phase is efficient.

17.22 Not to order lie detector tests, and to fire the treasurer.

17.23 To test market, then to go national only if test is highly or moderately successful.

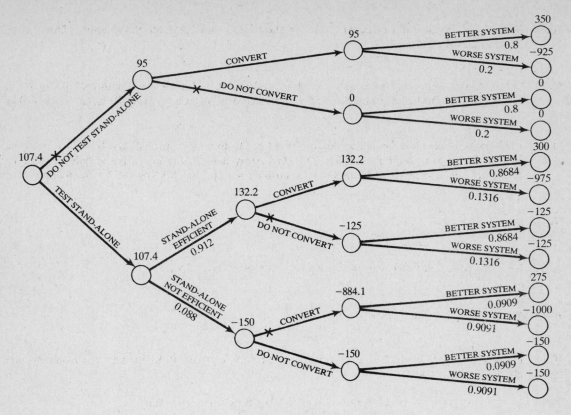

Fig. A-1

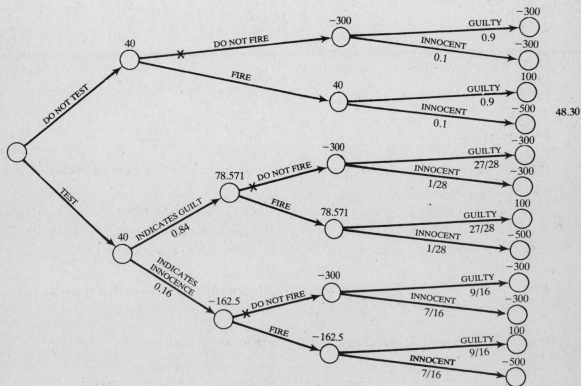

Fig. A-2

17.24 $82 250.

17.25   The test has value zero; see Fig. A-2 (gains in thousands of dollars).

17.26   Estimate $u(-15) = 0$, $u(-14) = 0.07$, $u(-4) = 0.31$, $u(-3) = 0.32$, $u(19) = 0.42$, $u(20) = 0.425$, $u(49) = 0.87$, and $u(50) = 1$.   Same answer as Problem 17.23.

17.27 $u_2 = 85$, $u_3 = 55$, $u_4 = -20$.

17.28 $C(0.34) = -$2 000 000$, $R(0.34) = $8 460 000$.

17.29   Risk-averse on $[-15, 10)$, risk-indifferent on $(10, 31)$, risk-seeking on $(31, 50]$.

17.30   Consider the risk-averse situation.   Let M_i $(i = 1, 2, \ldots, n)$ designate the dollar gain associated with the ith state of nature, S_i, for a specific decision D.   Denote the utility of M_i by u_i and the probability of S_i by p_i.   Since the utility function is strictly concave, its inverse, $M = f(u)$, is strictly convex.   Therefore,

$$C = f(p_1u_1 + p_2u_2 + \cdots + p_nu_n) \le p_1f(u_1) + p_2f(u_2) + \cdots + p_nf(u_n) = E(D)$$

the expected dollar gain of the decision.   Hence, $R = E(D) - C \ge 0$.   The risk-seeking case is proved similarly.

17.31

	S_1	S_2	S_3
D_1	-130	-45	0
D_2	-90	-15	-45
D_3	-20	0	-110
D_4	0	-5	-125

17.32   With a regret table, choose D_2 under minimax, either D_1 or D_2 under optimistic, and D_2 under middle-of-the-road.

CHAPTER 18

18.6 $m_1(8) = 77.40, with a 3, 2, 3 policy.

18.7   Let the state u be the number of thousand-dollar units at hand.   Then $m_1(2) = 2600, under the optimal policy

u / d	0	1	2	3	4	5	6
$d_1(u)$	$\cdots$	$\cdots$	A, B	$\cdots$	$\cdots$	$\cdots$	$\cdots$
$d_2(u)$	$\cdots$	A, B	A, B	A, B	A, B	$\cdots$	$\cdots$
$d_3(u)$	O	B	A, B	A, B	A, B	A, B	A, B

Here, O represents the decision to make no investment.

18.8 $m_1(2) = 0.352$, for the policy

	0	1	2	3	4	5	6
$d_1(u)$	$\cdots$	$\cdots$	A	$\cdots$	$\cdots$	$\cdots$	$\cdots$
$d_2(u)$	$\cdots$	A	A	O, A, B	A	$\cdots$	$\cdots$
$d_3(u)$	$\cdots$	$\cdots$	$\cdots$	A	A	O	O

18.9   Minimize the probability of not finding oil.   Then the maximum probability of finding oil is

$$1 - m_1(8) = 1 - 0.6 = 0.4$$

with all money allocated to site 1.

18.10   The state u is the number of units of work yet to be accomplished.   Then, $m_1(10) = 5.0368$, with one of many optimal policies being

d \ u	0	1	2	3	4	5	6	7	8	9	10
$d_1(u)$	$\cdots$	$\cdots$	$\cdots$	$\cdots$	$\cdots$	$\cdots$	$\cdots$	$\cdots$	$\cdots$	$\cdots$	2
$d_2(u)$	0	1	1	1	1	1	1	2	2	3	3
$d_3(u)$	0	1	1	1	1	2	2	3	3	4	4
$d_4(u)$	0	1	1	4	4	5	5	6	$\cdots$	$\cdots$	$\cdots$

18.11   Take as the state u the age of the current machine.   Then, $m_1(1) = \$3118.83$, under a policy that always retains the current (operable) machine.

18.12   The state u is the number of computers in inventory.   Then $m_1(0) = \$127\,110$, under the policy

d \ u	−5	−4	−3	−2	−1	0	1	2	3	4	5	6
$d_1(u)$	$\cdots$	$\cdots$	$\cdots$	$\cdots$	$\cdots$	3	$\cdots$	$\cdots$	$\cdots$	$\cdots$	$\cdots$	$\cdots$
$d_2(u)$	$\cdots$	4	4	4	3	3	0	0	0	$\cdots$	$\cdots$	$\cdots$
$d_3(u)$	4	4	3	3	2	0	0	0	0	0	0	0
$d_4(u)$	4	4	3	2	1	0	0	0	0	0	0	0
$d_5(u)$	$\cdots$	$\cdots$	$\cdots$	$\cdots$	1	0	0	0	0	0	0	0

18.13   Maximum reliability of 0.351, from 3 physical units of component 1, 2 units of component 2, and 1 unit of component 3.

18.14   Subcontractors 1, 2, and 3 assigned components 2, 1, and 3, respectively.

18.15   Set

$u \equiv$ antibody units still required to make up a total of 6 (from 0 to 6, in tenths)
$m_j(u) \equiv$ minimum expected number of workdays lost beginning at stage (day) j in state u
$x \equiv$ number of pills taken in a day (from 0 to 5; *why?*)
$f(x) \equiv$ units of antibody absorbed from x pills
$p(x) \equiv$ probability of missing work the next day (which is equivalent to the expected number of days missed from work) if x pills are taken

Then, for $j = 1, 2, 3, 4,$

$$m_j(u) = \min_{x=0,\dots,5} [p(x) + m_{j+1}(u - f(x))]$$

with $m_j(u) \equiv 0$ for $u < 0$ $(j = 2, 3)$ and

$$m_5(u) = \begin{cases} 0 & u \le 0 \\ 10\,000 & u > 0 \end{cases}$$

18.16   Set

$u \equiv$ number of work units needed to complete project 1 (from 0 to 16, in tenths)
$v \equiv$ number of work units needed to complete project 2 (from 0 to 23, in tenths)
$m_j(u, v) \equiv$ minimum expected cost to complete both projects beginning at stage (day) j in state (u, v)
$f_i(z) \equiv$ number of work units completed by z crews on project i $(i = 1, 2)$
$x_i \equiv$ number of contractor's own crews assigned to project i $(i = 1, 2)$
$y_i \equiv$ number of subcontracted crews assigned to project i $(i = 1, 2)$

Then, for $j = 1, \dots, 5$,

$$m_j(u, v) = (0.9)(5000) + (0.1)(4000) + \min [1500(y_1 + y_2) + m_{j+1}(u - g_1(x_1, y_1), v - g_2(x_2, y_2))]$$

where

$$g_1(x_1, y_1) = \begin{cases} f_1(x_1 + y_1) & x_1 = 0, 1, 2, 3, 4 \\ 0.9f_1(5 + y_1) + 0.1f_1(4 + y_1) & x_1 = 5 \end{cases}$$

$$g_2(x_2, y_2) = \begin{cases} f_2(y_2) & x_2 = 0 \\ 0.9f_2(x_2 + y_2) + 0.1f_2(x_2 + y_2 - 1) & x_2 = 1, 2, 3, 4, 5 \end{cases}$$

and the minimum is taken over all nonnegative integral values of x_1, x_2, y_1, y_2 such that

$$x_1 + x_2 = 5 \qquad x_1 + y_1 \le 6 \qquad x_2 + y_2 \le 6$$

The end condition is

$$m_6(u, v) \equiv \begin{cases} 0 & u \le 0 \text{ and } v \le 0 \\ 1\,000\,000 & u > 0 \text{ or } v > 0 \end{cases}$$

18.17   Set

$u \equiv$ number of money units remaining for allocation
$v \equiv$ number of votes already won
$m_j(u, v) \equiv$ maximum probability of gaining at least 100 votes starting at stage (primary) j in state (u, v)
$V_j \equiv$ number of votes at stake in stage j
$p_j(x) \equiv$ probability of winning V_j if x money units are spent in stage j

Then

$$m_j(u, v) = \max_{0 \le x \le \min \{u, 7\}} \{p_j(x)m_{j+1}(u - x, v + V_j) + [1 - p_j(x)]m_{j+1}(u - x, v)\}$$

for $j = 1, \dots, 5$, with

$$m_6(u, v) \equiv \begin{cases} 0 & v < 100 \\ 1 & v \ge 100 \end{cases}$$

The possible values for v are 0 for stage 1; 0 and 89 for stage 2; 0, 69, 89, and 158 for stage 3; and so on.

CHAPTER 19

19.15   Stochastic, not regular, ergodic; $\mathbf{L} = \begin{bmatrix} 1 & 0 \\ 1 & 0 \end{bmatrix}$.

19.16   Not stochastic.

19.17 Not stochastic.

19.18 Stochastic, not regular, not ergodic.

19.19 Stochastic, not regular, ergodic;

$$L = \begin{bmatrix} 1 & 0 & 0 & 0 \\ 0 & 3/8 & 0 & 5/8 \\ 0 & 0 & 1 & 0 \\ 0 & 3/8 & 0 & 5/8 \end{bmatrix}$$

19.20 Stochastic, regular, ergodic;

$$L = \frac{1}{45} \begin{bmatrix} 19 & 17 & 9 \\ 19 & 17 & 9 \\ 19 & 17 & 9 \end{bmatrix}$$

19.21 Stochastic, not regular, ergodic;

$$L = \begin{bmatrix} 1 & 0 & 0 \\ 1 & 0 & 0 \\ 1 & 0 & 0 \end{bmatrix}$$

19.22 3/11.

19.23 (a) 0.7625, (b) 0.8.

19.24 4/13, or approximately 31 percent of the time.

19.25 0.2, 0.14, 0.154, 0.151, and 0.15162.

19.26 (a) Approximately 34 discharged, 31 ambulatory, 18 bedridden, and 17 dead. (b) Approximately 65 discharged and 35 dead.

19.27 7/12 in good condition, 5/12 in average condition.

19.28 (a) 1, (b) none, (c) 1 and 3, (d) 1.

19.29 Designate one of the absorbing states as state 1. Then P has a 1 in the (1, 1)-position and zeros in the rest of the first row. Any power of P will have this same first row.

19.32 Because $\lambda = 1$ is an eigenvalue of P^T, it is also an eigenvalue of P (the two matrices have the same characteristic equation).

19.33 First prove, by induction, that eigenvectors belonging to distinct eigenvalues of P are linearly independent. Then construct M out of N linearly independent eigenvectors.

19.34 See Problem 19.15.

CHAPTER 20

20.13 Any bird kept more than 5 weeks can bring no more than 7¢ above a 5-week-old chicken.   This is less than the 10¢ differential profit obtained from replacing a 5-week-old bird by a newborn chick and selling it after 1 week.   The optimal policy is to sell when birds are 3 weeks old.   Here the weekly interest rate, obtained by solving $(1 + i)^{52} = 1.09$, is $i = 0.0016586374$; hence

$$\alpha = \frac{1}{1+i} = 0.998344109$$

20.14

State	2	3	4	5
Decision	0	3	4	5

20.15 State 1: enter a year with a 1-year-old company machine
State 2: enter a year with a 2-year-old company machine
State 3: enter a year with a leased 1-year-old machine
State 4: enter a year with a leased 2-year-old machine

State	1	2	3	4
Decision	KEEP	LEASE	KEEP	LEASE

20.16 If $\mathbf{I}$ denotes the $N \times N$ identity matrix and $\mathbf{Y} \equiv [PV(1), PV(2), \dots, PV(N)]^T$, (20.2) may be written as

$$\left(\frac{1}{\alpha}\mathbf{I} - \mathbf{P}\right)\mathbf{Y} = \frac{1}{\alpha}\mathbf{C}$$

The coefficient matrix on the left could be singular only if $1/\alpha$ were equal to λ, an eigenvalue of $\mathbf{P}$.   But

$$\frac{1}{\alpha} = 1 + i > 1$$

while (Theorem 19.1) $|\lambda| \le 1$.

20.17 $PV(1) = \$12\,665$, $PV(2) = \$13\,065$, $PV(3) = \$13\,565$.

20.18

i	1	2	3
d_i	2	4	4

20.19 Adjust the machine whenever it is not in state 1.

20.20 States are the number of mufflers in stock Saturday night, before any new ones are ordered.

State	0	1	2	3	4
Decision	3	0	0	0	0

20.21

i	1	2	3
$\bar{d}_i$	0	4	4

20.22

State	0	1	2	3	4
Decision	3	0	0	0	0

20.23 To promote only those shows having a 16, 17, or 18 rating.

CHAPTER 21

21.10 0.5204, 8.166, 81.66.

21.11 0.9272, 66.69, 666.9.

21.12 0.0621, 3.1, 12.1.

21.13 20.25.

21.14 132 805 cars.

21.15 7 days.

21.16 0.029.

21.17 0.5064, 2.48.

21.18 0.9000, 1.23.

21.19 0.0341, 4.30.

21.20 $\mu = (2/3)$ min^{-1}, $1 - p_0(12) = 0.4530$.

21.21 0.1034.

21.22 0.1815.

21.23 $\lambda = 1/4$, $\mu = 2/7$, 48.95 members.

21.25 (a) n/λ, (b) yes.

21.26 $\lambda_1 \Delta t + \lambda_2 \Delta t = (\lambda_1 + \lambda_2)\Delta t$.

CHAPTER 22

22.6 (a) individuals seeking food; (b) food dispensers and cashier; (c) single queue, multiple servers in series, FIFO, infinite capacity if waiting is allowed outside the cafeteria.

22.7 (a) individuals seeking barber service; (b) barbers; (c) two servers, FIFO, finite capacity of seven.

22.8 (a) individuals seeking gasoline; (b) customers at the pumps; (c) three servers, FIFO, finite capacity if no waiting is permitted outside the station.

22.9 (a) airplanes waiting to land; (b) runways; (c) generally one server, priority to planes requiring emergency landings (otherwise FIFO), infinite capacity.

22.10 (a) automobiles; (b) toll collectors; (c) as many servers as collectors, FIFO, infinite capacity.

22.11 (a) jobs to be typed; (b) typists; (c) as many servers as typists, queue discipline may be FIFO or PRI (with priority given to jobs submitted by top management or with rush designations), infinite capacity.

22.12 (a) troops; (b) individual spaces on troop carriers; (c) as many servers as there are spaces, PRI by rank, infinite capacity.

22.13 (a) cases; (b) judge; (c) single server, usually FIFO, infinite capacity.

22.14 (a) $9:30$, $10:18$; (b) 1.033; (c) 2.533.

22.15 (a) 4, (b) 16 (not including the three jobs that arrive at the moment the shift ends).

22.16 20 min.

22.17 Five (not including the customer denied entrance at the 60-min mark).

CHAPTER 23

23.14 (a) 2.25, (b) 4.5 min, (c) 0.062, (d) 0.25.

23.15 (a) 2, (b) 1.33, (c) 1 h, (d) 0.368.

23.16 (a) 2.25, (b) 2.25 min, (c) 3 min, (d) 0.178.

23.17 (a) 0.9, (b) 1.5, (c) 0.7364, (d) 0.07776.

23.18 (a) 0.528, (b) 0.2, (c) 0.632.

23.19 $16.80.

23.20 Yes, with expected daily savings of $105.

23.21 110 ft^2.

23.22 None on L or L_q; W is reduced by $1/2$.

23.23 $\rho^{n-2}(1-\rho)$.

23.24 $(1-\rho)^{-1}$.

23.26 The expected rate of transitions into state n is $\lambda p_{n-1} + \mu p_{n+1}$ (or μp_1, if $n = 0$); the expected rate of transitions out of state n is $\lambda p_n + \mu p_n$ (or λp_0, if $n = 0$). Equating these and dividing through by μ gives (1) and (2) of Problem 23.7.

23.27
$$F(z) = \frac{p_0}{1-\rho z}$$

23.28 By Theorem 21.1, the departure stream is a Poisson process *while the server is busy*. This is the case a fraction ρ of the time; hence, the expected number of departures in a unit time interval is

$$\rho\mu + (1-\rho)(0) = \lambda$$

CHAPTER 24

24.11 (a) 1/3, (b) 16/45.

24.12 (a) 23.5 s, (b) 0.1420, (c) 3.987.

24.13 With the new system, each teller's idle time drops from 66.67 to 60 percent and L decreases from $2(\frac{1}{2}) = 1$ to 0.9524.

24.14 (a) 0.025, (b) 0.3, (c) 0.675.

24.15 (a) 2.5, (b) 8 min, (c) $25 per hour.

24.16 (a) 13 h 4 min, (b) $495.48 per day.

24.17 No. New cost would be $213.33 from returning unserviced buses, plus $300 for new crew.

24.18 (a) 53 percent, (b) 1.32 per day.

24.19 (a) 2.90, (b) 46.4 s, (c) 50.4 h^{-1}.

24.20 (a) 2.089, (b) 6 min 48 s.

24.21 (a) 2.77, (b) 2.94 min.

24.22
$$p_0 = \frac{1 - 0.8\rho}{1 + 0.2\rho} \quad \text{and} \quad p_n = (0.8)^{n-1}\rho^n p_0 \quad (n = 1, 2, \ldots)$$

24.23 (a) 1.53, (b) 4.72 min.

24.24 (a) 1.51, (b) 3 min 14 s, (c) $3.72 per hour.

24.25 According to (24.1), the criterion for a steady state (see Problem 23.26) is satisfied if merely steps *up* into state n and steps *down* from state n occur at the same expected rate.

24.30 $p_0 = 0.0450$, $p_1 = 0.1350$, $p_2 = p_3 = 0.2024$, $p_4 = 0.1518$, $p_5 = 0.1139$, $p_6 = 0.0854$, $p_7 = 0.0641$.

24.31 $L = \rho$, $W = L/\lambda = 1/\mu$, $W_q = 0$, $L_q = 0$.

24.32 (a) 350, (b) 0.368.

24.33

$$p_0 = \left[\frac{s^s \rho^{s+1}}{s!} \sum_{n=s+1}^{N_0} \frac{N_0!}{(N_0-n)!} \rho^{n-(s+1)} + \sum_{n=0}^{s} \binom{N_0}{n} (s\rho)^n \right]^{-1}$$

$$p_n = \begin{cases} \binom{N_0}{n} (s\rho)^n p_0 & (n = 1, \ldots, s) \\[2mm] \dfrac{N_0!}{(N_0-n)!} \dfrac{s^s \rho^n}{s!} p_0 & (n = s+1, s+2, \ldots, N_0) \end{cases}$$

As $N_0 \to \infty$, these expressions go over into (24.5) and (24.6), provided $\rho < 1$.

24.35 (a) 5.87, (b) 16 percent.

24.36 Let S_n be the number of customers in service when the state is n ($n = 1, 2, \ldots$).

$$\frac{1}{\mu} = W - W_q = \frac{1}{\lambda}(L - L_q) = \frac{1}{\lambda}\left[\sum_{n=1}^{\infty} n p_n - \sum_{n=1}^{\infty} (n - S_n) p_n \right]$$

$$= \frac{1}{\lambda} \sum_{n=1}^{\infty} S_n p_n = \frac{1}{\lambda}(1 - p_0) \sum_{n=1}^{\infty} S_n \frac{p_n}{1 - p_0} = \frac{1}{\lambda}(1 - p_0)\hat{S}$$

Index

Absolute optimum, 97
Absorbing state, 232
A posteriori criterion, 198
A priori criterion, 198
Arc of network, 169
Arrival pattern, 266
Arrival rate, 256
  for an M/M/1 system, 273
Artificial variable, 18, 33
Assignment problem, 84
Assumption of stationarity, 234
Average arrival rate, M/M/1 system, 273
Average service rate, M/M/1 system, 273

Balance equations, M/M/1 system, 278
Balking, 266
  function, 283
Basic feasible solution, 25
Basic variable, 25
Bayes' criterion, 198
Bayes' theorem, 198, 201
Big M method, 39
Birth, in a growth process, 255
  in a queueing system, 266
Birth rate, 256
Bounding, 55
Branch and bound algorithm, 54
Branching, 54
Branch of network, 169

Capacity, of branch, 171
  of queueing system, 266
Certainty equivalent, 209
Cheapest-path problems, 170
Complementary slackness principle, 44, 51
Concave function, 99, 113
Connected branches, 169
  network, 169
Constraint, 1
Constraint qualification, 128
Convex combination, 24
  function, 99, 113
  set, 24
Critical point (*see* Stationary point)
Cut, 182
Cut algorithms, 63

D (queueing notation), 268
Dantzig cut algorithm, 67
Death, in a growth process, 255
  in a queueing system, 266
Death rate, 256
Decision, 154
  with an unbounded horizon, 234

Decision theory, 197
  tree, 198
Degenerate solution, 26, 72
Destinations, 70
Deterministic multistage processes, 154
Directional derivative, 116, 117
Discounted value (*see* Present value)
Discount factor, 156
Discounting, 156
Distribution vector, 224
Dominance, 187
Duality, 44
Duality theorem, 44
Dummy (*see* Fictitious destination or source)
Dynamic programming, deterministic, 154
  with discounting, 156
  stochastic, 213

E_k (queueing notation), 268
Equivalence probability, 199
Ergodic matrix, 225
Erlang distribution, 268 (*See also* Gamma distribution)
Euler's constant, 264
Expected return per period, 235, 236
Exploratory moves, 112
Exponential distribution, 258
Extreme point, 25

Fair game, 196
Feasible directions, method of, 128
Feasible region, 3
Fibonacci search, 99, 108
  sequence, 99, 109
Fictitious destination or source, 70
FIFO queue discipline, 268
Finite-capacity queue, 268, 284
Finite decision processes, 154
Finite-source queueing systems, 295
First approximation to an integer program, 54
Fixed point, 224
Fletcher-Powell, method of, 112
Frank and Wolfe, method of, 144
Functional equation, 234

G (queueing notation), 268
Gain matrix, 197
Game, 184
  fair, 196
  stable, 185
  unstable, 186
Gamma distribution, 279
Global optimum, 97, 110
Golden-mean search, 99

Gomory cut algorithm, 63
Gradient vector, 110

Hessian matrix, 110
Hidden conditions, 2
Hooke-Jeeves' pattern search, 112
    modified, 113
Hungarian method, 85

Infinite-capacity queue, 268
Integer program, 2
    solution of, 54, 63, 70, 84
Interarrival time, 258
    for an M/M/1 system, 273
    for a queueing system, 266

Jacobian matrix, 127
Junction, 84, 171

Kendall's notation, 268
Knapsack problem, 59
Kolmogorov equations, 256
Kuhn-Tucker conditions, 128, 143

L (number in queueing system), 273
L_q (queue length), 273
Lagrange multiplier, 127
Least-squares exponential curve, 125
LIFO queue discipline, 268
Limiting state distribution, 225
Linear combination, 26
Linear dependence, 24
Linear independence, 24
Linear Markovian growth process, 256, 257
Linear program, 1 (*See also* Simplex method)
    basic feasible solution of, 25
    duality, 44
    initial solution of, 18
    for matrix games, 186
    standard form of, 19
Line segment, 24
Link, 169
Little's formulas, 274, 282
Local optimum, 97, 110
Loop, 72
Lottery, 199

M (queueing notation), 268
Markov chain, 224
    absorbing state of, 232
    with discounting, 235
Markov process, 224
    birth-death, 255
Mathematical programming, 1
Matrix game, 184
Max-flow, min-cut theorem, 183
Maximal flow problems, 171
Maximin strategy, 185

Measures of effectiveness, 273
    for an M/M/1 system, 274
Memoryless property, 275
Middle-of-the-road criterion, 198
Minimax criterion, 185, 198
    strategy, 185
    theorem, 186
Minimum-span problems, 170
Mixed strategy, 184
M/M/1 system, 273
M/M/1/K system, 284
M/M/∞ system, 295
M/M/s system, 283
M/M/s/K system, 284
Move of a game, 184, 188
Multistage decision process, 154
    stochastic, 213
    with an unbounded horizon, 234

Naive decision criteria, 198
Nearest-neighbor method, 91
"Near-optimal" algorithms, 86
Negative (semi-) definite matrix, 111
Network, 169
Newton-Raphson method, 112, 127
Node, 169
Nondegenerate solution, 26
Nonlinear program, 1
    multivariable, constrained, 126
    multivariable, unconstrained, 110
    single-variable, 97
Nonnegativity condition, 17
Normalized utility, 199
Northwest corner rule, 71

Objective, 1
$o(\Delta t)$, 255
Optimistic decision criterion, 198
Optimization problems, 1
Oriented branch, 169

Path, 169
Pattern search, 112
Payoff matrix, 184
Penalty cost, 18
    function, 127
    weight, 127
Permutations, 84
Pessimistic decision criterion, 198
Pivot element, 33
Poisson distribution, 258
Poisson growth process, 257, 258
Policy, 154
Policy table, 213
Population, 255
Portfolio problem, 144, 145
Positive definite matrix, 119
Present value, 156

Primal, 44
Principle of optimality (Bellman's), 155
Probability generating function, 261
Production problems, 84
Pure birth process, 255
   linear, 256
   Poisson, 257
Pure death process, 255
   linear, 256
   Poisson, 258
Pure strategy, 184
   dominated, 187

Quadratic program, 2, 143
   with equality constraints, 153
Queue discipline, 268
Queueing systems, 266
   finite-source, 295
   $M/M/1$, 273
   $M/M/1/K$, 284
   $M/M/\infty$, 295
   $M/M/s$, 283
   $M/M/s/K$, 284

Regret matrix, 212
Regular matrix, 225
Reneging, 266
   function, 283
Risk-averse, 212
   -indifferent, 212
   -seeking, 212
Risk premium, 210
Rolle's theorem, 101
Rosenbrock function, 125

Scheduling models, 84
Sequential-search techniques, 98
Service pattern, 266
Service time, 266
   for an $M/M/1$ system, 273
Shadow costs, 44
Shortest-route problems, 170
Simplex method, 33
   tableau, 32
Sink, 170
SIRO queue discipline, 268
Slack variable, 17
Source, in network, 170
   in transportation problem, 70
Stable game, 185
Stage, 154
Standard form, of a constrained nonlinear program, 126
   of a linear program, 19
   of a quadratic program, 143
   of a transportation problem, 70

State, of a decision process, 154
   of a growth process, 255
   of a Markov process, 224
   of nature, 197
   of a queueing system, 266
State-dependent queueing systems, 282
State-transition diagram, 229
Stationarity, 234
Stationary point, 98, 111
Steady-state probabilities, 273, 282
   for an $M/M/1$ system, 273
   for an $M/M/1/K$ system, 284
   for an $M/M/s$ system, 283
   for an $M/M/s/K$ system, 285
Steepest ascent, method of, 111
Stochastic matrix, 224
Strategies, 184
   dominated, 187
   mixed, 184, 185
   pure, 184
Strictly convex (concave) function, 100, 113
Surplus variable, 17
Symmetric dual, 44
Symmetric game, 196
System capacity, 266

Three-point interval search, 99
Traffic intensity, 273
Transition matrix, 224
Transportation algorithm, 70
Transportation problem, 170
Transshipment problems, 84
Traveling salesman problem, 85, 86
   first approximation for, 86
Tree, 169
   for a decision process, 198, 211
   for an integer program, 56
Two-person game, 184
Two-phase method, 33

Unbounded horizon, 234
Unconstrained mathematical programs, 1, 110
Unimodal function, 98
Unstable game, 186
Unsymmetric dual, 45
Utility, 198
   von Neumann, 199
   normalized, 199
Utilization factor, 273

Value, of a game, 185, 186
   of a test, 211
Variance, 145
Vogel's method, 71
Von Neumann utilities, 199

W (time in queueing system), 274
W_q (waiting time), 274
Weierstrass theorem, 29, 111
Work column, 33

$W(t)$ (probability distribution function), 274
$W_q(t)$ (probability distribution function), 274

Zero-sum game, 184

Catalog

If you are interested in a list of SCHAUM'S
OUTLINE SERIES send your name
and address, requesting your free catalog, to:

SCHAUM'S OUTLINE SERIES, Dept. C
McGRAW-HILL BOOK COMPANY
1221 Avenue of Americas
New York, N.Y. 10020